Y0-ELJ-581

CASES AND MATERIALS ON

CALIFORNIA COMMUNITY PROPERTY

Sixth Edition

By

Gail Boreman Bird
Professor of Law
University of California, Hastings College of the Law

AMERICAN CASEBOOK SERIES®

WEST PUBLISHING CO.
ST. PAUL, MINN., 1994

American Casebook Series, the key symbol appearing on the front cover and the WP symbol are registered trademarks of West Publishing Co. Registered in the U.S. Patent and Trademark Office.

COPYRIGHT © 1966, 1971, 1977, 1983, 1988 WEST PUBLISHING CO.
COPYRIGHT © 1994 By WEST PUBLISHING CO.

610 Opperman Drive
P.O. Box 64526
St. Paul, MN 55164–0526
1–800–328–9352

All rights reserved
Printed in the United States of America

Library of Congress Cataloging-in-Publication Data

Bird, Gail Boreman, 1945–
   Cases and materials on California community property / by Gail
Boreman Bird. — 6th ed.
      p.   cm. — (American casebook series)
   Rev. ed. of: Cases and materials on California community property
/ Harold E. Verrall. 5th ed. 1988.
   Includes index.
   ISBN 0–314–03491–9
   1. Community property—California—Cases. I. Verrall, Harold E.
Cases and materials on California community property. II. Title.
III. Series.
KFC125.C6V4   1994
346.79404′2—dc20
[347.940642]   94–6691
                                                            CIP

ISBN 0–314–03491–9

TEXT IS PRINTED ON 10% POST
CONSUMER RECYCLED PAPER

Printed with Printwise
Environmentally Advanced Water Washable Ink

Bird, Calif.Comm.Prop. 6th ACB
1st Reprint–1996

To Gilbert and Virginia Boreman
in the fiftieth year of their marriage

*

Preface

The primary aim of this casebook is to give law students a practical understanding of the California marital property system. The historical development of the community property concept and some basic principles are traced in Chapter 1. The author believes that the classification process is the heart of the community property system, and that students should come to grips with this process early on in the course. Thus, Chapter 2 introduces the basic classification principles. Limitations on the classification process are explored in Chapter 3, and more specialized applications of the classification principles are treated in Chapter 4. The remaining chapters deal with the consequences flowing from the classification of property as community or separate, including management and control rights and responsibilities, creditors' rights and distribution of property on the termination of the community.

The pattern of earlier editions of the casebook, giving a textual overview of a particular area, followed by the appropriate statutes and cases, has been continued in this edition. Further ramifications and problems are explored in the notes to the cases. Case and statute citations as well as footnotes have been omitted from certain of the principal cases without so specifying. Numbered footnotes within cases are from the original materials and retain their original numbering.

I wish to express my appreciation to student research assistants John Zecca, Carol Federighi and Kim Bellomo for their research contributions to this edition.

GAIL BOREMAN BIRD

*

Summary of Contents

Table of Contents

*

Table of Cases

The principal cases are in bold type. Cases cited or discussed in the text are roman type. References are to pages. Cases cited in principal cases and within other quoted materials are not included.

Statutory Cross Reference Table

This casebook contains the principal cases defining and implementing the California community property system. Many of these cases make reference to Civil Code sections prior to the enactment of the Family Code in 1994. The following cross reference tables are provided for the convenience of the reader.

Civil Code	Family Code
480(pt.)	3515
4100	300
4101	200
4101(a)	301
4101(b)	302
4101(c)	304
4102	200
	212
	303
4103	305
4104	308
4200	306
4201(2d snt.)	353
4201(a)(1st pt.)	350
4201(a)(last pt.)	351
4201(b)(1st snt.)	352
4201(b)(3d–last snt.)	354
4201(c)–(d)	355
4205	400
4205.1	401
4205.5	402
4206	420 (a)
4206.5	420 (b)
4207	421
4208(a)	422
4208(b)	423
4209	424
4210	425
4212	200
	309
4400	2200
4401	2201
4425	2210
4426	2211
4429	2212 (a)
4450	200
	2250
4451	2212 (b)
4452(1st–3d snt.)	2251
4452(last snt.)	2252
4454	2253
4455	2254
4456	2255
4457(a)	2080
4457(b)	2082
4457(c)	2081
4458	2045
4501	2300
4503	200

Civil Code	Family Code
4503(1st snt.)	2330 (a)
4503(last snt.)	2331
4506	2310
4507	2311
4508(a)(1st snt.)	2333
4508(a)(2d snt.–end)	2334
4508(b)(1st snt.)	2345
4508(b)(last snt.)	2347
4509	2335
4510(a)	2312
4510(b)	2313
4510(c)–(d)	2332
4511	2336
4512	2338
4513	2346
4514(a)(1st snt.)	2339
4514(a)(2d snt.)	2340
4514(a)(last snt.)	2341 (a)
4514(b)	2341 (b)
4514(c)	2342
4514(d)	2344
4514(e)	2343
4515	2337
4516	2045
4530(a)	2320
4530(b)	2321
4531	2322
4700.10(a)	3800
4700.10(b)(1st snt.)	3801 (a)
4700.10(b)(2d snt.)	3801 (b)
4700.10(b)(3d snt.)	3801 (c)
4700.10(b)(4th snt.–end)	3802 (a)–(b)
4700.10(c)(1st snt.)	3802 (a)
4700.10(c)(2d snt., 1st pt.)	3803
	3804
4700.10(c)(last snt.)	3805
4700.10(d)	3806
4700.10(e)(1)	3807
4700.10(e)(2)	3808
4700.10(f)	3809
4700.10(g)	3810
4800(a)(1st para., 1st snt.)	2550
	2552

Civil Code	Family Code	Civil Code	Family Code
5126(a)(last para.)	Omitted	5128	1103
5127	1102	5131	4302
		5132(1st snt.)	4301

*

CASES AND MATERIALS ON
CALIFORNIA COMMUNITY PROPERTY

Sixth Edition

*

Chapter 1

DEVELOPMENT OF THE CALIFORNIA COMMUNITY PROPERTY SYSTEM

SECTION 1. MARITAL PROPERTY: AN OVERVIEW

Marital property law in the United States is traceable to two primary sources: the English common law and the civil law system prevailing on the continent. The so called "common law" system was adopted in forty-two of the American jurisdictions, while the community property system derived from the civil law prevailed in the remaining eight. The most fundamental distinction between these basic types of marital property systems has been ascribed to two rather different ways of looking at property holding within the family unit.[1] In the common law system, the husband and wife own all property individually except that which they expressly agree to hold jointly, while in the community property system the spouses own a significant portion of their property jointly unless they have agreed to hold it separately.[2]

Under the English common law model as originally imported to the majority of American jurisdictions, the husband and wife were not recognized as individuals, but were viewed as "one person in law." According to Blackstone, this meant that "the very being or legal existence of the woman is suspended during the marriage, or at least is incorporated or consolidated into that of the husband."[3] Consequently a married woman could not own personal property (whatever personal property she owned prior to marriage was vested absolutely in the husband),[4] and although she retained separate ownership of her real property, her ownership was subject to the husband's rights to take the rents and profits during the marriage, to sell the property without her

---

1. Donahue, What Causes Fundamental Legal Ideas: Marital Property in England and France in the Thirteenth Century, 78 Mich.L.Rev. 59 (1979).

2. Id. Professor Donahue posits several explanations for the divergence of these "fundamental legal ideas," including legal and political developments, social institu-

tions, and cultural attitudes towards the family.

3. 1 W. Blackstone, Commentaries 442 (10th ed. 1787).

4. 2 W. Blackstone, Commentaries 433 (10th ed. 1787).

consent, and to curtesy rights upon her death.[5] A married woman was under various other legal disabilities, including the inability to enter into contracts with either third persons or her husband.[6]

Beginning in the mid-nineteenth century, the American jurisdictions which had adopted the common law system began to remove many of the legal disabilities of married women by enacting married women's property acts. The major effect of these statutes was to separate the spouses into two legal persons by restoring the wife's capacity to own and manage property and to enter into contracts.[7] By the end of the nineteenth century all states had enacted some form of married women's property legislation.[8] These reforms ultimately resulted in a "title theory" to marital property: each spouse was entitled to ownership and control of all property standing in his or her name. Variations of this modified common law system [9] remained in force in most American jurisdictions until the middle of this century.

Largely due to early Spanish and French colonization influences, eight American jurisdictions adopted some version of the community property system developed under civil law. Under the civil law system, the spouses were recognized as separate legal persons while the marriage was regarded as an economic partnership under the husband's management.[10] Each spouse was deemed a co-owner of property acquired during marriage, regardless of the value of his or her actual contributions to the acquisition. The community property system was (and continues to be) a classification based system: all assets owned by married persons may be classified as community or separate. The usual definition of separate property includes property owned prior to marriage and property acquired by gift or inheritance. Any other assets acquired during marriage may be deemed community property, owned equally by both spouses.

The dividing line between the common law marital property system and the community property system has become increasingly blurred in recent years, largely due to the development of the equitable distribution concept in the common law jurisdictions. The great majority of common

---

5. Donahue, What Causes Fundamental Legal Ideas: Marital Property in England and France in the Thirteenth Century, 78 Mich.L.Rev. 59, 64–65 (1979).

6. 1 W. Blackstone, Commentaries 442 (10th ed. 1787). The nineteenth century French legal historian Jean Baptiste Brissaud, in writing of the English common law system, stated "Marriage is for the woman a sort of civil death." Jean Baptiste Brissaud, *A History of French Private Law*, Rapelje Howell, ed. and trans. (Boston, 1912, reprinted 1968), quoted in August, *The Spread of Community Property Law to the Far West,* 3 Western Legal History 35, 36 (1990)

7. Younger, Marital Regimes: A Story of Compromise and Demoralization, To-gether with Criticism and Suggestions for Reform, 67 Cornell L.Rev. 45, 63–64 (1981).

8. Id.

9. The traditional common law system as modified by the married women's property acts is sometimes referred to as "reformed common law." See Prager, The Persistence of Separate Property Concepts in California's Community Property System, 1849–1975, 24 UCLA L.Rev. 1, 4 (1976).

10. Younger, Marital Regimes: A Story of Compromise and Demoralization, Together with Criticism and Suggestions for Reform, 67 Cornell L.Rev. 45, 48 (1981).

law jurisdictions have abandoned the idea that legal title to property is determinative of its ownership, and have adopted the view that marriage is a shared enterprise or partnership, whose assets should be distributed equitably upon dissolution.[11] The equitable distribution doctrine does not admit of precise definition, but generally refers to the authority of the courts to award property legally owned by one spouse to the other spouse in the context of divorce or dissolution proceedings.[12] The doctrine permits a spouse who has made material contributions towards the acquisition of property to claim an equitable interest in such property even though title is in the name of the other spouse.[13] Many states now recognize the contributions of a spouse as homemaker, parent and general contributor to the well-being of the family, and consider such contributions in making an "equitable distribution."[14]

Equitable distribution systems may be broadly grouped into two general categories or types. In some jurisdictions, the divorce courts have the power to divide all property owned by either or both spouses regardless of its source in order to "do equity" between them at divorce. In other jurisdictions, the divorce court may divide only the "marital property," which is usually defined to exclude gifts, inheritances and premarital acquisitions.[15]

The development of the equitable distribution concept is widely viewed as a movement towards the shared enterprise view of marriage, bringing many common law jurisdictions close to a "deferred community property" approach to divorce.[16] Many commentators find this salutary: "Marriage produces a transition between the territorial selfish blob of flesh born on this planet to a sharing human being. In marriage, couples come together to form a new economic entity with sharing as the paradigm."[17] Others are more cautionary: "Compulsory sharing, and the kind of restraints that even deferred community property puts on the freedom of each spouse to deal with his own property, may come to be seen by increasing numbers of spouses as undesirable, in much the same way that the French revolutionaries felt that marriage, if conceived of as an indissoluble undertaking, was incompatible with the principle of individual liberty."[18]

Notes

1. The English common law marital property system underwent similar reforms and modifications in common law jurisdictions outside the

11. Annotation, Divorce: Equitable Distribution Doctrine, 41 ALR 4th 481, 486 (1985).

12. Id. at 484.

13. Freed & Walker, Family Law in the Fifty States: An Overview, 19 Family Law Quarterly 331 (1986).

14. Id. at 360.

15. Goldstein, Classifying Property in "Dual Property" States, 7 Equitable Distribution Reporter 1 (1987).

16. Commentary, UMPA: The Uniform Marital Property Act, 10 Community Property Journal 279, 280 (1983).

17. Remarks of William Cantwell, Uniform Laws Commissioners' UMPA Reporter, quoted in Winter, UMPA Fights for Recognition, 10 ABA Journal 76, 77 (1984).

18. Glendon, Is There a Future for Separate Property?, VIII Family Law Quarterly 315, 327 (1974).

United States. Judge McCall of the Family Court of Western Australia states that following the enactment of married women's property legislation in the late nineteenth century, a system of separation developed in both Australia and New Zealand. Under this "separation system," each spouse retains the property owned before marriage and each retains separately the property acquired by him or her during marriage. Upon breakdown of the marriage, however, this separation system is replaced by a statutory equitable distribution mechanism: "In exercising this power the court redistributes the property in accordance with what it currently considers necessary to achieve justice between the parties. It is with the exercise of this power that it is possible to say that there is, in a broad way, a principle of an embryo deferred community of property or equalisation of assets system emerging." McCall, *Dissolving the Economic Partnership of Marriage*, 14 U.W.Australia L.Rev. 365, 377 (1982).

2. Professor Glendon's expressed wariness of the deferred community property model stems in part from the experience of Sweden and Germany where the model was first developed and implemented. Professor Glendon reports that the legislatures of Sweden and West Germany are reexamining the deferred community property system in response to public expressions of discontent.

"In both West Germany and Sweden, the feeling is being expressed in some quarters that legal devices developed for the situation where one spouse works outside and the other works inside the home are increasingly inappropriate. In Sweden, the exclusively housewife marriage is said now to be becoming uncommon. In West Germany the two-earner marriage (*Doppelverdienerehe*) is said to have replaced *Hausfrauenehe* as the dominant pattern. The official policy statement of the Social Democratic Party and government sponsored legislation are designed to reflect and respond to the changing social situation. Already, many West German couples are going to the trouble to contract out of the deferred community in favor of separation of assets."

Glendon, *Is There a Future for Separate Property?*, VIII Family Law Quarterly 315, 322–323 (1974); see also M. Glendon, State, Law and Family 158–164 (1977).

3. The National Conference of Commissioners on Uniform State Laws has promulgated the Uniform Marital Property Act (UMPA) for consideration by state legislatures. UMPA is essentially a community property proposal which would introduce the "immediate shared ownership concept" of community property to the common law states and offer an "improved version" to the existing community property states. Commentary, UMPA: The Uniform Marital Property Act, 10 Community Property Journal 279, 286 (1983). Under UMPA, property acquired during marriage is classified as "marital property" in which each spouse has a present undivided one-half interest. Property acquired prior to marriage or by gift or inheritance is classified as "individual property" owned wholly by the acquiring spouse. Wisconsin was the first common law state to adopt an UMPA type of system, and may now be regarded as the ninth community property jurisdiction. See Freed & Walker, *Family Law in the Fifty States: An Overview*, 19 Family Law Quarterly 331, 355 (Table IV) (1986); Winter, *UMPA Fights for*

Recognition, 70 ABA Journal 76 (1984). The UMPA has met significant resistance in many common law jurisdictions. The President of the Indiana Bar Association states that the "UMPA goes far beyond the recognized inequalities and would create far more problems than any it can solve. The side effects of this medicine make the cure worse than the disease." Grayson, *UMPA—The Bad Penny Comes Back,* 33 Res Gestae 573 (June, 1990).

4. In reviewing the history and present status of American marital property systems, Professor Judith Younger concludes that the current systems are "neither rigid nor judgmental," but faults them for omitting "an important moral message about the welfare of minor children." She would reform the current systems by adding a new marital status—the marriage for minor children. This status would be accorded to all couples on the birth of their first child and continue until the youngest child reached the age of majority. Divorce from this marriage would be difficult to obtain; the couple seeking a divorce would have to establish that continuance of the marriage would be more detrimental to the minor children than divorce would be. With respect to property, during the children's minority, each spouse would be an equal owner and joint manager of all the earnings and property of both, whenever and however acquired. In support of this proposal, Professor Younger states: "If children need both parents in order to grow up right, the law should give parents that message and encourage them to heed it. Children deserve the opportunity to grow up in the best possible environment. A special legal status might provide it more often, and thus, the marriage for minor children deserves a chance." Younger, *Marital Property Regimes: A Story of Compromise and Demoralization, Together with Criticism and Suggestions for Reform,* 67 Cornell L.Rev. 45, 90–94, 102 (1981).

SECTION 2. DEVELOPMENT OF THE CALIFORNIA SYSTEM

The community property concept, which constitutes the foundation of the California marital property system, is based on the idea that a portion of the property held by a married person is dedicated to the economic security of the family. That portion is community property, which must be distinguished from the remaining property, called separate property. During the period of the marriage the exploitation of the two types of property is subject to different controls, both decisional and statutory. Different rules govern the distribution of community and separate property upon termination of the marriage. An understanding of the community property system requires a consideration of the problems of the classification of property as separate or community, the problems involved in the use of that property, and the problems of distribution of property on termination of the marital community by death or dissolution. In assessing the operation of the community property system, we must determine what the objectives of the system are, and must test those objectives, with the attendant controls of classification, exploitation and distribution, against the realistic needs and concerns of the business world, against the reasonable expectations of family members and against the rights and concerns of the property owner. There is also a growing need to coordinate the community property system with federal and state social welfare programs.

Many of the problems and tensions inherent in our present-day community property system are more easily understood when viewed in the context of the evolution of the system in California. The community property system is not of common law origin; rather it originated in the custom of the Visigothic tribes of Europe and was given written form in the early codes of Spain. Centuries later it was carried to the Spanish territories and from there to eight states of the United States.[19]

At the time California was annexed to the United States the marital property law of the area was the Spanish–Mexican community property system.[20] This system continued in effect under the Treaty of Guadalupe Hidalgo [21] and the first constitution of California, the Constitution of 1849.[22] The constitutional provision was in the form of a guarantee of the separate property of a married woman and a directive to the legislature to pass laws more clearly defining the rights of married women in "separate" and "common" property.[23]

The first legislature of the State of California put into statutory form the basic principles of the Spanish–Mexican community property system [24] and expressly provided that the common law of dower and curtesy should not be part of California common law.[25] The California Constitution of 1879 continued the recognition of the community property system, with a provision defining and guaranteeing the separate

19. The origins and history of the community property concept are admirably covered in de Funiak and Vaughn, Principles of Community Property (2d ed. 1971) Chapters 1–4.

20. Background materials include: Kirkwood, Historical Background and Objectives of the Law of Community Property in the Pacific Coast States, 11 Wash.L.Rev. 1 (1936); Lobingier, The Marital Community: Its Origin and Diffusion, 14 A.B.A.J. 211 (1928); McMurray, The Beginnings of the Community Property System in California and the Adoption of the Common Law, 3 Cal.L.Rev. 359 (1915); Loewy, The Spanish Community of Acquests and Gains and its Adoption and Modification by the State of California, 1 Cal.L.Rev. 32 (1912); Ballinger, Community Property, c. 1, sec. 1 (1895); Schmidt, The Civil Law of Spain and Mexico, Book 1, Tit. 1, c. 4 (1851).

21. Treaty of Guadalupe Hidalgo, Art. VIII and Art. IX, as amended (1848). See 5 Miller, Treaties and Other International Acts of the United States of America, 217–219, 241–242 (1937).

22. Constitution of the State of California, 1849, Art. XI, sec. 14. The source of

this section was the Texas Constitution, 1845, Art. VII, sec. 19. See Selover v. American Russian Commercial Co., 7 Cal. 266, 270 (1857). Debate on the California provision is reported in Brown, Debates in the Convention of California on the Formation of the State Constitution, 257–269 (1850).

23. An interesting discussion of the debates is contained in McGinty, Common Law and Community Property: Origins of the California System, 51 Cal.St.B.J. 478 (1976).

24. The Act of Apr. 17, 1850, Cal.Stats. 1849–50, c. 103, p. 254. The California statute like the constitutional provision shows the Texas influence. See The Act of Jan. 20, 1840, 2 Gammel Laws of Texas, p. 177 (1898); The Act of Mar. 13, 1848, Texas Laws 1848, c. 79, p. 77.

25. Section 10 of Cal.Stats. 1849–50, p. 254. This section became West's Ann.Cal.Civil Code § 173 and is now West's Ann.Cal.Civil Code § 5129. A very limited qualification of this section is found in West's Ann.Cal.Probate Code § 201.6.

property rights of both spouses.[26]

CALIFORNIA CONSTITUTION
1849 Art. XI, Sec. 14

All property, both real and personal, of the wife, owned or claimed by her before marriage, and that acquired afterwards by gift, devise, or descent, shall be her separate property; and laws shall be passed more clearly defining the rights of the wife, in relation as well to her separate property, as to that held in common with her husband. Laws shall also be passed providing for the registration of the wife's separate property.

CALIFORNIA CONSTITUTION
1879 Art. XX, Sec. 8

All property, real and personal, owned by either husband or wife before marriage, and that acquired by either of them afterwards by gift, devise, or descent, shall be their separate property.

CALIFORNIA CONSTITUTION
Amendment 1974, Art. I, Sec. 21

Property owned before marriage or acquired during marriage by gift, will, or inheritance is separate property.

Act of April 17, 1850 [27]

AN ACT *defining the rights of Husband and Wife*

Passed April 17, 1850

The People of the State of California, represented in Senate and Assembly, do enact as follows:

§ 1. All property, both real and personal, of the wife, owned by her before marriage, and that acquired afterwards by gift, bequest, devise, or descent, shall be her separate property; and all property, both real and personal, owned by the husband before marriage, and that acquired by him afterwards, by gift, bequest, devise, or descent, shall be his separate property.

§ 2. All property acquired after the marriage by either husband or wife, except such as may be acquired by gift, bequest, devise, or descent, shall be common property.

§ 3. A full and complete inventory of the separate property of the wife shall be made out and signed by the wife, acknowledged or proved in the manner required by law for the acknowledgment or proof of a conveyance of land, and recorded in the office of the Recorder of the county in which the parties reside.

§ 4. If there be included in the inventory any real estate lying in other counties, the inventory shall also be recorded in such counties.

26. Constitution of the State of California, 1879, Art. XX, Sec. 8.

27. The California Supreme Court has stated that this original community property statute accurately reflects the Spanish–Mexican community property system from which it was derived. The modern statutes defining the system are reprinted at appropriate stages throughout the book. The current statutes treat more specifically the problems of classification, control and management and distribution than did the original Act of 1850.

§ 5.   The filing of the inventory in the Recorder's office shall be notice of the title of the wife, and all property belonging to her, included in the inventory, shall be exempt from seizure or execution for the debts of her husband.

§ 6.   The husband shall have the management and control of the separate property of the wife, during the continuance of the marriage; but no sale or other alienation of any part of such property can be made, nor any lien or incumbrance created thereon, unless by an instrument in writing, signed by the husband and wife, and acknowledged by her upon an examination separate and apart from her husband, before a Justice of the Supreme Court, Judge of the District Court, County Judge, or Notary Public, or if executed out of the State, then so acknowledged before some Judge of a Court of Record, or before a Commissioner, appointed under the authority of this State to take acknowledgment of deeds.

§ 7.   When any sale shall be made by the wife of any of her separate property, for the benefit of her husband, or when he shall have used the proceeds of such sale with her consent in writing, it shall be deemed a gift, and neither she nor those claiming under her shall have any right to recover the same.

§ 8.   If the wife has just cause to apprehend that her husband has mismanaged or wasted, or will mismanage or waste, her separate property, she, or any other person in her behalf, may apply to the District Court for the appointment of a trustee, to take charge of and manage her separate estate: such trustee may, for good cause shown, be from time to time removed by the Court, and another appointed in his place.   Before entering upon the discharge of his trust, he shall execute a bond, with sufficient surety or sureties, to be approved by the Court, for the proper performance of his duties.   In case of the appointment of a trustee for the wife, he shall account for and pay over to the husband and wife, or either of them, the income and profits of the wife's estate, in such manner and proportion as the Court may direct.

§ 9.   The husband shall have the entire management and control of the common property, with the like absolute power of disposition as of his own separate estate.   The rents and profits of the separate property of either husband or wife shall be deemed common property.

§ 10.   No estate shall be allowed to the husband as tenant by courtesy upon the decease of his wife, nor any estate in dower be allowed to the wife upon the decease of her husband.

§ 11.   Upon the dissolution of the community by the death of either husband or wife, one half of the common property shall go to the survivor, and the other half to the descendants of the deceased husband or wife, subject to the payment of the debts of the deceased.   If there be no descendants of the deceased husband or wife, the whole shall go to the survivor, subject to such payment.

§ 12.   In case of the dissolution of the marriage, by the decree of any Court of competent jurisdiction, the common property shall be equally divided between the parties, and the Court granting the decree shall make such order for the division of the common property, or the sale and equal distribution of the proceeds thereof, as the nature of the case may require.

§ 13.   The separate property of the husband shall not be liable for the debts of the wife contracted before the marriage, but the separate property of the wife shall be and continue liable for all such debts.

§ 14.   In every marriage hereafter contracted in this State, the rights of husband and wife shall be governed by this Act, unless there is a marriage contract, containing stipulations contrary thereto.

§ 15. The rights of husband and wife, married in this State prior to the passage of this Act, or married out of this State, who shall reside and acquire property herein, shall also be determined by the provisions of this Act, with respect to such property as shall be hereafter acquired, unless so far as such provisions may be in conflict with the stipulations of any marriage contract.

§ 16. All marriage contracts shall be in writing, and executed and acknowledged or proved, in like manner as a conveyance of land is required to be executed and acknowledged or proved.

§ 17. When a marriage contract shall be acknowledged or proved, it shall be recorded in the office of the Recorder of the County in which the parties reside, and also in the office of the Recorder of every County in which any real estate may be situated, which is conveyed or affected by such marriage contract.

§ 18. When any marriage contract is deposited in the Recorder's office for record, it shall, as to all property affected thereby, in the county where the same is deposited, impart full notice to all persons of the contents thereof.

§ 19. No marriage contract shall be valid, or affect any property, except between the parties thereto, until it shall be deposited for record with the Recorder of the County where the parties reside, and if it relates to real estate in other counties, with the Recorder of the County wherein such property is situated.

§ 20. A minor, capable of contracting matrimony, may enter into a marriage contract, and the same shall be as valid as if he was of full age: Provided, it be assented to, in writing, by the person or persons whose consent is necessary to his marriage.

§ 21. A marriage contract may be altered at any time before the celebration of the marriage, but not afterwards.

§ 22. The parties to any marriage contract shall enter into no agreement, the object of which shall be to alter the legal order of descent, either with respect to themselves in what concerns the inheritance of their children or posterity, or with respect to their children between themselves, nor derogate from the rights given by law to the husband, as to the head of the family, or to the surviving husband or wife, as the guardian of their children.

§ 23. No stipulation of any marriage contract shall be valid, which shall derogate from the rights given by law to the husband, over the persons of his wife and children, or which belong to the husband, as the head of the family, or to the surviving husband or wife, as the guardian of their children.

———

The community property system is thus a bit of foreign law superimposed on the common law of California. The assimilation of this system into the California legal structure has produced certain inconsistencies and an occasional warping of basic community property principles. Legislators, judges and lawyers schooled in the common law tradition have been responsible for the modification and interpretation of the California community property system over the years since its adoption in 1849, and they have not always shown an understanding of the basic tenets of the community property concept and its fundamental differences from common law marital property principles.

The character and extent of the statutes defining the California system and a course of decisional law peculiar to California have resulted in a community property system substantially different from that of the Spanish–Mexican parent system and substantially different from that of any of the seven other community property states. It has become *sui generis,* and is so different from the parent system that reference to Spanish or Mexican authority is of little persuasive value.[28] For similar reasons, the California Supreme Court has indicated that the decisions of sister states may be less than forceful precedents.[29]

The development of California's existing community property system may be ascribed in large part to the development by the California courts and legislature of three basic principles that underlie and permeate the system. One of these is the tracing principle whereby property acquisitions are traced back to their original source. Another is the concept of equality of interests; i.e., that community property is family property in which both spouses have equal interests. A third underlying concept is that married persons may modify operation of the community property system by inter-spousal agreements. These three underlying principles are introduced in the following sections of this chapter. Their application to specific situations is developed more fully in the succeeding chapters dealing with classification, management and control, and division of property on termination of the marriage.

SECTION 3. DEVELOPMENT OF THE TRACING PRINCIPLE

The statutes establishing and defining the California community property system indicate that a married person can hold property either as separate or as community, and that different rules govern the management and distribution of the two types of property. It is therefore necessary to classify property held by a married person as either community or separate. This classification is essential to the resolution of all disputes between married persons involving property.

The drafters of the California Constitution, in adopting the community property system, saw fit to define only separate property. Property not within the ambit of that definition is presumably community property.[30] The statutes implementing the constitutional provision take a similar approach: the Civil Code first defines separate property and then states that all other property is community property.

WEST'S ANNOTATED CALIFORNIA FAMILY CODE

§ 760. Community property defined

Except as otherwise provided by statute, all property, real or personal, wherever situated, acquired by a married person during the marriage while domiciled in this state is community property.

---

28. A similar development has occurred in the law of a sister state. See Lyons, Development of Community Property Law in Arizona, 15 Louisiana L.Rev. 512 (1955).

29. See Grolemund v. Cafferata, 17 Cal.2d 679, 688, 111 P.2d 641, 645 (1941); Ottinger v. Ottinger, 141 Cal.App.2d 220, 296 P.2d 347 (1956).

30. "It is rather easier to define separate than community property, and one may thereafter say, to cover up his difficulty, that all other is community." Evans, The Ownership of Community Property, 35 Harv.L.Rev. 47 (1921).

(Stats.1992, c. 162 (A.B. 2650), § 10, operative Jan. 1, 1994.)

§ 770. Separate property of married person

(a) Separate property of a married person includes all of the following:

(1) All property owned by the person before marriage.

(2) All property acquired by the person after marriage by gift, bequest, devise, or descent.

(3) The rents, issues, and profits of the property described in this section.

(b) A married person may, without the consent of the person's spouse, convey the person's separate property.

(Stats.1992, c. 162 (A.B. 2650), § 10, operative Jan. 1, 1994.)

§ 771. Earnings and accumulations during period of separation

The earnings and accumulations of a spouse and the minor children living with, or in the custody of, the spouse, while living separate and apart from the other spouse, are the separate property of the spouse.

(Stats.1992, c. 162 (A.B. 2650), § 10, operative Jan. 1, 1994.)

§ 772. Earnings or accumulations after entry of judgment of legal separation

After entry of a judgment of legal separation of the parties, the earnings or accumulations of each party are the separate property of the party acquiring the earnings or accumulations.

(Stats.1992, c. 162 (A.B. 2650), § 10, operative Jan. 1, 1994.)

———

Note that the statutory definitions of separate property include the "rents, issues and profits" of such property. This was not always the case. The original California statute, in accordance with the parent Spanish–Mexican system, provided that the rents, profits and income of separate property were deemed community property. Thus under the parent system and the original California statute the spouses contributed to the community not only the products of their time, energy and skill during marriage, but also the use of any separate property owned by either of them. One rationale offered for this rule was "the conception that, although each spouse retained ownership of his or her separate property, each unselfishly and unhesitantly had at heart the success and well-being of the marital union and that, accordingly, the fruits and income of all property of each naturally were to be devoted to the benefit of the marital union." [31]

The early statutory provision was at issue in the case of George v. Ransom, reprinted in this section. The court rejected the Spanish rule

---

31. De Funiak & Vaughn, Principles of Community Property (2d ed. 1971) § 71.

A more pragmatic explanation is that the production of returns from separate property necessarily involves the time, energy or skill of the property owner, i.e. a community contribution, and it would be impractical to weigh this contribution against the separate property.

of classifying income from separate property as community property on state constitutional grounds. Separate property continues to be separate property despite changes in form and produces separate property on exploitation.

Community property is rather loosely defined in the statute. Essentially it encompasses all property not falling within the definition of separate property. Thus community property naturally includes all property acquired by a married person through the use of his or her time, energy and skill. We may indeed view the time, energy and skill of a married person as the primary community property asset. In essence then community property includes any acquisition traceable to this primary asset.

When property classified as community property is used to purchase another acquisition, the new asset is community property.[32] Similarly, when property classified as community property produces rents, profits, income, and increases in value, these products are community property.[33] These examples are simply variations on the basic tracing idea of the community property system: when exploited, community property produces community property.

GEORGE v. RANSOM

Supreme Court of California, 1860.

15 Cal. 322, 76 Am.Dec. 490.

BALDWIN, J., delivered the opinion of the Court—FIELD, C.J., concurring.

This question arises from the record in this case: can a creditor of the husband subject the proceeds or dividends of the separate estate of the wife to his claim? In this case the property sought to be subjected was the dividends of certain stock purchased by the wife with her separate funds.

By the fourteenth section of article eleven of the Constitution, it is provided: "All property, both real and personal, of the wife, owned or claimed by her before marriage, and that acquired afterward by gift, devise, or descent, shall be her separate property; and laws shall be passed, more clearly defining the rights of the wife, in relation as well to her separate property as to that held in common with her husband. Laws shall also be passed, providing for the registration of the wife's separate property."

By section nine of the act regulating the relation of husband and wife, (Wood's Dig. 488) it is enacted: "The husband shall have the entire management and control of the common property, with the like absolute power of disposition, as of his own separate estate; and the rents and profits of the separate estate of either husband or wife shall be deemed

32. Boyd v. Oser, 23 Cal.2d 613, 145 P.2d 312 (1944); see also Stewart v. Stewart, 199 Cal. 318, 249 P. 197 (1926).

33. Id.

common property, unless, in the case of the separate property of the wife, it shall be provided by the terms of the instrument whereby such property may have been bequeathed, devised, or given to her, that the rents and profits thereof shall be applied to her sole and separate use— in which case, the entire management and disposal of the rents and profits of such property shall belong to the wife, and shall not be liable for the debts of the husband.''

We think the Legislature has not the Constitutional power to say that the fruits of the property of the wife shall be taken from her, and given to the husband or his creditors. If the Constitutional provision be not a protection to the wife against the exercise of this authority, the anomaly would seem to exist, of a right of property in one, divested of all beneficial use—the barren right to hold in the wife, and the beneficial right to enjoy in the husband. One object of the provision was, to protect the wife against the improvidence of the husband; but this object would wholly fail, in many instances, if the estate of the wife were reduced to a mere reversionary interest, to be of no avail to her except in the contingency of her surviving her husband.

It has been seen that the provision of the Constitution is, that the property acquired by the wife by devise, bequest, etc., shall be her separate property. This term ''separate property'' has a fixed meaning in the common law, and had in the minds of those who framed the Constitution, the large majority of whom were familiar with, and had lived under that system. By the common law, the idea attached to separate property in the wife, and which forms a portion of its definition, is, that it is an estate, held as well in its use as in its title, for the exclusive benefit and advantage of the wife. The common law recognized no such solecism as a right in the wife to the estate, and a right in some one else to use it as he pleased, and to enjoy all the advantages of its use. It is not perceived that property can be in one, in full and separate ownership, with a right in another to control it and enjoy all of its benefits. The sole value of property is in its use; to disassociate the right of property from the use in this class of cases, would be to preserve the name—the mere shadow—and destroy the thing itself—the substance. It would be to make the wife the trustee for the husband, holding the legal title, while he held the fruits of that title. This could no more be done, in consistency with our ideas of property, during the lifetime of the wife, than for all time.

This was the view taken by the Judge below, and his judgment is affirmed.

Notes

1. The holding in George v. Ransom has been severely criticized over the years, primarily on the ground that the court confused community property principles with common law notions of ownership. See Bruch, *The Definition and Division of Marital Property in California: Towards Parity and Simplicity,* 33 Hastings L.J. 769, 779–81 (1982). The court also ignored the legal history of California as well as that of Texas and Louisiana, which

had similar statutes. August, *The Spread of Community Property to the Far West,* 3 Western Legal History 35, 53 (1990). Nevertheless, it remains a leading case in the development of the tracing principle in California: the fruits of separate property are traced to the source and classified accordingly. This rule encompasses not only changes in form, such as proceeds from the sale or exchange of a separate property asset, but also the rents, profits or other forms of income derived from separate property. The rule of George v. Ransom was subsequently codified not only in California, but also in Washington, Nevada, Arizona and New Mexico. "These states struck out on a quite different path toward development of basic principles of community property law from that followed generally in the states adhering to the Spanish rule." Reppy, *Major Events in the Evolution of American Community Property Law,* 23 Family Law Quarterly 163, 172 (1989).

2. The tracing principle, which applies with equal force to community property, became exceedingly complicated due to the earlier decision of the California Supreme Court in the Spreckels case. See Spreckels v. Spreckels, 116 Cal. 339, 48 P. 228, 36 L.R.A. 497, 58 Am.St.Rep. 170 (1897). Under the *Spreckels* rule, which remained in force from 1897 to 1976, the incidents and characteristics of existing community property could not be changed by amendments to the statutes of the community property system. The amendments applied only to new acquisitions. As a result there were many different types of community property. Transmutations in form did not change the type of community property, and the products of each type took on the character of the wealth which produced them. The *Spreckels* rule, which established that changes in the community property system affecting "vested interests" could not be constitutionally applied retroactively, was called into question and rejected by the California Supreme Court in the later cases of Addison v. Addison, 62 Cal.2d 558, 43 Cal.Rptr. 97, 399 P.2d 897 (1965), and Marriage of Bouquet, 16 Cal.3d 583, 128 Cal.Rptr. 427, 546 P.2d 1371 (1976), reprinted in Chapter 3. More recent decisions, however, appear to have revitalized the *Spreckels* rule. See, e.g., Marriage of Buol, 39 Cal.3d 751, 218 Cal.Rptr. 31, 705 P.2d 354 (1985), reprinted in Chapter 2 and Marriage of Fabian, 41 Cal.3d 440, 224 Cal.Rptr. 333, 715 P.2d 253 (1986), reprinted in Chapter 3.

3. Under the basic tracing principle developed in California, it is established that separate property produces separate property, and community property produces community property. Suppose that wife W owns a farm as her separate property. Her husband H carries on farming operations which produce a crop. The crop is sold. Are the proceeds of the sale community property or separate property? See Lewis v. Johns, 24 Cal. 98, 85 Am.Dec. 49 (1864). This type of problem is explored more fully in Chapter 4. *at most could be reimbursed if there were a Ⓡ.*

SECTION 4. DEVELOPMENT OF THE EQUALITY PRINCIPLE

A second basic idea underlying the community property system is the principle of equality of interest; that is, the idea that the spouses have equal ownership interests in the community property. Most acquisitions of community property involve the direct contribution of the time, energy and skill of married persons or may be traced to such a contribution. In addition, the spouses contribute equally to those acquisitions by performing the many acts of a family partner.[34] The relative values of these direct and indirect contributions cannot be put in issue,[35] and because the contributions are considered of equal value, the interests of the husband and wife are equal.[36] Equality of ownership was a primary tenet of the parent system, and is recognized by all American community property jurisdictions today. This was not always the case in California.

The statutes adopting the community property system in California followed the Spanish–Mexican precedents, and placed the husband in control and management of the community property. He had the power to possess and exploit the property, while the wife had no such rights. The fact that the husband had the major incidents of ownership led California courts to say that during the marriage, the husband had "practical ownership" of the community property, and the wife merely a "protected expectancy." Legislative amendments eroding the once total and exclusive management powers of the husband and giving the wife greater control did not alter the California courts' characterization of the wife's interest.

In the case of Stewart v. Stewart,[37] the wife argued that statutory changes limiting the husband's ability to make gifts of community property or conveyances of community real estate should be deemed to create a vested interest in an undivided one-half of the community property. The California Supreme Court rejected the argument, reasoning that the Legislature did not clearly state any purpose to create vested interest in the wife. Shortly thereafter, the legislature did speak plainly, and decreed that the interests of the spouses in the community property are "present, existing and equal." This provision was the first enacted in 1927 and is now contained at California Family Code Section 751, reprinted below.[38]

With respect to community property acquired after 1927, the courts no longer use the expressions "practical ownership" and "protected expectancy." Still they have continued to find the exploitation rights as defined prior to 1927 unchanged except to the extent that the legislature has made specific changes.[39] The position of the spouses in the areas of gift, estate and income taxation has certainly changed.[40] The 1927

34. See Coats v. Coats, 160 Cal. 671, 118 P. 441, 36 L.R.A. (N.S.) 844 (1911).

35. Id.

36. See Stewart v. Stewart, reprinted in this Section. See also Coats v. Coats, 160 Cal. 671, 118 P. 441, 36 L.R.A. (N.S.) 844 (1911); In re Marriage of Pilatti, 96 Cal. App.3d 63, 157 Cal.Rptr. 594 (1979), certiorari denied 445 U.S. 916, 100 S.Ct. 1276, 63 L.Ed.2d 600 (1980); In re Marriage of Brigden, 80 Cal.App.3d 380, 145 Cal.Rptr. 716 (1978).

37. Stewart v. Stewart, 199 Cal. 318, 249 P. 197 (1926).

38. The California Supreme Court's response was to declare that the statute could not be applied retroactively to community property acquired before 1927. Stewart v. Stewart, 204 Cal. 546, 269 P. 439 (1928). The problem of retroactivity is explored in greater depth in Chapter 3, Section 3.

39. See Grolemund v. Cafferata, 17 Cal.2d 679, 111 P.2d 641 (1941).

40. United States v. Malcolm, 282 U.S. 792, 51 S.Ct. 184, 75 L.Ed. 714 (1931). Half of the community property is in the estate of the decedent. United States v. Stewart, 270 F.2d 894 (9th Cir.1959), cer-

statute also had the effect of qualifying the wife as a party plaintiff in quiet title actions,[41] and produced several changes in the rules of procedure. But in the main, the effect of the 1927 statute has been less than sweeping. In many cases where the statute would seem to bear directly on the determination of problems involved, it has been ignored, and the courts have followed the early precedents.[42]

It is not too surprising that California courts had difficulty in recognizing the equality of ownership principle, given the fact that many of the major incidents of ownership—the rights to possession, management and control—were vested by statute in the husband. Piecemeal limitations on the husband's rights were added from time to time, but it was not until 1975 that these major incidents of ownership as well as ownership itself were shared equally by both spouses. This reform is considered in more detail in Chapter 5, which considers the management and control of community property.

WEST'S ANNOTATED CALIFORNIA FAMILY CODE

§ 751. Community property; interests of parties

The respective interests of the husband and wife in community property during continuance of the marriage relation are present, existing, and equal interests.

(Stats.1992, c. 162 (A.B. 2650), § 10, operative Jan. 1, 1994.)

STEWART v. STEWART
Supreme Court of California, 1926.
199 Cal. 318, 249 P. 197.

[Mrs. Stewart brought an action against her husband under the provisions of section 1060 of the Code of Civil Procedure, to quiet her title to an undivided half interest in real property, record title to which was in Mrs. Stewart. The property was community property and the marriage was still subsisting. The trial court quieted the title of Mrs. Stewart. From this judgment an appeal was taken.]

Richard J. [After quoting the constitutional provision adopting the community property system and the principal sections of the Act of April 17, 1850, setting up the system, the opinion continued:] The first judicial reference to the foregoing provisions of this act occurs in the case of Panaud v. Jones, 1 Cal. 488. * * *

* * *

The opinion refers to the said act of 1850 as * * * containing a clear and succinct statement of the Spanish law respecting the community

---

tiorari denied 361 U.S. 960, 80 S.Ct. 588, 4 L.Ed.2d 542; Bank of America National Trust and Savings Association v. Rogan, 33 F.Supp. 183 (D.C.Cal.1940); Crocker First National Bank v. United States, 183 F.2d 149 (9th Cir.1950).

41. Horton v. Horton, 115 Cal.App.2d 360, 252 P.2d 397 (1953).

42. See Estate of Kurt, 83 Cal.App.2d 681, 189 P.2d 528 (1948); Colden v. Costello, 50 Cal.App.2d 363, 122 P.2d 959 (1942).

property of husband and wife. It then proceeds to show that, under the Spanish and Mexican law quoted from several authorities which purport to give the text thereof, it was provided that the husband during the continuance of the marriage might freely alienate and dispose of the community property without the consent of the wife, and that such alienation should be valid unless it be proved that it was made with intention to defraud her. Among these authorities, the author of the opinion quotes from Febrero as follows:

> " 'The wife,' says Febrero (1 Feb.Mej. 225, § 19), 'is clothed with the revocable and feigned dominion and possession of one-half of the property acquired by her and her husband during the marriage; but after his death, it is transferred to her effectively and irrevocably, so that, by his decease, she is constituted the absolute owner in property and possession of the half which he left.' "

He further quotes:

> " 'The husband needs not the dissolution of the marriage to constitute him the real and veritable owner of all the Gananciales, since, even during the marriage, he has in effect the irrevocable dominion, and he may administer, exchange, sell and alienate them at his pleasure, provided there exist no intention to defraud the wife. For this reason, the husband living, and the marriage continuing, the wife cannot say that she has any Gananciales, nor interfere with the husband's free disposition thereof, under pretext that the law concedes the half to her, for the concession is intended for the cases expressed and none other.' "

[The court then reviewed all important cases of the next fifty years.]

In the case of Spreckels v. Spreckels, supra, it was earnestly urged that by the amendment to section 172 of the Civil Code in 1891 the status of the husband as invested with the sole ownership of the community property had been changed, and that the wife had thereby become invested with an ownership in the undivided one-half thereof. The court did not, however, deem it necessary to dispose of that question in that case, confining itself to the declaration that any legislative attempt to encroach upon the vested ownership by the husband of the property of the community so as to be retroactive upon such property owned by him prior thereto would be unconstitutional, as an interference with his vested rights in such property. In the second case of Spreckels v. Spreckels, 172 Cal. 775, 158 P. 537, the question as to the effect of such amendment to section 172 of the Civil Code was directly presented and this court, after the painstaking manner of Mr. Justice Shaw, went again over the ground covered by its former decisions from the beginning of our judicial history, reviewing all of the cases wherein it had been laid down as the established doctrine in this state that, under our statutes as they existed prior to 1891, the husband was, during the marriage "the sole and exclusive owner of all the community property, and that the wife had no title thereto, nor interest or estate therein, other than a mere expectancy as heir, if she survived him." Having so again held, the court proceeded to say:

"We are satisfied that the proviso of 1891 does not render a gift of community property by the husband without the consent of the wife void as to him, nor confer upon him, in his lifetime, or upon his personal representatives after his death, any right or power to revoke the gift or recover the property. There is nothing in the language to express the idea that the title does not, as before, remain wholly in him. The provision is merely for a limitation upon his power to dispose of it. He is bound by his own gift as fully as if it was of his separate estate. * * * Neither does the proviso purport to vest in the wife, during the marriage, any present interest or estate in the community property given away by the husband without her written consent. In view of the long-settled doctrine that the entire estate therein is in the husband during the marriage relation, a doctrine that had become a fixed and well understood rule of property, it is not to be supposed that the Legislature would have made a change of so radical a character without plain language to that effect. We do not find in the proviso such language, nor anything that can reasonably be so construed. If it confers upon her, during the marriage, any right respecting such gifts, it is nothing more than a right to revoke the gift and, if necessary, sue to recover the property, not as her separate estate, but to reinstate it as a part of the community property, with the title vested in the husband and subject to sale by him, as before. We do not find it necessary to determine whether this right accrues to her at once when the gift is made, or whether it remains in abeyance until her expectancy in the community property becomes vested by the dissolution of the marriage by death or divorce. In either case, upon the facts alleged, the present action must fail."

[The court then noticed the enactment of additional restraints on the husband's rights of management and control in 1917.]

It is most earnestly contended by and on behalf of the respondent herein that the changes in the laws relating to community property effectuated by these two latter amendments were such as to create in the wife, if such had not theretofore existed, a vested interest in an undivided one-half of the community property immediately upon the acquisition of such property by the spouses or either of them, and to continue thereafter during the existence of the marriage relation. We are unable for the following reasons to give our approval to that contention. The Legislature in framing these two amendments which, taken together, worked a revision of the former section 172 of the Civil Code did not state therein "in plain language," as it was pointed out in the second Spreckels Case it might easily have done, "that the purpose of these amendments was to vest in the wife during the marriage a present interest or estate in the community property." The Legislature did not even by said amendments to the Civil Code go as far as it had done in its revision of the inheritance tax law, coincidently adopted, so as to state that:

> The "one-half of the community property which goes to the surviving wife on the death of the husband * * * shall not be deemed to pass to her as heir of her husband but shall * * * be deemed to go, pass, or be transferred to her for valuable and adequate consideration."

Had the Legislature seen fit to so declare in the language employed by it in the coincident statute, no doubt could have existed as to its intent to work such a radical change in the former and long-established status as to render the interest of the wife in the community property thereafter to be acquired a present vested estate and interest therein from the date of its acquisition. The Legislature did not do this nor anything like it. All that the Legislature by these amendments did do, or attempt to do, was to cast about the interest of the wife in both the real and personal property of the community during the continued existence of the marriage relation added safeguards and protection against the fraudulent or inconsiderate acts of the husband in the exercise of his control and dominion over these properties of the nature of those already provided for in earlier statutes and especially in and by the 1891 amendment to section 172 of the Civil Code.

It follows, to our minds, irresistibly that the same reasoning which was applied to the earlier amendment of section 172 of the Civil Code equally applies to those changes in and revision thereof accomplished by the Legislature in 1917. Additional force is, if needed, given to this conclusion when the particular provisions of section 172a as added to the Code in that year are subjected to careful consideration; for it is made to therein appear that the sole lease, contract, mortgage, or deed of the husband holding the record title to community real property to a lessee, purchaser, or incumbrancer in good faith, without knowledge of the marriage relation, shall be presumed to be valid and shall be so valid unless an action to avoid such instrument shall be commenced within one year from the recordation thereof. This provision renders the conveyance of the whole of the community real estate to a purchaser or incumbrancer thereof in good faith voidable but not void; a condition entirely inconsistent with the existence of a present and vested ownership in the wife of an undivided one-half of such property, and also with an intent on the part of the Legislature by said amendments to effectuate such a radical change in a long-established rule of property. We are, therefore, clearly of the opinion that the amendments to the Civil Code, adopted in 1917, did not operate to change such rule to the extent of creating in the wife a present vested interest in the property of the community during the continuance of the marriage relation.

In what has been heretofore said in this opinion we are not unmindful of the fact that in certain of the other states which have been designated as "community property states," or, in other words, states which immediately derived or have mediately adopted their laws relating to community property from the laws of Spain and Mexico, a different interpretation of those laws and of the statutes based thereon has prevailed and that much emphasis has been laid during the presentation of this cause in the argument and briefs of counsel upon the divergence existing between the decisions of California and in these several other jurisdictions. Discussions of this character are interesting, but are by no means controlling in dealing with questions involving conflicts in laws. California was as much entitled as New Mexico or Texas or Washington to adopt and to persist in its own interpretation of the meaning and effect of the Spanish and Mexican laws in relation to the wife's interest in the community property. Having made and persisted in its own interpretation of these originals through all these years, and having by so doing created and consistently adhered to such interpretation as to render the same a fully established rule of property, it is for the Legislature, but not for this court, to depart from such rule. Up to and including the year 1917, the Legislature has not, in our opinion, seen fit so to do. The parties to this action acquired the property affected by this litigation during the year 1918.

* * *

We wish to say in conclusion that we are in accord with the intimations from time to time reflected by this court in the long line of its past decisions to the effect that the interest of the wife in the property of the community during the continuance of the marriage relation, while it has not yet reached the status of a vested interest therein, is, and has always been from a time reaching back into the Spanish and Mexican originals of our community property laws, a much more definite and present interest than is that of an ordinary heir. She has, by virtue of the share which in her own sphere she has contributed toward the acquisition and conservation of such properties, rights therein which have been always safeguarded against the fraudulent or inconsiderate acts of her husband with relation thereto, and for the assertion and safeguarding of which she has been given access to appropriate judicial remedies both before and after the time when her said rights and interests would ripen and become vested through the death of the husband or other severance of the marriage relation, whenever such rights and ultimate interests were affected by or threatened with such forms of invasion. The instant case is not, however, such a case. In her complaint herein the plaintiff expressly alleges that she and the defendant, her husband, "are now and ever since their said marriage have been peacefully and happily living together as husband and wife." She nowhere alleges therein that her said husband is attempting or threatening to deal with or dispose of said property fraudulently or inconsiderately or otherwise so as to affect or in anywise endanger her legal rights and interests therein. He could not do so in fact, even if he did so desire, since the legal title to said property stands of record in the plaintiff's name.

The trial court was clearly in error in adjudging that the interest of the plaintiff in said property was that of "the owner of an undivided one-half valid present vested interest in and to the within described property."

The judgment is reversed.

Note

The postponement of the full recognition of the wife's half interest in community property resulted in many doctrines seemingly inconsistent with the idea of equality between the spouses. As the *Stewart* case indicates, the husband could qualify as a party plaintiff in an action to quiet title, while the wife could not. The creditors of the husband could get satisfaction out of the community property, but those of the wife could not. Grolemund v. Cafferata, 17 Cal.2d 679, 111 P.2d 641 (1941). Tax treatment was also disparate; all of the income was taxable to the husband. See United States v. Robbins, 209 U.S. 315, 46 S.Ct. 148, 70 L.Ed. 285 (1926). The wife was not wholly bereft of rights, however. During the marriage the wife's interests were protected against fraud and mismanagement, and at the termination of the marriage the wife took her half as an owner, and not simply as a successor to her husband's interest. See Estate of Pezzola, 112 Cal.App.3d 752, 169 Cal.Rptr. 464 (1980); Estate of Piatt, 81 Cal.App.2d 348, 183 P.2d 919 (1947).

SECTION 5. THE PRINCIPLE OF CONTRACTUAL MODIFICATION

A third major tenet of the California community property system is the fact that the operation of the system may be modified or limited by an agreement between the spouses. The original Act of 1850 and the statutes now defining the system specifically provide that it is subject to antenuptial and postnuptial contractual modification.[43] The principle of contractual modification is subject to certain public policy limitations. The cases of *In re Marriage of Noghrey* and *Borelli v. Brusseau,* reprinted in this Section, examine these policy limitations.

Under the principle of contractual modification the spouses themselves can determine how their property will be classified; they can agree that what would generally be classified as community will be the separate property of one or the other, and conversely, they can transmute separate property to community property by agreement. In effect, they can contract themselves out of the community property system.

A major issue that has arisen in connection with the principle of contractual modification involves the degree of formality required for a valid transmutation agreement. Prior to 1985 the statutes did not expressly refer to transmutation agreements, but provided that "all contracts for marriage settlements must be in writing, and executed and acknowledged * * * in like manner as a grant of land."[44] Case law, however, established that "husbands and wives may contract to change

---

43. West's Ann.Cal. Family Code §§ 721, 850–53, 1500–1620.

44. Cal.Stats.1850, c. 103, p. 255, § 16.

property from community to separate or from separate to community and this may be done before marriage if the contract is in writing or if an oral contract is fully executed." [45] Furthermore, a premarital oral agreement could be deemed executed by the marriage itself or by other acts of ratification thereafter. The courts used a similar approach in dealing with the applicability of the general statute of frauds to transmutation agreements. [46] In addition to enforcing interspousal oral agreements, the California courts were also willing to find and enforce implied-in-fact agreements between the spouse altering the character of their property.

The historical willingness of the California courts to recognize and enforce informal interspousal contracts made the contractual modification principle an exceedingly important component of California community property law. The principle of contractual modification is also closely related to the various classification presumptions derived from the form of title, which are considered in detail in Chapter 2. Courts have frequently indicated that the taking of title in a certain form raises a presumption that a particular classification of the property was intended by the spouses. For example, when a married man participated in a transaction resulting in the vesting of a title in his wife, the courts said that he must have intended to accomplish something and that his intent could only have been to make the property her separate property. The transaction was deemed to raise a presumption of separate property. [47] Similarly, when the spouses took title to property as joint tenants, the courts said that presumptively the property was their separate property. [48] Such presumptions were held not to be rebuttable by simple tracing but were rebuttable by evidence of a different understanding. [49] The courts used the language of presumption in these situations, but realistically, they were recognizing that the facts raise very strong inferences of implied-in-fact contracts classifying the properties involved. [50]

Due to the burdensome tracing problems inherent in many of the classification and apportionment doctrines, [51] the recognition of informal and implied-in-fact contracts between spouses was of prime importance, and provided a faster and less costly means of resolving many classification problems. [52] On the other hand, it was asserted that transmutation

---

45. In re Wahlefeld's Estate, 105 Cal. App. 770, 288 P. 870 (1930).

46. Id.; Woods v. Security First National Bank, 46 Cal.2d 697, 299 P.2d 657 (1956).

47. Taylor v. Opperman, 79 Cal. 468, 21 P. 869 (1889).

48. See Chapter 2, Section 4.

49. See In re Marriage of Lucas, 27 Cal.3d 808, 166 Cal.Rptr. 853, 614 P.2d 285 (1980), reprinted in Chapter 2, Section 4.

50. See the language of contract in Socol v. King, 36 Cal.2d 342, 223 P.2d 627 (1950).

51. See Chapter 4, Sections 1 and 2.

52. In Benom v. Benom, 173 Cal.App.2d 286, 343 P.2d 632 (1959), the tracing of small sums of separate property resulted in a 2,000 page transcript. Perhaps an implied-in-fact contract could have avoided such expensive evidence.

was "dangerously easy" in California, leading to the twisting of casual comments into agreements or even to perjury by a divorcing spouse.[53]

The legislative response has been to strengthen the formalities required for premarital and interspousal transmutation agreements. With certain limited exceptions, transmutations of real or personal property made on or after January 1, 1985 must be in writing.[54] Premarital agreements, defined as agreements between prospective spouses made in contemplation of marriage and to be effective upon marriage, are now subject to the Uniform Premarital Agreement Act which requires a writing signed by both parties. The Uniform Act applies to any premarital agreement executed on or after January 1, 1986.[55] The legislative writing requirements have been described as part of a growing trend to "commercialize" the marital relationship, so that each spouse will know his or her rights more fully on dissolution. The imposition of a writing requirement as a requisite to establishing property rights will also tend to reduce the evidentiary quagmire of "pillow talk."[56]

WEST'S ANNOTATED CALIFORNIA FAMILY CODE

§ 720. Mutual obligations

Husband and wife contract toward each other obligations of mutual respect, fidelity, and support. *means nothing*

(Stats.1992, c. 162 (A.B.2650), § 10, operative Jan. 1, 1994.)

§ 721. Contracts with each other and third parties; fiduciary relationship

(a) Subject to subdivision (b), either husband or wife may enter into any transaction with the other, or with any other person, respecting property, which either might if unmarried.

(b) Except as provided in Sections 143, 144, 146, and 16040 of the Probate Code, in transactions between themselves, a husband and wife are subject to the general rules governing fiduciary relationships which control the actions of persons occupying confidential relations with each other. This confidential relationship imposes a duty of the highest good faith and fair dealing on each spouse, and neither shall take any unfair advantage of the other. This confidential relationship is a fiduciary relationship subject to the same rights and duties of nonmarital business partners, as provided in Sections 15019, 15020, 15021, and 15022 of the Corporations Code, including the following:

(1) Providing each spouse access at all times to any books kept regarding a transaction for the purposes of inspection and copying.

(2) Rendering upon request, true and full information of all things affecting any transaction which concerns the community property. Nothing in this section is intended to impose a duty for either spouse to keep detailed books and records of community property transactions.

---

53. W. Reppy, Community Property in California 39 (1980).

54. West's Ann.Cal. Family Code §§ 850–853.

55. West's Ann.Cal. Family Code §§ 1500–1620.

56. 1 Calif. Family Law Monthly 171 (Jan.1985).

(3) Accounting to the spouse, and holding as a trustee, any benefit or profit derived from any transaction by one spouse without the consent of the other spouse which concerns the community property.

(Stats.1992, c. 162 (A.B.2650), § 10, operative Jan. 1, 1994.)

§ 850. Transmutation by agreement or transfer

Subject to Sections 851 to 853, inclusive, married persons may by agreement or transfer, with or without consideration, do any of the following:

(a) Transmute community property to separate property of either spouse.

(b) Transmute separate property of either spouse to community property.

(c) Transmute separate property of one spouse to separate property of the other spouse.

(Stats.1992, c. 162 (A.B.2650), § 10, operative Jan. 1, 1994.)

§ 851. Transmutation subject to fraudulent transfer laws

A transmutation is subject to the laws governing fraudulent transfers.

(Stats.1992, c. 162 (A.B.2650), § 10, operative Jan. 1, 1994.)

§ 852. Validity of transmutations; application of section

(a) A transmutation of real or personal property is not valid unless made in writing by an express declaration that is made, joined in, consented to, or accepted by the spouse whose interest in the property is adversely affected.

(b) A transmutation of real property is not effective as to third parties without notice thereof unless recorded.

(c) This section does not apply to a gift between the spouses of clothing, wearing apparel, jewelry, or other tangible articles of a personal nature that is used solely or principally by the spouse to whom the gift is made and that is not substantial in value taking into account the circumstances of the marriage.

(d) Nothing in this section affects the law governing characterization of property in which separate property and community property are commingled or otherwise combined.

(e) This section does not apply to or affect a transmutation of property made before January 1, 1985, and the law that would otherwise be applicable to that transmutation shall continue to apply.

(Stats.1992, c. 162 (A.B.2650), § 10, operative Jan. 1, 1994.)

§ 853. Characterization of property in will; admissibility in proceedings commenced before death of testator

(a) A statement in a will of the character of property is not admissible as evidence of a transmutation of the property in a proceeding commenced before the death of the person who made the will.

(b) A waiver of a right to a joint and survivor annuity or survivor's benefits under the federal Retirement Equity Act of 1984 (Public Law 98–397) is not a transmutation of the community property rights of the person executing the waiver.

(c) A written joinder or written consent to a nonprobate transfer of community property on death that satisfies Section 852 is a transmutation and is governed by the law applicable to transmutations and not by Chapter 2 (commencing with Section 5010) of Part 1 of Division 5 of the Probate Code.

§ 1500. Effect of premarital agreements and other marital property agreements

The property rights of husband and wife prescribed by statute may be altered by a premarital agreement or other marital property agreement.

post marital
Post-marital

(Stats.1992, c. 162 (A.B.2650), § 10, operative Jan. 1, 1994.)

§ 1501. Agreements by minors

A minor may make a valid premarital agreement or other marital property agreement if the minor is emancipated or is otherwise capable of contracting marriage.

(Stats.1992, c. 162 (A.B.2650), § 10, operative Jan. 1, 1994.)

§ 1502. Recording of agreements

(a) A premarital agreement or other marital property agreement that is executed and acknowledged or proved in the manner that a grant of real property is required to be executed and acknowledged or proved may be recorded in the office of the recorder of each county in which real property affected by the agreement is situated.

(b) Recording or nonrecording of a premarital agreement or other marital property agreement has the same effect as recording or nonrecording of a grant of real property.

(Stats.1992, c. 162 (A.B.2650), § 10, operative Jan. 1, 1994.)

§ 1503. Law applicable to preexisting premarital agreements

Nothing in this chapter affects the validity or effect of premarital agreements made before January 1, 1986, and the validity and effect of those agreements shall continue to be determined by the law applicable to the agreements before January 1, 1986.

(Stats.1992, c. 162 (A.B.2650), § 10, operative Jan. 1, 1994.)

§ 1600. Short title

This chapter may be cited as the Uniform Premarital Agreement Act.

(Stats.1992, c. 162 (A.B.2650), § 10, operative Jan. 1, 1994.)

§ 1601. Effective date of chapter

This chapter is effective on and after January 1, 1986, and applies to any premarital agreement executed on or after that date.

(Stats.1992, c. 162 (A.B.2650), § 10, operative Jan. 1, 1994.)

§ 1610. Definitions *Pre-nup*

As used in this chapter:

(a) "Premarital agreement" means an agreement between prospective spouses made in contemplation of marriage and to be effective upon marriage.

(b) "Property" means an interest, present or future, legal or equitable, vested or contingent, in real or personal property, including income and earnings.

(Stats.1992, c. 162 (A.B.2650), § 10, operative Jan. 1, 1994.)

§ 1611. Form and execution of agreement; consideration

A premarital agreement shall be in writing and signed by both parties. It is enforceable without consideration.

(Stats.1992, c. 162 (A.B.2650), § 10, operative Jan. 1, 1994.)

§ 1612. Subject matter of premarital agreements

(a) Parties to a premarital agreement may contract with respect to all of the following:

(1) The rights and obligations of each of the parties in any of the property of either or both of them whenever and wherever acquired or located.

(2) The right to buy, sell, use, transfer, exchange, abandon, lease, consume, expend, assign, create a security interest in, mortgage, encumber, dispose of, or otherwise manage and control property.

(3) The disposition of property upon separation, marital dissolution, death, or the occurrence or nonoccurrence of any other event.

(4) The making of a will, trust, or other arrangement to carry out the provisions of the agreement.

(5) The ownership rights in and disposition of the death benefit from a life insurance policy.

(6) The choice of law governing the construction of the agreement.

(7) Any other matter, including their personal rights and obligations, not in violation of public policy or a statute imposing a criminal penalty.

(b) The right of a child to support may not be adversely affected by a premarital agreement.

(Stats.1992, c. 162 (A.B.2650), § 10, operative Jan. 1, 1994.)

§ 1613. Effective date of agreements

A premarital agreement becomes effective upon marriage.

(Stats.1992, c. 162 (A.B.2650), § 10, operative Jan. 1, 1994.)

§ 1614. Amendment or revocation of agreements

After marriage, a premarital agreement may be amended or revoked only by a written agreement signed by the parties. The amended agreement or the revocation is enforceable without consideration.

(Stats.1992, c. 162 (A.B.2650), § 10, operative Jan. 1, 1994.)

§ 1615. Unenforceable agreements

(a) A premarital agreement is not enforceable if the party against whom enforcement is sought proves either of the following:

(1) That party did not execute the agreement voluntarily.

(2) The agreement was unconscionable when it was executed and, before execution of the agreement, all of the following applied to that party:

(A) That party was not provided a fair and reasonable disclosure of the property or financial obligations of the other party.

(B) That party did not voluntarily and expressly waive, in writing, any right to disclosure of the property or financial obligations of the other party beyond the disclosure provided.

(C) That party did not have, or reasonably could not have had, an adequate knowledge of the property or financial obligations of the other party.

(b) An issue of unconscionability of a premarital agreement shall be decided by the court as a matter of law.

(Stats.1992, c. 162 (A.B.2650), § 10, operative Jan. 1, 1994.)

§ 1616. Void marriage, effect on agreement

If a marriage is determined to be void, an agreement that would otherwise have been a premarital agreement is enforceable only to the extent necessary to avoid an inequitable result.

(Stats.1992, c. 162 (A.B.2650), § 10, operative Jan. 1, 1994.)

§ 1617. Limitations of actions; equitable defenses including laches and estoppel

Any statute of limitations applicable to an action asserting a claim for relief under a premarital agreement is tolled during the marriage of the parties to the agreement. However, equitable defenses limiting the time for enforcement, including laches and estoppel, are available to either party.

(Stats.1992, c. 162 (A.B.2650), § 10, operative Jan. 1, 1994.)

§ 1620. Contracts altering legal relations of spouses; restrictions

Except as otherwise provided by law, a husband and wife cannot, by a contract with each other, alter their legal relations, except as to property.

(Stats.1992, c. 162 (A.B.2650), § 10, operative Jan. 1, 1994.)

A. Policy Considerations

IN RE MARRIAGE OF NOGHREY

California District Court of Appeal, 1985.
169 Cal.App.3d 326, 215 Cal.Rptr. 153.

FOLEY, ASSOCIATE JUSTICE.

Kambiz Noghrey appeals from a decision finding valid a premarital agreement. We reverse.

BACKGROUND

Kambiz and Farima were married for seven and one-half months when Farima filed for divorce. Her petition alleged the existence of an antenuptual agreement setting forth the property rights of the parties. The issue of the existence and validity of the agreement was bifurcated from the dissolution proceeding and heard first.

Frances and Charles Kandel had known Farima for several years prior to her marriage. Farima lived with the Kandels for the two years preceding the wedding.

Mrs. Kandel testified that when she and her family arrived for the Noghrey wedding Farima and Kambiz were not yet present, nor were Farima's parents. As she entered the hotel where the wedding was to take place, Mrs. Kandel was met by Kambiz' brother, Jamshid, who asked Mrs. Kandel and her husband to step aside. He handed Mrs. Kandel a piece of paper and pen and then began, with Kambiz' cousin, dictating terms of a premarital agreement.

Mrs. Kandel remembered writing "I, Kambiz Noghrey, agree to settle on Farima Human, the house * * * [i]n Sunnyvale, * * * [a]nd $500,000.00 or one-half of my assets, whichever is greater, in the event of a divorce." The agreement was written on the reverse side of the ceremonial wedding certificate which Mrs. Kandel believes was given to the rabbi.[1]

Mrs. Kandel then brought the completed document to Kambiz for his signature. Kambiz indicated he knew what the document was and that he wanted to sign the agreement. Mrs. Kandel testified she cautioned Kambiz to be very careful and to read the document because he would be giving his wife half of every thing he had. She inquired whether Kambiz wanted to sign the document. According to Mrs. Kandel, Kambiz indicated he would gladly give the property to his bride-to-be and he appeared serious when making the statement. Kambiz and Farima then signed the document, with Mr. Kandel and Kambiz' cousin signing as witnesses.

Farima testified that she signed the document because a husband has to give some protection to a new wife in case of divorce. She explained that it is hard for an Iranian woman to remarry after a divorce because she is no longer a virgin. In return for the premarital agreement, Farima gave Kambiz assurances that she was a virgin and was medically examined for that purpose.

Kambiz testified that he did not wish to sign the agreement but was coerced into doing so by Farima's mother. Kambiz claimed he told Mrs. Human he did not want to sign the agreement but she forced him into doing so by stating there would be no wedding if he did not sign. Kambiz' brother, Jamshid also testified that Farima's mother coerced Kambiz into signing the agreement. Jamshid testified he did not dictate terms to Mrs. Kandel and she was told by Farima's parents what to put into the agreement prior to the wedding date. Kambiz testified he believed Farima's mother or father told Mrs. Kandel what to put into the agreement. However, Jamshid admitted he did not observe Mr. or Mrs. Human giving instructions or dictating terms to Mrs. Kandel at the wedding and Mrs. Kandel testified she did not discuss the terms of the agreement with the bride's mother.

---

1. Kambiz and his brother testified that the document was given to Farima's father. In any event, the document could not be found for trial.

DISCUSSION

Of the many issues raised by Kambiz in this appeal, we find the first dispositive. We are in accord with his view that the antenuptial agreement on which this case centers encourages and promotes divorce. It is hence contrary to the public policy of this state and unenforceable.

As previously noted, the issues of the agreement's existence and validity were bifurcated from the remaining issues in the case and tried separately. Following trial of these issues the trial court filed the following Memorandum of Decision: "It is the opinion of the Court that the petitioner and respondent entered into a written antenuptial agreement, also known as 'Katuba' [sic], prior to their marriage.[2] The terms of the agreement were as follows: 'I, Kambiz Noghrey, agree to settle on Farima Human the house in Sunnyvale and $500,000 or one-half my assets, whichever is greater, in the event of a divorce. The said agreement should be found to be a valid, binding, and enforceable agreement.'"

An antenuptial agreement, the terms of which encourage or promote divorce, is against public policy and is unenforceable. This state's highest court has stated the matter thusly: "Contracts which facilitate divorce or separation by providing for a settlement only in the event of such an occurrence are void as against public policy. [Citations.]" (*In re Marriage of Higgason* (1973) 10 Cal.3d 476, 485, 110 Cal.Rptr. 897, 516 P.2d 289.)

* * *

We wish it understood that not all antenuptial agreements violate public policy. Such agreements by which the parties provide for their property rights are not *ipso facto,* illegal and void. Antenuptial agreements dealing with property owned prior to marriage and property and earnings accumulated subsequent to marriage are generally valid. (*In re Marriage of Dawley* (1976) 17 Cal.3d 342, 351, 131 Cal.Rptr. 3, 551 P.2d 323.) *Dawley,* nevertheless, reaffirmed the rule that such contracts are offensive to the public policy of this state if the "terms of the contract 'facilitate,' 'encourage,' or 'promote' divorce or dissolution. (*Id.,* at p. 350, 131 Cal.Rptr. 3, 551 P.2d 323.) The court further pointed out that the term "facilitate" should not be misconstrued so as to render illegal agreements that merely define the property rights of spouses, thereby

2. The *kethuba* is a marriage document which represents the obligation of the husband under the Jewish faith to, inter alia, provide for his wife upon divorcing her. Since the husband could apparently divorce his wife at will, the *kethuba* was a device created to provide economic security for the wife; but was also intended to discourage divorce by making it costly and undesirable for the husband. The wife, on the other hand, was not as free to divorce and was subject to loss or reduction of her rights should she divorce her husband on certain grounds. ("Kethuba" by Rachel Bernstein Wischnitzer, *The Universal Jewish Encyclopedia* (1942) Vol. 6, pp. 367–372.)

Although the very roots of the *kethuba* are embedded in religious doctrine, we do not reach the issue of whether a civil court, applying neutral principles of law, could interpret and construe such a document and resolve the property issues in question without running afoul of the Establishment clauses of the federal and state constitutions.

simplifying the issues and reducing the costs of a dissolution proceeding. "[P]ublic policy does not render property agreements unenforceable merely because such agreements simplify the division of marital property; it is only when the agreement encourages or promotes dissolution that it offends the public policy to foster and protect marriage." (*Id.,* at p. 350, fn. 5, 131 Cal.Rptr. 3, 551 P.2d 323.)

The agreement before us, however, is not of the type that seeks to define the character of property acquired after marriage nor does it seek to ensure the separate character of property acquired prior to marriage. This agreement is surely different and speaks to a wholly unrelated subject. It constitutes a promise by the husband to give the wife a very substantial amount of money and property, *but only upon the occurrence of a divorce.* No one could reasonably contend this agreement encourages the husband to seek a dissolution. Common sense and fiscal prudence dictate the opposite. Such is not the case with the wife. She, for her part, is encouraged by the very terms of the agreement to seek a dissolution, and with all deliberate speed, lest the husband suffer an untimely demise, nullifying the contract, and the wife's right to the money and property.

* * *

In this case, the primary focus at trial was on the existence *vel non* of the agreement with Kambiz contending he had been coerced into signing it just moments prior to the ceremony and Farima disputing this with a version that had Kambiz volunteering the document immediately before the ceremony as a token of his honor and good intentions. In all fairness to the trial court we note the existence issue overshadowed the issues of validity and public policy with the result that little evidence was introduced relative to the latter.[4] Farima did testify that neither she nor her parents possessed great wealth. The prospect of receiving a house and a minimum of $500,000 by obtaining the no-fault divorce available in California would menace the marriage of the best intentioned spouse.

DISPOSITION

The judgment of the trial court is reversed.

PANELLI, P.J., and AGLIANO, J., concur.

BORELLI v. BRUSSEAU

Court of Appeals, First District, 1993.
12 Cal.App.4th 647, 16 Cal.Rptr.2d 16.

PERLEY, ASSOCIATE JUSTICE.

Plaintiff and appellant Hildegard L. Borelli (appellant) appeals from a judgment of dismissal after a demurrer was sustained without leave to

---

4. In further deference to the trial court we note substantial evidence supports the court's finding as to the existence and content of the agreement, and, the lack of any coercion, duress or fraud in its derivation. It should also be noted that neither Appellant's present trial counsel, nor counsel who represented him on appeal, were involved at the trial of this matter.

amend to her complaint against defendant and respondent Grace G. Brusseau, as executor of the estate of Michael J. Borelli (respondent). The complaint sought specific performance of a promise by appellant's deceased husband Michael J. Borelli (decedent) to transfer certain property to her in return for her promise to care for him at home after he had suffered a stroke.

Appellant contends that the trial court erred by sustaining the demurrer on the grounds that the "alleged agreement [appellant] seeks to enforce is without consideration and the alleged contract is void as against public policy." We conclude that the contention lacks merit.

F<small>ACTS</small>

The only "facts" we can consider on this appeal from the sustaining of a demurrer are those "material facts properly pleaded, but not contentions, deductions or conclusions of fact or law." (*Blank v. Kirwan* (1985) 39 Cal.3d 311, 318, 216 Cal.Rptr. 718, 703 P.2d 58.) Since both parties' briefs wander far from the allegations of the complaint we will set out those allegations in some detail.

On April 24, 1980, appellant and decedent entered into an antenuptial contract. On April 25, 1980, they were married. Appellant remained married to decedent until the death of the latter on January 25, 1989.

In March 1983, February 1984, and January 1987, decedent was admitted to a hospital due to heart problems. As a result, "decedent became concerned and frightened about his health and longevity." He discussed these fears and concerns with appellant and told her that he intended to "leave" the following property to her.

1. "An interest" in a lot in Sacramento, California.

2. A life estate for the use of a condominium in Hawaii.

3. A 25 percent interest in Borelli Meat Co.

4. All cash remaining in all existing bank accounts at the time of his death.

5. The costs of educating decedent's step-daughter, Monique Lee.

6. Decedent's entire interest in a residence in Kensington, California.

7. All furniture located in the residence.

8. Decedent's interest in a partnership.

9. Health insurance for appellant and Monique Lee.

In August 1988, decedent suffered a stroke while in the hospital. "Throughout the decedent's August, 1988 hospital stay and subsequent treatment at a rehabilitation center, he repeatedly told [appellant] that he was uncomfortable in the hospital and that he disliked being away from home. The decedent repeatedly told [appellant] that he did not want to be admitted to a nursing home, even though it meant he would need round-the-clock care, and rehabilitative modifications to the house, in order for him to live at home."

"In or about October, 1988, [appellant] and the decedent entered an oral agreement whereby the decedent promised to leave to [appellant] the property listed [above], including a one hundred percent interest in the Sacramento property.... In exchange for the decedent's promise to leave her the property ... [appellant] agreed to care for the decedent in his home, for the duration of his illness, thereby avoiding the need for him to move to a rest home or convalescent hospital as his doctors recommended. The agreement was based on the confidential relationship that existed between [appellant] and the decedent."

Appellant performed her promise but the decedent did not perform his. Instead his will bequeathed her the sum of $100,000 and his interest in the residence they owned as joint tenants. The bulk of decedent's estate passed to respondent, who is decedent's daughter.

DISCUSSION

"It is fundamental that a marriage contract differs from other contractual relations in that there exists a definite and vital public interest in reference to the marriage relation. The 'paramount interests of the community at large,' quoting from the *Phillips* case *supra,* is a matter of primary concern." (*Hendricks v. Hendricks* (1954) 125 Cal. App.2d 239, 242, 270 P.2d 80.)

"The laws relating to marriage and divorce (Civ.Code, §§ 55–181) have been enacted because of the profound concern of our organized society for the dignity and stability of the marriage relationship. This concern relates primarily to the status of the parties as husband and wife. The concern of society as to the property rights of the parties is secondary and incidental to its concern as to their status." (*Sapp v. Superior Court* (1953) 119 Cal.App.2d 645, 650, 260 P.2d 119.)

"Marriage is a matter of public concern. The public, through the state, has interest in both its formation and dissolution.... The regulation of marriage and divorce is solely within the province of the Legislature except as the same might be restricted by the Constitution." (*Haas v. Haas* (1964) 227 Cal.App.2d 615, 617, 38 Cal.Rptr. 811.)

In accordance with these concerns the following pertinent legislation has been enacted: Civil Code section 242—"Every individual shall support his or her spouse...." Civil Code section 4802—"[A] husband and wife cannot, by any contract with each other, alter their legal relations, except as to property...." Civil Code section 5100—"Husband and Wife contract toward each other obligations of mutual respect, fidelity, and support." Civil Code section 5103—"[E]ither husband or wife may enter into any transaction with the other ... respecting property, which either might if unmarried." Civil Code section 5132—

"[A] married person shall support the person's spouse while they are living together...." *

The courts have stringently enforced and explained the statutory language. "Although most of the cases, both in California and elsewhere, deal with a wife's right to support from the husband, in this state a wife also has certain obligations to support the husband." (*In re Marriage of Higgason* (1973) 10 Cal.3d 476, 487, 110 Cal.Rptr. 897, 516 P.2d 289, disapproved on other grounds in *In re Marriage of Dawley* (1976) 17 Cal.3d 342, 352, 131 Cal.Rptr. 3, 551 P.2d 323.)

"Indeed, husband and wife assume mutual obligations of support upon marriage. These obligations are not conditioned on the existence of community property or income." (*See v. See* (1966) 64 Cal.2d 778, 784, 51 Cal.Rptr. 888, 415 P.2d 776.) "In entering the marital state, by which a contract is created, it must be assumed that the parties voluntarily entered therein with knowledge that they have the moral and legal obligation to support the other." (*Department of Mental Hygiene v. Kolts* (1966) 247 Cal.App.2d 154, 165, 55 Cal.Rptr. 437.)

Moreover, inter-spousal mutual obligations have been broadly defined. "[Husband's] duties and obligations to [wife] included more than mere cohabitation with her. It was his duty to offer [wife] his sympathy, confidence [citation], and fidelity." (*In re Marriage of Rabie* (1974) 40 Cal.App.3d 917, 922, 115 Cal.Rptr. 594.) When necessary, spouses must "provide uncompensated protective supervision services for" each other. (*Miller v. Woods* (1983) 148 Cal.App.3d 862, 877, 196 Cal.Rptr. 69.)

Estate of Sonnicksen (1937) 23 Cal.App.2d 475, 479, 73 P.2d 643, and *Brooks v. Brooks* (1941) 48 Cal.App.2d 347, 349–350, 119 P.2d 970, each hold that under the above statutes and in accordance with the above policy a wife is obligated by the marriage contract to provide nursing type care to an ill husband. Therefore, contracts whereby the wife is to receive compensation for providing such services are void as against public policy and there is no consideration for the husband's promise.

Appellant argues that *Sonnicksen* and *Brooks* are no longer valid precedents because they are based on outdated views of the role of women and marriage. She further argues that the rule of those cases denies her equal protection because husbands only have a financial obligation toward their wives, while wives have to provide actual nursing services for free. We disagree. The rule and policy of *Sonnicksen* and *Brooks* have been applied to both spouses in several recent cases arising in different areas of the law.

Webster's New Collegiate Dictionary (1981) p. 240, defines consortium as "The legal right of one spouse to the company, affection, and service of the other." Only married persons are allowed to recover

* [Author's note: now see California Family Code Sections 1620, 720, 721, 4300, 4301.]

damages for loss of consortium. (*Elden v. Sheldon* (1988) 46 Cal.3d 267, 277, 250 Cal.Rptr. 254, 758 P.2d 582.)

Rodriguez v. Bethlehem Steel Corp. (1974) 12 Cal.3d 382, 115 Cal.Rptr. 765, 525 P.2d 669, held that a wife could recover consortium damages. The Supreme Court's reasoning was as follows. "But there is far more to the marriage relationship than financial support. 'The concept of consortium includes not only loss of support or services, it also embraces such elements as love, companionship, affection, society, sexual relations, solace and more.' [Citation.] As to each, 'the interest sought to be protected is personal to the wife' (*ibid*)...." (*Rodriguez v. Bethlehem Steel Corp., supra,* at pp. 404–405, 115 Cal.Rptr. 765, 525 P.2d 669.) "The deprivation of a husband's physical assistance in operating and maintaining the family home is a compensable item of loss of consortium." (*Id.* at p. 409, fn. 31, 115 Cal.Rptr. 765, 525 P.2d 669.)

In *Krouse v. Graham* (1977) 19 Cal.3d 59, 66–67, 137 Cal.Rptr. 863, 562 P.2d 1022, an action for the wrongful death of the wife, the husband was allowed to recover consortium damages "for the loss of his wife's 'love, companionship, comfort, affection, society, solace or moral support, any loss of enjoyment of sexual relations, or any loss of her physical assistance in the operation or maintenance of the home.' " The wife "had recently retired as a legal secretary in order to care for her husband, Benjamin, whose condition of emphysema, in turn, caused him to retire and necessitated considerable nursing services."

The principal holding of *Watkins v. Watkins* (1983) 143 Cal.App.3d 651, 192 Cal.Rptr. 54, was that a marriage did not extinguish a woman's right to recover the value of her homemaker services rendered prior to the marriage. Much of the opinion is devoted to a discussion of *Sonnicksen* and *Brooks*. Those cases are approved by the court but not expanded to cover the period before marriage. (*Id.* at pp. 654–655, 192 Cal.Rptr. 54.)

Vincent v. State of California (1971) 22 Cal.App.3d 566, 99 Cal.Rptr. 410, held that for purposes of benefit payments spouses caring for each other must be treated identically under similar assistance programs. In reaching such conclusion the court held: "Appellants suggest that one reason justifying denial of payment for services rendered by ATD attendants who reside with their recipient spouses is that, by virtue of the marriage contract, one spouse is obligated to care for the other without remuneration. (Civ.Code, § 5100; *Estate of Sonnicksen* (1937) 23 Cal. App.2d 475, 479, 73 P.2d 643.) Such pre-existing duty provides a constitutionally sound basis for a classification which denies compensation for care rendered by a husband or wife to his spouse who is receiving welfare assistance. [Citations.] ... [¶] ... But insofar as one spouse has a duty created by the marriage contract to care for the other without compensation when they are living together, recipients of aid to the aged, aid to the blind and aid to the disabled are similarly situated." (*Vincent v. State of California, supra,* 22 Cal.App.3d at p. 572, 99 Cal.Rptr. 410.)

These cases indicate that the marital duty of support under Civil Code sections 242, 5100, and 5132 includes caring for a spouse who is ill. They also establish that support in a marriage means more than the physical care someone could be hired to provide. Such support also encompasses sympathy (*In re Marriage of Rabie, supra,* 40 Cal.App.3d at p. 922, 115 Cal.Rptr. 594) comfort (*Krouse v. Graham, supra,* 19 Cal.3d at pp. 66–67, 137 Cal.Rptr. 863, 562 P.2d 1022) love, companionship and affection (*Rodriguez v. Bethlehem Steel Corp., supra,* 12 Cal.3d at pp. 404–405, 115 Cal.Rptr. 765, 525 P.2d 669). Thus, the duty of support can no more be "delegated" to a third party than the statutory duties of fidelity and mutual respect (Civ.Code, § 5100). Marital duties are owed by the spouses personally. This is implicit in the definition of marriage as "a personal relation arising out of a civil contract between a man and a woman." (Civ.Code, § 4100.)

We therefore adhere to the longstanding rule that a spouse is not entitled to compensation for support, apart from rights to community property and the like that arise from the marital relation itself. Personal performance of a personal duty created by the contract of marriage does not constitute a new consideration supporting the indebtedness alleged in this case.

We agree with the dissent that no rule of law becomes sacrosanct by virtue of its duration, but we are not persuaded that the well-established rule that governs this case deserves to be discarded. If the rule denying compensation for support originated from considerations peculiar to women, this has no bearing on the rule's gender-neutral application today. There is as much potential for fraud today as ever, and allegations like appellant's could be made every time any personal care is rendered. This concern may not entirely justify the rule, but it cannot be said that all rationales for the rule are outdated.

Speculating that appellant might have left her husband but for the agreement she alleges, the dissent suggests that marriages will break up if such agreements are not enforced. While we do not believe that marriages would be fostered by a rule that encouraged sickbed bargaining, the question is not whether such negotiations may be more useful than unseemly. The issue is whether such negotiations are antithetical to the institution of marriage as the Legislature has defined it. We believe that they are.

The dissent maintains that mores have changed to the point that spouses can be treated just like any other parties haggling at arm's length. Whether or not the modern marriage has become like a business, and regardless of whatever else it may have become, it continues to be defined by statute as a personal relationship of mutual support. Thus, even if few things are left that cannot command a price, marital support remains one of them.

Disposition

The judgment is affirmed. Costs to respondents.

ANDERSON, P.J., concurs.

POCHÉ, ASSOCIATE JUSTICE, dissenting.

A very ill person wishes to be cared for at home personally by his spouse rather than by nurses at a health care facility. The ill person offers to pay his spouse for such personal care by transferring property to her. The offer is accepted, the services are rendered and the ill spouse dies. Affirming a judgment of dismissal rendered after a general demurrer was sustained, this court holds that the contract was not enforceable because—as a matter of law—the spouse who rendered services gave no consideration. Apparently, in the majority's view she had a pre-existing or pre-contract nondelegable duty to clean the bed pans herself. Because I do not believe she did, I respectfully dissent.

The majority correctly read *Estate of Sonnicksen* (1937) 23 Cal. App.2d 475, 73 P.2d 643 and *Brooks v. Brooks* (1941) 48 Cal.App.2d 347, 119 P.2d 970 as holding that a wife cannot enter into a binding contract with her husband to provide "nursing type care" for compensation. (Majority opn., *ante,* p. 19.) It reasons that the wife, by reason of the marital relationship, already has a duty to provide such care, thus she offers no new consideration to support an independent contract to the same effect. (See Civ.Code, §§ 1550, 1605.) The logic of these decisions is ripe for reexamination.

Sonnicksen and *Brooks* are the California Court of Appeal versions of a national theme. (See, e.g., *Bohanan v. Maxwell* (1921) 190 Iowa 1308, 181 N.W. 683; *Foxworthy v. Adams* (1910) 136 Ky. 403, 124 S.W. 381; *Martinez v. Martinez* (1957) 62 N.M. 215, 307 P.2d 1117; *Ritchie v. White* (1945) 225 N.C. 450, 35 S.E.2d 414; *Oates v. Oates* (1945) 127 W.Va. 469, 33 S.E.2d 457.) Excerpts from several of these decisions reveal the ethos and mores of the era which produced them.

" 'It would operate disastrously upon domestic life and breed discord and mischief if the wife could contract with her husband for the payment of services to be rendered for him in his home; if she could exact compensation for services, disagreeable or otherwise, rendered to members of his family; if she could sue him upon such contracts and establish them upon the disputed and conflicting testimony of the members of the household. To allow such contracts would degrade the wife by making her a menial and a servant in the home where she should discharge marital duties in loving and devoted ministrations, and frauds upon creditors would be greatly facilitated, as the wife could frequently absorb all her husband's property in the payment of her services, rendered under such secret, unknown contracts.' " (*Brooks v. Brooks, supra,* 48 Cal.App.2d 347 at p. 350, 119 P.2d 970 [quoting *Coleman v. Burr* (1883) 93 N.Y. 17, 25]; accord, *Bohanan v. Maxwell, supra,* 181 N.W. 683 at p. 687.)

"A man cannot be entitled to the services of his wife for nothing, by virtue of a uniform and unchangeable marriage contract, and at the same time be under obligation to pay her for those services.... She cannot be his wife and his hired servant at the same time.... That would be inconsistent with the marriage relation, and disturb the reciprocal duties of the parties." (*In re Callister's Estate* (1897) 153 N.Y. 294, 47 N.E. 268, 270.)

"[I]t is not within the power of husband and wife to contract with each other for the payment for such services.... It is the duty of husband and wife to attend, nurse, and care for each other when either is unable to care for himself. It would be contrary to public policy to permit either to make an enforceable contract with the other to perform such services as are ordinarily imposed upon them by the marital relations, and which should be the natural prompting of that love and affection which should always exist between husband and wife." (*Foxworthy v. Adams, supra,* 124 S.W. 381 at p. 383.)

Statements in two of these cases to the effect that a husband has an entitlement to his wife's "services" (e.g., *In re Callister's Estate, supra,* 47 N.E. 268 at pp. 269–270; *Ritchie v. White, supra,* 35 S.E.2d 414 at pp. 416–417) smack of the common law doctrine of coverture which treated a wife as scarcely more than an appendage to her husband. According to the United States Supreme Court, "At the common law the husband and wife were regarded as one. The legal existence of the wife during coverture was merged in that of the husband, and, generally speaking, the wife was incapable of making contracts, of acquiring property or disposing of the same without her husband's consent. They could not enter into contracts with each other, nor were they liable for torts committed by one against the other." (*Thompson v. Thompson* (1910) 218 U.S. 611, 614–615, 31 S.Ct. 111, 111, 54 L.Ed. 1180; see 1 Blackstone's Commentaries 442; 2 Blackstone's Commentaries 433.) The same court subsequently denounced coverture as "peculiar and obsolete" (*United States v. Yazell* (1966) 382 U.S. 341, 351, 86 S.Ct. 500, 506, 15 L.Ed.2d 404), "a completely discredited ... archaic remnant of a primitive caste system" (*id.* at p. 361, 86 S.Ct. at 511 (dis. opn. of Black, J.)) founded upon "medieval views" which are at present "offensive to the ethos of our society." (*United States v. Dege* (1960) 364 U.S. 51, 52–53, 80 S.Ct. 1589, 1591, 4 L.Ed.2d 1563.) One of the characteristics of coverture was that it deemed the wife economically helpless and governed by an implicit exchange: " 'The husband, as head of the family, is charged with its support and maintenance, in return for which he is entitled to the wife's services in all those domestic affairs which pertain to the comfort, care, and well-being of the family. Her labors are her contribution to the family support and care.' " (*Ritchie v. White, supra,* at pp. 416–417 [citation omitted].) But coverture has been discarded in California (see 11 Witkin, Summary of Cal.Law (9th ed. 1990) Husband and Wife, § 1, p. 13), where both husband and wife owe each other the duty of support. (Civ.Code, §§ 242, 5100, 5132.)

Not only has this doctrinal base for the authority underpinning the majority opinion been discarded long ago, but modern attitudes toward marriage have changed almost as rapidly as the economic realities of modern society. The assumption that only the rare wife can make a financial contribution to her family has become badly outdated in this age in which many married women have paying employment outside the home. A two-income family can no longer be dismissed as a statistically insignificant aberration. Moreover today husbands are increasingly involved in the domestic chores that make a house a home. Insofar as marital duties and property rights are not governed by positive law, they may be the result of informal accommodation or formal agreement. (See Civ.Code, § 5200 et seq.) If spouses cannot work things out, there is always the no longer infrequently used option of divorce. For better or worse, we have to a great extent left behind the comfortable and familiar gender-based roles evoked by Norman Rockwell paintings. No longer can the marital relationship be regarded as "uniform and unchangeable." (*In re Callister's Estate, supra,* 47 N.E. 268 at p. 270.)

It is true that public policy seeks to foster and protect that institution (*Glickman v. Collins* (1975) 13 Cal.3d 852, 857, 120 Cal.Rptr. 76, 533 P.2d 204) in recognition that the structure of society itself depends in large part upon the institution of marriage (*Marvin v. Marvin* (1976) 18 Cal.3d 660, 684, 134 Cal.Rptr. 815, 557 P.2d 106). Yet the recognition that marriage is "intimate to the degree of being sacred" (*Griswold v. Connecticut* (1965) 381 U.S. 479, 486, 85 S.Ct. 1678, ___, 14 L.Ed.2d 510) does not mean that the law is oblivious to what occurs within that relationship. Solicitude for domestic harmony is no longer synonymous with blindness to crimes spouses commit against each other (see *People v. Pierce* (1964) 61 Cal.2d 879, 40 Cal.Rptr. 845, 395 P.2d 893), even when those crimes involve the previously sacrosanct realm of sexual relations. (See Pen.Code, § 262.) Similarly, civil actions are allowed for intentional or negligent torts committed by one spouse against the other. (See Civ.Code, § 5113; *Klein v. Klein* (1962) 58 Cal.2d 692, 26 Cal.Rptr. 102, 376 P.2d 70; *Self v. Self* (1962) 58 Cal.2d 683, 26 Cal.Rptr. 97, 376 P.2d 65.)[1] The same is true for breached contracts. (See *Wilson v. Wilson* (1868) 36 Cal. 447; *In re Marriage of McNeill* (1984) 160 Cal.App.3d 548, 206 Cal.Rptr. 641.) Thus, when the simple justice of redressing obvious wrongs is involved, the arguments for domestic harmony have been rejected and are now in full retreat, not only in California (see *Gibson v. Gibson, supra,* 3 Cal.3d 914 at pp. 917–920, 92 Cal.Rptr. 288, 479 P.2d 648 and authorities cited), but throughout the entire nation. (See, e.g., Harper, James & Gray, The Law of Torts (2d ed. 1986) §§ 8.10–8.11, pp. 562–569, 573–578; Prosser & Keeton on Torts (5th ed. 1984) § 122, pp. 902–906; Rest.2d Torts, § 895F, com. f.)

Restraints on interspousal litigation are almost extinct. With the walls supposedly protecting the domestic haven from litigation already reduced to rubble, it hardly seems revolutionary to topple one more brick. Furthermore, in situations such as this, where one spouse has died, preserving " 'domestic life [from] discord and mischief' " (*Brooks v. Brooks, supra,* 48 Cal.App.2d 347 at p. 350, 119 P.2d 970) seems an academic concern that no modern academic seems concerned with.

1. A related development was the abolition of the comparable immunity granted parents from such suits by their children. (See *Gibson v. Gibson* (1971) 3 Cal.3d 914, 92 Cal.Rptr. 288, 479 P.2d 648; *Emery v. Emery* (1955) 45 Cal.2d 421, 289 P.2d 218.)

Fear that a contract struck between spouses "degrades" the spouse providing service, making him or her no better than a "hired servant" justifies the result in several cases. (E.g., *Brooks v. Brooks, supra,* 48 Cal.App.2d 347 at p. 350, 119 P.2d 970; *In re Callister's Estate, supra,* 47 N.E. 268 at p. 270.) Such fears did not prevent California from enacting a statute specifying that "either husband or wife may enter into any transaction with the other, or with any other person, respecting property, which either might if unmarried." (Civ.Code, §§ 5103, subd. (a), 4802.) This is but one instance of "the utmost freedom of contract [that] exists in California between husband and wife...." (*Perkins v. Sunset Tel. and Tel. Co.* (1909) 155 Cal. 712, 720, 103 P. 190.)

Reduced to its essence, the alleged contract at issue here was an agreement to transmute Mr. Borelli's separate property into the separate property of his wife.[2] Had there been no marriage and had they been total strangers, there is no doubt Mr. Borelli could have validly contracted to receive her services in exchange for certain of his property. The mere existence of a marriage certificate should not deprive competent adults of the "utmost freedom of contract" they would otherwise possess.

Then there is the concern about "frauds upon creditors." (E.g., *Brooks v. Brooks, supra,* 48 Cal.App.2d 347 at p. 350, 119 P.2d 970.) Our Supreme Court has repeatedly rejected the notion that the mere possibility of interspousal fraud or collusion at the expense of third parties bars an entire category of interspousal litigation. Instead, the truth finding role of the judiciary has been deemed adequate to deal with the problem in individual cases. In other words, whether or not a contract was induced by fraud is decided not by demurrer, but by human beings called jurors after they hear evidence. (See *Klein v. Klein, supra,* 58 Cal.2d 692 at pp. 694–696, 26 Cal.Rptr. 102, 376 P.2d 70; *Emery v. Emery, supra,* 45 Cal.2d 421 at pp. 431–432, 289 P.2d 218; see also *Hoeck v. Greif* (1904) 142 Cal. 119, 75 P. 670.) This modern approach completely undercuts one more of the doctrinal underpinnings of *Sonnicksen* and *Brooks* and is obviously applicable here. Since this shift in the law occurred after those cases were decided, it is one more reason to reconsider them and to reject their contemporary force. As Justice Holmes put it: "It is revolting to have no better reason for a rule of law than that so it was laid down in the time of Henry IV. It is still more revolting if the grounds upon which it was laid down have vanished long

---

2. Plaintiff makes reference in her complaint to a "1980 written antenuptial contract" that she alleges she "signed ... one day before her wedding." Although the record does not include a copy of this contract, it seems obvious from the context of this litigation that its general import was to segregate and preserve substantial assets as to Mr. Borelli's separate property.

The possibility that the agreement is ineffective to transmute the character of Mr.

Borelli's property because of noncompliance with various statute of frauds provisions (see Civ.Code, §§ 1624, 5110.730; Code Civ. Proc., §§ 1971–1972) need not be addressed here in light of plaintiff's allegation that defendants are estopped to claim the benefit of these provisions. (See 5 Witkin, Cal.Procedure (3d ed. 1985) Pleading, § 735, p. 182.)

since, and the rule simply persists from blind imitation of the past." (Justice Oliver Wendell Holmes, Collected Legal Papers (1920) p. 187.)

No one doubts that spouses owe each other a duty of support or that this encompasses "the obligation to provide medical care." (*Hawkins v. Superior Court* (1979) 89 Cal.App.3d 413, 418–419, 152 Cal.Rptr. 491.) There is nothing found in *Sonnicksen* and *Brooks,* or cited by the majority, which requires that this obligation be *personally* discharged by a spouse except the decisions themselves. However, at the time *Sonnicksen* and *Brooks* were decided—before World War II—it made sense for those courts to say that a wife could perform her duty of care only by doing so personally. That was an accurate reflection of the real world for women years before the exigency of war produced substantial employment opportunities for them. For most women at that time there was no other way to take care of a sick husband except personally. So to the extent those decisions hold that a contract to pay a wife for caring personally for her husband is without consideration they are correct only because at the time they were decided there were no other ways she could meet her obligation of care. Since that was the universal reality, she was giving up nothing of value by agreeing to perform a duty that had one and only one way of being performed.

However the real world has changed in the fifty-six years since *Sonnicksen* was decided. Just a few years later with the advent of World War II *Rosie the Riveter* became not only a war jingle but a salute to hundreds of thousands of women working on the war effort outside the home. We know what happened thereafter. Presumably in the present day husbands and wives who work outside the home have alternative methods of meeting this duty of care to an ill spouse. Among the choices would be: (1) paying for professional help; (2) paying for non professional assistance; (3) seeking help from relatives or friends; and (4) quitting one's job and doing the work personally.

A fair reading of the complaint indicates that Mrs. Borelli initially chose the first of these options, and that this was not acceptable to Mr. Borelli, who then offered compensation if Mrs. Borelli would agree to personally care for him at home. To contend in 1993 that such a contract is without consideration means that if Mrs. Clinton becomes ill President Clinton must drop everything and personally care for her.

According to the majority, Mrs. Borelli had nothing to bargain with so long as she remained in the marriage. This assumes that an intrinsic component of the marital relationship is the *personal* services of the spouse, an obligation that cannot be delegated or performed by others. The preceding discussion has attempted to demonstrate many ways in which what the majority terms "nursing-type care" can be provided without either husband or wife being required to empty a single bedpan. It follows that, because Mrs. Borelli agreed to supply this personal involvement, she was providing something over and above what would fully satisfy her duty of support. That personal something—precisely because it was something she was not required to do—qualifies as valid consideration sufficient to make enforceable Mr. Borelli's reciprocal promise to convey certain of his separate property.

Not only does the majority's position substantially impinge upon couples' freedom to come to a working arrangement of marital responsibilities, it may also foster the very opposite result of that intended. For example, nothing compelled Mr. Borelli and plaintiff to continue living together after his physical afflictions became known. Moral considerations notwithstanding, no legal force could have stopped plaintiff from leaving her husband in his hour of need. Had she done so, and had Mr. Borelli promised to give her some of his separate property should she come back, a valid contract would have arisen upon her return. Deeming them contracts promoting reconciliation and the resumption of marital relations, California courts have long enforced such agreements as supported by consideration. (E.g., *Bowden v. Bowden* (1917) 175 Cal. 711, 167 P. 154; *Braden v. Braden* (1960) 178 Cal.App.2d 481, 3 Cal.Rptr. 120.) Here so far as we can tell from the face of the complaint, Mr. Borelli and plaintiff reached largely the same result without having to endure a separation.[3] There is no sound reason why their contract, which clearly facilitated continuation of their marriage, should be any less valid. It makes no sense to say that spouses have greater bargaining rights when separated than they do during an unruptured marriage.

What, then, justifies the ban on interspousal agreements of the type refused enforcement by *Sonnicksen, Brooks,* and the majority? At root it appears to be the undeniable allure of the thought that, for married persons, "to attend, nurse, and care for each other ... should be the natural prompting of that love and affection which should always exist between husband and wife." (*Foxworthy v. Adams, supra,* 124 S.W. 381 at p. 383.) All married persons would like to believe that their spouses would cleave unto them through thick and thin, in sickness and in health. Without question, there is something profoundly unsettling about an illness becoming the subject of interspousal negotiations conducted over a hospital sickbed. Yet sentiment cannot substitute for common sense and modern day reality. Interspousal litigation may be unseemly, but it is no longer a novelty. The majority preserves intact an anomalous rule which gives married persons less than the utmost freedom of contract they are supposed to possess. The majority's rule leaves married people with contracting powers which are more limited than those enjoyed by unmarried persons or than is justified by legitimate public policy. In this context public policy should not be equated with coerced altruism. Mr. Borelli was a grown man who, having amassed a sizeable amount of property, should be treated—at least on demurrer—as competent to make the agreement alleged by plaintiff. The public policy of California will not be outraged by affording plaintiff the opportunity to try to enforce that agreement.

3. Plaintiff's allegation in her complaint that she forewent the opportunity "to live an independent life in consideration of her agreement" with Mr. Borelli carries the clear implication that she would have separated from him but for the agreement.

B. Formalities

IN RE ESTATE OF MacDONALD

Supreme Court of California, 1990.
51 Cal.3d 262, 272 Cal.Rptr. 153, 794 P.2d 911.

PANELLI, JUSTICE.

Civil Code section 5110.730 [now Family Code section 852] provides: "A transmutation of real or personal property is not valid unless made in writing by an express declaration that is made, joined in, consented to, or accepted by the spouse whose interest in the property is adversely affected."

In this case we are asked to decide what type of writing is necessary to satisfy the statute's requirements. In our view, section 5110.730(a) must be construed to preclude reference to extrinsic evidence in the proof of transmutations. Accordingly, we conclude a writing is not an "express declaration" for the purposes of section 5110.730(a) unless it contains language which expressly states that a change in the characterization or ownership of the property is being made. Thus, we affirm the judgment of the Court of Appeal.

FACTS AND PROCEEDINGS BELOW

Decedent Margery M. MacDonald ("Margery" or "decedent") married respondent Robert MacDonald ("Robert") in 1973. Both had been married previously, and each had children by a previous spouse. Robert was president of R.F. MacDonald Company ("the company"), where he participated in a defined benefit pension plan.

In August 1984, Margery learned that she had terminal cancer, and she and Robert made plans to divide their property into separate estates. Wishing to leave her property to her own four children, Margery divided the couple's jointly held stock, sold her half, and placed the proceeds in her separate account. The MacDonalds thereafter consulted with their personal accountant and attorney regarding the division of their jointly held real property. These properties were appraised and divided; Robert paid Margery $33,000 to equalize the division.

Robert was covered by a company defined benefit pension plan which came into existence on January 1, 1977. The designated beneficiary of Robert's interest in the pension plan was a revocable living trust he had established in 1982. The terms of the trust left the bulk of the corpus to Robert's children. In November, 1984 Robert turned 65 and his defined pension plan was terminated. On March 21, 1985, Robert received a disbursement of $266,557.90 from the plan. It is undisputed that Margery possessed a community property interest in the plan's benefits.[1] The pension funds were not divided or otherwise accounted

---

1. The dissent erroneously states (post, at p. 166 of 272 Cal.Rptr., at p. 924 of 794 P.2d) that the pension funds "... were essentially the product of Robert's 35 years in business, most of which preceded his marriage to decedent...." Actually, as

for at the time of the couple's previous division of their jointly held assets. These community funds were deposited into IRA accounts at three separate financial institutions.

The IRA accounts were opened solely in Robert's name, the designated beneficiary of each being the revocable living trust which had been designated as beneficiary of the pension plan. The three form documents prepared by the financial institutions for signature by IRA account holders, each entitled "Adoption Agreement and Designation of Beneficiary" ("adoption agreements"), provided space for the signature of a spouse not designated as the sole primary beneficiary to indicate consent to the designation.[2] Robert signed the adoption agreements, indicating his agreement to the terms of the IRA account agreements and designating his trust as beneficiary; Margery signed the consent portions of the adoption agreements ("consent paragraphs").

Margery died on June 17, 1985, bequeathing the residue of her estate to her four children. Executrix Judith Bolton filed a petition to determine title to personal property (Prob.Code, § 851.5), seeking to establish decedent's community property interest in the funds held in the IRA accounts. The trial court found that, in signing the consent paragraphs of the adoption agreements, decedent intended to waive any community property interest in the pension funds and to transmute her community property share of those funds into Robert's separate property. The court denied Bolton's petition, ruling that decedent had either waived her community property interest in the pension funds or, alternatively, transmuted it to Robert's separate property.

The Court of Appeal reversed, holding that the adoption agreements did not satisfy section 5110.730(a). (The court also declined to apply the "terminable interest rule" to the pension funds. Robert's petition for review does not challenge the Court of Appeal's opinion in this regard.) A dissenting justice argued that because decedent, in signing the consent paragraphs, had taken "specific, clear and final [action to] accomplish both [a] transfer and a subsequent transmutation[, t]he language and purpose of the statutory requirement were fully satisfied."

We granted review to construe section 5110.730(a).

DISCUSSION

It is undisputed that Margery possessed a community property interest in Robert's pension funds at the time they were disbursed to

---

noted above, the pension fund did not even come into existence until 1977, more than three years *after* Robert married decedent. Thus all payments into the plan occurred during the marriage of the parties.

2. The adoption agreements are one page long. They provide space for the entry of "General Information" (where Robert entered his name, address, and other personal data), for "Designation of Beneficiary," for "Consent of Spouse," for "General Provisions" (relating to payout procedures upon the participant's death) and for "Adoption of Plan" (which Robert signed, agreeing to participate in the particular financial institutions' retirement account plans). The consent portions of the adoption agreements each provided in full: "If participant's spouse is not designated as the sole primary beneficiary, spouse must sign consent. Consent of Spouse: Being the participant's spouse, I hereby consent to the above designation."

him. However, in California, married persons may by agreement or transfer, with or without consideration, transmute community property to separate property of either spouse.[3]

In this case, the trial court made a *factual finding* that "[d]ecedent, in executing the Adoption Agreement[s] for the three IRA's, intended to waive any community right she had in those IRA's and in fact to transmute her share of that community property asset to the separate property of Respondent." However, we defer to a trial court's factual findings only when they are supported by substantial evidence. (*Crawford v. Southern Pacific Co.* (1935) 3 Cal.2d 427, 429, 45 P.2d 183.)

Our close review of the record reveals that no substantial evidence supported the finding that Margery intended a transmutation.[4] The Court of Appeal incorrectly stated that Robert presented his own testimony and that of decedent's accountant as to decedent's state of mind when she signed the adoption agreements. In fact, there is absolutely no record evidence relating to Margery's intentions or state of mind when she signed the adoption agreements. The only testimony presented as to her state of mind during her estate planning activities relates to when she and her husband arranged an equal division of their jointly held real properties. The couple's accountant testified that she did not assist them in the division of any other assets.

Even if the trial court's findings as to Margery's intent were supported by substantial evidence, however, they would not support a finding of transmutation in this case. The statute providing for transmutation by transfer is by its own terms "[s]ubject to Sections 5110.720 to 5110.740, inclusive" (Civ.Code, § 5110.710), including, obviously, section 5110.730(a). Section 5110.730(a) invalidates attempts to transmute real or personal property unless certain conditions are met. We must therefore determine whether Margery's actions, whether or not they were *intended* to transfer her interest in the pension funds, were effective under section 5110.730(a) to transmute those funds from com-

---

3. Civil Code section 5110.710 provides: "Subject to Sections 5110.720 to 5110.740, inclusive, married persons may by agreement or transfer, with or without consideration, do any of the following: (a) Transmute community property to separate property of either spouse. (b) Transmute separate property of either spouse to community property. (c) Transmute separate property of one spouse to separate property of the other spouse."

4. No substantial evidence supports several other "factual findings" which the trial court incorporated into its judgment. The record contains no substantial evidence that Margery was "aware of the financial decisions being made in [her husband's] business, particularly in terms of the pension plan itself." The plan was stipulated to

have been established in 1977, before Margery became active in her husband's business. (She was bookkeeper in the years 1978–1980.) The record does not support the conclusion she was aware of its terms; at best she knew of its existence. Nor is there any evidence that she was "aware of the terms of the Living Trust [established by Robert MacDonald and made by him the beneficiary of his pension plan when the plan was established, and later named by him beneficiary of the IRA accounts]." The living trust was established in 1982, when Margery was no longer bookkeeper for R.F. MacDonald Company. In short, the record discloses no evidence that Margery even knew she had a community property interest in the pension plan proceeds.

munity property to Robert's separate property. We are of the opinion that they were not.[5]

Section 5110.730(a) requires that a valid transmutation be made, not just in writing, but in "writing by an *express declaration* that is made, joined in, consented to, or accepted by the spouse whose interest in the property is adversely affected." (§ 5110.730(a) emphasis added.) There is no dispute that the consent paragraphs in the adoption agreements, and decedent's signatures thereon, are "made in writing." These writings are manifestly "made, joined in, consented to or accepted by the spouse whose interest in the property is adversely affected," viz., decedent. Thus, the sole remaining issue to be decided is whether they constitute "an express declaration" for the purposes of section 5110.-730(a).

It is a fundamental rule of statutory construction that a court "should ascertain the intent of the Legislature so as to effectuate the purpose of the law." (*Select Base Materials, Inc. v. Board of Equalization* (1959) 51 Cal.2d 640, 645, 335 P.2d 672.) In determining such intent "[t]he court turns first to the words themselves for the answer." (*People v. Knowles* (1950) 35 Cal.2d 175, 182, 217 P.2d 1.)

It is not immediately evident from a reading of section 5110.730(a) what is meant by the phrase "an express declaration." Examination of the words of the statute and their arrangement reveals only that the "express declaration" called for is to be one "by" which "[a] transmutation of real or personal property" is "made." The statute does not state what words such an "express declaration" must include, what information it must convey, or even what topics it should discuss.

Since the words of section 5110.730(a) themselves, including the phrase "an express declaration," are unclear and ambiguous, it is necessary to resort to other indicia of the intent of the Legislature to determine what meaning the statute should be given. (*Lungren v. Deukmejian* (1988) 45 Cal.3d 727, 735, 248 Cal.Rptr. 115, 755 P.2d 299; *In re Lance W.* (1985) 37 Cal.3d 873, 886, 210 Cal.Rptr. 631, 694 P.2d 744.) In doing so, we consider the historical circumstances of the statute's enactment, as well as its legislative history. (*California Mfrs. Assn. v. Public Utilities Comm.* (1979) 24 Cal.3d 836, 844, 157 Cal.Rptr. 676, 598 P.2d 836.)

Section 5110.730(a) was adopted in 1984. (Stats.1984, ch. 1733, § 3, p. 6302.) Both parties refer to a 1983 report of the California Law Revision Commission ("Commission") to ascertain the intent of the Legislature in enacting section 5110.730(a). In recommending that the

---

5. We decline to treat respondent's IRA accounts as decedent's will substitute, as urged by respondent. Respondent has argued that Civil Code section 5110.730 does not apply to testamentary dispositions and/or to dispositions made by will substitutes. He further alleges that the IRA consent forms signed by Margery were a will substitute. We disagree. The record contains no substantial evidence that Margery or Robert intended that the IRA accounts would be so regarded. Moreover, consideration of respondent's will substitute theory, advanced for the first time in this court, would be contrary to our established policy. (See Cal.Rules of Court, rule 29(b).)

Legislature enact that statute, the Commission described "[s]ection 5110.730 [as] impos[ing] formalities on interspousal transmutations for the purpose of increasing certainty in the determination whether a transmutation has in fact occurred." (Recommendation Relating to Marital Property Presumptions and Transmutations, 17 Cal.Law Revision Com.Rep. (1984) ("Commission report") pp. 224–225.) The Commission report goes on to state that section 5110.730 overrules existing case law that permitted oral transmutation of personal property. (Commission report, supra, at pp. 224–225.)

In its discussion of the law then governing transmutations (Commission report, supra, at pp. 213–215), the Commission observed that "[u]nder California law it is quite easy for spouses to transmute both real and personal property; a transmutation can be found based on oral statements or implications from the conduct of the spouses." (Id., at p. 213.)

The Commission further observed that "the rule of easy transmutation has also generated extensive litigation in dissolution proceedings. It encourages a spouse, after the marriage has ended, to transform a passing comment into an 'agreement' or even to commit perjury by manufacturing an oral or implied transmutation." (Commission report, supra, at p. 214.) The Commission concluded its discussion of transmutation law by saying that "California law should continue to recognize informal transmutations for certain personal property gifts between the spouses, but should require a writing for a transmutation of real property or other personal property." (Ibid.) Unfortunately, the Commission did not explicitly expand upon the question of what such a writing should be required to contain, except to warn that "[t]he requirement of a writing should not be satisfied by a statement in a married person's will of the community character of the property, until the person's death." (Ibid.) The Commission stated only that its recommendations would be effectuated by the enactment of certain measures, including section 5110.730(a). (Commission report, supra, at p. 217.)

It thus appears from an examination of the Commission report that section 5110.730(a) was intended to remedy problems which arose when courts found transmutations on the basis of evidence the Legislature considered unreliable. To remedy these problems the Legislature decided that proof of transmutation should henceforth be in writing, and therefore enacted the writing requirement of section 5110.730(a).

There is no question that the Legislature intended, by enacting section 5110.730(a), to invalidate all solely oral transmutations. (Commission report, supra, at pp. 224–225.) By definition, *any* writing requirement would accomplish this limited goal. It is equally clear, however, that the Legislature intended that section 5110.730(a) would invalidate some transmutations which, under then-prevailing case law, would have been upheld on the basis of evidence other than oral statements. (Id., at p. 214 ["... easy transmutation ... encourages a spouse ... to commit perjury by manufacturing an oral *or* implied transmutation...." (Emphasis added.)].)

In our view, the Legislature cannot have intended that *any* signed writing whatsoever by the adversely affected spouse would suffice to meet the requirements of section 5110.730(a). First, to so construe that statute would render mere surplusage all the language following the words "unless made in writing," including the phrase "an express declaration." A construction rendering some words surplusage is to be avoided. (*People v. Black* (1982) 32 Cal.3d 1, 5, 184 Cal.Rptr. 454, 648 P.2d 104; *Watkins v. Real Estate Commissioner* (1960) 182 Cal.App.2d 397, 400, 6 Cal.Rptr. 191.) Second, as respondent acknowledges, some of the "easy transmutation" cases which section 5110.730 was intended to overturn involved non oral conduct or signed writings.[6] Therefore, it seems reasonable to assume that the Legislature intended section 5110.730(a) to invalidate some claimed transmutations even though some form of writing existed.

Thus, to construe section 5110.730(a) so that it does not contain mere surplusage, as well as to effect legislative intent, we must fashion a test by which courts may judge the adequacy of particular writings for section 5110.730(a) purposes.[7]

* * *

6. For a detailed analysis of existing transmutation law, the Commission referred the Legislature to Reppy, Debt Collection from Married Californians: Problems Caused by Transmutations, Single-Spouse Management, and Invalid Marriage, 18 San Diego L.Rev. 143 (1981) ("Reppy article"). (Commission report, supra, at p. 213, fn. 20.) Examples of objectionable transmutation cases discussed in the Reppy article include *Nevins v. Nevins* (1954) 129 Cal.App.2d 150, 276 P.2d 655. There, a husband filed his separate federal income tax return (which at that time called for him to report half the community income) without including half of his wife's income. Since he was aware of the existence of his wife's income, the court found that the husband's signed tax return, which did not include it, was highly probative of the husband having transmuted his community property interest in his wife's income to his wife's separate property. Another example discussed in the Reppy article is *In re Marriage of Lucas* (1980) 27 Cal.3d 808, 166 Cal.Rptr. 853, 614 P.2d 285. There, a motor home purchased by a couple during marriage was declared to have been transmuted to the wife's separate property when a purchase contract was made out in the husband's name only, but title and registration were made out in the wife's name only. (27 Cal.3d at pp. 817–818, 166 Cal.Rptr. 853, 614 P.2d 285; Reppy article, supra, at pp. 156–157, fns. 48–53.) See also *Pacific Mutual Life Insurance Co. v. Cleverdon* (1940) 16 Cal.2d 788, 791, 108 P.2d 405 [transmutation of wife's community earnings when husband "borrowed" and repaid some of them] and *O'Connor v. Traveler's Insurance Co.* (1959) 169 Cal.App.2d 763, 337 P.2d 893 [transmutation of wife's community earnings when husband made no objection to her giving some of them to her son], both discussed in the Reppy article.

7. The only reported California decision to consider the adequacy of a signed writing to meet the requirements of section 5110.730(a) concluded that the writing in question was not sufficient. (*Estate of Blair* (1988) 199 Cal.App.3d 161, 167–168, 244 Cal.Rptr. 627.) In *Blair*, a surviving husband disputed a probate order that he pay his deceased wife's estate one-half of the net proceeds from the sale of the family residence, which had been purchased by the couple during their marriage and held in joint tenancy. The probate court had found that there had been a transmutation of the property from joint tenancy to community property "as a result of an agreement or understanding" between the spouses during the course of their subsequent separation. The agreement was said to consist in the wife having listed the residence as community property in her petition for legal sepa-

[W]e conclude that a writing signed by the adversely affected spouse is not an "express declaration" for the purposes of section 5110.730(a) *unless* it contains language which expressly states that the characterization or ownership of the property is being changed.

Our conclusion honors each of the principles of statutory construction we have discussed. First, it interprets "express declaration," so as to give significance to all the words of section 5110.730(a). Second, it effects the intent of the Legislature to create a writing requirement which enables courts to validate transmutations without resort to extrinsic evidence and, thus, without encouraging perjury and the proliferation of litigation. Third, it is consistent with our interpretation of the similar requirement in section 683.[8]

We must now consider whether the writing involved in this case satisfies section 5110.730(a). Decedent signed paragraphs consenting to the designation of a beneficiary on three standard bank-form adoption agreements. These paragraphs read in full: "If participant's spouse is not designated as the sole primary beneficiary, spouse must sign consent. Consent of spouse: Being the participant's spouse, I hereby consent to the above designation. [Signature.]"

Obviously, the consent paragraphs contain no language which characterizes the property assertedly being transmuted, viz., the pension funds which had been deposited in the account. It is not possible to tell from the face of the consent paragraphs, or even from the face of the adoption agreements as a whole, whether decedent was aware that the legal effect of her signature might be to alter the character or ownership of her interest in the pension funds. There is certainly no language in the consent paragraphs, or the adoption agreements as a whole, expressly stating that decedent was effecting a change in the character or ownership of her interest. Thus, we agree with the Court of Appeal that these writings fail to satisfy the "express declaration" requirement of section 5110.730(a).

We do not hold that section 5110.730(a) requires use of the term "transmutation" or any other particular locution. Although a writing

---

ration and the husband having signed a deposition in the dissolution proceeding which said that he "believed" the residence was community property. The Court of Appeal held that the husband's deposition was not sufficient to satisfy Civil Code section 5110.730 because, although in writing, it did "not necessarily show the parties' separate agreement that the jointly held property was actually community property." (*Estate of Blair,* supra, 199 Cal.App.3d at pp. 165–168, 244 Cal.Rptr. 627.)

8. Following the filing of his petition for review, Robert submitted a letter to court asking to amend his petition for review to include the issue of whether the adoption agreements constituted a valid written consent to the disposal of a community proper-

ty asset under Civil Code section 5125, subdivision (b). Apparently, respondent's request amounted to a reformulation of his alternative argument in the Court of Appeal that decedent "waived" her interest in the IRA funds. The Court of Appeal found this argument to be "merely another means of circumventing the requirements of section 5110.730 ... allowing transmutations by oral agreement or conduct." We agree with the view of the Court of Appeal and, for the same reasons, reject Robert's waiver contention. In any event, Robert's letter seeking to amend his petition was never filed or approved by the court and, accordingly, our grant of review was limited to the issue of construing Civil Code section 5110.-730(a).

sufficient to satisfy the "express declaration" requirement of section 5110.730(a) might very well contain the words "transmutation," "community property," or "separate property," it need not. For example, the paragraph signed by decedent here would have been sufficient if it had included an additional sentence reading: "I give to the account holder any interest I have in the funds deposited in this account." [9]

We are aware that section 5110.730(a), construed as we have construed it today, may preclude the finding of a transmutation in some cases, where some extrinsic evidence of an intent to transmute exists. But, as previously discussed, it is just such reliance on extrinsic evidence for the proof of transmutations which the Legislature intended to eliminate in enacting the writing requirement of section 5110.730(a).

Manifestly, there are policy considerations weighing both in favor of and against any type of transmutation proof requirement. On the one hand, honoring the intentions of the parties involved in a purported transmutation may suggest that weight should be given to *any* indication of these intentions. On the other hand, the desirability of assuring that a spouse's community property entitlements are not improperly undermined, as well as concern for judicial economy and efficiency, support somewhat more restrictive proof requirements. The Legislature, in enacting section 5110.730(a), apparently thought it unwise to rely on some kinds of evidence to effect transmutations. It is not for us to question that legislative conclusion. Accordingly, the judgment of the Court of Appeal is affirmed.

LUCAS, C.J., and BROUSSARD, EAGLESON and KENNARD, JJ., concur.

MOSK, JUSTICE, concurring.

I concur in the judgment. I agree with the majority's ultimate conclusion that the purported "transmutations" in this case are not valid. But I do not agree with their construction of the controlling statute.

Civil Code section 5110.730, subdivision (a) (hereinafter section 5110.730(a)), provides: "A transmutation of real or personal property is not valid unless made in writing by an express declaration that is made, joined in, consented to, or accepted by the spouse whose interest in the property is adversely affected."

First, section 5110.730(a) establishes a *formal* requirement for the validity of transmutations. The majority appear to interpret the provision merely as a rule governing *proof.* But such an interpretation founders on the very words of the code section: "A transmutation . . . *is not valid* unless" the requirement imposed is met. The language is clear. There is no reason for a court to look beyond the provision's

---

9. Married persons who decide to open IRA accounts with community funds, of course, may or may not, in individual cases, wish to transmute those funds. Thus we do not assume that drafters of IRA account adoption agreements will want to revise their standard forms so that a spouse's signature consenting to a designation of beneficiary will always effect a transmutation.

words. But if it did so, there is certainly no reason to depart from their plain meaning.

Second, section 5110.730(a) lays down a formal requirement *of definite content.* The majority discern ambiguity in the language of the provision. I do not. It states: "A transmutation . . . is not valid unless made in writing by an express declaration" that is binding on the adversely affected spouse. With these words the code section unmistakably, albeit impliedly, requires an express declaration *of transmutation.*

In sum, although I do not agree with the majority's construction of section 5110.730(a), I do indeed agree with their result: the purported "transmutations" here are invalid. Therefore, I concur in the judgment.

ARABIAN, JUSTICE, dissenting, to opinion by PANELLI, JUSTICE.

INTRODUCTION

If the decedent in extremis had in her last breath uttered the question, "Oh death, where is thy sting?," the majority garbed in grim shrouds would have whispered, "At probate."

It has been said that no good deed goes unpunished. Unhappily, there is a kernel of truth in this otherwise cynical aphorism, perfectly illustrated in the majority opinion, which begins its journey attempting to protect spouses against questionable transmutations of community property, and ends by negating the estate plan of the decedent herein, and of others who, like decedent, can no longer dictate their intentions. Worse, in exalting form over substance, the majority impose unnecessarily rigid requirements on the drafting and interpretation of future transfers between spouses. In the process, they undermine the deference that trial courts deserve and merit on review. Therefore, I must respectfully dissent.

BACKGROUND

In August 1984, Margery MacDonald (hereafter Margery or decedent) sadly learned that she had terminal cancer. Faced with mortality, she undertook the labor of finalizing her estate. Fortunately, it was a task to which she was well suited.

Margery had worked for many years as a bookkeeper with the accounting firm of Hemming–Morse in San Mateo. Indeed, it was there that she met her second husband, Robert MacDonald, who employed the firm to oversee the corporate accounts of his business, Robert F. MacDonald Company. After the couple married in 1973 (it was a second marriage for Robert, as well), Margery became employed as the bookkeeper for her husband's firm. In that capacity she kept the books, the balance sheets, the income statements, tax returns and payroll. In addition, she took responsibility for the couple's personal finances and was exceptionally aware of their assets.

Both Margery and Robert had children from their prior marriages. Margery wished to leave the bulk of her estate to her four children. Accordingly, the couple's immediate goal became the apportionment of their property into separate estates. To that end, the MacDonalds consulted with their personal accountant, Elizabeth Gommel, regarding their holdings and the division of assets. As Ms. Gommel recalled, "[Decedent's] immediate objective was to separate her assets . . . and have an entirely separate estate. . . . She wanted it as easy to administer as it possibly could be, that all assets would be separate, so there would be no reason for difficulties to arise between her heirs and Mr. MacDonald."

The MacDonalds divided their stock holdings and Margery sold her half and placed the proceeds into her separate account. In addition, she prepared a schedule of all the couple's real property holdings (in addition to their home in Hillsborough, the couple owned residences in Foster City, Pacific Grove, San Carlos, Sacramento and Roseville), valued the properties and divided them with her husband; Robert paid $33,000 in cash to equalize the division.

Several months later, in November 1984, Robert reached the age of 65 and his company pension plan was terminated. On March 21, 1985, he received his pension disbursement of over $266,000; the money was immediately deposited into three IRA accounts in separate financial institutions. These pension funds had not been previously addressed in the couple's efforts to divide their estate, although it was undisputed that Margery was aware of their existence.

The three IRA accounts were opened solely in Robert's name. The designated beneficiary of each was a living trust that Robert had established in 1982. The terms of the trust gave the bulk of the corpus to Robert's children from his earlier marriage. Each of the three IRA documents, entitled "Adoption Agreement and Designation of Beneficiary" (agreement), provided space for the signature of a spouse not designated as the sole primary beneficiary to allow consent for the designation. Margery signed the consent portion of each agreement.

Three months later, on June 17, 1985, Margery died. Her will bequeathed the residue of her estate to her four children. Thereafter, her daughter and executrix of her estate, Judith Bolton, filed a petition to establish decedent's community property interest in the IRA funds. Following a probate hearing, the trial court denied the petition, concluding that the IRA funds were not assets of decedent's estate. The court's conclusion was based on the following express findings: "1. Decedent Margery MacDonald, both because of her occupation and as a result of advice received from professionals was both competent to [sic] and sophisticated in the administration of her assets; [¶] 2. [¶] Decedent was active in the business of Respondent Robert F. MacDonald and was aware of the financial decisions being made in that business, particularly in terms of the pension plan itself; [¶] 3. Decedent was aware of the terms of the Living Trust which left the bulk of Respondent's estate to Respondent's children and left Decedent a life interest in the estate; [¶] 4. Decedent made conscious and substantial choices regarding her assets and sought to put her estate in order to eliminate the possibility of any dissension between her children and her spouse; [¶] 5. Decedent, in executing the Adoption Agreement for the three IRA's, intended to waive any community property right she had in those IRA's and in fact to transmute her share of that community property asset to the separate property of Respondent."

The Court of Appeal, with one justice dissenting, reversed. A majority of the court concluded that decedent's consent to the IRA agreements did not satisfy the provisions of Civil Code section 5110.730, subdivision (a),[1] which requires that transmutations of property be "made in writing by an express declaration that it is made, joined in, consented to, or accepted by the spouse whose interest in the property is adversely affected." Justice Holmdahl, in dissent, would have held that the IRA agreements satisfied both the language and purpose of section 5110.730, subdivision (a).

DISCUSSION

The narrow issue presented is whether, in order to satisfy the requirements of section 5110.730, subdivision (a), a writing must expressly state that the writer is effecting a transmutation of property. Conceding that the statutory language yields no ready answer, the majority turn to legislative history. From their reading of the pertinent sources, they conclude that the statute was intended to foreclose the courts from the use of extrinsic evidence to ascertain the writer's intent. An examination of those same historical sources, however, reveals that the majority's conclusion is fundamentally flawed; the plain evidence shows that the Legislature intended a simple writing requirement akin to the statute of frauds—a formality that would admit the use of collateral evidence to clarify the writer's meaning.

The primary source relied on by the majority is the California Law Revision Commission (Commission) report to the Legislature recommending enactment of section 5110.730. (Recommendations Relating to Marital Property Presumptions and Transmutations, 17 Cal.Law Revision Com.Rep. (1984) ("Commission report") pp. 205–227.) The Commission report is indeed enlightening, although it leads to a conclusion precisely the opposite of that reached by the majority. The salient portion of the Commission report reads as follows:

"Under California law it is quite easy for spouses to transmute both real and personal property; a transmutation can be found based on *oral statements or implications from the conduct of the spouses.* [Fn. omitted.] [¶] California law permits an oral transmutation or transfer of property between the spouses *notwithstanding the statute of frauds.* [Fn. omitted.] ... It encourages a spouse, after the marriage has ended, to transform a passing comment into an 'agreement' or even to commit perjury by manufacturing an oral or implied transmutation. [¶] Most people would find an oral transfer of such property, even between spouses, to be suspect and probably fraudulent, either as to creditors or

---

1. Unless otherwise indicated, all statutory references are to the Civil Code.

between each other. [¶] California law should continue to recognize informal transmutations for certain personal property gifts between the spouses, but should require *a writing* for the transmutation of real property or other personal property." (Commission report, *supra,* at pp. 213–214, italics added.)

As the text of the Commission report thus makes clear, the statute was designed to overrule those decisions that had permitted transmutations "based on oral statements or implications from the conduct of the spouses." The Commission report's frequent references to "oral" agreements and the possibility of "fraudulent" conveyances demonstrate that the purpose of section 5110.730 was to "require a writing" in the nature of the "statute of frauds." (Commission report, *supra,* at pp. 213–215.)

The Commission comment accompanying the text of section 5110.-730 makes that intent even more plain: "Section 5110.730 imposes formalities on interspousal transmutations for the purpose of increasing certainty in the determination whether a transmutation has in fact occurred. Section 5110.730 makes clear that the *ordinary rules and formalities applicable to real property transfers apply also to transmutations of real property between the spouses. See Civil Code §§ 1091 and 1624 (statute of frauds). . . .* This overrules existing case law. See, e.g., *Woods v. Security First Nat'l Bank,* 46 Cal.2d 697, 701, 299 P.2d 657, 659 (1956). *Section 5110.730 also overrules existing law that permits oral transmutations of personal property. . . ."* (Commission report, *supra,* at pp. 224–225, italics added.)

The Commission's explicit reference to "the ordinary rules and formalities applicable to real property transfers," in conjunction with its express citation to the statute of frauds (§ 1624), leaves no doubt as to the nature of the writing requirement contemplated by the statute's authors. The plain statement of intention to overrule *Woods v. Security-First Nat. Bank,* (1956) 46 Cal.2d 697, 299 P.2d 657 (transmutation of real property based on oral agreement of the spouses) and the Commission report's explicit criticism of *In re Marriage of Lucas* (1980) 27 Cal.3d 808, 166 Cal.Rptr. 853, 614 P.2d 285 (finding a transmutation on the basis of a mobilehome document of title) underscore the legislative intent to create a simple writing requirement analogous to the statute of frauds. (Commission report, *supra,* at pp. 211, 222.)

That goal is evidenced further by the Commission's favorable reference to Reppy, *Debt Collection from Married Californians: Problems Caused by Transmutations, Single–Spouse Management, and Invalid Marriage* (1980) 18 San Diego L.Rev. 143 (hereafter Reppy). Like the Commission report itself, this article criticizes California's case law tradition of "easy transmutation," singling out for particular censure such cases as *Lucas, supra,* and *Woods, supra,* as well as *Pacific Mutual Life Insurance Co. v. Cleverdon* (1940) 16 Cal.2d 788, 108 P.2d 405 (husband's act of depositing funds into wife's separate account supports finding of intent to transmute to wife's separate property) and *O'Connor v. Travelers Insurance Co.* (1959) 169 Cal.App.2d 763, 337 P.2d 893 (wife's deposit of earnings to her separate account transmutes funds to her separate property). Consistent with the Commission's ultimate recommendation, the article calls for legislative enactment of a "statute of frauds" to govern transmutations of property between spouses. (Reppy, *supra,* at p. 240.)

Thus, the historical sources—the *very* sources cited and relied on by the majority—demonstrate irrefutably that the underlying purpose of section 5110.730 was to overrule decisions permitting transmutations "based on oral statements or implications from the conduct of the spouses" (Commission report, *supra,* at p. 213), and to create the equivalent of a statute of frauds to govern transmutations of property between spouses. (Id. at p. 222.) [2]

California's general statute of frauds provides that certain specified contracts are invalid "unless they, or some note or memorandum thereof, are in writing and subscribed by the party to be charged or by the party's agent." (§ 1624.) To satisfy the statute, it is well settled that a writing must contain only the essential terms of an agreement, and that what is essential depends on the particular agreement and its context. (*Seaman's Direct Buying Service, Inc. v. Standard Oil Co.* (1984) 36 Cal.3d 752, 762–763, 206 Cal.Rptr. 354, 686 P.2d 1158.)

The modern trend of the law favors a liberal construction of writings in order to carry out the intentions of the parties. (*Sunset–Sternau Food Co. v. Bonzi* (1964) 60 Cal.2d 834, 838, fn. 3, 36 Cal.Rptr. 741, 389 P.2d 133; *Okun v. Morton* (1988) 203 Cal.App.3d 805, 817, 250 Cal.Rptr. 220; *Hennefer v. Butcher* (1986) 182 Cal.App.3d 492, 500–501, 227 Cal.Rptr. 318.) Ultimately, if the parties have completed a transaction in which it appears that they intended to make a contract, "the court should not frustrate their intention if it is possible to reach a fair and just result, even though this requires a choice among conflicting mean-

---

2. In response to the obvious thrust of the Commission report and the Reppy article, the majority advance two arguments. Neither is persuasive. First, they suggest that a simple writing requirement analogous to the statute of frauds would render mere surplusage the statutory language, "unless made in writing *by an express declaration ....*" (§ 5110.730, subd. (a).) This begs the question, of course, since the very issue we must decide is, an "express declaration" of *what?* The majority would require specific language stating that the writer is effecting a transmutation of property. The legislative history, however, demonstrates that the purpose was simply to impose a statute-of-frauds equivalent; as explained in the discussion which follows, any writing that evidences an *intent* to alter the character of property fulfills this requirement.

The majority also assert that the Legislature "cannot have intended that *any* signed

writing whatsoever" would suffice, because some of the cases the statute was designed to overrule involved writings. Of course, the Commission report does not suggest that "any" signed writing would satisfy the statute, only those that meet the formalities of the statute of frauds. Moreover, the cases cited by the majority, *Nevins v. Nevins* (1954) 129 Cal.App.2d 150, 276 P.2d 655 and *In re Marriage of Lucas, supra,* 27 Cal.3d 808, 166 Cal.Rptr. 853, 614 P.2d 285, plainly fail to meet this standard. Neither involved a writing that even remotely evidenced, on its face, an intent to change the character of property. *Nevins* held that a husband's intent to transfer his community property could be inferred from his income tax return. *Lucas,* as noted earlier, inferred an intent to transmute property from the title document to a mobilehome. Neither of the writings at issue in *Nevins* and *Lucas* would have complied with section 5110.730.

ings and the filling of some gaps that the parties have left." (*Okun v. Morton, supra,* 203 Cal.App.3d at p. 817, 250 Cal.Rptr. 220, quoting 1 Corbin on Contracts (1963) § 95, p. 400.) As we have previously explained, an " 'agreement will not be held deficient [under the statute of frauds] for the failure to express that which is clearly *implied* when the writing is interpreted in accordance with the intentions of the parties.' [Citations.]" (*Seaman's Direct Buying Service, Inc. v. Standard Oil Co., supra,* 36 Cal.3d at p. 763, 206 Cal.Rptr. 354, 686 P.2d 1158, quoting *Seck v. Foulks* (1972) 25 Cal.App.3d 556, 568, 102 Cal. Rptr. 170, original italics.)

In light of these settled principles, it is evident that the Legislature could *not* have contemplated the strict test for compliance with section 5110.730 formulated by the majority. As noted, the legislative history reveals an intent to apply the "ordinary rules and formalities" associated with the statute of frauds. (Commission report, *supra,* at p. 225.) The Legislature, therefore, *must* have envisaged the introduction of extrinsic evidence where the writing, "interpreted in accordance with the intentions of the parties" (*Seaman's Direct Buying Service, Inc. v. Standard Oil Co., supra,* 36 Cal.3d at p. 763, 206 Cal.Rptr. 354, 686 P.2d 1158), demonstrates at least *an intent to transmute property pursuant to section 5110.730.*

Applying this test to the case at bar, it is clear that such an intention is readily discernible from the face of the IRA agreements. The transfer of the pension disbursement to Robert's IRA accounts involved a transfer of community property funds. The agreements contained an express declaration that the funds were being placed in Robert's name only. Decedent, the spouse whose interest was adversely affected, expressly consented to the designation of Robert's living trust, not herself, as the beneficiary. Thus, as contemplated by section 5110.-730, the IRA documents plainly involved a transfer of property and contained an express consent to that transfer by the spouse whose interests were adversely affected.

To be sure, the agreements did not explicitly describe the pension funds as community property or expressly state that decedent intended to transfer her interest to Robert. By requiring her consent, however, the documents clearly alerted decedent to the fact that she had an interest in the funds for which a waiver was required.

The majority, nevertheless, assert that there is *no* substantial evidence to support the trial court's finding that decedent knew she had a community property interest in the pension funds and intended to waive or transmute that interest. This is a patently selective reading of the record, contrary to the fundamental rule that a reviewing court must indulge all reasonable inferences in favor of the judgment. (*People v. Johnson* (1980) 26 Cal.3d 557, 576, 162 Cal.Rptr. 431, 606 P.2d 738.) The trial court found, and the undisputed evidence showed, that decedent had worked as a bookkeeper for her husband's business and had managed the family's financial affairs. She was aware of her husband's pension plan. She consented to the designation of Robert's living trust as the beneficiary of the IRA funds. The amount was in excess of $250,000. For what conceivable reason would an intelligent and financially sophisticated woman consent to relinquish so large an interest to which she was not even entitled? It is an insult to the decedent, and a distortion of the appellate review process, to insinuate that decedent was ignorant of her interest in the IRA funds.

In applying the "ordinary rules and formalities" to transfers under section 5110.730, the Legislature intended to preserve the traditional rules that govern the interpretation of writings where the intent of the parties is in dispute and may depend, in part, on the evaluation of extrinsic evidence. (See *Parsons v. Bristol Development Co.* (1965) 62 Cal.2d 861, 44 Cal.Rptr. 767, 402 P.2d 839.) The trial court here was in the best position to judge decedent's purpose, construed in light of the documents, the evidence, and the testimony and demeanor of the witnesses. In overruling that court's considered judgment, we not only contravene the legislative intent, but repudiate the necessary deference accorded trial courts in making such difficult determinations.

Worse, however, is the injury that the majority visits upon the decedent and others similarly situated. As her personal accountant testified, Margery's overriding interest, upon learning of her impending death, was to effect a clear allocation of assets in order to avoid any possibility of acrimony between Robert and her children. Her children were well provided for, having received substantial separate property and stock assets. The pension funds, though community property, were essentially the product of Robert's 35 years in business, most of which preceded his marriage to decedent; thus, Margery's election to waive and transfer any interest in those funds was eminently reasonable.[3]

There is no evidence of overreaching here, nor any hint of exploitation. There is only an effort by an obviously intelligent and courageous woman to set her estate in order before her passing, to effectuate a clear and fair allocation of her assets. Her intentions were good, but as Shakespeare observed, "The evil men do lives after them; the good is oft interred with their bones."[4] The majority, sadly, prove the truth of that statement.

Notes

1. West's Ann.Cal. Family Code § 721, which specifically permits married persons to enter into agreements respecting property, indicates that inter-spousal agreements are controlled by the general rules governing fiduciary relationships which control the actions of persons occupying confidential relations. Problems concerning the fairness of particular inter-

---

3. Robert's defined benefit pension plan became effective in January 1977 and matured seven years later, in 1984; the distribution came to over $250,000. Although the payments into the plan occurred during the course of his marriage to decedent, Robert's substantial contributions during the seven short years that the plan was in existence were plainly the product of his three decades in business, most of which *preceded* his second marriage.

4. Shakespeare, Julius Caesar, act III, scene 2.

spousal agreements, which involves the confidential nature of the husband-wife relationship, frequently arise in connection with property settlements at the breakdown of the marriage relationship. These problems will be considered in Chapter 7, dealing with the division of property on dissolution of the marriage.

2. Under general principles of contract law, consideration is essential to the enforceability of an agreement. However, in cases involving inter-spousal agreements, the courts indicated that the only consideration required is the mutual consent of the spouses. This principle is now codified at West's Ann.Cal. Family Code §§ 850 and 1611. Therefore an agreement transmuting community property to separate, or separate property to community may be essentially a donative transaction.

3. Where an inter-spousal agreement purports to create survivorship rights, the courts have been less willing to forego the requirement of a writing. For example, an oral agreement between a husband and wife to the effect that existing community property was to belong to the survivor was held within the statute of frauds and not enforceable against the husband's estate or the devisees under the husband's will. Estate of Baglione, 65 Cal.2d 192, 53 Cal.Rptr. 139, 417 P.2d 683 (1966). Similarly, in California Trust Co. v. Bennett, 33 Cal.2d 694, 204 P.2d 324 (1949), an oral understanding that the wife's separate property would be joint tenancy property was denied recognition.

4. Suppose that as a twenty-fifth wedding anniversary gift H, using his earnings, purchased a $100,000 diamond necklace for his wife. Shortly thereafter both spouses executed reciprocal wills each containing the provision that "all property standing in the name of either spouse is community property." A few years later, H files for dissolution and contends that the necklace is community property. What result? See West's Ann.Cal. Family Code §§ 850, 853.

5. West's Ann.Cal. Family Code § 852 appears to put an end to implied-in-fact transmutation agreements (with the possible exception of interspousal gifts of clothing, jewelry etc.). Note, though that the statute applies only to transmutation agreements made after January 1, 1985. Thus oral or implied-in-fact agreements made before that date are enforceable after that date. See, e.g., Marriage of Schoettgen, 183 Cal.App.3d 1, 227 Cal.Rptr. 758 (1986).

6. Suppose that one spouse claims that the separate property of the other spouse has been transmuted to community property. What is the proper standard of proof for establishing transmutation? In Marriage of Weaver, 224 Cal.App.3d 478, 273 Cal.Rptr. 696 (1990), the reviewing court indicated that at least under certain circumstances, the higher evidentiary standard of clear and convincing evidence should apply.

7. One of the major criticisms levelled against the *MacDonald* case is that the court failed to consider what may have been the most significant issue raised by the facts: Whether Mrs. MacDonald's consent to the beneficiary designations, even though not a waiver or transmutation, was sufficient to constitute a gift of her community interest in the IRAs effective on Mr. MacDonald's death. Subsequent to the *MacDonald* decision, clarifying legislation was enacted which specifically provides that although "a spouse's

written consent to a provision for a nonprobate transfer of community property on death is not necessarily transmutation of the consenting spouse's interest in the property," the spouse's written consent (although revocable during marriage or at dissolution) becomes irrevocable on the death of either spouse. The consenting spouse may also revoke or modify the consent by making a contrary disposition of the property in his or her will. The statute also specifies that a written consent which meets the requirements of Family Code Section 852 would constitute a transmutation. See California Probate Code Section 5000 et seq., effective January 1, 1993. For a general discussion of this problem, see Kasher, *Donative and Interspouse Transfers of Community Property in California,* 23 Pacific L.J. 361 (1992). The subject of community property gifts is covered in Chapter 5, infra, dealing with management and control.

Chapter 2

THE CLASSIFICATION OF PROPERTY AS COMMUNITY OR SEPARATE

SECTION 1. THE SIGNIFICANCE OF CLASSIFICATION

A married person may hold a particular item of property as community property or as separate property. The classification of any given asset as either separate or community is a critical determination due to the consequences which flow from such classification. Different rules govern separate and community property with respect to spousal management and control rights, creditors' rights, succession rights on the death of one of the spouses, and division of the property on dissolution. A thorough knowledge of the classification process is essential to an understanding and application of the community property system.

As a general rule, the classification of property as separate or community cannot be made simply by reference to title documents. Classification depends on a variety of factors, including the facts and circumstances surrounding the acquisition of the particular item, or an understanding or agreement between the spouses as to the property's character. In the absence of this type of evidence, classification may be made solely on the basis of a presumption. California courts have long been aided by various presumptions in the solution of classification problems. Indeed, the requirement that every item of wealth owned by a married person be classified as community or separate would be administratively impossible but for the existence of presumptions.

When a particular acquisition falls within one of the statutory definitions of separate property the courts state that it is presumed to be separate property. Where the acquisition falls outside the scope of these definitions the courts hold that it is presumed to be community property. Acquisitions which literally fit into one or the other of these two types sometimes fall within some special presumption because of the form of the title or because of a particular statute. The general presumption of community property is considered in Section 2 of this Chapter; the common presumptions of separate property in Section 3; and the special statutory and title presumptions in Section 4.

In addition to the various presumptions, courts may be aided in the classification process by finding an agreement between the spouses concerning the characterization of their property. As indicated in the preceding chapter, one of the hallmarks of the California community property system is that it is subject to contractual modification by the parties. Moreover the special statutory and judicial presumptions based on the form of title bear a close relationship to the principle of contractual modification.

SECTION 2. PRESUMPTION THAT ACQUISITION DURING MARRIAGE IS COMMUNITY PROPERTY

A preliminary step in the classification process involves determining whether the particular item of property is capable of being classified as community property; that is, whether it is within the scope of the community property system.[1] The next stage of the process requires an inquiry as to the time of the acquisition: was the item at issue acquired before marriage or during marriage? California courts, in accordance with the parent Spanish–Mexican system,[2] have declared that there is a general presumption that an acquisition during the period of marriage is community property. Conversely, if the item is shown to have been acquired before marriage, it falls within one of the statutory definitions of separate property, and is presumed to be separate property.

When an item was acquired during marriage, but the evidence shows that its acquisition was by gift, inheritance or testamentary disposition to one spouse, the case is said to be taken out of the general presumption of community property and put within the common presumption of separate property. Similarly, when the evidence shows that the acquisition falls within one of the special statutory presumptions, the case is taken out of the general presumption.[3] All of the presumptions are true presumptions, requiring a holding in keeping with the presumption in the absence of rebuttal evidence.[4]

A. *Raising the General Presumption of Community Property*

The general presumption comes into play when the fact of acquisition during marriage is established. But suppose that there is little or no evidence as to the manner or time of acquisition. How should the

---

1. This issue and related problems are considered in Chapter 3.

2. Illustrative is the translation of the commentary of Matienzo on that part of the Nueva Recopilacion which treats of community property:

"All property, movable or immovable, or whatsoever it may be, is presumed to be common to husband and wife and to have been acquired during marriage, unless the contrary is shown."

Gloss. 11 to Law 1 of Book 5, Title 9. Robbins, Community Property Laws, p. 16 (1940).

3. Rosenthal v. Rosenthal, 215 Cal. App.2d 140, 30 Cal.Rptr. 49 (1963); see also In re Marriage of Ashodian, reprinted in Section 4 of this Chapter.

4. Estate of Jolly, reprinted in this Section; see also In re Marriage of Ashodian, reprinted in Section 4 of this Chapter.

court approach the classification process in such a situation? Compare the court's reasoning in the *Mahoney* case with that of *Wilson*.

FIDELITY & CASUALTY CO. OF NEW YORK v. MAHONEY

California District Court of Appeal, 1945.
71 Cal.App.2d 65, 161 P.2d 944.

PARKER WOOD, JUSTICE.

On June 28, 1943, in Louisville, Kentucky, J.B. Mahoney, Sr., a resident of Los Angeles, purchased an airplane-travel accident insurance policy from the plaintiff insurance company and mailed it to the beneficiary named therein, J.B. Mahoney, Jr., of Los Angeles, his sixteen-year-old son by a former marriage. Soon after the policy was purchased, the insured boarded an airplane for the purpose of going to Los Angeles, and within an hour thereafter the airplane fell in Kentucky and as a result thereof he was killed.

Patricia Mahoney and the insured had been married about two months preceding the airplane accident, and at all times during their marriage they were domiciled in California. She made a demand on the insurance company for one-half the proceeds of the policy on the ground that the policy was purchased with community property.

The insurance company filed this action in interpleader, and upon stipulation an interlocutory decree was entered wherein it was ordered that upon deposit in court by the insurance company of $4989.50 (being the amount of the policy less $10.50 for costs) it would be released from liability under the policy, and it was further ordered that J.B. Mahoney, Jr., and Patricia Mahoney litigate between themselves to determine who was entitled to receive the amount so deposited. The insurance company made the deposit.

Defendant Patricia Mahoney alleged, among other things, that she was the widow of J.B. Mahoney, deceased; that the premium on said policy was paid by J.B. Mahoney from community property funds owned by him and her; and that as his widow she was entitled to one-half of said $5000.

Defendant J.B. Mahoney, Jr., alleged, among other things, that he was the beneficiary named in the policy; that the $5000 was not community property; that Patricia Mahoney had no right, title or interest in said $5000; and that the policy was purchased with the separate property of the deceased J.B. Mahoney.

The court found that the $5000 was not community property; that Patricia Mahoney had no right, title or interest therein; and that the policy was purchased with the separate property of deceased J.B. Mahoney. The court concluded that J.B. Mahoney, Jr., was entitled to a judgment ordering that the funds deposited with the court be paid to his guardian. The judgment was that J.B. Mahoney, Jr., by his guardian, recover judgment as against defendant Patricia Mahoney, and that he, by his guardian, was entitled to the sum of $2494.75 deposited in court by plaintiff. Defendant Patricia Mahoney appeals from the judgment, and contends that the findings of fact are not supported by the evidence.

In the statement on appeal it is recited: "There is no evidence as to the nature or extent of the decedent's estate, whether separate or community, except that it is shown the decedent earned a gross monthly salary in an undetermined amount during the period of his second marriage and that he had a bank account in his own name. There was no evidence on behalf of either of the defendants as to whether or not the premium paid for said policy of insurance came from the separate estate or the community estate of the decedent." The record does not show what amount was paid for the policy, but since it was stated in the written opinion of the trial judge and in the briefs that the amount was $1, it will be assumed herein that $1 was the amount of the premium.

Appellant's theory is that the insurance premium was paid by the insured from community funds, that such payment was a gift by the husband of community funds, and that such gift, being without her written consent, was a nullity under the provisions of Section 172 of the Civil Code as to her one-half interest in the premium money, and therefore she is entitled to one-half the proceeds of the policy.

Section 172 of the Civil Code provides: "The husband has the management and control of the community personal property, with like absolute power of disposition, other than testamentary, as he has of his separate estate; provided, however, that he cannot make a gift of such community personal property * * * without the written consent of the wife." If the insurance premium was paid from the husband's separate funds the wife was not entitled to any part of the proceeds of the policy, it being provided in Section 157 of the Civil Code that "Neither husband nor wife has any interest in the property of the other. * * *" In Mundt v. Connecticut Gen. Life Ins. Co., 1939, 35 Cal.App.2d 416, 95 P.2d 966, wherein the husband had paid the premiums on his life insurance policy from community funds without the wife's consent, the question was whether the wife, who was not the named beneficiary, was entitled to one-half the proceeds of the policy. In that case the court said, 35 Cal.App.2d at page 421, 95 P.2d at page 969: " * * * the only test applied to this problem had been whether the premiums (on a policy issued on the life of a husband after coverture) are paid entirely from community funds. If so, the policy becomes a community asset and the nonconsenting wife may recover an undivided one-half thereof * * *." See also Bazzell v. Endriss, 1940, 41 Cal.App.2d 463, 107 P.2d 49. The court was required to find whether the money used in paying the premium was paid from community funds. As above shown, there was no oral or documentary evidence as to whether the money used in paying the premium was community property or separate property. As to appellant's contention that the findings were not supported by the evidence, she argues that, since there was no evidence to the contrary, the presumption, under Section 164 of the Civil Code that property acquired after marriage (other than by gift, devise, or descent) is community property, is determinative that the money used to pay the insurance premium was community property. There is a presumption that property acquired after marriage, other than by gift, devise, or descent, is community property. In re Estate of Duncan, 9 Cal.2d 207, 217, 70 P.2d 174. Where the marriage relation has existed a short period of time the presumption that property acquired after marriage is community property is of less weight than in the case of a long-continued marriage relation. In re Estate of Duncan, supra, 9 Cal.2d at page 217, 70 P.2d 174; Falk v. Falk, 48 Cal.App.2d 762, 767, 120 P.2d 714; 41 C.J.S., Husband and Wife, § 189, p. 1031. There is no presumption, however, as to when property was acquired. Scott v. Austin, 57 Cal.App. 553, 556, 207 P. 710; 3 Cal.Jur.Supp. 554. The marriage relation had existed about two months. The husband had a bank account in his own name. It was not shown at the trial whether his bank account was large or small or whether the bank account had been in existence a long or short time, and it was not shown whether his monthly salary was large or small. It would seem that proof of such matters was available. Such proof would have been of material assistance to the trial court in determining whether the $1 used in paying the premium was acquired before or after the marriage, especially in view of the short time of marriage and in view of the small amount of the premium. The appellant had alleged in her answer that the premium was paid from community funds, but she did not allege that it was paid without her consent. Even if the premium had been paid from community funds, the gift of the $1 would not be invalid unless it was made without her consent. Although she was in the best position to know and to prove whether she had so consented, she offered no evidence as to whether she had consented to such payment. She was the one who was asserting an interest in the proceeds of a policy wherein she was not a named beneficiary. The $5000 was not property which had been in actual possession of the husband or wife. In the transaction whereby the husband expended $1 and acquired the accident insurance policy he did not dispose of property in possession of the value of $5000 or of any value in excess of $1. If the $1 was community property, and if the payment of it was an invalid gift because she had not consented thereto, her only interest therein during his lifetime would have been a one-half interest in the cash surrender value of the policy, namely, some amount less than fifty cents. There was no evidence that it had any surrender value. It was only upon the death of the insured that the expenditure of the $1 became the basis of a fixed right to recover $5000. The appellant was not entitled to a portion of the $5000 unless, as above stated, the premium was paid from community funds, and unless she had not consented to such payment. It was necessary therefore to determine the source of the $1 used in paying the premium. The burden was upon appellant to prove that the $1 premium was paid from community funds. Also the burden was upon her to prove that she did not consent to the payment of the premium. She failed to carry the burden in both respects.

As above indicated, only one-half of the amount deposited in court was in dispute. Before judgment was rendered, counsel stipulated and the court ordered that the other half of the amount deposited in court be paid to defendant, J.B. Mahoney, Jr.

The judgment is affirmed.

DESMOND, P.J., and SHINN, J., concur.

WILSON v. WILSON

California District Court of Appeal, 1946.
76 Cal.App.2d 119, 172 P.2d 568.

PETERS, PRESIDING JUSTICE. Defendant appeals from an interlocutory decree of divorce granted to his wife after an extended and bitterly contested trial.

* * *

The parties were married in New York on January 15, 1931. Shortly thereafter they established their domicile in San Francisco, and resided here until they separated on December 28, 1940. They have no children. This action was filed by the wife on January 19, 1942. The complaint charged the husband with extreme cruelty and desertion. * * *

The trial court found that the residence of the parties in San Francisco was community property and awarded the plaintiff a one-half interest therein, together with the exclusive right of use and occupancy.

* * *

The testimony in reference to the residence is not as clear as might be desired, but this condition of the record was caused by defendant's failure to be frank and fair with the trial court. Admittedly the house was purchased in 1938, some seven years after the marriage, and admittedly title was taken and still stands in defendant's name. Admittedly the house cost $20,000. Defendant testified that he paid for the house in cash and that the funds used for the purchase were the accumulations of dividends from property owned by him before marriage. Based on this evidence defendant urges as his principal contention on this appeal that it was error to find that the house was community property. In this connection he argues that since he testified that his sole community income was $6,000 a year, and since his wife testified that she estimated their living expenses at $3,500 to $4,000 per month, obviously the community funds were more than exhausted in paying the living expenses, and therefore the house must have been purchased with his separate funds. * * *

* * * The defendant, however, was in a much better position to know the exact living costs of the parties because he paid most of the household bills in cash. He testified that his wife's testimony as to their living expenses was "absolutely false" (R.T. 515) and that actually it cost them $300 to $800 a month for living expenses. (R.T. 516.) Obviously, if the $300 figure was believed by the trial court there was a substantial part of the $6,000 a year salary that could have been used to buy the house. The trial court was entitled to disbelieve the defendant's testimony as to the source of the funds, but to believe his testimony as to their living costs. It was entitled to disbelieve his testimony in part or in toto. Moreover, there is substantial evidence that after marriage, plaintiff, who is an artist, sold some of her art creations for substantial sums, and that the money so received was treated as community property. There is, therefore, in the record some evidence, weak though it may be from which it may reasonably be inferred that community funds were used to buy the house. This testimony, without the necessity of relying on presumptions, supports the challenged finding.

In addition the finding is supported by the strong presumption that all property acquired after marriage (except that acquired by a married woman, or by a married woman and another, by an instrument in writing) is community property. This presumption is fundamental in the community property system and is an integral part of the community property law not only of this state but of other states and countries where the system is in operation. See discussion and many cases collected and commented upon 3 Cal.Jur.Supp. p. 553, § 61 et seq. Coupled with this presumption is the elementary but fundamental rule that the burden rests upon the person asserting that the property is separate to establish that fact.

* * *

The presumption is, of course, a rebuttable one. But whether the evidence adduced to overcome the presumption is sufficient for the purpose is a question for the trial court. As in other cases of presumptions, the rule is that the presumption may outweigh the evidence adduced against it and that notwithstanding controverting testimony the presumption alone will support a finding in accordance therewith. See cases collected 3 Cal.Jur.Supp. p. 557, § 63.

Counsel for defendant, while giving lip service to these well settled rules, contends that they have no application here for at least two reasons—first, that the evidence controverts the presumption as a matter of law, and, secondly, that the presumption has no place in the present case at all. So far as the first contention is concerned, little need be said. Obviously, whether defendant's evidence rebutted the presumption was a question for the trial court. In view of what has already been said about defendant's testimony, obviously the trial court was justified in disregarding his testimony on this issue and finding in accordance with the presumption.

Defendant's second argument is that evidence that the house was bought in 1938 after marriage was not sufficient to raise the presumption—that in addition plaintiff was under a duty to show that the funds used in the purchase were acquired after marriage. In the absence of such evidence, says defendant, there is no evidentiary basis for the presumption. There is no such limitation on the rule—if there were, there would be but little room for the operation of the presumption. Obviously, if a litigant had to trace the funds used in each purchase to funds acquired after marriage there would be few cases indeed to which the presumption could apply. The true rule is that the burden is on the party asserting the separate character of the property, and that the presumption applies when the one claiming that the property is community offers evidence that that property was acquired after marriage.

* * *

ESTATE OF JOLLY
Supreme Court of California, 1925.
196 Cal. 547, 238 P. 353.

SEAWELL, J. This is a contest between the heirs at law of John Jolly and Margaret Jolly, husband and wife, both deceased, as to whether the property, real and personal, ordered distributed, was the separate property of Margaret Jolly or was the community property of John Jolly and his said wife, Margaret. No children were born as the issue of the marriage. The judge of the probate court found that John Jolly died on or about the 11th day of February, 1912, leaving no estate whatever, and that Margaret Jolly died intestate on April 4, 1922, leaving as her separate estate, the property in controversy consisting of real property of the value of $9,000 and money in bank and other personal property of the value of about $19,418.90, and accordingly ordered that distribution of the whole of said estate be made to the heirs at law of said Margaret Jolly to the exclusion of the heirs of said predeceased husband, John Jolly. The appeal is taken from that order. It is the claim of appellants that the estate is the community property of said marriage, and one half thereof should be distributed to the heirs at law of John Jolly, and the other half to the heirs of Margaret Jolly, as provided by section 1386, subd. 8, Civil Code.

* * *

The only evidence to be found in the record on the subject tends to show that John was a man of unusual earning ability, and that he was sturdy and frugal in his habits, industrious, a good and dependable workman, and had saved quite a sum of money before he left England for this country. The couple resided for a time at or near Johnstown, Pa. John was engaged in working in the mining districts of Pennsylvania. Afterwards they went to Illinois, then to Virginia City, Nev. He arrived at Virginia City in the early '70's. At that time the gold-mining industry was at its height. He worked as foreman and miner in the Comstock gold mines of Nevada for a period of about 20 years. He commanded good wages, receiving as much as $9 per day. * * * The record is silent as to what property he owned at the time of his death, or what disposition was made of his estate at the time of or prior to his demise. The widow died 10 years thereafter, April 4, 1922, leaving in her own name the estate in controversy, all of which was personal property, except a few parcels of realty, situated in San Diego, acquired by her August 8, 1918, and January 11, 1922, respectively, aggregating $9,000. The entire estate was appraised at $28,418.95.

Counsel in the case stipulated as follows:

"* * * At the time of his [John Jolly's] death, he and Margaret Jolly were husband and wife, and after his death Margaret Jolly did not engage in any occupation, and was in a poor condition of health from the date of the death of John Jolly until her own death, and not able to work."

The record contains affirmative evidence to the effect that Margaret Jolly had at no time, before or after marriage, ever engaged in any business or occupation or performed any duties, except household or domestic duties in her mother's family and in her marital relation. It does not appear that she ever owned or possessed a separate estate or an independent income from any source whatsoever, or that she had acquired any property by gift, devise, bequest, or descent.

* * *

The probate court found from the facts herein narrated that it was not true, as claimed by the heirs of John Jolly, that the property ordered distributed was accumulated subsequent to the marriage of the said parties, or that it was community property, but, on the contrary, found that the said John Jolly left no estate whatever at the time of his death, and that there was no community property belonging to either spouse at the time of his death, and that all of the property owned by the said Margaret Jolly or found in her possession at the time of her death was her separate property and estate. The question, therefore, is whether the evidence sustains the conclusion reached by the probate court, to wit, that all of said property was the separate estate of Margaret Jolly. In weighing the evidence, consideration must be given to all of the well-established presumptions of law affecting the acquisition or the possession of real and personal property by the spouse during coverture, and the increase thereof, as well as property found in the possession of the survivor, in the light of the circumstances appearing in each particular case. That portion of section 164, Civil Code, which prescribes the rules of presumptions in community property cases, provides as follows:

"All other property acquired after marriage by either husband or wife, or both, * * * is community property."

"The disputable presumption raised by section 164, Civil Code, is a form of evidence under section 1957, Code Civ.Proc. It may be controverted by other evidence, direct or indirect; but, unless so controverted, the court or jury is bound to find according to the presumption." Stafford v. Martinoni, 192 Cal. 724, 221 P. 919. The community [property] generically embraces all property belonging to the spouses, except such as the statute specifically removes from its operation. Community property is the rule, separate property the exception thereto.

Hence the presumption * * * follows.   * * * Ballinger on Community Property, p. 213.

No evidence of sufficient strength was adduced at the trial to overcome the presumption created by section 164 of the Civil Code. * * * The presumption of the wife's community interest in property acquired after marriage can be overcome only by the production of clear and satisfactory proof that the property in question was the separate property of the husband." Estate of Rolls, 193 Cal. 594, 226 P. 608; Dimmick v. Dimmick, 95 Cal. 326, 30 P. 547; Rowe v. Hibernia Sav. & Loan Soc., 134 Cal. 403, 66 P. 569; Freese v. Hibernia Sav. & Loan Soc., 139 Cal. 392, 73 P. 172; 5 Cal.Jur. 311, 312, 313.

It will be remembered that every possible method or means by which the property in question could have been acquired by the wife since the husband's death has been stipulated out of the case, except the bare possibility of gift, devise, bequest, or descent. There is no evidence tending to show or presumption of law tending to support a claim that she acquired any property in the four ways or means last above mentioned, and from the situation of the parties before marriage an inference of fact arises that the wife did not possess or own any property whatever before or at the time of marriage, and that the estate was therefore accumulated during coverture. Any other inference would be untenable under the uncontradicted evidence in the case. John Jolly and his wife, Margaret, enjoyed a matrimonial companionship for a period of about 40 years. They had no children, and the husband was an industrious, capable miner of economical habits, and as before stated it nowhere appears that the wife possessed or owned any separate estate before or after marriage. The fact would seem to be that she and the mother were in poor circumstances. Valuable property was found in her possession at the close of a span of life of about 75 years in duration, 40 years of which was passed in the marital state, and the last 10 years in widowhood, broken in health. Admittedly she engaged in no occupation during the latter period of her life.

Under the affirmative evidence of the case, aided by the usual presumptions of law, and with no evidence offered to overcome said presumptions, we must conclude that the estate ordered distributed to the heirs of Margaret Jolly as her separate property was the community property of said Margaret Jolly and her predeceased husband. * * *

Respondents insist that there is no evidence showing that the property was acquired during coverture. Admitting that there is no direct evidence on the question, but indirect or circumstantial only, this does not strengthen the weakness of respondent's position, as there is neither evidence of any kind or presumptions or inferences to support the conclusion that the property was acquired as separate property. The property in the possession of one of the spouses at the close of a long marital relation must be presumed to be community, unless a better right can be established by the spouse claiming it to be his or her separate property.

Respondents take the position that, in order for the presumption of section 164, Civil Code, to apply, it must be shown by direct evidence that the property was acquired during coverture; that is to say, it is not sufficient, in the absence of any evidence whatever as to the character of the property, to show merely that it was in the possession of the spouse during marriage, unless the circumstances of its possession are such as to definitely indicate the character of the property upon the death of the other. Our attention has been called to no case in this state where this precise question has been passed upon. "Acquired" and "possessed" are used rather interchangeably in many of the decisions of this court. It must be admitted, however, that in all the cases of this state in which the word "possession" was used as synonymous with "acquired" the facts were that the property actually came to either spouse during coverture. Estate of Bollinger, 170 Cal. 381, 149 P. 995, presents such an example. See, also, 5 Cal.Jur. 311, 312.

While the law strongly favors the indulgence of the presumption of community interest under ordinary circumstances of coverture, we do not think it necessary to extend the presumption prescribed by section 164, Civil Code, beyond the language of the section for the reason that the conclusion compelled in the instant case by the process of elimination and by the force of indirect evidence, forecloses any other conclusion but the sole one that the estate is not shown to be the separate estate of either spouse, and must for the reasons herein assigned be regarded as community property. The respondents failed to meet the burden of proof which the law casts upon them.

Respondents place emphasis on the fact that certain real property was purchased by the wife in 1918 and 1922. The grantee in those conveyances was the wife, the husband having been dead some years prior to the execution of said conveyances. This is not such a transaction as is dealt with in Fanning v. Green, 156 Cal. 279, 104 P. 308, or other cases in which one of the spouses deeded to the other, or where one is made the grantee by a third party during coverture. Here there was but one surviving spouse; therefore the rule announced in those cases cannot be applied to the facts of the present case. From what we have said as to the character of the property, it must follow that the realty purchased by the wife since the death of the husband must have been purchased with community funds. The fact that community property is sold and other property bought with the proceeds, or that such property is exchanged for other property, does not change the original character of the property; its character is determined by reference to the nature of the funds with which it is purchased, and so long as its source can be traced it retains the character of that source. 5 Cal.Jur. 294. The funds or property that purchased the realty in question can only be traced to a community source.

The order distributing the whole of the estate to the heirs of Margaret Jolly is hereby reversed.

Note

The fact of acquisition during marriage may be established by direct or by circumstantial evidence. Is evidence of possession during marriage sufficient to support the conclusion that the property is presumptively community property? Fidelity and Casualty Co. of New York v. Mahoney suggests not. Compare Wilson v. Wilson, reprinted supra; Estate of Bryant, 3 Cal.2d 58, 43 P.2d 529 (1935); Gaines v. California Trust Co., 48 Cal. App.2d 709, 121 P.2d 28 (1941); Lynam v. Vorwerk, 13 Cal.App. 507, 110 P. 355 (1910). In any event, proper preparation of a case for trial should alleviate this problem.

B. Rebuttal of the General Presumption by Tracing

The usual method of rebutting the general presumption is to trace the asset at issue back to a separate property source. For example, one spouse may show that the item was purchased with funds acquired by gift or inheritance, or which were earned prior to marriage, or while living separate and apart from the other spouse. The development of the tracing principle is outlined in Chapter 1. Its application is illustrated by the following case.

FREESE v. HIBERNIA SAVINGS & LOAN SOCIETY

Supreme Court of California, 1903.
139 Cal. 392, 73 P. 172.

ANGELLOTTI, J. Plaintiff administrator brought this action to recover the sum of $1,000, which, it was alleged, belonged to the estate of his intestate, and had been converted by the defendants to their own use. The action was tried without a jury, and the court granted a motion for a nonsuit, on the ground that the money sued for was not shown to have been the separate property of Ellen Denigan. From the judgment entered in favor of the defendants, plaintiff appeals, and the only ground alleged for reversal is that the court erred in granting the motion for a nonsuit.

The facts shown by the evidence, material to this controversy, are as follows, viz.: Ellen Denigan was, prior to her marriage, Ellen McCabe. She and Francis Denigan (whose name was also pronounced "Donegan" or "Dunnigan"), intermarried on the 19th day of January, 1862, and they continued to be husband and wife to the time of her death, which occurred July 3, 1896. At the time of her marriage, she was the owner of two parcels of real estate in San Francisco, one on Bryant street, conveyed to her in May, 1860, and one on Shipley street, conveyed to her in September, 1861. By a deed executed August 13, 1884, she and her husband conveyed the Shipley street lot for $2,000 cash. On August 18, 1884, there was deposited with Father Maraschi, treasurer at St. Ignatius College, to the credit of "Frank or Ellen Dunigan," the sum of $1,800. No other deposit was ever made on this account, and on July 6, 1886, the balance of principal remaining viz., $1,700, was withdrawn. On the same day July 6, 1886, account No. 133,269 was opened by the Hibernia

Savings & Loan Society with "Frank Denigan or Ellen Denigan" by a credit of cash of $1,700. On February 24, 1888, she conveyed the Bryant street land for a consideration of $6,750, which was paid her in cash, and on Monday, February 27, 1888, a deposit of $1,300 was made to the credit of said account. This account (133,269) continued to October 19, 1896, a little over three months after the death of Ellen Denigan when it was closed, the balance at that date being $2,413.33. The only two deposits made to the credit of this account were the $1,700 deposit of July 6, 1886, and the $1,300 deposit of February 27, 1888, all the other credits being dividends of interest earned by these two deposits. On the day this account was closed with a payment by the bank of the balance of $2,413.33 (October 19, 1896), account No. 212,145 was opened by the defendant bank with "Francis Denigan or James Denigan," by a credit of cash, $2,413.33, the Francis Denigan therein mentioned being the surviving husband of said Ellen Denigan. The only other deposit to the credit of said account was one of $250 on July 9, 1897, the other credits being of interest dividends. On November 29, 1897, there was paid by the bank on this account to defendant M.D. Connolly, on the written order of said Francis Denigan, dated November 28, 1897, the sum of $1,000. It is not disputed, and cannot well be under the decisions, that a motion for a nonsuit should not be granted where plaintiff's evidence is such that, if the case had gone to a jury on that evidence and a verdict had been rendered for him the evidence would be held sufficient to support the judgment upon the verdict. The rules as to nonsuit are the same whether the trial is by the court or by a jury. Goldstone v. Merchants' I. & C.S. Co., 123 Cal. 625, 56 P. 776.

The question then is whether, if the court below had, upon the evidence hereinbefore set forth, found that the property in question was the separate property of Ellen Denigan, such finding could be held to be supported by the evidence. We entertain no doubt that this question must be answered in the affirmative. While the presumption attending the possession of property by either husband or wife is that it is community property, such presumption is a disputable one, and may be controverted by other evidence. Respondents contend that the evidence of plaintiff was not legally sufficient to overcome this presumption. They rely upon expressions of this court in various cases to the effect that the fact that property is separate property of one of the spouses must be affirmatively established "by clear and decisive proof," "by clear and satisfactory evidence," and "by clear and convincing evidence." Speaking of expressions of this nature, some of which were stronger in terms than any used by this court, such as "clear and conclusive proof," and "conclusive proof," Ballinger, in his work on Community Property, says, in section 167: "It is not believed, however, that these terms should be considered as going to the length that their general meaning might import. Certainly it is not required that the proof to destroy this presumption should be any more than sufficient to satisfy the mind of court or jury that its weight is enough to cause a reasonable person, under all the circumstances, to believe in its sufficiency, in order to counterbalance the naked presumption that the property was acquired with the funds of the community. The property is merely considered as the property of the community until the contrary is shown by legal proof, and legal proof would seem to be a preponderance of the testimony under all the facts and circumstances of the particular case." See, also, 6 Am. & Eng.Ency. of Law (2d Ed.) p. 327. Clearly, it was never intended by this court to lay down a rule requiring demonstration in such matters; that is, such a degree of proof as, excluding possibility of error, produces absolute certainty. Civ.Code Proc. § 1826. Such proof is never required. Generally, moral certainty only is required, or that degree of proof which produces conviction in an unprejudiced mind; and evidence which ordinarily produces such conviction is satisfactory. Id. §§ 1826, 1835. Even in criminal cases, where life and personal liberty are involved, the law goes no further than to require that guilt shall be proved beyond a reasonable doubt, the accepted definition of which is that state of the case which, after an entire comparison and consideration of all the evidence, leaves the minds of the jury in that condition that they cannot say that they feel an abiding conviction, to a moral certainty, of the truth of the charge. We are of the opinion that it is incumbent on the party seeking to overcome the presumption of community property to do no more than to produce such legal evidence as, under all the circumstances of the particular case, would ordinarily produce conviction in an unprejudiced mind, and that in the face of such evidence the naked presumption, unsupported by any testimony, must fall. In considering whether or not such a degree of proof has been attained, we have the right to consider such presumptions and inferences as are authorized by the law of evidence. That a presumption declared by law has its place in such a dispute was acknowledged by this court in Denigan v. San Francisco Savings Union, 127 Cal. 142, 147, 59 P. 390, 78 Am.St.Rep. 35. An inference is simply a deduction which the reason of the judge or jury makes from the facts proved, and, in considering a question of the character here involved, we have the same right to make such reasonable deduction from the facts proved as we have in considering other questions. Measured by these rules, it is difficult to understand how it can be held that the evidence given on the trial was not legally sufficient to support a finding that the property was separate property. There was not a single circumstance shown by the evidence in aid of the presumption of community property, unless it be the form in which the account was kept, and, in view of what was said by this court in Denigan v. Hibernia S. & L. Soc., 127 Cal. 137, 59 P. 389, a case involving the deposit here in question, and Denigan v. S.F. Sav. Union, supra, it is apparent that the form in which the deposits were made does not materially assist.

It was established beyond doubt by the evidence that Ellen Denigan was the owner of two parcels of real estate at the time of her marriage, and that the same were therefore her separate property. It is presumed by direction of law that they continued to be her separate property as long as she owned them, and that the proceeds of the sale thereof were and continued to be her separate property. The only question, then concerning which there could be the slightest doubt, is as to whether these proceeds were sufficiently traced into the account with the defendant bank that existed at the time of her death, for, under the evidence in the record, there can be no reasonable doubt in the mind of any unprejudiced person that the account opened October 19, 1896, with "Francis Denigan or James Denigan," with a credit of $2,413.33, was opened by a deposit of the $2,413.33 that day taken from that account. That account, prior to the death of Ellen Denigan, had exclusive of interest dividends, but two credit items, one of July 6, 1886, of $1,700, and one of February 27, 1888, of $1,300. It is fairly inferable, from the circumstances shown, that the first deposit was the $1,700 on the same day withdrawn from the account of "Frank or Ellen Denigan" with Father Maraschi, and that the second was a portion of the proceeds of the sale made February 24, 1888, of Ellen Denigan's Bryant street property, and such, we think, would be the natural conclusion from the uncontradicted facts. It is also fairly inferable, from the evidence before the court, that the $1,800 deposited with Father Maraschi, to the credit of "Frank or Ellen Dunigan," on August 18, 1884, and which was the only credit item except a dividend for interest, was a portion of the $2,000 paid her not earlier than August 13, 1884, for her Shipley street property. In the absence of evidence of circumstances the effect of which would be to impair the showing made, we are satisfied that the proceeds of the sales of the separate property have been traced clearly enough to support a finding that the money on deposit with defendant bank at the time of Ellen Denigan's death was her separate property. It appears that $250 was deposited to the credit of the "Francis Denigan or James Denigan" account on July 9, 1897, and it is said that this certainly was not the separate property of Ellen Denigan, and that this must be held to be a part of the $1,000 paid to defendant Father Connolly. If this be granted, it would simply reduce plaintiff's claim by $250, and would not take away his right of recovery of the remaining $750. It is suggested by appellant that the $250 was probably deposited in this account to partially compensate for $600 withdrawn from the original account after the death of Ellen Denigan, but it is doubtful if any such inference is warranted by the evidence in the record. There was no merit in either of the other grounds specified in the motion for nonsuit. Plaintiff is the administrator of the estate of Ellen Denigan, and, so far as appears, the only administrator that said estate has ever had, and, as such, he is entitled to the possession of all her personal property as against the world.

The judgment is reversed, and the cause remanded for further proceedings.

Notes

1. Over the years the courts have stated that rebuttal requires "clear and satisfactory" evidence to overcome the general presumption of community property. They used such language when the only burden of proof in

civil cases was by a preponderance of the evidence, i.e., enough "to satisfy an unprejudiced mind." Thomassett v. Thomassett, 122 Cal.App.2d 116, 264 P.2d 626 (1953). The California Evidence Code now makes provision for two different evidentiary standards in civil cases: the preponderance of the evidence standard and the more stringent standard of "clear and convincing proof." West's Ann.Cal.Evid.Code § 502. No statute mandates the application of the higher standard in community property cases, but the language of some recent cases suggests that the higher standard may be judicially required. See In re Marriage of Ashodian, reprinted in Section 4 of this Chapter.

2. Tracing an asset back to a separate property source may be accomplished by direct evidence or more indirectly by circumstantial evidence. For example, it may be possible to rebut the general presumption by showing that at the time the item was acquired, there were no community property funds available. Evidence of the extent of community earnings and of family expenses, coupled with the presumption that family expenses are paid from community property, may show that there was no community wealth which could have been used to finance the acquisition. This type of evidence can be most successfully used in cases where the accounting period is relatively short and the community expenses exceeded community earnings continuously throughout the accounting period. We will consider the application of the "indirect tracing" method of rebuttal more fully in the materials on commingled funds in Chapter 4.

3. Family Code Section 802 provides as follows:

> The presumption that property acquired during marriage is community property does not apply to any property to which legal or equitable title is held by a person at the time of the person's death if the marriage during which the property was acquired was terminated by dissolution of marriage more than four years before the death.

(Stats.1992, c. 162 (A.B. 2650), § 10, operative Jan. 1, 1994.)

SECTION 3. THE COMMON STATUTORY PRESUMPTIONS RESPECTING SEPARATE PROPERTY

In addition to the general community property presumption, there are various common separate property presumptions. These are derived from the statutory definitions of separate property. Assets falling within one of these statutory categories are presumed to be separate property.

WEST'S ANNOTATED CALIFORNIA FAMILY CODE

§ 770. Separate property of married person

(a) Separate property of a married person includes all of the following:

(1) All property owned by the person before marriage.

(2) All property acquired by the person after marriage by gift, bequest, devise, or descent.

(3) The rents, issues, and profits of the property described in this section.

(b) A married person may, without the consent of the person's spouse, convey the person's separate property.

(Stats.1992, c. 162 (A.B. 2650), § 10, operative Jan. 1, 1994.)

§ 771. Earnings and accumulations during period of separation

The earnings and accumulations of a spouse and the minor children living with, or in the custody of, the spouse, while living separate and apart from the other spouse, are the separate property of the spouse.

(Stats.1992, c. 162 (A.B. 2650), § 10, operative Jan. 1, 1994.)

§ 772. Earnings or accumulations after entry of judgment of legal separation

After entry of a judgment of legal separation of the parties, the earnings or accumulations of each party are the separate property of the party acquiring the earnings or accumulations.

(Stats.1992, c. 162 (A.B. 2650), § 10, operative Jan. 1, 1994.)

———

One major category of separate property is based on the nature of the acquisition. Under Family Code Section 770, property acquired by one spouse by way of gift, bequest, devise or descent is presumptively separate property. This category of separate property is probably derived from the distinction drawn by the Spanish parent system between lucrative and onerous acquisitions. Property acquired by the spouses during marriage through the direct or indirect exploitation of the primary community property asset, that is, the time, energy and skill of husband and wife, was said to be acquired by "onerous title." Property acquired gratuitously, such as by a gift or inheritance, was deemed acquired by "lucrative title." Generally speaking, acquisitions by onerous title are community property, while an asset acquired by one spouse by lucrative title is separate property.[5]

Two other major categories of separate property are determined by the time of acquisition. Property acquired before marriage and property acquired after separation of the spouses or termination of the marriage is presumptively separate property. With respect to the former category, the primary issue is generally the timing of the acquisition, while cases involving the latter category frequently turn on the definition of separation.

ESTATE OF CLARK
California District Court of Appeal, 1928.
94 Cal.App. 453, 271 P. 542.

[In 1923 Edwin Clark died testate in Oklahoma. His father Dillard Clark, who would have been his sole heir if the will was invalid, began

---

5. De Funiak & Vaughn, Principles of Community Property (2d ed. 1971) § 62 at 127–28.

proceedings to contest the will. He won the contest action in the probate court but the proponents appealed and under Oklahoma practice a trial de novo was had in the district court and the will was held valid. While the case was pending in the district court Dillard Clark and the proponents of the will compromised their differences and agreed that Dillard Clark should be paid one-half the value of the estate. The contest was withdrawn and thereafter Dillard Clark was paid about $150,000. After the death of his son in 1923 and before the filing of the contest Dillard Clark married. When he died in 1926, his widow claimed the settlement money was community property in which she had a half interest against the will of her husband. The trial court held the property to be the separate property of decedent. On appeal the question was: did Dillard Clark prior to marriage have property which he exchanged for the $150,000 cash or did he merely find himself in a position where he could acquire the $150,000 by exploiting the nuisance value of that position? If the latter then the acquisition would be during marriage and community property.]

CRAIL, JUSTICE PRO TEM. * * *

The Supreme Court has construed the definition of separate property contained in section 163, Civil Code, to include "property taken in exchange for, or in the investment, or as the price of the property so originally owned or acquired." Meyer v. Kinzer, 12 Cal. 247, 73 Am.Dec. 538; Smith v. Smith, 12 Cal. 216, 73 Am.Dec. 533.

In case the will was held to be invalid, Major Clark was the sole heir of his son, and his right to contest the will was cast upon him immediately upon the death of his son. He claimed that his son's will was not a valid will. In this contention he had been sustained by the county court of Noble county, Okl. By way of compromise, however, he consented to the dismissal of his contest and to the admission of the will to probate. The terms of the compromise contemplated, however, that in consideration of withdrawing his contest, Major Clark should receive the half of his son's estate. It is this property and the profits thereof which are involved in this litigation. Had the will been rejected, he would have received all of his son's estate, and beyond doubt it would have been his separate property. The question is whether what he did receive is any the less his separate property because it came to him through the compromise that was effected. It would not be questioned that if, instead of acquiring a clear title to half of his son's estate by withdrawing his contest to the will, Major Clark had adopted the method of having the appeal dismissed and the will denied probate, and then transferring to the legatees and devisees one-half of the property, this property would be his separate property.

Did Major Clark transfer to the devisee under the will a property interest in return for that which was received by him under the terms of the compromise?

* * *

The right of an heir to transfer his inheritance, even though there is a will or purported will in existence, is recognized by our courts. At the instant of his son's death Major Clark had a property right which he could assign or transfer or surrender for a consideration acceptable to him, and also the statutory right, which of itself is a property right, to contest his son's will. In re Baker, 170 Cal. 578, 150 P. 989. This right was a right vested in him prior to his marriage, and therefore was his separate property. The property involved in this litigation came to Major Clark in exchange or in payment for such property, and was likewise his separate property.

* * *

While the mere expectancy of an heir is not usually regarded as property, the moment the ancestor has died, that expectancy is changed into a vested interest in property. It becomes thus vested by virtue of the death.

Much reliance is placed by appellant upon the case of Pancoast v. Pancoast, 57 Cal. 320. This case involved a situation where a man before his marriage intruded, without any right, on certain land, and after his marriage made a deed and gave up possession of a portion of the same to the rightful owner, in consideration whereof the owner conveyed to the trespasser the rest of the tract in fee. In this case the court held that as the trespasser had nothing before marriage except the mere ability to give trouble and cause expense to the true owners, the title which the latter conveyed to him after his marriage was something wholly new and did not fall within any of the classes of new acquisitions enumerated in the statute as being separate property, and was in law community property. There are some features of the case which are similar to the instant case; but there is this difference: That in the Pancoast Case the occupation does not appear to have been founded on any claim of right at all, but was a naked trespass, and the court refused to recognize a mere trespass as property; whereas Major Clark's claim to his son's estate was made in good faith on a bona fide contention that his son's will was invalid, and the Oklahoma court approved the settlement and found that it was free from fraud and duress and was for the best interest of the proponents of the will. In other words, that the contest was brought on probable cause. But above the good faith and above the probable cause, as steadfast as the rock of Gibraltar, stands out this element of differentiation—that his contest was the assertion of a statutory right amounting to property.

It is the contention of appellant that the will was declared to be a valid will by the Oklahoma court, and that it was therefore a valid will ab initio. The facts are that at the time of the settlement the will had not yet been declared to be a valid will; that it was the subject of a contest brought by Major Clark, a contest which the statute specifically authorized him to bring; that the will was an unnatural will in that it excluded by its provisions the only person who was the natural object of the bounty of the decedent; that the contest had been successful in the county court, and it was only by the prosecution of an appeal that the executors and legatees would have been able to obtain anything out of the estate; that no order of a probate court of Oklahoma had yet been entered admitting the will to probate; and that a will may be ever so valid, but until it is admitted to probate it is of no value as evidence of title. Roberts v. Roberts, 168 Cal. 307, 142 P. 1080; Estate of Patterson, 155 Cal. 626, 102 P. 941; Estate of Christensen, 135 Cal. 674, 68 P. 112. Thereafter the will was admitted to probate after the only person who was adversely interested had withdrawn his contest.

* * *

It is true that the property in litigation was acquired by Major Clark during the time he was married to appellant, but it was acquired by way of the compromise of a statutory right which was in itself property and which he owned prior to his marriage. Property acquired by compromise is separate property if the right compromised is separate. The right compromised is the consideration for the property obtained by the compromise, and the principle is the same as where property is purchased with separate funds. 31 Cor.Jur. 24, § 1099.

Judgment affirmed.

DOWNER v. BRAMET

California District Court of Appeal, 1984.
152 Cal.App.3d 837, 199 Cal.Rptr. 830.

OPINION

KAUFMAN, ASSOCIATE JUSTICE.

Plaintiff Gloria Alice Bramet Downer (hereinafter referred to as former wife) appeals from a judgment of nonsuit on her complaint for the determination of her rights in certain property and for fraud. She claims a community property interest in the proceeds of sale of a one-third interest in a ranch conveyed to her former husband George Keith Bramet by his employer after the parties separated. At the close of former wife's case, former husband moved for nonsuit. The motion was granted and judgment entered accordingly.

Facts

The parties were married in 1953, and separated in 1971. Former husband was an accountant and a tax expert. He worked for Chilcott Enterprises before, during and after the marriage, beginning in 1943. Chilcott Enterprises consisted of several businesses and corporations owned and operated by Edward Chilcott and his wife. Former husband was an officer of several of the corporations and acted as secretary-treasurer, accountant and recordkeeper for all of the Chilcotts' operations. Mr. Chilcott considered former husband his "righthand man."

Chilcott Enterprises had no retirement program of any kind for its employees. According to former wife's testimony, sometime in the mid–1960's former husband told her that Mr. Chilcott was going to give to him and two other employees a ranch in Oregon in lieu of retirement benefits. Nothing further was thereafter said about the ranch.

The parties separated in November 1971. In December 1972, after some exchange of drafts between the parties and their counsel, a marital settlement agreement was executed. The agreement, which was later incorporated in the judgment of dissolution, provided that all income and earnings of former husband or former wife after March 4, 1972, should be the separate property of the acquirer and that each party released any claim to such earnings or after acquired property. However, the agreement also contained a warranty "that neither party is now possessed of any property of any kind or description whatsoever, other than the property specifically mentioned in this Agreement" and a provision reading: "If it shall hereafter be determined by a Court of competent jurisdiction that one party is now possessed of any community property not set forth herein * * * such party hereby covenants and agrees to pay to [the other on demand an amount equal to one-half of the then] or present fair market value of such property, whichever is greater."

In August 1972, before the parties executed the agreement, but after the March 4 date specified in the settlement agreement, the Chilcotts deeded the W–4 Ranch in Oregon to former husband and two other employees. Former husband did not mention his interest in the ranch at the time he executed the settlement agreement in December 1972.

Former husband continued working for Chilcott Enterprises after the dissolution until he became disabled after suffering a stroke in 1976. In 1978, the ranch was sold for over $1,350,000 and former husband's interest in the sale proceeds was turned over to his conservator. This action was instituted in 1980 shortly after former wife learned of the conveyance of the ranch to former husband and the other employees.

Mr. Chilcott testified in essence that the conveyance to the three employees was a gift—the reason he deeded the ranch to the three employees was that he did not need the money and he just felt like giving it away.

Additional facts will be included in the discussion of the propriety of the nonsuit.

* * *

The Nonsuit

A nonsuit may be granted only when, " ' * * * disregarding conflicting evidence and giving to plaintiff's evidence all the value to which it is legally entitled, herein indulging in every legitimate inference which may be drawn from that evidence, the result is a determination that there is no evidence of sufficient substantiality to support a verdict in favor of the plaintiff if such a verdict were given.' " (*Estate of Lances* (1932) 216 Cal. 397, 400, 14 P.2d 768.) The question is thus whether there was substantial evidence that would have supported a verdict in favor of former wife on the issue of her interest in the ranch (or, more correctly, the proceeds from the sale of the ranch).

Former wife contends there was substantial evidence the transfer of the ranch interest to former husband was in lieu of pension benefits, and is therefore community property. Former husband contends there is no substantial evidence the ranch constituted a retirement benefit and argues the transfer of the ranch interest was a gift, and thus, separate property pursuant to Civil Code section 5108.[4] The trial court agreed with former husband that the transfer of the interest in the ranch to him was a gift and concluded therefore that it was his separate property.

We agree with the trial court and former husband that the Chilcotts' transfer of a one-third interest in the ranch to former husband was legally in the form of a gift. Civil Code section 1146 defines a gift as "a transfer of personal property, made voluntarily, and without consideration." The evidence establishes that that is precisely what was done in the case at bench. There is no evidence the ranch was transferred pursuant to a legal obligation to do so on the part of the Chilcotts. There is no evidence of any bargained-for contractual obligation nor of any detrimental reliance by former husband sufficient to invoke the doctrine of promissory estoppel. There is nothing to show, for example, that former husband was induced to stay in the Chilcotts' employ by the statement assertedly made by Mr. Chilcott that the ranch was going to be conveyed to the three employees in lieu of a pension program. There being no evidence of any legal obligation to convey the ranch, its conveyance can only have been a gift.

However, the conclusion the conveyance was legally a gift does not resolve the ultimate question of the characterization of the ranch interest or the proceeds of its sale as community or separate. Although Civil Code section 5108 provides that property acquired by the husband after marriage by gift is his separate property, the language of section 5108 must be read in the context of the entire marital property scheme. Earnings or property attributable to or acquired as a result of the labor, skill and effort of a spouse during marriage are community property. (Civ.Code, § 5110; cf. Civ.Code, § 5118.) Even though the transfer of the ranch interest was legally a gift, there is substantial, indeed strong, evidence the gift was made by former husband's employer in recognition of former husband's devoted and skillful services during his lifelong employment at Chilcott Enterprises.

The evidence shows former husband began working for Chilcott Enterprises in 1943. He became Mr. Chilcott's righthand man, did all the accounting for the various Chilcott operations, was responsible for all the tax planning, advice, and filing of returns, handled sales contracts and recordkeeping, served as officer in several of the corporate entities and supervised the ranch operations in California, Arizona and Oregon. For over 30 years, he was the Chilcotts' loyal and trusted employee. By contrast, there was no evidence of any social or personal relationship

4. Civil Code section 5108 reads in pertinent part: "All property owned by the husband before marriage, and that acquired afterwards by *gift*, bequest, devise, or descent, with the rents, issues, and profits thereof, is his separate property." (Emphasis added.)

between former husband and the Chilcotts. The Bramets never went out socially with the Chilcotts, and former husband never played golf or other sports with Mr. Chilcott, never took a social trip, played cards or anything of that sort with the Chilcotts. The Bramets went to the Chilcotts' house once to attend the wedding of the Chilcotts' oldest daughter, and one time former husband took care of the Chilcotts' home while they were away on vacation. Otherwise, former husband never went to the Chilcotts' home socially. Mr. Chilcott testified that, except for their business relationship, he had practically no contact with former husband.

Thus, although the conveyance of the ranch interest to former husband was in the form of a gift, the evidence would support, indeed strongly suggests, that it was in whole or part a remuneratory gift in recognition of former husband's loyal and skilled efforts for and services to his employer. (*Holby v. Holby* (1981) 131 Ariz. 113 [638 P.2d 1359, 1360]; de Funiak and Vaughn, Principles of Community Property (2d ed. 1971) § 70, pp. 157–160.) To the extent it was and to the extent the efforts and services were rendered during the marriage (see *In re Marriage of Poppe* (1979) 97 Cal.App.3d 1, 8–9, 158 Cal.Rptr. 500; *In re Marriage of Judd* (1977) 68 Cal.App.3d 515, 522–523, 137 Cal.Rptr. 318), the ranch interest conveyed to former husband and the proceeds of its sale were community property. (*Holby v. Holby, supra,* 131 Ariz. 113 [638 P.2d 1359, 1360]; de Funiak and Vaughn, Principles of Community Property (2d ed. 1971) § 70, pp. 157–160.)

It was error therefore to grant the nonsuit as to the cause of action to establish former wife's interest in the proceeds of sale of the ranch interest.

* * *

MORRIS, P.J., and RICKLES, J., concur.

LORING v. STUART

Supreme Court of California, 1889.
79 Cal. 200, 21 P. 651.

BELCHER, C.C. Action to foreclose a mortgage. Defense, that the defendant was a married woman when she executed the mortgage, and that the mortgaged property was community property, and the mortgage therefore void. The court found that at the date of the mortgage, and for more than ten years prior thereto, defendant was the wife of one Robert Stuart, but that she and her husband had lived separate and apart from each other for nearly two years, and that the mortgaged premises were the earnings of defendant while so living separate from her husband, and were her separate property. Judgment was entered foreclosing the mortgage, and from that judgment and an order denying her a new trial defendant appealed.

* * *

There was testimony tending to show that the defendant had been living separate from her husband for nearly five years when the case was tried. It appeared that the parties were living together in Rocklin, Placer county, in April, 1883; that in that month he went away to Forrest City, in Sierra county, and had ever since resided there; that she continued to live in Rocklin, and had kept boarders, and done other work to support herself and children; that she had never visited him nor he her, though he had twice passed through Rocklin; that he had written several letters to her and the children, and had three or four times sent small sums of money to the children. He testified: "The immediate cause of my leaving Rocklin was domestic infelicity, and such infelicity has not been healed by reconciliation. I do not intend to resume intimate marital relations with my wife, but my intentions in that regard did not exist on the 1st of January, 1885. It is only within the past six months that I fully determined in my own mind not to resume intimate marital relations with my wife again, but I have never ceased, nor do I intend to cease, performing my obligations to my family, while I have strength to do so. I left my wife, and did not inform her when, if ever, I would return, and did not acquaint my wife about my future intentions as to living with her." We think this shows a "separate" living within the meaning of section 169 of the Civil Code, and that the judgment cannot be reversed on this ground.

* * *

PER CURIAM. For the reasons given in the foregoing opinion the judgment and order are affirmed.

Notes

1. Under the Spanish–Mexican community property system, a spouse who in violation of marital obligations separated from the other spouse lost any claim to have new acquisitions during the period of separation classified as community property, and indeed under some circumstances, forfeited any claim to share in accumulations as of the time of separation. The innocent spouse, however, continued to benefit from new acquisitions of the guilty spouse. All American community property states have departed from this rule either by statute or case law. De Funiak & Vaughn, Principles of Community Property (2d ed. 1971) §§ 189–90 at 443–50. California statutes originally provided that the wife's earnings while living separate and apart from her husband were her separate property. This rule applied even if the wife was living separate and apart from her husband "through her own fault." Spreckels v. Spreckels, 116 Cal. 339, 342, 48 P. 228, 229, 36 L.R.A. 497, 500, 58 Am.St.Rep. 170, 172 (1897). There was no comparable provision controlling the earnings and accumulations of a married man living separate from his wife, and these therefore remained community property. In 1971 the legislature amended the statute, making it equally applicable to both spouses.

2. The term "living separate and apart" contained in West's Ann.Cal. Family Code § 771 is not statutorily defined, and thus has been open to judicial interpretation. Early on California courts rejected the contention

that the statute should be read literally, holding that it did not cover cases involving a temporary separation short of a family breakdown. Tobin v. Galvin, 49 Cal. 34 (1874). The courts required something more than mere physical separation. In Makeig v. United Security Bank & Trust Co., 112 Cal.App. 138, 296 P. 673 (1931), the husband and wife did not live together during their 14–year marriage due to economic and health considerations. The court held that they were not living separate and apart within the meaning of the statute:

> "Living separate and apart, however, as contemplated by said section * * * does not apply to a case where a man and wife are residing temporarily in different places due to economic or social reasons, but applies to a condition where the spouses have come to a parting of the ways and have no present intention of resuming the marital relations and taking up life together under the same roof."

In Kerr v. Kerr, 182 Cal.App.2d 12, 18, 5 Cal.Rptr. 630, 634 (1960), the court reached a similar conclusion: "In the instant case the evidence shows that there was no parting of the ways nor an intention not to resume marital relations and take up life together under the same roof until January 1, 1956, when appellant refused to permit respondent's return to their home. It is clear that respondent left for New Mexico because of his fear of being reincarcerated in the Stockton State Hospital. That did not mean that he was running away from his wife."

3. If physical separation is not determinative, what factors should the court consider in deciding whether or not the parties have been living separate and apart for purposes of West's Ann.Cal. Family Code § 771? Should the court apply a purely objective standard, or should the subjective intent of either spouse be taken into consideration? Consider In re Marriage of Baragry, which follows.

IN RE MARRIAGE OF BARAGRY
California Court of Appeal, 1977.
73 Cal.App.3d 444, 140 Cal.Rptr. 779.

FLEMING, ASSOCIATE JUSTICE.

Wife appeals that part of the interlocutory judgment of dissolution which fixes the date of the parties' separation as 4 August 1971, the date husband moved out of the family home. She contends the date should be 14 October 1975, the date husband filed his petition for dissolution, and, alternatively, that husband is estopped to contend the separation took place before 14 October 1975.

The facts are undisputed, and the issue is the legal conclusion that should flow from the facts. The parties were married in September 1956, and have two daughters, now thirteen and ten. Husband is an eye physician and surgeon. After a quarrel with wife, husband moved out of the family residence on 4 August 1971 and stayed for a time on his boat. Thereafter he took an apartment, into which his 28–year–old girlfriend and employee, Karen Lucien, moved and in which both now live. Although not sleeping in the family residence, husband maintained continuous and frequent contacts with his family. He ate dinner at home with wife almost every night in 1971 and 1972 and thereafter ate at home at least three to five times a week. He maintained his mailing address at the home. In 1971 and 1972, he took wife and daughters to Yosemite and San Francisco. On Christmas Eve, 1971, he slept at home. Throughout 1972 and 1973, he took his family to all UCSB basketball games. In 1973, he went with his wife to Sun Valley for a week without the children. He frequently took wife to social occasions—parties at friends' homes, dinners for professional and academic groups, outings with other doctors and their wives. He sent wife numerous Christmas, birthday, and anniversary cards throughout the years 1971 to 1975, including a card stating, "I love you" in 1973, and an anniversary card with a huge box of flowers in September 1975. In 1974 he filed an enrollment card at their daughter's private school stating that she lived at home with both parents. The parties continued to file joint income tax returns, and husband maintained his voting registration at the home address. He paid all the household bills and supported his family. He regularly brought his laundry home to wife, who washed and ironed it twice a month.

The parties had no sexual relations after 4 August 1971. Wife knew husband was living with Karen but wife desired a reconciliation, and continued to hope husband would return. Husband did not tell her he was never coming back. Husband testified he took wife on outings in order to preserve social appearances and to keep in touch with his children, who otherwise would not come to see him. He delayed filing for divorce because his "solid mid-Western upbringing" made him reluctant to file for divorce. Both parties agree that their relationship was entirely amicable but non-sexual after August 1971 and that they maintained the habits and appearance of a married couple except that husband slept with Karen. For four years husband maintained the facade of a marital relationship, but he now claims to have been legally separated from his wife. As proof he tenders his extra-marital activities.

What little law defines separation under Civil Code section 5118 [now Family Code Section 771] holds that "living separate and apart" refers to "that condition when spouses have come to a parting of the ways with no present intention of resuming marital relations." (In re Marriage of Imperato (1975) 45 Cal.App.3d 432, 435–436, 119 Cal.Rptr. 590, 592.) That husband and wife may live in separate residences is not determinative. (Makeig v. United Security Bank & Trust Co. (1931) 112 Cal.App. 138, 143, 296 P. 673; Tobin v. Galvin (1874) 49 Cal. 34.) The question is whether the parties' conduct evidences a complete and final break in the marital relationship. Here the only evidence of such a break is the absence of an active sexual relationship between the parties and husband's cohabitation elsewhere with a girlfriend. In our view such evidence is not tantamount to legal separation.

At bench the bone of contention is the community property character of husband's earnings from 1971 to 1975. To determine whether the conduct of the parties was such as to transmute the nature of that property from community to separate, we briefly recall the basic nature of the community property system. Property acquired during a legal marriage is strongly presumed to be community property. (Melny v. Melny (1949) 90 Cal.App.2d 672, 677, 203 P.2d 588; Falk v. Falk (1941) 48 Cal.App.2d 762, 767, 120 P.2d 714; Fountain v. Maxim (1930) 210 Cal. 48, 51, 290 P. 576; Wilson v. Wilson (1946) 76 Cal.App.2d 119, 126, 172 P.2d 568.) That presumption is fundamental to the community property system (In re Duncan's Estate (1937) 9 Cal.2d 207, 217, 70 P.2d 174), and stems from Mexican–Spanish law which likens the marital community to a partnership. Each partner contributes services of value to the whole, and with certain limitations and exceptions both share equally in the profits. (Stewart v. Stewart (1926) 199 Cal. 318, 342–343, 249 P. 197.) So long as wife is contributing her special services to the marital community she is entitled to share in its growth and prosperity. (In re Marriage of Lopez (1974) 38 Cal.App.3d 93, 107, 113 Cal.Rptr. 58.) "Under principles of community property law, the wife, by virtue of her position as wife, made to that value the same contribution as does a wife to any of the husband's earnings and accumulations during marriage. She is as much entitled to be recompensed for that contribution as if it were represented by the increased value of stock in a family business." (Referring to valuation of goodwill.) (Golden v. Golden (1969) 270 Cal.App.2d 401, 405, 75 Cal.Rptr. 735, 738.)

At bench, husband was presumably enjoying a captain's paradise, savoring the best of two worlds, and capturing the benefits of both. Wife was furnishing all the normal wifely contributions to a marriage that husband was willing to accept and most of the services normally furnished in a twenty-year-old marriage. Husband was reaping the advantages of those services and may be presumed to owe part of his professional success during that four-year period to wife's social and domestic efforts on his behalf. One who enjoys the benefit of a polygamous lifestyle must be prepared to accept its accompanying financial burdens. (Marvin v. Marvin (1976) 18 Cal.3d 660, 134 Cal.Rptr. 815, 557 P.2d 106; Civ.Code, § 3521.) During the period that spouses preserve the appearance of marriage, they both reap its benefits, and their earnings remain community property. To hold otherwise would be tantamount to saying that because husband slept on the living room couch for four years, or because he regularly slept elsewhere with another woman, wife can be deprived of her share in the household earnings.

Because there is no sufficient evidence to rebut the presumptive status of a legal marriage continuing until 14 October 1975, the judgment is reversed, and the cause is remanded for further proceedings. Costs to wife.

ROTH, P.J., and BEACH, J., concur.

Notes

1. The fact that the wife moved out of the family home and filed a petition for dissolution of marriage has been held not to establish as a

matter of law that the parties were living separate and apart within the meaning of the statute. This evidence was countered by the wife's testimony that although she filed a dissolution petition, she did not want a divorce and that she wanted to work out the parties' difficulties. In addition, there was evidence that the parties continued their sexual relationship, saw a marriage counselor, and traveled together. In re Marriage of Marsden, 130 Cal.App.3d 426, 181 Cal.Rptr. 910 (1982).

2. The term "accumulations" used in West's Ann.Cal. Family Code § 771 has caused considerably less difficulty than the phrase "living separate and apart." In a case involving the predecessor statute to § 771, "accumulations" was interpreted as follows:

> "* * *. When one speaks generally of accumulation of property, he is understood to refer to any property which a person acquires and retains, without regard to the means by which it is obtained. Of course if it were acquired by the wife by purchase with community funds, or in exchange for other community property, it would not be accumulated in the sense here involved. Such an acquisition would be a mere exchange and it would have the character possessed by that given in exchange for it. But where the wife, while living separate from her husband, through her own industry, labor, skill, or efforts of any kind, obtains property and holds it in possession, it is what would ordinarily be called an accumulation of property, and, under the rules stated in section 169, it would be a part of her separate estate."

The Court held that the acquisition of title by adverse possession was an accumulation within the meaning of the statute. Union Oil Co. v. Stewart, 158 Cal. 149, 156, 110 P. 313, 316 (1910). In the case of In re Marriage of Wall, 29 Cal.App.3d 76, 105 Cal.Rptr. 201 (1972), the court held that the proceeds of an Irish Sweepstakes Ticket purchased with support payments while living separate and apart were an accumulation within the meaning of West's Ann.Cal.Family Code § 771.

SECTION 4. SPECIAL PRESUMPTIONS BASED ON THE FORM OF TITLE

A. Acquisitions by a Married Woman

Family Code Section 803 raises a presumption of separate property when a title in writing was acquired by a married woman prior to January 1, 1975. No such provision covers a title acquired thereafter. The reason for this special presumption was the need to protect the married woman and persons dealing with her during the period when the husband had control and management of the community property. When the wife was given equal rights to control and manage community property there was no further need for the presumption, hence the present form of legislation. The presumption is rebuttable except against a person dealing in good faith and for a valuable consideration with the married woman, her legal representatives or successors.[6] The

---

6. In 1889 the code provision made the presumption conclusive in favor of a purchaser or encumbrancer in good faith and for a valuable consideration. Cal.Stats. 1889, c. 219, p. 328; Randall v. Washington, 161 Cal. 59, 118 P. 425 (1911); Gilmour v.

presumption was commonly applied where the husband, having management and control of the community property, put title to certain property in the name of his wife.[7] The underlying rationale for the presumption was that when a married man executed a conveyance of property to his wife, he must have intended to change the property rights of himself and his wife, not merely to indulge in an idle ceremony.[8] Should the presumption be applied where a married woman, although having no statutory rights of management and control, did in fact use community funds to negotiate a transaction and acquire written title in her name alone? Note that after 1951 a married woman had management and control rights over her earnings. Should the presumption be applied where the wife used her earnings to acquire property in her name alone?

WEST'S ANNOTATED CALIFORNIA FAMILY CODE

§ 803. Property acquired by married woman before January 1, 1975; conclusiveness of presumptions

Notwithstanding any other provision of this part, whenever any real or personal property, or any interest therein or encumbrance thereon, was acquired before January 1, 1975, by a married woman by an instrument in writing, the following presumptions apply, and are conclusive in favor of any person dealing in good faith and for a valuable consideration with the married woman or her legal representatives or successors in interest, regardless of any change in her marital status after acquisition of the property:

(a) If acquired by the married woman, the presumption is that the property is the married woman's separate property.

(b) If acquired by the married woman and any other person, the presumption is that the married woman takes the part acquired by her as tenant in common, unless a different intention is expressed in the instrument.

(c) If acquired by husband and wife by an instrument in which they are described as husband and wife, the presumption is that the property is the community property of the husband and wife, unless a different intention is expressed in the instrument.

(Stats.1992, c. 162 (A.B. 2650), § 10, operative Jan. 1, 1994.)

HORSMAN v. MADEN

California District Court of Appeal, 1941.
48 Cal.App.2d 635, 120 P.2d 92.

SPENCE, JUSTICE. Plaintiffs, as executors of the last will of Emile Maden, deceased, brought this action against defendant, the widow of

North Pasadena Land & Water Co., 178 Cal. 6, 171 P. 1066 (1918). In 1927 the language was changed to include a purchaser, encumbrancer, payor, or any other person dealing with such married woman in good faith and for a valuable consideration. Cal.Stats.1927, c. 487, p. 826. In 1941 the present language was adopted. Cal.Stats. 1941, c. 455, p. 1752. Cases do not indicate that the change in the statutory language resulted in any change in effect. See De

Boer v. De Boer, 111 Cal.App.2d 500, 244 P.2d 953 (1952); Attebury v. Wayland, 73 Cal.App.2d 1, 165 P.2d 524 (1946).

7. See, e.g., Hogevoll v. Hogevoll, 59 Cal.App.2d 188, 138 P.2d 693 (1943); Holmes v. Holmes, 27 Cal.App. 546, 150 P. 793 (1915).

8. Taylor v. Opperman, 79 Cal. 468, 21 P. 869 (1889); Johnson v. Johnson, 214 Cal.App.2d 29, 29 Cal.Rptr. 179 (1963).

claim on property

determine all actions

said deceased, seeking to quiet title to certain real and personal property and to obtain an accounting with respect to such of the property as had been disposed of by defendant. The cause was tried by the court sitting without a jury and, at the close of plaintiffs' case, the court granted defendant's motion for a nonsuit and entered a judgment of dismissal. Plaintiffs appeal from said judgment.

π

The controversy involved the issue of whether the property in question was the community property of Mr. and Mrs. Maden or the separate property of Mrs. Maden at the time of the death of Mr. Maden in 1939. The complaint alleged that the property was acquired as community property and that it remained community property at all times. The answer admitted that practically all of the property was acquired as community property but alleged that such property became the separate property of defendant by reason of certain transfers.

It appears from the evidence that Mr. and Mrs. Maden were married in 1914 and that certain real property together with certain stocks and bonds were acquired as community property during their married life. Some of the property was acquired in the name of Mr. Maden while other property was acquired in the names of both Mr. and Mrs. Maden. Said parties kept their securities in a joint safe deposit box and they also kept funds in joint bank accounts.

In the latter part of 1933, domestic difficulties arose after Mr. Maden had become interested in another woman. Mrs. Maden removed said securities from said joint safe deposit box and retained them in a safe deposit box of her own. * * *

Thereafter the parties attempted a reconciliation and took a three months' cruise to the Orient. Mrs. Maden retained possession of the securities. No permanent reconciliation resulted and, after their return from the Orient, the parties separated. Disputes arose over the matter of the support of Mrs. Maden. Apparently the dividends on the stocks were being sent to Mr. Maden and it was Mrs. Maden's desire to have the stocks transferred into her name in order that she would receive the dividends directly. Mrs. Maden testified that she requested such transfer as a matter of precaution for both herself and Mr. Maden. Mrs. Maden threatened to bring suit and to create a scandal unless the securities were so transferred. In October, 1934, Mr. Maden met his wife at the bank, endorsed the securities and permitted her to retain them. He also agreed to give Mrs. Maden $100 per month from his salary. In 1935, he also executed and delivered to her a deed to their home, title to which had previously stood in both their names, but he told her not to record said deed. Mrs. Maden did record the deed in 1937, however, and she testified she did so because she "thought it was better business to record it". The parties were never divorced and Mr. Maden made a will shortly before his death declaring all of said property to be community property and purporting to dispose of it as such.

Upon the trial, it was the theory of plaintiffs that there had been no intention upon the part of Mr. Maden to make a gift or to change the status of said property to separate property of Mrs. Maden and that said property therefore remained the community property of the spouses at the time of Mr. Maden's death. It was the theory of defendant that said transfers constituted executed gifts to Mrs. Maden and that said property was her separate property at all times after said transfers had been made. It appears that there was no written agreement between the parties concerning the status of said property and that there was no recital in any of the transfers stating that the property was transferred to Mrs. Maden as her separate property.

In support of their case, plaintiffs called several witnesses including Mrs. Maden, who was called under section 2055 of the Code of Civil Procedure. Plaintiffs endeavored to show by the declarations of Mr. Maden, made both before and after the transfers, that Mr. Maden had no intention to make a gift or to change the status of said property to the separate property of Mrs. Maden and that Mr. Maden had always treated the property as community property. Objection was made to the introduction of such evidence and practically all evidence of said declarations was excluded by the trial court. Some evidence covering such declarations was stricken out upon motion. Repeated offers were made and repeated objections were sustained. The view of the trial court was expressed as follows: "Here the question of intent on the part of the donor is not involved on the trial of this case at all." And finally the trial court said, "There is no use talking any further, counsel. This is a point where we have to stop. There will be no further testimony of any kind, oral or in the form of written declarations by the deceased, conveyed to this witness or anybody else, relative to the conversations occurring after the transactions with his wife."

On this appeal, plaintiffs contend that the trial court erred in granting the motion for nonsuit and that the trial court committed prejudicial error in its rulings excluding evidence of the declarations of the deceased which tended to show that he had no intention of making a gift to defendant or of changing the status of the property to separate property of defendant. In our opinion, both of these contentions must be sustained.

* * *

But in any event the error of the trial court in ruling upon the admissibility of evidence would require a reversal of the judgment. We are dealing here with a situation in which the property in question was admittedly acquired with community funds and in which it is claimed by defendant that said property became the separate property of defendant by virtue of executed gifts by the deceased. While there is a presumption that any property acquired by the defendant by an instrument in writing became her separate property, Civ.Code, sec. 164, such presumption is not conclusive between the parties but is disputable. Salveter v. Salveter, 206 Cal. 657, 275 P. 801; In re Estate of Bruggemeyer, 115 Cal.App. 525, 2 P.2d 534.

Property may be regarded as community property regardless of whether the record title stands in the name of the husband or of the wife or in the names of both the husband and the wife, and the courts are invested with full power to determine the status of any such property. Salveter v. Salveter, 206 Cal. 657, 275 P. 801; Jansen v. Jansen, 127 Cal.App. 294, 15 P.2d 777. And where it is claimed that an instrument in writing, executed by the husband to the wife, constituted a gift to the wife and changed the status of community property to that of separate property of the wife, the question of the intention of the husband in executing such instrument becomes "the all-important and controlling question". Ruiz v. Dow, 113 Cal. 490, 45 P. 867, 869; see, also, Fanning v. Green, 156 Cal. 279, 104 P. 308; In re Estate of Bruggemeyer, 115 Cal.App. 525, 2 P.2d 534. In determining this question of intention, the declarations of the alleged donor, made either before or after the transfer, are admissible and such declarations need not have been made in the presence of the adverse party. Ruiz v. Dow, supra; In re Estate of Hall, 154 Cal. 527, 98 P. 269; O'Dea v. Hibernia Savings & Loan Society, 119 Cal.App. 622, 7 P.2d 318; In re Estate of Carson, 184 Cal. 437, 194 P. 5, 17 A.L.R. 239. These last-mentioned authorities demonstrate the error of the trial court in excluding evidence of such declarations and our review of the record convinces us that such error was prejudicial to plaintiffs.

The only authorities cited by respondent which come reasonably close to approaching the problem presented here are Miller v. Brode, 186 Cal. 409, 199 P. 531, and Dale v. Dale, 87 Cal.App. 359, 262 P. 339. These cited cases are clearly distinguishable, however, as each of the instruments involved in said cases expressly recited that the property was conveyed to the wife as her separate property. We may further state that respondent's brief is based upon the premise that "the only issue in the case" was "whether or not there was an express oral agreement at the time of the transfer". As above stated, we do not believe that the allegation, found in one count of the complaint, that there was an oral agreement between the spouses at the time of the transfer was an essential allegation under the authorities hereinbefore cited. Proof that there was no intention on the part of the husband to make a gift or to change the status of the property was all that would have been required to sustain a finding, in conformity with the allegations of the complaint, that the property was at all times the community property of the spouses. Proof that there was an oral agreement at the time of the transfer would have been helpful to plaintiffs but it was not essential to make out their case. The allegation relating to the existence of such oral agreement should therefore have been treated as surplusage and the mere absence of evidence to prove such oral agreement did not justify the granting of the motion for nonsuit.

It is probably unnecessary but we deem it appropriate to state that this court should not be understood as indicating any view with respect to the ultimate determination of the issues of fact which may be presented in this controversy. The only questions before us on this appeal are the questions of law above discussed.

The judgment is reversed.

DONZE v. DONZE

California District Court of Appeal, 1928.
88 Cal.App. 769, 264 P. 294.

THOMPSON, JUSTICE PRO TEM. This is an appeal from that portion of an interlocutory judgment of divorce decreeing a certain house and lot standing in the name of appellant to be the community property of the respective spouses.

Appellant and respondent intermarried at Santa Barbara on July 29, 1909. In consideration of the sum of $100, the mother and father of respondent executed a deed of conveyance April 27, 1922, to lot 2, block 102, of said city of Santa Barbara, to appellant, Hattie Genevieve Donze, "as her separate property." A dwelling house was thereafter constructed on this lot at a cost of $2,800, which was borrowed from the building and loan association on a note and mortgage executed by these parties as a lien upon said premises. This money was subsequently paid in installments from the earnings acquired during coverture. Domestic trouble arose. In August, 1924, respondent brought suit against the appellant for divorce, alleging that said lot was their community property. * * * The court also found that the house and lot in question was community property, and awarded it to the spouses as "tenants in common." An appeal was taken from that portion of the decree which finds that this house and lot is community property, on the ground that this finding is unsupported by the evidence, and that oral testimony as to the title was incompetent to vary the terms of the deed.

The evidence is without conflict to the effect that all of the purchase price of said lot, together with the cost of construction of the dwelling house, was paid from community funds; the deed was executed by the father and mother of respondent to the appellant. Following the name of the grantee in this deed was the recital that the lot was conveyed "as her separate property." This deed was delivered to the appellant, who had it recorded, and afterward kept it among her private papers; the respondent never afterward saw the instrument. Over the objection of appellant that the evidence was incompetent and tended to vary the terms of a written instrument, the respondent was permitted to testify in effect that the deed was taken in the name of his wife as a matter of convenience. * * *

The evidence is undisputed that the deed was executed to appellant with the consent and at the request of respondent. There was no contention in this case that it was executed through fraud or mistake.

Where land is conveyed from a husband to his wife the presumption is that it was intended as a gift. So, also, where property is conveyed to a wife, from a third party, with the knowledge and consent of the husband, whether the consideration is paid by the husband from his separate property or from their community property the presumption is that it was intended as her separate property. Civ.Code, § 164; Sanchez v. Grace M.E. Church, 114 Cal. 295, 46 P. 2; Stafford v. Martinoni, 192 Cal. 724, 221 P. 919; 13 Cal.Jur. 854, § 50. The intention must ordinarily be inferred from all the surrounding circumstances, including the acts, declarations, and conduct of the interested parties at the time of the transaction. Gilmour v. N. Pasadena L. Co., 178 Cal. 6, 171 P. 1066; Fanning v. Green, 156 Cal. 279, 104 P. 308; Cohn v. Smith, 37 Cal.App. 764, 174 P. 682. But where a deed of conveyance to real property is made from a third party to the wife with the knowledge and consent and pursuant to directions from the husband, and the deed contains an express declaration that the property is conveyed to her as her separate property, regardless of whether the consideration is paid from his separate property or from the community funds the presumption that it was intended as a gift to the wife is conclusive, except when that intent is challenged on the trial by an issue of fraud or mistake. 13 Cal.Jur. 855, § 50; Miller v. Brode, 186 Cal. 409, 199 P. 531; Estate of McCauley, 138 Cal. 546, 71 P. 458; Swain v. Duane, 48 Cal. 358.

In the case of Miller v. Brode, supra, it is said:

"* * * The deed by which the ranch was acquired conveyed it to the decedent as sole grantee, and described it as her separate property, and was so made with the consent of her husband, who participated in the transaction. This definitely establishes the character of the property as her separate property. * * * Such a conveyance would be nothing more nor less than an express gift by the husband to the wife of community property. Swain v. Duane, 48 Cal. 358; Shanahan v. Crampton, 92 Cal. 9, 28 P. 50. There is no impediment to a husband making such a gift if he desires, and, if he does it, the property at once becomes the wife's separate property, and the effect of the conveyance in this respect cannot be avoided except by avoiding the conveyance itself. This, of course, cannot be done except for fraud, mistake, or some similar ground. In the absence of such ground for setting aside the transaction it is wholly immaterial that the property was community property before the husband conveyed it to the wife, or in case it were conveyed to her by a third person that the consideration given for it was community property. Its character is changed at once by the conveyance to the wife as her separate property either by the husband directly or by a third person with his consent."

The foregoing language seems to fit the instant case exactly. This deed was made to the wife at the request of the husband, and it recited that the property was conveyed to appellant "as her separate property." There was no fraud or mistake charged with relation to its execution. Under such facts the house and lot in question is conclusively presumed to be the separate property of the appellant.

The evidence as to the intent with which the deed was executed in the name of the appellant varied the terms of the written instrument, and, in the absence of appropriate allegations, was incompetent. The objection to this evidence should have been sustained. * * * It is true that in transactions between a husband and wife the law presumes the existence of a confidential relationship. Civ.Code, § 158. This fiduciary relationship also precludes either spouse from procuring an unfair advantage over the other by means of fraud, mistake, or undue influence. During the existence of this relationship, where an unfair advantage has been obtained, under appropriate pleadings, the transaction will be deemed to have been secured without consideration and by means of undue influence. Civ.Code, § 2235; 13 Cal.Jur. 860, § 54. Where such undue influence and advantage is alleged the burden is cast upon him who has the advantage to show that it was fair and free from fraud or undue influence. * * * But the mere existence of the relationship of husband and wife does not create a presumption of fraud or undue influence, in the absence of the procuring of an undue advantage, nor does it constitute a prima facie showing of such conduct. Before this presumption may be indulged it must appear that the marital confidence was violated and that an undue advantage was thereby secured. * * * But, manifestly, relief from such a fraudulent transaction may be secured only in a proceeding which presents the issue of fraud by specific pleadings. We have been pointed to no decision in the California Reports, nor elsewhere, holding that this serious charge of fraud may be raised without pleading the fiduciary relationship, the circumstances of the fraud, and the undue advantage secured. Upon the contrary, the cases cited indicate that the issues of fraud, lack of consideration, and undue influence were invariably raised by definite pleadings.

We therefore conclude that where a deed of conveyance is made to a wife, in which deed the character of the property is specifically declared to be "separate property," a rebuttable presumption is thereby created to the effect that it is her separate property, and that she holds the legal title thereto. This presumption may be overcome by the husband only on the theory that the deed is not what it purports to be, and was executed through fraud, mistake, or undue influence, and that the wife therefore holds but an equitable title for the benefit of the community. The invariable rule under such circumstance requires these issues to be raised by appropriate pleadings.

For the foregoing reasons the portion of the judgment determining property rights is reversed, and the cause is remanded for a new trial upon the sole issue as to the property rights. Inasmuch as the trial court was of the opinion that although the legal title to the property was in the wife, yet she held it for the community, and that the equitable title was in the community, it is directed that the plaintiff be permitted to amend his complaint upon timely and proper application therefor adding appropriate allegations of fraud, mistake, or undue influence, presenting the issue of the equitable ownership of the property, if he be so advised.

IN RE MARRIAGE OF ASHODIAN
California Court of Appeal, 1979.
96 Cal.App.3d 43, 157 Cal.Rptr. 555.

STEPHENS, ASSOCIATE JUSTICE.

Plaintiff husband appeals that portion of interlocutory judgment of dissolution of marriage which found certain real and personal property to be the separate property of defendant wife.

Husband and wife were married in 1943 and separated in 1974 after 31 years of marriage. Husband was a bus driver throughout the marriage; wife was a licensed real estate broker for approximately 15 years before the parties separated. Wife operated a business known as Belle Realty. Between 1962 and 1965, the parties bought and sold two properties in both their names. Husband then told wife he did not have the time to keep up maintenance and repair of the properties as she requested; that he didn't understand the business or want to be bothered with it. Wife thereafter bought and sold numerous properties in her own name and did not discuss them with husband; he did not know she held title to them solely in her name until after the parties separated. However, on her request he signed grant deeds to two of the properties and also knew tax problems were presented by the wife's business.

Husband filed a petition for dissolution of marriage in 1975, alleging that all the real property involved was community. The court rejected wife's contention that the parties had agreed the proceeds from her business would be her separate property. Wife then asserted the presumption in effect prior to 1975 that property acquired by a married woman by an instrument in writing is her separate property. (Civ.Code, § 5110.) Husband testified that he did not intend a gift to wife of his interest in the property; he had assumed it was all family property. The court found that the separate property presumption did apply and that husband had failed to rebut it. In ruling that husband made a gift of his community interest in the realty to his wife, the court stated: "It's quite apparent that Mr. Ashodian sort of abandoned his wife to practice in the field of real estate and didn't want to be bothered by it. And I think that constitutes sufficient evidence of a gift. And I don't believe that he's met the burden which the law requires him to meet to establish anything to the contrary." The disputed properties and proceeds from their sale were confirmed to wife as her separate property. This appeal followed.

The issue before us is whether a wife could use her community property earnings to purchase real estate in her own name prior to 1975 and then invoke a presumption that the property belongs to her alone. The answer here is yes.

The separate property presumption found in Civil Code section 5110, which applies only to property acquired by a married woman prior to 1975 by an instrument in writing, is rebuttable as to all except bona fide purchasers. We are required initially by the Evidence Code to characterize a rebuttable presumption as one affecting either the burden of proof or the burden of producing evidence (Evid.Code, § 601), where the statutory or decisional law creating the presumption has failed to so specify. A presumption affecting the burden of proof is one established to implement a public policy other than to facilitate the determination of the particular action in which the presumption is to be applied. (Evid. Code, § 605.) The presumptions in Civil Code section 5110 come within this definition; our case law has classified the community property presumption and the joint tenancy presumption in section 5110 as presumptions affecting the burden of proof. (Hansford v. Lassar (1975) 53 Cal.App.3d 364, 371–372, 125 Cal.Rptr. 804 [joint tenancy]; Baron v. Baron (1970) 9 Cal.App.3d 933, 939, 88 Cal.Rptr. 404 [community property].) Likewise, the separate property presumption therein is one affecting the burden of proof.

The public policy reason supporting this presumption was originally the protection of a married woman's title to property in her own name when the husband had exclusive management and control of the spouses' community property prior to 1975. When Civil Code section 5125 was amended to give the wife joint management and control of community property as of 1975, the separate property presumption in section 5110 was no longer needed and was accordingly abolished as to property acquired by a married woman after 1974. We mention these policy reasons because our courts will still be dealing with this presumption for some years to come, in cases involving property acquired by a married woman before 1975.

Since the separate property presumption is one affecting the burden of proof, the effect of the presumption is to impose on the party against whom it operates the burden of proving the nonexistence of the presumed fact. The presumed fact here is that wife owned the property as her separate property. Husband in this case thus had to rebut the presumption by proving that the ownership interests were community property.

Once it is ascertained that a rebuttable presumption affects the burden of proof, we are next required by the Evidence Code to determine the applicable burden of proof standard; the question is whether the particular presumption must be rebutted by a preponderance of the evidence, clear and convincing proof, or proof beyond a reasonable doubt. (Evid.Code, §§ 115, 190.) Unless otherwise provided by law, the appropriate standard is proof by a preponderance of the evidence. (Evid.Code, § 115.) In this case, however, the long history of our decisional law has already established that the strong presumptions of separate property and community property found in Civil Code section 5110, unlike the joint tenancy presumption therein, must be rebutted by clear and convincing evidence. (Estate of Duncan (1937) 9 Cal.2d 207, 217, 70 P.2d 174; Estate of Jolly (1925) 196 Cal. 547, 553, 238 P. 353; Nevins v.

Nevins (1954) 129 Cal.App.2d 150, 154, 276 P.2d 655; Attebury v. Wayland (1946) 73 Cal.App.2d 1, 5, 165 P.2d 524.) [1]

We are not here faced with conflicting presumptions, because the separate property presumption in Civil Code section 5110 is an exception to the general presumption that all property acquired after marriage is community property. (7 Witkin, Summary of Cal. Law (8th ed. 1974) Community Property, § 41, p. 5133.) Thus, where this particular separate property presumption is raised, the general community property presumption does not apply. (Nevins v. Nevins, supra, 129 Cal.App.2d at 154, 276 P.2d 655.) This is in contrast to the familiar rule in recent commingling cases, where the community property presumption controls and the party asserting otherwise carries the burden of proving the property was separate. (Estate of Murphy (1976) 15 Cal.3d 907, 917, 126 Cal.Rptr. 820, 544 P.2d 956; In re Marriage of Mix (1975) 14 Cal.3d 604, 610–611, 122 Cal.Rptr. 79, 536 P.2d 479; See v. See (1966) 64 Cal.2d 778, 783, 51 Cal.Rptr. 888, 415 P.2d 776.) We emphasize that this basic rule is the correct approach to the presumptions and burden of proof in the absence of the statutory separate property presumption in section 5110. Even without a commingling issue, this rule was well settled before the Civil Code was amended in 1889 to add the special separate property presumption. (Morgan v. Lones (1888) 78 Cal. 58, 62, 20 P. 248, citing Ramsdell v. Fuller (1865) 28 Cal. 37; Meyer v. Kinzer (1859) 12 Cal. 247; Smith v. Smith (1859) 12 Cal. 216.) Now that the separate property presumption has been abolished as to property acquired by a married woman after 1974, the general rule with its proper allocations of the burden of proof should once again apply to such property, which is presumed community unless proven otherwise by clear and convincing evidence. In this case, however, all the disputed property was purchased by wife in her name alone prior to 1975 and there is no commingling issue before us, so we are squarely within the mandate of the separate property presumption with its concomitant burden of proof on husband claiming the property for the community.

We must therefore inquire what kinds of facts are to be considered in determining whether or not the presumption has been rebutted. Such facts, established by case law, include the following: (1) lack of an agreement between husband and wife to transmute community property into separate property (Civ.Code, § 5103); See v. See, supra, 64 Cal.2d 778, 51 Cal.Rptr. 888, 415 P.2d 776; Louknitsky v. Louknitsky (1954) 123 Cal.App.2d 406, 410, 266 P.2d 910; (Halloran v. Isaacson (1949) 95 Cal.App.2d 357, 360–361, 213 P.2d 19); (2) husband had no intent to make a gift of separate or community property to wife (See v. See, supra, 64 Cal.2d 778, 783, 51 Cal.Rptr. 888, 415 P.2d 776; Geller v. Anolik (1954) 127 Cal.App.2d 21, 26, 273 P.2d 29; DeBoer v. DeBoer (1952) 111

---

1. This is understandable in light of the fact that many married couples take title to property as joint tenants for survivorship purposes, without intending to negate their community property interests or under- standing the inconsistency of joint tenancy and community property interests. It follows, then, that a lesser burden of proof should suffice to overcome the joint tenancy presumption.

Cal.App.2d 500, 505, 244 P.2d 953); (3) wife used community property funds to purchase property in her own name with husband's knowledge but he intended no gift (Steward v. Paige (1949) 90 Cal.App.2d 820, 825, 203 P.2d 858; Estate v. Baer (1947) 81 Cal.App.2d 830, 835, 185 P.2d 412); and (4) wife used community property funds to purchase property in her own name without husband's knowledge (Louknitsky v. Louknitsky, supra, 123 Cal.App.2d 406, 410, 266 P.2d 910).[2] These facts may be proved by direct or circumstantial evidence. (Nichols v. Mitchell (1948) 32 Cal.2d 598, 605, 197 P.2d 550; Guerin v. Guerin (1957) 152 Cal. App.2d 696, 704, 313 P.2d 902; Nevins v. Nevins, supra, 129 Cal.App.2d 150, 154, 276 P.2d 655.) Since a presumption is no longer evidence in California (Evid.Code, § 600) we must examine the record to determine whether any substantial evidence (Evid.Code, § 140) supports the finding of the court below. The record shows that (1) she used her real estate earnings to buy these properties, (2) husband did not know at the time of purchases that she took title in her own name, (3) there was no agreement that wife's earnings were her separate property, (4) husband did know wife was buying and selling real property and that he was not concerned therewith, (5) husband knew that he executed two grant deeds to aid in the transfer of properties, and (6) husband knew income from real estate transactions were considered at the time income tax returns were drafted and he made no inquiry as to it.

Here, the court's ruling that husband intended a gift by "abandoning" wife to practice real estate was correct since it is supported by the evidence albeit conflicting. The finding that there was no agreement between the parties, as found by the trial court, (3) above, is supportable under items (1) and (2) above. There remains the question as to whether a gift resulted under the facts of the case. The inference that husband intended a gift of his interest to wife where he executed grant deeds, (5) above, is warranted. His knowledge that an accountant and wife had income tax problems with property transactions and he sought no information as to them, (4) and (6) above, additionally confirms his abandonment of any interest therein. While pursuit of separate careers by spouses who do not discuss their business with each other cannot be deemed "abandonment" without more, here the disavowal of having anything to do with the wife's transactions and the signing of grant deeds to such properties constitutes sufficient evidence of a gift. The factual finding by the trial court on conflicting evidence is binding upon this court.

The judgment is affirmed.

KAUS, P.J., and ASHBY, J., concur.

2. In commingling cases, of course, there are two established methods for rebutting the community property presumption and carrying the burden of proof to show property purchased during marriage was separate: (1) tracing the purchase to a separate property source, and (2) proving that at the time of purchase all community income was exhausted by family expenses. (Estate of Murphy, supra, 15 Cal.3d 907, 918, 126 Cal.Rptr. 820, 544 P.2d 956; In re Marriage of Mix, supra, 14 Cal.3d 604, 611–612, 122 Cal.Rptr. 79, 536 P.2d 479; See v. See, supra, 64 Cal.2d 778, 783, 51 Cal.Rptr. 888, 415 P.2d 776.)

Hearing denied; MOSK, CLARK and MANUEL, JJ., dissenting.

Notes

1. In several cases involving transactions antedating 1975, where a married woman alone negotiated a transaction and used community funds to acquire a title in writing in her name, the courts rebelled against giving effect to the special presumption. On one pretext or another they took the case out of the special presumption or found it rebutted without more facts than those showing the nature of the transaction. See, e.g., Louknitsky v. Louknitsky, 123 Cal.App.2d 406, 266 P.2d 910 (1954); In re Marriage of Mix, reprinted in Chapter 4, Section 1.

2. Where the instrument not only puts title in the name of a married woman, but also specifically provides "as her separate property," there would seem to be no occasion to raise a presumption and the issue should be whether parol evidence can show a different meaning absent fraud, mistake or undue influence. Miller v. Brode, 186 Cal. 409, 199 P. 531 (1921); Donze v. Donze, 88 Cal.App. 769, 264 P. 294 (1928). Code of Civil Procedure Section 1856 which limits the admissibility of extrinsic evidence ostensibly controls this problem but its operation has been greatly restricted. See Note, *Chief Justice Traynor and the Parol Evidence Rule*, 22 Stanford Law Review 547 (1970).

3. The fact that there is no statutory presumption when the transaction involves a conveyance to a married woman after January 1, 1975 does not necessarily mean that a presumption of separate property could not be raised. Cases involving transactions prior to the enactment of the statutory presumption in 1889 raised a presumption of separate property where a married man conveyed community property to his wife or used community funds to purchase property in his wife's name. The courts reasoned that he must have intended some change in the property rights of himself and his wife in the wealth involved. Taylor v. Opperman, 79 Cal. 468, 21 P. 869 (1889). The ending of the statutory presumption for transactions after January 1, 1975 does not necessarily affect this judicial presumption, which is a contractual type of presumption based on the form of the title. Such a presumption is rebuttable by evidence negating any implied understanding to create separate property in the spouse but is not rebuttable by mere tracing. For example, in Marriage of Lucas, 27 Cal.3d 808, 166 Cal.Rptr. 853, 614 P.2d 285 (1980), title to a motor home was taken in the wife's name alone after January 1, 1975. Although a portion of the purchase price was traceable to community funds, the court concluded that the trailer was the wife's separate property on the basis of the judicial inference that a gift was created by the husband's acquiescence in the form of title. Other aspects of the *Lucas* case are examined in the next section.

B. Tenancy in Common and Joint Tenancy

The presumption that property interests acquired prior to 1975 by a married woman by written instrument are her separate property is also applicable to undivided interests held by a married woman with another person. Early cases applying this presumption held that where title was taken by husband and wife as tenants in common, the wife's interest was presumptively her separate property, while the husband's interest was presumed to be community property. This meant that on termination of the community the wife in effect had a three-fourths interest in the property.[9] This result was changed by statute in 1935.[10] Family Code Section 803 now provides that property acquired by a husband and wife by an instrument in which they are described as husband and wife is presumptively community property, unless the instrument expresses a different intention. Whether the instrument sufficiently describes the parties as husband and wife seems primarily a matter of grammar.[11] Whether an instrument expresses a different intention is a more difficult question. Language sufficient to create a joint tenancy has been held to express such an intention.[12]

Despite the fact that California is a community property jurisdiction, most married couples in California hold most of their property as joint tenants.[13] Various reasons have been advanced for the popularity of the joint tenancy form of ownership. One is the survivorship feature of joint tenancy; the property passes by operation of law to the survivor, without the necessity of probate administration. Another more pragmatic reason is the fact that real estate and stock brokers frequently direct their clients to take title in joint tenancy.

The legal consequences of a husband and wife holding title as joint tenants to what would otherwise be community property are by no means clear. The underlying problem involves fitting this common law form of tenure into the California community property system, and the fit has not yet been perfected.

Because the legal incidents of the forms of ownership differ, California courts have repeatedly held that a community estate and a joint tenancy cannot co-exist in the same item of property.[14] The property must be determined to be either community property or joint tenancy; it cannot be both. In making this determination, the California Supreme Court in Siberell v. Siberell initially held that "[t]he use of community funds to purchase the property and the taking of title thereto in the names of the spouses as joint tenants is tantamount to a binding agreement between them that the same shall not thereafter be held as community property, but instead as a joint tenancy with all the characteristics of such an estate." [15] The court further held that parol evidence

9. Dunn v. Mullan, 211 Cal. 583, 296 P. 604, 77 A.L.R. 1015 (1931); Estate of Regnart, 102 Cal.App. 643, 283 P. 860 (1929).

10. Cal.Stats.1935, c. 707, p. 1912.

11. See Cooke v. Tsipouroglou, 59 Cal.2d 660, 31 Cal.Rptr. 60, 381 P.2d 940 (1963); Wilcox v. Berry, 32 Cal.2d 189, 195 P.2d 414 (1948); Cardew v. Cardew, 192 Cal.App.2d 502, 514, 13 Cal.Rptr. 620, 626 (1961).

12. See Turknette v. Turknette, 100 Cal.App.2d 271, 223 P.2d 495 (1950).

13. Eighty-five per cent of the real property held by married persons in California is held in joint tenancy. Bayse, Joint Tenancy: A Reappraisal, 30 Cal.St.Bar J. 504 (1955); see also Sterling, Joint Tenancy and Community Property in California, 14 Pac.L.J. 927 (1983).

14. Siberell v. Siberell, 214 Cal. 767, 7 P.2d 1003 (1932); Tomaier v. Tomaier, 23 Cal.2d 754, 146 P.2d 905 (1944); Gudelj v. Gudelj, 41 Cal.2d 202, 259 P.2d 656 (1953).

15. Siberell v. Siberell, 214 Cal. 767, 7 P.2d 1003 (1932).

at variance with this agreement was not admissible.[16]

These rules were affirmed in Watson v. Peyton,[17] where the court noted that the testimony of one joint tenant could not be admitted to vary the terms of the deed, and held that having participated in the transaction, the wife could not testify that she intended to preserve her community property interest: "The wife having requested in writing the execution of the joint tenancy deed, she cannot defeat her act by testimony of a hidden intention not disclosed to the other party at the time of the execution of the document." [18]

The approach taken by the Supreme Court in the *Siberell* and *Watson* cases was substantially modified in Tomaier v. Tomaier.[19] The court rejected the notion that simply taking title in joint tenancy constituted a binding agreement that the property would be separate and not community, and indicated that such a transaction would merely raise a presumption of joint tenancy ownership. The court suggested that the use of common law forms of conveyance should not be permitted to alter the community character of property contrary to the intention of the parties.[20] The court did not disavow, however, the idea that joint tenancy and community property ownership were inherently inconsistent, nor did it reject the determination in Watson v. Peyton that the hidden undisclosed intention of one spouse was inadmissible to prove that the parties intended that the property remain community property.[21]

Litigation involving the question of joint tenancy versus community property has been extensive in the years since *Tomaier* was decided. Dozens of cases have attempted to define the presumption and to determine how it can be rebutted. Unfortunately, they offer little guidance in determining whether property will be deemed community or joint tenancy in any particular case. Ameliorative legislation has been enacted, but it applies only in the dissolution context, and its application has been further limited by judicial decision.

The legislature first attempted to address the joint tenancy problem in 1965 by enacting a special presumption that "when a single family residence of a husband and wife is acquired by them during marriage as joint tenants, for the purpose of the division of such property upon dissolution of marriage or legal separation only, the presumption is that such single family residence is the community property of the husband and wife." [22] Rebuttal of this special community property presumption was at issue in *Marriage of Lucas,* reprinted in this section.

16. Id.

17. Watson v. Peyton, 10 Cal.2d 156, 73 P.2d 906 (1937).

18. Id.

19. Tomaier v. Tomaier, 23 Cal.2d 754, 146 P.2d 905 (1944).

20. Id.

21. Id.

22. This presumption was originally included in Civil Code Section 5510. See Cal.Stats.1965, c. 1710, p. 3843. It has since been repealed and a broader version is now contained at West's Ann.Cal. Family Code § 2580.

The *Lucas* decision was perceived as unfair by many family law practitioners and scholars largely because it tended to deny any form of credit or compensation to a spouse who had contributed separate property to a joint tenancy asset. Legislation was subsequently enacted to remedy this perceived injustice. The single family residence proviso of Civil Code Section 5110 was removed and replaced by Sections 4800.1 and 4800.2. Section 4800.1 greatly strengthened the community property presumption by allowing only written rebuttal evidence, while Section 4800.2 provided for reimbursement to the spouse making separate property contributions, thereby ameliorating the harsh effects of *Lucas*. When originally enacted, Section 4800.1 applied only to joint tenancy property, but it was later revised to include all forms of concurrent ownership. The "anti-*Lucas*" legislation is now contained at Family Code Sections 2580, 2581 and 2640.

Under Section 2581 property acquired by the parties during marriage in any joint form is presumed to be community property for the purpose of division at dissolution. This presumption affects the burden of proof, and may only be rebutted by a clear statement in the title documents that the property is separate or by proof of a written agreement. Note that the statute applies only in the dissolution context; where the marriage is terminated by death, the judicially developed presumptions will continue to apply. The major problem that has arisen under this legislation involves the constitutionality of its retroactive application. This problem is raised in the *Buol* and *Hilke* cases reprinted in this section.

The first two cases in this section involve the judicial treatment of the joint tenancy-community property problem in the absence of legislation. The remaining cases involve the judicial interpretation and limitation of the various statutory "solutions" to the problem.

LOVETRO v. STEERS

California District Court of Appeal, 1965.
234 Cal.App.2d 461, 44 Cal.Rptr. 604.

[An action by a widow on a promissory note executed by defendants to a married man and his wife as joint tenants. The husband had released the defendants from part of their promise. If the note was community property or if the husband was agent of his wife in the release transaction, then the release reduced the obligation of the defendants. The court found for the defendants on both points. Only that part of the opinion relating to the classification of the asset is reprinted.]

MOLINARI, J. * * * We deal first with the theory that the subject note was in actuality an asset of the community.

When property is conveyed to a husband and wife as joint tenants, the form of the conveyance is such as to destroy the statutory presumption that the property is community even though the consideration for such conveyance consists of community funds or assets; such an instrument creates a tenancy in which the interests of the husband and wife are separate property. (Siberell v. Siberell, 214 Cal. 767, 773, 7 P.2d 1003; Mears v. Mears, 180 Cal.App.2d 484, 500, 4 Cal.Rptr. 618.) However, the form of the instrument under which a husband and wife hold title is not conclusive as to the status of the property; property acquired as joint tenants may be shown to be actually community property or the separate property of one spouse according to the intention, understanding or agreement of the parties. (Gudelj v. Gudelj, 41 Cal.2d 202, 212, 259 P.2d 656; Socol v. King, 36 Cal.2d 342, 345, 223 P.2d 627; Tomaier v. Tomaier, 23 Cal.2d 754, 758–759, 146 P.2d 905; Delanoy v. Delanoy, 216 Cal. 23, 26, 13 P.2d 513; Mears v. Mears, supra, 180 Cal.App.2d p. 500, 4 Cal.Rptr. 618.) In Socol, we find the following language: "When there is an oral or written agreement as to the ownership of the property [citations], or where such an understanding may be inferred from the conduct and declarations of the spouses [citations], it is true that the terms of the [joint tenancy] deed are not controlling. But where such circumstances do not exist, a true joint tenancy is created by a conveyance to husband and wife in that form, although the property is purchased with community funds [citations]." (36 Cal.2d p. 346, 223 P.2d p. 630.)

The evidence presented against the presumption arising from the form of the deed is not restricted solely to evidence of the source of the funds used to purchase the property but may consist of any substantial credible and relevant evidence showing the intention, understanding or agreement of the parties. (Gudelj v. Gudelj, supra, 41 Cal.2d p. 212, 259 P.2d 656; Socol v. King, supra, 36 Cal.2d p. 346, 223 P.2d 627; Mears v. Mears, supra, 180 Cal.App.2d p. 500, 4 Cal.Rptr. 618.) The presumption, however, cannot be overcome by testimony of a hidden intention not disclosed to the other grantee or transferee at the time of the execution of the conveyance or instrument in question. (Gudelj v. Gudelj, supra, 41 Cal.2d p. 212, 259 P.2d 656; Socol v. King, supra, 36 Cal.2d p. 346, 223 P.2d 627.) Whether the evidence is sufficient to overthrow the presumption arising from the form of the instrument is a question of fact. (Gudelj v. Gudelj, supra, 41 Cal.2d p. 212, 259 P.2d 656; DeBoer v. DeBoer, 111 Cal.2d 500, 504, 244 P.2d 953.) Subsequent to Socol, a number of decisions emanating from the District Courts of Appeal have analyzed the particular facts before them in order to determine whether a finding that the joint tenancy presumption had been rebutted found support in the evidence. (Among these are: Jenkins v. Jenkins, 147 Cal.App.2d 527, 305 P.2d 289; Bowman v. Bowman, 149 Cal.App.2d 773, 308 P.2d 906; Blankenship v. Blankenship, 212 Cal.App.2d 736, 28 Cal.Rptr. 176; Taliaferro v. Taliaferro, 217 Cal. App.2d 211, 31 Cal.Rptr. 690.) Of particular interest, insofar as the present case is concerned are the Jenkins and Blankenship cases. In Jenkins, the spouses acquired property in joint tenancy with funds derived from the husband's earnings. The parties took title in joint tenancy at the suggestion of friends and the escrow clerk to avoid probate proceedings in the event of the death of either of them. Neither of the spouses knew the difference between joint tenancy and community property, and they had had no discussion or previous understanding concerning the taking of title in joint tenancy. The appellate court held that the evidence was sufficient to justify a finding that title was taken in joint tenancy for the sole purpose of facilitating its transfer upon the death of one of the spouses. The reviewing court stated as follows: "If the evidence is sufficient to convince the court that the parties had no agreement and no intention to alter the community character of the property it may properly be determined that it remains community property notwithstanding the fact that title was knowingly taken in joint tenancy. [Citations.]" (147 Cal.App.2d p. 529, 305 P.2d p. 290.)

In Blankenship, two parcels of property were acquired with community funds by joint tenancy deeds. At the trial the plaintiff husband admitted that he did not know " 'what joint tenancy property is' " or " 'what community property is' "; that he never discussed with his wife how title to either of the parcels was to be taken, and that he did not learn that title was taken in joint tenancy until he was so advised by his counsel. (212 Cal.App.2d p. 740, 28 Cal.Rptr. p. 176.) He admitted that he intended each parcel in turn to be a home for himself and his wife. The defendant wife testified that there were no written agreements between the plaintiff and herself relating to the title to their community property and that up to the time of their present difficulties " 'there was never any question about property. We assumed that we owned everything together. Both of our names were on everything—cars included.' " (P. 741, 28 Cal.Rptr. p. 179.) There was also testimony of other witnesses to the effect that both of the spouses referred to the respective parcels as " 'our home,' " " 'our house' " and " 'our property.' " (P. 741, 28 Cal.Rptr. p. 176.) These facts were held by this court to constitute substantial evidence of the intention and understanding of both parties to continue to hold the real property in question as their community property despite the joint tenancy form of the deeds. Justice Sullivan, writing for this court, stated as follows: "We are presented here with the everyday situation of a husband and wife purchasing property with community funds and taking title as joint tenants. * * * [I]t is common knowledge that this form of ownership is adopted in order to provide for automatic and inexpensive survivorship on death. When the conduct of the spouses shows that they regard the property as their marital property and where, as here, it appears that they never actually understood the characteristics and effect of a joint tenancy there is a sound basis for a trier of fact to conclude that they never intended to change the character of their property." (P. 742, 28 Cal.Rptr. p. 180.)

Before turning to the facts of the present case in the light of the foregoing principles, we should here point out that we are bound by the trial court's finding that the subject note was community property if there is substantial evidence in the record to support such finding. (Mears v. Mears, supra, 180 Cal.App.2d 484, 500–501, 4 Cal.Rptr. 618.) The finding of a trial court that property is either separate or community in character is binding and conclusive on the appellate court if it is supported by sufficient evidence, or if it is based on conflicting evidence or upon evidence that is subject to different inferences; and if a trial court determines that a presumption has been overcome such determination will not be disturbed on appeal if there is substantial conflict in the evidence, or, although there is no conflict, if different inferences might fairly be drawn from the evidence. (In re Rauer's Collection Co., 87 Cal.App.2d 248, 256, 196 P.2d 803; Rogers v. Rogers, 86 Cal.App.2d 817, 820, 195 P.2d 890; Mears v. Mears, supra, 180 Cal.App.2d pp. 500–501, 4 Cal.Rptr. 618; Veronin v. Veronin, 131 Cal.App.2d 298, 300, 280 P.2d 173; Stauffer v. Stauffer, 135 Cal.App.2d 515, 518–519, 287 P.2d 518.)

The evidence in the record on this issue is as follows: Plaintiff testified that she and her husband at no time agreed, either orally or in writing, to hold the promissory note in some manner other than the form in which it was written, and that she was ignorant of the legal distinction between title taken in joint tenancy and that taken in community property; the consideration furnished for the note consisted of Sam's partnership interest; the installment payments made on the note were never divided into separate shares, but were deposited in the Lovetros' joint commercial banking account, which account was used by the Lovetros to pay family living expenses; the testimony by plaintiff that "this money that was being paid on this note for the sale of his [Sam's] partnership interest, that was all considered part of the family pot"; and plaintiff's affirmative answer to the question: "As far as you were concerned however, the sale of this business of your husband's interest in this auto parts business, that money was for both you and your husband * * * And because you were husband and wife?"

In addition to this testimony the trial court had before it the presumption that Sam's partnership interest was community property. The record is devoid of any evidence as to whether such interest was community or separate property. In the absence of any such evidence, and in the light of Joan's testimony, the trial court was entitled to presume that such interest was community property since all property which is acquired after marriage, other than that specified in sections 162 and 163, is community property and the burden is on the party seeking to establish that such property is in fact separate. (§ 164; Falk v. Falk, 48 Cal.App.2d 762, 768, 120 P.2d 714; Kenney v. Kenney, 128 Cal.App.2d 128, 135, 274 P.2d 951.) In the present case no claim was made by plaintiff that the partnership interest was separate property. The record shows that Sam and Joan were married for 25 years, that Sam went into business with Gene about two years before he died, that they were in business together about a year, and that Sam had been in the auto parts business between one and two years prior to going into business with Gene. From this evidence the trial court was entitled to infer that the partnership business was acquired during the marriage. We conclude, therefore, that Joan's testimony, when coupled with the presumption that the partnership interest was community property, constitutes substantial evidence of the intention of both Sam and Joan to continue to hold the subject note representing the proceeds from the sale of such interest as their community property despite the joint tenancy form of the note.

We find no merit, moreover, to plaintiff's argument that because many of plaintiff's acts on which the court relied in determining that the Lovetros held the note as community property took place after the execution of the release and concerned the proceeds of the note rather than the note itself, therefore these acts cannot be considered by the court for the purpose of rebutting the joint tenancy presumption. In many of the cases which we have reviewed with respect to the issue here before us, the court found the property in question to be a community asset based in part on evidence relating to the acts or declarations of the spouses concerning not only the property itself, but also its source, and its use. Furthermore, in many of these same cases, the acts and declarations relied on by the court took place after the spouses had acquired the subject property. In other words, although the crucial issue in these cases involves the intention of the parties as to the manner in which they were holding the particular property, there can be no doubt that the acts or declarations of the parties prior to, contemporaneous with, and subsequent to the acquisition of this property, and concerning as well the source and proceeds of the property can be of probative value in determining such intent.

Notes

1. In Gudelj v. Gudelj, 41 Cal.2d 202, 213–14, 259 P.2d 656, 663–664 (1953), the husband used his separate funds and community funds to acquire residential real property. Title was taken in joint tenancy. The husband testified that he did not intend to make a gift of his separate property to his wife. The trial court accepted this evidence, and determined the respective interests of the spouses in the property on the basis of the sources of funds used to purchase it. The Supreme Court reversed, declaring:

> Applying the rule of the Socol case to the facts here shown, John's testimony as to his undisclosed intention not to make a gift of a present interest in the property is not evidence of a mutual understanding or agreement negativing the express terms in the deed. It is of no significance that John was unaware of the legal effect of the deed. Nor is it material that the home was purchased primarily from John's separate funds, Catherine being aware of their source. All of these facts, taken together, provide no basis for an inference of a mutual understanding or agreement between John and Catherine that the separate and community nature of the funds used in the purchase was to be preserved. Therefore, there being no substantial evidence tending to rebut the presumption created by the joint tenancy deed, the property is owned by the parties in joint tenancy.

2. If one party understands the implications of taking title in joint tenancy, and the other does not, is evidence of the ignorance of one spouse admissible to rebut the presumption arising from the joint tenancy form of title? Some cases seem to turn on the degree of participation in the transaction by the ignorant spouse. For example, in Palazuelos v. Palazue-

los, 103 Cal.App.2d 826, 230 P.2d 431 (1951), the wife apparently did not participate in or interfere with her husband's investment of community funds, and was ignorant of the meaning of joint tenancy. Her undisclosed intention that the property remain community was held admissible. In Schindler v. Schindler, 126 Cal.App.2d 597, 272 P.2d 566 (1954), the wife signed the papers involved in the purchase of the property. The court stated that in so doing, she consented to the transfer of community funds to joint tenancy property and the fact that she was unaware of or mistaken about the legal effect of the deed was of no significance.

ESTATE OF LEVINE
California Court of Appeal, 1981.
125 Cal.App.3d 701, 178 Cal.Rptr. 275.

HASTINGS, ASSOCIATE JUSTICE.

This case illustrates one of the pitfalls of "how to avoid probate." The appeal concerns a family residence held in joint tenancy although one of the spouses, secretly as it turned out, considered it community property. The court held the property to be joint tenancy and this appeal followed.

Phillip and Estelle Levine were married on January 1, 1974. They had been neighbors for 20 years on Saturn Avenue in Los Angeles, and their respective spouses had predeceased them by several years. Both had children from their prior marriages, all of whom were adults at the time Phillip and Estelle married.

In April of 1975, Phillip and Estelle purchased a home on Lindbrook Avenue in Los Angeles ("the Lindbrook home"), taking title as joint tenants.

Phillip died on November 26, 1977. His will named as co-executors his attorney, Samuel Leemon, and his son Murray Levine. Murray filed a petition in the probate court seeking to have the Lindbrook home declared to be community property of Phillip and Estelle. After hearing testimony, the court determined that the home was joint tenancy property, and denied the petition.

At the hearing, attorney Leemon testified in support of the petition. His testimony was as follows: He and Phillip were cousins and lifelong acquaintances, and he had handled Phillip's legal affairs in recent years. Shortly after he married Estelle in January of 1974, Phillip came to Leemon and asked him to prepare a will. Since Phillip planned to sell his home on Saturn Avenue and purchase a new home with the proceeds, he wanted his Will to reflect his intention with respect to the character of the property: the new home was to be considered community property, but would be held in joint tenancy for convenience only. The reason for this was twofold. First, Phillip wanted to be able to devise his one-half of the house to his children, Murray and Iris, which he would be able to do if the home were community property. However, if Estelle predeceased him he also wanted to prevent Estelle from devising her one-half of their community property to her children and wanted to avoid a lengthy probate administration, both of which he could accomplish by holding the property in joint tenancy. Phillip's banker advised him that he could achieve what he wanted by holding the new home in joint tenancy but calling it community property. Leemon advised against this, and told Phillip that unless he had some agreement with Estelle that the home was to be community property, it would be considered joint tenancy property and would pass to Estelle if Phillip predeceased her. Phillip was adamant, however, and said there was no problem because he and Estelle had such an agreement. Accordingly, the will was drafted with the following language:

> "FIFTH: I hereby declare that I am selling my home at 9707 Saturn, Los Angeles, California, and will use part of the proceeds of sale to purchase a new home.

> "The new home is to be considered community property although of record, for convenience only, the title will be shown and taken in Joint Tenancy."

After Leemon drafted the will, he did not have any further contact with Phillip before the Lindbrook home was purchased, and did not know what agreement, if any, Phillip and Estelle had with regard to the character of the property.

Estelle testified that she never had any discussions with Phillip as to what would happen to their property if one of them died, and Phillip never told her that he wanted his half to go to his children. She never knew Phillip had a will until after he died. When questioned about her knowledge of the meaning of "joint tenancy," she said that she had a joint will with her former husband, they held their home on Saturn Avenue in joint tenancy, and the house passed to her upon his death. She thought that joint tenancy was the only way title to property could be held, and never doubted that she would get the Lindbrook home if Phillip died first.

Estelle also testified that when she and Phillip bought the Lindbrook home, they met with the bank escrow officer and Phillip instructed that the deed should be prepared showing Phillip and Estelle as joint tenants. They had a similar conversation with the real estate broker who handled the sale. She said that Phillip made the down payment and mortgage payments, while she contributed approximately $10,000 towards remodeling the home.

In rebuttal, Murray testified that he had four separate conversations with his father alone in which Phillip told him that Murray and his sister Iris would inherit half the proceeds of the Saturn Avenue house upon Phillip's death.

Based upon the testimony presented at the hearing, the court concluded that, although Phillip intended that the Lindbrook home be considered community property, he never disclosed his intention to Estelle. Accordingly, the court found that the Lindbrook home was joint tenancy property, and denied the petition. Murray, the appellant, contends that the court's finding was not supported by substantial evidence.

The law on the issue before us is quite clear. For the purpose of determining the character of real property upon the death of a spouse, there is a rebuttable presumption that the character of the property is as set forth in the deed. (Schindler v. Schindler, 126 Cal.App.2d 597, 601–602, 272 P.2d 566.) The presumption still applies where the property was purchased with the separate funds of one spouse. (Gloden v. Gloden, 240 Cal.App.2d 465, 468–469, 49 Cal.Rptr. 659.) The burden is on the party seeking to rebut the presumption to establish that the property is held in some other way; this may be done by a showing that the character of the property was changed or affected by an agreement or common understanding between the spouses. Such agreement may be oral or written, or may be inferred from the conduct and declarations of the spouses. However, there must be an agreement of some sort; the presumption may not be overcome by testimony about the hidden intention of one spouse, undisclosed to the other spouse at the time of the conveyance. (Socol v. King, 36 Cal.2d 342, 346, 223 P.2d 627; Gudelj v. Gudelj, 41 Cal.2d 202, 212, 259 P.2d 656; Schindler v. Schindler, supra, 126 Cal.App.2d at p. 603, 272 P.2d 566.) Whether the presumption is rebutted is a question of fact for resolution by the trial court, and we are bound by that court's finding if it is supported by substantial evidence. (In re Marriage of Wall, 30 Cal.App.3d 1042, 1046, 106 Cal.Rptr. 690; In re Marriage of Smith, 79 Cal.App.3d 725, 742, 145 Cal.Rptr. 205.)

The crucial question, therefore, was whether Phillip communicated his intention to Estelle, and whether they had some agreement or understanding that the property would be other than a joint tenancy. Aside from Phillip's statement to his lawyer that "there wouldn't be any problem," the only evidence presented concerning any such agreement was Estelle's testimony that there wasn't one. It was Murray's burden to show that the character of the property was as Phillip intended; absent such an agreement, Murray cannot meet his burden and overcome the presumption created by the deed that the Lindbrook home was joint tenancy property.

Murray contends that the above rule of law unfairly deprives Phillip's children of part of their inheritance. He suggests that we adopt the statutory law applied in marriage dissolution cases where the single family residence acquired during marriage and held in joint tenancy is presumed to be community property. (Civ.Code, § 5110.) This argument, however, should be directed to our Legislature, since it specifically limited the presumption in section 5110 to division of such property in dissolution of marriage or legal separation cases only.

The judgment is affirmed.

STEPHENS, ACTING P.J., and ASHBY, J., concur.

Hearing denied; Kaus, J., did not participate.

Notes

1. Suppose that husband and wife use community funds to purchase a parcel of real property. Both spouses are ignorant of title implications and title is taken in joint tenancy solely at the instigation of the real estate broker. The wife dies first. Her will purports to leave one half of the parcel to her children from a former marriage. What result? Note that even where joint tenancy ownership is intended and established, it is possible for one joint tenant to effect a severance of the joint tenancy, resulting in a tenancy in common. In Riddle v. Harmon, 102 Cal.App.3d 524, 162 Cal. Rptr. 530 (1980), the court held that severance could be accomplished simply by one joint tenant making a grant to himself, thus obviating the "strawman" requirement. See also Estate of Carpenter, 140 Cal.App.3d 709, 189 Cal.Rptr. 651 (1983). It has been suggested that a joint tenant's attempted devise of his or her interest to a third party should be similarly effective: "What one can accomplish by the formality of conveyance to oneself and a subsequent devise should be possible by direct testamentary statement." Bruch, *The Definition and Division of Marital Property in California: Towards Parity and Simplicity,* 33 Hastings L.J. 769, 835 n. 251 (1982). See Civil Code Section 683.2 for the statutory requirements regarding severance of a joint tenancy.

2. In Estate of England, 233 Cal.App.3d 1, 6, 284 Cal.Rptr. 361, 364 (1991) the husband died, leaving a holographic will that expressly attempted to sever his joint tenancy interest in residential property owned by himself and his wife as joint tenants. He desired to devise his interest to his son. The appellate court, in affirming the trial court's decision, stated:

> Section 683.2, subdivision (c), requires that a document unilaterally severing a joint tenancy be recorded in order to give the other joint tenants constructive notice of the severance and to avoid fraud. Accordingly, subdivision (a)'s inclusion of "other means" to sever a joint tenancy may not be read to include a will which has not been recorded as required by subdivision (c).

3. Because of the frequent confusion and uncertainty engendered by the situation where married persons use community funds to acquire an asset in joint tenancy, the California Law Revision Commission has indicated that the legal interrelation of joint tenancy and community property is in need of further clarification. The Commission has tentatively recommended that any property of married persons derived from community property sources be presumed to remain community even though title is in joint tenancy. The presumption would apply for tax purposes, creditor's rights, dissolution, and death. The presumption could be overridden by an express written agreement or declaration. *California Law Revision Commission, Tentative Recommendation, Effect of Joint Tenancy on Community Property* (January 1993).

IN RE MARRIAGE OF LUCAS

Supreme Court of California, 1980.
27 Cal.3d 808, 166 Cal.Rtpr. 853, 614 P.2d 285.

MANUEL, JUSTICE.

Gerald E. Lucas appeals from an interlocutory judgment dissolving his marriage to Brenda G. Lucas, awarding child custody, fixing spousal and child support and dividing property. Gerald contests only the trial court's determination of the parties' ownership interests in their residence and in a vehicle, both of which were purchased with a combination of community and separate funds. In this case we must resolve a conflict among the Courts of Appeal regarding the proper method of determining separate and community property interests in a single family dwelling acquired during the marriage with both separate property and community property funds.

Brenda and Gerald were married in March 1964 and lived together continuously until their separation in December 1976. At the time of their marriage Brenda was beneficiary of a trust. The trust corpus was distributed to her free of the trust in September 1964. She immediately established a revocable *inter vivos* trust of which she was trustor and beneficiary. The trust, conceded by Gerald to be Brenda's separate property, had a value of approximately $44,000 at the time of trial.

In November 1968, Brenda and Gerald bought a house for $23,300. Brenda used $6,351.57 from her trust for the down payment, and they assumed a loan of $16,948.43 for the balance of the purchase price. Title to the house was taken as "Gerald E. Lucas and Brenda G. Lucas, Husband and Wife as Joint Tenants." Brenda paid $2,962 from her trust funds for improvements to the property; the remainder of the expenses on the property was paid for with community funds. At the time of trial the residence had a fair market value of approximately $56,250 and a loan balance of approximately $14,600, leaving a net equity of approximately $41,650. The community had reduced the principal by $2,052.32 and paid $6,801.14 in interest and $5,146.20 for taxes.

The trial court findings describe the parties' intent regarding ownership of the residence as follows: "The only discussions with regard to taking joint tenancy title to the property related to wife's understanding that title would pass to husband upon her death and that the children would benefit from this result; further, the parties contemplated that, taking title in this manner would result in favorable tax consequences due to husband's veterans status. Wife did not intend to make a gift to the husband of any interest in the home purchased with her separate funds, nor did she know of any other legal significance of taking title to real property in the manner it was taken. Neither did husband intend to make a gift to wife of the payments made on the home from community funds during the period of ownership."

Brenda testified that she and Gerald did not discuss where the down payment would come from except to the extent that the payments would be higher if they did not use her trust fund and instead took a second trust deed on the house. Brenda said they had no agreement regarding the manner in which she would be disposing of the trust funds and that they did not discuss keeping the funds separate or using them to exhaust community debts. Brenda also testified that it was her intention at the time of the purchase to acquire the house for herself but that she did not discuss this with her husband.

In the interlocutory judgment entered in April 1978, the trial court deducted Brenda's $2,962 payment for improvements from the equity of $41,650.50 and then awarded a community property interest in the residence of 24.42 percent with a value of $9,477.50. A separate property interest of 75.58 percent with a value of $29,241 was confirmed to Brenda.

The Courts of Appeal have taken conflicting approaches to the question of the proper method for determining the ownership interests in a residence purchased during the parties' marriage with both separate and community funds. In In re Marriage of Bjornestad (1974) 38 Cal.App.3d 801, 113 Cal.Rptr. 576, the Court of Appeal allowed only reimbursement for separate property contributions to the down payment on the purchase of the parties' residence. In In re Marriage of Aufmuth (1979) 89 Cal.App.3d 446, 152 Cal.Rptr. 668, the Court of Appeal developed a scheme of pro rata apportionment of the equity appreciation between the separate and community property contributions to the purchase price. The Court of Appeal in In re Marriage of Trantafello (1979) 94 Cal.App.3d 533, 156 Cal.Rptr. 556, however, held that the residence was entirely community in nature in the absence of any evidence of an agreement or understanding between the parties to the contrary.

The beginning point of analysis in each case was the nature of title taken by the parties. In *Bjornestad* and *Trantafello,* title was taken by husband and wife as joint tenants; in *Aufmuth,* it was taken as community property. Until modified by statute in 1965, there was a rebuttable presumption that the ownership interest in property was as stated in the title to it. (Machado v. Machado (1962) 58 Cal.2d 501, 25 Cal.Rptr. 87, 375 P.2d 55; Gudelj v. Gudelj (1953) 41 Cal.2d 202, 259 P.2d 656; Socol v. King (1950) 36 Cal.2d 342, 223 P.2d 627; Tomaier v. Tomaier (1944) 23 Cal.2d 754, 146 P.2d 905.) Thus a residence purchased with community funds, but held by a husband and wife as joint tenants, was presumed to be separate property in which each spouse had a half interest. (See Socol v. King, supra, 36 Cal.2d at pp. 345–347, 223 P.2d 627.) The presumption arising from the form of title could be overcome by evidence of an agreement or understanding between the parties that the interests were to be otherwise. (Ibid.; Gudelj v. Gudelj, supra, 41 Cal.2d at p. 212, 259 P.2d 656; Machado v. Machado, supra, 58 Cal.2d at p. 506, 25 Cal.Rptr. 87, 375 P.2d 55.) It could not be overcome, however, "solely by evidence as to the source of the funds used to purchase the property." (Gudelj v. Gudelj, supra, 41 Cal.2d at p. 212, 259 P.2d at p. 662.) Nor could it "be overcome by testimony of a hidden intention not disclosed to the other grantee at the time of the execution of the conveyance." (Ibid.; Socol v. King, supra, 36 Cal.2d at p. 346, 223 P.2d 627; Machado v. Machado, supra, 58 Cal.2d at p. 506, 25 Cal.Rptr. 87, 375 P.2d 55.)

The presumption arising from the form of title created problems upon divorce or separation when title to the parties' residence was held in joint tenancy. (Review of Selected 1965 Code Legislation (Cont.Ed. Bar) p. 40; Final Rep. of Assem. Interim Com. on Judiciary Relating to Domestic Relations (1965) pp. 121–122, 2 Appen. to Assem.J. (1965 Reg.Sess.) hereafter referred to as Domestic Relations Rep.) Unless the presumption of separate property created by the form of title could be overcome by evidence of a common understanding or agreement to the contrary, a house so held could not be awarded to the wife as a family residence for her and the children. (Ibid.) In 1965 the Legislature considered various proposals to remedy this problem. The Legislature also noted that "husbands and wives take property in joint tenancy without legal counsel but primarily because deeds prepared by real estate brokers, escrow companies and by title companies are usually presented to the parties in joint tenancy form. The result is that they don't know what joint tenancy is, that they think it is community property, and then find out upon death or divorce that they didn't have what they thought they had all along and instead have something else which isn't what they had intended." (Domestic Relations Rep., p. 124.)

In 1965, in an attempt to solve these problems, the Legislature added the following provision to Civil Code section 164: "[W]hen a single family residence of a husband and wife is acquired by them during marriage as joint tenants, for the purpose of the division of such property upon divorce or separate maintenance only, the presumption is that such single family residence is the community property of said husband and wife." (Stats.1965, ch. 1710, p. 3843; see now Civ.Code § 5110.)[2] The effect of this provision was to change the presumptive form of ownership to that more closely matching the intent and assumptions of most spouses who acquire and hold their residence in joint tenancy. (Review of Selected 1965 Code Legislation (Cont.Ed.Bar) pp. 40–41; Domestic Relations Rep., pp. 124–125.) There is no indication that the Legislature intended in any way to change the rules regarding the strength and type of evidence necessary to overcome the presump-

2. Section 164 was repealed in 1969 in connection with the enactment of the Family Law Act. (Stats.1969, ch. 1608, § 3, p. 3313.) It was replaced by section 5110 which contains an almost identical provision: "When a single-family residence of a husband and wife is acquired by them during marriage as joint tenants, for the purpose of the division of such property upon dissolution of marriage or legal separation only, the presumption is that such single-family residence is the community property of the husband and wife."

Although section 164 was the applicable statute when the parties in this case purchased their house, as a matter of convenience, future references in this opinion will be to the current statute, section 5110.

tion arising from the form of title. (See Domestic Relations Rep., p. 124.)

The presumption arising from the form of title is to be distinguished from the general presumption set forth in Civil Code section 5110 that property acquired during marriage is community property. It is the affirmative act of specifying a form of ownership in the conveyance of title that removes such property from the more general presumption. (See Socol v. King, supra, 36 Cal.2d at p. 346, 223 P.2d 627.) It is because of this express designation of ownership that a greater showing is necessary to overcome the presumption arising therefrom than is necessary to overcome the more general presumption that property acquired during marriage is community property. In the latter situation, where there is no written indication of ownership interests as between the spouses, the general presumption of community property may be overcome simply by tracing the source of funds used to acquire the property to separate property. (See In re Marriage of Mix (1975) 14 Cal.3d 604, 608–612, 122 Cal.Rptr. 79, 536 P.2d 479; Estate of Murphy (1976) 15 Cal.3d 907, 917–919, 126 Cal.Rptr. 820, 544 P.2d 956; See v. See (1966) 64 Cal.2d 778, 783, 51 Cal.Rptr. 888, 415 P.2d 776.) It is not necessary to show that the spouses understood or intended that property traceable to separate property should remain separate.

The rule requiring an understanding or agreement comes into play when the issue is whether the presumption arising from the form of title has been overcome. It is supported by sound policy considerations, and we decline to depart from it. To allow a lesser showing could result in unfairness to the spouse who has not made the separate property contribution. Unless the latter knows that the spouse contributing the separate property expects to be reimbursed or to acquire a separate property interest, he or she has no opportunity to attempt to preserve the joint ownership of the property by making other financing arrangements. The act of taking title in a joint and equal ownership form is inconsistent with an intention to preserve a separate property interest. Accordingly, the expectations of parties who take title jointly are best protected by presuming that the specified ownership interest is intended in the absence of an agreement or understanding to the contrary. We therefore resolve the conflict in Court of Appeal opinions by following *Trantafello* and disapproving *Aufmuth* and *Bjornestad* to the extent they are inconsistent with this opinion.

In the present case there is no evidence of an agreement or understanding that Brenda was to retain a separate property interest in the house. Nor is there any finding by the trial court on the question. The only findings in this regard are that neither party intended a gift to the other. Such evidence and findings are insufficient to rebut the presumption arising from title set forth in Civil Code section 5110. The trial court's determination must therefore be reversed.

Neither the parties nor the court applied the correct rules to this case, and it is possible that had they done so the proof might have been different. In the interest of justice, therefore, the matter of the community or separate property character of the residence must be remanded for reconsideration in light of these rules.

If on reconsideration the house is found to be entirely community in nature, Brenda would also be barred from reimbursement for the separate property funds she contributed in the absence of an agreement therefor. It is a well-settled rule that a "party who uses his separate property for community purposes is entitled to reimbursement from the community or separate property of the other only if there is an agreement between the parties to that effect." (See v. See, supra, 64 Cal.2d at p. 785, 51 Cal.Rptr. at p. 893, 415 P.2d at p. 781; Weinberg v. Weinberg (1967) 67 Cal.2d 557, 570, 63 Cal.Rptr. 13, 432 P.2d 709; In re Marriage of Epstein (1979) 24 Cal.3d 76, 82–86, 154 Cal.Rptr. 413, 592 P.2d 1165.) While the parties are married and living together it is presumed that, "unless an agreement between the parties specifies that the contributing party be reimbursed, a party who utilizes his separate property for community purposes intends a gift to the community." (In re Marriage of Epstein, supra, 24 Cal.3d at p. 82, 154 Cal.Rptr. at p. 417, 592 P.2d at p. 1169.)

For guidance in the event that on reconsideration the court finds there was an understanding or agreement that Brenda was to retain a separate property interest in the residence, we discuss briefly the question of the proper method of calculating the community and separate interests. In these inflationary times when residential housing is undergoing enormous and rapid appreciation in value, we believe that the most equitable method of calculating the separate and community interests when the down payment was made with separate funds and the loan was based on a community or joint obligation is that set forth by Justice McGuire in In re Marriage of Aufmuth, supra, 89 Cal.App.3d at pp. 456–457, 152 Cal.Rptr. 668. In brief, the *Aufmuth* formula gives the spouse who made the separate property down payment a separate property interest in the residence in the proportion that the down payment bears to the purchase price; the community acquires that percentage of the residence which the community loan bears to the purchase price.[3]

3. The value of those interests is computed by first determining the amount of capital appreciation, which is computed by subtracting the purchase price from the fair market value of the residence. The separate property interest would be determined by adding the amount of capital appreciation attributable to separate funds to the amount of equity paid by separate funds. The community interest would be the amount of capital appreciation attributable to community funds plus the amount of equity paid by community funds; the amount of equity paid by community funds is represented by the amount by which the principal balance on the loan has been reduced.

These principles may be exemplified by considering a house purchased for $100,000, with the wife paying the entire down payment of $20,000 from separate property funds and the community contributing the rest of the purchase price in the amount of a loan for $80,000. There would be a 20 percent separate property interest and an 80 percent community property interest in the house. Assume that the fair market value of the house at the time of trial is $175,000, resulting in a capital appreciation of $75,000, and the mortgage balance at the time of separation was $78,000. The value of the separate property interest would be $35,000, which represents the amount of capital appreciation attributable to the sep-

If the trial court finds no agreement or understanding that Brenda was to retain a separate property interest in the residence, Brenda's contribution of $2,962 of separate funds for improvements should have no effect on the determination of the parties' interests, and the presumption of section 5110 is controlling. (See v. See, supra, 64 Cal.2d at p. 783, 51 Cal.Rptr. 888, 415 P.2d 776.) If there was an understanding that Brenda's separate interest should be maintained, but no separate understanding with respect to improvements, Brenda should receive no additional credit for her expenditure for improvements, for it may be presumed that she intended that they redound to both the community and her separate interest in the property. (Cf., See v. See, supra, 64 Cal.2d at p. 785, 51 Cal.Rptr. 888, 415 P.2d 776.)

* * *

The judgment is reversed insofar as it determines the respective interests of the parties in the residence and divides the community property. It is affirmed in all other respects.

BIRD, C.J., and TOBRINER, MOSK, CLARK, RICHARDSON and NEWMAN, JJ., concur.

Notes

1. The apportionment aspects of the *Lucas* decision are considered in Section 3 of Chapter 4.

2. We saw earlier that one of the most common methods of rebutting the general community property presumption is to trace the asset at issue to a separate property source. Why should not this method of rebuttal be equally applicable to the special presumption of community property where the family residence is held in joint tenancy? *Lucas* indicates that tracing evidence alone will not negate the presumed intent of the parties. Why not? *Gift to Community*

3. The *Lucas* holding was extended in In re Marriage of Cademartori, 119 Cal.App.3d 970, 174 Cal.Rptr. 292 (1981). There the husband owned certain real property as his separate property. He sold the real property in 1966, and ultimately invested the proceeds in a warehouse, taking title as "John P. Cademartori and Sandy Cademartori, his wife." The title designation put the case within the special presumption that where title is taken by husband and wife as husband and wife, the property is presumptively community property. The reviewing court held that the tracing of the warehouse back to a separate property source and the husband's testimony that he never intended to make a gift, although sufficient to rebut the general presumption, were not sufficient to rebut the special statutory presumption.

WEST'S ANNOTATED CALIFORNIA FAMILY CODE

§ 2580. Legislative findings and declarations

The Legislature hereby finds and declares as follows:

arate funds (20 percent of $75,000) added to the amount of equity paid by separate funds ($20,000). The net value of the community property interest would be $62,000, which represents the amount of capital apprecia-tion attributable to community funds (80 percent of $75,000) added to the amount of equity paid by community funds ($80,000 minus $78,000).

(a) It is the public policy of this state to provide uniformly and consistently for the standard of proof in establishing the character of property acquired by spouses during marriage in joint title form, and for the allocation of community and separate interests in that property between the spouses.

(b) The methods provided by case and statutory law have not resulted in consistency in the treatment of spouses' interests in property they hold in joint title, but rather, have created confusion as to which law applies to property at a particular point in time, depending on the form of title, and, as a result, spouses cannot have reliable expectations as to the characterization of their property and the allocation of the interests therein, and attorneys cannot reliably advise their clients regarding applicable law.

(c) Therefore, a compelling state interest exists to provide for uniform treatment of property. Thus, former Sections 4800.1 and 4800.2 of the Civil Code, as operative on January 1, 1987, and as continued in Sections 2580 and 2640 of this code, apply to all property held in joint title regardless of the date of acquisition of the property or the date of any agreement affecting the character of the property, and those sections apply in all proceedings commenced on or after January 1, 1984. However, those sections do not apply to property settlement agreements executed before January 1, 1987, or proceedings in which judgments were rendered before January 1, 1987, regardless of whether those judgments have become final.

§ 2581. Community property presumption for property held in joint form

For the purpose of division of property on dissolution of marriage or legal separation of the parties, property acquired by the parties during marriage in joint form, including property held in tenancy in common, joint tenancy, or tenancy by the entirety, or as community property, is presumed to be community property. This presumption is a presumption affecting the burden of proof and may be rebutted by either of the following:

(a) A clear statement in the deed or other documentary evidence of title by which the property is acquired that the property is separate property and not community property.

(b) Proof that the parties have made a written agreement that the property is separate property.

§ 2640. Separate property contributions to property acquisition

(a) "Contributions to the acquisition of the property," as used in this section, include downpayments, payments for improvements, and payments that reduce the principal of a loan used to finance the purchase or improvement of the property but do not include payments of interest on the loan or payments made for maintenance, insurance, or taxation of the property.

(b) In the division of the community estate under this division, unless a party has made a written waiver of the right to reimbursement or has signed a writing that has the effect of a waiver, the party shall be reimbursed for the party's contributions to the acquisition of the property to the extent the party traces the contributions to a separate property source. The amount reimbursed shall be without interest or adjustment for change in monetary values and shall not exceed the net value of the property at the time of the division.

IN RE MARRIAGE OF BUOL

Supreme Court of California, 1985.
39 Cal.3d 751, 218 Cal.Rptr. 31, 705 P.2d 354.

REYNOSO, JUSTICE.

May legislation requiring a writing to prove, upon dissolution of marriage, that property taken in joint tenancy form is the separate property of one spouse constitutionally be applied to cases pending before its effective date? We conclude that it may not. Applied retroactively, the statute impairs vested property rights without due process of law.

Esther and Robert Buol married in 1943 and separated in 1977. The Buols had three children together and Esther had one child from a previous marriage.

Robert worked as a laborer until 1970 when he was fired, at least in part, due to alcoholism. He began receiving Social Security total disability payments in 1973. Esther began working in 1954 as a housekeeper, a babysitter and an attendant to elderly women. Since 1959 she has been employed as a nursing attendant at a local hospital.

With Robert's knowledge and consent, Esther put her earnings in a separate bank account. Esther used the money to support the family, and in 1963, purchased a home in San Rafael. Although title was taken in joint tenancy on the advice of the realtor handling the sale, Esther made all mortgage, tax, insurance and maintenance payments out of her separate account. Robert contributed nothing. The original purchase price was $17,500. The home is now valued at approximately $167,500.

The sole issue at trial was the status of the home as separate or community property. Esther testified that she purchased the home with her earnings which Robert had emphasized numerous times were hers to do with what she pleased. She also testified that she never would have gone to work without such an agreement because "that would be more money for him to put into gambling and drinking." In addition, she testified that he had always maintained that the house was hers and that he wanted no responsibility for it, until after he moved out and started demanding that she sell it so that he could have a share of the proceeds.

Esther's testimony was corroborated by two of the Buol's children, Roy and Judith, Judith's husband, and Esther's brother-in-law. Each remembered many conversations with Robert, alone or in family gatherings, in which he confirmed that the house was Esther's. Robert offered conflicting testimony, but conceded that he considered Esther's earnings to be hers alone, that he borrowed from her occasionally and that she made all the house payments out of her separate account.

Finding that the parties had an enforceable oral agreement (*In re Marriage of Lucas* (1980) 27 Cal.3d 808, 166 Cal.Rptr. 853, 614 P.2d 285) that the earnings and the home were Esther's separate property, the court entered judgment awarding the home to Esther. Robert appealed, contending that there was insufficient evidence to support the finding of an oral agreement.

While the appeal was pending, Civil Code section 4800.1 was enacted. Under that section the only means of rebutting the presumption that property acquired during marriage in joint tenancy is community property is by providing evidence of a written agreement that the property is separate property.[4] No writing exists in the instant case.

I

We must determine whether section 4800.1 may be given retroactive effect without offending the state Constitution. It appears that the Legislature intended section 4800.1 to apply retroactively to cases such as the one at bench. Section 4 of Assembly Bill No. 26 states, "This act applies to the following proceedings: [¶] (a) Proceedings commenced on or after January 1, 1984. [¶] (b) Proceedings commenced before January 1, 1984, to the extent proceedings as to the division of property are not yet final on January 1, 1984." (Stats.1983, ch. 342, § 4.) As the trial court's judgment awarding the $167,500 residence to Esther as her separate property was on appeal as of section 4800.1's January 1, 1984, effective date, the division of property was not yet final. (Code Civ. Proc., § 1049. See *In re Marriage of Brown* (1976) 15 Cal.3d 838, 126 Cal.Rptr. 633, 544 P.2d 561.) Presumably, therefore, section 4800.1 would operate to defeat Esther's separate property interest to the extent it is unprotected by section 4800.2's formula for reimbursing separate property contributions to community assets.[5] Under section 4800.2, only $17,500 would be credited as Esther's separate property; the remaining $150,000 would be attributed to the community.

Legislative intent, however, is only one prerequisite to retroactive application of a statute. Having identified such intent, it remains for us to determine whether retroactivity is barred by constitutional con-

4. Section 4800.1 provides: "For the purpose of division of property upon dissolution of marriage or legal separation, property acquired by the parties during marriage in joint tenancy form is presumed to be community property. This presumption is a presumption affecting the burden of proof and may be rebutted by either of the following:

"(a) A clear statement in the deed or other documentary evidence of title by which the property is acquired that the property is separate property and not community property.

"(b) Proof that the parties have made a written agreement that the property is separate property."

5. Section 4800.2, also adopted as part of Assembly Bill No. 26, provides: "In the division of community property under this part unless a party has made a written waiver of the right to reimbursement or signed a writing that has the effect of a waiver, the party shall be reimbursed for his or her contributions to the acquisition of the property to the extent the party traces the contributions to a separate property source. The amount reimbursed shall be without interest or adjustment for change in monetary values and shall not exceed the net value of the property at the time of the division. As used in this section, 'contributions to the acquisition of the property' include down payments, payments for improvements, and payments that reduce the principal of a loan used to finance the purchase or improvement of the property but do not include payments of interest on the loan or payments made for maintenance, insurance or taxation of the property."

straints. We have long held that the retroactive application of a statute may be unconstitutional if it is an ex post facto law, if it deprives a person of a vested right without due process of law, or if it impairs the obligation of a contract. (*Rosefield Packing Co. v. Superior Court* (1935) 4 Cal.2d 120, 122, 47 P.2d 716; *San Bernadino County v. Indus. Acc. Com.* (1933) 217 Cal. 618, 628, 20 P.2d 673. See *In re Marriage of Bouquet* (1976) 16 Cal.3d 583, 592, 128 Cal.Rptr. 427, 546 P.2d 1371; *Robertson v. Willis* (1978) 77 Cal.App.3d 358, 365, 143 Cal.Rptr. 523.)

Retroactive application of section 4800.1 would operate to deprive Esther of a vested[6] property right without due process of law. (Cal. Const., art. I, § 7.) At the time of trial, Esther had a vested property interest in the residence as her separate property. (Cf. *Bouquet*, supra, 16 Cal.3d at p. 591, 128 Cal.Rptr. 427, 546 P.2d 1371; *Addison v. Addison* (1965) 62 Cal.2d 558, 566, 43 Cal.Rptr. 97, 399 P.2d 897.) The law had long recognized that "separate property . . . [might] be converted into community property or *vice versa* at any time by oral agreement between the spouses. [Citations.]" (*Woods v. Security–First National Bank* (1956) 46 Cal.2d 697, 701, 299 P.2d 657. See also *Beam v. Bank of America* (1971) 6 Cal.3d 12, 25, 98 Cal.Rptr. 137, 490 P.2d 257.)

The Buols had such an agreement as to Esther's earnings and the home she purchased and maintained with those earnings.[7] "The status of property as community or separate is normally determined at the time of its acquisition." (*Bouquet*, supra, 16 Cal.3d at p. 591, 128 Cal.Rptr. 427, 546 P.2d 1371; *Trimble v. Trimble* (1933) 219 Cal. 340, 343, 26 P.2d 477.) Such status is not dependent on the form in which title is taken. (*Machado v. Machado* (1962) 58 Cal.2d 501, 506, 25 Cal.Rptr. 87, 375 P.2d 55.)

At all relevant times—when Esther purchased the home, during trial and when the trial court entered judgment for Esther—proof of an oral agreement was all that was required to protect Esther's vested separate property interest. (See *Lucas*, supra, 27 Cal.3d 808, 166 Cal.Rptr. 853, 614 P.2d 285; *Machado*, supra, 58 Cal.2d 501, 25 Cal. Rptr. 87, 375 P.2d 55.) Section 4800.1's requirement of a writing

---

6. "The word vested assumes different meanings in different contexts. [Citation.] We use the word vested here to describe property rights that are not subject to a condition precedent." (*Bouquet*, supra, 16 Cal.3d at p. 591, fn. 7, 128 Cal.Rptr. 427, 546 P.2d 1371.)

7. Robert contends that the record does not support the trial court's finding that the parties had such an agreement. This contention is without merit. "In reviewing the sufficiency of the evidence. * * * 'the power of the appellate court begins and ends with a determination as to whether there is any substantial evidence, contradicted or uncontradicted' to support the trial court's findings. [Citations.]" *Estate*

of Leslie (1984) 37 Cal.3d 186, 201, 207 Cal.Rptr. 561, 689 P.2d 133.

Esther and several family members testified to countless statements on Robert's part that the money and the house belonged to Esther. Even Robert himself testified that he considered Esther's earnings to be her property and borrowed from her with that understanding. It is undisputed that Esther made the downpayment and all the house payments from her separate account. Despite Robert's testimony that he had no agreement with Esther that the house was her separate property, the trial court's conclusion to the contrary is supported by substantial evidence.

evidencing the parties' intent to maintain the joint tenancy asset as separate property operates to substantially impair that interest.

Two Courts of Appeal have summarily rejected the contention that section 4800.1 directly impairs vested property rights, finding instead that the measure "merely alters the evidentiary burden of proof when a husband and wife take property by a joint tenancy deed." (*In re Marriage of Martinez* (1984) 156 Cal.App.3d 20, 30, 202 Cal.Rptr. 646; See also *In re Marriage of Taylor* (1984) 160 Cal.App.3d 471, 474, 206 Cal.Rptr. 557; *In re Marriage of Benart* (1984) 160 Cal.App.3d 183, 188, fn. 2, 206 Cal.Rptr. 495.) [8] This literal reading of the statute without due consideration for its practical application to proceedings initiated prior to its effective date, unnecessarily exalts form over substance, substantially impairing vested property rights along the way.

While the Legislature generally is free to apply changes in rules of evidence or procedure retroactively when no vested rights are involved, it is not so unrestrained when these changes directly affect such rights.

* * *

The answer to the question whether a particular statute is "merely evidentiary" or "purely procedural" is not always to be found in the statutory language. " 'Alteration of a substantial right * * * is not merely procedural, even if the statute takes a seemingly procedural form.' " (*People v. Smith* (1983) 34 Cal.3d 251, 260, 193 Cal.Rptr. 692, 667 P.2d 149, quoting *Weaver v. Graham* (1981) 450 U.S. 24, 29, fn. 12, 101 S.Ct. 960, 964, fn. 12, 67 L.Ed.2d 17.) "Destroying enforcement of a vested right is, * * * tantamount to destroying the right itself." (*Baldwin v. City of San Diego* (1961) 195 Cal.App.2d 236, 240, 15 Cal.Rptr. 576.) We must, therefore, extend our analysis beyond the Legislature's chosen evidentiary language—"this presumption is a presumption affecting the burden of proof"—and focus upon the realities of retroactive application of the statute.

Applied retroactively, section 4800.1 unquestionably is substantive. A statute is substantive in effect when it "imposes a new or additional liability and substantially affects existing rights and obligations." (*Aetna Cas. & Surety Co. v. Ind. Acc. Com.* (1947) 30 Cal.2d 388, 395, 182 P.2d 159.) Section 4800.1 imposes a statute of frauds where there was none before, penalizing the unwary for relying upon the law as it existed at the time the property rights were created rather than at the time dissolution proceedings were already underway. This paradoxical approach is aptly illustrated by the *Martinez* court's gratuitous offer to remand that case "in fairness to [the husband] * * * for a hearing at which he shall have the opportunity to prove a written agreement in

8. Several Courts of Appeal have assumed section 4800.1 applies retroactively without addressing the issue whether such application is constitutional. (See, e.g., *In re Marriage of Huxley* (1984) 159 Cal. App.3d 1253, 206 Cal.Rptr. 291; *In re Mar-* *riage of Koppelman* (1984) 159 Cal.App.3d 627, 205 Cal.Rptr. 629; *In re Marriage of Anderson* (1984) 154 Cal.App.3d 572, 201 Cal.Rptr. 498; *In re Marriage of Neal* (1984) 153 Cal.App.3d 117, 200 Cal.Rptr. 341.)

accordance with section 4800.1." (*Id.*, 156 Cal.App.3d at p. 30, 202 Cal.Rptr. 646.) Understandably, the court refrains from suggesting just how the husband might go about creating the document that is missing solely because it was never required to prove a separate property interest under former law.

The statute does much more than simply articulate the means by which the community property presumption might be rebutted. Insofar as it applies retroactively, the statute imposes an irrebuttable presumption barring recognition of the vested separate property interest. In the case at bar, and all similar proceedings instituted prior to January 1, 1984, the time for executing a written agreement as to the character of joint tenancy marital property has long passed. By eliminating the means by which one might prove the existence of the vested property right, imposing instead an evidentiary requirement with which it is impossible to comply, section 4800.1 affects the vested property right itself.

* * *

Section 4800.2s' provision for reimbursement of the separate property contributions to what now is conclusively presumed to be community property regardless of the parties' intent, does little to neutralize section 4800.1's adverse effect on vested property rights. In the instant case, the trial court ruled that the $167,500 home was Esther's separate property. Retroactive application of the new statutory scheme would decrease that separate property interest to only $17,500. Esther would not be reimbursed for interest payments on the mortgage (which would have constituted virtually all of her monthly payments during the early years of the loan), taxes, insurance payments or maintenance costs. The remaining $150,000 would be credited to the community, an interest which arose only after judgment was entered by the trial court. Robert would thus receive a windfall of $75,000. Moreover, because the house represents the full extent of Esther's property, she would be forced to sell it to satisfy Robert's claim. As this case all too painfully demonstrates, section 4800.2 may provide only superficial protection against section 4800.1's potentially devastating impact upon vested property rights.

II

We turn to the question whether impairment of Esther's vested property right violates due process of law. Vested rights are not immutable; the state, exercising its police power may impair such rights when considered reasonably necessary to protect the health, safety, morals and general welfare of the people. (*Bouquet*, supra, 16 Cal.3d at p. 592, 128 Cal.Rptr. 427, 546 P.2d 1371.) In determining whether a given provision contravenes the due process clause we look to "the significance of the state interest served by the law, the importance of the retroactive application of the law to the effectuation of that interest, the extent of reliance upon the former law, the legitimacy of that reliance, the extent of actions taken on the basis of that reliance, and the extent to which the retroactive application of the new law would disrupt those actions." (*Ibid.*)

Where "retroactive application is necessary to subserve a sufficiently important state interest" (*Bouquet,* supra, 16 Cal.3d at p. 593, 128 Cal.Rptr. 427, 546 P.2d 1371), the inquiry need proceed no further. (See *Addison,* supra, 62 Cal.2d at p. 567, 43 Cal.Rptr. 97, 399 P.2d 897.) In *Bouquet,* where we validated retroactive application of an amendment to Civil Code section 5118 making the postseparation earnings of both spouses, not just those of the wife, separate property, we emphasized that "[t]he state's interest in the equitable dissolution of the marital relationship supports this use of the police power to abrogate rights in marital property that derived from the patently unfair former law." (*Bouquet,* supra, 16 Cal.3d at p. 594, 128 Cal.Rptr. 427, 546 P.2d 1371.) As noted in *Bouquet,* we reached the same conclusion in *Addison,* supra, 62 Cal.2d 558, 43 Cal.Rptr. 97, 399 P.2d 897, wherein we upheld the constitutionality of retroactive application of quasi-community property legislation despite its interference with the husband's vested property rights.

In both *Bouquet* and *Addison* we identified an important state interest in the "equitable dissolution of the marital relationship" and stressed that retroactive application was necessary to remedy "the rank injustice of the former law." (*Bouquet,* supra, 16 Cal.3d at p. 594, 128 Cal.Rptr. 427, 546 P.2d 1371; *Addison,* supra, 62 Cal.2d at p. 567, 43 Cal.Rptr. 97, 399 P.2d 897.) Thus, these cases support the proposition that the state's paramount interest in the equitable dissolution of the marital partnership justifies legislative action abrogating rights in marital property where those rights derive from manifestly unfair laws. No such compelling reason exists for applying section 4800.1 retroactively. Section 4800.1 cures no "rank injustice" in the law and, in the retroactivity context, only minimally serves the state interest in equitable division of marital property, at tremendous cost to the separate property owner.

As evidence of legislative intent, the Senate reprinted the California Law Revision Commission's Report Concerning Assembly Bill No. 26 in the Senate Journal. (See Sen.Com. on Judiciary Rep. on Assembly Bill No. 26 (July 14, 1983) 3 Sen.J. (1983 Reg.Sess.) pages 4865–4867.) While the report sheds no light on the Legislature's decision to give the measure retrospective effect, it does elucidate the reasoning behind enactment of section 4800.1. The Senate was concerned that because marital partners often use community property funds to acquire assets taken in joint tenancy without knowledge of the legal distinctions between the two, and the courts are without jurisdiction to divide joint tenancy property upon dissolution, absent section 4800.1's community property presumption, the courts may be precluded from making "the most sensible disposition of all the assets of the parties." (*Id.,* at p. 4865.) Although section 5110 already contained such a presumption for the single-family residence, the Senate wanted to extend the presumption to all marital property taken in joint tenancy because "spouses frequently hold substantial amounts of their wealth in joint tenancy form, including bank accounts, stocks, and other real property." (*Ibid.*) In addition, the report states that a writing satisfying the statute of frauds is necessary to rebut the community property presumption, but fails to set forth the reasoning underlying that conclusion. (*Id.,* at pp. 4865–4866.)

From this statement of intent we can infer that the Legislature's primary motivation in enacting section 4800.1 was to promote the state's interest in equitable distribution of marital property upon dissolution. We are at a loss to explain, however, how retroactive application of the statute is "necessary to subserve" that interest.

Retroactive application of the writing requirement does not advance the goal of insuring equitable division of community property where, as here, the asset in question is the separate property of one spouse. Moreover, because the writing requirement only applies to joint tenancy property, it fails to achieve uniformity in the division of marital property. The presumption that property taken as "husband and wife" is community property (§ 5110) may still be rebutted by evidence of a contrary oral agreement. (See *Lucas,* supra, 27 Cal.3d at p. 816, 166 Cal.Rptr. 853, 614 P.2d 285.) Nontitle property acquired during marriage is presumed to be community property (§ 5110), but may be proved otherwise by tracing alone. (*In re Marriage of Mix* (1975) 14 Cal.3d 604, 608–612, 122 Cal.Rptr. 79, 536 P.2d 479.)

Thus, whether or not a spouse will be able to prove that certain property is separate may well depend on happenstance alone.[9] The Legislature and the courts have long been aware that " 'husbands and wives take property in joint tenancy without legal counsel but primarily because deeds prepared by real estate brokers, escrow companies and by title companies are usually presented to the parties in joint tenancy form.' [Citation.]" (*Lucas,* supra, 27 Cal.3d at p. 814, 166 Cal.Rptr. 853, 614 P.2d 285.) Given the lack of uniformity in treatment of marital property presumptions, it seems manifestly unfair to apply section 4800.1 to penalize one marital partner after all is said and done, for making an uninformed legal decision at the insistence of a real estate

9. For example, in *Neal,* supra, 153 Cal. App.3d 117, 200 Cal.Rptr. 341, the wife converted the form of title to her home to joint tenancy at the insistence of the lending institution refinancing the property. After the trial court ruled that the home, and a car and some furnishings purchased with the loan proceeds were the wife's separate property, section 4800.1 was enacted and the Court of Appeal reversed. The court held that the house was community property, but found that because the lender was relying on the equity in the home, rather than the parties' income, in making the loan, and the parties had an oral *Lucas* agreement, the loan proceeds were the wife's separate property. Accordingly, the court concluded that the furniture was her separate property. Without access to the vehicle registration, however, the court was uncertain whether the car was separate property. If the registration reads "Patricia *or* Henry" then the car would be deemed to be held in joint tenancy (Veh. Code, §§ 4150.5, 5600.5) and section 4800.1 would apply. If, on the other hand, it reads "Patricia *and* Henry," then section 4800.1 would not apply and the parties' oral agreement would control.

agent, where retroactivity of the statute advances no sufficiently compelling state interest.

The extent and legitimacy of Esther's reliance on former law is, of course, difficult to gauge with certainty. However, the record is clear that Esther and Robert considered the house to be her property despite the joint tenancy form of title. The decision to take the property as joint tenants was made solely at the suggestion of a realtor. Had existing law required the parties to execute a writing as proof that the property was to remain separate, the likelihood that Esther and Robert would have done so appears great. As it stands, retroactive application of section 4800.1 vitiates Esther and Robert's oral agreement, which the trial court found to be valid and enforceable under existing law, and imposes a new writing requirement with which Esther cannot possibly comply. The parties' legitimate expectations, therefore, are substantially disregarded in favor of needless retroactivity.

Two other policy considerations work against retroactive application of section 4800.1. First, " * * * to the extent the statute furthers a policy of evidentiary convenience, that policy is not served by application of the statute to cases already tried." (*Taylor,* supra, 160 Cal.App.3d 471, 478, 206 Cal.Rptr. 557 (Sims, J. dis.).) This is particularly true in cases, such as the one at bench, where the trial court correctly applied existing law in determining the asset to be separate property. Second, the manifest interest in finality pervading this sensitive area of the law is thwarted by retroactive application of the statute. "The net effect of retroactive legislation is that parties to marital dissolution actions cannot intelligently plan a settlement of their affairs nor even conclude their affairs with certainty after a trial based on then-applicable law." (*Id.,* at p. 479, 206 Cal.Rptr. 557 (Sims, J. dis.).)

We conclude that retroactive application of section 4800.1 would substantially impair Esther's vested property right without due process of law.[10] The state interest in equitable dissolution of the marital partnership is not furthered by retroactive effect. Retroactivity only serves to destroy Esther's legitimate separate property expectations as a penalty for lack of prescience of changes in the law occurring after trial. Due process cannot tolerate such a result.

The judgment is affirmed.

BIRD, C.J., and MOSK, KAUS, BROUSSARD, GRODIN and LUCAS, JJ., concur.

IN RE MARRIAGE OF HILKE

Supreme Court of California, In Bank, 1992.
4 Cal.4th 215, 14 Cal.Rptr.2d 371, 841 P.2d 891.

PANELLI, JUSTICE.

For the purpose of division of property upon dissolution of marriage, property acquired by the parties during marriage in joint tenancy form

10. Holdings to the contrary in the following cases are disapproved: *Taylor,* supra, 160 Cal.App.3d 471, 206 Cal.Rptr. 557; *Benart,* supra, 160 Cal.App.3d 183, 206 Cal. Rptr. 495; *Martinez,* supra, 156 Cal.App.3d 20, 202 Cal.Rptr. 646; *Anderson,* supra, 154 Cal.App.3d 572, 201 Cal.Rptr. 498; *Neal,* supra, 153 Cal.App.3d 117, 200 Cal.Rptr. 341.

is presumed to be community property. (Civ.Code, § 4800.1, subd. (b).)[1] This case requires us to determine the character of a marital residence—title to which was held by the spouses in joint tenancy—when, after entry of a judgment dissolving the marital relationship, followed by the wife's death, the trial court exercised its reserved jurisdiction to divide the marital property. The trial court applied the presumption set forth in section 4800.1 and found the residence to be community property. The Court of Appeal reversed, reasoning that the wife's death intervened before that statute could be applied, so that the husband's right of survivorship as a joint tenant prevailed. We reverse.

FACTUAL BACKGROUND

Robert and Joyce Hilke married in 1955. In 1969 they purchased a residence, taking title as "husband and wife, as joint tenants." On January 27, 1989, Mrs. Hilke filed a petition to dissolve the marriage.

1. Civil Code section 4800.1 provides as follows:

"(a) The Legislature hereby finds and declares as follows:

"(1) It is the public policy of this state to provide uniformly and consistently for the standard of proof in establishing the character of property acquired by spouses during marriage in joint title form, and for the allocation of community and separate interests in that property between spouses.

"(2) The methods provided by case and statutory law have not resulted in consistency in the treatment of spouses' interests in property which they hold in joint title, but rather, have created confusion as to which law applies at a particular point in time to property, depending on the form of title, and, as a result, spouses cannot have reliable expectations as to the characterization of their property and the allocation of the interests therein, and attorneys cannot reliably advise their clients regarding applicable law.

"(3) Therefore, the Legislature finds that a compelling state interest exists to provide for uniform treatment of property; thus the Legislature intends that the forms of this section and Section 4800.2, operative on January 1, 1987, shall apply to all property held in joint title regardless of the date of acquisition of the property or the date of any agreement affecting the character of the property, and that that form of this section and that form of Section 4800.2 are applicable in all proceedings commenced on or after

January 1, 1984. However, the form of this section and the form of Section 4800.2 operative on January 1, 1987, are not applicable to property settlement agreements executed prior to January 1, 1987, or proceedings in which judgments were rendered prior to January 1, 1987, regardless of whether those judgments have become final.

"(b) For the purpose of division of property upon dissolution of marriage or legal separation, property acquired by the parties during marriage in joint form, including property held in tenancy in common, joint tenancy, tenancy by the entirety, or as community property is presumed to be community property. This presumption is a presumption affecting the burden of proof and may be rebutted by either of the following:

"(1) A clear statement in the deed or other documentary evidence of title by which the property is acquired that the property is separate property and not community property.

"(2) Proof that the parties have made a written agreement that the property is separate property."

Further statutory references are to the Civil Code, unless otherwise noted.

Effective January 1, 1994, section 4800.1 has been repealed and replaced with an equivalent provision in the Family Code. (Stats.1992, ch. 162, §§ 3, 10; see Fam.Code, § 2580 (effective Jan. 1, 1994).)

The parties stipulated to an order bifurcating the proceeding, terminating their marital status, and reserving jurisdiction over all other issues, including support and property division.

Before any of the property issues were adjudicated, Mrs. Hilke died.[2] Thereafter, the administrator of her estate was substituted as a party. (Code Civ.Proc., § 385; *Kinsler v. Superior Court* (1981) 121 Cal.App.3d 808, 812, 175 Cal.Rptr. 564.) There had been no change in the title to the property between its acquisition and the date of Mrs. Hilke's death.

The trial court denied Mr. Hilke's motion for summary adjudication of the property's character. The matter proceeded to trial on the undisputed facts set forth in the preceding two paragraphs. Neither party contended there had been any contributions of separate property toward purchase of the residence, and there was no claim of an agreement that the property would be the separate property of either spouse. The trial court determined it retained jurisdiction to decide all of the real property issues that could have been decided had they been presented at the time the parties' marital status was dissolved. It then held that the residence was the parties' community property. The Court of Appeal reversed, and we granted review to address the effect of section 4800.1 on the present situation.

ANALYSIS

A discussion of the development of the statute with which we are concerned will assist our resolution of this dispute. Before 1966, California courts applied a rebuttable presumption that ownership interest in property was as stated in the title. Thus, a residence purchased with community funds, but held by a husband and wife as joint tenants, was presumed to be separate property in which each spouse had a one-half interest. The presumption arising from the form of title created difficulties upon divorce or separation when the parties held title to their residence in joint tenancy. A court could not award a house so held to one spouse for use as a family residence for that spouse and the children, unless the presumption arising from the joint tenancy title could be rebutted by evidence of an agreement or understanding to the contrary. (*In re Marriage of Lucas* (1980) 27 Cal.3d 808, 813–814, 166 Cal.Rptr. 853, 614 P.2d 285.)

To remedy the problem, the Legislature in 1965 added the following provision to former section 164:

> "[W]hen a single family residence of a husband and wife is acquired by them during marriage as joint tenants, for the purpose of the division of such property upon divorce or separate maintenance only, the presumption is that such single family residence is the community property of said husband and wife." (Stats.1965, ch. 1710, § 1, pp. 3843–3844.)

---

2. In her will, Mrs. Hilke left her share of the parties' community property to her children.

Former section 164 was repealed in 1969 in connection with the enactment of the Family Law Act. (Stats.1969, ch. 1608, § 3, p. 3313; *In re Marriage of Lucas, supra,* 27 Cal.3d 808, 814, fn. 2, 166 Cal.Rptr. 853, 614 P.2d 285.) Effective January 1, 1970, an almost identical provision in section 5110 replaced the substance of former section 164. (Stats.1969, ch. 1608, § 8, p. 3339.)

Section 5110, in turn, was amended in 1983, and the presumption regarding marital property held in joint tenancy form for the purpose of division of property upon dissolution of marriage was moved to newly adopted section 4800.1. The presumption was expanded to cover all property acquired during marriage in joint tenancy form. (Stats.1983, ch. 342, § 1, p. 1538.)

In an effort to ensure application of the presumption to marital property held in joint tenancy form, no matter when acquired (see *In re Marriage of Buol* (1985) 39 Cal.3d 751, 218 Cal.Rptr. 31, 705 P.2d 354; *In re Marriage of Fabian* (1986) 41 Cal.3d 440, 224 Cal.Rptr. 333, 715 P.2d 253), the Legislature in 1986 amended section 4800.1 to include its finding that "[i]t is the public policy of this state to provide uniformly and consistently for the standard of proof in establishing the character of property acquired by spouses during marriage in joint title form, and for the allocation of community and separate interests in that property between the spouses." (Stats.1986, ch. 539, § 1, p. 1924; § 4800.1, subd. (a)(1).) The Legislature found that a compelling state interest exists to provide for uniform treatment of property, and accordingly amended the statute to provide that section 4800.1 shall apply to all property held in joint title regardless of the date of acquisition of the property or the date of any agreement affecting the character of the property. (§ 4800.1, subd. (a)(3).)

The nub of this case is whether the community property presumption of section 4800.1 applies to the residence owned by Mr. and Mrs. Hilke. If it does not, then the presumption arising from the form of title is that the spouses were joint tenants and Mr. Hilke consequently succeeds to the property by right of survivorship, absent a transmutation. * * *

* * *

Mr. Hilke argues that section 4800.1 * * * may not, consistently with due process, be applied retroactively to the marital residence the parties acquired in 1969. In support of this contention, he cites *In re Marriage of Buol, supra,* 39 Cal.3d 751, 218 Cal.Rptr. 31, 705 P.2d 354, and *In re Marriage of Fabian, supra,* 41 Cal.3d 440, 224 Cal.Rptr. 333, 715 P.2d 253. He contends that if a community property presumption applies at all in this case, it can be only that form of the presumption that existed when the parties bought their residence in 1969. Former section 164 allowed rebuttal of the presumption by *any* understanding or agreement, oral or written, that the property was to be held as indicated in the title. Thus, he reasons, his declaration in support of his motion for summary adjudication—that the spouses desired the survivorship feature of joint tenancy when they acquired the property, and never made any contrary agreement—sufficed to rebut the presumption. (*In re Marriage of Lucas, supra,* 27 Cal.3d 808, 166 Cal.Rptr. 853, 614 P.2d 285.)

We disagree with his initial premise. Section 4800.1 may be applied on the facts of this case even though the property was acquired before its enactment.

There can be no doubt that the Legislature intended courts to apply section 4800.1 in a division of property upon dissolution of marriage, regardless of the date of acquisition of the property, for the statute expressly says so. (§ 4800.1, subd. (a)(3) ["[T]he Legislature intends that the forms of this section and Section 4800.2, operative on January 1, 1987, shall apply to all property held in joint title regardless of the date of acquisition of the property or the date of any agreement affecting the character of the property. . . ."].) Unless there are constitutional impediments to its application, therefore, we may not refuse the statutory mandate.

Retroactive legislation may not be applied when it constitutes an ex post facto law or an impairment of an existing contract, or when to do so would impair a vested property right without due process of law. (*In re Marriage of Fabian, supra,* 41 Cal.3d at p. 447, 224 Cal.Rptr. 333, 715 P.2d 253.) We are concerned in this case only with the question of whether section 4800.1 impairs a vested property right.

As we have recognized in a similar context, a vested property right is one that is not subject to a condition precedent. (*In re Marriage of Buol, supra,* 39 Cal.3d at p. 757, fn. 6, 218 Cal.Rptr. 31, 705 P.2d 354; *In re Marriage of Bouquet* (1976) 16 Cal.3d 583, 591, fn. 7, 128 Cal.Rptr. 427, 546 P.2d 1371.) Mr. Hilke's claim fails at the threshold, for his survivorship interest in the marital residence is plainly subject to the condition precedent that he survive Mrs. Hilke. As Mr. Hilke himself notes in his brief on a collateral point, severance of a joint tenancy—by eliminating the survivorship characteristic of the joint tenancy form of ownership—theoretically affects the expectancy interest of the other joint tenant, but does not involve a diminution of his or her present vested interest. Put another way, a joint tenant has no vested interest in being the surviving tenant. The community property presumption of section 4800.1 therefore may be applied retroactively in the circumstances of this case.

The factual distinctions between this case, on one hand, and *Buol* and *Fabian,* on the other, bear emphasis. In *Buol,* the spouses had an oral agreement that the wife's earnings and the house she purchased and maintained with them were her separate property; at all relevant times—when she purchased the house and throughout the trial—proof of an oral agreement was all that was required to protect her separate property interest. (*In re Marriage of Buol, supra,* 39 Cal.3d at p. 757, 218 Cal.Rptr. 31, 705 P.2d 354.) Section 4800.1, requiring for the first time a writing to establish a separate interest in property held in joint tenancy form, was enacted *during the pendency of the husband's appeal.* To determine whether retroactive application of section 4800.1 would contravene due process, we examined factors enumerated in *In re Marriage of Bouquet, supra,* 16 Cal.3d at page 592, 128 Cal.Rptr. 427, 546 P.2d 1371; the significance of the state interest served by the law, the importance of the retroactive application of the law to the effectuation of that interest, the extent of reliance on the former law, the legitimacy of that reliance, the extent of actions taken on the basis of that reliance, and the extent to which the retroactive application of the new law would disrupt those actions. (*In re Marriage of Buol, supra,* 39 Cal.3d at pp. 761–763, 218 Cal.Rptr. 31, 705 P.2d 354.) On consideration of those factors, we concluded that application of section 4800.1 to a proceeding *commenced before the effective date of the statute* would impair the wife's vested property rights without due process of law. (39 Cal.3d at p. 763, 218 Cal.Rptr. 31, 705 P.2d 354.)

In *Fabian,* we addressed the issue of the retroactivity of section 4800.2, a companion measure to section 4800.1 that provides for reimbursement of separate property contributions to community property unless there is a signed writing waiving reimbursement. During their marriage, Mr. and Mrs. Fabian purchased a motel, taking title as "husband and wife as community property." (*In re Marriage of Fabian, supra,* 41 Cal.3d at p. 443, 224 Cal.Rptr. 333, 715 P.2d 253.) The husband invested in the motel some $275,000 of his separate assets. The parties had no agreement that he would be reimbursed for that sum. The trial court found that the motel was community property and, applying then-current law, that the husband had made a gift to the community of his contribution. *During the pendency of the husband's appeal,* section 4800.2 was enacted, in effect reversing the presumption of the prior law and resurrecting the husband's separate property interest. (41 Cal.3d at pp. 443–444, 224 Cal.Rptr. 333, 715 P.2d 253.) Analyzing the *Bouquet–Buol* factors, we held that retroactive application of section 4800.2 would unconstitutionally impair the wife's vested interest in the property. (41 Cal.3d at pp. 448–451, 224 Cal.Rptr. 333, 715 P.2d 253.)

In both *Buol* and *Fabian,* a spouse's *vested* property interests were infringed without due process by retroactive legislation enacted during the pendency of the appeal. In the present case, by contrast, Mr. Hilke's interest was not vested but rather contingent on his surviving his former wife.[4] We need not engage in extensive analysis of the *Bouquet–Buol* factors as they might apply in this situation, because in the absence of a vested interest, retroactive legislation does not violate due process.

Application of section 4800.1 to this case yields the conclusion that the residence was community property. The statute delineates two ways of rebutting the presumption, but neither is available: the deed does not

4. An additional difference between this case, on one hand, and *Fabian* and *Buol,* on the other, is that section 4800.1 was enacted well before Mrs. Hilke filed the petition for dissolution.

contain a clear statement that the residence is separate property and not community property, and the record contains no proof that the parties made a written agreement that the residence was separate property. (§ 4800.1, subd. (b).) It follows that the trial court properly ordered the residence sold and the proceeds divided equally between the parties. (See § 4800, subd. (a).)

* * *

DISPOSITION

The judgment of the Court of Appeal is reversed.

LUCAS, C.J., and MOSK, KENNARD, ARABIAN, BAXTER and GEORGE, JJ., concur.

Notes

1. The reaction of the family law bench and bar to the *Buol* decision was summarized by the appellate court in Marriage of Delgado, 176 Cal. App.3d 666, 222 Cal.Rptr. 119 (1986), as follows:

> Effective January 1, 1984, section 4800.1 establishes a presumption that "property acquired by the parties during marriage in joint tenancy form is presumed to be community property." This presumption is rebuttable only by a statement in the documentary evidence of title or by a written agreement that the property is separate property, neither of which were present here. By uncodified language and legislative history the statute was made applicable to all proceedings which were not final as of the statute's effective date. (Stats.1983, ch. 342, § 4.) However, for the first time in more than 50 years our Supreme Court has found a family law statute unconstitutional, determining that retroactive application of section 4800.1 would deny due process. (*In re Marriage of Buol* (1985) 39 Cal.3d 751, 218 Cal.Rptr. 31, 705 P.2d 354.)

> The decision in *Buol* has created confusion and consternation in the Family Law Bench and Bar by failing to answer the question of when section 4800.1 becomes operative. Is it applicable only to cases filed after its effective date of January 1, 1984, only to cases tried after that date, or only to cases where the judgment was entered after that date? The legal analysis of due process in *Buol* supports the argument that section 4800.1 is inapplicable to cases when an oral agreement or understanding took place prior to the effective date of the statute. Until our Supreme Court supplies the answer, the Family Law Bench and Bar is left to speculate.

The California Law Revision Commission asked the California Supreme Court to clarify the scope of its decision. The court denied the modification request and ordered the *Buol* decision final forthwith. Subsequently the Legislature enacted Assembly Bill 625, an urgency statute effective April 10, 1986, providing that Civil Code Sections 4800.1 and 4800.2 would apply to all proceedings commenced on or after January 1, 1984 regardless of the date of acquisition of the property. The urgency measure stated:

> "SECTION 1. Section 4 of Chapter 342 of the Statutes of 1983 is amended to read:

"SEC. 4. This act applies to proceedings commenced on or after January 1, 1984, regardless of the date of acquisition of property subject to the proceedings or the date of any agreement affecting the property.

"SEC. 2. This act is an urgency statute necessary for the immediate preservation of the public peace, health, or safety within the meaning of Article IV of the Constitution and shall go into immediate effect. The facts constituting the necessity are:

"Sections 4800.1 and 4800.2 of the Civil Code were enacted by Chapter 342 of the Statutes of 1983 and applied immediately to all family law proceedings not yet final on January 1, 1984, its effective date, in order to cure a serious problem in the law governing division of assets at dissolution of marriage (See Report of Senate Committee on Judiciary on Assembly Bill 26, 83 Senate Journal 4865, July 14, 1983). The Supreme Court in In re Marriage of Buol, 39 Cal.3d 751, 705 P.2d 354, 218 Cal.Rptr. 31 (1985), held that this legislation cannot be applied to pending litigation in some circumstances, but the precise scope of the decision is unclear.

"The Buol decision has caused confusion among family law judges and lawyers as to what law governs in a heavily litigated area in which important property rights are affected. The decision also frustrates the intent of the Legislature to correct a serious problem in the law that is causing inequitable treatment of many parties.

"This act is intended to resolve the confusion caused by Buol and to reaffirm the need for immediately applicable legislation, to the extent constitutionally permissible, in order to assure all litigants of equitable treatment upon dissolution of marriage. Any further delay will accentuate unreasonably the current confusion and problems in this area of the law."

This legislation was held unconstitutional in Marriage of Griffis, 187 Cal. App.3d 156, 231 Cal.Rptr. 510 (1986). Thereafter the amended version of Civil Code Sections 4800.1 and 4800.2 was enacted, now contained at West's Ann.Cal. Family Code §§ 2580–81 and 2640.

2. Does *Marriage of Hilke* help resolve the retroactivity problems raised in *Buol*? Note the court's footnote suggestion that an additional distinction between *Hilke* and *Buol* "is that section 4800.1 was enacted well before Mrs. Hilke filed for dissolution." Does this mean that the statute may be constitutionally applied to dissolutions filed after 1984, as the current statutory language mandates? Professor Grace Blumberg states that "*Hilke* may be understood to suggest that the courts of appeal may have read *Buol* * * * too broadly when they settled on transactions as the marker for unconstitutional retroactive application." G. Blumberg, *Community Property in California* 227 (1993). When the Family Code was originally enacted in 1992, the legislature conceded the constitutional point. The current version, however, reiterates the 1984 effective date.

3. The holding in *Buol* applied only to Civil Code Section 4800.1. In Marriage of Fabian, 41 Cal.3d 440, 224 Cal.Rptr. 333, 715 P.2d 253 (1986), the retroactive application of Section 4800.2 was held constitutionally defec-

tive for similar reasons. Retroactivity problems are discussed in more detail in Chapter 3 of the casebook.

4. If a couple acquires property taking title in joint tenancy prior to marriage, but makes payments on the purchase price during marriage using community funds, should the property be deemed community property for purposes of dissolution? See Marriage of Leversee, 156 Cal.App.3d 891, 203 Cal.Rptr. 481 (1984), indicating that the presumptions contained in West's Ann.Cal. Family Code § 2581 are not applicable to premarriage acquisitions.

Chapter 3

LIMITATIONS ON THE CLASSIFICATION PROCESS

In the preceding Chapters, we considered the basic principles involved in the classification of property as community or separate. We will now examine certain limitations that have been imposed on the operation of the classification process. These include limits on the types of property that may be classified as community property, limits on the persons within the coverage of the community property system, and certain constitutional limitations on the operation of the community property system. In Chapter 4 we will consider some specialized applications of the classification process.

SECTION 1. PROPERTY WITHIN THE SYSTEM

A married person can use his time, energy and skill or existing community funds to acquire various items of property, both tangible and intangible. Most types of legally recognized and protected property interests fit into the community property system without difficulty. There are certain relationships of economic value, however, which the courts have removed from the community property system. For example, the value of a professional education acquired by a spouse during marriage has been held not to be property within the system.[1] Similarly, the right to practice a particular profession such as medicine or law is a valuable property right but is not classifiable as community property.[2] By contrast, the professional practice itself, including the goodwill element of the practice, is property within the system.[3]

The cases have stated many times that a court cannot divide the nonexistent. But such statements should not mean that items of wealth

---

1. Todd v. Todd, reprinted in this section; In re Marriage of Aufmuth, 89 Cal. App.3d 446, 152 Cal.Rptr. 668 (1979).

2. Franklin v. Franklin, 67 Cal.App.2d 717, 155 P.2d 637 (1945).

3. In re Marriage of Lopez, reprinted in this Section.

having value cannot be community property merely because present division in kind is impracticable, or merely because there is no market for the item so that placing a present dollar value on it is difficult, or merely because some condition remains to be satisfied before it can be deemed a vested interest. Where a relationship of value is produced by the expenditure of a community asset, it should be community property even if it is forfeitable or otherwise subject to termination, or even if it is temporarily inchoate and contingent, or even if its valuation may have to be postponed to some future day. So long as it realistically has substantial potential value there is no reason to exclude it from the system. These ideas are reflected in the cases involving contingent fee agreements,[4] term life insurance policies,[5] and pension plan benefits.[6]

Other types of property interests, potentially classifiable as community property, may be taken out of that category under certain circumstances or conditions. In the preceding chapter, we saw that the earnings and accumulations of a spouse during separation are that spouse's separate property. Personal injury damages, although classified as community property, are treated much like separate property on dissolution of the marriage.[7] Community property earnings are not available to satisfy certain pre-marital debts,[8] and there is also preferential treatment of assets for the satisfaction of tort claims.[9] These matters will be considered in succeeding Chapters dealing with creditors' rights and the division of property on dissolution.

TODD v. TODD
California District Court of Appeal, 1969.
272 Cal.App.2d 786, 78 Cal.Rptr. 131.

BRAY, ASSOCIATE JUSTICE (assigned). Plaintiff appeals from portions of an interlocutory decree of divorce granting her a divorce, dividing the community property, and awarding her alimony, child support and attorneys' fees.

Plaintiff also appeals from a minute order date February 1, 1967, denying attorneys' fees and costs on appeal.

QUESTIONS PRESENTED

A. Appeal from the decree:

4. Waters v. Waters, 75 Cal.App.2d 265, 170 P.2d 494 (1946).

5. Estate of Logan, 191 Cal.App.3d 319, 236 Cal.Rptr. 368 (1987); In re Marriage of Gonzalez, 168 Cal.App.3d 1021, 214 Cal. Rptr. 634 (1985); Biltoft v. Wootten, 96 Cal.App.3d 58, 157 Cal.Rptr. 581 (1979); Modern Woodmen of America v. Gray, 113 Cal.App. 729, 299 P. 754 (1931).

6. Many of the pension plan cases decided prior to 1975 voiced ideas inconsistent with these conclusions, holding that non-

vested retirement benefits were excluded from the community property system. The effect of these cases was to make suspect all contingent property interests. This line of cases was ultimately overruled by the California Supreme Court in the case of In re Marriage of Brown, reprinted in this Section.

7. West's Ann.Cal.Family Code § 2603.

8. West's Ann.Cal.Family Code § 911.

9. West's Ann.Cal.Family Code § 1000.

1. Was plaintiff entitled to an award based upon the value of the husband's education?

2. In dividing the community property, did the court improperly value the husband's law practice?

RECORD

Plaintiff and defendant were married January 25, 1947. They separated December 26, 1964.

1. *Husband's Education*

Three months before the marriage, defendant, a high school graduate and having spent one semester at Sacramento Junior College before service in the armed forces, reenrolled at that college under the educational benefits of the Cal–Vet and G.I. programs. Without finishing his college course he was admitted to the University of San Francisco Law School, graduating therefrom with an LLB degree in June 1951, and was admitted to the State Bar. He started to practice law in Grass Valley. His assets at that time, other than his license to practice law, were practically nil. By March 1, 1965, the community had accumulated net assets in excess of $200,000, and his law practice was bringing in approximately $23,412 net per year.

Plaintiff was working prior to the marriage; she continued working the entire time defendant was in school and for several years after he started practicing law. Her earnings were treated as community income and were used to supplement defendant's veteran's benefits to keep defendant in college and law school, and thereafter for general community purposes. The court at the time of dividing the community property valued the law practice at $9,866.47 and awarded plaintiff no portion thereof. The value was based upon accounts receivable, moneys in various banks, and goodwill valued at $1,000.

Plaintiff contended and now contends that defendant's education, partially paid for by community funds, is a community asset and that in terms of its existing economic potential it has a substantial worth which must be taken into account in evaluating the community estate for divorce purposes. The court made a finding, "EDUCATION OF DEFENDANT: * * * the value of this claimed asset is nothing $_0__."

Testimony was admitted on the value of an education, and on the value of defendant's education. A witness for the plaintiff, Philip Eden, testified that he had examined statements of defendant's earnings as an attorney since being admitted to practice and pointed out that defendant was in good health and could reasonably be expected to work until retirement age of 65; that his life expectancy was beyond that; that his average annual earnings from the law practice were $23,412, excluding business investments, stock dividends, interest, etc.; and that defendant, until he reached the age of 65, could be expected to earn $519,746. This figure did not include allowance for retirement, fringe benefits or future increases in prices and earnings. Eden then testified to factors which would cause greatly increased earnings which would make the total earnings greater than the above estimate. He then placed the value of defendant's education and law degree at $308,000.

If a spouse's education preparing him for the practice of the law can be said to be "community property," a proposition which is extremely doubtful even though the education is acquired with community moneys, it manifestly is of such a character that a monetary value for division with the other spouse cannot be placed upon it.

In Franklin v. Franklin (1945) 67 Cal.App.2d 717, 155 P.2d 637, which held that a husband's cause of action for personal injuries is not considered "property" for community division in a divorce action, the court stated (at p. 725, 155 P.2d at p. 641), "the word 'property,' as used in the code sections relating to community property, does not encompass every property right acquired by either husband or wife during marriage * * *. The right to practice medicine and similar professions, for instance, is a property right but it is not one which could be classed as community property."

At best, education is an intangible property right, the value of which, because of its character, cannot have a monetary value placed upon it for division between spouses.

Plaintiff has cited no case law holding that the education of a spouse acquired in whole or in part with community moneys is tangible property, the value of which may be divided with the other spouse.

It should be pointed out that the assets of the community were the results of defendant's legal education and that in a sense plaintiff realized the value therefrom in the award to her of a value of $111,-500.97 in those assets. (The court awarded defendant $89,116.35 in assets.)

2. *The Law Practice*

While the right to practice law is a property right which cannot be classed as community property, the value of the practice at the time of dissolution of the community is community property. (Franklin v. Franklin, supra, p. 725, 155 P.2d 637.)

In Brawman v. Brawman (1962) 199 Cal.App.2d 876, 19 Cal.Rptr. 106, the defendant appealed from a decree denying her alimony. The plaintiff was a lawyer who had commenced his law practice one year before the marriage and whose income from it was $26,000 net at the time of the divorce action. The court said that on divorce and dissolution of the community "a professional practice goes automatically to the spouse licensed to practice it. * * * Effectually, it is the case of a silent partner withdrawing from a going business. And, if such partner is to receive fair compensation for her share, on her enforced retirement, it should be so evaluated." The court stated further that where a lucrative law business had been built by the husband during the marriage, "the business is community property and it has a substantial value." (P. 882, 19 Cal.Rptr. p. 109.) The court then pointed out that the appeal was not from the community property division but from denial of alimony.

"* * * Therefore, discussion of the value of the law business has application only to respondent's contention that denial of alimony is to be justified on the basis of the court's generosity in the award of property to the wife. Considering the value of the law practice for this limited purpose, it becomes clear that the wife here received not more, but less, in value of the community property than did the husband." (Brawman v. Brawman, supra, p. 882, 19 Cal.Rptr. p. 110.)

"On divorce and dissolution of the community a professional practice perforce remains in the hands of the spouse licensed to practice it. Nevertheless, in terms of its existing economic potential, it may have a substantial worth which must be taken into account in evaluating the community estate for divorce purposes." (Fritschi v. Teed (1963) 213 Cal.App.2d 718, 726, 29 Cal.Rptr. 114, 119.)

In Fritschi v. Teed, supra, at pages 726–727, 29 Cal.Rptr. 114, the court pointed out that the practice of the medical doctor husband had netted more than $40,000 per year for several years preceding the divorce, and that during the period subsequent to the interlocutory decree his net professional annual income was almost $47,000. "Thus, at the time the divorce court was formulating the property division, the expectation of future professional income was a valuable asset of the marital community." The controversy was over the interpretation of the interlocutory decree as to whether it reserved the right to divide the husband's post-interlocutory earnings with the wife, and held that it did not.

While, of course, the division of community property is a matter in the discretion of the trial court, where, as here, the court has failed to give consideration to certain of the community property and has failed to evaluate it for division purposes, the cause must be returned to the trial court for consideration thereof.

The court did not segregate the accounts receivable from the other community accounts receivable. In fact, it failed to go into the question of what were the accounts receivable of the law practice.

In evaluating the law practice, the court accepted the Carlisle Report of $8,866.47 depreciated book value, which included the "Bank Control" of $1,704.05 and added $1,000 thereto for goodwill. The goodwill of a law practice—even one in which the husband will remain and in which there is to be a continuity of practice—is no doubt difficult to evaluate. It depends upon a variety of factors. On the record of this case we cannot say that the trial court erred in its valuation of goodwill. We see no good reason to disturb the court's finding as to the value of the goodwill, but the value of the practice as a business is another matter.

It was stipulated that the valuation date of all the property was March 1, 1965.

The parties separated December 26, 1964. Within the week defendant sold half of the law business to Bishop for $3,126.93. At that time some $11,494.27 had been advanced to clients. The court did not find accounts receivable in the law firm separately from the accounts receivable from transactions outside the law practice. The finding of total accounts receivable was $6,906.53. Of this, only $1,444.33 belonged to the law firm. No consideration was given to the $11,494.27 owing from clients for moneys advanced, except the $1,444.33. Moreover, in valuing the law business only matters which had been concluded and charged on the books were considered. Here was a law practice that in 1963 and 1964 produced $16,209 and $21,188 respectively, and in March 1965 defendant's half was valued at less than one-half of the 1963 income, without considering most of the advances for clients, the value of the partly completed accounts in the office and the law books. Defendant testified that there were many cases pending in the office at the time of the formation of the partnership. Plaintiff's accountant placed a value on the practice of $49,420.

Incidentally, there appears to be no evidence of what became of the $3,126.93 paid by Bishop to defendant for his interest in the partnership formed January 1, 1965.

Mr. Dodini was appointed by the court to examine the books of Todd and Bishop for the year 1965. Although Todd testified that many of the old cases were terminated that year, Dodini was unable to find in them what fees and costs were paid to Todd. Todd testified that in 1966 "we were still able to liquidate some of the old accounts receivable from the law practice as an individual."

Plaintiff, who kept the books for the law practice from the beginning until the separation of the parties, testified that a partial examination of the clients cards disclosed accounts receivable as of December 1964 in the sum of $22,148.14. Plaintiff gave a list of these to Dodini, who testified that he could not find most of them in his investigation of the 1965 records.

Considering the small amount for which defendant sold one-half of his law practice and the condition of its books when investigations were made, an inference arises that defendant did considerable covering up of the financial condition of the practice. The cause will have to be remanded to the trial court for a reappraisal of the value of defendant's law practice on March 1, 1965, which should include all accounts receivable and all business then in the office.

So much of the interlocutory decree as relates to the value of the law practice is reversed with directions to the trial court to reevaluate the same in accordance with this opinion and to divide the same between the parties in the same proportions as the balance of the community property was divided.

Notes

1. What is the basis for the court's determination that an education acquired by the expenditure of community assets is not property within the

community property system? A professional education can be valued, and that value could be divided in some way on dissolution. Perhaps the court's underlying concern was that in valuing and dividing such an asset, reference would have to be made to post-marital acts of the educated spouse. Post-marital acts are not acts for the benefit of the community. This concern was voiced in In re Marriage of Aufmuth, 89 Cal.App.3d 446, 461, 152 Cal.Rptr. 668, 678 (1979):

> The value of a legal education lies in the potential for increase in the future earning capacity of the acquiring spouse made possible by the law degree and innumerable other factors and conditions which contribute to the development of a successful law practice. A determination that such an "asset" is community property would require a division of post-dissolution earnings to the extent that they are attributable to the law degree, even though such earnings are by definition the separate property of the acquiring spouse. As the court observed in In re Marriage of Fortier (1973) 34 Cal.App.3d 384, 388, 109 Cal.Rptr. 914, 918: "Since the philosophy of the community property system is that a community interest can be acquired only during the time of the marriage, it would then be inconsistent with that philosophy to assign to any community interest the value of the post-marital efforts of either spouse."

2. In *Todd* the parties separated after an eighteen year marriage. As a further rationale for its decision denying the wife any community property interest in her husband's education, the court noted that the other assets of the community were the fruits of the husband's legal education, and that therefore the wife had essentially realized the values therefrom by the award to her of half the value of the other assets. Suppose though that the husband had filed for dissolution shortly after receiving his law school degree, and that his spouse had supported the community during the three years of his legal training. In this situation the community has not received the expected benefit of the husband's higher earnings attributable to the law degree; furthermore, there may be no community property to divide if all the community assets were used to finance the student spouse's education. The unfairness of this situation has prompted many jurisdictions to develop some form of compensatory award for the working spouse. See L. Weitzman, The Divorce Revolution 124–129 (1985).

3. Although California courts have declined to treat the value of education or a professional license as a community property asset, they have on occasion given the spouse of the professional reimbursement for personal and monetary contributions toward such education and professional license. In Aarons v. Brasch, 229 Cal.App.2d 197, 40 Cal.Rptr. 153 (1964), the trial court awarded the wife $7,500 as compensation for the years in which she provided the means by which the husband could pursue academic studies. When required to characterize this award as a property division or support, the appellate court deemed it support, there being no other basis for it.

4. In 1984 the California legislature responded to the professional education problem by the enactment of West's Ann.Cal.Family Code § 2641, reprinted below. Under this statute, the community is entitled to reimbursement for "community contributions to education or training of a party that substantially enhances the earning capacity of the party." In recom-

mending the enactment of this provision, the California Law Revision Commission noted:

> The Commission does not believe that it would be either practical or fair to classify the value of the education, degree, or license, or the enhanced earning capacity, as community property and to divide the value upon marriage dissolution. Classification of these items as community property would create problems involving management and control, creditor's rights, taxation, and disposition at death, not to mention the complexities involved in valuation at dissolution. The complexities are exacerbated in the typical case where part of the student spouse's education is received before marriage and part during marriage. Moreover, to give the working spouse an interest in half the student spouse's increased earnings for the remainder of the student spouse's life because of the relatively brief period of education and training received during marriage is not only a windfall to the working spouse but in effect a permanent mortgage on the student spouse's future. Such an approach would certainly discourage the student spouse from marriage until his or her education is complete. And, if the student spouse desired further education during marriage, such a rule would force the student spouse and working spouse to arrive at a fair determination of their rights by means of a marital agreement and might encourage a dissolution of the marriage. Such a rule—one that most people would think is unfair and the effect of which they would try to avoid—should not be codified in the law.

> All factors considered, a more equitable solution, in the Commission's judgment, is to require the student spouse to reimburse the community for the community expenditures for his or her education and training. This solution in effect gives the working spouse the same amount the student spouse was given for the education. The working spouse can use the money for his or her own education or any other purpose. It puts the parties on equal footing without generating a windfall for the working spouse or permanently impairing the student spouse's future. It takes from the student spouse only what was actually given and restores to the working spouse only what he or she actually lost. It addresses the basic inequity with a minimum of disruption to the community property system.

Recommendations Relating to Family Law, 17 Cal.L.Revision Comm'n Reports 201, 234–235 (1984).

WEST'S ANNOTATED CALIFORNIA FAMILY CODE

§ 2627. Educational loans; liabilities for death or injuries; assignment

Notwithstanding Sections 2550 to 2552, inclusive, and Sections 2620 to 2624, inclusive, educational loans shall be assigned pursuant to Section 2641 and liabilities subject to paragraph (2) of subdivision (b) of Section 1000 shall be assigned to the spouse whose act or omission provided the basis for the liability, without offset.

(Stats.1992, c. 162 (A.B. 2650), § 10, operative Jan. 1, 1994.)

§ 2641. Community contributions to education or training

(a) "Community contributions to education or training" as used in this section means payments made with community or quasi-community property for education or training or for the repayment of a loan incurred for education or training, whether the payments were made while the parties were resident in this state or resident outside this state.

(b) Subject to the limitations provided in this section, upon dissolution of marriage or legal separation of the parties:

(1) The community shall be reimbursed for community contributions to education or training of a party that substantially enhances the earning capacity of the party. The amount reimbursed shall be with interest at the legal rate, accruing from the end of the calendar year in which the contributions were made.

(2) A loan incurred during marriage for the education or training of a party shall not be included among the liabilities of the community for the purpose of division pursuant to this division but shall be assigned for payment by the party.

(c) The reimbursement and assignment required by this section shall be reduced or modified to the extent circumstances render such a disposition unjust, including, but not limited to, any of the following:

(1) The community has substantially benefited from the education, training, or loan incurred for the education or training of the party. There is a rebuttable presumption, affecting the burden of proof, that the community has not substantially benefited from community contributions to the education or training made less than 10 years before the commencement of the proceeding, and that the community has substantially benefited from community contributions to the education or training made more than 10 years before the commencement of the proceeding.

(2) The education or training received by the party is offset by the education or training received by the other party for which community contributions have been made.

(3) The education or training enables the party receiving the education or training to engage in gainful employment that substantially reduces the need of the party for support that would otherwise be required.

(d) Reimbursement for community contributions and assignment of loans pursuant to this section is the exclusive remedy of the community or a party for the education or training and any resulting enhancement of the earning capacity of a party. However, nothing in this subdivision limits consideration of the effect of the education, training, or enhancement, or the amount reimbursed pursuant to this section, on the circumstances of the parties for the purpose of an order for support pursuant to Section 4320.

(e) This section is subject to an express written agreement of the parties to the contrary.

(Stats.1992, c. 162 (A.B.2650), § 10, operative Jan. 1, 1994.)

IN RE MARRIAGE OF WATT

Court of Appeals, First District, 1989.
214 Cal.App.3d 340, 262 Cal.Rptr. 783.

* * *

I. BACKGROUND

The parties married on June 17, 1972, and separated nine and one-half years later on December 15, 1981. In 1974 they moved to Hawaii so David could continue his studies there. The couple had no children.

David was a full-time student for the entire nine and one-half years of the marriage, advancing from an undergraduate program to postgraduate studies and finally medical school; he received his medical degree five months after separation. Elaine worked full time during the marriage, using all of her income for family expenses.

For the years 1975 through 1981 (exclusive of 1977, for which we have no information), the parties' combined gross income was $81,-779.92, of which Elaine contributed $66,923.92 in earnings and David contributed $14,856. David's student loans for the same period totalled $26,642. David used at least $3,000 in loan funds for direct educational expenses (tuition, books, fees), leaving approximately $23,642 for the couple's living expenses.

For the past 17 years Elaine has worked for Kaiser Foundation Hospital (Kaiser), first as a pharmacy clerk and, since 1979, as a pharmacy technician. Following separation, Elaine held two part-time jobs, working sometimes 60 hours per week to meet monthly living expenses. In 1986 she assumed a full-time position at Kaiser.

Elaine became interested in nutrition and culinary arts and started taking cooking classes in 1981. She testified that during their marriage, she talked with David about the possibility of attending school after he finished his education and stated, "that's when I decided I would like to go into culinary arts." Shortly after the couple separated, Elaine borrowed $500 from David's mother to pursue a junior college education in the field of nutrition. After two semesters she abandoned that effort because she could not "make it" working part time or being on call, and had to take another job. She later repaid the loan.

At trial Elaine explained she would like to enroll in the 16–month program at the California Culinary Academy in San Francisco. Her aspiration is to start her own catering business.

David now is an anesthesiologist with the Permanente Medical Group. In 1987 his annual salary was approximately $94,000. With overtime, his actual income has been much higher.

* * *

II. THE TRIAL COURT DECISION

The trial court issued a detailed statement of decision which included the following findings pertinent to this appeal: (1) the extent to which Elaine contributed to David's attainment of an education, training, career position or license "was minimal to the point of 'de minimis non curat lex'"; (2) Elaine evidenced no need for spousal support, retraining or education to obtain more marketable skills/employment;

and (3) the couple's standard of living during the marriage did not exceed Elaine's present standard of living.

The court also found that Elaine's gross income was higher than the income she indicated was "achievable" as a chef and concluded, "a need to change [jobs] has not been shown.... [Elaine is] self supporting, beyond the standard of living attained by the parties while married, and in no need of support...."

On the matter of reimbursement for the expenses of David's education, the court determined there were no community contributions which should be reimbursed. Finally, the court ordered David to assume full responsibility for repayment of all student loans (nothing had been repaid during the marriage).

III. ELAINE'S APPEAL

On appeal Elaine contends the trial court abused its discretion in denying spousal support and erred in ruling that the community made no reimbursable contributions to David's education.

Elaine's arguments concern interpretation of amendments to the Family Law Act which the Legislature enacted in 1984 to provide for (1) reimbursement of the community's contributions for the education or training of a spouse under specified circumstances and (2) consideration of the nonstudent spouse's contributions to the attainment of that education or training when awarding spousal support.

* * *

A. *Spousal Support*

The Family Law Act vests broad discretion in the trial court to decide the propriety of a spousal support award. (*In re Marriage of Wilson* (1988) 201 Cal.App.3d 913, 916, 247 Cal.Rptr. 522.) A reviewing court will not disturb this exercise of discretion unless "it can fairly be said that no judge would reasonably make the same order under the same circumstances." (*In re Marriage of Sinks* (1988) 204 Cal.App.3d 586, 591, 251 Cal.Rptr. 379.)

Section 4801 [now Family Code Section 4320] establishes the criteria a court must follow in fashioning an appropriate support order. The court must not simply recognize these criteria, it must also apply them in arriving at its decision. (*In re Marriage of Fransen* (1983) 142 Cal.App.3d 419, 425, 190 Cal.Rptr. 885.)

Elaine asserts we must reverse the judgment because the trial court based its decision on incorrect legal or factual conclusions about (1) her potential income as a chef; (2) her economic needs; (3) the contributions she made to David's career and (4) the couple's lifestyle. We discuss each of these concerns and conclude that the lower court did err in applying the third and fourth concerns.

(1) Retraining

* * *

[T]he court concluded Elaine had no need for retraining or education to acquire more marketable skills. In connection with this conclusion the court found that her then-current income was higher than would be "achievable" as a chef. Elaine claims the evidence does not support this finding, and, in turn, the court erroneously determined she did not need retraining.

The evidence shows Elaine's gross annual income to be $26,156.00. The brochure for the California Culinary Academy indicates graduates report an average annual starting salary of $25,000. A newspaper article included in the record states that graduates attaining top executive chef status earn at least $50,000 annually plus a percentage of the business. From the record it is apparent that starting out, Elaine in fact would be no better off economically for completing the program than she is now, although her earning potential might be higher.

Elaine also argues that the court's finding is misleading because the $26,156 is pay for a 60–hour, not a 40–hour week. True, Elaine testified she worked 60 hours a week "on and off" for the last five years. She also testified that in 1985 or 1986 she took a full time job at Kaiser. We do not know when she quit her second job, or how much of the $26,156 would be related to working in excess of a 40–hour week. Further, we do not know how many hours a chef works.

We think the reasonable inference from the facts presented is that the career change anticipated by Elaine would not immediately or necessarily result in a material increase in income and, thus, Elaine did not demonstrate a present need for retraining or education to attain more marketable skills. Substantial evidence supports this conclusion.

(2) Needs

Elaine next urges that the court should have awarded spousal support based on need. The trial court found her monthly net income to be between $1,400 and $1,600, with monthly expenses running approximately $1,400. Under these facts, Elaine was earning just enough to get by.

Elaine disputes the monthly expense finding. Her income and expense declaration filed July 22, 1987, listed monthly expenses of $2,409, as contrasted with $1,359 as of December 17, 1986. During cross-examination, it became apparent that certain items such as rent, transportation and incidentals, although substantially higher on the second statement, either had not changed at all, or had not changed as much. Further, the balance listed for several loans remained the same on the July statement, when in fact they were lower because of payments made during the intervening seven months. And of the $1,686.47 balance showing for "Attorneys–Hawaii," most was owed by David, not Elaine.

It appears the trial court in weighing the evidence and, in particular, the discrepancies brought out during cross-examination, chose to accept the earlier financial statement as more accurately reflecting Elaine's true monthly expenses. This is within the province of the trial court, and we conclude that its finding concerning Elaine's monthly expenses is supported by substantial evidence. Thus the court did not abuse its discretion in failing to award spousal support based on need.

(3) Contributions

Elaine additionally argues that the trial court erroneously found she had made a "de minimis" contribution to David's attainment of an education and career position. The evidence shows that all of David's direct, out-of-pocket educational expenses, such as tuition, books and lab fees, were paid for with proceeds from student loans and grants. However, Elaine shouldered approximately 64 percent of the community's living expenses for the period 1975–1981. In dollar terms, she paid $28,426 more than David did—an amount which is not so minimal that the law does not accord it notice.

The court's conclusion is either factually wrong and, therefore, not supported by the evidence, or is based on an interpretation of section 4801 that does not take living expenses into account when examining the extent to which the nonstudent spouse "contributed to the attainment of" the student spouse's education and career.

We begin our analysis by pointing out that the operative * * * language is ambiguous because the concept of "contributing to the attainment" of an education is open-ended and nowhere defined in the statutory scheme. As such, the language is subject to conflicting interpretations.

Thus, some discussion of the legislative history * * * is appropriate here. In November 1983, the Assembly Committee on Judiciary held a public hearing on legislative proposals to resolve community property/career asset issues presented in the high profile case of *In re Marriage of Sullivan,* then pending before the Supreme Court. In that case, Janet Sullivan argued that her husband obtained his medical education by virtue of the couple's joint efforts and sacrifices, it was their greatest asset, and both should share in its benefits upon dissolution. The committee inquired whether existing law allowed for adequate compensation for the spouse who assisted his or her mate in attaining an education. At the hearings, a spokesperson for the California Law Revision Commission (CLRC) discussed the commission's legislative proposal for a reimbursement solution.

Assembly Bill 3000 was drafted after the hearings and enacted by the Legislature in August 1984; it incorporated the CLRC proposal and additionally expanded the spousal support criteria * * * to include consideration of the nonstudent spouse's contribution to the student spouse's education or training. Thus, the new legislative scheme afforded two remedies, as appropriate, in cases where one spouse worked to put the other through school: (1) reimbursement and (2) support.

The new spousal support guideline is a companion to, but not duplicative of, the * * * right of reimbursement for community contributions to the student spouse's education. (See Hogoboom & King, Cal. Practice Guide: Family Law (The Rutter Group 1989), §§ 6:88.2–6:88.4, pp. 6–90—6–91.) Although section 4800.3, subdivision (d), specifically states that reimbursement and loan assignment is the exclusive remedy for the education or enhanced earning capacity of a spouse, it also clarifies that nothing therein "shall limit consideration of the effect of the education, training, or enhancement, or the amount reimbursed . . . the circumstances of the parties for the purpose of an order for support * * *." (*Id.*, at pp. 6–91.)

We agree that [the statute] should be interpreted broadly to require consideration of *all* of the working spouse's efforts to assist the student spouse in acquiring an education and enhanced earning capacity. Where the nonstudent helped the student through school and into a higher earning career position, that spouse's contributions should be given weighty consideration by the trial court in deciding the propriety and extent of a spousal support award.

Nothing in the statutory language indicates that one spouse's contribution to the attainment of the other's education or career is limited to direct education expenses. The notion of "contributing to the attainment" of an education is broader than the * * * concept of "payments made for" education or training. Common sense tells us that more goes into contributing to the attainment of an education than the mere cost of tuition, books and supplies. Many students who seriously pursue education or training forego full-time or even part-time remunerative employment, relying instead on other sources to provide for their necessities of life. Certainly, these other sources contribute to the student's attainment of an education. We thus hold that in the case of a career threshold marriage where the working spouse provided a far greater share of living expenses while the student spouse acquired a professional degree, section 4801 requires the trial court to consider the totality of the nonstudent's contributions and efforts toward attainment of that degree, including contributions for ordinary living expenses.

* * *

We conclude the judgment must be reversed insofar as it denied Elaine spousal support.

* * *

B. Reimbursement for Contribution To His Education

Elaine's second attack concerns the trial court's ruling that there were no reimbursable community contributions to David's education. The record reveals that direct education expense were paid from loan and grant funds. Elaine asserts that section 4800.3 [now Family Code section 2641] does not limit "payments made with community property for education or training" to direct costs, and should be construed broadly with its remedial purpose in mind to include living expenses over the nine and one-half years of marriage.

Section 4800.3 remedies the injustice that often occurred when a couple separated on the eve of, or shortly after, a spouse's graduation or other educational accomplishment, long before that education could benefit the community. (*In re Marriage of Slivka* (1986) 183 Cal.App.3d 159, 167, 228 Cal.Rptr. 76.)   Prior to its enactment, there was no right of the community to reimbursement for expenditures made for education or training. The new remedy, however, is not unlimited.

The CLRC comment to section 4800.3 explains that the purpose of the provision is to authorize reimbursement of community expenditures for educational expenses that have benefited primarily one party to the marriage. It goes on to state: "Subdivision (a) does not detail the expenditures that might be included within the concept of 'community contributions.' These expenditures would at lease include cost of tuition, fees, books and supplies, and transportation." (CLRC com., West's Ann.Code, § 4800.3 (1989 pocket supp.) p. 95.)

From this comment, as well as the definition of community contributions to education or training, it is evident that the thrust of section 4800.3 is to require reimbursement for expenses that are related to the education experience itself. The married couple would incur ordinary living expenses regardless of whether one spouse is attending school, staying home, or working.

Elaine has pursued her reimbursement claim on the theory that section 4800.3 entitles the community to full reimbursement for *all* its contributions to living expenses over the nine and one-half-year period. She has failed to show what expenses, if any, were specially connected to David's education. There was no evidence produced at trial that the community paid for any education-related expenses, such as tuition, fees, or special living expenses incurred because of the education experience. Based upon such a lack of evidence, we conclude the trial court correctly ruled that the community made no reimbursable contributions pursuant to section 4800.3.

Elaine further argues that unless we construe section 4800.3 as encompassing reimbursement for all living expenses "it must be declared unconstitutional." In that event, she urges us to characterize the professional degree as community property, subject to valuation and distribution.

Elaine maintains that anything short of her proposed interpretation leads to due process and equal protection violations. Not so. There is no constitutionally recognized property interest in the form of a right to reimbursement for community property earnings which a spouse voluntarily spends for the couple's living expenses during marriage. Nor, as Elaine argues, does our construction of section 4800.3 impermissibly treat spouses differently according to whether the community benefits financially from the education or not. Whether the community benefits economically from the educated spouses's enhanced opportunities depends on the parties and the timing of career development relative to the date of separation, not on section 4800.3. Furthermore, section 4800.3

by its terms mandates a more favorable result for the nonstudent spouse when the community reaps *no* advantage from the education. Where the community has already benefited substantially from the education of one spouse, section 4800.3 requires the court to *reduce or modify* reimbursement as necessary to prevent an unjust disposition. (§ 4800.3, subd. (c).)

Finally, we reject Elaine's suggestion that this court declare David's medical degree community property. Section 4800.3, subdivision (d), makes it abundantly clear that reimbursement is the *only* remedy in California. The CLRC Comment further explains: "Although the education, degree or license or the resulting enhanced earning capacity is not 'property' subject to division, community expenditures for them are properly subject to reimbursement." (CLRC com., West's Annotated Code, § 4800.3 (1989 pocket supp.) p. 95.)

* * *

V. Conclusion

The judgment is affirmed in part and reversed in part, with directions to conduct further proceedings consistent with this opinion. David to pay costs on appeal.

CHANNELL and PERLEY, JJ., concur.

Note

West's Ann.Cal.Family Code § 2641 by its terms makes reimbursement the exclusive remedy for professional education or training received during marriage, thus precluding further litigation on the question of whether a professional education and concomitant enhanced earning capacity are susceptible of classification and division as community property. However, the legislation also provides that it is subject to an express written agreement of the parties. Moreover the "exclusive remedy" language of the statute does not appear to preclude both reimbursement and spousal support. 1 Calif. Family Law Monthly 170 (1985).

IN RE MARRIAGE OF LOPEZ
Court of Appeal, 1974.
38 Cal.App.3d 93, 113 Cal.Rptr. 58.

CARTER, JUSTICE. Husband is an attorney, having received his law degree in 1952, passed the Bar Examination in October 1952 and was admitted to practice in California in January 1953. On August 8, 1957, while thus engaged in the practice of law, husband and wife were married.

On January 1, 1970, husband formed a law partnership with two of his associates, Donald R. Kennedy and Robert L. Srite, at which time Srite paid the sum of $53,500 cash for a 25 percent interest in husband's law practice. This cash was deposited in Account Nos. 12 and 4239 (4324), Bank of Redding, in husband's name. At the same time, Kennedy paid husband $13,500 in cash and executed an unsecured promissory note in the sum of $40,000 for the purchase of 25 percent of husband's law business. Documents entitled "Agreement for the Sale of an Interest in Fixtures, Equipment, Library and Goodwill of a Law Practice," dated January 1, 1970, were executed by husband and his new partners. Each agreement provided that husband sell an undivided 25 percent interest in and to the fixtures, equipment and law library to each partner for the sum of $1,224.32, respectively. A 25 percent interest in the law practice goodwill which husband sold to each of his new partners was valued at $52,275.68 in both agreements.

Concurrently, husband and his partners executed a partnership agreement which specified that the beginning capital of the partnership was $214,000 of which $209,895.72 was designated as goodwill. This agreement provided for a schedule of payments to be made to a partner withdrawing voluntarily, with no payment on return of capital investment if voluntary withdrawal occurred the first year (1970). Repayment of capital was provided in varying increments upon voluntary withdrawal by a partner during the ensuing five years.

During the trial, husband testified: "Every year at the end of the year or during the year I withdrew every penny of my income from the practice and used it for the benefit of the community. If there was at the end of the year say ten or fifteen thousand dollars in the office account, I would take that out and put it into a savings account or something such as that, or acquire—make an investment with it for the community." Husband confirmed that there were no cash reserves in his law practice because of this conduct, and that the assets of his law practice consisted only of a library, office equipment and accounts receivable.

Husband was awarded as his separate property the bank accounts which contained the balance of the cash payments made by Kennedy and Srite, the unpaid balance of the Kennedy note, and a 50 percent interest in the law partnership of Lopez, Kennedy and Srite.

1. *Husband's interest in his law partnership and the proceeds from the sale of a one-half interest therein were erroneously found to be all separate property.*

For reasons hereafter set forth, we hold that the trial court erred in determining that the 50 percent interest of the husband in his law practice and the proceeds paid him by his two law partners were separate property (Findings 20 and 21). Husband asserts in his brief as follows: "It is clear from the uncontradicted evidence, that the law practice of the respondent at the time he opened his office on October 1, 1957, was a continuance of his already existing practice, and it was the sole and separate property of the respondent, and remained the same throughout the marriage." Husband further argues that any community interest in his law practice was withdrawn each year and that he applied the income earned therefrom to community investments. The trial court accepted this approach. However, such position ignores the law as stated in two earlier decisions of this court.

In Brawman v. Brawman (1962) 199 Cal.App.2d 876, 19 Cal.Rptr. 106, we had occasion to comment on the proper classification of a law practice commenced one year before a marriage which lasted 21 years. During his practice husband built up a substantial earning capacity. The divorce decree was silent as to ownership of the law practice; on appeal, wife contended that she was improperly denied alimony. This court therein stated at page 882, 19 Cal.Rptr. at page 109: "The law business was a substantial part of the community, but was given no valuation by the judge who, in declaring the parties to have been 'marital partners' evidently did not feel that the partnership relationship covered the law business. Where, as here, respondent had commenced the practice of law just one year before his marriage and had built up a lucrative law business by his industry and professional ability, a practice producing $24,000 a year net, the business is community property and it has a substantial value. [Citation.] In considering this value, consideration must be given to the fact that, on divorce and dissolution of the community, a professional practice goes automatically to the spouse licensed to practice it. He is not selling out or liquidating, but continuing in business. Effectually, it is the case of a silent partner withdrawing from a going business. And, if such partner is to receive fair compensation for her share, on her enforced retirement, it should be so evaluated."

In Todd v. Todd (1969) 272 Cal.App.2d 786, 791, 78 Cal.Rptr. 131, 135, we again held that "While the right to practice law is a property right which cannot be classed as community property, the value of the practice at the time of dissolution of the community is community property."

It is generally settled that the efforts, time and skills of the husband are community assets. (Somps v. Somps (1967) 250 Cal.App.2d 328, 332–333, 58 Cal.Rptr. 304.) Assuming that husband commenced his law practice with certain monies earned by him prior to his marriage which were his separate property, the primary value of his practice was derived from his own individual efforts after marriage, rather than from the negligible sum of money initially invested in his law business. The approach urged by husband on appeal gives the worth of his separate property used in his law practice an exaggerated importance. In the instant case, the value of the law practice was clearly one and the same as the husband's energy, skill, judgment, intelligence and personality as a practicing attorney. Even though, as argued at trial, the retirement and death of other attorneys in the Redding area may have contributed to the growth of husband's practice, these factors cannot be deemed the "other favorable business factors" which were determinative in *Somps.*

2. *Existence and valuation of goodwill and assets of husband in his law practice.*

Several serious questions have been raised as to the valuation of husband's interest in his law partnership. Pursuant to section 4800 of the Civil Code (1970 Family Law Act), a trial court is now required to "divide the community property and the quasi-community property of the parties * * * equally." In order to do this, the trial court *must make specific findings of fact* as to the nature and value of the specific property of the parties. (May v. May (1969) 275 Cal.App.2d 264, 79 Cal.Rptr. 622; Hong v. Hong (1965) 237 Cal.App.2d 239, 241, 46 Cal. Rptr. 710; Cardew v. Cardew (1961) 192 Cal.App.2d 502, 13 Cal.Rptr. 620; Cal.Rules of Court, tit. IV, div. I, ch. 2, rule 1242.)

It has been urged that there can be no "goodwill" in husband's professional law business upon dissolution. Neither Lyon v. Lyon (1966) 246 Cal.App.2d 519, 524, 54 Cal.Rptr. 829 nor Heywood v. Sooy (1941) 45 Cal.App.2d 423, 114 P.2d 361, are applicable to the case at bench, since both cases involved dissolutions of law partnerships between practicing attorneys. The case before us deals solely with a marital dissolution and not a law partnership dissolution. The court in Golden v. Golden (1969) 270 Cal.App.2d 401, 405, 75 Cal.Rptr. 735, 737, noted the crucial distinction: "Where, as in *Lyon,* the firm is being dissolved, it is understandable that a court cannot determine what, if any, of the goodwill of the firm will go to either partner. But, in a matrimonial matter, the practice of the sole practitioner husband will continue, with the same intangible value as it had during the marriage. Under principles of community property law, the wife, by virtue of her position of wife, made to that value the same contribution as does a wife to any of husband's earnings and accumulations during marriage. She is as much entitled to be recompensed for that contribution as if it were represented by the increased value of stock in a family business." *[handwritten: wifes cont.]*

Consistent with this principle of community property law, if "goodwill" in a professional practice as a going business is found to exist as an asset at the time of a marital dissolution, such asset is subject to the innumerable consequences of the Family Law Act of 1970. In such cases, professional goodwill may thus be separate property, community property, or varying degrees of both depending upon the particular circumstances. The fact that "professional goodwill" may be elusive, intangible, difficult to evaluate and will ordinarily require special disposition, is not reason to ignore its existence in a proper case.

It has been aptly stated: "Accountants, writers on accounting, economists, engineers, and courts, have all tried their hands at defining goodwill, at discussing its nature, and at proposing means of valuing it. The most striking characteristic of this immense amount of writing is the number and variety of disagreements reached." (John B. Canning, Ph.D., The Economics of Accountancy (N.Y.1929), p. 28, The Ronald Press Co.)

Mindful of the nebulous area into which we venture, we believe that for purposes of a marital dissolution, the parties are primarily concerned with the existence, value and consequences of the "goodwill" of a professional business in an *economic sense,* as distinguished from legal or accounting concepts. As stated by Professor Norton M. Bedford, University of Illinois:

"It seems to be well established in the literature of economics that the economic value of any asset depends upon the future net receipts which the asset will produce. While these receipts to a consumer are receipts of satisfactions, to a business firm the receipts are cash or cash equivalent (more broadly, purchasing power equivalent). *Since the future is unknown, different individuals and business entities will have different expectations as to what these future receipts will be. Thus, there is no certainty in any one valuation of an asset. To the contrary, a considerable amount of uncertainty attaches to any valuation. But subject to this variability, the conceptual view of the economic value of any asset is based on the future receipts which the asset will produce.* Because individual assets are not used in isolation but as a part of an organized entity containing a variety of distinct assets, the economic concept of goodwill is introduced when the future receipts of the organization cannot be assigned as a contribution of a finite list of specific assets. That is, the search to assign a specific cause, in the form of a specific asset, for the expected future receipts requires the introduction of goodwill as an asset." ("Goodwill," Norton M. Bedford, Prof. of Accountancy and Business Administration, Univ. of Ill., Handbook of Modern Accounting (1970) by Sidney Davidson, McGraw–Hill Book Co., ch. 19, p. 19–5.) (Emphasis added.)

We think it follows that *in marital cases the expectancy of future earnings is not synonymous with, nor should it be the basis for, determining the value of "goodwill" of a professional practice, but is simply a factor to consider in deciding if such an asset exists.* A community property interest can only be acquired during the marriage, and it would be inconsistent with that philosophy to assign values to the postmarital efforts of either spouse. In re Marriage of Fortier (1973) 34 Cal.App.3d 384, 387–388, 109 Cal.Rptr. 915.

We emphasize that no rigid or unvarying rule has been enunciated by our courts for determining the existence or value of the "goodwill" of a law practice or any other profession as a going business, and therefore each case must be determined upon its own facts. Whatever the result in a given case, we hold that where the issue is raised in a marital dissolution action, the trial court must make a specific finding as to the existence and value of the "goodwill" of a professional business as a going concern whether related to that of a sole practitioner, a professional partnership or a professional corporation. (Golden v. Golden, supra, 270 Cal.App.2d 401, 75 Cal.Rptr. 735 (sole medical practitioner); Todd v. Todd, supra, 272 Cal.App.2d 786, 78 Cal.Rptr. 131 (sole legal practitioner); Brawman v. Brawman, supra, 199 Cal.App.2d 876, 19 Cal.Rptr. 106 (sole legal practitioner).)

In so holding, we do not imply that every professional business as a going concern necessarily has a valuable goodwill, or that if found to exist the value thereof may be precisely fixed in terms of so many dollars. Instead, there are certain factors, assuredly not all inclusive, which may tend to provide the trial court with broad latitude in resolving these questions, with one objective being the determination of the fair economic value of all the community property for equal division purposes. (Civ.Code, § 4800.) In addition, if the trial court were to find in a proper case that the asset of professional goodwill is the separate property of the practitioner, where spousal or child support is an issue, a specific finding as to value is required, since it may directly affect the question of ability to meet those obligations. (In re Marriage of Cosgrove (1972) 27 Cal.App.3d 424, 433–434, 103 Cal.Rptr. 733.)

Certain matters merit consideration which may be said reasonably to contribute to, diminish, or affect the intangible value of professional goodwill at the time of dissolution and the continuity and retention of the benefits thereof which the professional practitioner will continue to enjoy after the marital dissolution. In that context some such factors are the practitioner's age, health, past demonstrated earning power, professional reputation in the community as to his judgment, skill, knowledge, his comparative professional success, and the nature and duration of his business as a sole practitioner or as a member of a partnership or professional corporation to which his professional efforts have made a proprietary contribution. In addition, consideration should be given to the *value* of the "fixed" and "other assets" of the professional business with which the "goodwill" is to continue its relationship.

While "market value" and the value for marital dissolution purposes of "professional goodwill" may be synonymous, in our view such value should be determined with *considerable care and caution,* since it is a unique situation in which the continuing practitioner is *judicially forced to buy an intangible asset at a judicially determined value and compelled to pay a former spouse her share in tangible assets.* (Civ.Code, § 4800.) Asset values and liabilities should be determined as near to the date of trial as reasonably practicable (Randolph v. Randolph (1953) 118 Cal. App.2d 584, 258 P.2d 547), with the reservation, however, that since the enactment of Civil Code section 5118, effective March 4, 1972, any portion of the law practice assets including goodwill which are attributable to the earnings and accumulations of a spouse living separate and apart are the separate property of the spouse earning or accumulating the same. This could be significant where the earnings of a professional person are substantial and the time lapse from separation to trial is considerable.

In determining the value of a law practice or interest therein, the trial court should determine the existence and value of the following: (a) fixed assets, which we deem to include cash, furniture, equipment, supplies and law library; (b) other assets including properly aged accounts receivable, costs advanced with due regard for their collectability; work in progress partially completed but not billed as a receivable, and work completed but not billed; (c) goodwill of the practitioner in his law business as a going concern; and (d) liabilities of the practitioner related to his business.

In the case at bench, husband and his two law partners arrived at an agreed value of $209,895.72 for goodwill in husband's law business as of January 1, 1970, some 14 months prior to the husband's filing for a dissolution of the marriage. On remand, the trial court should give careful weight to that agreement, with the observation, however, that the agreement allocated the sum of $4,897.28 to the value of the furniture, equipment and law library. There is no mention in the agreement of the "other assets" of a law practice such as accounts receivable, costs advanced, work in progress not billed, or work completed and not billed. As properly urged by the wife, the value of these "other assets" should be determined, along with the question whether the partners contemplated the inclusion of their value in the $209,895.72 goodwill item. Finally, in light of such findings, the trial court should determine the value of the "goodwill," if any, in husband's law partnership business.

We note that at the time of trial husband's capital account in his law partnership was in excess of $120,000. Whatever its determined amount and ultimate nature, this item, along with the $40,000 Kennedy note and the $67,000 paid to husband by his partners must be considered in the determination of the extent of the community property of the parties.

Notes.

1. Given the *Aufmuth* court's rationale for excluding the value of a professional education from the community property system, and given the economic definition of goodwill used by the Lopez court, what is the justification for the classification of the goodwill component of a professional practice as community property? Is the item being labelled "goodwill" really property, or is it merely part of the professional practitioner's post-separation earnings and therefore reachable only as support? See Lurvey, *Professional Goodwill on Marital Dissolution: Is it Property or Another Name for Alimony?* 52 Cal.St.B.J. 27 (1977); Norton, *Professional Goodwill—Its Value in California Marital Dissolution Cases,* 3 Community Property Journal 9 (1976).

2. Once the existence of goodwill is established as a component of a business or a professional practice, it must be valued. It has been stated that "[b]ecause many factors affect goodwill, there appear to be almost as many formulas as there are accountants," and California courts have utilized a wide variety of valuation techniques. Bruch, *The Definition and Division of Marital Property in California: Towards Parity and Simplicity,* 33 Hastings L.J. 769, 810–12 (1982). Some cases indicate that because it is impermissible to classify post-separation earnings as community property, the value of goodwill must be established without reference to the potential or continuing net income of the professional practitioner. See, e.g., In re Marriage of Fortier, 34 Cal.App.3d 384, 109 Cal.Rptr. 915 (1973); In re Marriage of Foster, 42 Cal.App.3d 577, 117 Cal.Rptr. 49 (1974). "[A] proper means of arriving at the value of goodwill contemplates any legitimate method of evaluation that measures its present value by taking into account

some past result. * * * To some degree, goodwill always contemplates continuity of business (*Foster, supra.*). However continuity of a business being assumed does *not* mean that the post-separation results of husband's efforts can, or should, be included in the goodwill formula * * *." Marriage of King, 150 Cal.App.3d 304, 309–310, 197 Cal.Rptr. 716, 719–720 (1983). Valuation problems will be explored further in the materials in Chapter 7 dealing with the division of community property on dissolution.

3.   In the *Lopez* case, the appellate court indicated that on remand, the trial court should give "careful weight" to the husband's partnership agreement in valuing the goodwill of the practice. Suppose that a partnership agreement provides for specified withdrawal rights, and that the partner spouse subsequently withdraws from the partnership, receiving the amount specified in the withdrawal rights clause. Should the community value of the partnership interest be limited to the contractual withdrawal right in subsequent dissolution proceedings between the partner spouse and the other spouse? See Marriage of Slater, 100 Cal.App.3d 241, 160 Cal.Rptr. 686 (1979).

4.   Could the right of publicity be analogized to goodwill in the event that one of the spouses is a celebrated public figure? Consider the following excerpt from Miller, *Divorce in the Entertainment Industry—Some Special Problems,* 5 Comm/Ent.L.J. 43, 54–57 (1982), reprinted by permission of the publisher.

Consider the following hypothetical situation. An unmarried actor works for a local television station in Los Angeles, performing the principal role in a "soap opera." After two years of broadcasts, the show and the actor have developed a substantial local following. The actor is hired for a national television version of the show aired from Los Angeles by CBS Television. He marries. Within three months the show begins to enjoy increasing national popularity. An enterprising businessman identifies the actor as a rising television "star" and uses the actor's likeness on a "celebrity calendar." No consent for the use is secured. Sales of the calendar are phenomenal, and the profits are substantial. The actor immediately sues in the Los Angeles Superior Court, and a $200,000 settlement is negotiated. At the same time the actor and his wife agree that their short marriage has been a mistake and seek a dissolution of the marriage. The question presented in the divorce is whether the proceeds of the settlement are community property or simply separate property of the actor. If community property, the proceeds are subject to equal division in the proceeding for dissolution of the marriage.

A threshold question regarding the nature of the right of publicity must be asked. What is the nature of the right? Is it a property right or one grounded in tort law? The question has evoked different answers over the years.

* * *

If the nature of the interest in protecting and exploiting name and likeness is derived solely from the notion of "privacy," then it would appear to be an interest grounded in tort law. If so, under California law, such characterization would likely have as a consequence that money received as compensation for an *invasion* of such privacy right would (except in limited cases) be awarded solely to the "injured" spouse upon a divorce. No equivalent award of property would be made to the other spouse. On the other hand, if the right of publicity is proprietary in character, that is, if its essence is "property," then to the extent that such property is generated as a result of the efforts of a spouse during marriage, it should be divisible upon a divorce as community property.

* * *

Is the "right of publicity" more evanescent than "goodwill"? Perhaps. The hypothetical example posed at the beginning of this section avoids a valuation issue by presenting the asset as having an established settlement value. But suppose there were no such benchmark. Suppose the celebrity had not yet succeeded in exploiting his "right" at the time of the divorce, or suppose the celebrity recoiled from *ever* exploiting his or her fame and simply wanted to be left alone. Must he or she be judicially forced to buy back from the other spouse his or her community interest in a right never exercised or to be exercised? It has been suggested that there are a number of ways to evaluate this asset, with the most readily adaptable being a market value determination without deduction for any restraints on exploitation which the celebrity might impose.

The hypothetical example also suggests yet another problem. How does one determine whether the asset had its source in separate or community origins? The example suggests that there may have to be a tracing or allocation of some kind between the premarital (separate property) component and that resulting from the marital (community property) efforts. That exercise is bound to present formidable difficulties, not the least of which is persuading a trial court that there is a credible basis for making such an allocation.

Given the number of "celebrities" residing in California and the state's divorce statistics, it is surprising that no California appellate court has dealt directly with the issue of celebrity good will. New York and New Jersey courts have considered the question and concluded that good will based on celebrity status could be treated as a marital asset subject to equitable distribution. See Piscopo v. Piscopo, 232 N.J.Super. 559, 557 A.2d 1040 (1989); Golub v. Golub, 139 Misc.2d 440, 527 N.Y.S.2d 946 (1988).

IN RE MARRIAGE OF WORTH

California District Court of Appeal, 1987.
195 Cal.App.3d 768, 241 Cal.Rptr. 135.

RACANELLI, PRESIDING JUSTICE.

This appeal presents the novel issue whether the marital community has an interest in a copyright. We conclude that it does, and we affirm the judgment.

Facts

During the marriage, appellant husband wrote and published several books, including two books on trivia: The Complete Unabridged Super Trivia Encyclopedia (1977) and The Complete Super Trivia Encyclopedia, Volume II (1981). In their 1982 divorce decree, husband and wife agreed to divide the royalties from those books equally.

In 1984, husband filed an action in federal court against the producers of the board game, "Trivial Pursuit," alleging copyright infringement claiming that certain questions used in the board game were plagiarized from husband's books. Thereafter, wife sought an order from the superior court declaring that she would be entitled to one-half of any proceeds derived from that lawsuit based upon the terms of the interlocutory decree. The trial court granted wife's request and ordered husband restrained from disbursing the proceeds of any verdict or settlement until wife's portion was accounted for. Husband now appeals.[1]

Discussion

I

Copyright Law

Preliminarily, we undertake a brief odyssey into the somewhat arcane domain of copyright law. Patent and copyright protection is rooted in our federal Constitution: "The Congress shall have power * * *

" * * *

"To promote the progress of science and useful arts, by securing for limited times to authors and inventors the exclusive right to their respective writings and discoveries." (U.S. Const., art. I, § 8, cl. 8.)

Congress has implemented its constitutional power through enactment of a copyright statute, most recently rewritten and codified as the Copyright Act of 1976 (17 U.S.C. § 101 et seq.).[2] The Act provides broad protection to any creation expressed in tangible form. (§ 102(a).)

The Act grants to a copyright holder exclusive rights over his own work to copy, perform, display, distribute for sale, and prepare derivative works. (§ 106.) Any person who infringes upon the copyright and copies, sells, or creates derivative works without permission is subject to both civil and criminal action. (§§ 501, 506.) The copyright holder may grant a license to others to make use of the copyrighted work (§ 201(d))

1. During the pendency of this appeal, the federal district court ruled that husband has no claim of copyright infringement; that ruling was affirmed on appeal. (*Worth v. Selchow & Righter Company* (9th Cir.1987) 827 F.2d 569 [87 Daily Journal D.A.R. 6036].) Husband has since informed this court of his intention to pursue further appeal. In view of the pending status of the federal litigation, we have elected to reach the merits of the present appeal. Of course, should the federal opinion be affirmed without any material modification, the present lawsuit would become moot.

2. Unless otherwise indicated, all further section references are to the Copyright Act of 1976, title 17 of the United States Code.

customarily in exchange for the copyright holder's right to receive royalties.[3]

Unlike patents or trademarks, copyright protection is self-executing. No registration or prior approval is needed, and the copyright exists as soon as the work is created. (§§ 102(a), 302(a).) However, registration and an affixed copyright notice are required before the owner can bring suit for copyright infringement. (§§ 401, 408, 411(a).)

In a suit for copyright infringement, the copyright holder may obtain injunctive relief, impoundment of the infringing materials and damages. (§§ 502(a), 503, 504.) Recoverable damages include the copyright holder's actual damages plus any profits of the infringer not comprising a component of actual damages. (§ 504.)

II

Copyright as Community Property

Husband points out that under the Act a copyright in a protected work "vests initially in the author or authors of the work." (§ 201(a).) Thus, he argues, the copyright belongs only to the author. We disagree.

Our analysis begins with the general proposition that all property acquired during marriage is community property. (Civ.Code, § 5110.) Thus, there seems little doubt that any artistic work created during the marriage constitutes community property. (See *Lorraine v. Lorraine* (1935) 8 Cal.App.2d 687, 701, 48 P.2d 48 [patent is community property]; *Frankenheimer v. Frankenheimer* (1964) 231 Cal.App.2d 101, 41 Cal. Rptr. 636 [no spousal interest in husband's literary property acquired after divorce]; *Herwig v. United States* (1952) 105 F.Supp. 384, 122 Ct.Cl. 493 [proceeds from sale of film rights to wife's book taxable to each spouse].)

The fact that husband alone authored the trivia books is not determinative. The principles of community property law do not require joint or qualitatively equal spousal efforts or contributions in acquiring the property; it is enough that the skill and effort of one spouse expended during the marriage resulted in the creation or acquisition of a property interest.

"California community property law is based on a partnership model in which each spouse contributes to and shares in the prosperity of the marriage (*In re Marriage of Brigden* (1978) 80 Cal.App.3d 380, 389 [145 Cal.Rptr. 716]). The community property concept recognizes the important role of each spouse in the success of the community and places husband and wife on an equal footing with respect to property accumulated during marriage (*Meyer v. Kinzer and Wife* (1859) 12 Cal. 247, 251). Each spouse's effort, time and skill are community assets (*In re Marriage of Lopez* (1974) 38 Cal.App.3d 93, 105 [113 Cal.Rptr. 58]; *Somps v. Somps* (1967) 250

3. A royalty is generally defined to mean compensation given to the copyright owner for permission to use the copyrighted work. (Black's Law Dict. (5th ed. 1979) p. 1195.)

Cal.App.2d 328, 332 [58 Cal.Rptr. 304]; *Strohm v. Strohm* (1960) 182 Cal.App.2d 53, 62 [5 Cal.Rptr. 884]), and any benefit derived therefrom belongs to both (*Estate of Gold* (1915) 170 Cal. 621, 623 [151 P. 12])."

(*In re Marriage of Hillerman* (1980) 109 Cal.App.3d 334, 337–338, 167 Cal.Rptr. 240.)

In the present case, husband conceived, wrote and published the trivia books during the marriage. Thus, the conclusion is inescapable that such literary works constituted community property. Indeed, at the time of the interlocutory decree, husband virtually conceded that the books were community property. Under the terms of the stipulated judgment (drafted by husband's attorney), it is provided in pertinent part: "The parties agree that future royalties from the books * * * listed on the Petition, along with all reprints shall be paid equally to Petitioner and Respondent. The parties agree that the literary agent for Respondent shall be joined as a party and that the agent shall pay directly to Petitioner her one-half interest in the royalties. The parties agree that the court shall reserve jurisdiction over any issues that may subsequently arise regarding the distinction between a re-edition or complete reworking of any book which is community property." The reference in the final sentence to "any book which is community property" strongly indicates the parties' understanding and agreement that the listed books, which include the trivia books, were community property.

Moreover, husband's agreement to divide the royalties manifests further acknowledgement that the books were considered to be community property. Under the community property doctrine, rents, issues and profits have the same character as the property source itself. (Civ.Code, §§ 5107, 5108.) In agreeing to wife's entitlement to one-half of the royalties, husband has at least tacitly conceded the community property nature of the books themselves.

If the artistic work is community property, then it must follow that the copyright itself obtains the same status. Under copyright legislation, a copyright is automatically acquired upon expression of the work. (§§ 102(a), 302(a).) Here, husband registered the copyrights as well. Since the copyrights derived from the literary efforts, time and skill of husband during the marriage, such copyrights and related tangible benefits must be considered community property. (See 1 Nimmer on Copyright (1987), § 6.13[B], p. 6–37.)

Moreover, the Act expressly provides for the transfer of a copyright by contract, will "or by operation of law." (§ 201(d)(1).) Consequently, notwithstanding that the copyright "vests *initially*" in the authoring spouse (§ 201(a), emphasis added), the copyright is automatically transferred to both spouses by operation of the California law of community property.

Of course, a copyright itself is an intangible interest separate and distinct from the tangible creative work. (§ 202.) Although a copyright is " ' * * * an intangible incorporeal right in the nature of a privilege or franchise * * * ' " (*Remick Music Corp. v. Interstate Hotel Co. of Nebraska* (D.Neb.1944) 58 F.Supp. 523, 542, affd., 157 F.2d 744 (8th Cir.1946), cert. den., 329 U.S. 809, 67 S.Ct. 622, 91 L.Ed. 691 (1947)), it is nevertheless personal property. (*Stuff v. La Budde Feed & Grain Co.* (E.D.Wis.1941) 42 F.Supp. 493.) And the community property doctrine encompasses *intangible* as well as tangible property. (*In re Marriage of Lopez* (1974) 38 Cal.App.3d 93, 107, 113 Cal.Rptr. 58, disapproved on other grounds in *In re Marriage of Morrison* (1978) 20 Cal.3d 437, 453, 143 Cal.Rptr. 139, 573 P.2d 41 [goodwill of professional practice]; *Golden v. Golden* (1969) 270 Cal.App.2d 401, 75 Cal.Rptr. 735 [same].) The fact that a copyright is intangible will not affect its community character or the community nature of any tangible benefits directly associated with the copyright.

We are, of course, cognizant of those decisions which determined that a law school *education* acquired during the marriage is not a divisible community asset. (See *In re Marriage of Aufmuth* (1979) 89 Cal.App.3d 446, 461, 152 Cal.Rptr. 668, disapproved on another point in *In re Marriage of Lucas* (1980) 27 Cal.3d 808, 815, 166 Cal.Rptr. 853, 614 P.2d 285; *Todd v. Todd* (1969) 272 Cal.App.2d 786, 791, 78 Cal.Rptr. 131.) In *In re Marriage of Aufmuth,* this court (Division Four) reasoned that classification of a legal education, represented by a law degree, as a community "asset" would run counter to settled community property principles by requiring division of attributable postdissolution earnings which, by definition, constitute the separate property of the acquiring spouse.[4] (89 Cal.App.3d at p. 461, 152 Cal.Rptr. 668.)

We think a copyright is analytically distinguishable. A copyright *has* a present value based upon the ascertainable value of the underlying artistic work. Its value normally would not depend on the postmarital efforts of the authoring spouse but rather on the tangible benefits directly or indirectly associated with the literary product.

In short, we conclude that a copyright on a literary work produced during the marriage is as much a divisible community asset as the underlying artistic creation itself.

* * *

IN RE MARRIAGE OF BROWN
Supreme Court of California, 1976.
15 Cal.3d 838, 126 Cal.Rptr. 633, 544 P.2d 561.

TOBRINER, JUSTICE. Since French v. French (1941) 17 Cal.2d 775, 778, 112 P.2d 235, California courts have held that nonvested pension

---

4. The underlying rationale has been impliedly validated by the Legislature in enacting Civil Code section 4800.3, which provides not for a division of the value of the degree but only for reimbursement to the community for contributions to a spouse's education and training. (See *In re Marriage of Sullivan* (1984) 37 Cal.3d 762, 209 Cal.Rptr. 354, 691 P.2d 1020.)

rights are not property, but a mere expectancy, and thus not a community asset subject to division upon dissolution of a marriage. Two years ago we granted a hearing in In re Marriage of Wilson (1974) 10 Cal.3d 851, 112 Cal.Rptr. 405, 519 P.2d 165, to reconsider "the current viability of the rule of French v. French" (10 Cal.3d at p. 853, 112 Cal.Rptr. at p. 406, 519 P.2d at p. 166), but upon examination of the record in *Wilson* we discovered that the *French* issue had been waived by the nonemployee spouse. Properly raised in the present case by appellant Gloria Brown, the issue of division of nonvested pension rights upon dissolution of a marriage again confronts this court.

Upon reconsideration of this issue, we have concluded that French v. French should be overruled and that the subsequent decisions which rely on that precedent should be disapproved. As we shall explain, the *French* rule cannot stand because nonvested pension rights are not an expectancy but a contingent interest in property; furthermore, the *French* rule compels an inequitable division of rights acquired through community effort. Pension rights, whether or not vested, represent a property interest; to the extent that such rights derive from employment during coverture, they comprise a community asset subject to division in a dissolution proceeding.

Before we turn to the facts of this appeal we must devote a few words to terminology. Some decisions that discuss pension rights, but do not involve division of marital property, describe a pension right as "vested" if the employer cannot unilaterally repudiate that right without terminating the employment relationship. (See Strumsky v. San Diego County Employees Retirement Ass'n (1974) 11 Cal.3d 28, 45, 112 Cal. Rptr. 805, 520 P.2d 29; Kern v. City of Long Beach (1947) 29 Cal.2d 848, 855, 179 P.2d 799; Dryden v. Board of Pension Commrs. (1936) 6 Cal.2d 575, 579, 59 P.2d 104.) As we explain later, we believe that these decisions correctly define the point at which a pension right becomes a property interest. In divorce and dissolution cases following French v. French, however, the term "vested" has acquired a special meaning; it refers to a pension right which is not subject to a condition of forfeiture if the employment relationship terminates before retirement. We shall use the term "vested" in this latter sense as defining a pension right which survives the discharge or voluntary termination of the employee.

As so defined, a vested pension right must be distinguished from a "matured" or unconditional right to immediate payment. Depending upon the provisions of the retirement program, an employee's right may vest after a term of service even though it does not mature until he reaches retirement age and elects to retire. Such vested but immature rights are frequently subject to the condition, among others, that the employee survive until retirement.

The issue in the present case concerns the nonvested pension rights of respondent Robert Brown. General Telephone Company, Robert's employer, maintains a noncontributory pension plan in which the rights of the employees depend upon their accumulation of "points," based upon a combination of the years of service and the age of the employee. Under this plan, an employee who is discharged before he accumulates 78 points forfeits his rights; an employee with 78 points can opt for early retirement at a lower pension, or continue to work until age 63 and retire at an increased pension.

Gloria and Robert Brown married on July 29, 1950. When they separated in November of 1973, Robert had accumulated 72 points under the pension plan, a substantial portion of which is attributable to his work during the period when the parties were married and living together. If he continues to work for General Telephone, Robert will accumulate 78 points on November 30, 1976. If he retires then, he will receive a monthly pension of $310.94; if he continues his employment until normal retirement age his pension will be $485 a month.

Relying on the *French* rule, the trial court held that since Robert had not yet acquired a "vested" right to the retirement pension, the value of his pension rights did not become community property subject to division by the court. It divided the remaining property, awarding Gloria the larger share but directing her to pay $1,742 to Robert to equalize the value received by each spouse. The court also awarded Gloria alimony of $75 per month. Gloria appeals from the portion of the interlocutory judgment that declares that Robert's pension rights are not community property and thus not subject to division by the court.

As we have stated, the fundamental theoretical error which led to the inequitable division of marital property in the present case stems from the seminal decision of French v. French, supra, 17 Cal.2d 775, 112 P.2d 235. Mrs. French claimed a community interest in the prospective retirement pay of her husband, an enlisted man in the Fleet Reserve. The court noted that "under the applicable statutes the [husband] will not be entitled to such pay until he completes a service of 14 years in the Fleet Reserve and complies with all the requirements of that service." (P. 778, 112 P.2d p. 236.) It concluded that "At the present time, his right to retirement pay is an expectancy which is not subject to division as community property." (Ibid.)

In 1962 the Court of Appeal in Williamson v. Williamson, 203 Cal.App.2d 8, 21 Cal.Rptr. 164, explained the *French* rule, asserting that "To the extent that payment is, at the time of the divorce, subject to conditions which may or may not occur, the pension is an expectancy, not subject to division as community property." (203 Cal.App.2d at p. 11, 21 Cal.Rptr. at p. 167.)

Subsequent cases, however, have limited the sweep of *French,* holding that a vested pension is community property even though it has not matured (In re Marriage of Martin (1975) 50 Cal.App.3d 581, 584, 123 Cal.Rptr. 634; In re Marriage of Ward (1975) 50 Cal.App.3d 150, 123 Cal.Rptr. 234; In re Marriage of Bruegl (1975) 47 Cal.App.3d 201, 205, fn. 4, 120 Cal.Rptr. 597; Bensing v. Bensing, supra, 25 Cal.App.3d 889, 893, 102 Cal.Rptr. 255), or is subject to conditions within the employee's control (Waite v. Waite (1972) 6 Cal.3d 461, 472, 99 Cal.Rptr. 325, 492

P.2d 13; In re Marriage of Peterson (1974) 41 Cal.App.3d 642, 650–651, 115 Cal.Rptr. 184.) But although we have frequently reiterated the *French* rule in dictum (see, e.g., Marriage of Jones (1975) 13 Cal.3d 457, 461, 119 Cal.Rptr. 108, 531 P.2d 420; In re Marriage of Fithian (1974) 10 Cal.3d 592, 596, 111 Cal.Rptr. 369, 517 P.2d 449; Phillipson v. Board of Administration (1970) 3 Cal.3d 32, 40–41, 89 Cal.Rptr. 61, 473 P.2d 765; cf. Smith v. Lewis (1975) 13 Cal.3d 349, 355, 118 Cal.Rptr. 621, 530 P.2d 589), we have not previously had occasion to reexamine the merits of that rule.

Throughout our decisions we have always recognized that the community owns all pension rights attributable to employment during the marriage. (See Phillipson v. Board of Administration, supra, 3 Cal.3d 32, 39, 89 Cal.Rptr. 61, 473 P.2d 765; French v. French, supra, 17 Cal.2d 775, 778, 112 P.2d 235; Marriage of Ward, supra, 50 Cal.App.3d 150, 153, 123 Cal.Rptr. 234.) The *French* rule, however, rests on the theory that nonvested pension rights may be community, but that they are not property; classified as mere expectancies, such rights are not assets subject to division on dissolution of the marriage.

We have concluded, however, that the *French* court's characterization of nonvested pension rights as expectancies errs. The term expectancy describes the interest of a person who merely foresees that he might receive a future beneficence, such as the interest of an heir apparent (Civ.Code, § 700; see Estate of Perkins (1943) 21 Cal.2d 561, 569, 134 P.2d 231), or of a beneficiary designated by a living insured who has a right to change the beneficiary (see Morrison v. Mutual L. Ins. of N.Y. (1940) 15 Cal.2d 579, 583, 103 P.2d 963; Mayfield v. Fidelity & Casualty Co. (1936) 16 Cal.App.2d 611, 619, 61 P.2d 83). As these examples demonstrate, the defining characteristic of an expectancy is that its holder has no *enforceable right* to his beneficence.

Although some jurisdictions classify retirement pensions as gratuities, it has long been settled that under California law such benefits "do not derive from the beneficence of the employer, but are properly part of the consideration earned by the employee." (In re Marriage of Fithian, supra, 10 Cal.3d 592, 596, 111 Cal.Rptr. 369, 371, 517 P.2d 449, 451.) Since pension benefits represent a form of deferred compensation for services rendered (In re Marriage of Jones, supra, 13 Cal.3d 457, 461, 119 Cal.Rptr. 108, 531 P.2d 420), the employee's right to such benefits is a contractual right, derived from the terms of the employment contract. Since a contractual right is not an expectancy but a chose in action, a form of property (see Civ.Code, § 953; Everts v. Will S. Fawcett Co. (1937) 24 Cal.App.2d 213, 215, 74 P.2d 815), we held in Dryden v. Board of Pension Commrs., supra, 6 Cal.2d 575, 579, 59 P.2d 104, that an employee acquires a property right to pension benefits when he enters upon the performance of his employment contract.

Although *Dryden* involved an employee who possessed vested pension rights, the issue of nonvested rights came before us in Kern v. City of Long Beach, supra, 29 Cal.2d 848, 179 P.2d 799. There a city employee contended that the city's repeal of a pension plan unconstitutionally impaired the obligation of contract. The city defended on the ground that the employee's pension rights had not vested at the time of the abrogation of the plan.

Ruling in favor of the employee, we stated in *Kern* that: "[T]here is little reason to make a distinction between the periods before and after the pension payments are due. It is true that an employee does not earn the right to a full pension until he has completed the prescribed period of service, but he has actually earned some pension rights as soon as he has performed substantial services for his employer. [Citations omitted.] He * * * has then earned certain pension benefits, the payment of which is to be made at a future date. * * * [T]he mere fact that performance is in whole or in part dependent upon certain contingencies does not prevent a contract from arising, and the employing governmental body may not deny or impair the contingent liability any more than it can refuse to make the salary payments which are immediately due. Clearly, it cannot do so after all the contingencies have happened, and in our opinion it cannot do so at any time after a contractual duty to make salary payments has arisen, since a part of the compensation which the employee has at that time earned consists of his pension rights." (29 Cal.2d at p. 855, 179 P.2d at p. 803.)

Since we based our holding in *Kern* upon the constitutional prohibition against impairment of contracts, a prohibition applicable only to public entities, the private employer in Hunter v. Sparling (1948) 87 Cal.App.2d 711, 197 P.2d 807 contended that it could repudiate an employee's nonvested pension rights without liability. Rejecting that contention, the Court of Appeal cited the language from *Kern* quoted above and concluded that once the employee performed services in reliance upon the promised pension, he could enforce his right to a pension either under traditional contract principles of offer, acceptance and consideration or under the doctrine of promissory estoppel. (87 Cal.App.2d at p. 725, 197 P.2d 807.) In subsequent years the courts have repeatedly reaffirmed that a nonvested pension right is nonetheless a contractual right, and thus a property right.

Although, as we have pointed out, supra, courts have previously refused to allocate this right in a nonvested pension between the spouses as community property on the ground that such pension is contingent upon continued employment, we reject this theory. In other situations when community funds or effort are expended to acquire a conditional right to future income, the courts do not hesitate to treat that right as a community asset. For example, in Waters v. Waters (1946) 75 Cal. App.2d 265, 170 P.2d 494, the attorney husband had a contingent interest in a suit pending on appeal at the time of the divorce; the court held that his fee, when and if collected, would be a community asset. Indeed in the several recent pension cases the courts have asserted that vested but immature pensions are community assets although such pensions are commonly subject to the condition that the employee survive until retirement. (See Smith v. Lewis, supra, 13 Cal.3d 349,

355, fn. 4, 118 Cal.Rptr. 261, 530 P.2d 589; In re Marriage of Martin, supra, 50 Cal.App.3d 581, 123 Cal.Rptr. 634; Marriage of Bruegl, supra, 47 Cal.App.3d 201, 205, 120 Cal.Rptr. 597.)

We conclude that French v. French, and subsequent cases erred in characterizing nonvested pension rights as expectancies and in denying the trial courts the authority to divide such rights as community property. This mischaracterization of pension rights has, and unless overturned, will continue to result in inequitable division of community assets. Over the past decades, pension benefits have become an increasingly significant part of the consideration earned by the employee for his services. As the date of vesting and retirement approaches, the value of the pension right grows until it often represents the most important asset of the marital community. (See Thiede, op. cit., supra, U.S.F.L.Rev. 635.) A division of community property which awards one spouse the entire value of this asset, without any offsetting award to the other spouse, does not represent that equal division of community property contemplated by Civil Code section 4800.

The present case illustrates the point. Robert's pension rights, a valuable asset built up by 24 years of community effort, under the French rule would escape division by the court as a community asset solely because dissolution occurred two years before the vesting date. If, as is entirely likely, Robert continues to work for General Telephone Company for the additional two years needed to acquire a vested right, he will then enjoy as his separate property an annuity created predominately through community effort. This "potentially whimsical result," as the Court of Appeal described a similar division of community property in In re Marriage of Peterson, supra, 41 Cal.App.3d 642, 651, 115 Cal.Rptr. 184, cannot be reconciled with the fundamental principle that property attributable to community earnings must be divided equally when the community is dissolved.

Respondent does not deny that if nonvested pension rights are property, the French rule results in an inequitable division of that property. He maintains, however, that any inequity can be redressed by an award of alimony to the nonemployee spouse. Alimony, however, lies within the discretion of the trial court; the spouse "should not be dependent on the discretion of the court * * * to provide her with the equivalent of what should be hers as a matter of absolute right." (In re Marriage of Peterson, supra, 41 Cal.App.3d 642, 651, 115 Cal.Rptr. 184, 191.)

Respondent and amicus further suggest that a decision repudiating the French rule would both impose severe practical burdens upon the courts and restrict the employee's freedom to change his place or terms of employment. We shall examine these contentions and point out why they do not justify a continued refusal by the courts to divide nonvested pension rights as a community asset.

In dividing nonvested pension rights as community property the court must take account of the possibility that death or termination of employment may destroy those rights before they mature. In some cases the trial court may be able to evaluate this risk in determining the present value of those rights. (See De Revere v. De Revere, supra, 5 Wash.2d 741, 491 P.2d 249; *Thiede,* op. cit. supra, 9 U.S.F.L.Rev. 635, 654.) But if the court concludes that because of uncertainties affecting the vesting or maturation of the pension that it should not attempt to divide the present value of pension rights, it can instead award each spouse an appropriate portion of each pension payment as it is paid. This method of dividing the community interest in the pension renders it unnecessary for the court to compute the present value of the pension rights, and divides equally the risk that the pension will fail to vest. (See Cohan & Fink, Is the Non–Employee Community Interest in Qualified Deferred Compensation a Hidden Asset or a Latent Liability? (1974) 1 Com.Prop.J. 7, 13; Note, op. cit., supra, 24 Hastings L.J. 347, 356–357.)

As respondent points out, an award of future pension payments as they fall due will require the court to continue jurisdiction to supervise the payments of pension benefits. Yet this obligation arises whenever the court cannot equitably award all pension rights to one spouse, whether or not such rights are vested; the claim of mere administrative burden surely cannot serve as support for an inequitable substantive rule which distinguishes between vested and nonvested rights. Despite the administrative burden such an award imposes, courts in the past have successfully divided vested pension rights by awarding each spouse a share in future payments. (See Marriage of Wilson, supra, 10 Cal.3d 851, 855–856, 112 Cal.Rptr. 405, 519 P.2d 165; Bensing v. Bensing, supra, 25 Cal.App.3d 889, 892, 102 Cal.Rptr. 255.) Courts can divide nonvested pension rights in like fashion.

Moreover, the practical consequence of the *French* rule has been historically that the court must often award alimony to the spouse who, deprived of any share in the nonvested pension rights, lacks resources to purchase the necessities of life. (Article, op. cit., supra, 6 U.C.Davis L.Rev. 26, 32.) Judicial supervision of alimony awards, undertaken in the past, entails far more onerous a burden than supervision of future pension payment.

As to the claim that our present holding will infringe upon the employee's freedom of contract, we note that judicial recognition of the nonemployee spouse's interest in vested pension rights has not limited the employee's freedom to change or terminate his employment, to agree to a modification of the terms of his employment (including retirement benefits), or to elect between alternative retirement programs. We do not conceive that judicial recognition of spousal rights in nonvested pensions will change the law in this respect. The employee retains the right to decide, and by his decision define, the nature of the retirement benefits owned by the community.

Robert finally contends that any decision overruling French v. French, supra, 17 Cal.2d 775, 112 P.2d 235 should be given purely prospective effect. Although as we explain our decision cannot be accorded complete retroactivity without upsetting final judgments of long standing, we believe the decision may properly govern any case in which no final judgment dividing the marital property has been rendered.

Although as a general rule "a decision of a court of supreme jurisdiction overruling a former decision is retrospective in its operation" (County of Los Angeles v. Faus (1957) 48 Cal.2d 672, 680–681, 312 P.2d 680, 685), we have recognized exceptions to that proposition when considerations of fairness and public policy preclude full retroactivity (see Westbrook v. Mihaly (1970) 2 Cal.3d 765, 800–801, 87 Cal.Rptr. 839, 471 P.2d 487; Forster Shipbldg. Co. v. County of L.A. (1960) 54 Cal.2d 450, 459, 6 Cal.Rptr. 24, 353 P.2d 736). In Neel v. Magana, Olney, Levy, Cathcart & Gelfand (1971) 6 Cal.3d 176, 193, 98 Cal.Rptr. 837, 848, 491 P.2d 421, 432, we observe that the resolution of this issue of prospective application turns primarily on two factors: "the extent of public reliance upon the former rule, * * * [and] the ability of litigants to foresee the coming change in the law." In the present case both factors militate against a purely prospective overruling of French v. French. It is unlikely that a layman would rely upon the *French* rule, or even know of that doctrine; attorneys familiar with the decision in French v. French would also realize from our opinion in Marriage of Wilson, supra, 10 Cal.3d 851, 112 Cal.Rptr. 405, 519 P.2d 165 that the *French* rule was ripe for reconsideration. The unjust distribution of property engendered by the *French* rule should not be perpetuated by denial of any retrospective effect to our decision.

On the other hand, if we accord complete retroactivity of our decision today we might reopen controversies long settled by final judgment. Undoubtedly in the 35 years since the rendition of French v. French, counsel, relying on that decision, have often failed to list nonvested pension rights as among the community assets of the marriage. In some cases the inability of the nonemployee spouse to assert an interest in nonvested pension rights may have induced the court to award additional alimony. Yet under settled principles of California community property law, "property which is not mentioned in the pleadings as community property is left unadjudicated by decree of divorce, and is subject to future litigation, the parties being tenants in common meanwhile." (In re Marriage of Elkins (1972) 28 Cal.App.3d 899, 903, 105 Cal.Rptr. 59, 61.) Consequently full retroactivity poses the danger that a nonemployee spouse might upset a settled property distribution by a belated assertion of an interest as a tenant in common in the employee's nonvested pension rights.

We conclude that our decision today should not apply retroactively to permit a nonemployee spouse to assert an interest in nonvested pension rights when the property rights of the marriage have already been adjudicated by a decree of dissolution or separation which has become final as to such adjudication, unless the decree expressly reserved jurisdiction to divide such pension rights at a later date (see

Civ.Code, § 4800). Our decision will apply retroactively, however, to any case in which the property rights arising from the marriage have not yet been adjudicated, to such rights if such adjudication is still subject to appellate review, or if in such adjudication the trial court has expressly reserved jurisdiction to divide pension rights.

For the foregoing reasons we conclude that the holding of French v. French, supra, 17 Cal.2d 775, 112 P.2d 235 that nonvested pension rights cannot constitute community property subject to division upon dissolution of the marriage must be overruled.

In sum, we submit that whatever abstract terminology we impose, the joint effort that composes the community and the respective contributions of the spouses that make up its assets, are the meaningful criteria. The wife's contribution to the community is not one whit less if we declare the husband's pension rights not a contingent asset but a mere "expectancy." Fortunately we can appropriately reflect the realistic situation by recognizing that the husband's pension rights, a contingent interest, whether vested or not vested, comprise a property interest of the community and that the wife may properly share in it.

The judgment of the superior court is reversed and the cause remanded for further proceedings consistent with the views expressed herein.

Notes

1. Employment during marriage permits the classification of pensions as community property. Included are pensions under public employees' retirement systems. Statutory restrictions on the assignment and attachment of such pensions does not prevent their division on dissolution of the marriage. See Phillipson v. Board of Administration, 3 Cal.3d 32, 89 Cal.Rptr. 61, 473 P.2d 765 (1970).

Where, however, these benefits are created by federal legislation, the Supremacy Clause of the United States Constitution may preclude their classification as community property. The United States Supreme Court has ruled that California community property laws cannot be applied to certain federally created benefits. These decisions are considered in Section 3 of this Chapter.

2. The principles espoused by the court in *Brown* have been used to bring other types of employee benefits within the operation of the California community property system. In the case of In re Marriage of Shea, 111 Cal.App.3d 713, 716, 169 Cal.Rptr. 490, 491 (1980), the court summarized the legislation establishing Veteran's Educational Benefits and continued: "The veteran's educational allowances provided by this statutory scheme are a form of employee benefits, similar in nature to the wide variety of fringe benefits—for example, employer-paid life insurance, tuition reimbursement programs, and pensions—furnished by public and private employers. Like other types of employee benefits, the veteran's education allowance is designed to attract prospective employees, and entitlement to these benefits can be attained only by service with the employer. Consequently, the general principles governing characterization of fringe benefits flowing from

the employment relationship determine whether veterans' education benefits are community property.''

3. Note that the Supreme Court expressly held that its decision in *Brown* was not to be given retroactive effect. In Shaver v. Shaver, 107 Cal.App.3d 788, 165 Cal.Rptr. 672 (1980), the husband's nonvested pension was not divided in 1967 dissolution proceedings. Because of the non-retroactivity policy, the nonvested pension was not property within the operation of the community property system, and could never become divisible property.

4. Further problems involving the classification of various employment benefits are considered in Chapter 4.

IN RE MARRIAGE OF SPENGLER
Court of Appeals, Third District, 1992.
5 Cal.App. 4th 288, 6 Cal.Rptr.2d 764.

SIMS, ASSOCIATE JUSTICE.

In this postjudgment marital dissolution proceeding, petitioner below, Barbara Ann Spengler (wife), filed a complaint in joinder against claimant Rose G. Spengler (beneficiary) in which wife claimed a community property interest in proceeds received by beneficiary from a term life insurance policy upon the death of wife's former husband, Daniel F. Spengler, Sr. (husband). The trial court found the policy was an omitted community asset (Civ.Code, § 4353[1]) and entered judgment awarding half the proceeds to wife. The issue on appeal is whether an employment-related group term life insurance policy is community property subject to division in a marital dissolution. The narrower question is whether such policy's provision of a right to renewed coverage without proof of current insurability is a valuable community asset subject to division in a marital dissolution where the insured spouse becomes uninsurable during the marriage, such that the existing policy provides future coverage the insured spouse could not otherwise obtain. We will conclude the employment-related group term life insurance policy is not a community property asset beyond expiration of the term acquired with community efforts, and this result is unaffected by uninsurability if the insured employee has no enforceable right to compel the employer to renew the policy. We will therefore reverse the judgment.

FACTUAL AND PROCEDURAL BACKGROUND

Wife and husband were married in 1967.

---

1. Undesignated statutory references are to the Civil Code.

Section 4353 provides: ''In any action for legal separation or dissolution or annulment of a marriage, the court has continuing jurisdiction to award community property or community debts to the parties that has not been previously adjudicated by a judgment therein. A party may file a postjudgment motion or order to show cause in the proceeding in order to obtain adjudication of any community asset or debt omitted or not adjudicated by the judgment. In these cases, the court shall equally divide the omitted or unadjudicated community asset or debt, unless the court finds upon good cause shown that the interests of justice require an unequal division of the asset or debt.''

In 1980, husband began working for Mid–Valley Dairy Company. The employer provided various life insurance benefits to employees, apparently as fringe benefits. The policy at issue in this case was a group term life insurance plan that insured employees for the amount of their salary up to $180,000. The insured group was large enough so that employees were not required to undergo a physical examination or submit proof of insurability. This coverage continued, though underwritten by different insurers, until husband's death.

In 1982, husband was diagnosed with prostate cancer. According to testimony of an insurance expert, a person in husband's situation would have been "uninsurable," i.e., unable to obtain individual life insurance.

Husband and wife separated in 1986. The marriage was dissolved by bifurcated judgment from which wife appealed.

* * *

After dissolution, the insurance coverage continued under a policy issued by Hartford Life Insurance Company in September 1989. That same month, husband married Rose Spengler and named her as his beneficiary under the policy.

Three months later, husband died.

Beneficiary received approximately $100,000 as designated beneficiary of the subject policy. Wife filed a complaint in joinder, seeking half the proceeds as a community asset.

* * *

Following a bench trial, the trial court concluded the insurance policy was community property and was an omitted asset under Civil Code section 4353 (fn. 1, *ante*). The court entered judgment in favor of wife for one-half of the policy proceeds.

DISCUSSION

I

Beneficiary contends a term life insurance policy is not a community asset subject to division under the Family Law Act and does not become a community asset by virtue of the insured spouse becoming uninsurable during the marriage. We agree.

We now turn to the merits.

The Courts of Appeal are split on the issue of whether a term life insurance policy is community property. The Second District has held that a term life insurance policy, having no cash surrender value, is not "property" within the meaning of the community property laws. (*In re Marriage of Lorenz* (1983) 146 Cal.App.3d 464, 467, 194 Cal.Rptr. 237.) The Fourth District has held that, even though term life insurance lacks cash surrender value, it may have replacement value subject to community property division where insurability is lessened by advancing age or declining health of the insured spouse. (E.g., *In re Marriage of Gonzalez* (1985) 168 Cal.App.3d 1021, 1025, 214 Cal.Rptr. 634.) The First District has held that, as long as the insured spouse remains insurable, term life insurance has no divisible community property value upon expiration of the term acquired with community funds/efforts. (*Estate of Logan* (1987) 191 Cal.App.3d 319, 325, 236 Cal.Rptr. 368.) However, according to dictum in *Logan,* if the insured becomes uninsurable during the marriage, the policy's renewal rights to continued coverage that cannot otherwise be purchased is a community asset to be divided upon dissolution. (*Id.* at p. 326, 236 Cal.Rptr. 368.) As will appear, we agree with *Logan's* holding but disagree with its dictum.

Logan, supra, 191 Cal.App.3d 319, 236 Cal.Rptr. 368 was an action against an estate, in which a former wife sought a share in the proceeds of her deceased former husband's employment-related term life insurance policy, for which preseparation premium payments had been paid with community funds. Because *Logan* contains a cogent analysis of the issue and relevant case law, we quote extensively from that decision:

"The first case to consider a closely related issue was *Biltoft v. Wootten* (1979) 96 Cal.App.3d 58 [157 Cal.Rptr. 581] [ ] which involved a contributory group term life insurance policy available through the insured's employment and paid with biweekly deductions from his pay. After separation, but before dissolution, decedent had changed the beneficiary under the policy from his spouse to his children. On appeal the issue was whether the proceeds were community or separate property. The court held the proceeds were part community and part separate according to the proportion that the amount of premiums paid with community property bore to the total amount of premiums paid. The reasoning underlying the decision was that each premium payment did not purchase a new contract of insurance because, if the decedent had tried to purchase the policy after separation, 'it is unlikely that he would have been able to obtain the same coverage for the same premium on the same terms of eligibility' and 'The decedent's community efforts for the 20 years prior to the separation maintained the policy in force.' (*Id.* at p. 61 [157 Cal.Rptr. 581].) The court's opinion does not indicate what evidence, if any, was presented to support the conclusion that it was 'unlikely' decedent could have purchased the identical policy after separation.

"*Lorenz* [*supra,* 146 Cal.App.3d 464, 194 Cal.Rptr. 237] distinguished *Biltoft* as a case dealing with the right to proceeds from term insurance upon the death of the insured spouse prior to dissolution.[3] The *Lorenz* analysis was that many fringe benefits of employment such as use of an employer's health club facilities, reduced prices at the company cafeteria or discounts on purchases of an employer's products were of value to an employee, but did not constitute community property divisible upon dissolution. *Lorenz* held that although the benefits of

---

3. Although *Biltoft* was distributing proceeds, the court noted that the court in a dissolution action need not reserve jurisdiction until the policyholder dies but could determine value of the policy in the same way it determines value of other community property rights. (*Biltoft v. Wootten* (1979) 96 Cal.App.3d 58, 62, 157 Cal.Rptr. 581.)

term life insurance have a value, until those benefits become payable, the policy itself is worthless and is not divisible as community property.

"The *Gonzalez* [*supra,* 168 Cal.App.3d 1021, 214 Cal.Rptr. 634] court concluded, '*Lorenz* is simply incorrect in the assertion that assets such as term life insurance and accrued vacation time have no economic value. . . .' [Citation.] *Gonzalez* reasoned that the spouses had acquired rights because the policy had been obtained during marriage with community funds. The court concluded, with no indication what evidence existed in the record to support its conclusion, 'Undoubtedly the premium rate was very favorable, and pursuant to federal statute, husband was not required to establish medical eligibility for coverage. [Citation.] We are confident the same policy acquired today, assuming husband is still insurable, would cost considerably more.' [Citation.]

"To say that '[t]he *Gonzalez* decision has been subject to criticism by members of the Bar' (Cal. Family Law Service, § 23:138) is putting it mildly. In addition to placing another roadblock in the way of simplified dissolution of marriage, the requirements of this decision would also significantly increase the cost of dissolution by requiring each side to employ expert witnesses to testify to the value of term life insurance policies. We suspect that in most cases the cost to the parties of expert witnesses would be greater than the value of the term life insurance policy. We believe the *Gonzalez* and *Bowman* decisions result from an erroneous analysis of the nature of term life insurance policies." (*Logan, supra,* 191 Cal.App.3d at pp. 322–324, 236 Cal.Rptr. 368, fn. omitted.)

The *Logan* court explained the nature of term life insurance policies as follows:

" 'Term insurance is life insurance written for a fixed or specified term. To reflect the increasing risk of death as the insured increases in age, term insurance policies either have increasing premiums from year to year or provide decreasing death benefits paid on the insured's death. At the expiration of the term of years, the policy expires without retaining cash value. One advantage of term insurance is its cost. Since it does not retain cash value, the premium cost for comparable coverage is less than it is with whole life insurance. Some forms of term insurance may be converted into permanent or whole life policies or may be automatically renewable at regular intervals at a higher premium.' (5A Markey, Cal. Family Law, Practice and Procedure, § 122.03[2][b].) Term life insurance policies typically contain two elements, dollar coverage payable in the event of death and a right to renewal for future terms without proof of current medical eligibility.

"As to the element of dollar coverage, term life insurance simply provides for protection against the contingency of the death of the insured during the term of the policy. If the premium for the next term is not paid, the policy is not renewed. In this respect, it is the same as automobile or health insurance. Thus when the premium is paid with community funds, the policy is community property for the period covered by that premium. This is true whether the premium is paid as a fringe benefit by the insured's employer, paid for by the insured, or a combination of both. The policy provides dollar coverage only for the specific term for which the premium was paid. Thus, as to dollar coverage, term life insurance upon which premiums were paid from community funds has no value after the term has ended without the insured having become deceased.

"With respect to the element of the right to renew coverage for additional terms, term life insurance has either a significant value or no value at all. The right to renewal upon payment of the premium for the next term is significant because the insured possesses the right even if he or she has become uninsurable in the meantime. Usually, as Markey points out, policies require increasing premiums and/or decreasing amounts of coverage as the insured gets older. If, as is usually the case, the insured is insurable at the end of the term purchased with community funds, the renewed policy, that is, the term policy purchased by the payment of the premium with postseparation earnings which are separate property pursuant to Civil Code section 5118,[4] or by the employer as a postseparation fringe benefit, changes character from community to separate property.

"At this time, if the insured is insurable, the community has fully received everything it bargained for, dollar protection against the contingency of death during the term paid for with community funds and the right to renew without proof of insurability for an additional term. If the insured remains insurable, the right to renew the policy has no value since the insured could obtain comparable term insurance for a comparable price in the open market. The community having received everything it bargained for, there is no longer any community property interest in the policy and no community asset left to divide.

"We believe the courts in *Biltoft*, *Gonzalez* and *Bowman*[5] came to incorrect conclusions because they made unsupported and erroneous assumptions about the nature of term life insurance and the availability to the insured of other comparable insurance. In *Biltoft*, the court assumed 'it is unlikely that [decedent] would have been able to obtain the same coverage for the same premium on the same terms of eligibility.' (*Biltoft v. Wootten, supra*, 96 Cal.App.3d at p. 61 [157 Cal.Rptr. 581].) In *Gonzalez* the court assumed '[u]ndoubtedly the premium rate was very favorable' and 'husband was not required to establish medical eligibility for coverage,' and concluded, 'We are confident the same policy today, assuming husband is still insurable, would cost considerably more.' (*In re Marriage of Gonzalez, supra*, 168 Cal.App.3d at p. 1026 [214 Cal.Rptr. 634].) To this we ask, where was the evidence to support

---

4. Civil Code section 5118 provides: "The earnings and accumulations of a spouse and the minor children living with, or in the custody of, the spouse, while living separate and apart from the other spouse, are the separate property of the spouse."

5. *Bowman v. Bowman* (1985) 171 Cal. App.3d 148, 217 Cal.Rptr. 174 was decided by the same court that decided *Gonzalez* and simply followed the *Gonzalez* holding.

these assumptions? For all we know, by the time of the appeal, Mr. Gonzalez or Mr. Bowman might well have changed jobs and gotten new employment in the private sector which provided greater term life insurance coverage paid for by the employer. Such coverage is usually available even if the employed might be otherwise uninsurable, since new employees are usually covered under the employer's group life insurance plans without evidence of insurability. The group insurance with the former employers would have ceased when the insured changed employment.

"We believe the correct rule to be that term life insurance covering a spouse who remains insurable is community property only for the period beyond the date of separation for which community funds were used to pay the premium. If the insured dies during that period the proceeds of the policy are fully community. Otherwise, the insured remaining insurable, a term policy does not constitute a divisible community asset since the policy is of no value and the community has fully received what it bargained for. If the insured becomes uninsurable during the term paid with community funds, then the right to future insurance coverage which cannot otherwise be purchased is a community asset to be divided upon dissolution." (*Logan, supra,* 191 Cal.App.3d at pp. 324–326, 236 Cal.Rptr. 368, fns. omitted.)

A concurring justice in *Logan* noted that the dictum regarding an exception in the event the insured spouse becomes uninsurable was an issue that had not been fully briefed and was not ripe for decision. (*Logan, supra,* 191 Cal.App.3d at p. 327, 236 Cal.Rptr. 368, conc. opn. of Haning, J.)

We agree with *Logan's* holding that an employment-related term life insurance policy is not a community property asset after expiration of the term acquired with community funds/efforts. We respectfully disagree, however, with *Logan's* dictum finding an exception where the insured spouse becomes uninsurable during the marriage.

In our view, the fallacy of classifying the renewal right in this case as community property is that it is based on the faulty premise that during the marriage husband was able to acquire a policy that could not thereafter be taken away. But that is not the case. The right to continued insurance protection under an employment-related insurance policy is not inexorably earned by the investment of community funds/efforts in acquiring the policy. It depends on the insured's continuing to work at that employment *and* on the employer's continuing to provide the group insurance plan.

In order to qualify as community property, an asset or interest must be "property" within the meaning of the community property laws. (*Lorenz, supra,* 146 Cal.App.3d at p. 467, 194 Cal.Rptr. 237.) Thus, the question is whether the isolated interest in this case—the renewal right— is "property" as opposed to a mere expectancy. (See *In re Marriage of Brown* (1976) 15 Cal.3d 838, 846, fn. 8, 126 Cal.Rptr. 633,

544 P.2d 561, citing § 697 [contingent future interest is property] and § 700 [expectancy is not to be deemed an interest of any kind].)

We recognize that "Fringe benefits [6] are not a gift from the employer but are earned by the employee as part of the compensation for services. [Citations.] Thus fringe benefits such as ... employer-paid life insurance ... are community property to the extent they are earned by the time, skill and effort of a spouse during marriage. [Citations.] Fringe benefits consisting of *contractual rights* to future benefits after separation, though unvested and unmatured, are property subject to allocation between community and separate interests at the time of dissolution. [Citation.]" (*In re Marriage of Harrison* (1986) 179 Cal. App.3d 1216, 1226, 225 Cal.Rptr. 234, emphasis added [community interest in qualified stock options], citing inter alia *Polk v. Polk* (1964) 228 Cal.App.2d 763, 781, 39 Cal.Rptr. 824 [community interest in insurance proceeds].)

The fact that a benefit is subject to contingencies does not preclude a finding of a divisible property interest. (*In re Marriage of Brown*, supra, 15 Cal.3d at p. 846, fn. 8, 126 Cal.Rptr. 633, 544 P.2d 561.) A contract right, though contingent, may be a valuable property right if it is "subject only to conditions within the control of the [holder of the right]." (*In re Marriage of Fonstein* (1976) 17 Cal.3d 738, 745–746, 131 Cal.Rptr. 873, 552 P.2d 1169 [right to withdraw from partnership]; see also *In re Marriage of Skaden* (1977), 19 Cal.3d 679, 139 Cal.Rptr. 615, 566 P.2d 249 [employment termination benefits contained in written contract were property interest, though extent of benefits was contingent on compliance with contract conditions]; see also cases cited in *In re Marriage of Kilbourne* (1991) 232 Cal.App.3d 1518, 1524, fn. 5, 284 Cal.Rptr. 201 [that husband's right to receive fees from law practice was contingent on future events did not negate status as community assets].)

To be distinguished from the *contract rights* referenced in the preceding paragraphs is a "mere expectancy," which does not constitute a property interest under community property laws. Thus, our Supreme Court has indicated that a benefit contingent on continued employment may or may not be "property" subject to the community property laws depending on whether it is a mere expectancy or a contract right. (*In re Marriage of Brown*, supra, 15 Cal.3d 838, 126 Cal.Rptr. 633, 544 P.2d 561 [nonvested pension rights are property].) "The term expectancy describes the interest of a person who merely foresees that he might receive a future beneficence, such as the interest of an heir apparent [citations], or a beneficiary designated by a living insured who has a right to change the beneficiary [citations].... [T]he defining characteristic of an expectancy is that its holder has no *enforceable right* to his beneficence." (*Id.* at pp. 844–845, 126 Cal.Rptr. 633, 544 P.2d 561, original emphasis, fn. omitted.) *Brown* concluded that nonvested pension rights, though contingent on continued employment, are not mere

---

6. The parties cite no evidence as to who paid the premiums on the policy, but the stipulated facts state the employer "provided" the insurance benefits, and wife does not dispute beneficiary's characterization of the policy as a fringe benefit.

expectancies but represent a form of deferred compensation for services rendered—a contractual right derived from the employment contract. "Since a contractual right is not an expectancy but a chose in action, a form of property [citations], ... an employee acquires a property right to pension benefits when he enters upon the performance of his employment contract." (*Ibid.*)

Applying the above principles, we conclude that the isolated interest in this case—the renewal right—was a mere expectancy rather than a contingent property interest. We emphasize that the interest we are examining is *only* the renewal right, *not* the coverage element of the policy. The renewal right depended not only on continued employment by husband but also on continued offering of the plan by the employer. Although there was no testimony about the specifics of husband's employment terms, the insurance expert testified that any group term life insurance policy can be terminated by the employer at any time, with 30 days notice. He further testified that continued coverage for the uninsurable employee depended both on the employee continuing the employment *and* the employer continuing the policy. Wife does not dispute this evidence, nor does she contend that anything in husband's employment contract prevented the employer from discontinuing the group plan. Thus, although there is a contingent contract right to policy *proceeds* in the event of death during the term, there is no right on the part of husband to compel the employer to *renew* the coverage upon expiration of the term. In other words, the prospect of renewal of the policy by the employer was a beneficence to which husband had no enforceable right.

Thus, while the renewal right has potential value, we conclude that in the absence of a right by the insured spouse to enforce that value, the renewal right is not "property" within the meaning of the community property laws. (*In re Marriage of Brown*, supra, 15 Cal.3d at pp. 844–845, 126 Cal.Rptr. 633, 544 P.2d 561.) That the policy *was* renewed in this case is immaterial, because this is not a question to be answered in hindsight. As a matter of law, the renewal right aspect of an employment-related group term life insurance policy is not property subject to division in marital dissolution where the employee has no enforceable right to renewal.

This result is equitable, because the community has received the full benefit of its bargain—continued coverage protection throughout the course of the marriage. There is no carry-over right from the days of the marriage. There is no right to insurance that transcends the separation.

We conclude the trial court erred in finding the insurance policy in this case to be a community property asset.

DISPOSITION

The judgment is reversed. Appellant will recover her costs on appeal.

PUGLIA, P.J., and NICHOLSON, J., concur.

Notes

1. Note that there is a basic distinction between whole life insurance and a policy of term insurance: A whole life policy has an investment component in addition to death benefits. California courts have traditionally recognized this "cash surrender value" as divisible community property in dissolution proceedings. See, e.g., In re Marriage of Holmgren, 60 Cal. App.3d 869, 871, 130 Cal.Rptr. 440, 441 (1976).

2. Suppose that after separation a spouse incurs lower premiums on his term life insurance for future policies because of his prior relationship with the same insurance company during marriage. It could be argued that the lowered rate is attributable to the purchase of earlier policies by the community. Should the community receive some form of compensation on the basis of this factor? See 3 Calif. Family Law Monthly 434 (1987).

3. Where a policy of term insurance is continued in effect until the death of the insured by the payment of premiums traceable to both separate and community funds, it has been held that the proceeds of the policy should be apportioned between the separate and community estates in the same ratio that the amount of the community funds paid for the premiums bears to the amount of separate funds paid for such purpose. Modern Woodmen of America v. Gray, 113 Cal.App. 729, 299 P. 754 (1931).

SECTION 2. PERSONS WITHIN THE SYSTEM

A. The Valid Marriage Requirement

Some community property jurisdictions hold that a community can exist when a man and woman in good faith enter into a marital relationship even though the marriage is legally void. This approach is consonant with the Spanish–Mexican community property system.[10] In California, however, a valid marriage is prerequisite to the existence of a marital community, and hence there can be no community property without a legally binding marriage. Marriage is statutorily defined as "a personal relation arising out of a contract between a man and a woman, to which the consent of the parties capable of making that contract is necessary."[11] The California position is in line with the views of common law courts denying marital property rights to putative spouses. The marriage required for the existence of a community in California does not have to be of any special type. It need only be a marriage recognized by the state.[12]

Although the common law did not extend the coverage of its marital property system to a putative spouse, it did afford protection in appropri-

---

10. 1 de Funiak and Vaughn, Principles of Community Property, § 56, p. 96 (1971); 2 de Funiak, Id., pp. 74, 168–169 (1943); Smith v. Smith, 1 Tex. 621, 46 Am.Dec. 121 (1846).

11. West's Ann.Cal.Family Code § 300.

12. The requirements for a legal marriage are contained at West's Ann.Cal.Fam-ily Code §§ 300–594. West's Ann.Cal.Family Code § 308 provides that "all marriages contracted without this state, which would be valid by the laws of the jurisdiction in which the same were contracted, are valid in this state."

ate cases by application of the principles of contract, tort, quasi-contract and restitution.[13] California courts have given similar types of protection. In addition, the California courts developed an equitable community property system analogous to the legal system. This judicially created equitable system initially recognized the earnings and accumulations of the putative relationship as equitable community property.[14] Later cases extended the concept, recognizing a putative spouse as a "surviving spouse" for purposes of intestate succession,[15] as a "widow" within the State Employees' Retirement System,[16] the Workmen's Compensation Act[17] and the Social Security Act,[18] and as an "heir" within the Wrongful Death Act.[19]

The equitable community property system was partially codified in 1969 by the addition of Family Code Section 2251. This provision recognizes the equitable system in dissolution cases, characterizing the equitable community property as "quasi-marital property," and providing for its division on dissolution of the putative marriage. Where the putative relationship is brought to an end by death rather than by annulment or other dissolution proceedings, it is presumed that the judicially created system will continue to apply.

One problem raised by the statutory recognition of the putative marriage relationship involves spousal support claims. Family Code Section 2254 now provides for temporary and permanent support of a putative spouse. Case law had previously permitted restitutional recovery by a putative spouse for certain services rendered during the relationship.[20] The impact of this statute, if any, on an action for restitution is not clear.[21]

The equitable community property system was created to protect a person who entered into a marital relationship with a good faith belief that a marriage existed. It did not apply to a meretricious relationship.[22]

---

13. See: West's Ann.Cal.Civil Code, §§ 5118 and 5119; Randolph v. Randolph, 118 Cal.App.2d 584, 258 P.2d 547 (1953); Ottinger v. Ottinger, 141 Cal.App.2d 220, 296 P.2d 347 (1956).

14. Coats v. Coats, reprinted in this Section.

15. Estate of Leslie, reprinted in this Section.

16. Adduddell v. Board of Adm. Pub. Emp. Retirement System, 8 Cal.App.3d 243, 87 Cal.Rptr. 268 (1970); but see Allen v. Western Conference of Teamsters Pension Trust Fund, 788 F.2d 648 (9th Cir.1986).

17. Brennfleck v. Workmen's Compensation App. Board, 3 Cal.App.3d 666, 84 Cal.Rptr. 50 (1970).

18. Aubrey v. Folsom, 151 F.Supp. 836 (N.D.Cal.1957).

19. Kunakoff v. Woods, 166 Cal.App.2d 59, 332 P.2d 773 (1958).

20. Sanguinetti v. Sanguinetti, 9 Cal.2d 95, 69 P.2d 845 (1937); Lazzarevich v. Lazzarevich, 88 Cal.App.2d 708, 200 P.2d 49 (1949).

21. It has been argued that the statutory provision precludes a quasi-contractual recovery for services. See Luther and Luther, Support and Property Rights of the Putative Spouse, 24 Hastings L.J. 311 (1973). Such a contention seems inconsistent with the general principle against repeal of established doctrines by implication and with inferences from the language of the opinion in the Marvin case. The Supreme Court considered both the cases concerning restitutional recovery for rendered services and the alimony statute without mentioning any potential conflict between them.

22. See Vallera v. Vallera reprinted in this Section.

After the enactment of the Family Law Act which eliminated any consideration of fault in dissolution cases, and with an increasing social acceptance of non-marital cohabitation relationships, doubts developed as to whether a good faith belief in the existence of a marriage would continue to be a requisite for the application of quasi-marital property principles. The California Supreme Court in Marvin v. Marvin settled the question by expressly holding that the equitable system applied only to relationships based on such a good faith belief.[23] The court also made clear, however, that contractual and restitutional principles should be liberally applied to property claims between persons living in meretricious relationships.[24]

WEST'S ANNOTATED CALIFORNIA FAMILY CODE

§ 300. Consent; issuance of license and solemnization

Marriage is a personal relation arising out of a civil contract between a man and a woman, to which the consent of the parties capable of making that contract is necessary. Consent alone does not constitute marriage. Consent must be followed by the issuance of a license and solemnization as authorized by this division, except as provided by Section 425 and Part 4 (commencing with Section 500).

§ 301. Adults; capability to consent to and consummate marriage

An unmarried male of the age of 18 years or older, and an unmarried female of the age of 18 years or older, and not otherwise disqualified, are capable of consenting to and consummating marriage.

(Stats.1992, c. 162 (A.B. 2650), § 10, operative Jan. 1, 1994.)

§ 305. Proof of consent and solemnization

Consent to and solemnization of marriage may be proved under the same general rules of evidence as facts are proved in other cases.

(Stats.1992, c. 162 (A.B. 2650), § 10, operative Jan. 1, 1994.)

§ 2200. Incestuous marriages

Marriages between parents and children, ancestors and descendants of every degree, and between brothers and sisters of the half as well as the whole blood, and between uncles and nieces or aunts and nephews, are incestuous, and void from the beginning, whether the relationship is legitimate or illegitimate.

(Stats.1992, c. 162 (A.B. 2650), § 10, operative Jan. 1, 1994.)

§ 2201. Bigamous and polygamous marriages; exceptions; absentees

(a) A subsequent marriage contracted by a person during the life of a former husband or wife of the person, with a person other than the former husband or wife, is illegal and void from the beginning, unless:

23. Marvin v. Marvin, 18 Cal.3d 660, 134 Cal.Rptr. 815, 557 P.2d 106 (1976), reprinted in this Section.

24. This ruling was foreshadowed by the dissenting opinions in Vallera v. Vallera, reprinted in this Section, and Keene v. Keene 57 Cal.2d 657, 21 Cal.Rptr. 593, 371 P.2d 329 (1962).

(1) The former marriage has been dissolved or adjudged a nullity before the date of the subsequent marriage.

(2) The former husband or wife (i) is absent, and not known to the person to be living for the period of five successive years immediately preceding the subsequent marriage, or (ii) is generally reputed or believed by the person to be dead at the time the subsequent marriage was contracted.

(b) In either of the cases described in paragraph (2) of subdivision (a), the subsequent marriage is valid until its nullity is adjudged pursuant to subdivision (b) of Section 2210.

(Stats.1992, c. 162 (A.B. 2650), § 10, operative Jan. 1, 1994.)

§ 2210. Annulment, causes for

A marriage is voidable and may be adjudged a nullity if any of the following conditions existed at the time of the marriage:

(a) The party who commences the proceeding or on whose behalf the proceeding is commenced was without the capability of consenting to the marriage as provided in Section 301 or 302, unless, after attaining the age of consent, the party for any time freely cohabited with the other as husband and wife.

(b) The husband or wife of either party was living and the marriage with that husband or wife was then in force and that husband or wife (1) was absent and not known to the party commencing the proceeding to be living for a period of five successive years immediately preceding the subsequent marriage for which the judgment of nullity is sought or (2) was generally reputed or believed by the party commencing the proceeding to be dead at the time the subsequent marriage was contracted.

(c) Either party was of unsound mind, unless the party of unsound mind, after coming to reason, freely cohabited with the other as husband and wife.

(d) The consent of either party was obtained by fraud, unless the party whose consent was obtained by fraud afterwards, with full knowledge of the facts constituting the fraud, freely cohabited with the other as husband or wife.

(e) The consent of either party was obtained by force, unless the party whose consent was obtained by force afterwards freely cohabited with the other as husband or wife.

(f) Either party was, at the time of marriage, physically incapable of entering into the marriage state, and that incapacity continues, and appears to be incurable.

(Stats.1992, c. 162 (A.B. 2650), § 10, operative Jan. 1, 1994.)

§ 2251. Status of putative spouse; division of community or quasi-community property

(a) If a determination is made that a marriage is void or voidable and the court finds that either party or both parties believed in good faith that the marriage was valid, the court shall:

(1) Declare the party or parties to have the status of a putative spouse.

(2) If the division of property is in issue, divide, in accordance with Division 7 (commencing with Section 2500), that property acquired during the union which would have been community property or quasi-community property if the union had not been void or voidable. This property is known as "quasi-marital property".

(b) If the court expressly reserves jurisdiction, it may make the property division at a time after the judgment.

(Stats.1992, c. 162 (A.B. 2650), § 10, operative Jan. 1, 1994.)

§ 2252. Liability of quasi-marital property for debts of parties

The property divided pursuant to Section 2251 is liable for debts of the parties to the same extent as if the property had been community property or quasi-community property.

(Stats.1992, c. 162 (A.B. 2650), § 10, operative Jan. 1, 1994.)

§ 2254. Order for support; putative spouse

The court may, during the pendency of a proceeding for nullity of marriage or upon judgment of nullity of marriage, order a party to pay for the support of the other party in the same manner as if the marriage had not been void or voidable if the party for whose benefit the order is made is found to be a putative spouse.

(Stats.1992, c. 162 (A.B. 2650), § 10, operative Jan. 1, 1994.)

§ 2255. Attorney's fees and costs

The court may grant attorney's fees and costs in accordance with Part 5 (commencing with Section 270) of Division 2 in proceedings to have the marriage adjudged void and in those proceedings based upon voidable marriage in which the party applying for attorney's fees and costs is found to be innocent of fraud or wrongdoing in inducing or entering into the marriage, and free from knowledge of the then existence of any prior marriage or other impediment to the contracting of the marriage for which a judgment of nullity is sought.

(Stats.1992, c. 162 (A.B. 2650), § 10, operative Jan. 1, 1994.)

COATS v. COATS

Supreme Court of California, 1911.
160 Cal. 671, 118 P. 441, 36 L.R.A., N.S., 844.

SLOSS, J. The plaintiff and the defendant intermarried in November, 1887. In January, 1906, the defendant, Lee B. Coats, obtained a judgment annulling the marriage, on the ground of the physical incapacity of the plaintiff, Ida H. Coats. After such judgment had become final, this action was commenced to obtain a division of the property which had been accumulated by the parties during the existence of the marriage. The court below gave the plaintiff judgment for $10,000. From this judgment, the defendant appeals. The appeal is taken on the judgment roll alone.

The findings are as follows:

[The court's statement of the findings follows in summary form: Plaintiff, in good faith belief of her physical capacity to enter into marriage, married the defendant in 1887. She continued in good faith in that belief for the full eighteen years of the marriage relationship. From 1887 to 1900 defendant engaged in farming operations and plaintiff rendered the normal services of a farmer's wife in maintaining the home, cooking for farm employees and assisting in the farming operations. In

1897 defendant entered into a partnership business in the buying and selling of horses. During the period from 1887 to 1900 substantial wealth was accumulated by defendant but by 1900 this was all lost except for a $2500 interest in the partnership business. From 1901 to the annulment of the marriage in 1906, plaintiff and defendant lived in hotels and apartments with plaintiff performing the normal services of a wife. During this period from a monetary point of view her services were of no pecuniary value in the accumulation of wealth by the defendant. At the time of the annulment defendant possessed assets of about $70,000 value, the product of the $2500 partnership interest above mentioned and his business skills. The trial court decreed that equitably plaintiff was entitled to a $10,000 share of this wealth.]

Passing, for the moment, the consideration of certain subsidiary problems which arise on the particular facts found, this appeal presents for determination, primarily, the question whether a woman, who has in good faith entered into a marriage which may be avoided at the instance of the other party, is entitled, upon or after annulment, to any participation in the property which has been accumulated by the efforts of both parties during the existence of the supposed marriage, and while she in good faith believed that such marriage was valid. The mere statement of the question would seem to be sufficient to require an answer in the affirmative. To say that the woman in such case, even though she may be penniless and unable to earn a living, is to receive nothing, while the man with whom she lived and labored in the belief that she was his wife, shall take and hold whatever he and she have acquired, would be contrary to the most elementary conceptions of fairness and justice. This marriage was not void in the extreme sense. Estate of Gregorson, 116 Pac. 60. The defendant had the right to attack it, and to have it annulled, but, in the absence of such attack, it was good as against everybody. Third parties could not question its validity in any way, and even the husband himself was bound by it, until and unless he undertook to set it aside by means of an action for annulment.

The argument of appellant in this connection is that, while a voidable marriage is valid, unless annulled, yet, where there has been a decree of annulment, the decree determines that no marriage ever existed, and renders it void ab initio. Accordingly, upon the making of the decree, the children become illegitimate (except for statutory provisions, like section 84 of our Civil Code), and property rights of either party in so far as they depend upon marriage, are at an end. There is ample authority supporting the proposition that the effect of a decree of nullity is to declare that the marriage was void from the beginning. 2 Nelson, Div. & Sep. § 566; 1 Bish.Mar., Div. & Sep. §§ 259, 277, 1596; 26 Cyc. 919, 920; 19 A. & E.Enc.L. 1220; Matter of Eichhoff, 101 Cal. 600, 36 P. 11; Chase v. Chase, 55 Me. 21. So, too, it is generally held that when a marriage is annulled property rights dependent upon the existence of the marriage, such as dower and curtesy, are terminated and annulled. 19 A. & E.Enc.L. 1221; Chase v. Chase, supra; Price v. Price, 124 N.Y. 589, 27 N.E. 383, 12 L.R.A. 359. But these decisions, and others cited by the appellant, deal with the rights of one of the parties in property owned by the other. An interest in such property, dependent solely upon marriage, cannot exist after an adjudication that there has been no marriage. If, as is suggested by the appellant, the annulment is to be treated as analogous to a rescission, it should properly enough be accompanied by a restoration to the parties of what they respectively had before marriage, and what they would have had in the absence of a marriage.

Here, however, the question is a different one. The controversy is, not over the property owned by the defendant prior to marriage, or acquired by him alone thereafter, but has to do with the acquisitions of the two parties after marriage, and before annulment. If both have contributed to such acquisitions, each has an interest which did not exist at the time of the marriage. The status quo could not be restored upon annulment, without making some provision for the equitable division of this property. In the absence of fraud or other ground affecting the right to claim relief, there can be no good reason for saying that either party should by reason of the annulment, be vested with title to all of the property acquired during the existence of the supposed marriage.

* * * Even though it may be true that, strictly speaking, there is no "community property" where there has not been a valid marriage (Chapman v. Chapman, 11 Tex.Civ.App. 392, 32 S.W. 564; see 68 Am.St.Rep. p. 376, note), the courts may well, in dividing gains made by the joint efforts of a man and a woman living together under a voidable marriage which is subsequently annulled, apply, by analogy, the rules which would obtain with regard to community property, where a valid marriage is terminated by death of the husband or by divorce. The apportionment of such property between the parties is not provided by any statute. It must therefore be made on equitable principles. In the absence of special circumstances, such as might arise through intervening claims of third persons, we can conceive of no more equitable basis of apportionment than an equal division. Until the making of the annulment decree, the marriage was valid, and the property in question was impressed with the community character. Upon annulment, such property, even though it be no longer community property, should be divided as community property would have been upon a dissolution of the marriage by divorce or the death of the husband.

If these views be sound, it is entirely immaterial that the bulk of the property was acquired between the years 1900 and 1906, and that the plaintiff's services in its accumulation were "of no monetary value." She is not suing to recover for services rendered under a contract for labor, nor to establish the value of her interest in a business partnership. What she did, she did as a wife, and her share of the joint accumulations must be measured by what a wife would receive out of community property on the termination of the marriage. "The law will not inquire * * * whether the acquisition was by the joint efforts of the husband and wife, or attempt to adjust their respective rights in proportion to the amount each contributed thereto. The law will not concern itself with such an inquiry, but will leave the parties to share in the property in the same proportion as though the marriage contract was what the wife had every reason to believe it to be, i.e., a valid marriage." F.W. & R.G.R. Co. v. Robertson, supra. If then, the facts would have justified an allotment to the wife of one-half of the property acquired by the parties, there can be no complaint of the allowance of $10,000 which was much less than one-half.

The judgment is affirmed.

Notes

1. The equitable community doctrine developed in *Coats v. Coats* was subsequently applied to a void, as contrasted with a voidable, putative marriage. Schneider v. Schneider, 183 Cal. 335, 191 P. 533, 11 A.L.R. 1386 (1920).

2. Note that in defining the property rights of a putative spouse, the court in *Coats* stressed the essentially equitable character of the doctrine, and cautioned that it should not be applied where an injustice would result, particularly where its application would deprive third persons of vested property rights. Aside from this qualification, the division of equitable community property (now labeled quasi-marital property) is analogous to the division of legal community property. For example, in Estate of Krone, 83 Cal.App.2d 766, 189 P.2d 741 (1948), the court held that the putative spouse received all of the equitable community property on the death of her ostensible husband intestate. Presumably, only one-half of the quasi-marital property would be subject to testamentary disposition by a person in a putative marriage relationship. West's Ann.Cal.Code § 2251, governing division of quasi-marital property on annulment of the putative marriage, mandates that it be treated in the same fashion as community property.

3. *Coats v. Coats* and *Estate of Krone* dealt only with the earnings and accumulations arising during the putative relationship, i.e., the equitable community property or quasi-marital property. Should the putative spouse be accorded the rights of a spouse with respect to other types of property or claims? Suppose that one party to the putative marriage dies intestate, leaving substantial separate property in addition to quasi-marital property. Should the survivor receive the same intestate share of such separate property that a surviving spouse would receive? Consider *Estate of Leslie*, reprinted below.

4. A good faith belief in the validity of the marriage relationship is a requisite to the operation of the quasi-marital property system. It has been stated that the term "good faith belief" is a legal term of art, and must be tested by an objective standard. A proper assertion of putative spouse status must rest on facts that would cause a reasonable person to harbor a good faith belief in the existence of a valid marriage. See Marriage of Vryonis, 202 Cal.App.3d 712, 248 Cal.Rptr. 807 (1988), indicating that attempted solemnization is a "major factor to be considered in the calculus of good faith." Could this requirement be fulfilled by a good faith belief in the invalidity of a divorce? In the case of In re Marriage of Monti, 135 Cal.App.3d 50, 185 Cal.Rptr. 72 (1982), the parties entered into a valid marriage. Two years later they were divorced, and a final decree was

entered. While the divorce proceedings were pending, the parties reconciled and lived together for some eleven years. In 1981 the "wife" filed for dissolution, and then discovered that she was not legally married. The appellate court held that she was a putative spouse. She had relied on her former husband's statement that the pending divorce would not become final unless he appeared in court, and hence believed that a second marriage was unnecessary because she was his lawful wife. She therefore had a good faith belief that a valid marriage existed. See also Lazzarevich v. Lazzarevich, 88 Cal.App.2d 708, 200 P.2d 49 (1948).

ESTATE OF LESLIE
Supreme Court of California, 1984.
37 Cal.3d 186, 207 Cal.Rptr. 561, 689 P.2d 133.

BIRD, CHIEF JUSTICE.

Is a surviving putative spouse entitled to succeed to a share of his or her decedent's separate property under the Probate Code?

On April 22, 1972, William Garvin and Fay Reah Leslie were married in Tijuana, Mexico. The marriage was invalid because it was never recorded as required by Mexican law. However, Garvin believed that he and Leslie were validly married. The couple lived together as husband and wife for almost nine years, until Leslie's death in 1981. Throughout this period, they resided in a house in Mira Loma. The house had been purchased by Leslie, Mike Bosnich, her former husband, and respondent Alton B. Smith, a son from a prior marriage who lived next door. This case concerns the administration and distribution of Leslie's estate.

* * *

On February 6, 1981, Leslie died intestate. She was survived by Garvin, her son Smith, and three other adult children from a prior marriage.

Smith filed a petition for letters of administration in the estate of his deceased mother. Garvin objected to Smith's petition, filed his own petition for letters of administration, and sought a determination as to who was entitled to distribution of the estate.

* * *

In January 1982, a court trial was held to determine the appointment of the administrator and the distribution of the property in the estate. The trial court found that a putative marriage had existed between Garvin and Leslie, denied Garvin's petition for letters of administration, and determined that he was not entitled to any of decedent's separate property. The court also found that some of the property was quasi-marital and some was separate.

* * *

The principal issue presented by this case is whether a putative spouse is entitled to succeed to a share of his or her decedent's separate property. Although this court has not directly confronted this question, the conclusions of other courts on this and analogous questions are instructive.

* * *

A number of Court of Appeal decisions support the conclusion that a putative spouse is entitled to succeed to a share of the decedent's separate property. *Estate of Goldberg* (1962) 203 Cal.App.2d 402, 21 Cal.Rptr. 626, is one such case. Sam Goldberg died intestate, survived by Edith, his putative spouse, and three children from a prior marriage. The trial court found that Edith was both Sam's actual and putative spouse. She was awarded all of the community property as well as one-third of Sam's separate property. The other two-thirds of the separate property was awarded to Sam's children. (*Id.,* 203 Cal.App.2d at p. 404, 21 Cal.Rptr. 626; see § 221, *ante,* fn. 6.) The children appealed.

The Court of Appeal agreed with the trial court's finding that there was insufficient evidence that Edith was Sam's actual wife, but sufficient evidence that she was Sam's putative wife. (203 Cal.App.2d at pp. 411–412, 21 Cal.Rptr. 626.) As a putative spouse, Edith was entitled "to the same share of the 'community' property as she would receive as an actual wife." (*Id.,* 203 Cal.App.2d at p. 412, 21 Cal.Rptr. 626.)

Although the *Goldberg* court was silent on the question of Edith's right as a putative spouse to succeed to Sam's *separate* property, the court did affirm the trial court's award of one-third of that property to Edith. By such action, the Court of Appeal implicitly recognized the right of a surviving putative spouse to an intestate share of the decedent's separate property.

Similarly in *Garrado v. Collins* (1955) 136 Cal.App.2d 323, 288 P.2d 620, the trial court awarded the putative husband one-third of the decedent's separate property. The decedent's two children from a previous marriage appealed, arguing that the putative husband was not entitled to any of the separate property. (*Id.,* 136 Cal.App.2d at pp. 324–325, 288 P.2d 620.)

The Court of Appeal did not reach the merits of the trial court's award. Instead, it held that the children lacked standing as aggrieved parties and dismissed the appeal. (136 Cal.App.2d at pp. 325–326, 288 P.2d 620.) In dictum, the court noted that the children could not inherit the separate property at issue because that property would descend either to the legal husband, who was still living, or to the surviving putative husband. (*Ibid.*) That observation is significant, since the court recognized the possibility that the putative husband may have been awarded the "surviving spouse's" share of the separate property even as against the legal husband.

Finally, there is *Estate of Shank* (1957) 154 Cal.App.2d 808, 316 P.2d 710. Claire Shank married her legal husband in 1944, then obtained a Mexican divorce, and subsequently married her putative husband. In 1953, she died intestate, leaving an estate consisting entirely of separate property. She was survived by a putative husband, a legal husband, and three adult siblings. (*Id.,* 154 Cal.App.2d at pp. 809–810, 316 P.2d 710.)

The trial court found that the Mexican divorce was invalid and awarded all the separate property to the siblings. The court also found that the legal husband had acquiesced in and relied upon the Mexican divorce and had conducted himself as if that decree were valid. He was, therefore, estopped from asserting that he was the surviving spouse for the purpose of inheriting the decedent's separate property. In addition, the trial court found that the decedent's marriage to her putative husband was invalid because she was still married to her legal husband at the time of the second "marriage." (154 Cal.App.2d at pp. 810–811, 316 P.2d 710.) Both the legal and putative husbands appealed. (*Id.,* 154 Cal.App.2d at p. 811, 316 P.2d 710.)

The Court of Appeal affirmed the award as to the legal husband, concluding that as against the putative husband, the former was estopped from contending that the divorce was invalid. (154 Cal.App.2d at pp. 811–812, 316 P.2d 710.) However, the court concluded that the putative husband was entitled to one-half of the separate property. Since the decedent was estopped from denying the validity of the Mexican divorce during her life as against the putative husband, her heirs, in privity with her, were also estopped. The court noted that a second marriage is presumed to be valid. (*Id.,* 154 Cal.App.2d at p. 812, 316 P.2d 710.) Although the result in *Shank* rests on estoppel principles, it provides yet another example of a putative spouse who was permitted to succeed to a share of the decedent's separate property.

In many analogous contexts, California courts, as well as federal courts applying California law, have accorded surviving putative spouses the same rights as surviving legal spouses. Examples abound.

In *Kunakoff v. Woods, supra,* 166 Cal.App.2d 59, 67–68, 332 P.2d 773, a surviving putative spouse was held to be an heir for the purposes of Code of Civil Procedure section 377. As such, she was entitled to bring an action for the wrongful death of her deceased partner. The Court of Appeal noted that the term "spouse" may include a putative spouse. (*Kunakoff v. Woods, supra,* 166 Cal.App.2d at p. 63, 332 P.2d 59.) The court reasoned that since a putative spouse is an heir for purposes of succession, she is an heir for purposes of maintaining an action for wrongful death. (*Id.,* 166 Cal.App.2d at pp. 67–68, 332 P.2d 773.)

A surviving putative spouse has also been held to be a surviving spouse within the meaning of Government Code section 21364. (*Adduddell v. Board of Administration, supra,* 8 Cal.App.3d 243, 87 Cal.Rptr. 268.) That statute entitles a surviving spouse to special death benefits under the Public Employees' Retirement Law. In *Adduddell,* the court indicated that it would be "illogical and inconsistent" for the Legislature to intend that a putative spouse is a surviving spouse under section 201, but not a surviving spouse under Government Code section 21364. (8 Cal.App.3d at pp. 249–250, 87 Cal.Rptr. 268.)

A surviving putative spouse has also been held to be a "surviving widow" within the meaning of a former version of Labor Code section 4702 (Stats.1969, ch. 65, § 1, p. 187), and thus entitled to recovery of workers' compensation death benefits. (*Brennfleck v. Workmen's Comp. App. Bd., supra,* 3 Cal.App.3d 666, 84 Cal.Rptr. 50; see also *Neureither v. Workmen's Comp. App. Bd.* (1971) 15 Cal.App.3d 429, 433, 93 Cal. Rptr. 162.)

Finally, it is noteworthy that putative spouses have been awarded spousal benefits under the civil service retirement statute (5 U.S.C. § 8341, *Brown v. Devine* (N.D.Cal.1983) 574 F.Supp. 790, 792), under the Longshoremen's and Harbor Workers' Compensation Act (33 U.S.C. § 901 et seq., *Powell v. Rogers* (9th Cir.1974) 496 F.2d 1248, 1250, cert. den., 419 U.S. 1032, 95 S.Ct. 514, 42 L.Ed.2d 307; *Holland America Insurance Company v. Rogers* (N.D.Cal.1970) 313 F.Supp. 314, 317–318), and under the Social Security Act (42 U.S.C. § 416, *Aubrey v. Folsom* (N.D.Cal.1957) 151 F.Supp. 836, 840; *Speedling v. Hobby* (N.D.Cal.1955) 132 F.Supp. 833, 836).

The foregoing authority compels but one conclusion: a surviving putative spouse is entitled to succeed to a share of his or her decedent's separate property.[11] This result is inherently fair. By definition, a putative marriage is a union in which at least one partner believes in good faith that a valid marriage exists. As in this case, the couple conducts themselves as husband and wife throughout the period of their union. Why should the right to separate property accorded to legal spouses be denied to putative spouses?

Further, to deny a putative spouse the status of surviving spouse for the purposes of succeeding to a share of the decedent's separate property would lead to anomalous and unjust results. For example, where the decedent is survived by a putative spouse and children of the putative marriage, such a rule would deny the spouse succession rights to separate property even though the children are accorded such rights.[12] Such a rule would also deny succession rights to a putative spouse who lived with the decedent for many years, while according these rights to the legal spouse, even if that spouse's partner died the day the couple were married. (Laughran & Laughran, *Property and Inheritance Rights of Putative Spouses in California: Selected Problems and Suggested Solutions* (1977) 11 Loyola L.A.L.Rev. 45, 68.) Surely, the Legislature never intended such results.

---

11. There may be cases in which two or more surviving spouses each claim an intestate share of the decedent's separate property. However, that scenario is not before this court and need not be resolved at this time.

12. By statute, children of a putative marriage possess the right of intestate succession to the separate property of their deceased parents. (See § 255; Civ.Code, § 7002.)

There is one Court of Appeal decision which has reached a conclusion contrary to that reached by this court today. That decision must therefore be addressed. *In Estate of Levie* (1975) 50 Cal.App.3d 572, 123 Cal.Rptr. 445, the trial court awarded the putative spouse all of the quasi-marital property as well as an intestate share of the decedent's separate property. (*Id.,* 50 Cal.App.3d at p. 574, 123 Cal.Rptr. 445.) One of the decedent's children from a prior marriage appealed. The Court of Appeal reversed the separate property determination, rejecting the argument that a putative spouse is entitled to a surviving spouse's share of the decedent's separate property. (*Id.,* 50 Cal.App.3d at pp. 576–577, 123 Cal.Rptr. 445.)

The *Levie* court articulated three reasons in support of its holding. First, it noted that there appeared to be no California decision suggesting that a putative spouse is entitled to succeed to an interest in the decedent's separate property. Second, it declared that the equities connected with quasi-marital property do not apply to a decedent's separate property because the joint efforts of the putative spouses did not contribute to the acquisition of that property. Lastly, the court observed that to give the putative spouse an interest in a decedent's separate property would "unjustifiably disregard the statutory scheme governing intestate succession of separate property." (50 Cal.App.3d at pp. 576–577, 123 Cal.Rptr. 445.)

Levie has been severely criticized by the commentators and for good reasons. (See, e.g., Laughran & Laughran, *op. cit. supra,* 11 Loyola L.A.L.Rev. at pp. 64, 66–68, 78, 85; Bruch, *The Definition and Division of Marital Property in California: Towards Parity and Simplicity* (1982) 33 Hastings L.J. 771, 825, fn. 224; Reppy, *Debt Collection from Married Californians: Problems Caused by Transmutations, Single–Spouse Management, and Invalid Marriage* (1981) 18 San Diego L.Rev. 143, 218, fn. 283.) Not only are the *Levie* court's reasons unpersuasive, but its conclusion leads to anomalous, absurd and unjust results.

Levie's first reason is plainly in error. Numerous California decisions *have* suggested that a putative spouse is entitled to succeed to a share of a decedent's separate property. (See *ante,* at pp. 566–567 of 207 Cal.Rptr., pp. 138–139 of 689 P.2d.) For example, the result in *Estate of Krone, supra,* 83 Cal.App.2d 766, 189 P.2d 741 (*ante,* at pp. 565–566 of 207 Cal.Rptr., pp. 137–138 of 689 P.2d) suggests that a putative spouse should also be considered a surviving spouse for purposes of other sections in the same division of the Probate Code. Moreover, a surviving putative spouse has been accorded the same rights as a surviving legal spouse in many analogous contexts. (See *ante,* at pp. 567–568, of 207 Cal.Rptr., pp. 139–140 of 689 P.2d.) Clearly, *Levie's* first reason is without basis in fact.

Equally unpersuasive are the other two reasons given in *Levie.* Two commentators have aptly addressed these reasons in their article concerning the rights of putative spouses. (See Laughran & Laughran, *op. cit. supra,* 11 Loyola L.A.L.Rev. at pp. 66–68.) As the Laughrans observe, "[w]hile it is true that the joint efforts of putative spouses do not contribute to the acquisition of separate property, it is equally true that the efforts of a legally married person do not contribute to the acquisition of separate property of the other spouse. It therefore begs the question to state that the 'equities' of a putative spouse differ depending upon whether rights of succession to quasi-marital or separate property are at issue, since the same distinction applies to the 'equities' of a legally married person with respect to rights of succession to community and separate property. Thus, as to rights of intestate succession to separate property of the decedent, the 'equitable' position of a surviving legal spouse and a surviving putative spouse is the same." (*Id.,* at p. 67.)

Further, language within the *Levie* opinion contradicts its ultimate conclusion. *Levie* stated that a putative spouse's right to succeed to quasi-marital property is derived from " '[e]quitable considerations arising from the reasonable expectation of the continuation of benefits attending the status of marriage entered into in good faith * * *.' [Citations.]" (50 Cal.App.3d at p. 576, 123 Cal.Rptr. 445.) As the Laughrans convincingly assert, "[t]hat very language dictates a decision in favor of the surviving putative spouse in cases involving succession to *separate* property, since the rights of a 'surviving spouse' [to succeed to separate property under the Probate Code] are 'benefits attending the status of marriage.' " (Laughran & Laughran, *op. cit. supra,* 11 Loyola L.A.L.Rev. at p. 67, italics added.)

To accord a surviving putative spouse rights to the decedent's separate property honors rather than disregards the statutory scheme governing intestate succession. (Laughran & Laughran, *op. cit. supra,* 11 Loyola L.A.L.Rev. at p. 67; but see *Levie, supra,* 50 Cal.App.3d at p. 577, 123 Cal.Rptr. 445.) Since the right to succession is not an inherent or natural right, but purely a creature of statute (*Estate of Simmons* (1966) 64 Cal.2d 217, 221, 49 Cal.Rptr. 369, 411 P.2d 97), a surviving legal spouse inherits a decedent's separate property "only because the statutes provide that a person having the status of 'surviving spouse' takes a certain share." (Laughran & Laughran, *op. cit. supra,* 11 Loyola L.A.L.Rev. at p. 67.) To accord a surviving putative spouse the status of "surviving spouse" simply recognizes that a good faith belief in the marriage should put the putative spouse in the same position as a survivor of a legal marriage. (*Id.,* at p. 68.) Thus, contrary to *Levie,* to permit a surviving putative spouse to succeed to a share of the decedent's separate property in no way upsets the statutory scheme of intestate succession.

Levie is "wrong in its analysis of the 'equities,' wrong as a matter of statutory construction, and * * * ignores compelling analogous precedents." (Laughran & Laughran, *op. cit. supra,* 11 Loyola L.A.L.Rev. at p. 78.) Therefore, to the extent that it is inconsistent with this opinion, *Levie* is disapproved.

* * *

Virtually every court which has considered the issue has accorded a surviving putative spouse the same rights as a surviving legal spouse. The one court which has decided against such benefits did so in a poorly reasoned and unsound decision. Moreover, as in most putative spouse cases, the couple involved here lived together for a substantial period of time, conducting themselves as husband and wife throughout their union. To deny one of their members an intestate share of the decedent's separate property while permitting him to succeed to the quasi-marital property defies logic and leads to unjust results. Therefore, this court holds that a surviving putative spouse is entitled to succeed to a share of the decedent's separate property. Similar reasoning supports the conclusion that a surviving putative spouse is entitled to first preference for letters of administration.

Accordingly, the portion of the trial court's judgment denying Garvin an interest in decedent's separate property and letters of administration in decedent's estate is reversed. In all other respects, the judgment is affirmed.

MOSK, KAUS, BROUSSARD, REYNOSO, GRODIN and LUCAS, JJ., concur.

Notes

1. On occasion the putative spouse situation is complicated by the presence of a legal spouse. For example, in Estate of Vargas, 36 Cal.App.3d 714, 111 Cal.Rptr. 779 (1974), Juan Vargas lived a double life as a husband and father to two different families, neither of which knew of the other's existence. This "terrestrial paradise" lasted for 24 years, ending only when Juan died intestate. Both "spouses" asserted the right to succeed to Juan's estate as his surviving spouse. The appellate court upheld the trial court's decision to divide the estate equally between the legal and putative spouses, concluding:

> In the present case, depending on which statute or legal theory is applied, both Mildred, as legal spouse, and Josephine, as putative spouse, have valid or plausible claims to at least half, perhaps three-quarters, possibly all, of Juan's estate. The court found that both wives contributed in indeterminable amounts and proportions to the accumulations of the community. (Vallera v. Vallera, 21 Cal.2d 681, 683, 134 P.2d 761.) Since statutes and judicial decisions provide no sure guidance for the resolution of the controversy, the probate court cut the Gordian knot of competing claims and divided the estate equally between the two wives, presumably on the theory that innocent wives of practicing bigamists are entitled to equal shares of property accumulated during the active phase of the bigamy. No injury has been visited upon third parties, and the wisdom of Solomon is not required to perceive the justice of the result.

2. In the *Leslie* case, the California Supreme Court recognized that "there may be cases in which two or more surviving spouses each claim an intestate share of the decedent's separate property," but indicated that that particular scenario was not before them and therefore need not be resolved. Such a scenario was presented in Estate of Hafner, reprinted in this Section.

3.   For a case of overlapping relationships but involving successive and therefore not conflicting claims, see Patillo v. Norris, 65 Cal.App.3d 209, 135 Cal.Rptr. 210 (1976).

ESTATE OF HAFNER
California District Court of Appeal, 1986.
184 Cal.App.3d 1371, 229 Cal.Rptr. 676.

DANIELSON, ASSOCIATE JUSTICE.

* * *

FACTUAL BACKGROUND AND PROCEEDINGS BELOW

Joan Hafner (Joan) and the decedent Charles J. Hafner (Charles) were married on June 12, 1954, in the State of New York; it was the first marriage for each of them.   Following their marriage they took up residence in College Point, New York.   Joan has continued to live in or near College Point ever since.   The marriage between Joan and Charles produced three daughters, all of whom are now living: Catherine Kotsay, born December 25, 1955; Lillian Mayorga, born November 18, 1956; and Dorothy Hafner, born November 16, 1957.

In February or March of 1956 Joan learned that she was pregnant with her second child and told Charles.   In April or May of 1956 Charles left Joan, without prior notice and without letting her know where he would be.   At that time their first child, Catherine, was sick and Joan moved back to her parents, who supported her; she received no support from Charles.

Joan and Charles were reunited briefly in early 1957.   Charles left Joan for the last time in February 1957.   Joan, then pregnant with their third child, encountered Charles on the street in New York in May 1957. He told her, "I hear you are going to have another baby", and asked her whether she would like to go to California.   Joan replied, "What guarantees would I have that you won't leave me pregnant again?"   Charles replied, "There's no guarantees."

In 1956 and 1958, Joan filed support proceedings against Charles in the New York family court.   In 1956, she obtained a $12 per week child support order and in 1958 she obtained a similar order for $20 per week. Charles made four support payments in 1958 but never made any other payments.   In 1958, Joan consulted an attorney in New York on the support matters, but, because of the expense required to locate Charles in California, she did not pursue the matter.   In 1961, Joan abandoned any further efforts to obtain support warrants in the New York family court because such efforts caused her to lose time on her job.

Joan last saw Charles in the New York family court in 1958 when he was brought before the court on a support warrant.   Shortly after that appearance, an acquaintance told Joan that Charles had gone to California.   From 1958 until his death in 1982, Joan and Charles never saw or communicated with each other again. Joan knew that Charles was in California but did not know where in California.

Beginning in 1961, and continuously thereafter, Joan considered her marriage to Charles for all practicable purposes to have ended and that they would never reconcile or even see each other again.

Except for short intervals to have their babies, Joan was employed at all times following her marriage to Charles, and was so employed at the time of the trial below. She reared the three daughters of herself and decedent.

In August, 1953, shortly after graduating from high school, Joan commenced working at a magazine company and continued until August, 1955, when she left because she was pregnant with her first daughter. In April, 1957, she went to work on the assembly line of a rubber company, on a machine putting snaps on baby pants. Except for a three-month lay-off to have her third baby she stayed on that machine for about 12 years, when the company moved away. She started at the minimum wage and later became a piece worker. After two weeks of unemployment she went to work for a glove manufacturing company, starting as an order picker, filling orders, and later as a stock supervisor, making sure that the orders were picked and sent out. She was still so employed at the time of the trial of the within action and had then been working at the glove factory for 14 and a half years.

Joan never sought a divorce from Charles; it is unclear whether she did not seek a divorce because of religious convictions, the lack of financial resources, or a lack of interest. At no time from their marriage in 1954 until his death on December 25, 1982, did Charles ever file proceedings to dissolve his marriage to Joan. Their marriage was still in full force and effect at the time of Charles' death.

Respondent Helen L. Hafner (Helen) met Charles in 1962 when he was a patron at a beer bar where she was working as a barmaid. Helen had separated from her second husband, Eldon Pomeroy, in November, 1961.

Charles told Helen that he had divorced his wife, Joan, in New York on charges of adultery, that he had three children of that marriage with Joan, and that he had given up an interest in a house in lieu of child support. Charles further stated that the divorce records had been destroyed in a fire in New York. Helen, in good faith, relied on these representations and believed them to be true continuously thereafter; she had no actual knowledge or reasonable grounds to believe otherwise.

In July 1962, Helen and Charles went to Tijuana, Mexico, to enable Helen to obtain a divorce from Pomeroy and to participate in a marriage ceremony with Charles. Both of those objectives were accomplished. Helen, in good faith, believed that both the divorce and marriage were valid. Following their return from Tijuana in 1962, Helen and Charles lived as husband and wife.

Helen's second husband, Pomeroy, was killed in an accident on June 21, 1963. In June 1963, Helen consulted an attorney and was advised that her Mexican divorce from Pomeroy was invalid in California. Following Pomeroy's death Helen and Charles went to Las Vegas, Nevada, and participated in a marriage ceremony. After that marriage ceremony, on October 14, 1963, Helen and Charles returned to the Los Angeles area where they lived and held themselves out as husband and wife until Charles' death. They had one child, Kimberly Hafner, born December 10, 1964.[5]

On September 27, 1973, Charles was seriously injured in an automobile accident which left him with permanent physical disabilities and brain damage that rendered him incapable of employment.[6] During the nine months in the hospital and his subsequent recovery period, Helen faithfully attended to his needs as his wife and continued to do so for some nine years until his death.

Charles and Helen accumulated approximately $69,000 in hospital and doctor bills as a result of the accident. Those bills were not paid until Charles' personal injury action was settled for $900,000, in 1975, which netted decedent $600,000 after attorney's fees. Helen and her attorney, Charles Weldon, were appointed as Charles' co-conservators in 1975. The personal injury settlement was placed in conservatorship accounts and administered under court supervision. The conservatorship assets were subsequently transferred to Charles' probate administrator following Charles' death.

Charles Hafner died intestate on December 25, 1982, leaving an estate appraised at $416,472.40; his entire probate estate consists of the remainder of the proceeds of his personal injury settlement.

* * *

Helen filed a petition for determination of entitlement to estate (former § 1080), claiming to be the surviving wife of Charles and seeking to have the probate court determine the persons entitled to share in the distribution of Charles' estate.

Appellants (Joan and the three daughters) filed a response to the petition and a statement of interest, asserting their respective claims to a share of Charles' estate, as his surviving spouse and children, pursuant to section 221.

Kimberly Hafner, a child of Charles, also filed a statement of interest in the estate.

Appellants claimed that they, together with Kimberly, should succeed to Charles' entire estate under section 221, and that even if Helen

---

5. Kimberly Hafner filed a "protective" cross-appeal to protect her rights in the event of a reversal or modification of the judgment on appeal.

6. The trial court found that Charles' condition in 1974 was such that he could have communicated with Joan and their children had he desired to do so. Charles and Helen also visited his sister and attended his brother's wedding in San Jose in 1975.

were found to be a good faith putative spouse the court should, under equitable principles, divide the estate among them.

* * *

Helen's petition came on for a nonjury trial on January 12, 1984. Following the conclusion of the trial, the court rendered its statement of decision, on February 1, 1984, in which it concluded that Helen had a legal right to succeed to Charles' entire estate as his surviving spouse under Probate Code section 201. The court also concluded that Helen was Charles' good faith putative spouse and that it would be inequitable to deny her Charles' entire estate.

On February 27, 1984, the court made and entered its judgment determining entitlement to estate distribution and order for family allowance, in accordance with its statement of decision. Appellants and Kimberly Hafner filed timely notices of appeal from that judgment.

CONTENTIONS

Appellants contend that (1) the trial court erred in awarding the entire estate to the putative spouse, Helen, in the absence of an estoppel against the wife, Joan, and Charles' children; (2) the trial court improperly applied equities so as to disinherit the wife and children of the decedent in favor of his putative spouse; and (3) the trial court's decision as to the family allowance was erroneous as a matter of law, and was not supported by the evidence.

DISCUSSION

* * *

The Character of the Property

We must view the character of the property in Charles' intestate estate from the perspectives of the surviving wife and the surviving putative spouse.

(a) From the Perspective of Joan

As to Joan, the entire probate estate was the separate property of Charles, the decedent.

Charles was a married person, married to Joan, and was living separate from her at the time the money was received by him in 1975, pursuant to the settlement of his claim for damages for personal injury.

At the time Charles' personal injury settlement money was received, in 1975, Civil Code section 5126 provided in pertinent part: "(a) All money * * * received by a married person * * * for damages for personal injuries * * * pursuant to an agreement for the settlement or compromise of a claim for such damages is the separate property of the injured person if such money * * * is received * * *: [¶] * * * (2) While either spouse, if he or she is the injured person, is living separate from the other spouse."

Civil Code section 5126 is consonant with Civil Code section 5118 which provides, in pertinent part: "The earnings and accumulations of a spouse * * * while living separate and apart from the other spouse, are the separate property of the spouse."

(b) From the Perspective of Helen

As to Helen, the entire probate estate is quasi-marital property.

The trial court found that Helen was the putative spouse of Charles. At the time of the events of this case, former section 4452 of the Civil Code,[11] a part of The Family Law Act enacted in 1969, provided, in pertinent part: "Whenever a determination is made that a marriage is void or voidable and the court finds that either party or both parties believed in good faith that the marriage was valid, the court shall declare such party or parties to have the status of a putative spouse, and, if the division of property is in issue, shall divide, in accordance with Section 4800, that property acquired during the union which would have been community property or quasi-community property if the union had not been void or voidable. Such property shall be termed 'quasi-marital property.'"[12]

Principles Applicable to Intestate Succession to Quasi-Marital Property of a Void Marriage

It is settled that in the case of a void or voidable marriage, as between a putative spouse and the other spouse, or as between the surviving putative spouse and the heirs of his or her decedent other than the decedent's surviving legal spouse, the putative spouse is entitled to share in the property accumulated by the partners during their void or voidable marriage. It is also settled that the share to which the putative spouse is entitled is the same share of the quasi-marital property as the spouse would receive as an actual and legal spouse if there had been a valid marriage, i.e., it shall be divided equally between the parties. (*Estate of Leslie* (1984) 37 Cal.3d 186, 194, 207 Cal.Rptr. 561, 689 P.2d 133; Civ.Code, §§ 4452, 4800, subd. (a).)

The proportionate contribution of each of the parties to the property acquired during the void or voidable union is immaterial in this state because it is divided as community property would be divided upon the dissolution of a valid marriage. (*Vallera v. Vallera* (1943) 21 Cal.2d 681, 683–684, 134 P.2d 761.)

---

11. Civil Code section 4452 was amended by Statutes 1984, chapter 1671, section 2, page ___, effective January 1, 1985, to provide that the quasi-marital property of an annulled marriage is liable for debts of the parties. The 1984 amendment would have no effect upon the resolution of the issues presented by this case.

12. There can be no community property in the absence of a valid marriage. (Civ. Code, § 687, *Estate of Leslie*, (1984) 37 Cal.3d 186, 193, 207 Cal.Rptr. 561, 689 P.2d 133.) The putative marriage cases decided prior to the enactment of the Family Law Act have struggled with the term to be applied to property which cannot be "community property" since there is no valid marriage but which, otherwise, has all of the incidents of community property. In Civil Code section 4452, our Legislature has resolved this problem by directing that such property be termed "quasi-marital property." It is with considerable relief that we use that term here.

These principles were established by numerous judicial decisions, and were made a part of our positive law by the enactment, in 1969, of Civil Code section 4452, a part of the Family Law Act, effective January 1, 1970. There is no reason to believe that the Legislature, by that enactment, intended to change those principles. (Cf. *Marvin v. Marvin* (1976) 18 Cal.3d 660, 681, 134 Cal.Rptr. 815, 557 P.2d 106.)

The Trial Court Erred in Awarding the Entire Intestate Estate to the Putative Spouse

We have examined the cases cited by the trial court as authorities for its decision and find them wanting. None of the cited cases is authority for a decision on the facts and issues which were before the trial court in the case at bench.

* * *

As Between The Surviving Spouse And Children Of A Decedent And The Decedent's Putative Spouse, The Surviving Spouse And Children Are Entitled To Succeed To The Separate Property In An Intestate Decedent's Estate

We bear in mind that the issue presented in the case at bench is the proper resolution of the competing interests of the legal wife of a decedent, and his putative wife, for succession to his intestate estate.

In *Estate of Leslie* (1984) 37 Cal.3d 186, 207 Cal.Rptr. 561, 689 P.2d 133, our Supreme Court, in deciding a contest between the surviving putative spouse of an intestate decedent and the children of that decedent by a prior marriage, observed that "[t]here may be cases in which two or more surviving spouses each claim an intestate share of the decedent's separate property. However, that scenario is not before this court and need not be resolved at this time." (*Id.*, at p. 197, fn. 11, 207 Cal.Rptr. 561, 689 P.2d 133.) The case at bench is such a case, and we find substantial public policy and precedent to establish and protect the rights of the legal spouse, and the children of the legal community, in the estate of their spouse and parent.

We first note that marriage and the family are highly favored by the public policy of the State of California, as evidenced by statute and by countless decisions of our courts.

In decisions resolving competing claims of legal spouses of decedents and the decedents' putative spouses, as to the right to succeed to the decedent's estate, our courts have awarded one-half of the quasi-marital property to the putative spouse and the rest of the property to the decedent's legal heirs or as disposed of by decedent's will.

In *Estate of Ricci* (1962) 201 Cal.App.2d 146, 19 Cal.Rptr. 739, the contest was between Viola, the first and legal wife of Henry, and his putative spouse, Antoinetta. At issue was heirship to the property of decedent which had been acquired as the result of the joint efforts of decedent and Antoinetta during the years of their void marriage. Viola and Henry were married in Italy in 1907; that marriage was never terminated and remained in force until Henry's death in 1956. Meanwhile, Henry came to California. Antoinetta, in good faith, participated in a ceremonial marriage with Henry in 1919. Henry and Antoinetta lived together as husband and wife continuously thereafter until Henry died, intestate, in 1956. The trial court found, inter alia, that Antoinetta was the surviving putative wife of Henry, that the presumption of the validity of the second marriage had been overcome, and that there was no basis in the evidence for an estoppel against Viola. The trial court decreed that one-half of the property should be awarded to Viola and the other half to Antoinetta. The Court of Appeal concluded that the decision of the trial court was supported by the evidence and the law and affirmed the decree.

In its opinion, the reviewing court quoted extensively from *Burby, Family Law for California Laywers*, at pages 359–360, setting forth his comments on the problems arising in the distribution of property accumulated in a void or voidable marriage. Professor Burby had written:

" 'Some difficulty is presented if conflicting claims are asserted by a legally recognized spouse and a putative spouse. Of course the claim of a putative spouse must be limited to property acquired during the continuance of that relationship. It seems obvious that one-half of the property in question belongs to the putative spouse. The other half belongs to the legal community (husband and legally recognized spouse) and should be distributed as any other community property under the same circumstances.

" 'A putative marriage was involved in *Estate of Krone*. The property in question was acquired during the continuance of this relationship and was claimed by the putative wife after the death of the husband. Her claim was resisted by issue of a former marriage. The court held that all of the property in question passed to the putative spouse by force of Probate Code section 201, which provides: "Upon the death of either husband or wife, one-half of the community property belongs to the surviving spouse; the other half is subject to the testamentary disposition of the decedent, and in the absence thereof goes to the surviving spouse * * *." The conclusion reached by the court seems to be a proper one. The claimants (husband's issue by a former marriage) would be entitled to recover only on the theory that the property in question constituted a part of the husband's separate estate. But the property in question was not of that type.

" 'A much more difficult problem would be raised if a claim were asserted by a legally recognized spouse. That was the situation involved in *Union Bank & Trust Co. v. Gordon [supra]* 116 Cal.App.2d 681 [1254 P.2d 644]. The deceased husband devised and bequeathed one-half of the property acquired during the putative marriage to his putative wife, Elsie, and one-half to his children. The legally recognized wife claimed a right to share in his estate. This claim was denied. [The trial court held, inter alia, that the legal wife] was estopped to deny the validity of the putative marriage because after her purported divorce (it was void because secured by the husband in Nevada and without having established a sufficient domicile) she purported to enter into another marriage. In the absence of the argument that she was estopped to deny the validity of the husband's putative marriage, there is no sound reason for excluding the legally recognized spouse from her share in acquisitions made by her husband during a putative marriage. It is true that one-half of the property belongs to the putative spouse but the other half belongs to the legally recognized community and there is no basis upon which the legally recognized spouse can be excluded from a proper share therein.' " (*Estate of Ricci, supra,* 201 Cal. App.2d at pp. 148–150, 19 Cal.Rptr. 793.)

The *Ricci* court went on to say:

"The case of *Union Bank & Trust Co. v. Gordon, supra,* in which it was held that the legal wife was not entitled to share in the estate of her deceased husband was correctly decided on the basis of estoppel, but, as we analyze the authorities, the legal wife could not have been excluded without the estoppel. To do so could penalize an innocent wife who had been deserted by her husband, and would be contrary to section 201 of the Probate Code which states that 'Upon the death of either husband or wife, one-half of the community property belongs to the surviving spouse; * * *' Here there are no facts in the record justifying the application of the doctrine of estoppel." (*Id.,* at p. 150, 19 Cal.Rptr. 793.)

"In conclusion we agree with the following statement of the learned trial judge in his memorandum opinion: 'Yet under the case law of this state it seems clear that each of the two widows absent of the other is entitled to the whole estate. Thus, in a contest between them it would seem both logical and equitable to divide the property equally, awarding the putative wife the half to which she [presumably] contributed and giving to the legal but deserted wife the half over which the husband normally has testamentary control.' " (*Id.,* at pp. 151–152, 19 Cal.Rptr. 793.)

Sousa v. Freitas (1970) 10 Cal.App.3d 660, 89 Cal.Rptr. 485, was a contest between Maria, the legal wife of Manuel, and Catherine, his putative spouse, as to the property of Manuel's estate, all of which had been acquired by the joint efforts of Manuel and Catherine during their void marriage. Maria and Manuel Sousa were married in Portugal in 1905; they had one son. Manuel emigrated to California in 1908, changed his name to Freitas in 1915, and participated in a marriage ceremony with Catherine in 1919. Catherine believed in good faith that she was lawfully married to Manuel and lived with him as wife and husband until Manuel died in 1962. Manuel left a will devising and bequeathing all of his property to Catherine. The trial court awarded the estate one-half to Maria and one-half to Catherine. The Court of Appeal modified the judgment holding that Catherine was entitled to one-half, being her share as a good-faith putative spouse, and the other half belonged to the legal community of Manuel and Maria. Manuel had a right to dispose of one-half of that half by his will, but the other half, one-fourth of the gross estate, belonged to Maria. As authority, the Court of Appeal cited *Estate of Ricci* and quoted from Professor Burby's comments as set forth in *Ricci*, above.

Estate of Atherley (1975) 44 Cal.App.3d 758, 119 Cal.Rptr. 41, was a contest between Ruth, the legal wife of Harold, and his putative wife, Annette, for determination of heirship to Harold's intestate estate. Ruth and Harold were married in 1933 and had two children. Harold left Ruth in 1947 and joined Annette. Harold and Annette lived together from 1947 until Harold's death in 1969; they had no children. In 1961 Harold obtained an invalid divorce from Ruth in Mexico, and in 1962 Harold married Annette in Nevada. Ruth, Harold, and Annette were in touch with each other from time to time; they shared in common the knowledge of Harold's marriage with Ruth, his cohabitation with Annette, his invalid divorce from Ruth and his void marriage with Annette. Most of Harold's estate had been accumulated during the period of his cohabitation with Annette, both before and after the void Mexican divorce and Nevada marriage. The trial court held that Ruth was the surviving spouse and implicitly held that Annette was Harold's putative spouse. The estate was comprised of a mixture of real and personal property, including separate property and joint tenancy property. The Court of Appeal, applying the rule of *Sousa v. Freitas, supra,* held that Annette, the putative spouse, was entitled to one half of the total estate as well as those assets which were hers by separate ownership or joint tenancy survivorship, and that the rest of the estate was property of the legal marriage and passed by intestate succession; that Ruth had an interest in that property as the surviving spouse but, since Ruth and Harold had two children, the extent of her interest depended on whether it was community or separate property. The judgment was reversed in part with directions.

Estate of Vargas (1974) 36 Cal.App.3d 714, 111 Cal.Rptr. 779, was a contest between Mildred, the first and legal wife of Juan, and Josephine, Juan's putative wife, competing for Juan's intestate estate. Mildred and Juan were married in 1929, raised three children, and lived together continuously for 40 years until Juan's death in 1969. Juan and Josephine were married in 1945, raised four children, and lived together for 24 years until Juan's death in 1969. Neither Mildred nor Josephine knew of the existence of the other, though both "families" lived in the Los Angeles area. The trial court ruled that Josephine was Juan's putative spouse. Most of the assets were acquired after 1945, during the period of the dual-familial relationship. The Court of Appeal affirmed the trial court's division of the estate equally between the legal wife and the putative spouse on equitable principles, stating:

> "Since statutes and judicial decisions provide no sure guidance for the resolution of the controversy, the probate court cut the Gordian knot of competing claims and divided the estate equally

between the two wives, presumably on the theory that innocent wives of practicing bigamists are entitled to equal shares of property accumulated during the active phase of the bigamy. No injury has been visited upon third parties, and the wisdom of Solomon is not required to perceive the justice of the result." (*Id.*, at p. 719, 111 Cal.Rptr. 779.)

In the light of the foregoing it is clear that every court which has considered the issue of succession to a decedent's intestate estate, as between a surviving legal spouse and a surviving putative spouse, has awarded one-half of the quasi-marital property to the putative spouse and the other half to the legal spouse, or spouse and children, under the provisions of section 221.

It appears that Civil Code section 4452 was designed to provide for the division of quasi-marital property in accordance with section 4800, in the event of an annulment by the parties of their void or voidable marriage or their voluntary separation.

However, the enactment of section 4452 did not repeal or supersede former section 221 of the Probate Code nor sections 5126 and 5118 of the Civil Code.

There are no provisions in the Probate Code governing the distribution of quasi-marital property on the death of a party to a void or voidable marriage. However, Civil Code section 4452 officially recognizes the status of "putative spouse", creates the classification of "quasi-marital property", and provides for the division of that property, if necessary, pursuant to Civil Code section 4800, i.e. equal division. By analogy, recognition of the right of a putative spouse to an equal division of the quasi-marital property should be followed and applied in distributing that property on the death of a party to a void or voidable marriage.

If we were to apply the provisions of Civil Code sections 5126 and 5118 strictly, literally, and mechanically, Charles' entire intestate estate would be his separate property and, pursuant to former section 221 of the Probate Code, would be distributed to Joan and the four children, and Helen would receive nothing.

On the other hand, if we were to look only to Civil Code section 4452, and to give it the broadest possible construction, Charles' entire intestate estate would be treated as though it were the community property of Charles and Helen and, pursuant to former section 201 of the Probate Code, the entire estate would go to Helen, and Joan and the four children would receive nothing.

If the entire estate were distributed to Joan and the four children we would be ignoring and denying the purpose of Civil Code section 4452; and if the entire estate were distributed to Helen we would be ignoring and denying the purpose of Civil Code sections 5126 and 5118 and former section 221 of the Probate Code, as well as the strong public policy which favors and protects marriage and the family. The result in either such case would be grossly unfair and unconscionable.

It is clear that our statutes are not designed to provide for the unique circumstances present in this case. When statutes are in conflict, the requirements of some being in irreconcilable opposition to others, only the chancellor can protect the innocent and render justice.

Since a just distribution of the estate among the parties is not provided by any statute, this case cries out for the firm but fair hand of equity for its resolution.

> "Equity or chancery law has its origin in the necessity for exceptions to the application of rules of law in those cases where the law, by reason of its universality, would create injustice in the affairs of men. [Citations.]" (*Estate of Vargas, supra*, 36 Cal. App.3d 714, 718, 111 Cal.Rptr. 779.)

The first duty of equity is to be equitable. In this case equity demands, and we hold, that one-half of the estate should be distributed to Helen, the putative spouse, and the other half to Joan, the legal spouse, and the four children of Charles, as provided by former section 221 of the Probate Code. This result is inherently fair.

With this result we will have done equity to all of the parties and will have honored the spirit of all of the statutory provisions which apply.

* * *

The Granting Of A Family Allowance To The Putative Spouse Was Contrary To Law

Appellants contend that the trial court's award of a family allowance to Helen, a putative spouse, was error and contrary to law in that the authorizing statute provides for a family allowance to the "surviving spouse" of a decedent but does not so provide to a surviving putative spouse.

In 1984, former section 680 of the Probate Code provided, in pertinent part: "(a) The surviving spouse, minor children, and * * * are entitled to such reasonable allowance out of the estate as shall be necessary for their maintenance according to their circumstances, during the progress of the settlement of the estate."

The 1983 amendment to the Probate Code, effective January 1, 1985, rewrote those provisions in section 6540 of the Probate Code but made no substantial changes in the pertinent portion.

The word "spouse" means "One's wife or husband." (*Black's Law Dictionary* (5th Ed.) p. 1258; and see *Menchaca v. Farmers Insurance Exchange* (1976) 59 Cal.App.3d 117, 128, 130 Cal.Rptr. 607.) The statutes do not contemplate that a person have more than one spouse at one time. (Civ.Code, § 4401, subd. (1); Pen.Code, § 281.)

As we have noted, the trial court found that Joan and Charles were married in 1954 and that neither had taken any steps to dissolve that marriage.

Therefore, Joan was Charles' spouse at the time of his death.

The court also found that the marriage of Helen and Charles was invalid [void] in that Charles had never obtained a divorce from Joan. Helen was never Charles' spouse. Helen did qualify as a "putative spouse" under the "good faith" provisions of Civil Code section 4452.

The right to a family allowance is entirely statutory and is given by section 680 of the Probate Code. That section does not authorize the probate court to make an allowance for the benefit of persons other than the persons specified therein. (*Estate of Blair* (1954) 42 Cal.2d 728, 730, 269 P.2d 612.)

"It follows from the express provisions of section 680 that a prerequisite for family allowance is that the claimant be the decedent's widow." (*Estate of Casimir* (1971) 19 Cal.App.3d 773, 778, 97 Cal.Rptr. 623; *Estate of Brooks* (1946) 28 Cal.2d 748, 750, 171 P.2d 724.)

Appellants stated in their opening brief that they know of no reported decisions in California holding that a putative spouse is entitled to a family allowance. Respondent discusses the subject in her brief but cites no such case to us, and we have found none.

It is not the role of the courts to legislate. In a situation such as that before us, courts should exercise restraint and leave the power to legislate where our Constitution has placed it, in the Legislature. (Cal. Const., art. IV, § 1.) The Legislature enacted the Family Law Act, including Civil Code section 4452, which recognized and gave certain rights to putative spouses. It also rewrote substantial portions of the Probate Code in 1983, effective 1985, including the repeal of former section 680 and its re-enactment with amendments as section 6540 of the present Probate Code. In so amending those statutes the Legislature did not provide for a family allowance for a putative spouse though it easily could have done so if that had been its intent. We cannot attribute these facts to oversight.

The language of section 680 is not ambiguous; it clearly provides that a surviving spouse is entitled to a reasonable family allowance. The judicial decisions interpreting and applying section 680 declare that it does not authorize the probate court to make a family allowance for the benefit of persons other than those specified therein. A putative spouse is not one of the persons specified in section 680 and the court's award of a family allowance to a putative spouse is contrary to law.

* * *

CONCLUSION

On the basis of legal precedents, as set forth above, and equitable principles, we must reverse the judgment and remand the cause with instructions.

We find that the property of the estate of decedent Charles Hafner should be awarded one-half to his putative spouse, Helen Hafner, and the other half to be awarded to and divided among his legal and surviving spouse, Joan, and his four children, Catherine, Lillian, Dorothy and Kimberly, in accordance with former section 221 of the Probate Code.

The court shall also reconsider its previous decision as to a family allowance for Joan, Charles' legal wife, as well as for Helen, and shall order that any allowances paid to Joan or to Helen during the administration of this estate shall be charged against the amount of the distributive share of this estate to which Joan or Helen shall be entitled, as was agreed in the stipulation filed November 1, 1983.

DECISION

The judgment is reversed. The cause is remanded with instructions that the court make and enter a new and different judgment consistent with this opinion. Costs are awarded to appellants.

ARABIAN, J., concurs.

LUI, ACTING PRESIDING JUSTICE, dissenting.

The majority's decision fails to grant the surviving putative spouse, Helen Hafner, any share of the deceased's separate property. The majority thereby ignores our Supreme Court's decision in *Estate of Leslie* (1984) 37 Cal.3d 186, 207 Cal.Rptr. 561, 689 P.2d 133, and the statutory scheme set forth in former Probate Code section 221[1] governing intestate succession to separate property.

Intestate succession in California is governed exclusively by statute. The basic flaw in the majority's analysis is that it attempts to apply equitable principles in distributing the decedent's estate instead of following the statutory scheme.

The majority relies on decisions which predate the enactment of Civil Code section 4452 (section 4452). These appellate decisions applied equitable principles to establish the right of a surviving putative spouse to succeed to a distributive share of property accumulated during a putative union under former Probate Code sections 201 and 201.5 (dealing with community and quasi-community property respectively) as a "surviving spouse."[2] The equitable doctrines developed in the pre-

1. Former Probate Code section 221 provided that: "If the decedent leaves a surviving spouse, and only one child or the lawful issue of a deceased child, the estate goes one-half to the surviving spouse and one-half to the child or issue. If the decedent leaves a surviving spouse, and more than one child living or one child living and the lawful issue of one or more deceased children, the estate goes one-third to the surviving spouse and the remainder in equal shares to his children * * *."

2. The majority opinion at page 689 states: "[I]t is clear that every court which has considered the issue of succession to a decedent's intestate estate, as between a surviving legal spouse and a surviving puta-

tive spouse, has awarded one-half of the quasi-marital property to the putative spouse and the other half to the legal spouse, or spouse and children, under the provisions of [former Probate Code] section 221." The majority cites the *Estate of Ricci* (1962) 201 Cal.App.2d 146, 19 Cal.Rptr. 739; *Sousa v. Freitas* (1970) 10 Cal.App.3d 660, 89 Cal.Rptr. 485; *Estate of Atherley* (1975) 44 Cal.App.3d 758, 119 Cal.Rptr. 41; and the *Estate of Vargas* (1974) 36 Cal.App.3d 714, 111 Cal.Rptr. 779.

The decisions in *Estate of Ricci, supra,* 201 Cal.App.2d 146, 19 Cal.Rptr. 739, and *Sousa v. Freitas, supra,* 10 Cal.App.3d 660, 89 Cal.Rptr. 485, are distinguishable from the present appeal because these decisions

section 4452 line of cases did not alter the formula for intestate succession as set forth in the Probate Code. The majority's resolution of this case, however, does alter the statutory formula for intestate succession.

In enacting section 4452, the Legislature established the legal right of a surviving putative spouse to property acquired during the putative union which would have been community property or quasi-community property if the union had not been void or voidable, and termed this property "quasi-marital property."

Under section 4452, the putative spouse has a vested share of one-half of the quasi-marital property accumulated during the putative union. If the union is dissolved prior to the death of one spouse, each spouse is entitled to one-half of the quasi-marital property. Death of either spouse to a putative union does not terminate the surviving spouse's interest in quasi-marital property.

A surviving putative spouse's one-half interest in quasi-marital property is vested and not subject to intestate succession by any other person. Thus, the proper legal distribution of the decedent's estate gives the putative spouse one-half of the decedent's entire estate pursuant to section 4452.[3]

Purporting to apply general and equitable principles which are inapplicable, the majority then concludes that only the surviving legal spouse and the deceased's four children are entitled to share in the other half of the decedent's entire estate. The majority thus holds that the surviving putative spouse has no interest whatsoever in the decedent's separate property. The majority's holding violates former Probate Code section 221 and the *Estate of Leslie* and errs in attempting a resolution of this thorny problem by distributing decedent's separate property on an "all or nothing" basis.

In *Leslie*, the Supreme Court was confronted with the conflicting claims to a deceased wife's separate property asserted by her putative husband and a son by a prior marriage. The question presented in *Leslie* was whether the putative husband was entitled to succeed to a

predate the enactment of Civil Code section 5118. The decision in the *Estate of Atherley, supra*, 44 Cal.App.3d 758, 119 Cal.Rptr. 41, did not consider the applicability of section 5118 since that statute, as originally enacted, was not effective until after the decedent Harold Atherley's death in 1969. The decision in *Vargas, supra*, 36 Cal. App.3d 714, 111 Cal.Rptr. 779 is distinguishable under a unique factual situation not present in this appeal. In *Vargas*, two innocent women were victims of a man who had contemporaneously lived a double life. In this appeal, appellant had long been deserted by the decedent and had learned to live her life separate and apart from the decedent physically, emotionally, and financially.

Thus, none of the decisions from which the majority rests its conclusion considers the fact situation presented in this appeal and the impact of the enactment of Civil Code sections 4452 and 5118.

3. The majority concludes that the putative spouse is entitled to one-half of the decedent's estate but under a different analysis.

The trial court concluded that section 4452 allows the putative spouse to succeed to the decedent's entire estate. While the trial court's conclusion has arguable merit, I would interpret section 4452 as applying merit, only to the surviving putative spouse's one-half interest in the quasi-marital property if the deceased spouse also left a legal spouse and/or children.

share of the *deceased wife's separate property* under the Probate Code rather than under equitable principles. The court in *Leslie* concluded that the trial court had *incorrectly* determined that the husband was *not* the decedent's "surviving spouse" under former Probate Code section 221.

Leslie cited the decision in *Estate of Krone* (1948) 83 Cal.App.2d 766, 189 P.2d 741, and stated that "*Krone* has been read 'to recognize a putative [spouse] as a legal spouse for the purpose of succession,' " under Probate Code section 201, citing *Kunakoff v. Woods* (1958) 166 Cal. App.2d 59, 65–66, 332 P.2d 773, and "[t]hat reading is clearly applicable to the determination of the separate property rights of a putative spouse." (*Estate of Leslie, supra,* 37 Cal.3d at p. 194, 207 Cal.Rptr. 561, 689 P.2d 133.)

"To accord a surviving putative spouse rights to the decedent's separate property honors rather than disregards the statutory scheme governing intestate succession. (Laughran & Laughran [*Property and Inheritance Rights of Putative Spouses in California: Selected Problems and Suggested Solutions* (1977)] 11 Loyola L.A.L.Rev. [45] at p. 67 * * *.) *Since the right to succession is not an inherent or natural right, but purely a creature of statute* [citation], *a surviving legal spouse inherits a decedent's separate property 'only because the statutes provide that a person having the status of "surviving spouse" takes a certain share.'* (Laughran & Laughran, *op. cit. supra,* 11 Loyola L.A.L.Rev. at p. 67.) *To accord a surviving putative spouse the status of 'surviving spouse' simply recognizes that a good faith belief in the marriage should put the putative spouse in the same position as a survivor of a legal marriage.* (*Id.,* at p. 68.)" (*Estate of Leslie, supra,* 37 Cal.3d at p. 199, 207 Cal.Rptr. 561, 689 P.2d 133, emphasis added.)

Under the above-quoted reasoning of *Leslie,* a surviving putative spouse is entitled to a legal share of a deceased spouse's separate property. While the court in *Leslie* was not faced with the conflicting claims of two spouses, its reasoning that the rights of surviving putative and legal spouses should be given parity under the law is instructive to a resolution of this appeal. Putting their respective rights to the deceased spouse's separate property on par requires that the surviving putative and legal spouses share that portion of the deceased's separate property to which each is entitled to under former Probate Code section 221. The proper legal distribution of the decedent's estate in this case should result in the surviving putative spouse taking one-half of the decedent's entire estate pursuant to section 4452 as her quasi-marital property. As to the remainder of the decedent's estate, following the mandate in *Leslie,* the putative and legal spouses should be treated equally. Therefore, under former Probate Code section 221, the proper legal distribution of the remainder of the decedent's estate should be as follows: one-third of that portion of the estate should be divided equally between the surviving putative and legal spouses; the remaining two-thirds should be distributed in equal shares to the decedent's four children by both relationships.[4]

The majority concludes that the surviving putative spouse is not entitled to a family allowance because she is not a "surviving spouse" within the meaning of Probate Code section 6540 (section 6540). Section 6540 provides that the surviving spouse, minor children, and dependent adult handicapped children are entitled to an allowance necessary for their maintenance during the administration of the estate.

The majority's conclusion is unreasonable in view of the *Leslie* mandate which accords a putative spouse equal status with the legal spouse *for essentially all purposes.* (See *Estate of Leslie, supra*, 37 Cal.3d at pp. 195–196, 207 Cal.Rptr. 561, 689 P.2d 133.) The better resolution is to give both the surviving putative and legal spouses consideration for a family allowance should their circumstances warrant it. Following the majority's reasoning, if the decedent left only a putative spouse and no legal spouse, the putative spouse would *not* be entitled to a family allowance. It is unlikely that the Legislature intended such a narrow reading of section 6540.

I would remand the matter to the superior court for a modification of the judgment consistent with the distribution scheme set forth above. I would also require the trial court to consider the necessity of a family allowance to both spouses under section 6540.

VALLERA v. VALLERA
Supreme Court of California, 1943.
21 Cal.2d 681, 134 P.2d 761.

TRAYNOR, JUSTICE. Plaintiff brought this action for separate maintenance and for a division of community property, which she alleged was worth at least $60,000.

* * * The trial court found that plaintiff and defendant did not on December 16, 1938, or at any other time contract a common law marriage in Michigan or elsewhere; that they did not at any time enter into or attempt to enter into an agreement to take each other as husband and wife; that beginning in May, 1936, and for at least three years thereafter, plaintiff cohabited meretriciously with defendant; that between January, 1933, and December 15, 1938, defendant was married to Ethel Chippo Vallera; that plaintiff knew from the beginning of her relationship with defendant that he was married and under a legal disability to enter into a marriage contract with her; that while the marriage between defendant and Ethel Chippo Vallera was dissolved on December 15, 1938, neither plaintiff nor defendant learned of its dissolution until November, 1939; and that on July 6, 1940, defendant entered

4. It should be noted that the only difference between the distribution suggested here and that formulated by the majority is that the surviving spouse's share of the decedent's separate property would be divided by the surviving legal and putative spouses and not given entirely to the surviving legal spouse.

into a valid marriage with Lido Cappello. The court concluded that plaintiff and defendant had never been husband and wife; that plaintiff was not entitled to maintenance; and that there was no community property. It held, however, that all property acquired by the parties between December 16, 1938, and July 6, 1940, except such property as either might have acquired by gift, devise, bequest, or descent, was held by them as tenants in common, each owning an undivided one-half thereof, and defendant has appealed from this part of the judgment. He contends that since there was no marriage, no attempt to contract marriage, no belief in the existence of a valid marriage, no evidence of any agreement between the parties as to their property rights, and no evidence concerning the accumulation of property or contributions by the parties thereto, plaintiff could not acquire the rights of a cotenant in property acquired by him during the period of illicit cohabitation.

It is well settled that a woman who lives with a man as his wife in the belief that a valid marriage exists is entitled upon termination of their relationship to share in the property acquired by them during its existence. Feig v. Bank of Italy etc. Ass'n, 218 Cal. 54, 21 P.2d 421; Figoni v. Figoni, 211 Cal. 354, 295 P. 339; Schneider v. Schneider, 183 Cal. 335, 191 P. 533, 11 A.L.R. 1386; Coats v. Coats, 160 Cal. 671, 118 P. 441, 36 L.R.A., N.S., 844; see Knoll v. Knoll, 104 Wash. 110, 176 P. 22, 11 A.L.R. 1394. The proportionate contribution of each party to the property is immaterial in this state (Coats v. Coats, supra; Macchi v. La Rocca, 54 Cal.App. 98, 201 P. 143), for the property is divided as community property would be upon the dissolution of a valid marriage. Sanguinetti v. Sanguinetti, 9 Cal.2d 95, 69 P.2d 845, 111 A.L.R. 342; Feig v. Bank of America, etc., Ass'n, 5 Cal.2d 266, 54 P.2d 3; Schneider v. Schneider, supra; Coats v. Coats, supra; Macchi v. La Rocca, supra.

The essential basis of a putative marriage, however, is a belief in the existence of a valid marriage. Flanagan v. Capital Nat. Bank, 213 Cal. 664, 3 P.2d 307; see Evans, Property Interests Arising from Quasi–Marital Relations, 9 Corn.L.Q. 246; 20 Cal.L.Rev. 453. * * * The controversy is thus reduced to the question whether a woman living with a man as his wife but with no genuine belief that she is legally married to him acquires by reason of cohabitation alone the rights of a co-tenant in his earnings and accumulations during the period of their relationship. It has already been answered in the negative. Flanagan v. Capital Nat. Bank, 213 Cal. 664, 3 P.2d 307. Equitable considerations arising from the reasonable expectation of the continuation of benefits attending the status of marriage entered into in good faith are not present in such a case.

Plaintiff's lack of good faith in alleging the belief that she had entered into a valid marriage would not, however, preclude her from recovering property to which she would otherwise be entitled. If a man and woman live together as husband and wife under an agreement to pool their earnings and share equally in their joint accumulations, equity will protect the interests of each in such property. Bacon v. Bacon, 21 Cal.App.2d 540, 69 P.2d 884; Mitchell v. Fish, 97 Ark. 444, 134 S.W.

940, 36 L.R.A., N.S., 838; see Feig v. Bank of America etc. Ass'n, supra; Bracken v. Bracken, 52 S.D. 252, 256, 217 N.W. 192; Hayworth v. Williams, 102 Tex. 308, 116 S.W. 43, 132 Am.St.Rep. 879. Even in the absence of an express agreement to that effect, the woman would be entitled to share in the property jointly accumulated, in the proportion that her funds contributed toward its acquisition. Hayworth v. Williams, supra; Delamour v. Roger, 7 La.Ann. 152. There is no evidence that the parties in the present case made any agreement concerning their property or property rights. The meager evidence with respect to the accumulation of the alleged community property can support only the inference that the property consisted of defendant's earnings during the period in question, and there is no contention to the contrary. There is thus no support in the record for the trial court's finding that the parties each owned an undivided one-half of the property acquired by either of them between December 16, 1938, and July 5, 1940.

* * *

The part of the judgment appealed from is reversed.

CURTIS, JUSTICE (dissenting in part). * * * In the absence of any proof of any cash or property contribution by the plaintiff, the holding of the trial court that she owned a one-half interest in the property accumulated must have been based upon the conclusion that the value of her services as a housekeeper, cook, and homemaker was of sufficient value to warrant an equal division of the property. The majority opinion substitutes its own appraisal of the value of her services in the home as being of no more value than the cost of maintenance of herself and her two children. The holding of the trial court seems to me more reasonable.

* * *

MARVIN v. MARVIN
Supreme Court of California, 1976.
18 Cal.3d 660, 134 Cal.Rptr. 815, 557 P.2d 106.

TOBRINER, JUSTICE.

During the past 15 years, there has been a substantial increase in the number of couples living together without marrying.[1] Such nonmarital relationships lead to legal controversy when one partner dies or the couple separates. Courts of Appeal, faced with the task of determining property rights in such cases, have arrived at conflicting positions: two cases (In re Marriage of Cary (1973) 34 Cal.App.3d 345, 109 Cal.Rptr. 862; Estate of Atherley (1975) 44 Cal.App.3d 758, 119 Cal.Rptr. 41) have

---

1. "The 1970 census figures indicate that today perhaps eight times as many couples are living together without being married as cohabited ten years ago." (Comment, In re Cary: A Judicial Recognition of Illicit Cohabitation (1974) 25 Hastings L.J. 1226.)

held that the Family Law Act (Civ.Code, § 4000 et seq.) requires division of the property according to community property principles, and one decision (Beckman v. Mayhew (1975) 49 Cal.App.3d 529, 122 Cal.Rptr. 604) has rejected that holding. We take this opportunity to resolve that controversy and to declare the principles which should govern distribution of property acquired in a nonmarital relationship.

We conclude: (1) The provisions of the Family Law Act do not govern the distribution of property acquired during a nonmarital relationship; such a relationship remains subject solely to judicial decision. (2) The courts should enforce express contracts between nonmarital partners except to the extent that the contract is explicitly founded on the consideration of meretricious sexual services. (3) In the absence of an express contract, the courts should inquire into the conduct of the parties to determine whether that conduct demonstrates an implied contract, agreement of partnership or joint venture, or some other tacit understanding between the parties. The courts may also employ the doctrine of quantum meruit, or equitable remedies such as constructive or resulting trusts, when warranted by the facts of the case.

In the instant case plaintiff and defendant lived together for seven years without marrying; all property acquired during this period was taken in defendant's name. When plaintiff sued to enforce a contract under which she was entitled to half the property and to support payments, the trial court granted judgment on the pleadings for defendant, thus leaving him with all property accumulated by the couple during their relationship. Since the trial court denied plaintiff a trial on the merits of her claim, its decision conflicts with the principles stated above, and must be reversed.

1. The Factual Setting of This Appeal

Since the trial court rendered judgment for defendant on the pleadings, we must accept the allegations of plaintiff's complaint as true, determining whether such allegations state, or can be amended to state, a cause of action. (See Sullivan v. County of Los Angeles (1974) 12 Cal.3d 710, 714–715, fn. 3, 117 Cal.Rptr. 241, 527 P.2d 865; 4 Witkin, Cal.Procedure (2d ed. 1971) pp. 2817–2818.) We turn therefore to the specific allegations of the complaint.

Plaintiff avers that in October of 1964 she and defendant "entered into an oral agreement" that while "the parties lived together they would combine their efforts and earnings and would share equally any and all property accumulated as a result of their efforts whether individual or combined." Furthermore, they agreed to "hold themselves out to the general public as husband and wife" and that "plaintiff would further render her services as a companion, homemaker, housekeeper and cook to * * * defendant."

Shortly thereafter plaintiff agreed to "give up her lucrative career as an entertainer [and] singer" in order to "devote her full time to defendant * * * as a companion, homemaker, housekeeper and cook;"

in return defendant agreed to "provide for all of plaintiff's financial support and needs for the rest of her life."

Plaintiff alleges that she lived with defendant from October of 1964 through May of 1970 and fulfilled her obligations under the agreement. During this period the parties as a result of their efforts and earnings acquired in defendant's name substantial real and personal property, including motion picture rights worth over $1 million. In May of 1970, however, defendant compelled plaintiff to leave his household. He continued to support plaintiff until November of 1971, but thereafter refused to provide further support.

On the basis of these allegations plaintiff asserts two causes of action. The first, for declaratory relief, asks the court to determine her contract and property rights; the second seeks to impose a constructive trust upon one half of the property acquired during the course of the relationship.

* * *

2. PLAINTIFF'S COMPLAINT STATES A CAUSE OF ACTION FOR BREACH OF AN EXPRESS CONTRACT

In Trutalli v. Meraviglia (1932) 215 Cal. 698, 12 P.2d 430 we established the principle that nonmarital partners may lawfully contract concerning the ownership of property acquired during the relationship. We reaffirmed this principle in Vallera v. Vallera (1943) 21 Cal.2d 681, 685, 134 P.2d 761, 763, stating that "If a man and woman [who are not married] live together as husband and wife under an agreement to pool their earnings and share equally in their joint accumulations, equity will protect the interests of each in such property."

In the case before us plaintiff, basing her cause of action in contract upon these precedents, maintains that the trial court erred in denying her a trial on the merits of her contention. Although that court did not specify the ground for its conclusion that plaintiff's contractual allegations stated no cause of action,[3] defendant offers some four theories to sustain the ruling; we proceed to examine them.

Defendant first and principally relies on the contention that the alleged contract is so closely related to the supposed "immoral" character of the relationship between plaintiff and himself that the enforcement of the contract would violate public policy.[4] He points to cases

3. The colloquy between court and counsel at argument on the motion for judgment on the pleadings suggests that the trial court held the 1964 agreement violated public policy because it derogated the community property rights of Betty Marvin, defendant's lawful wife. Plaintiff, however, offered to amend her complaint to allege that she and defendant reaffirmed their contract after defendant and Betty were divorced. The trial court denied leave to amend, a ruling which suggests that the

court's judgment must rest upon some other ground than the assertion that the contract would injure Betty's property rights.

4. Defendant also contends that the contract was illegal because it contemplated a violation of former Penal Code section 269a, which prohibited living "in a state of cohabitation and adultery." (§ 269a was repealed by Stats.1975, ch. 71, eff. Jan. 1, 1976.) Defendant's standing to raise the issue is questionable because he alone was

asserting that a contract between nonmarital partners is unenforceable if it is "involved in" an illicit relationship (see Shaw v. Shaw (1964) 227 Cal.App.2d 159, 164, 38 Cal.Rptr. 520 (dictum); Garcia v. Venegas (1951) 106 Cal.App.2d 364, 368, 235 P.2d 89 (dictum), or made in "contemplation" of such a relationship (Hill v. Estate of Westbrook (1950) 95 Cal.App.2d 599, 602, 213 P.2d 727; see Hill v. Estate of Westbrook (1952) 39 Cal.2d 458, 460, 247 P.2d 19; Barlow v. Collins (1958) 166 Cal.App.2d 274, 277, 333 P.2d 64 (dictum); Bridges v. Bridges (1954) 125 Cal.App.2d 359, 362, 270 P.2d 69 (dictum)). A review of the numerous California decisions concerning contracts between nonmarital partners, however, reveals that the courts have not employed such broad and uncertain standards to strike down contracts. The decisions instead disclose a narrower and more precise standard: a contract between nonmarital partners is unenforceable only *to the extent* that it *explicitly* rests upon the immoral and illicit consideration of meretricious sexual services.

* * *

Although the past decisions hover over the issue in the somewhat wispy form of the figures of a Chagall painting, we can abstract from those decisions a clear and simple rule. The fact that a man and woman live together without marriage, and engage in a sexual relationship, does not in itself invalidate agreements between them relating to their earnings, property, or expenses. Neither is such an agreement invalid merely because the parties may have contemplated the creation or continuation of a nonmarital relationship when they entered into it. Agreements between nonmarital partners fail only to the extent that they rest upon a consideration of meretricious sexual services. Thus the rule asserted by defendant, that a contract fails if it is "involved in" or made "in contemplation" of a nonmarital relationship, cannot be reconciled with the decisions.

* * *

The principle that a contract between nonmarital partners will be enforced unless expressly and inseparably based upon an illicit consideration of sexual services not only represents the distillation of the decisional law, but also offers a far more precise and workable standard than that advocated by defendant. Our recent decision in In re Marriage of Dawley (1976) 17 Cal.3d 342, 551 P.2d 323, offers a close

---

married and thus guilty of violating section 269a. Plaintiff, being unmarried could neither be convicted of adulterous cohabitation nor of aiding and abetting defendant's violation. (See In re Cooper (1912) 162 Cal. 81, 85–86, 121 P. 318.)

The numerous cases discussing the contractual rights of unmarried couples have drawn no distinction between illegal relationships and lawful nonmarital relationships. (Cf. Weak v. Weak (1962) 202 Cal.

App.2d 632, 639, 21 Cal.Rptr. 9 (bigamous marriage).) Moreover, even if we were to draw such a distinction—a largely academic endeavor in view of the repeal of section 269a—defendant probably would not benefit; his relationship with plaintiff continued long after his divorce became final, and plaintiff sought to amend her complaint to assert that the parties reaffirmed their contract after the divorce.

analogy. Rejecting the contention that an antenuptial agreement is invalid if the parties contemplated a marriage of short duration, we pointed out in *Dawley* that a standard based upon the subjective contemplation of the parties is uncertain and unworkable; such a test, we stated, "might invalidate virtually all antenuptial agreements on the ground that the parties contemplated dissolution * * * but it provides no principled basis for determining which antenuptial agreements offend public policy and which do not." (17 Cal.3d 342, 352, 551 P.2d 323, 329.)

Similarly, in the present case a standard which inquires whether an agreement is "involved" in or "contemplates" a nonmarital relationship is vague and unworkable. Virtually all agreements between nonmarital partners can be said to be "involved" in some sense in the fact of their mutual sexual relationship, or to "contemplate" the existence of that relationship. Thus defendant's proposed standards, if taken literally, might invalidate all agreements between nonmarital partners, a result no one favors. Moreover, those standards offer no basis to distinguish between valid and invalid agreements. By looking not to such uncertain tests, but only to the consideration underlying the agreement, we provide the parties and the courts with a practical guide to determine when an agreement between nonmarital partners should be enforced.

Defendant secondly relies upon the ground suggested by the trial court: that the 1964 contract violated public policy because it impaired the community property rights of Betty Marvin, defendant's lawful wife. Defendant points out that his earnings while living apart from his wife before rendition of the interlocutory decree were community property under 1964 statutory law (former Civ.Code, §§ 169, 169.2)[7] and that defendant's agreement with plaintiff purported to transfer to her a half interest in that community property. But whether or not defendant's contract with plaintiff exceeded his authority as manager of the community property (see former Civ.Code, § 172), defendant's argument fails for the reason that an improper transfer of community property is not void *ab initio,* but merely voidable at the instance of the aggrieved spouse. (See Ballinger v. Ballinger (1937) 9 Cal.2d 330, 334, 70 P.2d 629; Trimble v. Trimble (1933) 219 Cal. 340, 344, 26 P.2d 477.)

In the present case Betty Marvin, the aggrieved spouse, had the opportunity to assert her community property rights in the divorce action. (See Babbitt v. Babbitt (1955) 44 Cal.2d 289, 293, 282 P.2d 1.) The interlocutory and final decrees in that action fix and limit her interest. Enforcement of the contract between plaintiff and defendant against property awarded to defendant by the divorce decree will not impair any right of Betty's, and thus is not on that account violative of

7. Sections 169 and 169.2 were replaced in 1970 by Civil Code section 5118. In 1972 section 5118 was amended to provide that the earnings and accumulations of *both* spouses "while living separate and apart

public policy.[8]

Defendant's third contention is noteworthy for the lack of authority advanced in its support. He contends that enforcement of the oral agreement between plaintiff and himself is barred by Civil Code section 5134, which provides that "All contracts for marriage settlements must be in writing * * *." A marriage settlement, however, is an agreement in contemplation of marriage in which each party agrees to release or modify the property rights which would otherwise arise from the marriage. (See Corker v. Corker (1891) 87 Cal. 643, 648, 25 P. 922.) The contract at issue here does not conceivably fall within that definition, and thus is beyond the compass of section 5134.[9]

Defendant finally argues that enforcement of the contract is barred by Civil Code section 43.5, subdivision (d), which provides that "No cause of action arises for * * * [b]reach of a promise of marriage." This rather strained contention proceeds from the premise that a promise of marriage impliedly includes a promise to support and to pool property acquired after marriage (see Boyd v. Boyd (1964) 228 Cal.App.2d 374, 39 Cal.Rptr. 400) to the conclusion that pooling and support agreements not part of or accompanied by promise of marriage are barred by the section. We conclude that section 43.5 is not reasonably susceptible to the interpretation advanced by defendant, a conclusion demonstrated by the fact that since section 43.5 was enacted in 1939, numerous cases have enforced pooling agreements between nonmarital partners, and in none did court or counsel refer to section 43.5.

In summary, we base our opinion on the principle that adults who voluntarily live together and engage in sexual relations are nonetheless as competent as any other persons to contract respecting their earnings and property rights. Of course, they cannot lawfully contract to pay for the performance of sexual services, for such a contract is, in essence, an agreement for prostitution and unlawful for that reason. But they may agree to pool their earnings and to hold all property acquired during the relationship in accord with the law governing community property; conversely they may agree that each partner's earnings and the property acquired from those earnings remains the separate property of the

from the other spouse, are the separate property of the spouse."

8. Defendant also contends that the contract is invalid as an agreement to promote or encourage divorce. (See 1 Witkin, Summary of Cal.Law (8th ed.) pp. 390–392 and cases there cited.) The contract between plaintiff and defendant did not, however, by its terms require defendant to divorce Betty, nor reward him for so doing. Moreover, the principle on which defendant relies does not apply when the marriage in question is beyond redemption (Glickman v. Collins (1975) 13 Cal.3d 852, 858–859, 120 Cal.Rptr. 76, 533 P.2d 204); whether or not

defendant's marriage to Betty was beyond redemption when defendant contracted with plaintiff is obviously a question of fact which cannot be resolved by judgment on the pleadings.

9. Our review of the many cases enforcing agreements between nonmarital partners reveals that the majority of such agreements were oral. In two cases (Ferguson v. Schuenemann, supra, 167 Cal.App.2d 413, 334 P.2d 668; Cline v. Festersen, supra, 128 Cal.App.2d 380, 275 P.2d 149), the court expressly rejected defenses grounded upon the statute of frauds.

earning partner.[10] So long as the agreement does not rest upon illicit meretricious consideration, the parties may order their economic affairs as they choose, and no policy precludes the courts from enforcing such agreements.

In the present instance, plaintiff alleges that the parties agreed to pool their earnings, that they contracted to share equally in all property acquired, and that defendant agreed to support plaintiff. The terms of the contract as alleged do not rest upon any unlawful consideration. We therefore conclude that the complaint furnishes a suitable basis upon which the trial court can render declaratory relief. (See 3 Witkin, Cal.Procedure (2d ed.) pp. 2335–2336.) The trial court consequently erred in granting defendant's motion for judgment on the pleadings.

3. PLAINTIFF'S COMPLAINT CAN BE AMENDED TO STATE A CAUSE OF ACTION FOUNDED UPON THEORIES OF IMPLIED CONTRACT OR EQUITABLE RELIEF

As we have noted, both causes of action in plaintiff's complaint allege an express contract; neither assert any basis for relief independent from the contract. In In re Marriage of Cary, supra, 34 Cal.App.3d 345, 109 Cal.Rptr. 862, however, the Court of Appeal held that, in view of the policy of the Family Law Act, property accumulated by nonmarital partners in an actual family relationship should be divided equally. Upon examining the *Cary* opinion, the parties to the present case realized that plaintiff's alleged relationship with defendant might arguably support a cause of action independent of any express contract between the parties. The parties have therefore briefed and discussed the issue of the property rights of a nonmarital partner in the absence of an express contract. Although our conclusion that plaintiff's complaint states a cause of action based on an express contract alone compels us to reverse the judgment for defendant, resolution of the *Cary* issue will serve both to guide the parties upon retrial and to resolve a conflict presently manifest in published Court of Appeal decisions.

Both plaintiff and defendant stand in broad agreement that the law should be fashioned to carry out the reasonable expectations of the parties. Plaintiff, however, presents the following contentions: that the decisions prior to *Cary* rest upon implicit and erroneous notions of punishing a party for his or her guilt in entering into a nonmarital relationship, that such decisions result in an inequitable distribution of property accumulated during the relationship, and that *Cary* correctly held that the enactment of the Family Law Act in 1970 overturned those prior decisions. Defendant in response maintains that the prior decisions merely applied common law principles of contract and property to persons who have deliberately elected to remain outside the bounds of

10. A great variety of other arrangements are possible. The parties might keep their earnings and property separate, but agree to compensate one party for services which benefit the other. They may choose to pool only part of their earnings and property, to form a partnership or joint venture, or to hold property acquired as joint tenants or tenants in common, or agree to any other such arrangement. (See generally Weitzman, Legal Regulation of Marriage: Tradition and Change (1974) 62 Cal.L.Rev. 1169.)

the community property system.[11] *Cary,* defendant contends, erred in holding that the Family Law Act vitiated the force of the prior precedents.

As we shall see from examination of the pre-*Cary* decisions, the truth lies somewhere between the positions of plaintiff and defendant. The classic opinion on this subject is Vallera v. Vallera, supra, 21 Cal.2d 681, 134 P.2d 761. Speaking for a four-member majority, Justice Traynor posed the question: "whether a woman living with a man as his wife but with no genuine belief that she is legally married to him acquires by reason of cohabitation alone the rights of a cotenant in his earnings and accumulations during the period of their relationship." (21 Cal.2d at p. 684, 134 P.2d at p. 762.) Citing Flanagan v. Capital Nat. Bank (1931) 213 Cal. 664, 3 P.2d 307, which held that a nonmarital "wife" could not claim that her husband's estate was community property, the majority answered that question "in the negative." (21 Cal.2d pp. 684–685, 134 P.2d 761.) *Vallera* explains that "Equitable considerations arising from the reasonable expectation of the continuation of benefits attending the status of marriage entered into in good faith are not present in such a case." (P. 685, 134 P.2d p. 763.) In the absence of express contract, *Vallera* concluded, the woman is entitled to share in property jointly accumulated only "in the proportion that her funds contributed toward its acquisition." (P. 685, 134 P.2d p. 763.) Justice Curtis, dissenting, argued that the evidence showed an implied contract under which each party owned an equal interest in property acquired during the relationship.

The majority opinion in *Vallera* did not expressly bar recovery based upon an implied contract, nor preclude resort to equitable remedies. But Vallera's broad assertion that equitable considerations "are not present" in the case of a nonmarital relationship (21 Cal.2d at p. 685, 134 P.2d 761) led the Courts of Appeal to interpret the language to preclude recovery based on such theories. (See Lazzarevich v. Lazzarevich (1948) 88 Cal.App.2d 708, 719, 200 P.2d 49; Oakley v. Oakley (1947) 82 Cal.App.2d 188, 191–192, 185 P.2d 848.)[12]

11. We note that a deliberate decision to avoid the strictures of the community property system is not the only reason that couples live together without marriage. Some couples may wish to avoid the permanent commitment that marriage implies, yet be willing to share equally any property acquired during the relationship; others may fear the loss of pension, welfare, or tax benefits resulting from marriage (see Beckman v. Mayhew, supra, 49 Cal.App.3d 529, 122 Cal.Rptr. 604). Others may engage in the relationship as a possible prelude to marriage. In lower socio-economic groups the difficulty and expense of dissolving a former marriage often leads couples to choose a nonmarital relationship; many unmarried couples may also incorrectly believe that the doctrine of common law marriage prevails in California, and thus that they are in fact married. Consequently we conclude that the mere fact that a couple have not participated in a valid marriage ceremony cannot serve as a basis for a court's inference that the couple intend to keep their earnings and property separate and independent; the parties' intention can only be ascertained by a more searching inquiry into the nature of their relationship.

12. The cases did not clearly determine whether a nonmarital partner could recover in quantum meruit for the reasonable value of services rendered. But when we affirmed a trial court ruling denying recovery in Hill v. Estate of Westbrook, supra, 39 Cal.2d 458, 247 P.2d 19, we did so in part

Consequently, when the issue of the rights of a nonmarital partner reached this court in Keene v. Keene (1962) 57 Cal.2d 657, 21 Cal.Rptr. 593, 371 P.2d 329, the claimant forwent reliance upon theories of contract implied in law or fact. Asserting that she had worked on her partner's ranch and that her labor had enhanced its value, she confined her cause of action to the claim that the court should impress a resulting trust on the property derived from the sale of the ranch. The court limited its opinion accordingly, rejecting her argument on the ground that the rendition of services gives rise to a resulting trust only when the services aid in acquisition of the property, not in its subsequent improvement. (57 Cal.2d at p. 668, 21 Cal.Rptr. 593, 371 P.2d 329.) Justice Peters, dissenting, attacked the majority's distinction between the rendition of services and the contribution of funds or property; he maintained that both property and services furnished valuable consideration, and potentially afforded the ground for a resulting trust.

This failure of the courts to recognize an action by a nonmarital partner based upon implied contract, or to grant an equitable remedy, contrasts with the judicial treatment of the putative spouse. Prior to the enactment of the Family Law Act, no statute granted rights to a putative spouse.[13] The courts accordingly fashioned a variety of remedies by judicial decision. Some cases permitted the putative spouse to recover half the property on a theory that the conduct of the parties implied an agreement of partnership or joint venture. (See Estate of Vargas (1974) 36 Cal.App.3d 714, 717–718, 111 Cal.Rptr. 779; Sousa v. Freitas (1970) 10 Cal.App.3d 660, 666, 89 Cal.Rptr. 485.) Others permitted the spouse to recover the reasonable value of rendered services, less the value of support received. (See Sanguinetti v. Sanguinetti (1937) 9 Cal.2d 95, 100–102, 69 P.2d 845.)[14] Finally, decisions affirmed the power of a court to employ equitable principles to achieve a fair division of property acquired during putative marriage. (Coats v. Coats (1911) 160 Cal. 671, 677–678, 118 P. 441; Caldwell v. Odisio (1956) 142 Cal.App.2d 732, 735, 299 P.2d 14.)[15]

on the ground that whether the partner "rendered her services because of expectation of monetary reward" (p. 462, 247 P.2d p. 21) was a question of fact resolved against her by the trial court—thus implying that in a proper case the court would allow recovery based on quantum meruit.

13. The Family Law Act, in Civil Code section 4452, classifies property acquired during a putative marriage as "quasi-marital property," and requires that such property be divided upon dissolution of the marriage in accord with Civil Code section 4800.

14. The putative spouse need not prove that he rendered services in expectation of monetary reward in order to recover the reasonable value of those services. (San-

guinetti v. Sanguinetti, supra, 9 Cal.3d 95, 100, 69 P.2d 845.)

15. The contrast between principles governing nonmarital and putative relationships appears most strikingly in Lazzarevich v. Lazzarevich, supra, 88 Cal.App.2d 708, 200 P.2d 49. When Mrs. Lazzarevich sued her husband for divorce in 1945, she discovered to her surprise that she was not lawfully married to him. She nevertheless reconciled with him, and the Lazzareviches lived together for another year before they finally separated. The court awarded her recovery for the reasonable value of services rendered, less the value of support received, until she discovered the invalidity of the marriage, but denied recovery for the same services rendered after that date.

Thus in summary, the cases prior to *Cary* exhibited a schizophrenic inconsistency. By enforcing an express contract between nonmarital partners unless it rested upon an unlawful consideration, the courts applied a common law principle as to contracts. Yet the courts disregarded the common law principle that holds that implied contracts can arise from the conduct of the parties.[16] Refusing to enforce such contracts, the courts spoke of leaving the parties "in the position in which they had placed themselves" (Oakley v. Oakley, supra, 82 Cal. App.2d 188, 192, 185 P.2d 848, 850), just as if they were guilty parties "in pari delicto."

Justice Curtis noted this inconsistency in his dissenting opinion in *Vallera,* pointing out that "if an express agreement will be enforced, there is no legal or just reason why an implied agreement to share the property cannot be enforced." (21 Cal.2d 681, 686, 134 P.2d 761, 764; see Bruch, Property Rights of De Facto Spouses Including Thoughts on the Value of Homemakers' Services (1976) 10 Family L.Q. 101, 117–121.) And in Keene v. Keene, supra, 57 Cal.2d 657, 21 Cal.Rptr. 593, 371 P.2d 329, Justice Peters observed that if the man and woman "were not illegally living together * * * it would be a plain business relationship and a contract would be implied." (Diss. opn. at p. 672, 21 Cal.Rptr. at p. 602, 371 P.2d at p. 338.)

Still another inconsistency in the prior cases arises from their treatment of property accumulated through joint effort. To the extent that a partner had contributed *funds* or *property,* the cases held that the partner obtains a proportionate share in the acquisition, despite the lack of legal standing of the relationship. (Vallera v. Vallera, supra, 21 Cal.2d at p. 685, 134 P.2d at 761; see Weak v. Weak, supra, 202 Cal.App.2d 632, 639, 21 Cal.Rptr. 9.) Yet courts have refused to recognize just such an interest based upon the contribution of *services.* As Justice Curtis points out "unless it can be argued that a woman's services as cook, housekeeper, and homemaker are valueless, it would seem logical that if, when she contributes money to the purchase of property, her interest will be protected, then when she contributes her services in the home, her interest in property accumulated should be protected." (Vallera v. Vallera, supra, 21 Cal.2d 681, 686–687, 134 P.2d 761, 764 (diss. opn.); see Bruch, op. cit. supra, 10 Family L.Q. 101, 110–114; Article, Illicit Cohabitation: The Impact of the Vallera and Keene

---

16. "Contracts may be express or implied. These terms, however, do not denote different kinds of contracts, but have reference to the evidence by which the agreement between the parties is shown. If the agreement is shown by the direct words of the parties, spoken or written, the contract is said to be an express one. But if such agreement can only be shown by the acts and conduct of the parties, interpreted in the light of the subject-matter and of the surrounding circumstances, then the con- tract is an implied one." (Skelly v. Bristol Sav. Bank (1893) 63 Conn. 83, 26 A. 474, 475, quoted in 1 Corbin, Contracts (1963) p. 41.) Thus, as Justice Schauer observed in Desny v. Wilder (1956) 46 Cal.2d 715, 299 P.2d 257, in a sense all contracts made in fact, as distinguished from quasi-contractual obligations, are express contracts, differing only in the manner in which the assent of the parties is expressed and proved. (See 46 Cal.2d at pp. 735–736, 299 P.2d 257.)

Cases on the Rights of the Meretricious Spouse (1973) 6 U.C. Davis L.Rev. 354, 369–370; Comment (1972) 48 Wash.L.Rev. 635, 641.)

Thus as of 1973, the time of the filing of In re Marriage of Cary, supra, 34 Cal.App.3d 345, 109 Cal.Rptr. 862, the cases apparently held that a nonmarital partner who rendered services in the absence of express contract could assert no right to property acquired during the relationship. The facts of *Cary* demonstrated the unfairness of that rule.

Janet and Paul Cary had lived together, unmarried, for more than eight years. They held themselves out to friends and family as husband and wife, reared four children, purchased a home and other property, obtained credit, filed joint income tax returns, and otherwise conducted themselves as though they were married. Paul worked outside the home, and Janet generally cared for the house and children.

In 1971 Paul petitioned for "nullity of the marriage." [17] Following a hearing on that petition, the trial court awarded Janet half the property acquired during the relationship, although all such property was traceable to Paul's earnings. The Court of Appeal affirmed the award.

Reviewing the prior decisions which had denied relief to the homemaking partner, the Court of Appeal reasoned that those decisions rested upon a policy of punishing persons guilty of cohabitation without marriage. The Family Law Act, the court observed, aimed to eliminate fault or guilt as a basis for dividing marital property. But once fault or guilt is excluded, the court reasoned, nothing distinguishes the property rights of a nonmarital "spouse" from those of a putative spouse. Since the latter is entitled to half the "quasi marital property" (Civ.Code, § 4452), the Court of Appeal concluded that, giving effect to the policy of the Family Law Act, a nonmarital cohabitator should also be entitled to half the property accumulated during an "actual family relationship." (34 Cal.App.3d at p. 353, 109 Cal.Rptr. 862.) [18]

17. The Court of Appeal opinion in In re Marriage of Cary, supra, does not explain why Paul Cary filed his action as a petition for nullity. Briefs filed with this court, however, suggest that Paul may have been seeking to assert rights as a putative spouse. In the present case, on the other hand, neither party claims the status of an actual or putative spouse. Under such circumstances an action to adjudge "the marriage" in the instant case a nullity would be pointless and could not serve as a device to adjudicate contract and property rights arising from the parties' nonmarital relationship. Accordingly, plaintiff here correctly chose to assert her rights by means of an ordinary civil action.

18. The court in *Cary* also based its decision upon an analysis of Civil Code section 4452, which specifies the property rights of a putative spouse. Section 4452 states that if the "court finds that either party or both parties believed in good faith that the marriage was valid, the court should declare such party or parties to have the status of a putative spouse, and shall divide, in accordance with Section 4800, that property acquired during the union * * *." Since section 4800 requires an equal division of community property, *Cary* interpreted section 4452 to require an equal division of the property of a putative marriage, so long as one spouse believed in good faith that the marriage was valid. Thus under section 4452, *Cary* concluded, the "guilty spouse" (the spouse who knows the marriage is invalid) has the same right to half the property as does the "innocent" spouse.

Cary then reasoned that if the "guilty" spouse to a putative marriage is entitled to one-half the marital property, the "guilty"

Cary met with a mixed reception in other appellate districts. In Estate of Atherley, supra, 44 Cal.App.3d 758, 119 Cal.Rptr. 41, the Fourth District agreed with *Cary* that under the Family Law Act a nonmarital partner in an actual family relationship enjoys the same right to an equal division of property as a putative spouse. In Beckman v. Mayhew, supra, 49 Cal.App.3d 529, 122 Cal.Rptr. 604, however, the Third District rejected *Cary* on the ground that the Family Law Act was not intended to change California law dealing with nonmarital relationships.

If *Cary* is interpreted as holding that the Family Law Act requires an equal division of property accumulated in nonmarital "actual family relationships," then we agree with Beckman v. Mayhew that *Cary* distends the act. No language in the Family Law Act addresses the property rights of nonmarital partners, and nothing in the legislative history of the act suggests that the Legislature considered that subject.[19] The delineation of the rights of nonmarital partners before 1970 had been fixed entirely by judicial decision; we see no reason to believe that the Legislature, by enacting the Family Law Act, intended to change that state of affairs.

But although we reject the reasoning of *Cary* and *Atherley,* we share the perception of the *Cary* and *Atherley* courts that the application of former precedent in the factual setting of those cases would work an unfair distribution of the property accumulated by the couple. Justice

partner in a nonmarital relationship should also receive one-half of the property. Otherwise, the court stated, "We should be obliged to presume a legislative intent that a person, who by deceit leads another to believe a valid marriage exists between them, shall be legally guaranteed half of the property they acquire even though most, or all, may have resulted from the earnings of the blameless partner. At the same time we must infer an inconsistent legislative intent that two persons who, candidly with each other, enter upon an unmarried family relationship, shall be denied any judicial aid whatever in the assertion of otherwise valid property rights." (34 Cal.App.3d at p. 352, 109 Cal.Rptr. at p. 866.)

This reasoning in *Cary* has been criticized by commentators. (See Note, op. cit., supra, 25 Hastings L.J. 1226, 1234–1235; Comment, In re Marriage of Carey [sic]: The End of the Putative–Meretricious Spouse Distinction in California (1975) 12 San Diego L.Rev. 436, 444–446.) The commentators note that Civil Code section 4455 provides that an "innocent" party to a putative marriage can recover spousal support, from which they infer that the Legislature intended to give only the "innocent" spouse a right to one-half of the quasi-marital property under section 4452.

We need not now resolve this dispute concerning the interpretation of section 4452. Even if *Cary* is correct in holding that a "guilty" putative spouse has a right to one-half of the marital property, it does not necessarily follow that a nonmarital partner has an identical right. In a putative marriage the parties will arrange their economic affairs with the expectation that upon dissolution the property will be divided equally. If a "guilty" putative spouse receives one-half of the property under section 4452, no expectation of the "innocent" spouse has been frustrated. In a nonmarital relationship, on the other hand, the parties may expressly or tacitly determine to order their economic relationship in some other manner, and to impose community property principles regardless of such understanding may frustrate the parties' expectations.

19. Despite the extensive material available on the legislative history of the Family Law Act neither *Cary* nor plaintiff cites any reference which suggests that the Legislature ever considered the issue of the property rights of nonmarital partners, and our independent examination has uncovered no such reference.

Friedman in Beckman v. Mayhew, supra, 49 Cal.App.3d 529, 535, 122 Cal.Rptr. 604, also questioned the continued viability of our decisions in *Vallera* and *Keene;* commentators have argued the need to reconsider those precedents.[20] We should not, therefore, reject the authority of *Cary* and *Atherley* without also examining the deficiencies in the former law which led to those decisions.

The principal reason why the pre-*Cary* decisions result in an unfair distribution of property inheres in the court's refusal to permit a nonmarital partner to assert rights based upon accepted principles of implied contract or equity. We have examined the reasons advanced to justify this denial of relief, and find that none have merit.

First, we note that the cases denying relief do not rest their refusal upon any theory of "punishing" a "guilty" partner. Indeed, to the extent that denial of relief "punishes" one partner, it necessarily rewards the other by permitting him to retain a disproportionate amount of the property. Concepts of "guilt" thus cannot justify an unequal division of property between two equally "guilty" persons.[21]

Other reasons advanced in the decisions fare no better. The principal argument seems to be that "[e]quitable considerations arising from the reasonable expectation of * * * benefits attending the status of marriage * * * are not present [in a nonmarital relationship]." (Vallera v. Vallera, supra, 21 Cal.2d at p. 685, 134 P.2d 761, 763.) But, although parties to a nonmarital relationship obviously cannot have based any expectations upon the belief that they were married, other expectations and equitable considerations remain. The parties may well expect that property will be divided in accord with the parties' own tacit understanding and that in the absence of such understanding the courts will fairly apportion property accumulated through mutual effort. We need not treat nonmarital partners as putatively married persons in order to apply principles of implied contract, or extend equitable remedies; we

20. See *Bruch,* op. cit., supra, 10 Family L.Q. 101, 113; Article, op. cit., supra, 6 U.C.Davis L.Rev. 354; Comment (1975) 6 Golden Gate L.Rev. 179, 197–201; Comment, op. cit., supra, 12 San Diego L.Rev. 4356; Note, op. cit., supra, 25 Hastings L.J. 1226, 1246.

21. Justice Finley of the Washington Supreme Court explains: "Under such circumstances [the dissolution of a nonmarital relationship], this court and the courts of other jurisdictions have, in effect, sometimes said, 'We will wash our hands of such disputes. The parties should and must be left to their own devices, just where they find themselves.' To me, such pronouncements seem overly fastidious and a bit fatuous. They are unrealistic and, among other things, ignore the fact that an unannounced (but nevertheless effective and binding) rule of law is inherent in any such terminal statements by a court of law. The unannounced but inherent rule is simply that the party who has title, or in some instances who is in possession, will enjoy the rights of ownership of the property concerned. The rule often operates to the great advantage of the cunning and the shrewd, who wind up with possession of the property, or title to it in their names, at the end of a so-called meretricious relationship. So, although the courts proclaim that they will have nothing to do with such matters, the proclamation in itself establishes, as to the parties involved, an effective and binding rule of law which tends to operate purely by accident or perhaps by reason of the cunning, anticipatory designs of just one of the parties." (West v. Knowles (1957) 50 Wash.2d 311, 311 P.2d 689, 692 (conc. opn.).)

need to treat them only as we do any other unmarried persons.[22]

The remaining arguments advanced from time to time to deny remedies to the nonmarital partners are of less moment. There is no more reason to presume that services are contributed as a gift than to presume that funds are contributed as a gift; in any event the better approach is to presume, as Justice Peters suggested, "that the parties intend to deal fairly with each other." (Keene v. Keene, supra, 57 Cal.2d 657, 674, 21 Cal.Rptr. 593, 603, 371 P.2d 329, 339 (dissenting opn.); see *Bruch,* op. cit., supra, 10 Family L.Q. 101, 113.)

The argument that granting remedies to the nonmarital partners would discourage marriage must fail; as *Cary* pointed out, "with equal or greater force the point might be made that the pre–1970 rule was calculated to cause the income producing partner to avoid marriage and thus retain the benefit of all of his or her accumulated earnings." (34 Cal.App.3d at p. 353, 109 Cal.Rptr. at p. 866.) Although we recognize the well-established public policy to foster and promote the institution of marriage (see Deyoe v. Superior Court (1903) 140 Cal. 476, 482, 74 P. 28), perpetuation of judicial rules which result in an inequitable distribution of property accumulated during a nonmarital relationship is neither a just nor an effective way of carrying out that policy.

In summary, we believe that the prevalence of nonmarital relationships in modern society and the social acceptance of them, marks this as a time when our courts should by no means apply the doctrine of the unlawfulness of the so-called meretricious relationship to the instant case. As we have explained, the nonenforceability of agreements expressly provided for meretricious conduct rested upon the fact that such conduct, as the word suggests, pertained to and encompassed prostitution. To equate the nonmarital relationship of today to such a subject matter is to do violence to an accepted and wholly different practice.

We are aware that many young couples live together without the solemnization of marriage, in order to make sure that they can successfully later undertake marriage. This trial period,[23] preliminary to marriage, serves as some assurance that the marriage will not subsequently end in dissolution to the harm of both parties. We are aware, as we have stated, of the pervasiveness of nonmarital relationships in other situations.

The mores of the society have indeed changed so radically in regard to cohabitation that we cannot impose a standard based on alleged moral considerations that have apparently been so widely abandoned by so many. Lest we be misunderstood, however, we take this occasion to point out that the structure of society itself largely depends upon the institution of marriage, and nothing we have said in this opinion should

---

22. In some instances a confidential relationship may arise between nonmarital partners, and economic transactions between them should be governed by the principles applicable to such relationships.

23. Toffler, Future Shock (Bantam Books, 1971) page 253.

be taken to derogate from that institution. The joining of the man and woman in marriage is at once the most socially productive and individually fulfilling relationship that one can enjoy in the course of a lifetime.

We conclude that the judicial barriers that may stand in the way of a policy based upon the fulfillment of the reasonable expectations of the parties to a nonmarital relationship should be removed. As we have explained, the courts now hold that express agreements will be enforced unless they rest on an unlawful meretricious consideration. We add that in the absence of an express agreement, the courts may look to a variety of other remedies in order to protect the parties' lawful expectations.[24]

The courts may inquire into the conduct of the parties to determine whether that conduct demonstrates an implied contract or implied agreement of partnership or joint venture (see Estate of Thornton (1972) 81 Wash.2d 72, 499 P.2d 864), or some other tacit understanding between the parties. The courts may, when appropriate, employ principles of constructive trust (see Omer v. Omer (1974) 11 Wash.App. 386, 523 P.2d 957) or resulting trust (see Hyman v. Hyman (Tex.Civ.App. 1954) 275 S.W.2d 149). Finally a nonmarital partner may recover in quantum meruit for the reasonable value of household services rendered less the reasonable value of support received if he can show that he rendered services with the expectation of monetary reward. (See Hill v. Estate of Westbrook, supra, 39 Cal.2d 458, 462, 247 P.2d 19.)[25]

Since we have determined that plaintiff's complaint states a cause of action for breach of an express contract, and, as we have explained, can be amended to state a cause of action independent of allegations of express contract,[26] we must conclude that the trial court erred in granting defendant a judgment on the pleadings.

The judgment is reversed and the cause remanded for further proceedings consistent with the views expressed herein.[27]

WRIGHT, C.J., and McCOMB, MOSK, SULLIVAN and RICHARDSON, JJ., concur.

CLARK, JUSTICE (concurring and dissenting).

24. We do not seek to resurrect the doctrine of common law marriage, which was abolished in California by statute in 1895. (See Norman v. Thomson (1898) 121 Cal. 620, 628, 54 P. 143; Estate of Abate (1958) 166 Cal.App.2d 282, 292, 333 P.2d 200.) Thus we do not hold that plaintiff and defendant were "married," nor do we extend to plaintiff the rights which the Family Law Act grants valid or putative spouses; we hold only that she has the same rights to enforce contracts and to assert her equitable interest in property acquired through her effort as does any other unmarried person.

25. Our opinion does not preclude the evolution of additional equitable remedies to protect the expectations of the parties to a nonmarital relationship in cases in which existing remedies prove inadequate; the suitability of such remedies may be determined in later cases in light of the factual setting in which they arise.

26. We do not pass upon the question whether, in the absence of an express or implied contractual obligation, a party to a nonmarital relationship is entitled to support payments from the other party after the relationship terminates.

27. We wish to commend the parties and amici for the exceptional quality of the briefs and argument in this case.

The majority opinion properly permits recovery on the basis of either express or implied in fact agreement between the parties. These being the issues presented, their resolution requires reversal of the judgment. Here, the opinion should stop.

This court should not attempt to determine all anticipated rights, duties and remedies within every meretricious relationship—particularly in vague terms. Rather, these complex issues should be determined as each arises in a concrete case.

The majority broadly indicates that a party to a meretricious relationship may recover on the basis of equitable principles and in quantum meruit. However, the majority fails to advise us of the circumstances permitting recovery, limitations on recovery, or whether their numerous remedies are cumulative or exclusive. Conceivably, under the majority opinion a party may recover half of the property acquired during the relationship on the basis of general equitable principles, recover a bonus based on specific equitable considerations, and recover a second bonus in quantum meruit.

The general sweep of the majority opinion raises but fails to answer several questions. First, because the Legislature specifically excluded some parties to a meretricious relationship from the equal division rule of Civil Code section 4452, is this court now free to create an equal division rule? Second, upon termination of the relationship, is it equitable to impose the economic obligations of lawful spouses on meretricious parties when the latter may have rejected matrimony to avoid such obligations? Third, does not application of equitable principles—necessitating examination of the conduct of the parties—violate the spirit of the Family Law Act of 1969, designed to eliminate the bitterness and acrimony resulting from the former fault system in divorce? Fourth, will not application of equitable principles reimpose upon trial courts the unmanageable burden of arbitrating domestic disputes? Fifth, will not a quantum meruit system of compensation for services—discounted by benefits received—place meretricious spouses in a better position than lawful spouses? Sixth, if a quantum meruit system is to be allowed, does fairness not require inclusion of all services and all benefits regardless of how difficult the evaluation?

When the parties to a meretricious relationship show by express or implied in fact agreement they intend to create mutual obligations, the courts should enforce the agreement. However, in the absence of agreement, we should stop and consider the ramifications before creating economic obligations which may violate legislative intent, contravene the intention of the parties, and surely generate undue burdens on our trial courts.

By judicial overreach, the majority perform a nunc pro tunc marriage, dissolve it, and distribute its property on terms never contemplated by the parties, case law or the Legislature.

Notes

1. Upon remand following the Supreme Court's decision in *Marvin,* the trial court found that no express contract was reached between the parties, nor was there any implied agreement. The judge concluded that Michelle should be awarded $104,000 for "rehabilitation purposes so that she may have the economic means to re-educate herself * * * and so that she may return from her status as a companion of a motion picture star to a separate, independent but perhaps more prosaic existence." The appellate court struck down this award on the ground that the issue of rehabilitation had not been raised in the pleadings and that there was no legal or equitable basis for it. Marvin v. Marvin, 122 Cal.App.3d 871, 176 Cal.Rptr. 555 (1981). A similar result obtained in Taylor v. Polackwich, 145 Cal.App.3d 1014, 1021, 194 Cal.Rptr. 8, 13 (1983), where the appellate court overturned a rehabilitative award, stating: [W]hile a rehabilitative award is a proper means of enforcing rights which cannot otherwise be adequately enforced, an equitable remedy may not be employed to grant rehabilitation to one who has no underlying right to relief on any theory."

2. In the event that the meretricious cohabitation relationship is terminated by the death of one of the parties, should the surviving party have any rights in the property earned or accumulated by the decedent during the period of the relationship? Presumably the survivor could file a creditor's claim against the estate, but it seems clear that the survivor is not an heir under the intestate succession statutes or statutory protective provisions. It has been held that a non-marital partner is not an heir for the purpose of bringing a wrongful death action. Aspinall v. McDonnell Douglas Corp., 625 F.2d 325 (9th Cir.1980), Harrod v. Pacific Southwestern Airlines, Inc., 118 Cal.App.3d 155, 173 Cal.Rptr. 68 (1981); Matuz v. Gerardin Corporation, 204 Cal.App.3d 128, 228 Cal.Rptr. 442 (1986).

3. Suppose that one partner in a cohabitation relationship sustains serious personal injuries due to the negligence of a third person. Should the non-injured partner be permitted to maintain a cause of action for loss of consortium? The California Supreme Court addressed this and related questions in Elden v. Sheldon, 46 Cal.3d 267, 250 Cal.Rptr. 254, 758 P.2d 582 (1988), holding that a person may not recover damages for loss of consortium or negligent infliction of emotional distress caused by the injury or death of his or her non-marital cohabitant. The Court recognized that there has been a significant increase during the past twenty years in the number of unmarried couples, and that such relationships may offer as much affection and emotional support as is provided by immediate family members, but concluded that the strong policy favoring the marriage relationship and the projected increase in litigation mitigated against allowing such lawsuits. In his dissenting opinion, Justice Broussard pointed out the majority's holding precludes gay or lesbian plaintiffs from stating a cause of action based on the partner's injury or death. "Clearly the state's interest in marriage is not advanced by precluding recovery to couples who could not in any case choose marriage." Id. at 46 Cal.3d 267, 250 Cal.Rptr. 254. For a critical discussion of the *Elden* case, see Cavanaugh, *A New Tort in California: Negligent Infliction of Emotional Distress (For Married Couples Only)*, 41 Hastings L.J. 447 (1990). For a discussion of *Marvin* in the same-sex cohabitation context, see Note, *Applying Marvin v. Marvin, to Same-Sex*

Couples: A Proposal for a Sex-Preference Neutral Cohabitation Contract Statute, 25 U.C. Davis L.R. 1029 (1992).

4. Note that with some limited exceptions, property agreements between legally married persons must now be evidenced by a writing. West's Ann.California Family Code §§ 850–853. Should a similar writing requirement be imposed for non-marital property agreements? Minnesota enacted legislation requiring that cohabitation agreements be in writing, but the Minnesota Supreme Court severely restricted the scope of the statute by holding it applicable only where the sole consideration for the contract is the contemplation of sexual relations out of wedlock. In re Estate of Eriksen, 337 N.W.2d 671 (Minn.1983); Prince, *Public Policy Limitations on Cohabitation Agreements: Unruly Horse or Circus Pony?* 70 Minn.Law Rev. 163, 200 (1985).

5. Where title to property is held solely in the name of one unmarried cohabitant, any contractual claim of the other cohabitant must be proved by "clear and convincing" evidence rather than merely by a preponderance of the evidence. Tannehill v. Finch, 188 Cal.App.3d 224, 232 Cal.Rptr. 749 (1986).

6. In the *Marvin* case, the court indicated that the cohabitation relationship could possibly be analogized to a joint venture. Presumably this analogy is applicable only to the parties inter se. In Planck v. Hartung, 98 Cal.App.3d 838, 159 Cal.Rptr. 673 (1979), the court held that non-marital partners living together as a family were not engaged in a joint venture so as to permit the negligence of one to be imputed to the other.

7. Suppose that a couple never actually resided together, but that there was mutual financial and emotional support in the context of an intimate relationship. Could an implied contract give rise to continuing support obligations? In Bergen v. Wood, 14 Cal.App. 4th 854, 18 Cal.Rptr.2d 75 (1993), the appellate court indicated that such an agreement would be "unenforceable because the parties did not cohabit and therefore no consideration * * * existed apart from the sexual relationship." The court reasoned that "if cohabitation were not a prerequisite to recovery, every dating relationship would have the potential for giving rise to such claims, a result no one favors." Compare Milian v. De Leon, 181 Cal.App.3d 1185, 226 Cal.Rptr. 831 (1986).

B. The Domicile Requirement

The Act of 1850, which established the community property system in California, provided that the system was to apply to the property of persons who contracted marriage in the state and to property acquired within the state by persons who were married elsewhere but moved to California.[25] No evidence has been found of any attempt to use this

---

25. Cal.Stats.1849–50, c. 103, p. 254,— "Sec. 14. In every marriage hereafter contracted in this State, the rights of husband and wife shall be governed by this Act. * * * Sec. 15. The rights of husband and wife, married in this State prior to the passage of this Act, or married out of this State, who shall reside and acquire property herein, shall also be determined by the provisions of this Act, with respect to such property as shall be hereafter acquired. * * *"

The above provisions were not directly incorporated into the Codes but the Code Commissioner did say Section 183 of the

provision to tie the operation of the system to the marriage contract. Rather the courts have consistently declared marital property rights to be controlled by the law of the domicile of the married persons at the time of the acquisition of wealth.[26]

Starting in 1917, the legislature attempted to modify the community property system to protect new California domiciliaries who had married and acquired property in a common law jurisdiction. The early legislation was ruled unconstitutional for reasons that are considered in Section 3 of this Chapter. Subsequent legislation resulted in the development of the quasi-community property concept: property which would have been community property had it been acquired in California would be categorized as quasi-community property and treated in a fashion similar to community property on termination of the marriage by death or dissolution. The constitutionality of the quasi-community property legislation was eventually upheld by the California Supreme Court.[27]

ROZAN v. ROZAN

Supreme Court of California, 1957.
49 Cal.2d 322, 317 P.2d 11.

TRAYNOR, JUSTICE. Plaintiff brought this action against her husband, Maxwell M. Rozan, for divorce, support, custody of their minor child, and division of their community property.

* * *

The first finding essential to the division of the property is that plaintiff and defendant "established their residence and domicile in California in May, 1948, and in any event not later than July, 1948" and "that ever since they have been and still are residents of and domiciled in the State of California." A determination of the domicile is essential, for marital interests in movables acquired during coverture are governed by the law of the domicile at the time of their acquisition. Schecter v. Superior Court, 49 Cal.2d 3, 314 P.2d 10; In re Estate of Bruggemeyer, 115 Cal.App. 525, 538, 2 P.2d 534; Justis v. Atchison, Topeka and Santa Fe Ry. Co., 12 Cal.App. 639, 644, 108 P. 328; Civil Code, § 164; see Rest., Conflict of Laws § 290; Stumberg, Conflict of Laws [2d ed. p. 313]; Goodrich, Conflict of Laws [3rd ed.] p. 385. Moreover, the interests of the spouses in movables do not change even though the movables are taken into another state or are used to purchase land in another state. Tomaier v. Tomaier, 23 Cal.2d 754, 759, 146 P.2d 905; Depas v. Mayo, 11 Mo. 314, 319; see also Beard's Ex'r v. Basye, 46 Ky. 133, 146; Avery

---

Proposed Civil Code came from Section 14 of the original Community Property Act. Lindley, Burch and Haymond, Civil Code of the State of California (1871). This became Section 177, and is now Section 5133 of the Civil Code.

26. See: Estate of Niccolls, 164 Cal. 368, 129 P. 278 (1912); Estate of Frees, 187 Cal. 150, 201 P. 112 (1921); Rozan v. Rozan, 49 Cal.2d 322, 317 P.2d 11 (1957), reprinted in this Section.

27. See Addison v. Addison and Paley v. Bank of America, reprinted in Section 3 of this Chapter.

v. Avery, 12 Tex. 54; Rest., Conflict of Laws §§ 290, 291; Stumberg, Conflict of Laws [2d ed.] p. 314; Goodrich, Conflict of Laws [3rd ed.] p. 378.

Defendant contends that there is no evidence that he was ever in California before July of 1948 and that sending his pregnant wife to California to make a home there in May of 1948 did not establish his domicile in California. See Sheehan v. Scott, 145 Cal. 684, 690, 79 P. 350; 17 Pitts.L.Rev. 97. It is unnecessary to determine whether defendant was domiciled in this state prior to July 1948, for all the property involved was acquired subsequent to that date.

[The court found that the evidence supported the finding of domicile not later than July, 1948.]

The next essential finding on which the division of property depends is "that after plaintiff and defendant became domiciled in California, as a result of defendant's work, efforts, ability, and skills as an oil broker and operator, they acquired some money and property but that in the latter part of 1948 and in any event before May 1949 they lost everything so acquired by them from the latter part of 1948 until May 1949 and had none thereof and that sometime between December 1948 and May 1949, Rozan was obliged to apply to the Veterans' Administration for a pension in order to furnish plaintiff and Rozan their necessary living expenses and necessities of life." This finding is substantiated by the testimony of plaintiff as well as that of defendant, who stated "At that time I was hard pressed. I had properties but no income."

The last finding on which the division of property depends is that the North Dakota properties "were acquired with community property and community property money." It is undisputed that these properties were acquired after 1949, at which time plaintiff and defendant had no funds. Defendant's testimony supports the finding that these properties were purchased with movables for he testified that he made a lot of money on his Canadian ventures as an oil operator and that it was with this money that the North Dakota properties were purchased. Both plaintiff's and defendant's testimony supports the finding that at the time of trial they still owned everything that they owned when they left Colorado in May of 1948, except two parcels that defendant transferred to a trust for his son and an interest that plaintiff sold. Plaintiff accounted for the expenditure of the proceeds received from the sale of that interest. It thus appears that the purchase money for the North Dakota properties was acquired by the efforts and skill of defendant as an oil operator subsequent to the establishment of the California domicile and was therefore community property. Schecter v. Superior Court, supra, 49 Cal.2d 3, 314 P.2d 10. Moreover there is a presumption that in the absence of evidence of gift, bequest, devise or descent, all property acquired by the husband after marriage is community property. Civ. Code, §§ 163, 164; In re Estate of Duncan, 9 Cal.2d 207, 217, 70 P.2d 174; In re Estate of Jolly, 196 Cal. 547, 553, 238 P. 353; Nilson v. Sarment, 153 Cal. 524, 527, 96 P. 315; Wilson v. Wilson, 76 Cal.App.2d

119, 125–126, 172 P.2d 568. There is no evidence that the purchase money was acquired by gift, bequest, devise, or descent. There is, therefore, substantial evidence to sustain the trial court's finding that the North Dakota properties were purchased with community property funds. It follows that the trial court could properly declare that the plaintiff was entitled to 65 per cent of such property as against the husband, for it was within the sound discretion of the trial court to assign the community property to the respective parties in such proportions as it deems just when a divorce is granted on the ground of extreme cruelty (Civ.Code, § 146).

Notes

1. The North Dakota courts accorded full faith and credit to the California judgment in so far as it established that the price paid for the North Dakota land was community property, but refused to recognize that portion of the judgment giving the wife a sixty-five percent interest in the property. Rozan v. Rozan, 129 N.W.2d 694 (N.D.1964).

2. West's Ann.Cal.Family Code § 2660, originally enacted in 1970, sets forth guidelines for the division of out-of-state real property acquired by a California domiciliary as community or quasi-community property. If possible the trial court should effect a division of the couple's community and quasi community property without changing the record title to out-of-state realty. If this is not possible, the section authorizes the court to require the parties to execute conveyances of the out-of-state realty or to award the equivalent money value of the property to the party who would have been benefitted by such conveyances. The application of these guidelines was considered by the Supreme Court in In re Marriage of Fink, 25 Cal.3d 877, 160 Cal.Rptr. 516, 603 P.2d 881 (1979), a case involving community property situated in Florida. The court did not discuss the application of the guidelines to out-of-state quasi-community property.

GRAPPO v. COVENTRY FINANCIAL CORPORATION

Court of Appeals, First District, 1991.
235 Cal.App.3d 496, 286 Cal.Rptr. 714.

MERRILL, ACTING PRESIDING JUSTICE.

Michael A. Grappo appeals from a judgment finding that he had no community property interest in certain real property located in Incline Village on Lake Tahoe in Nevada; that he was not entitled to the imposition of an equitable lien on the property; and that he had no interest in the property entitled to priority over the claims of respondents. It should be noted initially that in this proceeding appellant is not seeking to recover an indebtedness on the basis of a loan transaction but is claiming an interest in real property. We affirm the judgment.

FACTUAL AND PROCEDURAL HISTORY

Respondent Tillie D. Grappo and appellant Michael A. Grappo were married in 1974 and based on appellant's testimony the trial court found they separated in 1979.[1] Both parties had been married previously and had families from those marriages. Appellant had retired from his 25-year career as an agent of the Internal Revenue Service. He was an active real estate investor. Since his retirement, he actively managed a large number of real estate investments. Aside from the pension he received from the Internal Revenue Service, appellant received income in the form of rents from 25 parcels of real estate which he owned in his own name. Appellant was also an attorney, an accountant, and a licensed real estate broker.

In 1977, respondent acquired three unimproved lots on Lakeshore Drive, Incline Village, Nevada, one of which was 1046 Lakeshore Drive, the property at issue in this case. She acquired this property in her own name, as her separate property, with funds obtained by her through a bank loan. Appellant was aware of the fact that the property was acquired by respondent as her separate property, and acknowledged this fact at trial.

Appellant and respondent resided together in Alameda, California, until late 1979, when respondent moved to one of her properties on Lakeshore in Incline Village. Although from time to time the parties would visit each other at their respective residences in Alameda, California, and Incline Village, Nevada, appellant testified that he and respondent never resumed residence together after 1979. Appellant filed for a dissolution of the marriage in 1983, but did not prosecute it. According to appellant, he wanted the marriage to be terminated in 1979, and considered himself separated from respondent as of that time.

Appellant testified that since the beginning of this marriage with respondent, they had kept their property segregated, in order that their separate property would remain separate and not be commingled with or transmuted to community property. It was appellant's intention, which he made clear to respondent, that all property acquired by either of them during their marriage was to remain the separate property of the person acquiring it. In addition, appellant and respondent had "an explicit understanding" that any incremental increase in value to each party's separate property attributable to their personal time and effort spent managing and supervising such property would also be separate property, and not community property.

* * *

CHOICE OF LAW

Appellant next urges that in considering his claim of a community property interest the trial court erred in applying California rather than Nevada law. Appellant's argument is unpersuasive.

---

1. References to "respondent" in the singular are to respondent Tillie Grappo. References to "respondents" in the plural are to all of the respondent parties in this appeal. All other references to individual respondents other than Tillie Grappo will be by name.

It is true, as appellant states, "[t]he general rule is that questions relating to interests in real property are determined by the law of the situs." (*Barber v. Barber* (1958) 51 Cal.2d 244, 247, 331 P.2d 628.) However, as is pointed out in the very Supreme Court case cited by appellant for this principle, this rule does *not* apply "where the funds used for the purchase were acquired by spouses while domiciled in another state...." (*Ibid.*)

"Generally, the court looks to the domicile of the parties at the time the property was acquired to characterize the property as separate or community." (4A Powell on Real Property (1991) Community Property, ¶ 626[1], pp. 53–91—53–92, fn. omitted.) As a rule, marital interests in money and property acquired during a marriage are governed by the law of the domicile at the time of their acquisition, even when such money and property is used to purchase real property in another state. (*Rozan v. Rozan* (1957) 49 Cal.2d 322, 326, 317 P.2d 11; *Ford v. Ford* (1969) 276 Cal.App.2d 9, 11, 80 Cal.Rptr. 435; *Haws v. Haws* (1980) 96 Nev. 727, 615 P.2d 978, 980–981; 11 Witkin, Summary of Cal.Law (9th ed. 1990) Community Property, § 16, p. 387; 4A Powell on Real Property, *op. cit. supra*, ¶ 626[4], [5], pp. 53–96—53–97; McClanahan, *Community Property Law in the United States* (1982) Conflict of Laws, § 13.12, p. 601.) "Property rights are not lost simply because property is transported into another state and exchanged there for other property." (*Tomaier v. Tomaier* (1944) 23 Cal.2d 754, 759, 146 P.2d 905.) [4]

Here, the state in which appellant and respondent were domiciled during their marriage from 1974 to 1979, prior to their separation, was California. It was here that the parties were living at the time that respondent purchased the subject property. California was also the state in which appellant resided throughout the time that he supplied the money for the costs of construction of the house on the property, by means of loans to respondent of his own funds. Moreover, it is only appellant—a California resident—who has asked the court to apply Nevada law in this case. All of the individual parties to this action, with the possible exception of respondent Tillie Grappo, are also California residents. Respondent herself asks that California law be applied, and objects to the application of Nevada law. Under standard choice of law principles, it is apparent that California, and not Nevada, is the state which has the most significant relationship to the parties and issues in

---

4. The choice of law rules in Nevada would produce the same result. In *Haws v. Haws, supra*, 615 P.2d 978, the Nevada Supreme Court ruled that, contrary to the situs rule generally applicable to issues regarding interests in real property, community property issues are decided on the basis of the marital domicile rather than the physical location of the real property. As the court stated: "During oral argument, [wife's] counsel indicated that [wife] sought an adjudication of property rights in Nevada because she believed [husband's] real estate purchases in Nevada, following their separation, were community property. [¶] The division of the community property is governed by California law because California was the marital domicile and [wife's] residence at the time of the dissolution. California Civil Code § 5118 provides that earnings and accumulations of a spouse following separation are classified as separate property. Therefore, after separating from [wife] in 1973, [husband's] acquisitions were his separate property." (*Id.*, at p. 981.)

this case. (Rest.2d Conf. of Laws, §§ 6, 222.) In the instant case, we are not concerned with a conveyance transaction under real property law, but are determining the respective rights of married persons under family law.

Under the facts presented and the applicable choice-of-law rules, therefore, we conclude that the characterization of the parties' respective marital interests in the subject property must be determined under the community property law of California. (*Tomaier v. Tomaier, supra,* 23 Cal.2d at p. 759, 146 P.2d 905; *Haws v. Haws, supra,* 615 P.2d at pp. 980–981; 11 Witkin, Summary of Cal.Law, *op. cit. supra,* Community Property, § 16, p. 387; 4A Powell on Real Property, *op. cit. supra,* ¶ 626[4], [5], pp. 53–96—53–98; McClanahan, *Community Property Law in the United States, op. cit. supra,* § 13.12, p. 601.) Appellant himself states that his claim is not a contractual one, but is based on the fact that he was married to respondent and that he acquired a community interest as a result of his advancement of funds and his contribution of time, labor and skill to the property. Thus, the trial court's choice of California law was correct.

* * *

DISPOSITION

The judgment is affirmed.

STRANKMAN and CHIN, JJ., concur.

Notes

1. Where a non-California domiciliary acquires real property in California, courts have employed the tracing doctrine voiced in Rozan v. Rozan and have classified such property according to the law of the domiciliary jurisdiction. In Estate of Warner, 167 Cal. 686, 140 P. 583 (1914), an Illinois domiciliary sent money to California for the acquisition of California real property. On his death, the court held that the property was not community property.

2. Where a non-California domiciliary dies leaving a will that disposes of California real property, the surviving spouse has the same rights to elect against the will as are afforded by the domiciliary jurisdiction. West's Ann.Cal.Probate Code § 120.

SECTION 3. CONSTITUTIONAL LIMITATIONS

A. *The Due Process and Privileges and Immunities Clauses*

The California community property system has frequently been modified by legislative amendments. The general tendency of the earlier amendments was to enlarge the rights of the wife with respect to the community property. For example, in 1891, legislation was enacted prohibiting the husband from making a gift of the community property without his wife's consent.[28] In 1917, a statutory provision was enacted

28. Cal.Stats.1891, c. 220 p. 425, § 1, amending former West's Ann.Civ.Code § 172.

preventing the husband from conveying community real property unless his wife joined in the conveyance.[29] In 1923, the wife was given the power of testamentary disposition over her one-half of the community property.[30] In 1927, the wife was deemed to have a present, existing, equal interest in the community property, rather than a protected expectancy.[31] In 1951, the wife was given management and control over her community property earnings.[32] In the past, it was held that a statute which increased the wife's rights could not be retroactively applied so as to affect the vested rights of the husband in property previously acquired. This principle of non-retroactivity was first announced in the case of *Spreckels v. Spreckels*,[33] where the court held that the 1891 amendment denying the husband the right to make a gift of community property was unconstitutional as to property acquired prior to its effective date: "To deprive him of this power is certainly to divest him of a property right * * * counsel admit that, if the husband is the owner of the property, then a statute which makes the exercise of the right subject to the will of another is unconstitutional."[34] Over the years the *Spreckels* rule was gradually undermined, and appeared to have been laid to rest in *In re Marriage of Bouquet*, reprinted in this section. However, as *Marriage of Buol* and its progeny indicate, the California Supreme Court has given renewed vitality to the principle of non-retroactivity as a constitutional limitation on the community property system.

The *Spreckels* rule, although announced in a case involving the so-called vested rights of California domiciliaries in community property, also had a significant impact on the development of the quasi-community property concept. There was no difficulty in applying the concept to new acquisitions made by married persons *after* moving to and establishing a domicile in California. Difficulties arose when the legislature attempted to create marital property interests in wealth which had been acquired *prior* to moving to California. The right of the state, under its police power, to care for the economic needs of the immigrant families was never doubted. The problems arose because of the *Spreckels* rule that an amendment to the community property system could not be applied to wealth already acquired by the married person. Because this rule prevented the legislature from changing the classification of existing wealth of its own citizens, the California Supreme Court held that a legislative attempt to change the ownership incidents and characteristics

29. Former West's Ann.Civ.Code § 172a, added by Cal.Stats.1917, c. 583, p. 829, § 1.

30. Cal.Stats.1923, c. 18, p. 29, § 1, amending former West's Ann.Civ.Code § 1401.

31. Former West's Ann.Civ.Code § 161a, added by Cal.Stats.1927, c. 265, p. 484, § 1.

32. Former West's Ann.Civ.Code § 171c, added by Cal.Stats.1951, c. 1102, p. 2860, § 1.

33. Spreckels v. Spreckels, 116 Cal. 339, 48 P. 228, 36 L.R.A. 497, 58 Am.St.Rep. 170 (1897).

34. Id. For a critical analysis of Spreckels v. Spreckels and its progeny, see Reppy, Retroactivity of the 1975 California Community Property Reforms, 48 So.Cal.L.Rev. 977, 1044–1118 (1975).

of property brought into California by married persons becoming California domiciliaries would violate the constitutional privileges and immunities clause.[35]

The constitutionality of the quasi-community property concept in the dissolution context was reconsidered by the California Supreme Court in *Addison v. Addison*, reprinted in this section.

WEST'S ANNOTATED FAMILY CODE OF CALIFORNIA

§ 125. Quasi-community property

"Quasi-community property" means all real or personal property, wherever situated, acquired before or after the operative date of this code in any of the following ways:

(a) By either spouse while domiciled elsewhere which would have been community property if the spouse who acquired the property had been domiciled in this state at the time of its acquisition.

(b) In exchange for real or personal property, wherever situated, which would have been community property if the spouse who acquired the property so exchanged had been domiciled in this state at the time of its acquisition.

(Stats.1992, c. 162 (A.B.2650), § 10, operative Jan. 1, 1994.)

WEST'S ANNOTATED PROBATE CODE OF CALIFORNIA

§ 66. Quasi-community Property

As used in this code, "quasi-community property" means the following property, other than community property as defined in Section 28:

(a) All personal property wherever situated, and all real property situated in this state, heretofore or hereafter acquired by a decedent while domiciled elsewhere that would have been the community property of the decedent and the surviving spouse if the decedent had been domiciled in this state at the time of its acquisition,

(b) All personal property wherever situated, and all real property situated in this state, heretofore or hereafter acquired in exchange for real or personal property, wherever situated, that would have been the community property of the decedent and the surviving spouse if the decedent had been domiciled in this state at the time the property so exchanged was acquired.

(Added by Stats.1983, c. 842, § 21.)

35. Estate of Thornton, 1 Cal.2d 1, 33 P.2d 1, 92 A.L.R. 1343 (1934)—A married man on moving his home from Montana to California brought with him property which would have been community property had he been domiciled in California at the time of its acquisition. The court held unconstitutional a statute reclassifying such property as community property. The stated reasons were: "If the right of a husband, a citizen of California, as to his separate property, is a vested one and may not be impaired or taken by California law, then to disturb in the same manner the same property right of a citizen of another state, who chances to transfer his domicile to this state, bringing his property with him, is clearly to abridge the privileges and immunities of the citizen."

§ 101. Quasi-community Property

Upon the death of a married person domiciled in this state, one-half of the decedent's quasi-community property belongs to the surviving spouse and the other half belongs to the decedent.

(Added by Stats.1983, c. 842, § 22.)

ADDISON v. ADDISON

Supreme Court of California, 1965.
62 Cal.2d 558, 43 Cal.Rptr. 97, 399 P.2d 897.

[Footnotes to the opinion have been omitted.]

PETERS, JUSTICE. * * *

At the time of their marriage in Illinois in 1939, Morton, having previously engaged in the used car business, had a net worth which he estimated as being between $15,000 and $20,000. Leona, however, testified that her husband's net worth was almost nothing at the time of their marriage. In 1949 the Addisons moved to California bringing with them cash and other personal property valued at $143,000 which had been accumulated as a result of Morton's various Illinois business enterprises. Since that time Morton has participated in several California businesses.

On February 20, 1961, Leona filed for divorce and requested an equitable division of the marital property. On trial, Leona asserted two theories in support of her claim of property rights. The first was based upon statements Morton allegedly made to her indicating that she had a proprietary interest in property standing in his name alone, i.e., the theory of oral transmutation. In addition, Leona attempted to apply the recently enacted quasi-community property legislation by contending that the property presently held in Morton's name was acquired by the use of property brought from Illinois and that that property would have been community property had it been originally acquired while the parties were domiciled in California.

The trial court found no oral transmutation of Morton's separate property into community property, a finding amply supported by the record, and held the quasi-community property legislation to be unconstitutional.

The sociological problem to which the quasi-community property legislation addresses itself has been an area of considerable legislative and judicial activity in this state. One commentator has expressed this thought as follows: "Among the perennial problems in the field of community property in California, the status of marital personal property acquired while domiciled in another State has been particularly troublesome. Attempts of the Legislature to designate such personalty as community property uniformly have been thwarted by court decisions." (Comment (1935) 8 So.Cal.L.Rev. 221, 222.)

The problem arises as a result of California's attempts to apply community property concepts to the foreign, and radically different (in hypotheses) common-law theory of matrimonial rights. In fitting the common-law system into our community property scheme the process is of two steps. First, property acquired by a spouse while domiciled in a common-law state is characterized as separate property. (Estate of O'Connor, 218 Cal. 518, 23 P.2d 1031, 88 A.L.R. 856.) Second, the rule of tracing is invoked so that all property later acquired in exchange for the common-law separate property is likewise deemed separate property. (Kraemer v. Kraemer, 52 Cal. 302.) Thus, the original property, and all property subsequently acquired through use of the original property is classified as the separate property of the acquiring spouse.

One attempt to solve the problem was the 1917 amendment to Civil Code section 164 which had the effect of classifying all personal property wherever situated and all real property located in California into California community property if that property would not have been the separate property of one of the spouses had that property been acquired while the parties were domiciled in California. Insofar as the amendment attempted to affect personal property brought to California which was the separate property of one of the spouses while domiciled outside this state, Estate of Thornton, 1 Cal.2d 1, 33 P.2d 1, 92 A.L.R. 1343, held the section was unconstitutional. The amendment's effect upon real property located in California was never tested but generally was considered to be a dead letter as the section was never again invoked on the appellate level.

Another major attempt to alter the rights in property acquired prior to California domicile was the passage of Probate Code section 201.5. This section gave to the surviving spouse one half of all the personal property wherever situated and the real property located in California which would not have been the separate property of the acquiring spouse had it been acquired while domiciled in California. As a succession statute, its constitutionality was upheld on the theory that the state of domicile of the decedent at the time of his death has full power to control rights of succession. (In re Miller, 31 Cal.2d 191, 196, 187 P.2d 722.) In other words, no one has a vested right to succeed to another's property rights, and no one has a vested right in the distribution of his estate upon his death. Hence succession rights may be constitutionally altered. This theory was a basis of the dissent in *Thornton*.

In the present case, it is contended that *Estate of Thornton*, supra, 1 Cal.2d 1, 33 P.2d 1, is controlling and that the current legislation, by authority of Thornton, must be held to be unconstitutional. *Thornton* involved a situation of a husband and wife moving to California and bringing with them property acquired during their former domicile in Montana. Upon the husband's death, his widow sought to establish her community property rights in his estate as provided by the then recent amendment to Civil Code section 164. The majority held the section unconstitutional on the theory that upon acquisition of the property the husband obtained vested rights which could not be altered without violation of his privileges and immunities as a citizen and also that "to take the property of A and transfer it to B because of his citizenship and domicile, is also to take his property without due process of law. This is true regardless of the place of acquisition or the state of his residence." (Estate of Thornton, supra, 1 Cal.2d 1, 5, 33 P.2d 1, 3, 92 A.L.R. 1343.)

The underlying rationale of the majority was the same in *Thornton* as it had been since Spreckels v. Spreckels, 116 Cal. 339, 48 P. 228, 36 L.R.A. 497, which established, by a concession of counsel, that changes in the community property system which affected "vested interests" could not constitutionally be applied retroactively but must be limited to prospective application.

The constitutional doctrine announced in *Estate of Thornton*, supra, has been questioned. Justice (now Chief Justice) Traynor in his concurring opinion in Boyd v. Oser, 23 Cal.2d 613, at p. 623, 145 P.2d 312, at page 318, had the following to say: "The decisions that existing statutes changing the rights of husbands and wives in community property can have no retroactive application have become a rule of property in this state and should not now be overruled. It is my opinion, however, that the constitutional theory on which they are based is unsound. [Citations.] That theory has not become a rule of property and should not invalidate future legislation in this field intended by the Legislature to operate retroactively."

The underlying theory of *Thornton* has also been questioned by several legal authorities in this field. (Armstrong, "Prospective" Application of Changes in Community Property Control—Rule of Property or Constitutional Necessity? (1945) 33 Cal.L.Rev. 476; Schreter, "Quasi–Community Property" in the Conflict of Laws (1962) 50 Cal.L.Rev. 206; Comment, Community and Separate Property: Constitutionality of Legislation Decreasing Husband's Power of Control Over Property Already Acquired (1938) 27 Cal.L.Rev. 49, 51–55; see also Comment (1927) 15 Cal.L.Rev. 399.)

Thus, the correctness of the rule of *Thornton* is open to challenge. But even if the rule of that case be accepted as sound, it is not here controlling. This is so because former section 164 of the Civil Code has an entirely different impact from the legislation presently before us. The legislation under discussion, unlike old section 164, makes no attempt to alter property rights merely upon crossing the boundary into California. It does not purport to disturb vested rights "of a citizen of another state, who chances to transfer his domicile to this state, bringing his property with him * * *." (Estate of Thornton, supra, 1 Cal.2d 1, at p. 5, 33 P.2d 1, at p. 3.) Instead, the concept of quasi-community property is applicable only if a divorce or separate maintenance action is filed here after the parties have become domiciled in California. Thus, the concept is applicable only if, after acquisition of domicile in this state, certain acts or events occur which give rise to an action for divorce or separate maintenance. These acts or events are not necessarily connected with a change of domicile at all.

It cannot be successfully argued that the quasi-community property legislation is unconstitutional because of a violation of the due process clause of the federal Constitution. Morton has not been deprived of a vested right without due process. As Professor Armstrong has correctly pointed out in her article, supra: "Vested rights, of course, may be impaired 'with due process of law' under many circumstances. The state's inherent sovereign power includes the so called 'police power' right to interfere with vested property rights whenever reasonably necessary to the protection of the health, safety, morals, and general well being of the people. The annals of constitutional law are replete with decisions approving, as constitutionally proper, the impairing of, and even the complete confiscation of, property rights when compelling public interest justified it.

" * * *

"The constitutional question, on principle, therefore, would seem to be, not whether a vested right is impaired by a marital property law change, but whether such a change reasonably could be believed to be sufficiently necessary to the public welfare as to justify the impairment." (Armstrong, "Prospective" Application of Changes in Community Property Control—Rule of Property or Constitutional Necessity? (1945) supra, 33 Cal.L.Rev. 476, 495–496.)

Clearly the interest of the state of the current domicile in the matrimonial property of the parties is substantial upon the dissolution of the marriage relationship. This was expressly recognized by the United States Supreme Court in Williams v. State of North Carolina, 317 U.S. 287, at p. 298, 63 S.Ct. 207, at p. 213, 87 L.Ed. 279, where it was said: "Each state as a sovereign has a rightful and legitimate concern in the marital status of persons domiciled within its borders. The marriage relation creates problems of large social importance. Protection of offspring, property interests, and the enforcement of marital responsibilities are but a few of commanding problems in the field of domestic relations with which the state must deal."

In recognition of much the same interest as that advanced by the quasi-community property legislation, many common-law jurisdictions have provided for the division of the separate property of the respective spouses in a manner which is "just and reasonable" and none of these statutes have been overturned on a constitutional basis.

In the case at bar it was Leona who was granted a divorce from Morton on the ground of the latter's adultery and hence it is the spouse guilty of the marital infidelity from whom the otherwise separate property is sought by the operation of the quasi-community property legislation. We are of the opinion that where the innocent party would otherwise be left unprotected the state has a very substantial interest and one sufficient to provide for a fair and equitable distribution of the marital property without running afoul of the due process clause of the Fourteenth Amendment. For the same reasons sections 1 and 13 of article I of the California Constitution, substantially similar in language, are not here applicable.

Morton also asserts that there is an abridgment of the privileges and immunities clause of the Fourteenth Amendment citing Estate of Thornton, supra, 1 Cal.2d 1, 33 P.2d 1. As has been observed "The 'privileges and immunities' protected are only those that belong to citizens of the United States as distinguished from citizens of the States—those that arise from the Constitution and laws of the United States as contrasted with those that spring from other sources." (Hamilton v. Regents of the University of California, 293 U.S. 245, 261, 55 S.Ct. 197, 203, 79 L.Ed. 343, rehg. den. 293 U.S. 633, 55 S.Ct. 345, 79 L.Ed. 717.) Aside from the due process clause, already held not to be applicable, *Thornton* may be read as holding that the legislation there in question impinged upon the right of a citizen of the United States to maintain a domicile in any state of his choosing without the loss of valuable property rights. As to this contention, the distinction we have already noted between former Civil Code section 164 and quasi-community property legislation is relevant. Unlike the legislation in *Thornton*, the quasi-community property legislation does not cause a loss of valuable rights through change of domicile. The concept is applicable only in case of a decree of divorce or separate maintenance.

It is also argued that the legislation here under discussion may be unconstitutional under the privileges and immunities clause of section 2 of article IV of the United States Constitution. It is there provided that "The Citizens of each State shall be entitled to all Privileges and Immunities of Citizens in the several States." The argument is that under the doctrine of Spreckels v. Spreckels, supra, 116 Cal. 339, 48 P. 228, California has refused to tamper with vested marital property rights of its own citizens and must therefore accord the same treatment to citizens of other states. As the United States Supreme Court has observed, "Like many other constitutional provisions, the privileges and immunities clause is not an absolute. It does bar discrimination against citizens of other States where there is no substantial reason for the discrimination beyond the mere fact that they are citizens of other States. But it does not preclude disparity of treatment in the many situations where there are perfectly valid independent reasons for it. Thus the inquiry in each case must be concerned with whether such reasons do exist and whether the degree of discrimination bears a close relation to them. The inquiry must also, of course, be conducted with due regard for the principle that the States should have considerable leeway in analyzing local evils and in prescribing appropriate cures." (Toomer v. Witsell, 334 U.S. 385, 396, 68 S.Ct. 1156, 1162, 92 L.Ed. 1460, rehg. den. 335 U.S. 837, 69 S.Ct. 12, 93 L.Ed. 389.) In the case at bar, Leona, as a former nondomiciliary of California, is a member of a class of people who lost the protection afforded them in Illinois had they sought a divorce there before leaving that state. (See Marsh, Marital Property and Conflict of Laws (1st ed. 1952) pp. 233–234 and cases cited in fn. 22.) She has lost that protection, and is thus in need of protection from California. Hence, the discrimination, if there be such, is reasonable and not of the type article IV of the federal Constitution seeks to enjoin.

Additionally, it is urged that the quasi-community property legislation is not applicable to Morton because the legislation was enacted subsequent to the filing of the cause of action but prior to the judgment. This position is untenable. (See Peabody v. City of Vallejo, 2 Cal.2d 351, 363–364, 40 P.2d 486 (the law at the time of judgment is controlling); see also Tulare Dist. v. Lindsay–Strathmore Dist., 3 Cal.2d 489, 526–528, 45 P.2d 972.)

Nor is the statute being applied retroactively. That is so because the legislation here involved neither creates nor alters rights except upon divorce or separate maintenance. The judgment of divorce was granted after the effective date of the legislation. Hence the statute is being applied prospectively.

It follows that the trial court was in error in refusing to apply the quasi-community property legislation to the case at bar.

Traynor, C.J., and Tobriner, Peek, Burke, and Schauer, JJ., concur.

McComb, Justice (dissenting). I dissent. I would affirm the judgment for the reasons expressed by Mr. Justice Ford in the opinion prepared by him for the District Court of Appeal in Addison v. Addison, Cal.App., 40 Cal.Rptr. 330.

IN RE MARRIAGE OF ROESCH

California District Court of Appeal, 1978.
83 Cal.App.3d 96, 147 Cal.Rptr. 586.

[The parties married and were domiciled in Pennsylvania for approximately 27 years. During virtually the entire period of the marriage, the husband was employed by a Pittsburgh steel company and the wife was a homemaker. They acquired numerous assets in Pennsylvania, including the family home, automobile, insurance policies, and various investment properties. The husband ultimately received an offer of employment from Kaiser Industries Corporation of Oakland, California. He separated from his wife and moved to California, where he assumed the position of president and chief executive officer of Kaiser. Six months later, he filed for dissolution in Alameda County. The trial court characterized the Pennsylvania assets as quasi-community property and divided them accordingly.]

Christian, Associate Justice.

The marriage of Helen F. Roesch and William R. Roesch was dissolved by an interlocutory judgment. Wife appeals from certain portions of the judgment.

* * *

Wife contends that the trial court's division of certain assets which it characterized as quasi-community property was improper. Specially, she challenges the propriety of the trial court's order with respect to retirement benefits from Jones & Laughlin, certain insurance policies on respondent's life acquired by the parties during marriage, and certain income-producing assets.

In the absence of a statute to the contrary, personal property acquired by a spouse during marriage while domiciled in a common law state does not lose its character as the separate property of the acquiring spouse upon a change of domicile to a community property state. (Addison v. Addison (1965) 62 Cal.2d 558, 563, 43 Cal.Rptr. 97, 399 P.2d 897; see 14 A.L.R.3d 404, 411–416.) Furthermore, the rule of tracing is invoked so that all property later acquired in exchange for the common law separate property is likewise deemed separate property. (Id.)

The Legislature has twice attempted to alter the "domicile of acquisition" principle. A former statutory provision (Civ.Code, § 164 as amended in 1917 [now Civ.Code, § 5110]) attempted to treat as community property all personal property acquired during marriage by either husband or wife, or both, while domiciled elsewhere, which property would have been community property if acquired while domiciled in this state. In Estate of Thornton (1934) 1 Cal.2d 1, 33 P.2d 1, this provision was held ineffective, on the basis that changes in the community property system which would impair "vested interests" could not constitutionally be applied retrospectively.

The constitutional foundation of *Thornton*, supra, has arguably been undermined by subsequent decisions holding that vested property rights can be diminished by retrospective application of changes in marital property law if such application is demanded by a sufficiently important state interest. (In re Marriage of Bouquet (1976) 16 Cal.3d 583, 592, 128 Cal.Rptr. 427, 546 P.2d 1371; Addison v. Addison, supra, 62 Cal.2d 558, 567–569, 43 Cal.Rptr. 97, 399 P.2d 897; see generally Boyd v. Oser (1944) 23 Cal.2d 613, 623, 145 P.2d 312.) Thus, in Addison v. Addison, supra, 62 Cal.2d 558, 43 Cal.Rptr. 97, 399 P.2d 897, the court held that a 1961 enactment[1] expanding the definition of community property could constitutionally be applied in cases meeting two prerequisite conditions: (1) both parties have changed their domicile to California, and (2) subsequent to the change of domicile the spouses sought in a California court legal alteration of their marital status. Unless both of these conditions exist, the interest of the State of California in the status of the property of the spouses is insufficient to justify reclassification without violating the due process clause of the Fourteenth Amendment

1. "As used in this part, 'quasi-community property' means all real or personal property, wherever situated, heretofore or hereafter acquired in any of the following ways:

"(a) By either spouse while domiciled elsewhere which would have been community property if the spouse who acquired the property had been domiciled in this state at the time of its acquisition.

"(b) In exchange for real or personal property, wherever situated, which would have been community property if the spouse who acquired the property so exchanged had been domiciled in this state at the time of its acquisition."

(Civ.Code, § 4803, based on former Civ. Code, § 140.5 added by Stats.1961.)

and the privileges and immunities clause of article IV, section 2, of the federal Constitution. Additionally, reclassification based upon a mere change of domicile would abridge the privileges and immunities clause of the Fourteenth Amendment.

In the present case the parties lived in Pennsylvania for virtually their entire married life. *After* their separation, husband transferred his domicile to California; wife and the parties' minor son remained in Pennsylvania. Under these facts, the interest of California in the marital property of the parties is minimal, while that of Pennsylvania is substantial. Moreover, as a domiciliary of Pennsylvania, wife is entitled to the protection of the laws of that state. Application of California's quasi-community property statute was therefore improper. While no modification of the judgment is called for in the absence of an appeal by husband, wife cannot be heard to complain that the apportionment to her was insufficient, from assets which under governing Pennsylvania law were not subject to apportionment at all.

* * *

Notes

1. The applicability of West's Ann.Cal. Family Code § 125 in the split domicile situation was peripherally raised in the case of In re Marriage of Ben–Yehoshua, 91 Cal.App.3d 259, 154 Cal.Rptr. 80 (1979). There the husband and wife were married and domiciled in Israel. After 13 years of marriage, the wife came to California for a visit and filed for dissolution some six months later. The trial court determined that certain real and personal property located in Israel was quasi-community property, and awarded the wife a one-half interest. The appellate court sustained the classification and division of the Israel real property, stating: "In support of the judgment we interpret the decree as a mere declaration of entitlement to the property which has no direct effect on the title to the property in Israel." The propriety of applying Section 125 under choice of law principles was apparently not raised by the husband nor addressed by the court.

2. The appellate court in *Roesch* indicated that California's quasi-community property law should not be applied unless two requirements were met: (1) both spouses had changed their domicile to California and (2) subsequent to the change of domicile, the spouses sought alteration of their marital status in a California court. In Fransen v. Fransen, 142 Cal.App.3d 419, 190 Cal.Rptr. 885 (mod. 143 Cal.App.3d 357H) (1983), the court held that the second *Roesch* criterion is satisfied when *either* spouse initiates a legal proceeding to alter the marital status. The court reasoned that "[t]o require otherwise would enable one spouse to defeat a quasi-community property claim of the other spouse by merely refusing to seek a dissolution, annulment or legal separation."

3. Consent to jurisdiction has been held to satisfy the first *Roesch* criterion as an alternative to change of domicile. In re Marriage of Jacobson, 161 Cal.App.3d 465, 472, 207 Cal.Rptr. 512, 516 (1984).

PALEY v. BANK OF AMERICA NATIONAL TRUST & SAVINGS ASSOCIATION

California District Court of Appeal, 1958.
159 Cal.App.2d 500, 324 P.2d 35.

LILLIE, JUSTICE.

* * *

Plaintiff and Lillian were married in Illinois in 1906. They lived there until 1920 at which time they moved to Pennsylvania. Plaintiff became an American citizen in 1925. On January 1, 1936, the Paleys came to California where they took up residence in Los Angeles and remained until her death. While living in the common-law states of Illinois and Pennsylvania, plaintiff acquired substantial personal property. We are of the view that all of that property, under the law of the states of his then domicile, was his separate property and that Lillian had neither a present nor expectant interest therein. When the Paleys moved to California in 1936, plaintiff brought the property with him. Had that property been acquired by Paley while he was domiciled in California, it would have been community property, but having been his separate property in the state in which it was acquired, its character did not change when it was brought to California. It was plaintiff's separate property where it was acquired and it retained its separate character in this state.

Lillian died testate on January 2, 1954, survived by the plaintiff. On her death she owned real and personal property valued in excess of $1,750,000. At the time of Lillian's death, plaintiff was the owner of property having a value of about $8,000,000, none of which was community property, all having been acquired as aforesaid, as his sole and separate property. At the trial, defendant contended that under section 201.5 of the Probate Code, Lillian had a right to and did, by will, devise and bequeath to her beneficiaries (who did not include plaintiff) not only her own property but one-half of plaintiff's sole and separate property.

In rendering judgment for plaintiff, the trial court concluded (1) that section 201.5 of the Probate Code does not apply to, or affect the disposition of, or plaintiff's right, title and interest in any of his property; and (2) that if section 201.5 is applicable to the property of the surviving spouse (plaintiff) under the circumstances here involved, the section is unconstitutional.

Appellant seeks reversal of the judgment on the ground that factually the case falls within the provisions of Probate Code, Section 201.5 and that this section as applied to respondent herein is a valid enactment and should control. Its contention raises two main points:

(1) Does section 201.5 of the Probate Code give a predeceased spouse testamentary power over the separate and sole property of the surviving spouse?

(2) If it does, as applied to respondent, is the statute constitutional?

Section 201.5 of the Probate Code reads as follows:

"Upon the death of either husband or wife one-half of all personal property, wherever situated, heretofore or hereafter acquired after marriage by either husband or wife, or both, while domiciled elsewhere, which would not have been the separate property of either if acquired while domiciled in this state, shall belong to the surviving spouse; the other one-half is subject to the testamentary disposition of the decedent, and in the absence thereof goes to the surviving spouse, subject to the debts of the decedent and to administration and disposal under the provisions of Division 3 of this code."

We are satisfied that section 201.5, as applied to the facts in the instant case, will operate to take from a living person his sole and separately owned property, by the testamentary action of the predeceased spouse having no interest of any kind therein.

Respondent urges that such a purported testamentary disposition could not be a reasonable interpretation of the statute; first, because such an effect was not intended by our Legislature and second, because it would be unconstitutional in its operation.

The legislative history of section 201.5 and the obvious purpose for which it was enacted favor the interpretation placed on it by the trial court in its application to the facts in the instant case. Prior to the Supreme Court's decision in Estate of Thornton, 1934, 1 Cal.2d 1, 33 P.2d 1, 92 A.L.R. 1343, our Legislature made several unsuccessful attempts to change the interests of the spouses in property acquired during marriage outside of the State of California. The Thornton case arose out of the 1917 and 1923 amendments to sections 164 of the Civil Code. The husband died in 1929. Had the amendments been operative as against him, they would have had the effect of passing one-half of his property, separate when acquired in Montana, to his surviving spouse who under Montana law had no interest in it other than dower. The Supreme Court held that, as applied, they were unconstitutional for the reason that the limitation of the vested rights of one spouse in his separate property, found in the 1917 and 1923 amendments, was a denial of due process and an abridgement of the privileges and immunities of a citizen. Mr. Justice Langdon in his dissenting opinion agreed with the proposition that "absolutely owned personal property brought into this state by the husband cannot be taken from him, nor can his ownership or control over it be diminished or impaired by our statute," (1 Cal.2d 5–6, 33 P.2d 3), but in discussing the problem of succession to the property of a *deceased* spouse, he expressed the view that upon the death of a decedent, certain property owned by him and brought into this state may be subject to the same rules of testamentary disposition and succession as community property acquired here. It is clear that he had in mind a statute which would operate only to control the succession to the property of a decedent—a statute of succession. It is obvious that he had no thought of a statute which would permit a decedent to dispose of the other spouse's separate property.

In 1935 after the decision in the Thornton case and intending to follow the suggestion of Mr. Justice Langdon our Legislature enacted Probate Code, section 201.5. That it was intended to be strictly a statute of succession as suggested by the dissenting opinion and did not purport to rearrange property rights as between living spouses is borne out in a number of cases. In Re Miller, 31 Cal.2d 191, at page 196, 187 P.2d 722, at page 725, the Supreme Court said:

"Unlike the earlier legislation which had been declared unconstitutional, this statute (section 201.5) does not purport to rearrange property rights between living husbands and wives in marital property brought into this state upon their change of domicile to California. On the contrary, it is a succession statute apparently enacted in pursuance of the theory of the dissenting opinion in the Thornton case * * *"

Other courts have expressed a similar view that the section did not attempt to reclassify in the lifetime of the spouses any property coming within its terms (Paley v. Superior Court, 137 Cal.App.2d 450, 290 P.2d 617; In re Estate of Schnell, 67 Cal.App.2d 268, 154 P.2d 437).

From the authorities cited it is clear that from the beginning section 201.5 of the Probate Code was interpreted by our courts strictly as a succession statute governing the devolution, on death, of the property of the decedent and that it was not intended to operate in such a way as to dispose of the property of a living person which, in effect, would rearrange the property rights of the spouses during their lifetimes.

A fair reading of the statute itself bears this out. An analysis of its language makes it obvious that instead of applying to all property of both spouses, as contended by appellant, it applies to each spouse and to the property of that spouse upon his or her death. To shorten its wording, the Legislature used the disjunctive forms in referring first to the death of either husband or wife, and second, to property acquired after marriage by either husband or wife. This to show that the statute was to apply in exactly the same way; to each spouse and to the property of that spouse on his or her death. The first words, "Upon the death," qualify the entire section. Furthermore, the title of the Act plainly designates it as a statute of "Succession (Descent of Property)". Additional corroboration is supplied by the use of the word "goes" in specifying what occurs in the event decedent does not exercise the testamentary power provided for. In that event the property "goes" to the surviving spouse. As appellant seeks to apply this to a failure of a decedent to dispose of the property of the surviving spouse, there is nothing to "go" to the latter because the property is already and always has been vested in him as his sole and separate property. This is another indication of the legislative intent to deal only with the property of the deceased spouse and not with the sole and separate property of the surviving one.

We conclude from its history, its language and from prior judicial interpretation, that section 201.5 of the Probate Code is strictly a statute of succession which does not extend, nor purport to give, to one spouse the testamentary power to dispose of the surviving spouse's separate property, in which she has no interest, during the latter's lifetime. Otherwise construed and applied to the facts in the instant case, its operation would be unconstitutional.

A review of the authorities cited by both parties discloses no case in which the question of the constitutionality of section 201.5 of the Probate Code, as the statute is sought to be applied to the property of the surviving spouse, has been raised, decided or even discussed. The question is an open one.

Appellant's argument that the presumption of legislative validity operates in favor of section 201.5 is of little help when a direct challenge to its constitutionality is made, and it is overcome. The presumption of constitutionality may be overcome by a showing that the statute in question operates to deprive one of property without due process of law or that any of the guarantees of our constitution have been violated. This same point was argued without success in Re Estate of Thornton, supra. It is not the presumption that determines the constitutionality or unconstitutionality of a statute but the fact of its operation and effect in a given case.

When plaintiff came to California, he was already the sole and absolute owner of the property in question. His wife had no interest in it whatever, expectant or otherwise. The character of this property did not change when he brought it to this state. If section 201.5 is to be applied in the instant case, then it gave plaintiff's wife as soon as she became a California resident the right to dispose of her husband's separate property by will, thereby stripping him, while he is still living, of one-half of his sole and separate property. Can this application of section 201.5 constitutionally give to the wife such a power? We think not. If the statute has that effect, it clearly takes plaintiff's property without due process of law.

* * *

The due process clause, however, is not the only constitutional provision involved here. If applied in the manner urged by appellant, section 201.5 conditions the right to enter and settle in California upon the giving up of one's right to his own sole and separate property, which abridges the privileges and immunities of a citizen of the United States. Under Amendment XIV, section 1, United States Constitution, and a variety of Supreme court decisions, Mr. Paley had the right, accorded to all citizens of this country, to travel freely between the states and to become a resident of any one of them. If section 201.5 is applied in the manner urged by appellant, immediately upon his becoming a resident of California, plaintiff's separate property in which she has no interest whatever is subjected to the testamentary disposition of his wife. In other words in order to exercise his right guaranteed under the Constitution he must give up a substantial part of the incidents of the ownership of his property. This problem, too, was discussed by the Supreme Court in Re Estate of Thornton, 1 Cal.2d at page 5, 33 P.2d at page 3. Therein the court said: " * * * If the right of a husband, a citizen of California, as to his separate property, is a vested one and may not be impaired or taken by California law, then to disturb in the same manner the same property right of a citizen of another state, who chances to transfer his domicile to this state, bringing his property with him, is clearly to abridge the privileges and immunities of the citizen. * * * " It seems plain from this language our Legislature cannot constitutionally exact as the price of residence here that plaintiff give up vested rights in property which he acquired and which he owned before he came here.

We conclude that section 201.5 of the Probate Code, as it purports to give one person the power either to take the property of another or to curtail or diminish the owner's right in it during his lifetime, is arbitrary and unconstitutional as violative of the due process clause and that it abridges the privileges and immunities of a citizen. Appellant cites various California cases in support of its contention that the constitutionality of section 201.5 has already been upheld by the courts of this state. They neither raised the question of its constitutionality, nor was the section sought to be applied to take away the property of the surviving spouse. * * *

* * *

Although section 201.5 may be properly applicable to the property of the deceased spouse, it is quite a different matter when applied to a situation in which the separate property of a living person is subject to disposition by the will of a spouse having no interest in it. If the first application be constitutional there is nothing in the law to require a similar holding when the statute is applied to a materially different set of facts in which it may work an impairment of some right secured by the Constitution. The rule that a statute may be invalid as applied to one set of facts, yet valid as applied to another, is too well-known to require citation of authority. In this case, however, we have more of a question of the operation and effect of a statute and of how it affects the rights and interests of the various parties to whom it is sought to be applied rather than a question of severability. But its constitutionality in the first situation cannot prevent a contrary determination in the other if justified under the law. In other words, if section 201.5 is constitutional as applied to the property of an acquiring decedent, such a holding does not necessarily render it constitutional as applied to the property of the acquiring surviving spouse. Generally, when a statute is unconstitutional in part and the invalid part cannot be severed the entire statute is void. Therefore, if appellant is correct in its contention that section 201.5 is not severable the statute is not saved merely because it may, in part, be constitutional.

Nevertheless, section 201.5 appears to be severable. The purpose of the legislative enactment was to provide a rule of succession and it was designed to operate on the property of the decedent. If it be limited to this, as a succession statute, then it would be complete in itself and capable of being executed in accord with the legislative intent and the dominant purpose of the legislature. That being so, the constitutional part is clearly severable from the unconstitutional. The fact that a statute is unconstitutional in part does not necessarily invalidate it in its entirety. The remaining part of the statute may be preserved if it can be separated from the unconstitutional part without destroying the statutory scheme or purpose. * * *

Appellant's principal argument that section 201.5 is not a deprivation of property without due process of law centers around the proposition that it is a reasonable exercise of the police power of the state. This same argument advanced in Re Estate of Thornton, supra, was not successful. Appellant cites considerable authority to the effect that a modification or even abolition of marital property rights comes within the regulatory power of the state and that the police power can destroy vested rights. There are as many cases in which the court recognizes the principle that, however exercised, even the police power is subject to the constitutional limitation that it may not be exerted arbitrarily or unreasonably. Nashville, C. & St. L. Ry. v. Walters, 294 U.S. 405, 55 S.Ct. 486, 79 L.Ed. 949; McKay Jewelers v. Bowron, 19 Cal.2d 595, 122 P.2d 543, 139 A.L.R. 1188; Dobbins v. City of Los Angeles, 195 U.S. 223, 25 S.Ct. 18, 49 L.Ed. 169. Statutes which operate in a manner to give one person power over the property of another have been declared clearly arbitrary and a denial of due process, the police power notwithstanding (Carter v. Carter Coal Co., 298 U.S. 238, 56 S.Ct. 855, 80 L.Ed. 1160; State Board of Dry Cleaners v. Thrift–D–Lux Cleaners, 40 Cal.2d 436, 438, 254 P.2d 29; State of Washington ex rel. Seattle Title Trust Co. v. Roberge, 278 U.S. 116, 49 S.Ct. 50, 73 L.Ed. 210; Eubank v. City of Richmond, 226 U.S. 137, 33 S.Ct. 76, 57 L.Ed. 156). These cases involved various statutes which delegated the power to curtail or limit rights of ownership in property held by another. In the instant case section 201.5, if applied in the manner sought by appellant, delegates the power to take another's property away completely.

* * *

In the instant case, the entire rights to the property in question were fully vested in respondent alone, solely and exclusively, at the time he acquired the property and still were vested in him alone when section 201.5 was enacted and when he came to California. Lillian at no time ever had any kind of an interest in his property. The authorities cited by appellant seem to have little to do with our question—whether the wife who got no interest in the property when it was acquired can thereafter be given the right to dispose of it.

We hold that section 201.5, as applied to plaintiff, has the effect of taking his property without due process of law and abridging his privileges and immunities as a citizen of the United States. It is unconstitutional and void as applied to him. Section 201.5 of the Probate Code did not grant Mrs. Paley the testamentary power claimed for her.

The judgment is affirmed.

WHITE, P.J., and FOURT, J., concur.

Notes

1. The current probate definition of quasi-community property contained at Probate Code Section 66, in keeping with the *Paley* decision, more clearly limits the applicability of the quasi-community property remedy to the decedent's property than did the predecessor statute at issue in *Paley*.

2. The quasi-community property remedy is designed to alleviate the problems that can arise when a married couple moves from a common law jurisdiction to California. The converse situation, when Californians change their domicile to a common law jurisdiction, can give rise to similar problems. For a discussion of the various approaches taken by the common law jurisdictions to this problem, see Clausnitzer, *Property Rights of Surviving Spouses and the Conflict of Laws*, 18 Journal of Family Law 471, 491–497 (1979–80); Note, *Community Property and the Problems of Migrations*, 66 Wash. U.L.Q. 773 (1988).

IN RE MARRIAGE OF BOUQUET

Supreme Court of California, 1976.
16 Cal.3d 583, 128 Cal.Rptr. 427, 546 P.2d 1371.

TOBRINER, JUSTICE. Harry Bouquet appeals from certain provisions of an interlocutory judgment dissolving the marriage and determining the property rights of the parties.

Harry Bouquet and Ima Nell Bouquet married on June 9, 1941, and separated on March 2, 1969. On April 20, 1971, Ima petitioned for dissolution of marriage and determination of the property rights of the spouses. After trial on May 17 and 18, 1972, the court entered an interlocutory judgment dissolving the marriage and determining the property rights of the spouses on May 26, 1972.

On March 4, 1972, after the filing of the petition but before the entry of the interlocutory judgment, Civil Code, section 5118, [now Family Code Section 771] as amended in 1971, took effect. The amended legislation provides that the earnings and accumulations of *both* spouses while they live apart constitute separate property. Prior to the amendment of section 5118, the earnings and accumulations of the wife while the spouses lived apart were separate property although those of the husband were community property. With the trial court's permission, the husband amended his original response and insisted at trial that his earnings and accumulations subsequent to March 2, 1969, the date of separation, were his separate property. The trial court rejected the husband's contention and held that only the earnings and accumulations he acquired after March 4, 1972, the effective date of the amendment, constituted his separate property.

This case squarely poses an issue of first impression, namely whether amended section 5118 governs property rights acquired prior to the effective date of that amendment that have not been finally adjudicated by a judgment from which the time to appeal has elapsed. In resolving this question affirmatively we conclude that the amendment, properly construed, requires retroactive application and that such application does not constitute an unconstitutional deprivation of the wife's property.

We first address the issue of statutory construction: does the amendment to section 5118 of the Civil Code govern property acquired prior to its effective date. Although legislative enactments are generally presumed to operate prospectively and not retroactively, (Interinsurance Exchange v. Ohio Cas. Ins. Co. (1962) 58 Cal.2d 142, 149, 23 Cal.Rptr. 592, 373 P.2d 640; DiGenova v. State Board of Education (1962) 57 Cal.2d 167, 176, 18 Cal.Rptr. 369, 367 P.2d 865), this presumption does not defy rebuttal. We have explicitly subordinated the presumption against the retroactive application of statutes to the transcendent canon of statutory construction that the design of the Legislature be given effect. (Mannheim v. Superior Court (1970) 3 Cal.3d 678, 686, 91 Cal.Rptr. 585, 478 P.2d 17.) The central inquiry, therefore, is whether the Legislature intended the amendment to section 5118 to operate retroactively.

The language of the amendment does little to reveal the Legislature's intent regarding the amendment's prospective or retroactive application. But the statutory language does not furnish the only resource at our disposal. In In re Estrada, supra, 63 Cal.2d 740, 48 Cal.Rptr. 172, 408 P.2d 948, we clothed an amendment to the Penal Code with retroactive effect despite the silence of its language on the issue and the presumption against retroactive application. We explain: "That rule of construction, however, is not a straightjacket. Where the Legislature has not set forth in so many words what it intended, the rule of construction should not be followed blindly in complete disregard of factors that may give a clue to the legislative intent. It is to be applied only after, *considering all pertinent factors, it is determined that it is impossible to ascertain the legislative intent.*" (63 Cal.2d 740, at p. 746, 48 Cal.Rptr. 172, at p. 176, 408 P.2d 948, at p. 952 (emphasis added); accord City of Sausalito v. County of Marin (1970) 12 Cal.App.3d 550, 557, 90 Cal.Rptr. 843.)

Consistent with *Estrada's* mandate, we must address "all pertinent factors" when attempting to divine the legislative purpose. A wide variety of factors may illuminate the legislative design, "such as context, the object in view, the evils to be remedied, the history of the times and of legislation upon the same subject, public policy, and contemporaneous construction." (Alford v. Pierno (1972) 27 Cal.App.3d 682, 688, 104 Cal.Rptr. 110, 114; Estate of Ryan (1943) 21 Cal.2d 498, 133 P.2d 626.) The issue in the present case is a close one, but we conclude that the Legislature did intend the amendment to section 5118 to apply retroactively.

The husband suggests that one "pertinent factor" that supports the retroactivity of the present statute was the patent unconstitutionality of the former statute. The Legislature, the argument goes, surely intended as quickly as possible to substitute the new law for the prior constitutionally infirm law. This argument, though admittedly somewhat speculative, merits some weight in our calculus of legislative intent.

Although the constitutionality of former section 5118 is not directly before us in this case, we can nonetheless observe that it would be subject to strong constitutional challenge. Prior to the amendment, section 5118 blatantly discriminated against the husband during periods of separation: the earnings of the wife were her separate property while those of the husband belonged to the community. It seems doubtful that the state could conjure a rational relation between this unequal treatment and any legitimate state interest. It is even less likely that the state could sustain the greater showing required by our recognition that sex based classifications are inherently suspect. (Sail'er Inn, Inc. v. Kirby (1971) 5 Cal.3d 1, 95 Cal.Rptr. 329, 485 P.2d 529.)

The probable constitutional infirmity of the former law does lend some support to the conclusion that the Legislature intended the amendment to have retroactive effect. We assume that the Legislature was aware of judicial decisions (Buckley v. Chadwick (1955) 45 Cal.2d 183, 288 P.2d 12, 289 P.2d 242); we thus assume that the Legislature knew of the dubious constitutional stature of the sexually discriminating old law. We may reasonably infer, therefore, that the Legislature wished to replace the possibly infirm law with its constitutionally unobjectionable successor as soon as possible. While this inference is hardly conclusive, it is of some value in ascertaining the Legislature's intent.

The husband relies primarily upon a Senate resolution incorporating a letter written to the President Pro Tempore of the Senate by Assemblyman Hayes, the author of the amendment. In that letter, Assemblyman Hayes voiced his view that the amendment was intended to operate retroactively, and observed that he had so argued in obtaining passage of the bill. As we shall explain, although the letter is irrelevant to the extent that it merely reflects the personal views of Assemblyman Hayes, it is quite relevant to the extent that it evidences the understanding of the Legislature as a whole.

In construing a statute we do not consider the motives or understandings of individual legislators who cast their votes in favor of it. (In re Lavine (1935) 2 Cal.2d 324, 327, 41 P.2d 161, 42 P.2d 311; Bragg v. City of Auburn (1967) 253 Cal.App.2d 50, 54, 61 Cal.Rptr. 284.) Nor do we carve an exception to this principle simply because the legislator whose motives are proferred actually authored the bill in controversy. (Epstein v. Resor (N.D.Cal., 1969) 296 F.Supp. 214, 216); no guarantee can issue that those who supported his proposal shared his view of its compass. The understandings of Assemblyman Hayes, then, do not per se expose the Legislature's intent.

In the present case, however, the resolution incorporating the Hayes letter commands respect because it gives evidence of *more* than the personal understanding of the letter's author. First, the letter casts some light on the shrouded legislative history of the amendment. Assemblyman Hayes observed not only that he intended the bill to apply retroactively, but that he *argued* to that effect in obtaining the bill's passage. In Rich v. State Board of Optometry (1964) 235 Cal.App.2d 591, 45 Cal.Rptr. 512, the court accepted the testimony of an assemblyman as an indicator of legislative intent because the court was satisfied that the "testimony was not an expression of his own opinion * * * but a reiteration of the discussion and events which transpired in the Assembly committee hearing when the amendments * * * were under consideration." (235 Cal.App.2d 591, at p. 603, 45 Cal.Rptr. 512, at p. 520.) Although Assemblyman Hayes did articulate his personal view that the statute operated retroactively, he also alluded to the argument that he had presented in securing the passage of the amendment. Debates surrounding the enactment of a bill may illuminate its interpretation. (Sato v. Hall (1923) 191 Cal. 510, 519, 217 P. 520.) Consequently, the letter lends some support to the retroactive application of the amendment through the light it sheds upon legislative debates.

Second, the letter is relevant because it was printed pursuant to Senator Grunsky's motion to publish it as a "letter of legislative intent." The materiality of the letter is not lost merely because it was written and published after the effective date of the amendment; we may properly consider a subsequent expression of legislative intent regarding the construction of a prior statute. (California Employment Stabilization Commission v. Payne (1947) 31 Cal.2d 210, 213–214, 187 P.2d 702.) To be sure, Senator Grunsky's motion was technically a motion to print, not a motion of legislative intent. We are not prepared, however, to ignore completely his indication—clearly embodied in the resolution—that the letter be printed as a letter of legislative intent.

To say that the letter properly bears upon the issue of legislative intent is not to hold that it necessarily concludes that issue. In many cases the indicia of intent are in conflict, and the proper construction of the statute requires us to impute weight to expressions of intent in accord with their probative value. Thus, a motion to print a letter of legislative intent commands less respect than a formal resolution of legislative intent. Likewise, an individual legislator's recount of the argument preceding the passage of a bill probably merits less weight than extensive committee reports on the bill or a formal record of the legislative debates.

In the present case, however, such subtle balancing is unnecessary since we find no conflicting indicia against which to balance the probative value of the letter, the resolution adopting it, or the Legislature's appreciation of the probable unconstitutionality of the former law. While the language of the amendment does not evince a legislative desire that it operate retroactively, neither does it reveal a legislative intent that it operate prospectively only. Apart from the Hayes letter, the legislative history is silent on the issue of retroactivity. In short, the only indicators of legislative intent ascertainable in this case call for the retroactive application of the amendment.

Respondent must do more than merely point to the presumption against retroactive application as a counterweight. As *Estrada* counseled, the presumption should operate only when, looking at all the pertinent factors, we fail to detect the legislative intent. Given the Hayes letter and the absence of conflicting indicia, we cannot hold that "it is impossible to ascertain the legislative intent." (In re Estrada, ante, 63 Cal.2d 740, 746, 48 Cal.Rptr. 172, 176, 408 P.2d 948, 952.) We conclude, therefore that the Legislature intended amended section 5118 to apply retroactively.

We must now determine whether the retroactive application of amended section 5118 constitutes an unconstitutional deprivation of the property of the wife. The status of property as community or separate is normally determined at the time of its acquisition. (Trimble v. Trimble (1933) 219 Cal. 340, 343, 26 P.2d 477.) Consequently, the wife gained vested property rights when, prior to the effective date of amended section 5118, her husband earned income. The retroactive application of the amendment deprives the wife of her half share of the income that her husband had accumulated during that period. Notwithstanding the fact that it denudes the wife of certain vested property rights, we uphold the retroactive application of the amendment.

Retroactive legislation, though frequently disfavored, is not absolutely proscribed. The vesting of property rights, consequently, does not render them immutable: "Vested rights, of course, may be impaired 'with due process of law' under many circumstances. The state's inherent sovereign power includes the so called 'police power' right to interfere with vested property rights whenever reasonably necessary to the protection of the health, safety, morals, and general well being of the people. * * * The constitutional question, on principle, therefore, would seem to be, not whether a vested right is impaired by a marital property law change, but whether such a change reasonably could be believed to be sufficiently necessary to the public welfare as to justify the impairment." (Addison v. Addison, supra, 62 Cal.2d at p. 566, 43 Cal.Rptr. at p. 102, 399 P.2d at p. 902; quoting Armstrong, "Prospective" Application of Changes in Community Property Control—Rule of Property or Constitutional Necessity?" (1945) 33 Cal.L.Rev. 476, 495.)

In determining whether a retroactive law contravenes the due process clause, we consider such factors as the significance of the state interest served by the law, the importance of the retroactive application of the law to the effectuation of that interest, the extent of reliance upon the former law, the legitimacy of that reliance, the extent of actions taken on the basis of that reliance, and the extent to which the retroactive application of the new law would disrupt those actions. (See generally Reppy, Retroactivity of the 1975 California Community Property Reforms (1975) 48 So.Cal.L.Rev. 977, 1048–1049; Note, Retroactive

Application of California's Community Property Statutes (1966) 18 Stan. L.Rev. 514, 518–519, 521–522; Hochman, The Supreme Court and the Constitutionality of Retroactive Legislation, supra, 73 Harv.L.Rev. 692; Greenblatt, Judicial Limitations on Retroactive Civil Legislation (1956) 51 Nw.U.L.Rev. 540, 559.) The parties agree that amended section 5118 can be applied retroactively if such a retroactive application is necessary to subserve a sufficiently important state interest. (See Addison v. Addison, supra, 62 Cal.2d 558, 43 Cal.Rptr. 97, 399 P.2d 897; see generally Boyd v. Oser (1944) 23 Cal.2d 613, 623, 145 P.2d 312 (Traynor, J., concurring).) The wife, however, contends that the retroactive application of this amendment serves no such interest. We disagree.

Addison involved a factual pattern almost identical to that of the present case; it conclusively establishes the constitutionality of applying amended section 5118 retroactively. Prior to 1961, a wife could not, upon obtaining a decree of divorce or separate maintenance, secure any interest in property that her husband had acquired in a common law state. California's 1961 quasi-community property legislation (Stats. 1961, ch. 636, §§ 1–23, pp. 1838–1845) effectively reclassified as community property any common law separate property that would have been community property if it had been acquired by a California domiciliary. *Addison* upheld the constitutionality of applying that legislation to spouses who came to California, resided here, and then separated prior to the effective date of the legislation, so long as the trial was held subsequent to that date.

The application of the quasi-community property legislation to property acquired before its effective date clearly impaired the husband's vested property rights; prior to the enactment of the legislation he had been the sole owner of certain property and afterwards the property belonged to the community. Nevertheless, we deemed the retroactive application of the legislation a proper exercise of the police power. The state's paramount interest in the equitable distribution of marital property upon dissolution of the marriage, we concluded, justified the impairment of the husband's vested property rights. (See generally Williams v. North Carolina (1942) 317 U.S. 287, 298, 63 S.Ct. 207, 87 L.Ed. 279.)

The infringement of the wife's vested property rights in this case finds support in the same state interest that justified the retroactive application of the legislation in *Addison;* here, as in *Addison*, the Legislature reallocated property rights in the course of its abiding supervision of marital property and dissolutions. Moreover, the legislation sprang in both cases from an appreciation of the rank injustice of the former law. The calculus of the costs and benefits of the retroactive application of amended section 5118, therefore, does not differ significantly from that implicit in *Addison*. This peculiar congruence between the present case and *Addison* permits us to sustain the retroactive application of amended section 5118 without protracted discussion. The divestiture of the wife's property rights in the instant case is no more a taking of property without due process of law than was the divestiture of the husband's property rights in *Addison*. The state's interest in the equitable dissolution of the marital relationship supports this use of the police power to abrogate rights in marital property that derived from the patently unfair former law.

In sum, we hold that amended section 5118 governs all property rights, whenever acquired, that have not been finally adjudicated by a judgment from which the time to appeal has lapsed.

We reverse the judgment below and remand the case for proceedings consistent with the views expressed herein.

IN RE MARRIAGE OF BUOL

Supreme Court of California, 1985.
39 Cal.3d 751, 218 Cal.Rptr. 31, 705 P.2d 354.

[This case is reprinted supra at page 117.]

B. *The Supremacy Clause*

Another constitutional limitation upon the operation of the California community property system involves the supremacy clause of the United States constitution and the doctrine of federal preemption. Under this doctrine, state laws must yield to any conflicting federal law when Congress, in the proper exercise of a constitutionally granted source of power, has expressly or impliedly sought federal supremacy. One of the major issues that has arisen in connection with state marital property laws is whether various types of federally created benefits, such as retirement benefits, life insurance, and social security benefits, are precluded from classification and division as community property by virtue of federal preemption. Related issues, including jurisdictional questions, are seen in the bankruptcy cases.[36]

With the exception of social security benefits,[37] California courts have generally been reluctant to declare federal preemption of state community property laws, and even when preemption was mandated, the state courts tended to mitigate its effects.[38] However, as the following materials indicate, the federal courts have not always demonstrated such reluctance.

WISSNER v. WISSNER

Supreme Court of the United States, 1950.
338 U.S. 655, 70 S.Ct. 398, 94 L.Ed. 424.

MR. JUSTICE CLARK delivered the opinion of the Court.

We are to determine whether the California community property law, as applied in this case, conflicts with certain provisions of the

---

36. See, e.g., In re Teel, 34 B.R. 762 (Bkrtcy.App.1983)

37. See, e.g., In re Marriage of Hillerman, 109 Cal.App.3d 334, 167 Cal.Rptr. 240 (1980).

38. In re Marriage of Milhan, 13 Cal.3d 129, 117 Cal.Rptr. 809, 528 P.2d 1145 (1974); In re Marriage of Fithian, 10 Cal.3d 592, 111 Cal.Rptr. 369, 517 P.2d 449 (1974).

National Service Life Insurance Act of 1940;[1] and if so, whether the federal law is consistent with the Fifth Amendment to the Constitution of the United States. The cause is here on appeal from the final judgment of a California District Court of Appeal, the Supreme Court of California having denied a hearing. Reading the opinion below as a decision that the federal statute was unconstitutional, we noted probable jurisdiction. 28 U.S.C. § 1257(1), 28 U.S.C.A. § 1257(1).

The material facts are not in dispute. Appellants are the parents, and appellee the widow, of Major Leonard O. Wissner, who died in India in 1945 in the service of the United States Army. He had enlisted in the Army in November 1942 and in January 1943 subscribed to a National Service Life Insurance policy in the principal sum of $10,000, which policy was in effect at the date of his death. The opinion below indicates that the decedent and appellee were estranged at the time he entered the Army or shortly thereafter. In January 1943 he requested his attorney to "get an insurance policy away" from appellee. After six months in the service decedent stopped the allotment to his wife, and in September 1943 expressed the wish that he "could find some way of forcing plaintiff to a settlement and a divorce." It is not surprising, therefore, that, without the knowledge or consent of his wife, the Major named his mother principal and his father contingent beneficiary under his National Service Life Insurance policy. Since his death the United States Veterans' Administration has been paying his mother the proceeds of the policy in monthly installments.

In 1947 the Major's widow brought action against the appellants in the Superior Court for Stanislaus County, State of California, alleging that under California community property law she was entitled to one-half the proceeds of the policy. Appellants answered that their designation as beneficiaries was "final and conclusive as against any claimed rights" of appellee. The court found that the decedent and his widow had been married in 1930, and until the date of Major Wissner's death had been legally domiciled there and subject to the state's community property laws. Major Wissner's army pay, which was held to be community property under California law,[2] was the source of the premiums paid on the policy. But no claim was made for the premiums; the widow sought the proceeds of the insurance. The court concluded that, consistent with California law in the ordinary insurance case, the proceeds of this policy "were and are the community property" of the widow and the decedent, and entered judgment for appellee for one-half the amount of payments already received, plus interest, and required appellants to pay appellee one-half of all future payments "immediately upon the receipt thereof" by appellees or either thereof. The District Court of Appeal

---

1. 54 Stat. 1008, as amended, 38 U.S.C. § 801 et seq., 38 U.S.C.A. § 801 et seq. Amendments added in 1946, 60 Stat. 781, do not concern us here.

2. We assume the correctness of the lower court's statement of state law. See also French v. French, 1941, 17 Cal.2d 775, 112 P.2d 235, 134 A.L.R. 366. The view we take of this case makes it unnecessary to decide whether California is entitled to call army pay community property.

affirmed, 1949, 89 Cal.App.2d 759, 201 P.2d 837, holding that appellee had a "vested right" to the insurance proceeds, and the Supreme Court of California denied a hearing, one judge dissenting.

We are of the opinion that the decision below was incorrect. The National Service Life Insurance Act is the congressional mode of affording a uniform and comprehensive system of life insurance for members and veterans of the armed forces of the United States. A liberal policy toward the serviceman and his named beneficiary is everywhere evident in the comprehensive statutory plan. Premiums are very low and are waived during the insured's disability; costs of administration are borne by the United States; liabilities may be discharged out of congressional appropriations.

The controlling section of the Act provides that the insured "shall have the right to designate the beneficiary or beneficiaries of the insurance [within a designated class], * * * and shall * * * at all times have the right to change the beneficiary or beneficiaries * * *." 38 U.S.C. § 802(g), 38 U.S.C.A. § 802(g). Thus Congress has spoken with force and clarity in directing that the proceeds belong to the named beneficiary and no other. Pursuant to the congressional command, the Government contracted to pay the insurance to the insured's choice. He chose his mother. It is plain to us that the judgment of the lower court, as to one-half of the proceeds, substitutes the widow for the mother, who was the beneficiary Congress directed shall receive the insurance money. We do not share appellee's discovery of congressional purpose that widows in community property states participate in the payments under the policy, contrary to the express direction of the insured. Whether directed at the very money received from the Government or an equivalent amount, the judgment below nullifies the soldier's choice and frustrates the deliberate purpose of Congress. It cannot stand.

The judgment under review has a further deficiency so far as it ordered the diversion of future payments as soon as they are paid by the Government to the mother. At least in this respect, the very payments received under the policy are to be "seized," in effect, by the judgment below. This is in flat conflict with the exemption provision contained in 38 U.S.C. § 454a, 38 U.S.C.A. § 454a, made a part of this Act by 38 U.S.C. § 816, 38 U.S.C.A. § 816: Payments to the named beneficiary "shall be exempt from the claims of creditors, and shall not be liable to attachment, levy, or seizure by or under any legal or equitable process whatever, either before or after receipt by the beneficiary. * * *"

We recognize that some courts have ruled that this and similar exemptions relating to pensions and veterans' relief do not apply when alimony or the support of wife or children is in issue. See Schlaefer v. Schlaefer, 1940, 71 App.D.C. 350, 112 F.2d 177, 130 A.L.R. 1014; Tully v. Tully, 1893, 159 Mass. 91, 34 N.E. 79; Hodson v. New York City Employees' Retirement System, 1935, 243 App.Div. 480, 278 N.Y.S. 16; In re Guardianship of Bagnall, 1947, 238 Iowa 905, 29 N.W.2d 597, and cases therein cited. But cf. Brewer v. Brewer, 1933, 19 Tenn.App. 209,

84 S.W.2d 1022, 1040. We shall not attempt to epitomize a legal system at least as ancient as the customs of the Visigoths,[3] but we must note that the community property principle rests upon something more than the moral obligation of supporting spouse and children: the business relationship of man and wife for their mutual monetary profit. See de Funiak, Community Property, § 11 (1943). Venerable and worthy as this community is, it is not, we think, as likely to justify an exception to the congressional language as specific judicial recognition of particular needs, in the alimony and support cases. Our view of those cases, whatever it may be, is irrelevant here.[4] Further, Congress has provided in the National Service Life Insurance Act that the chosen beneficiary of the life insurance policy shall be, during life, the sole owner of the proceeds.

The constitutionality of the congressional mandate above expounded need not detain us long. Certainly Congress in its desire to afford as much material protection as possible to its fighting force could wisely provide a plan of insurance coverage. Possession of government insurance, payable to the relative of his choice, might well directly enhance the morale of the serviceman. The exemption provision is his guarantee of the complete and full performance of the contract to the exclusion of conflicting claims. The end is a legitimate one within the congressional powers over national defense, and the means are adapted to the chosen end. The Act is valid. McCulloch v. Maryland, 1819, 4 Wheat. 316, 421, 4 L.Ed. 579. And since the statute which made the insurance proceeds possible was explicit in announcing that the insured shall have the right to designate the recipient of the insurance, and that "No person shall have a vested right" to those proceeds, 38 U.S.C. § 802(i), 38 U.S.C.A. § 802(i), appellee could not, in law, contemplate their capture. The federal statute establishes the fund in issue, and forestalls the existence of any "vested" right in the proceeds of federal insurance. Hence no constitutional question is presented. However "vested" her right to the proceeds of nongovernmental insurance under California law, that rule cannot apply to this insurance. Compare W.B. Worthen Co. v. Thomas, 1934, 292 U.S. 426, 54 S.Ct. 816, 78 L.Ed. 1344, 93 A.L.R. 173; Lynch v. United States, 1934, 292 U.S. 571, 54 S.Ct. 840, 78 L.Ed. 1434. See Hines v. Lowrey, 1938, 305 U.S. 85, 59 S.Ct. 31, 83 L.Ed. 56; Norman v. Baltimore & Ohio R. Co., 1935, 294 U.S. 240, 55 S.Ct. 407, 79 L.Ed. 885, 95 A.L.R. 1352; Ruddy v. Rossi, 1918, 248 U.S. 104, 39 S.Ct. 46, 63 L.Ed. 148, 8 A.L.R. 843.

3. See Lobingier, An Historical Introduction to Community Property Law, 8 Nat.L.Rev. (No. 2), p. 45 (1928); de Funiak, Community Property, c. II (1943).

4. There are, of course, support aspects to the community property principle, and in some cases they may be of considerable importance. Likewise alimony may not be limited to the amount essential to support the divorced spouse. But we do not think the Congress would have intended decision to turn on factual variations in the spouse's need. If there is a distinction to be drawn, we think it must be based upon a generalization as to the dominating characteristics of a particular class of cases—alimony cases, support cases, community property cases. The alimony cases have uniformly been decided on that basis.

The judgment below is reversed.

Reversed.

MR. JUSTICE DOUGLAS took no part in the consideration or decision of this case.

MR. JUSTICE MINTON, dissenting.

MR. JUSTICE FRANKFURTER, MR. JUSTICE JACKSON, and I are unable to agree with the majority in this case. The husband's earnings are community property under § 161a, California Civil Code. The wife has a vested interest in one-half of such earnings. United States v. Malcolm, 282 U.S. 792, 51 S.Ct. 184, 75 L.Ed. 714; Bank of America Nat. Trust & Savings Ass'n v. Mantz, 4 Cal.2d 322, 49 P.2d 279; Cooke v. Cooke, 65 Cal.App.2d 260, 150 P.2d 514.

If the premiums on a policy in a private insurance company had been paid out of community property without the wife's consent, the wife could claim her proportionate share of the insurance. Grimm v. Grimm, 26 Cal.2d 173, 157 P.2d 841; Cooke v. Cooke, supra; Bazzell v. Endriss, 41 Cal.App.2d 463, 107 P.2d 49; Mundt v. Connecticut General Life Ins. Co., 35 Cal.App.2d 416, 95 P.2d 966.[1]

It is claimed that the exemption provision of the federal statute prevents the same rule from applying here. This provision, 49 Stat. 609, 38 U.S.C. § 454a, 38 U.S.C.A. § 454a, provides:

> "Payments of benefits due or to become due * * * shall be exempt from the claims of creditors, and shall not be liable to attachment, levy, or seizure by or under any legal or equitable process whatever, either before or after receipt by the beneficiary."

What did Congress contemplate by the enactment of this provision? I think the statute presupposes that the beneficiary is the undisputed owner of the proceeds, and that a creditor has sought to reach the fund on an independent claim. Under those circumstances the remedy is denied, for the statute immunizes the fund from levy or attachment. That is not the case before us. The nature of this dispute is a claim by the wife that she is the *owner* of a half portion of these proceeds because such proceeds are the fruits of funds originally hers.

And recognition of her status as an owner glaringly reveals the irrelevancy of the choice of beneficiary provision. 54 Stat. 1010, 38 U.S.C. § 802(g), 38 U.S.C.A. § 802(g). Congress stated that the serviceman was to have the right to designate his beneficiary. When he has done so all other persons than the one selected are foreclosed from claiming the proceeds as beneficiary. No further effect has the statute.

---

1. " * * * the only test applied to this problem has been whether the premiums (on a policy issued on the life of a husband after coverture) are paid entirely from community funds. If so, the policy becomes a community asset and the non-consenting wife may recover an undivided one-half thereof 'without regard' * * * to the disproportionate size of the premium when compared with the face of the policy." Mundt v. Connecticut General Life Ins. Co., 35 Cal.App.2d at page 421, 95 P.2d at page 969.

Here the wife makes no claim to rights as a beneficiary. I am not persuaded that either the choice of beneficiary or the exemption provision should carry the implication of wiping out family property rights, which traditionally have been defined by state law. Fully to respect the right which Congress gave the serviceman to designate his beneficiary does not require disrespect of settled family law and the incidents of the family relationship. As noted in the opinion of the Court, analogous occasions have found courts expressing greater reluctance to obliterate rights recognized by the states.[2]

Even accepting the Court's view that the exemption provision applies to the wife, it was intended to protect the fund from attachment, levy, or seizure only so long as it could be identified as a fund. No attachment, levy, or seizure is attempted here. This was an action at law for a money judgment. Appellee obtained a judgment for one-half of the payments that had been collected by the beneficiaries and for one-half of those to be collected thereafter. Payments received under the policy are only the measure of the recovery.

To allow such a judgment does not interfere with the fund or the free designation of the beneficiary by the serviceman. I cannot believe that Congress intended to say to a serviceman, "You may take your wife's property and purchase a policy of insurance payable to your mother, and we will see that your defrauded wife gets none of the money." Certainly Congress did not intend to upset the long-standing community property law of the states where it was not necessary for the protection of the Government in its relation to the soldier or to the integrity of the fund from "attachment, levy, or seizure." These are words of art. They have a definite meaning and usage in the law. This usage is not present here. I find nothing in the section that prohibits the beneficiary from being sued at any time on a matter growing out of the transaction by which the soldier acquired the insurance, at least where there is no attempt to attach, levy, or seize the fund. It was the fund Congress was interested in protecting, not the beneficiary. I would affirm.

Notes

1. Professor Reppy reports that "*Wissner* was such a jolt to community property principles that the attorneys general of California, Idaho, Nevada, Texas and Arizona filed briefs urging the granting of the wife's petition for a rehearing, but to no avail." Reppy, *Community Property in the U.S. Supreme Court—Why Such a Hostile Reception?* 10 Community Property Journal 93, 104 (1983). The California courts subsequently mitigated the

2. The Court has sought to distinguish, unsuccessfully I think, the many cases holding that payments received as pension, disability insurance, or veterans' compensation are not exempted from claims for alimony or family support by exemption statutes in the pattern of § 454a. Exhaustive discussions may be found in In re Bagnall's Guardianship, 238 Iowa 905, 29 N.W.2d 597; Schlaefer v. Schlaefer, 71 App.D.C. 350, 112 F.2d 177, 130 A.L.R. 1014. See also Gaskins v. Security–First Nat. Bank of Los Angeles, 30 Cal.App.2d 409, 86 P.2d 681; Hollis v. Bryan, 166 Miss. 874, 143 So. 687. Cf. Note, 11 A.L.R. 123 and succeeding annotations.

adverse impact of *Wissner* on the community property system by a narrow interpretation of the preemption holding. The opening paragraph of the California Supreme Court's decision in Marriage of Milhan, 13 Cal.3d 129, 130–131, 117 Cal.Rptr. 809, 528 P.2d 1145 (1974), is illustrative:

> In this case we determine the extent to which the trial court in a marriage dissolution proceeding may exercise jurisdiction over a National Service Life Insurance policy issued to one of the parties but paid for with community property funds. We conclude that, in view of federal law protecting an insured's interest in and control over such military policies, the trial court is without authority to divest the insured of such interest or control. Specifically, the court may not award the policy to the other spouse, may not deprive the insured of his right to change the beneficiary of the policy, and may not require the insured to surrender the policy in order to obtain, and thereupon divide and distribute, its cash value. We hold, however, that if sufficient community assets exist aside from the policy, the trial court may award the other spouse an amount therefrom equivalent to his or her community interest in the policy.

See also Marriage of Fithian, 10 Cal.3d 592, 111 Cal.Rptr. 369, 517 P.2d 449 (1974), indicating that "*Wissner* does not require community property states to classify the proceeds of National Service Life Insurance policies as separate property, but only to refrain from administering those incidents of community property law which would frustrate the congressional plan." However, the set-off approach developed by the California courts, whereby the dissolution court could value the community interest in the federal benefit and award the non-military spouse an equivalent amount of other community assets, was subsequently disapproved by the U.S. Supreme Court in the *Hisquierdo* and *McCarty* cases discussed below.

2. Employee retirement benefits have long been deemed property classifiable as community property under the California community property system. Under the *Brown* decision, previously considered, even non-vested pension benefits may be so classified. Where, however, the retirement benefits were created by federal legislation, a question arose concerning the propriety of their classification as community property. The assertion that the federal statutory schemes regarding military and other types of retirement benefits preempt state community property laws was decisively rejected by the California Supreme Court. In re Marriage of Fithian, 10 Cal.3d 592, 598, 111 Cal.Rptr. 369, 372, 517 P.2d 449, 452 (1974).

The issue was then taken to the United States Supreme Court. In Hisquierdo v. Hisquierdo, 439 U.S. 572, 99 S.Ct. 802, 59 L.Ed.2d 1 (1979), the Supreme Court ruled that California community property laws could not be applied to pensions created under the Railroad Retirement Act. In McCarty v. McCarty, 453 U.S. 210, 101 S.Ct. 2728, 69 L.Ed.2d 589 (1981), the court similarly held that military retirement benefits were outside the operation of the state community property system. The court first determined that the application of community property law would conflict with the federal military retirement scheme. Congress' use of the term "personal entitlement" with respect to military retired pay and the anti-attachment provisions of the federal legislation were deemed indicative of a conflict between the state community property system and the federal law. The Supreme Court concluded that "it is manifest that the application of community property principles to military retired pay threatens grave harm to 'clear and substantial federal interests,'" and held that federal law would preclude a state court from dividing military retired pay pursuant to state community property laws.

The *Hisquierdo* and *McCarty* decisions were severely criticized by community property scholars. See, e.g., Reppy, *Learning to Live with Hisquierdo*, 6 Community Property Journal 5 (1979); Kornfeld, *Supreme Court Majority Shoots Down Community Property Division of Military Retired Pay*, 8 Community Property Journal 187 (1981). In 1982, Congress enacted the Uniformed Services Former Spouses' Protection Act, which authorizes a state court to treat military retirement pay either as the property of the Armed Forces member or as property of the member and his spouse in accordance with the law of the jurisdiction of such court. 10 U.S.C.A. § 1408. The holding in *Hisquierdo* was similarly abrogated by the Railroad Retirement Solvency Act of 1983 (45 U.S.C.A. § 231m), which expressly authorizes a state court to divide railroad retirement benefits in dissolution proceedings under state law.

3. The Retirement Equity Act of 1984 [29 U.S.C.A. § 1056(d)] effective January 1, 1985, specifically addresses the possible preemption problems involved in the Employee Retirement Income Security Act, commonly known as ERISA. Because ERISA governs most private pension plans, these problems were seen as particularly acute. Under the Retirement Equity Act, "qualified domestic relations orders" of a state dissolution court are not preempted by ERISA. Furthermore, the spendthrift provisions contained in ERISA, which prohibit the assignment or alienation of benefits, do not apply to payments to alternate beneficiaries named in such orders. The Act defines a qualified domestic relations order to include any judgment, decree or order, including the approval of a property settlement agreement, that relates to marital property rights or support and is made pursuant to state law, including state community property law. The Act also establishes procedures to be followed by pension plan administrators in complying with the domestic relations order.

4. The United State Supreme Court confronted the preemption question again in *Mansell v. Mansell*, 490 U.S. 581, 109 S.Ct. 2023, 104 L.Ed.2d 675 (1989). The case involved the classification and diversion of military disability benefits elected by a spouse in lieu of retirement pay. California courts had treated such benefits as community property to the extent they represented a substitute for retirement pay. The U.S. Supreme Court held that the Former Spouses Protection Act retired pay provisions were not applicable, and that federal preemption was mandated by Congress' intent "both to create new benefits for former spouses and to place limits on state courts designed to protect military retirees." See Gilbert, *A Family Law Practitioner's Road Map to the Uniformed Services Former Spouses Protection Act,* 32 Santa Clara L.Rev. 61 (1992)

5. The preemption rationale of *Hisquierdo* and *McCarty* has been applied to Social Security benefits. In re Marriage of Hillerman, 109 Cal.App.3d 334, 167 Cal.Rptr. 240 (1980). Several courts had previously

reached the same result but on the theory that Social Security benefits were not legally cognizable property rights. See, e.g., In re Marriage of Nizenkoff, 65 Cal.App.3d 136, 135 Cal.Rptr. 189 (1976); see generally, Cohen, Federal Pension Benefits: The Reach of Preemption, 34 Hastings L.J. 293 (1982).

6. The preemption doctrine may have application in contexts other than federally created pension and insurance benefits. For example, under the federal bankruptcy laws, the filing of a bankruptcy vests the United States District Courts with exclusive jurisdiction over property of the bankruptcy estate. As a result, if one spouse files for bankruptcy, the bankruptcy court acquires exclusive jurisdiction over the community property of both spouses, even where dissolution proceedings are pending in state court. To the extent that there is any conflict between community property laws and the federal bankruptcy laws with respect to the disposition of the property, the federal laws will control under the supremacy clause. In re Teel, 34 B.R. 762 (Bkrtcy.App.1983). In Marriage of Cohen, 105 Cal.App.3d 836, 164 Cal.Rptr. 672 (1980), the court ruled that the husband's nonliability for his share of the community indebtedness as to which he had been discharged from liability in bankruptcy was required under the supremacy clause.

7. The California Court of Appeals has held that the federal Copyright Act does not preclude the characterization of a copyright as divisible community property: "We find no inconsistency between the federal Copyright Act and California's community property law so as to invoke the preemption doctrine." Marriage of Worth, 195 Cal.App.3d 768, 778, 241 Cal.Rptr. 135, 140 (1987).

*

Chapter 4

SELECTED PROBLEMS IN CLASSIFICATION

A large number of married persons do not keep their separate property and community property wholly segregated. They put both community funds and separate funds in a single bank account, or use a combination of separate funds and community funds in the purchase of a single asset, or expend community property assets, including their time, energy and skill, in the operation of a separate property business. They may use separate property to make improvements to community property, or vice versa. These kinds of situations can give rise to serious problems when the asset must be classified for purposes of distribution on death, division on dissolution, or attachment by creditors. This Chapter examines the classification process, particularly the basic tracing principle, in the context of these special problems.[1]

SECTION 1. COMMINGLED FUNDS

"Commingling" refers to the combining or intermixing of community and separate funds into a common mass or pool. The most frequent example involves the deposit of both community and separate funds in a single bank account during marriage. If the deposits are made at one time, and no withdrawals are made, and records are kept of the nature of the deposits, the classification process is relatively simple. The account can be viewed as an acquisition during marriage, and within the general presumption of community property. The spouse seeking to establish the separate character of a portion of the funds may rebut the general presumption by directly tracing that portion of the funds to a separate property source.

Where there are deposits and withdrawals over a period of time, and the commingled funds are used to purchase other assets, the problem of classifying the ownership interests in such property becomes more complicated. The controlling principles, however, remain the same.

---

1. For a discussion of this general problem area in both community property and common law contexts, see Reynolds, Increases in Separate Property and the Evolving Marital Partnership, 24 Wake Forest L.R. 239 (1989)

265

The property comes within the general presumption of community property, but it may be possible to rebut this presumption by directly tracing the asset to a separate property source. If direct evidence is lacking, as it may well be if the spouses have not kept accurate records of the nature of every deposit and withdrawal, a more indirect type of tracing may be used. This method of indirect tracing is aided by the judicial presumption that family expenses are paid from the community funds. If it can be established that at the time of the disputed acquisition, the community funds in the account had been exhausted by community expenses, then the balance in the account at the time the property was purchased was necessarily separate. Any item purchased with the remaining funds would then be deemed separate property.

Where it is impossible to trace either directly or indirectly the separate and community contributions to the commingled fund or assets purchased with commingled funds, the general presumption of community property controls. And even if the respective amounts of the community and separate contributions can be established, if the amount of the community property contribution is insignificant, the court may disregard it.

SEE v. SEE

Supreme Court of California, 1966.
64 Cal.2d 778, 51 Cal.Rptr. 888, 415 P.2d 776.

TRAYNOR, CHIEF JUSTICE. Plaintiff Laurance A. See and cross-complainant Elizabeth Lee See appeal from an interlocutory judgment that grants each a divorce. * * *

The parties were married on October 17, 1941, and they separated about May 10, 1962. Throughout the marriage they were residents of California, and Laurance was employed by a family-controlled corporation, See's Candies, Inc. For most of that period he also served as president of its wholly-owned subsidiary, See's Candy Shops, Inc. In the twenty-one years of the marriage he received more than $1,000,000 in salaries from the two corporations.

Laurance had a personal account on the books of See's Candies, Inc., denominated Account 13. Throughout the marriage his annual salary from See's Candies, Inc., which was $60,000 at the time of the divorce, was credited to this account and many family expenses were paid by checks drawn on it. To maintain a credit balance in Account 13, Laurance from time to time transferred funds to it from an account at the Security First National Bank, hereafter called the Security Account.

The funds deposited in the Security Account came primarily from Laurance's separate property. On occasion he deposited his annual $15,000 salary from See's Candy Shops, Inc. in that account as a "reserve against taxes" on that salary. Thus there was a commingling of community property and separate property in both the Security Account and Account 13. Funds from the Security Account were sometimes used to pay community expenses and also to purchase some of the assets held in Laurance's name at the time of the divorce proceedings.

Over Elizabeth's objection, the trial court followed the theory advanced by Laurance that a proven excess of community expenses over community income during the marriage establishes that there has been no acquisition of property with community funds.

Such a theory, without support in either statutory or case law of this state, would disrupt the California community property system. It would transform a wife's interest in the community property from a "present, existing and equal interest" as specified by Civil Code section 161a, into an inchoate expectancy to be realized only if upon termination of the marriage the community income fortuitously exceeded community expenditures. It would engender uncertainties as to testamentary and inter vivos dispositions, income, estate and gift taxation, and claims against property.

The character of property as separate or community is determined at the time of its acquisition. (In re Miller, 31 Cal.2d 191, 197, 187 P.2d 722; Siberell v. Siberell, 214 Cal. 767, 770, 7 P.2d 1003; Bias v. Reed, 169 Cal. 33, 42, 145 P. 516.) If it is community property when acquired, it remains so throughout the marriage unless the spouses agree to change its nature or the spouse charged with its management makes a gift of it to the other. (Odone v. Marzocchi, 34 Cal.2d 431, 435, 211 P.2d 297, 212 P.2d 233, 17 A.L.R.2d 1109; Mears v. Mears, 180 Cal.App.2d 484, 499, 4 Cal.Rptr. 618.)

Property acquired by purchase during a marriage is presumed to be community property, and the burden is on the spouse asserting its separate character to overcome the presumption. (Estate of Niccolls, 164 Cal. 368, 129 P. 278; Thomasset v. Thomasset, 122 Cal.App.2d 116, 123, 264 P.2d 626.) The presumption applies when a husband purchases property during the marriage with funds from an undisclosed or disputed source, such as an account or fund in which he has commingled his separate funds with community funds. (Estate of Neilson, 57 Cal.2d 733, 742, 22 Cal.Rptr. 1, 371 P.2d 745.) He may trace the source of the property to his separate funds and overcome the presumption with evidence that community expenses exceeded community income at the time of acquisition. If he proves that at that time all community income was exhausted by family expenses, he establishes that the property was purchased with separate funds. (Estate of Neilson, supra, at p. 742, 22 Cal.Rptr. 1, 371 P.2d 745; Thomasset v. Thomasset, supra, 122 Cal. App.2d at p. 127, 264 P.2d 626.) Only when through no fault of the husband, it is not possible to ascertain the balance of income and expenditures at the time property was acquired, can recapitulation of the total community expenses and income throughout the marriage be used to establish the character of the property. Thus, in Estate of Ades, 81 Cal.App.2d 334, 184 P.2d 1, relied on by plaintiff, this method of tracing was used to establish that assets discovered after the husband's death had been acquired before the marriage. The question was not presented as to the balance of income and expenditures at any specific time during the marriage. In Estate of Arstein, 56 Cal.2d 239, 14 Cal.Rptr. 809, 364 P.2d 33, relied on by plaintiff, the husband's skill and industry in managing his separate property was the source of all community income during the marriage. Not until the trial could a determination be made as to what proportion of the total income was attributable to the husband's skill and industry. In Thomasset v. Thomasset, supra, 122 Cal.App.2d 116, 264 P.2d 626, the court made clear that the time of acquisition of disputed property is decisive. "An accountant testified that at the time the various items adjudged to be defendant's separate property were purchased, there were no community funds available. * * * The evidence [shows] that at the time the property was purchased the community funds had been exhausted * * *." (Id. at p. 127, 264 P.2d at p. 633.) Anything to the contrary in Patterson v. Patterson, 242 A.C.A. 378, 51 Cal.Rptr. 339, is disapproved.

A husband who commingles the property of the community with his separate property, but fails to keep adequate records, cannot invoke the burden of record keeping as a justification for a recapitulation of income and expenses at the termination of the marriage that disregards any acquisitions that may have been made during the marriage with community funds. If funds used for acquisitions during marriage cannot otherwise be traced to their source and the husband who has commingled property is unable to establish that there was a deficit in the community accounts when the assets were purchased, the presumption controls that property acquired by purchase during marriage is community property. The husband may protect his separate property by not commingling community and separate assets and income. Once he commingles, he assumes the burden of keeping records adequate to establish the balance of community income and expenditures at the time an asset is acquired with commingled property.

The trial court also followed the theory that a husband who expends his separate property for community expenses is entitled to reimbursement from community assets. This theory likewise lacks support in the statutory or case law of this state. A husband is required to support his wife and family. (Civ.Code, §§ 155, 196, 242.) Indeed, husband and wife assume mutual obligations of support upon marriage. These obligations are not conditioned on the existence of community property or income. The duty to support imposed upon husbands by Civil Code section 155 and upon wives by Civil Code section 176 requires the use of separate property of the parties when there is no community property. There is no right to reimbursement under the statutes.

Likewise a husband who elects to use his separate property instead of community property to meet community expenses cannot claim reimbursement. In the absence of an agreement to the contrary, the use of his separate property by a husband for community purposes is a gift to the community. The considerations that underlie the rule denying reimbursement to either the community or the husband's separate estate for funds expended to improve a wife's separate property (Dunn v.

Mullan, 211 Cal. 583, 589, 296 P. 604, 77 A.L.R. 1015) apply with equal force here. The husband has both management and control of the community property. (Civ.Code, §§ 172, 172a) along with the right to select the place and mode of living. (Civ.Code, § 156.) His use of separate property to maintain a standard of living that cannot be maintained with community resources alone no more entitles him to reimbursement from after-acquired community assets than it would from existing community assets.

Nor can we approve the recognition of an exception, a right to reimbursement of separate funds expended for community purposes at a time when a community bank account is exhausted. (Kenney v. Kenney, 128 Cal.App.2d 128, 136, 274 P.2d 951; Thomasset v. Thomasset, supra, 122 Cal.App.2d 116, 126, 264 P.2d 626; Hill v. Hill, 82 Cal.App.2d 682, 698, 187 P.2d 28; cf. Mears v. Mears, supra, 180 Cal.App.2d 484, 508, 4 Cal.Rptr. 618.) Although this exception was restricted to recovery from the same community account when replenished, there is no statutory basis for it, and the court that first declared it cited no authority to support it. Such an exception conflicts with the long-standing rule that a wife who uses her separate funds in payment of family expenses without agreement regarding repayment cannot require her husband to reimburse her. (Ives v. Connacher, 162 Cal. 174, 177, 121 P. 394; Blackburn v. Blackburn, 160 Cal.App.2d 301, 304, 324 P.2d 971; Thomson v. Thomson, 81 Cal.App. 678, 254 P. 644; cf. Haseltine v. Haseltine, 203 Cal.App.2d 48, 21 Cal.Rptr. 238.) Nor is a wife required to reimburse her husband in the converse situation, particularly since the husband has the control and management of community expenses and resources. The basic rule is that the party who uses his separate property for community purposes is entitled to reimbursement from the community or separate property of the other only if there is an agreement between the parties to that effect. To the extent that they conflict with this rule Mears v. Mears, supra, 180 Cal.App.2d 484, 4 Cal.Rptr. 618; Kenney v. Kenney, supra, 128 Cal.App.2d 128, 274 P.2d 951; Thomasset v. Thomasset, supra, 122 Cal.App.2d 116, 264 P.2d 626, and Hill v. Hill, 82 Cal.App.2d 682, 187 P.2d 28, are disapproved.

Plaintiff has not met his burden of proving an excess of community expenses over community income at the times the other assets purchased during the marriage were acquired. The part of the judgment finding them to be his separate property is therefore reversed. Since the property issues were tried on the theory that the nature of the property could be determined by proving total community income and expenditures and since the parties may have additional evidence that would otherwise have been presented, plaintiff's failure to overcome the presumption that the assets are community property is not conclusive. We therefore remand the case for retrial of the property issues. Since the court considered the lack of community property a significant factor in determining the amount of the alimony award, that part of the judgment is also reversed.

Notes

1. In Estate of Murphy, 15 Cal.3d 907, 919, 126 Cal.Rptr. 820, 829, 544 P.2d 956 (1976), the Supreme Court indicated that the See v. See rule requiring adequate record keeping should apply with the same force in a case where the marriage was terminated by death: "Murphy had the opportunity during his lifetime to maintain adequate records for tracing the disposition of his separate income. His legatees are bound by the consequences of his failure to do so."

2. Although a spouse is not generally entitled to reimbursement for separate funds utilized to meet community obligations, the California Supreme Court in In re Marriage of Epstein, 24 Cal.3d 76, 154 Cal.Rptr. 413, 592 P.2d 1165 (1979) held that the See rule does not apply to expenditures subsequent to separation. The court noted that the rule denying reimbursement is based largely on the presumption that the paying spouse intended a gift, and that when the parties have separated, the rational basis for presuming a donative intent disappears. Thus the husband could claim reimbursement for sums expended after separation to preserve and maintain the family residence, unless such sums were paid to fulfill the husband's support obligations or unless there was an agreement that the payment would not be reimbursed.

IN RE MARRIAGE OF MIX

Supreme Court of California, 1975.
14 Cal.3d 604, 122 Cal.Rptr. 79, 536 P.2d 479.

[During her marriage to Richard Mix, Esther deposited separate property income and community property earnings in a bank account and withdrew funds from such account to purchase rental properties. The classification of such rental properties was put in issue in dissolution proceedings.]

SULLIVAN, JUSTICE. * * * During the marriage of Richard and Esther the law bestowed on Richard the management and control of the community personal property other than Esther's earnings and on Esther the management and control of her community property earnings and separate property rents, issues and profits, with other exceptions not here applicable. (§§ 5124, 5125, and see fn. 5, ante; see also §§ 5113.5, 5128.) Thus under the law and the undisputed facts Esther had the management and control of the commingled bank accounts at the California Bank. Because the presumption in section 5110 that any interest in property acquired by a married woman in writing is her separate property will have no further effect after the wife acquires joint management of all community property on January 1, 1975 (see fn. 6, ante), it should likewise not apply when the wife had management and control of the bank account in question. Otherwise, the wife managing a commingled account could by this device insulate herself from the rules applicable to commingling. We conclude therefore that the controlling presumption in this case is the one that property acquired during marriage is community property. (See v. See, supra, 64 Cal.2d 778, 783, 51 Cal.Rptr. 888, 415 P.2d 776.)

The presumption that all property acquired by either spouse during the marriage is community property may be overcome. (See v. See, supra, 64 Cal.2d at p. 783, 51 Cal.Rptr. 888, 415 P.2d 776; Estate of Niccolls (1912) 164 Cal. 368, 371, 129 P. 278; Patterson v. Patterson, supra, 242 Cal.App.2d 333, 341, 51 Cal.Rptr. 339; Thomasset v. Thomasset, supra, 122 Cal.App.2d 116, 123, 264 P.2d 626.) Whether or not the presumption is overcome is a question of fact for the trial court. (Machado v. Machado (1962) 58 Cal.2d 501, 506, 25 Cal.Rptr. 87, 375 P.2d 55; Gudelj v. Gudelj (1953) 41 Cal.2d 202, 212, 259 P.2d 656; Pack v. Vartanian (1965) 232 Cal.App.2d 466, 470, 42 Cal.Rptr. 729.) Generally speaking such post-marital property can be established to be separate property by two independent methods of tracing. The first method involves direct tracing. As the court explained in *Hicks:* "[S]eparate funds do not lose their character as such when commingled with community funds in a bank account so long as the amount thereof can be ascertained. Whether separate funds so deposited continue to be on deposit when a withdrawal is made from such a bank account for the purpose of purchasing specific property, and whether the intention of the drawer is to withdraw such funds therefrom, are questions of fact for determination by the trial court." (Hicks v. Hicks, supra, 211 Cal. App.2d 144, 157, 27 Cal.Rptr. 307, 315; 7 Witkin, Summary of Cal.Law (8th ed.) § 33, pp. 5126–5127.) The second method involves a consideration of family expenses. It is based upon the presumption that family expenses are paid from community funds. (Thomasset v. Thomasset, supra, 122 Cal.App.2d 116, 126, 264 P.2d 626; 7 Witkin, Summary of Cal.Law (8th ed.) § 42, pp. 5133–5136.) If at the time of the acquisition of the property in dispute, it can be shown that all community income in the commingled account has been exhausted by family expenses, then all funds remaining in the account at the time the property was purchased were necessarily separate funds. (See v. See, supra, 64 Cal.2d 778, 783, 51 Cal.Rptr. 888, 415 P.2d 776.)

The effect of the presumption and the two methods overcoming it are succinctly summarized in *See:* "If funds used for acquisitions during marriage cannot otherwise be traced to their source and the husband who has commingled property is unable to establish that there was a deficit in the community accounts when the assets were purchased, the presumption controls that property acquired by purchase during marriage is community property." (Id. at p. 784, 51 Cal.Rptr. at p. 892, 415 P.2d at p. 780.) Throughout the marriage Esther commingled her community property earnings from her law practice with the rents, issues and proceeds from her separate property in several bank accounts. She concedes that she made no attempt to trace the source of the property by resorting to the "family expense method." We are satisfied from our review of the evidence that Esther failed to keep adequate records to show that family expenses had exhausted community funds at the time of the acquisition of any of the property here in dispute.

Esther contends, however, that she introduced sufficient evidence to trace the source of the funds used to acquire each item of disputed property to her separate property in accordance with the "direct tracing test" described in Hicks v. Hicks, supra, 211 Cal.App.2d 144, 27 Cal. Rptr. 307 (see p. 84, ante), and that therefore the trial court's finding to that effect is supported by substantial evidence. In *Hicks* the husband introduced evidence of separate property deposits amounting to $267,-580.81, consisting of $91,610.90 from dividends, $66,266.70 in proceeds from sales of separate property assets, and $109,703.21 from loans secured by the credit of his separate property. He also introduced evidence of separate property withdrawals in the amount of $172,931.80 and an excess of total separate property deposits over separate property withdrawals in the amount of $94,649.01. The court held that this evidence in combination with evidence showing that the questioned withdrawals were intended to purchase the disputed property as separate property, supported the trial court's finding of separate property.

Esther introduced into evidence a schedule compiled by herself and her accountant from her records which itemized chronologically each source of separate funds, each expenditure for separate property purposes, and the balance of separate property funds remaining after each such expenditure. She received $99,632.02 attributable to her separate property; expended $42,213.79 for separate property purposes leaving an excess of separate property receipts over separate property expenditures in the amount of $57,418.23 throughout the course of the marriage. Each year from 1958 to 1968, excepting the year 1961, there was an excess of separate property receipts over separate property expenditures, leaving a balance of separate funds. The 1961 deficit did not, however, exhaust the balance of separate funds carried forward from prior years. The schedule demonstrated that Esther's expenditures for separate property purposes closely paralleled in time and amount separate property receipts and thus established her intention to use only her separate property funds for separate property expenditures.

Richard contends that the schedule contains a fatal flaw in that the entries of receipts and expenditures are not tied to any bank account or bank accounts. Therefore, he argues, the schedule shows merely the availability of separate funds on the given dates but fails utterly to demonstrate the actual expenditures of those funds for the enumerated separate purposes. Esther concedes that she was unable to support the schedule by correlating each itemized deposit and withdrawal on the schedule with an entry in a particular bank account due to the unavailability of various bank records as well as to the lack of such records of her own. Richard urges that this state of the evidence demonstrates that Esther has failed to meet her burden, that she has therefore not overcome the community property presumption, and that her claims to specific property as being her separate property must fall.

We agree that the schedule by itself is wholly inadequate to meet the test prescribed by Hicks v. Hicks, supra, 211 Cal.App.2d 144, 27 Cal. Rptr. 307, and to support the trial court's finding that Esther "identified and traced" the separate property. However, the schedule was not the only evidence introduced by Esther to effect the tracing. She personally testified that the schedule was a true and accurate record, that it accurately reflected the receipts and expenditures as accomplished through various bank accounts, although she could not in all instances correlate the items of the schedule with a particular bank account, and that it accurately corroborated her intention throughout her marriage to make these expenditures for separate property purposes, notwithstanding her use of the balance of her separate property receipts for family expenses.

The trial court evidently believed Esther. "The testimony of a witness, even the party himself, may be sufficient." (6 Witkin, Cal.Procedure (2d ed.) § 248, p. 4240.) Viewing this evidence in the light most favorable to Esther, giving her the benefit of every reasonable inference, and resolving all conflicts in her favor, as we must under the rules of appellate review (Crawford v. Southern Pac. Co. (1935) 3 Cal.2d 427, 429, 45 P.2d 183; 6 Witkin, Cal.Procedure (2d ed.) § 245, pp. 4236, 4237), we conclude that there is substantial evidence to support the trial court's finding that Esther traced and identified the source and funds of her separate property. We are satisfied that the trial court was warranted in inferring from this evidence that the bank records if introduced would fully verify the schedule as supported by Esther's testimony to the effect that "separate funds * * * continue[d] to be on deposit when a withdrawal [was] made * * * for the purpose of purchasing specific property, and * * * [that] the intention of the drawer * * * [was] to withdraw such funds therefrom * * *." (Hicks v. Hicks, supra, 211 Cal.App.2d 144, 157, 27 Cal.Rptr. 307, 315.)

Since we conclude that the judgment can be upheld on the basis of an adequate tracing of Esther's separate property, it is unnecessary for us to consider whether it can also be upheld on the independent basis of an agreement between Richard and Esther as to the separate character of the properties in controversy.

The judgment is affirmed.

IN RE MARRIAGE OF FRICK

California District Court of Appeal, 1986.
181 Cal.App.3d 997, 226 Cal.Rptr. 766.

[Prior to marriage Jerome owned real property which he used to operate the Mikado Hotel and Restaurant. During marriage he used certain funds to reduce the principal balance of an encumbrance on the real property. The trial court determined that the funds so used were community property. On appeal Jerome contended that these funds were his separate property.]

JOHNSON, J. * * *

Jerome incorporated the Mikado Hotel and Restaurant in September 1978. On October 1, 1978, Jerome entered into a lease between himself as lessor/landlord and the Mikado as lessee/tenant. The original lease called for payment to Jerome of $9,166 per month. The payments were reduced to $6,666 per month at the end of 1979. He deposited this amount into his personal account. Each month he made trust deed payments on the Mikado to Transamerica out of his personal account. In 1978, these payments were $5,000 per month. By the time of trial, these payments were $5,700 per month. Jerome contends the payments to Transamerica should not have been credited to the community since they were made contemporaneously or reasonably contemporaneously with his deposit of the monthly rental charge and, as such, the payments were traceable to a separate property source. We disagree.

While it is true, rents which are received from a separate property source are considered separate property (Civ.Code, § 5108.), Jerome commingled these funds with community property funds.[5] As Jerome testified, the Mikado Hotels, Inc. has two accounts, a general account and a payroll account. He also has a personal account. The income from the operation of the hotel and the restaurant is first deposited into the general account. He then takes some of the money from this account and puts it into the payroll account to meet his corporate payroll needs. He deposits his salary, community property, into his personal account. It is also into this account that he deposits the rent he receives from the corporation and it is from this account that Jerome makes payments to Transamerica.[6]

Where funds are paid from a commingled account, the presumption is that the funds are community funds. (*In re Marriage of Mix* (1975) 14 Cal.3d 604, 610–611, 122 Cal.Rptr. 79, 536 P.2d 479; *In re Marriage of Marsden, supra,* 130 Cal.App.3d at p. 441, 181 Cal.Rptr. 910.) In order to overcome this presumption, a party must trace the funds expended to a separate property source. (*Ibid.*) This issue presents a question of fact for the trial court and its finding will be upheld if supported by substantial evidence.

There are essentially two methods for tracing expended funds to a separate property source. The first method, relied upon by Jerome, is direct tracing. When separate funds deposited with community funds continue to be on deposit when the withdrawal is made and it is the intention of the drawer to withdraw separate funds specifically, the

---

5. We note this is not the typical case in which separate property is producing rent payments. In the case at bar, Jerome essentially paid himself rent. He was the owner of the corporation which paid the rent and the owner of the land, the recipient of the payments. He thus had complete control over the amount of rent payments that he required. Rent was originally $9,166 per month. He later reduced the rent to $6,666 per month since allegedly the corporation could not afford to pay the higher rate. It was thus very easy for Jerome unilaterally to manipulate that which he received as income payments and that which he received as rents. Thus, although we need not reach the issue be- cause of the commingling in his account, we question whether such rent payments should indeed be treated as Jerome's separate property.

6. The record is unclear as to what other deposits were made into this account and what other expenditures were made with funds from this account. Although in response to this court's inquiry, Jerome's counsel cited other possible sources of money which Jerome deposited into his personal account, we do not believe the record demonstrates these deposits were indeed made into this account.

We note it is also unclear from the record when Jerome opened his personal account.

separate property status of the withdrawn funds is established. Jerome contends he satisfied this test. He received rent payments each month of either $9,166 or $6,666 per month. He paid Transamerica $5,000 or $5,700 per month out of this account. Thus, he concludes, these payments have been traced to a separate property source. However, this testimony is not enough to satisfy the requirements in this context. "[T]he burden of establishing a spouse's separate interest in presumptive community property is not simply that of presenting proof at the time of litigation but also one of keeping adequate records. 'The husband may protect his separate property by not commingling community and separate assets and income. Once he commingles, he assumes the burden of keeping records adequate to establish the balance of community income and expenditures at the time an asset is acquired with commingled property.' (*See v. See, supra,* 64 Cal.2d [778] at p. 784 [51 Cal.Rptr. 888, 415 P.2d 776].)" (*Estate of Murphy, supra,* 15 Cal.3d at p. 919, 126 Cal.Rptr. 820, 544 P.2d 23.) The exact amount of money allocable to separate property and the exact amount of money allocable to community property must be ascertained before it can be said the money allocable to separate property is not so commingled that all funds in the account are community property. (*Thomasset v. Thomasset* (1953) 122 Cal.App.2d 116, 124–125, 264 P.2d 626, disapproved on other grounds in *See v. See* (1966) 64 Cal.2d at pp. 778, 785–786, 51 Cal.Rptr. 888, 415 P.2d 776; *Tassi v. Tassi* (1958) 160 Cal.App.2d 680, 689, 325 P.2d 872.)

In the case at bar, Jerome provided evidence he received a specific amount of separate property income each month which he deposited in a particular personal account. He also made loan payments from this account. However, he made no other showing of the activity that occurred in this account during this month. We are merely provided an isolated portion of the account's activity. For instance, Jerome provided no evidence of what other expenditures were made from this account, the nature of the funds used, and the time in which they were expended. (Compare *In re Marriage of Mix, supra,* 14 Cal.3d at pp. 613–614, 122 Cal.Rptr. 79, 536 P.2d 479; see Comment, *The Mix–Hicks Mix: Tracing Troubles Under California's Community Property System* (1979) 26 UCLA L.Rev. 1231, 1244–1245.) We are left in the dark as to the precise status and amount of separate property in Jerome's personal account at the time of these payments. As the court properly found, "* * * petitioner [Jerome] commingled community and separate funds so that no separate property funds could be found to be the source of the payments on the real estate after marriage." Moreover, we are not satisfied Jerome presented sufficient evidence to demonstrate it was his intent to use only separate property funds to make loan payments. As such, Jerome did not meet his burden of tracing the monthly loan payments to his separate property income.

* * *

Note

Other aspects of the *Frick* decision are considered in sections 2 and 3 of this chapter.

ESTATE OF CUDWORTH

Supreme Court of California, 1901.
133 Cal. 462, 65 P. 1041.

[At the time of his marriage Mr. Cudworth was possessed of substantial separate property. On his death more than twenty-one years later the probate court held that all the personal property possessed on death was community property. This appeal followed.]

HENSHAW, J. * * * From the time of his marriage until the time of his death the deceased had no trade, occupation, or employment whatsoever, excepting that during that period he employed his time in attending to looking after and caring for his separate property, in collecting the rents therefrom, in making sales thereof, and collecting interest on his mortgages, notes, and bonds, and dividends on his stock, and in making repairs and improvements upon his properties. The only property that he received or earned from any other source during all this time was the sum of $2,080, which he earned as an appraiser for the savings and loan society in the two years between September, 1876, and September, 1878. The widow testified that she had an income from her own separate property at the time she married the deceased. For the first six years after the marriage that income amounted to $68 per month. After that, until 1888, it was $90.58 per month, from 1888 until 1892 it was $48 per month, and from 1892 until October, 1893, it was $70.50 per month, and after that, until Mr. Cudworth's death, in May, 1898, it was $32.50 per month. "All the money that I received as income from my property was turned over by me to my husband, to be used for household purposes and as he wanted to."

These facts then establish that Cudworth was engaged in no employment, other than the care and preservation of his own property; that he received no property except from rents and incomes of that which he owned at the time of his marriage, and from the sales of it, except the trifling sum of $2,000, which he received in the course of two years as an appraiser for the loan society. At the time of his death his estate is worth $55,000 less than at the time of his marriage, and more than $90,000 less than the value of his estate at the time of his marriage, together with the rents and dividends which he received from his separate property during his marriage. When the computation is made as to the difference between the amounts which the wife gave to Cudworth monthly, as the income of her property, and the amount which monthly he gave back to her in the form of an allowance, it will be seen that she gave him a total of $15,847, and received back $11,880, leaving the net amount which she gave him $3,967, or the equivalent of a monthly gift to him of $15 for the period of 21 years. Upon the other hand, during that same time the actual cash which Cudworth received

from his separate property, derived from income and sales, was $150,-
000, or an average of $570 per month. Notwithstanding this, the court
decrees, in effect, that all of the personal property left by Cudworth at
the time of his death was community property, and distributes it
accordingly. Yet when Cudworth died his personal property was of the
value of only $58,000, or nearly two-thirds less than the amount of
actual cash that he had received from his separate estate during coverture. In support of this decree respondent relies upon the principle thus
enunciated by Ballinger in his work on Community Property: "When
the separate property or funds of either spouse is intermixed or commingled with community property, so that the separate property has lost its
identity and cannot be clearly traced or segregated, the community,
being the paramount estate, draws the whole mass to it, and it becomes
community property. The general rule laid down by the courts is that
such confusion works a forfeiture of the separate character of the
property so commingled." This principle, it may be said, is well supported by authority; but there is a modification of it equally important,
and peculiarly apposite to this case, and the same learned author thus
expresses it: "But, where the community interest is inconsiderable in
the property with which it has been intermingled, the community will
not draw to it the separate estate." It does not appear that there was
here any commingling of community funds with the separate estate of
the deceased; nor yet does it appear that there was any commingling of
funds of the separate property of the wife with the separate property of
the husband, such as could justify a decree that all must be considered
community property. As to community funds, it is shown that there
were none, saving the trifling amount of $2,000, earned by Cudworth as
an appraiser. Where a husband, charged with the support of a family,
has some income derived from his separate property, and some from his
earnings which are community property, there is no presumption that he
has supported the family out of the separate property and preserved
intact the community funds. He is at perfect liberty to devote all that is
necessary of the community earnings to the family support, and to
preserve his separate property intact. But if it be conceded, though it is
not shown, that there was any commingling of the separate funds of the
wife with the separate funds of the husband, it was commingling of such
a trifling sum with such a large amount as to make it to the last degree
inequitable to hold that the husband's property thereby lost its separate
character and became community. Clearly, under every principle of law
and justice, where the separate property of the husband can be traced, as
here it distinctly can, when it passes into his estate the original capital
and its transmutations are still separate property, equal with the rents,
income, and profits derived therefrom,—those profits, that is to say,
which have arisen naturally and without the active engagement by the
husband of his capital in some business or employment. In this case all
of the income of the property was derived from rents, interest, and
dividends, and was as wholly and purely separate property as was the
real estate, the stocks, bonds, and notes from which it flowed. But,
applying this principle, there were not only no profits from the transac-

tions of Cudworth during his lifetime which could be accounted community property, but the actual value of his personal property had shrunken greatly. Finally, Mrs. Cudworth testifies that she gave the money to her husband to pay household expenses, or do what he pleased with. There was nothing unnatural in her thus contributing from her separate funds this small proportionate amount towards family maintenance, and if, as she states, she did give this money to him to do as he pleased with, the gift itself made the property his separate property as much as any gift of property by him to her would have effectuated the same result. But if it should still be said that the property remained the property of the wife, and was given over merely to the custody of the husband, the utmost of her right would be a claim and demand upon his estate for this sum of $3,000. The order and decree setting the final account of the executor is therefore affirmed, while upon the appeal from that part of the decree of distribution judging the personal property of the deceased to be community property, and distributing it according to law, the decree is reversed, with directions to the trial court, upon the evidence adduced and the facts found, to adjudge and decree that the personal property in the estate of said decedent is separate property.

Notes

1. Note that at the time of the intermixing of community and separate funds during the first two years of the marriage in *Estate of Cudworth,* the community property contribution was not insignificant as compared to the separate property contributions, but as more and more separate property was added during the following eighteen years, the community contribution became relatively minimal. The court's conclusion is further buttressed by the family expense presumption. Family expenses were paid out of the inter-mixed property, and presumptively community property was first used to pay these expenses. See also Kershman v. Kershman, 192 Cal.App.2d 18, 13 Cal.Rptr. 288 (1961).

2. A reverse application of the *de minimis* principle was used by the court in In re Marriage of Shelton, 118 Cal.App.3d 811, 816–817, 173 Cal.Rptr. 629, 631–32 (1981). The husband contended that his post-separation gambling proceeds constituted his separate property because he acquired them after separation from his wife. He argued that the income arose from his separate "skill, efforts and industry," thus commingling community property and separate property, and that he should receive a fair share of the profits as his separate property. The argument was rejected:

> Husband's "skill, efforts, and industry" were minimal. Although perhaps involving some slight element of skill, successful gambling of the type afforded at the Lake Tahoe casinos depends mainly upon good luck. Kershman v. Kershman (1961) 192 Cal.App.2d 18, 21, 13 Cal.Rptr. 288, held where the community property portion in commingled community and separate property is inconsiderable compared to the separate property contribution, then the whole will be treated as separate property. There is no reason why the reverse should not be equally true. Here, husband's separate property contribution was the minimal skill and effort required at games of chance, an inconsiderable factor compared to

the community property contribution of $10,000. The entire winnings are therefore community property and the trial court's judgment was correct.

SECTION 2. BUSINESS PROFITS

When a married person uses both separate property and his or her time, energy and skill in operating a business, a rather complex classification problem may arise. Suppose, for example, that separate property is used as the capital of a business operated by one spouse during marriage. As time passes, the value of the business increases. The increase may be partly or wholly the result of a natural increase in the value of the capital due to general economic conditions; or it may be partly or wholly the result of added capital; or it may be partly or wholly attributable to profits left in the business. The problem is essentially one of tracing the gains and profits back to their source.

Under the basic tracing principle, separate property produces separate property and community assets produce community property. Where the two types of property combine in the production of something new, California courts have determined that the new production should be apportioned according to the relative separate and community contributions. The apportionment rule was first developed in cases involving the use of a spouse's time, energy and skill in connection with a separately owned business, but has since been extended to cover other types of activities including agricultural operations, real estate and securities investments.[1] The principle also has application where one spouse continues to manage a community property business while living separate and apart from the other spouse.[2]

If it is found that both separate and community property assets contributed to the business profits, it is then necessary to determine how such profits should be apportioned. If there is clear evidence of both the normal rate of return on the separate property capital and the value of the community services, no special apportionment formula is necessary. The profits may simply be apportioned ratably according to the relative established contributions.[3] But suppose that evidence of the value of the spouse's services or of the normal rate of return on the particular type of capital is incomplete or inconclusive. California courts have developed two different approaches to deal with this situation. One method, frequently called the *Pereira* approach after the case of Pereira v. Pereira[4] involves the allocation of a fair return on the spouse's separate property investment as separate income, and then the allocation of any excess to the community. The alternative approach, commonly referred

---

1. Estate of Neilson, 57 Cal.2d 773, 22 Cal.Rptr. 1, 371 P.2d 745 (1962); Beam v. Bank of America, 6 Cal.3d 12, 98 Cal.Rptr. 137, 490 P.2d 257 (1971); Weinberg v. Weinberg, 67 Cal.2d 557, 63 Cal.Rptr. 13, 432 P.2d 709 (1967).

2. In re Marriage of Imperato, reprinted in this Section.

3. Todd v. Commissioner of Internal Revenue, reprinted in this Section; see also Gudelj v. Gudelj, 41 Cal.2d 202, 259 P.2d 656 (1953).

4. Pereira v. Pereira, reprinted in this Section.

to as the *Van Camp* [5] approach and used in the *Tassi* case reprinted in this section, is to determine the reasonable value of the spouse's services, allocate that amount to community property, and treat the balance as separate property.

The various formulas stated in the business profits cases should not be viewed simply as alternative devices to be used according to some vague "fairness" standard. Rather, the determination as to which approach or formula is to be used in any given case should depend on the type of evidence available. There is language in several cases that the court should also consider whether the character of the separate capital or the community labor was the chief contributing factor in the realization of the profits in determining which approach to use.[6] A very broad review of the cases shows that the evidence in many of them permits a determination of the productivity of the invested separate property, either at the legal interest rate or at some proven rate of return, but does not permit a determination of the productivity of the community contribution of time, energy, and skill. In such cases the presumption that the profits are community property is partially rebutted, and an apportionment based on the *Pereira* approach is appropriate. In other cases the record contains evidence of the reasonable value of the contribution of time, energy, and skill and evidence that the separate property capital is highly productive. The reasonable inference from such evidence is that the separate property produced the entire excess over the reasonable value of the services. In this situation apportionment may be reasonably based on the *Van Camp* formula.

Thus we have cases in which the evidence is primarily directed to the productivity of separate property in capital, and the excess is deemed community property. We also have cases where the evidence is directed to the value of the spouse's management, and the excess is considered separate property. A third type of case is possible, where there is substantial evidence showing the value of the contributions of both the separate property capital and of the management by the married person. Where the established rates of productivity of both capital and management account for all of the profits realized, apportionment of the profits can simply be made accordingly.[7] Even where the profits exceed what the established productivity rates would normally produce, there seems to be no reason why the entire profits should not be apportioned according to the demonstrated productivity rates.[8] The cases in this section start with a case in which there is complete evidence of productivity of capital and management. Succeeding cases involve deficiencies in the evidence for one reason or another.

5. Van Camp v. Van Camp, 53 Cal.App. 17, 199 P. 885 (1921).

6. Beam v. Bank of America, 6 Cal.3d 12, 98 Cal.Rptr. 137, 490 P.2d 257 (1971).

7. See Gudelj v. Gudelj, 41 Cal.2d 202, 259 P.2d 656 (1953).

8. See Todd v. McColgan, 89 Cal.App.2d 509, 201 P.2d 414 (1949); see also Todd v. Commissioner of Internal Revenue, reprinted in this Section.

TODD v. COMMISSIONER OF INTERNAL REVENUE

Circuit Court of Appeals, Ninth Circuit, 1946.

153 F.2d 553.

(Petitioners were equal partners who on January 1, 1936 had invested $144,360.81 of their separate property in a lumber business. This capital was increased thereafter by plowing back much of the earnings. On January 1, 1940 the capital amounted to $226,890.77 and on January 1, 1941, to $285,678.98.)

DENMAN, CIRCUIT JUDGE. This is a review of a decision of the Tax Court determining deficiencies in the income taxes for the calendar years 1940 and 1941 of each of the petitioners, * * *.

The dispute between the parties concerns the portion of the income of these last two years attributable (a) to capital, the separate income of the husbands, and (b) the amount arising from the taxpayers' management of the business. All the income from capital contributed by the husbands is taxable to the husbands as separate property, plus one-half of the income from managing the business.

The Commissioner found that a very considerable portion of the increased capital came from leaving in the business, in each of the years from 1936 to 1939 inclusive, the money product of the capital as well as a portion of that from the managerial activities of the taxpayers, and the evidence sustains the finding.

It is contended by the taxpayers that despite this constantly increasing capital from both sources, the Commissioner and the Tax Court erred in refusing to hold that the limit of the separate capital investment for 1940 and 1942 was what it was on January 1, 1936, $144,360.81. With this we cannot agree. The income from the separate property left in the business remains separate property and is entitled to its share of the income thereafter.

Taxpayers further contend that the separate property capital is entitled to a return not exceeding the legal rate of interest in California of 7%, and that in no event is it entitled to a return exceeding 8% for either year.

Taxpayers properly summarize the law respecting the return on the separate capital of one of the California spouses:

"But the California rule of property law is that where the spouse has an investment in a business at the time of marriage which he continues to conduct during marriage, that investment continues to be his separate property. What part of the subsequent profits is separate income and what part thereof is community income is to be determined by the facts in the case. Whatever arises from the use of the capital by the community is separate property, and whatever arises from the personal activity, ability, or capacity of the spouse is community property."

The statement then continues:

"The California rule of property law is that where the separate capital investment of the spouse is definitely determined in amount as of the date of marriage, the income attributable thereto is interest thereon at a rate not in excess of the legal interest rate of seven percent unless the facts in the case show that it is entitled to a greater return than legal interest."

[In a footnote the court cited Pereira v. Pereira, 156 Cal. 1, 7, 11, 12, 103 P. 488, 23 L.R.A.,N.S., 880, 134 Am.St.Rep. 107.]

Under the federal income tax law it is the duty of the Commissioner of Internal Revenue to determine from "the facts in the case" the amount of the return on the taxpayer's capital. He has determined that the facts show that the product of the capital is not only in excess of 7%, the legal rate in California, but much more than 8%.

We think there is evidence from which the Commissioner and the Tax Court properly could find that the return on the capital exceeded the California legal rate of 7% for the tax years in question. There is evidence from which the Commissioner and Tax Court could infer that the lumber business is a highly fluctuating one of large profits, succeeded by large losses—that is, a merchandising business in which a higher rate of return is necessary in good years to offset the losses of bad years.

It also appears that in 1940 the war in Europe and war preparations in this country caused a constant increase in demand for lumber, and with it a corresponding increase in prices and in value of inventories.

It was stated by one of the partners that the money was left in the business as "a sort of investment" for the "inflation in inventory." They "let it lay there in the business in the way of inventory." He stated that the taxpayers could have done the same volume of business with half the inventories but the fact is that they preferred to take the war-caused increasing value in the inventories. Hence, as stated, the Commissioner and the Tax Court were warranted in inferring that there was a substantial gain in capital value of inventory as distinguished from earnings from new business obtained.

The Commissioner's method of allocation between the separate capital income and the managerial community earnings is a rational one. The capital of the business was constantly increasing. Eight percent of the average capital balance in each of these years is held the base of the capital earnings. Salaries for services are found annually for the base of the community earnings. The two are added together and the percentage each base bares to the total constitute the proportions of the total income attributable to capital and to services.

Beginning in 1936, when the capital on January 1st was admittedly $144,360.81, the average capital for the year was computed as $151,-980.71. Upon this the 8% was computed at $12,158.46. This was added to the $10,000 salary, making a total of $22,158.46. The percentage of the income attributable to capital earnings is 54.87%, and to managerial earnings is the remaining 45.13%.

54.87% of the 1936 partnership income of $26,990.92 is $14,809.92 attributable to capital earnings. This was left in the business and added to the partnership capital of 1937.

The 45.13% of $26,990.92 is $12,818 attributable to community earnings. However, all this was not left in the business. $11,763 of it was taken out as personal expenses—that is, under the California law presumed taken from the community income. Van Camp v. Van Camp, 53 Cal.App. 17, 25, 199 P. 885. The remainder was left in the business as community capital to share in the total earnings of future years as taxable community income.

Pursuing this method for the succeeding years, the Commissioner and the Tax Court found the partners' separate capital of the partnership in 1940 to be increased to $242,380.68 and that the community had left in the business, above withdrawals of living expenses, $13,904.19.

Applying the above formula of the shares of the 8% on capital added to an increased salary factor of $15,000, the Commissioner and the Tax Court fixed the taxes and deficiencies for each of the equal partners on the total partnership income of $46,204.96, as follows:

[The computation by the court showed a 1940 deficiency of $6436.84 with 54.62 percent of the income attributed to separate property capital, 3.13 percent to community property capital, and 42.25 percent to management services. The 1941 deficiency next mentioned in the opinion was on the findings that 57.51 percent of the income was attributable to separate property capital, 5.57 percent to community property capital, and 36.92 percent to management services.]

For 1941 there was a similar computation showing a deficiency in the husband's income of $8,515.97.

It is claimed that the figures showing the average of capital balances during the years 1940 and 1941 fail to show certain sums attributable to the separate and community shares of the capital. Since the Commissioner's plan of allocation is a rational one, the burden of showing error in computing in its application is upon the taxpayers. Helvering v. Taylor, 293 U.S. 507, 515, 55 S.Ct. 287, 79 L.Ed. 623; Lucas v. Kansas City Structural Co., 281 U.S. 264, 271, 50 S.Ct. 263, 74 L.Ed. 848; Welch v. Helvering, 290 U.S. 111, 115, 54 S.Ct. 8, 78 L.Ed. 212. This they have failed to do.

This case was argued and submitted to us by both parties on the theory that the findings in the following assignments of error were actually made by the Tax Court:

"6. The evidence does not support the *finding* that the capital invested in the partnership business had earned or was entitled to be credited with a return thereon for either of the years 1940 or 1941 greater than eight per cent which the Commissioner determined and the Court *found* to be a fair return thereon.

* * *

"8. The evidence does not support the *finding* that the capital invested in the partnership business had earned or was entitled to be credited with a return thereon for either of the years 1940 or 1941 greater than seven per cent." (Emphasis supplied.)

No such findings of fact were made by the Tax Court or findings substantially like them. The case is ordered remanded to the Tax Court to make findings with regard to the issue as to the respective amounts attributable to capital and to the petitioners' management of the business and its decision thereon, having in view the agreement of the parties here that such findings were made. Cf. Oliver v. Commissioner, Jan. 1, 1945, 4 T.C. 684.

Remanded.

Notes

1. In Gudelj v. Gudelj, 41 Cal.2d 202, 259 P.2d 656 (1953), the husband withdrew from the profits of the business $3,600, found to be the reasonable value of his services, and an average of $2,000 a year, found to be the reasonable return on the investment of $11,500. This investment was composed of $1,500 found to be the husband's separate property and $10,000 found to be borrowed money and community property. Thus complete evidence of the production of profits showed $3,600 a year came from management, a community asset, and $2,000 a year came from the invested capital which was $3/23$ separate property and $20/23$ community property.

2. The approach of the principal case was followed in Todd v. McColgan, 89 Cal.App. 509, 201 P.2d 414 (1949).

PEREIRA v. PEREIRA

Supreme Court of California, 1909.
156 Cal. 1, 103 P. 488, 23 L.R.A., N.S., 880, 134 Am.St.Rep. 107.

SHAW, J. The plaintiff obtained an interlocutory judgment of divorce on the ground of extreme cruelty. This judgment also declared that the plaintiff should have three-fifths of the community property when the divorce became final, that she should thereafter have custody of her minor child by the marriage, and it provided for theory that all of his gains received after marriage, from whatever sources, were to be classed as community property, and that no allowance was made in favor of his separate estate on account of interest or profit on the $15,500 invested in the business at the time of the marriage. This capital was undoubtedly his separate estate. The fund remained in the business after marriage and was used by him in carrying it on. The separate property should have been credited with some amount as profit on this capital. It was not a losing business, but a very profitable one. It is true that it is very clearly shown that the principal part of the large income was due to the personal character, energy, ability, and capacity of the husband. This share of the earnings was, of course, community property; but without capital he could not have carried on the business. In the absence of circumstances showing a different result, it is to be presumed that some of the profits were justly due to the capital invested. There is nothing to show that all of it was due to defendant's efforts alone. The probable contribution of the capital to the income should have been determined from all the circumstances of the case, and, as the business was profitable, it would amount at least to the usual interest on a long investment well secured. Boggess v. Richards, Adm'r, 39 W.Va. 576, 20 S.E. 599, 26 L.R.A. 537, 45 Am.St.Rep. 938; Trapnell v. Conkling, 37 W.Va. 252, 16 S.E. 570, 38 Am.St.Rep. 30; Penn v. Whitehead, 17 Grat. (Va.) 503, 94 Am.Dec. 478; Glidden v. Taylor, 16 Ohio St. 509, 91 Am.Dec. 98. We think the court erred in refusing to increase the proportion of separate property and decrease the community property to the extent of the reasonable gain to the separate estate from the earnings properly allowable on account of the capital invested.

* * *

The judgment as to the amount and value of the community property and as to the disposition thereof between the parties is reversed, and the cause is remanded for a new trial and judgment upon that issue alone. In all other particulars the judgment is affirmed.

ON REHEARING

PER CURIAM. Since the filing of the opinion in this case, the plaintiff has asked that, instead of remanding the case for a new trial of the issues as to the property, the judgment be modified in regard thereto, and has filed a written consent that the defendant be allowed, as part of his separate estate, out of the cash on hand, interest at the rate of 7 per cent. on the $15,500 found to be the capital invested in his business. This removes the objection to directing a modification of the judgment. The defendant introduced no evidence to show that the capital invested was entitled to a greater return than legal interest, and, in the absence of such evidence, the burden of proof being upon him, that would be the utmost he could claim. The wife would have been entitled to an opportunity to prove, if she could, that it earned a smaller proportion of the profits than legal interest, and, she being the respondent, it was for that reason considered necessary to order a new trial for that purpose. Her consent aforesaid avoids this necessity and leaves the case in such condition that a modification of the judgment will end the litigation with justice to both parties. Fox v. Hale & Norcross S. Min. Co., 122 Cal. 221, 54 P. 731.

Interest at 7 per cent. on the $15,500 from April 19, 1900, the date of the marriage, to November 3, 1905, the time of the trial, amounts to $6,012.70. Deducting this from $12,139.03, found to be the cash on hand at the time of the trial, leaves $6,126.33, as the part of the cash belonging to the community. The plaintiff's three-fifths of this is $3,675.86, and the defendant's two-fifths is $2,450.47.

It is ordered that the judgment be modified by changing the respective statements of the shares of each in the cash on hand therein, so that the part relating to the plaintiff's share shall read as follows: "Second. The sum of three thousand six hundred and seventy-five and 86–100 dollars ($3,675.86), in cash, being three-fifths of the sum of $6,126.33 in cash found by the Supreme Court to be community property of the plaintiff and defendant; and that no interest in defendant's separate property be awarded to plaintiff." And so that the part relating to the defendant's share shall read as follows: "Second. The sum of two thousand four hundred and fifty and 47–100 dollars ($2,450.47), in cash, being two-fifths of the sum found to be community property as aforesaid." And that as so modified the judgment stand affirmed; the plaintiff to recover all costs.

Notes

1. "Defendant contends that a 7 percent return is not currently considered to be a fair or adequate return on risk capital invested in a small, closely held corporation and that the increase in net worth of his wholly owned corporation was partially attributable to inflation and other general economic and business factors. Since he offered no evidence of current returns, however, the trial court correctly adopted the rate of legal interest. (Pereira v. Pereira, supra, 156 Cal. 1, 11–12; cf. Tassi v. Tassi (1958) 160 Cal.App.2d 680, 691, 325 P.2d 872.) Since he also offered no evidence of the effect of inflation and other economic factors on his corporations, the trial court properly disregarded those factors. (Cf. Logan v. Forster (1952) 144 Cal.App.2d 587, 601, 250 P.2d 730.)" Weinberg v. Weinberg, 67 Cal.2d 557, 63 Cal.Rptr. 13, 432 P.2d 709 (1967).

2. In In re Marriage of Folb, 53 Cal.App.3d 862, 126 Cal.Rptr. 306 (1975), the court found that the evidence supported a 12% return on capital and also determined that compounding that was not necessary and on the facts of the case would have denied substantial justice between the parties.

TASSI v. TASSI

California District Court of Appeal, 1958.
160 Cal.App.2d 680, 325 P.2d 872.

DOOLING, JUSTICE. Plaintiff Marjorie Tassi brought this action upon the death of her husband to recover from defendants one-half of various properties on the ground that these properties were gifts of community property made by her husband without her consent. She appeals from the judgment which held that 73% of the property was her husband's separate property at the time of the transfers.

Plaintiff-appellant's main attack is on the sufficiency of the evidence to support the allocation of earnings from the business in the ratio of 73% separate property and 27% community property. It is the duty of the court to allocate earnings from the business which is the separate property of a husband and in which the husband is actively employed, finding as separate property the portion of the earnings properly attributable to the business, and as community property the portion of the earnings properly attributable to the husband's efforts. The evidence showed that during the marriage decedent withdrew $447,805.75 from the business and paid living expenses of $44,093.16. No attempt was made by decedent to allocate these withdrawals between salary and business earnings. Decedent devoted full time to the management of the business.

Two approaches have ordinarily been made to the allocation of earnings in such cases: 1. to allow interest on the capital investment of the business, allocate such interest as separate property, and treat the balance as community earnings attributable to the efforts of the husband (Pereira v. Pereira, 156 Cal. 1, 103 P. 488, 23 L.R.A., N.S., 880); 2. to determine the reasonable value of the husband's services in the business, allocate that amount as community property, and treat the balance as separate property attributable to the normal earnings of the business. Huber v. Huber, 27 Cal.2d 784, 167 P.2d 708. The court adopted the latter formula.

There was evidence of witnesses familiar with the wholesale meat business that the reasonable salary for the general manager of such a business was from $10,000 to $15,000 per year. Plaintiff-appellant argues that the hypothetical questions on which this testimony was based were not based upon the evidence, particularly in that they did not include the factors that this was a small, wholly owned business. The court has a wide discretion in the admission of expert testimony (In re Guardianship of Jacobson, 30 Cal.2d 312, 313, 324, 182 P.2d 537; 19 Cal.Jur.2d, Evidence, § 288, p. 14) and the salary customarily paid to general managers of wholesale meat businesses is relevant and competent evidence of the reasonable value of such services in a particular business of that character. The difficulty of obtaining evidence limited to small wholly owned businesses is obvious. The salary allowed by such owners to themselves lies entirely in their own discretion and the surest standard would not be what such owners were accustomed to allow to themselves but rather what independent employers were in the habit of paying others for similar services in the free give and take of the open market. We find no error in the admission of this evidence.

The evidence is sufficient to support the trial court's conclusion that the reasonable value of decedent's services did not exceed $15,000 per year. Plaintiff-appellant argues that only where the husband has in fact allocated a portion of earnings to salary is the formula adopted by the court allowable. It is true that in Gilmore v. Gilmore, 45 Cal.2d 142, 150, 287 P.2d 769, and Harrold v. Harrold, 43 Cal.2d 77, 78, 80, 271 P.2d 489, there had been a fixed amount drawn by the husband-owner as salary. But in Huber v. Huber, supra, 27 Cal.2d 784, 167 P.2d 708, in which case the husband had drawn $150 from the business every two weeks, without allocating any part to salary, and there was testimony "that the business would warrant a salary of $150 per month to defendant" the court said (27 Cal.2d at page 792, 167 P.2d at page 713): "Under these circumstances the court was justified in reaching the conclusion that the earnings allocable to community property consisted of $1,800 per year * * *."

"In applying this principle of apportionment the court is not bound either to adopt a predetermined percentage as a fair return on business capital which is separate property nor need it limit the community interest only to the salary fixed as the reward for a spouse's service but may select whatever formula will achieve substantial justice between the parties. * * *

"It is primarily a question of fact 'for the court to determine what portion of the profits thereafter arises from the use of this (separate) capital and what part arises from the activity and personal ability of the husband.'" Logan v. Forster, 114 Cal.App.2d 587, 600, 250 P.2d 730, 738.

There was testimony that the period of World War II and the Korean War which followed it were years of high profits in the meat business, and an analysis of the customers' accounts showed that almost ⅓ of the total sales volume during the entire marriage was to purchasers who were already customers of the business when the parties were married. From this evidence the court was justified in finding that the business earnings were chiefly attributable to the business as such rather than to decedent's services. Plaintiff-appellant points to the scarcity of meat and rationing as off-setting factors to the high war time profits but the balancing of these factors is the appropriate function of the trial court and not of this court on appeal.

Since earnings were not allowed to accumulate in the business, and the business investment was the separate property of decedent we find no substance in the complaint that some part of the increase in the value of the business should have been allocated to community property.

Judgment affirmed.

Notes

1. In Beam v. Bank of America, 6 Cal.3d 12, 98 Cal.Rptr. 137, 490 P.2d 257 (1971), the parties were divorced after 29 years of marriage. The husband had inherited $1,629,129 in cash and securities. He was not employed during the marriage, but instead devoted his time to handling his separate estate investments. At the end of the marriage, the husband's estate was worth $1,850,507.33.

The wife contended that a portion of the increase should be attributed to the husband's efforts during marriage. She introduced evidence showing that a professional investment manager would charge an annual fee based on one percent of the corpus of the funds, and that the husband was an experienced investor. The trial court concluded from the circumstances of the case that the *Pereira* approach should be utilized, and adopted the legal interest rate of 7 percent simple interest as the reasonable rate of return on the husband's separate property. The result was that the entire increase in the estate's value over the 29 year period was attributable to the normal *Von Kamp* growth factor of the property itself, and was entirely the husband's separate property. The approach taken by the trial court was affirmed by the California Supreme Court: "We cannot under the facts before us condemn as unreasonable the judge's implicit decision that the modest increment of Mr. Beam's estate was more probably due to the 'character of the capital investment' than to the 'personal activity, ability, and capacity of the spouse.'"

The Supreme Court also noted that if the family expense presumption were applied, none of the increase could be attributable to community property, regardless of which accounting approach was used. Even if the husband's skills as an investment manager were worth $17,000 per year, this entire amount would have been exhausted by the family's living expenses, which averaged $24,000 per year.

2. It has been suggested that in deciding which approach to use (*Pereira* or *Van Camp*) the court should generally determine whether the increase in value during marriage was primarily due to a spouse's efforts or due to a separate property capital. If the former, the court should apply whichever approach will yield the greatest community gain. If capital is the most significant, the approach yielding the largest separate property gain should be chosen. Oldham, *Separate Property Businesses That Increase In Value During Marriage,* 1990 Wisconsin Law Review 585, 588–89 (1990).

IN RE MARRIAGE OF FRICK

California District Court of Appeal, 1986.
181 Cal.App.3d 997, 226 Cal.Rptr. 766.

[Jerome owned and operated the Mikado Hotel and restaurant business prior to marriage. The trial court found that the business had increased in value during the marriage in large part due to Jerome's labor, and applied the *Pereira* approach to the classification of the increased value of the business.]

JOHNSON, J. * * *

The trial court found the value of the going business of the hotel and restaurant increased from $131,000 at the time of the marriage to $290,000 at the time of the trial. Using a *Pereira* calculation, the court concluded Jerome's capital investment should have earned $99,850. The value of the business over and above this, $59,150, was community income. However, since Jerome supported himself, Hiroko, and her three children from a prior marriage, the court concluded the approximately $6,000 per year of community income ($59,150 divided by ten years of marriage) was exhausted by family expenses. As such no community property remained in existence.

Hiroko contends the trial court erred in making this determination since the court relied on figures presented by Jerome's expert witnesses and these figures were incomplete. We disagree.

Stein, a certified public account, prepared the appraisal which the trial court relied on in making its determination. He testified as to the documentation he used in reaching the conclusions in his appraisal of the business. The records reviewed included: general ledgers from

October 1, 1978, to June 30, 1982; purchase journals from November 1, 1979, to June 30, 1982; general journals from October 1, 1978, to June 30, 1982; corporation tax returns for fiscal years ending June 30, 1979 through 1982; cash receipts 1976 through December 31, 1982; cash disbursements 1976 through December 31, 1982; general journal 1976 through December 31, 1982; general ledger January 1976 through December 31, 1982; statement of revenues and expenses December 31, 1971, 1972, and 1973; and individual income tax returns 1971 through 1981.

Hiroko contends Jerome did not provide certain records, particularly with regard to the pre–1976 period, and without these records the opinions of experts such as Stein, must be deemed speculative and conjectural. However, Stein thoroughly described how he arrived at his conclusion and documented the sources used for reaching this conclusion. While it is true, Stein did make some assumptions due to the lack of certain documentation, the court could properly conclude the assumptions were reasonable. For instance in making the 1971 valuation, financial statements and the proprietorship's books were not available as of December 31, 1971. Thus, an assumption was made that the proprietorship would have had at least two cash banks of $500 each in order to operate, i.e., Jerome would have had at least $500 in the motel bank and $500 in the restaurant bank. Given this assumption, Stein included $1,000 in cash on the balance sheet. In addition, to determine the accounts receivable for 1971, Stein looked at the accounts receivable for 1976. Since the sales figure for 1971 was $354,764 or 59 percent of the 1976 sales of $600,286, he estimated the accounts receivable on hand in 1971 would reflect this same relationship. As Stein testified, based on experience, receivables will go up almost in direct proportion to one's increase in volume.

In her challenge to the court's determination, Hiroko also raises the difficulty her experts had in obtaining records. Be this as it may, we fail to see how this in any way affects the propriety of the court's reliance on Jerome's experts who were provided more thorough documentation.

Hiroko also contends since Jerome's expert testified as to his opinion solely based on figures provided to him by Jerome, the court should not have adopted the expert's testimony. However, the expert did not testify simply based on what Jerome told him. As discussed above, Jerome provided him substantial documentation. It was from this documentation that the expert reached his conclusions. Moreover, Jerome's testimony concerning his estimate of the value of the business was irrelevant to the conclusions reached by the expert.

Hiroko also challenges the court's conclusion the community income from the business was exhausted by the community's living expenses since Jerome supported himself, Hiroko and her children from a former marriage. We believe the court erred in this regard.

As discussed earlier, the trial court applied the *Pereira* method to apportion the profits of Jerome's business between Jerome and the community.　Pursuant to this method, the court allocated a fair return on Jerome's investment in the separate property and allocated the excess profits to the community property.　(*Pereira v. Pereira* (1909) 156 Cal. 1, 7, 103 P. 488.)　The court determined the community was entitled to $59,150.　However, the court then determined all the community income was exhausted due to community expenses incurred over the course of the marriage.[11]　As such, the community was not entitled to any of the profit from the business.　We believe the court erred in this latter respect.　During the course of the marriage, Jerome took out of the business whatever income he needed to meet the expenses of the community, i.e., disbursements from the business covered the community living expenses.　These disbursements represented community income since had these disbursements not been made, the value of the corporation would have increased, and under the *Pereira* formula, all of this increased value would have been community property.　As such, we are at a loss to understand why the community should be charged with community expenses twice.　Community expenses were met with disbursements from the business.　These disbursements in fact represented profits from the business which the community would have been entitled to under the *Pereira* formula had they not been withdrawn from the business.　A second family expense deduction is unwarranted and unfair to the community.　(Bodenheimer, *The Community Without Community Property: The Need for Legislative Attention to Separate–Property Marriages Under Community Property Laws* (1972) 8 Cal.Western L.Rev. 381, 396–403.)[12]

* * *

IN RE MARRIAGE OF IMPERATO
California District Court of Appeal, 1975.
45 Cal.App.3d 432, 119 Cal.Rptr. 590.

HASTINGS, ASSOCIATE JUSTICE.

STATEMENT OF FACTS

Louis J. Imperato (husband), appellant and Diana L. Imperato (wife), respondent, were married on June 27, 1959, in Phoenix, Arizona. They subsequently moved to California where they lived together with their two minor children until December 30, 1971, when they separated. The children stayed with husband.

On July 10, 1969, Personalized Data Delivery Service (PDD) was incorporated.　It specialized in data processing delivery.　The corpora-

---

11.　It is presumed the expenses of the family are paid from community funds rather than separate funds.　In the absence of contrary evidence, the community earnings are chargeable with these expenses.　(*Beam v. Bank of America, supra,* 6 Cal.3d at p. 20, 98 Cal.Rptr. 137, 490 P.2d 257.)

12.　We recognize the Supreme Court in *Beam v. Bank of America, supra,* 6 Cal.3d at p. 21, 98 Cal.Rptr. 137, 490 P.2d 257 stated that after a court ascertains the amount of community income under the *Pereira* approach, it deducts the community's living expenses from community income to determine the balance of community property.　However, this aspect of the court's decision was dicta, and as such, not binding on this court.

tion was actually an extension of a partnership between husband and his father, with husband becoming the sole shareholder, president and manager thereof. On the date of the separation, PDD had a net worth of $1,665.85. Husband continued to operate the corporation after separation, and on June 30, 1973, PDD had a net worth of $17,614.26. Trial was held on August 22, 1973. The trial court ruled the community property would be valued as of June 30, 1973, the date closest to the date of trial for which proof of value existed.[1] It was agreed husband would retain the business and pay wife her one-half interest therein. Husband argued the business should be valued as of date of separation.

ISSUES

1. In a marital dissolution action, should community property be valued as of date of separation or as near to date of trial as reasonably practicable?

2. Is PDD's appreciation in value between the dates of separation and trial the "earnings" or "accumulations" of husband for purposes of Civil Code section 5118?

ARGUMENT

1. The 1971 amendment to section 5118[2] of the Civil Code provides that the earnings and accumulations of a spouse, while living separate and apart from the other spouse, are the separate property of the spouse. Prior to said amendment, the earnings and accumulations of the wife were treated as her separate property, while the husband's were not. (The Family Law Act became effective January 1, 1970, and section 5118 adopted in full the language of former section 169.)

This change, husband urges, reflects legislative intent that community property should be valued as of the date of separation. His argument is based on a statement found in Randolph v. Randolph, 118 Cal.App.2d 584, 258 P.2d 547. In that case, there was almost a twenty-year period of separation, during which time the husband operated a floral business. The court held that valuation of the business must be taken on a date as near as possible to the date of dissolution of the marital community, but it said on page 586 of 118 Cal.App.2d, on page 548 of 258 P.2d: "It may also be pointed out that section 169, Civil Code, provides that when a wife lives separate from her husband her earnings and accumulations are her separate property but that no corresponding provision is made for the protection of a deserted husband. If such a provision would be desirable it would be the task of the legislature to make it. Until this is done the deserted husband can find protection in the diligent institution of a divorce suit only."

Husband claims the Legislature finally responded to the invitation of the *Randolph* court when it amended section 5118 to its present form.

---

1. The parties stipulated that PDD was community property.

2. Civil Code, § 5118 states: "The earnings and accumulations of a spouse and the minor children living with, or in the custo-

dy of, the spouse, while living separate and apart from the other spouse, are the separate property of the spouse." (Effective March 4, 1972.)

He further states: " ' * * * living separate and apart * * *' refers to that condition when spouses have come to a parting of the ways with no present intention of resuming marital relations. (Makeig v. United Security Bk. & T. Co. (1931) 112 Cal.App. 138 [296 P. 673].)" In light of the amendment, and the legal meaning given to the words "living separate and apart", husband contends logic would seem to dictate that valuation of the community property should be made at date of separation.[3] This date is particularly appropriate, he asserts, when it is the effort of one spouse that has caused an increase in valuation of a community asset, and this person should receive the increase as his or her separate property because division of the property equally at the higher valuation unfairly benefits the other spouse.[4]

While this appears to be a case of first impression on the theory propounded by husband, it is not the first case to consider the amendment to section 5118. In In Re Marriage of Lopez, 38 Cal.App.3d 93, at page 110, 113 Cal.Rptr. 58, at page 68, the court said: "Asset values and liabilities should be determined as near to the date of trial as reasonably practicable (Randolph v. Randolph (1953), 118 Cal.App.2d 584, 258 P.2d 547), *with the reservation, however, that since the enactment of Civil Code section 5118, effective March 4, 1972, any portion of the law practice assets including goodwill which are attributable to the earnings and accumulations of a spouse living separate and apart are the separate property of the spouse earning or accumulating the same. This could be significant where the earnings of a professional person are substantial and the time lapse from separation to trial is considerable.*" (Italics added.) The opinion reaffirms that the valuation date should be at date of trial or close thereto, but recognizes that both spouses keep their earnings and accumulations as their separate property after separation. If the earnings of a spouse in some manner increase the value of a community asset, the court must then determine what portion of the asset is community property and what portion is separate property. This is the only logical application to be given to the amendment. Valuation on date of separation is important only when it is used in conjunction with the final valuation for apportioning community and separate property. As we understand husband's argument, community property must be valued as of date of separation with all of the increase in value subsequent thereto passing to the spouse that devoted time and effort to its preservation. This formula overlooks the inherent growth factor found in many assets, investment and re-investment of capital, market fluctuations, and numerous other components that can increase

---

3. The date of separation here was December 30, 1971. At that time section 5118 provided that only wife's earnings and accumulations were separate. Until the effective date of the amendment (March 4, 1972), husband's earnings were still community property. Husband failed to note this item in his argument.

4. In the present case, husband had custody of the children during separation. He places great emphasis on this fact, claiming that use of the trial date for valuation purposes will injure the children. He rationalizes that the working spouse, not wishing to benefit the other spouse, will permit a community property business to deteriorate, thereby causing the children to suffer due to a reduction in the family income.

the value of most assets. Nor does husband consider the issue of loss in value often caused for various reasons. If his theory is adopted, logic compels the conclusion that the spouse devoting time to the asset must also stand the loss. In many situations this also would be very unfair.

The date for valuation of assets as stated in *Randolph* is not new in California, and has consistently been followed. (See Ottinger v. Ottinger, 141 Cal.App.2d 220, 224, 296 P.2d 347.) Section 5118, as it now reads, does not change the basic concept behind the rule. It merely takes the income and accumulations of the spouses out of "community property." Without further legislative expression, *Lopez*, supra, properly states how the section must be applied in apportioning community assets that have increased in value after separation of the parties.

2. Husband next argues that if the date of separation is not the proper valuation date, in this case the increase in net worth should be considered as earnings or accumulations within the meaning of section 5118. He reasons that he was the sole stockholder [5] of PDD and that he presented evidence to show that the corporate entity was nothing more than a style or business name, and therefore should be treated as a sole proprietorship for determining the rights of the parties in the business, after separation.

The word "earnings" is broader in scope than "wages" and "salary." It can encompass income derived from carrying on a business as a sole proprietor where the earnings are the fruit or award for labor and services without the aid of capital. In Romanchek v. Romanchek, 248 Cal.App.2d 337, 56 Cal.Rptr. 360, the wife owned and operated as a sole proprietorship a school in French design. This Division, on page 342, 56 Cal.Rptr. on page 364, said: "The school was small, and its activities consisted of plaintiff's teaching, designing, pattern making, and the like. Plaintiff was 'very active' and worked at the school 'all the time' as its sole worker. The income derived from this school resulted from the personal character, ability, energy and capacity of the plaintiff, and was community property while the parties lived together. (Civ.Code, § 146; Pereira v. Pereira, 156 Cal. 1, 103 P. 488, 134 Am.St.Rep. 107, 23 L.R.A., N.S., 880.) Until December of 1959 the parties lived together as husband and wife.

"From late 1959 until some time in early 1962 the parties lived separate and apart. During this period plaintiff's school income was her separate property."

In contrast, the earnings of a corporation are not, generally speaking, the earnings of the individual stockholder or stockholders, but are "profits" of the corporation to be distributed usually in the form of dividends. A stockholder-employee takes his earnings in salary, bonuses and other forms of benefits. Husband testified he paid himself a salary from the business during the period of separation, and the trial court

---

5. He does not refer to his wife as a stockholder in his brief, although of course she is by reason of her community interest.

considered this income as his total earnings. It was for this reason that husband argued that the court should disregard the corporate entity and treat the business as a sole proprietorship, as this would more realistically determine his earnings. The record indicates an effort by husband to place into evidence facts that would establish his alter ego theory. He presented checks drawn from both his personal bank account and PDD's bank account which were used to pay the personal expenses of the wife.[6] But it is apparent from the record that the court felt from the beginning of the trial that it was bound by the *Randolph* rule and other evidence was ruled inadmissible that would have been pertinent to this issue. In fairness to the trial court, *Lopez,* supra, had not been published at time of trial; thus, there was no direct decisional law to guide the court on this matter.

In the case at bar, the conflicting methods of the apportionment formulas used in the landmark cases of *Pereira* and *Van Camp*[7] would be applied in reverse. In those cases, the husband owned separate property but devoted his community time after marriage to managing and preserving the property. Here, we have community property acquired during marriage, and if the facts justify apportionment we seek to allocate increases of the community property occurring after separation into separate property. Assuming the trial court treats PDD as a sole proprietorship, the *Pereira* approach would allocate a fair return of the increase to the community property and the excess would be husband's separate property. The *Van Camp* formula would determine the reasonable value of husband's services (less the draws or salary taken) and allocate this additional sum, if any, to husband as his separate property and the balance of the increase to community property. We do not speculate on the formula to be used here.[8] If the trial court, after hearing the evidence, disregards the corporate entity, it must apply the theory that is deemed most appropriate. As stated in Beam v. Bank of America, supra, 6 Cal.3d 12, 18, 98 Cal.Rptr. 137, 141, 490 P.2d 257, 261:

6. See Schoenberg v. Romike Properties, 251 Cal.App.2d 154, 59 Cal.Rptr. 359, where husband and wife were sole stockholders and wrote checks for their personal expenses from the corporation bank account. The court considered this as important evidence that the corporation was the alter ego of husband and wife.

7. Over the years our courts have evolved two quite distinct, alternative approaches to allocating earnings between separate and community income. One method of apportionment, first applied in Pereira v. Pereira (1909), 156 Cal. 1, 7, 103 P. 488 and commonly referred to as the *Pereira* approach, "is to allocate a fair return on the [husband's separate property] investment [as separate income] and to allocate any excess to the community property as arising from the husband's efforts."

(Estate of Neilson, 57 Cal.2d 733, 740, 22 Cal.Rptr. 1, 5, 371 P.2d 745, 748.) The alternative apportionment approach, which traces its derivation to Van Camp v. Van Camp, 53 Cal.App. 17, 27–28, 199 P. 885, is " 'to determine the reasonable value of the husband's services * * *, allocate that amount as community property, and treat the balance as separate property attributable to the normal earnings of the [separate estate].' " (Beam v. Bank of America, 6 Cal.3d 12, 18, 98 Cal.Rptr. 137, 141, 490 P.2d 257, 261.)

8. As stated earlier, March 4, 1972, would be the first valuation date of the community property. However, it is left to the trial court's discretion to use a new valuation of PDD as of this date, or use a date as near to this date as is reasonably practical.

" 'In making such apportionment between separate and community property our courts have developed no precise criterion or fixed standard, but have endeavored to adopt that yardstick which is most appropriate and equitable in a particular situation * * * depending on whether the character of the capital investment in the separate property or the personal activity, ability, and capacity of the spouse is the chief contributing factor in the realization of income and profits [citations]. * * * [Par.] In applying this principle of apportionment the court is not bound either to adopt a predetermined percentage as a fair return on business capital which is separate property [the *Pereira* approach] nor need it limit the community interest only to [a] salary fixed as the reward for a spouse's service [the *Van Camp* method] but may select [whichever] formula will achieve substantial justice between the parties. [Citations.]' (Logan v. Forster (1952) 114 Cal.App.2d 587, 599–600, 250 P.2d 730, 737."

We are not unaware of the rule that an incorporator should be precluded from ignoring his own deliberately chosen corporate form.[9] (6 Witkin, Summary of Cal.Law (8th ed. 1974) Corporations, § 15, p. 4327.) However, there are numerous exceptions. * * *

* * * We believe a special situation exists when a husband and wife who are the sole stockholders of a corporation are dissolving their marriage and the other factors mentioned exist. One reason for justifying the alter ego doctrine is that it prevents injustice. If no third parties are affected, and the husband and wife have not treated the corporation as a separate entity, logic and fairness would permit the court to disregard the corporate entity when evidence offered by either party justifies such a finding, and it would enable a fair apportionment of the property.

We reiterate that we are not satisfied that the trial court gave due consideration to the alter ego theory and its effect on this case as expounded here. We believe husband was precluded from presenting all of his evidence on this issue. For this reason, the judgment is reversed and remanded to the trial court for the sole purpose of determining the issues as outlined in this opinion.

KAUS, P.J., and ASHBY, J., concur.

SECTION 3. INSTALLMENT AND CREDIT ACQUISITIONS

Married persons frequently use both separate and community property in the acquisition of major assets, particularly those acquired over time or on credit. For example, a life insurance policy may be taken out prior to marriage, but the premiums after marriage are paid with community earnings. Separate property may be used as the down payment for the purchase of a house or business, with later payments

---

9. Stated differently, a sole stockholder is estopped to deny the validity of his own corporation.

coming from community funds. A loan may be taken out before marriage, but repaid with the earnings of one spouse during marriage. While the marriage continues, most couples probably give little thought to their respective ownership interests in such assets, but on termination of marriage by death or dissolution, classification of the asset, including any appreciation in value, must be made. California courts have developed various allocation principles for the classification of installment acquisitions, borrowed funds and credit acquisitions. However no totally satisfactory rule or formula has yet been devised for dealing with modern complex credit transactions, which may involve a loan, the mortgage of existing or newly acquired property, and repayment of the loan over time.

A. Acquisitions in Installment Transactions

The California community property system requires that all acquisitions be classified as community or separate property. We have seen that when an asset is acquired during marriage, it is presumptively community property, but where the purchase price is traced to separate property, the asset may be classified according to its source. Any increase in the value of the asset would be classified on the same basis. In some transactions, however, ownership interests in an asset are realistically acquired on a piecemeal basis over time. Common examples include pensions, insurance, and real property acquired under an installment sales contract. The initial transaction in the acquisition of such an asset may have occurred prior to marriage, with the acquisition completed during marriage. Or the entire acquisition may have occurred during marriage, but have been accomplished at least partly with the separate funds of one or the other of the spouses. Different theories have been developed for the classification of such acquisitions.

The Spanish–Mexican parent system classified property at the "inception of the right," that is, when the first interest in the subject matter was acquired. If wealth of a different classification was subsequently used to complete the acquisition transaction, reimbursement was a possibility, but there was no apportionment of the subject matter itself.[9] Some of the early California cases followed the inception of the right doctrine, or were at least consistent with it.[10] In later cases, California courts evolved a quite different approach, reasoning that when an asset is acquired over time by installment payments, the asset should be apportioned on the basis of community and separate contributions to the total purchase price and classified accordingly. The apportionment theory has been utilized in a wide variety of installment acquisition cases, including land sale contracts,[11] insurance policies,[12] pensions,[13] and

9. See de Funiak & Vaughn, Principles of Community Property (2d ed. 1971) § 64, p. 130.

10. See Estate of Boody, 119 Cal. 402, 51 P. 634 (1897); Harris v. Harris, 71 Cal. 314, 12 P. 274 (1886); Lake v. Lake, 52 Cal. 428 (1877). For a more recent application of the inception of right theory, see Marriage of Joaquin, 193 Cal.App.3d 1529, 239 Cal.Rptr. 175 (1987).

11. Vieux v. Vieux, reprinted in this Section.

contingency fees.[14]

VIEUX v. VIEUX

California District Court of Appeal, 1926.
80 Cal.App. 222, 251 P. 640.

[Prior to marriage plaintiff and defendant agreed that a certain lot should be purchased. The agreement to purchase was executed by the plaintiff who made the original payment of $280. After marriage community property in the amount of $553.68 was used to make payments on the purchase price, to pay interest and taxes. The conveyance was in the name of the plaintiff. In divorce proceedings the trial court held the lot was plaintiff's separate property.]

HOUSER, J. * * * For the purpose of determining the respective property rights of the husband and the wife, the circumstances surrounding the purchase of the property should receive consideration. While no transcript of the evidence received on the trial of the action has been presented to this court, sufficient facts are set forth in the findings to enable this court to perceive that, prior to the marriage, the parties together viewed the property and concluded that it was desirable for community purposes. The fact that thereafter they may have used it in that manner, and applied community funds in payment of the purchase price of the property, confirms the thought that, as between the husband and the wife, the property was considered as "community" rather than "separate." The authorities are in accord that by agreement between husband and wife the status of any property owned by them may be changed from separate to community, and vice versa. While no finding of the court recites the fact that the parties were "agreed," either at the time of the purchase or at any time thereafter, that the property in question was "community," their action in the premises at least encourages the belief that before the marriage each of them considered the property as being prospectively "community" and after marriage the property was to be improved, sustained, supported and finally completely and absolutely owned by them by reason of their common and joint efforts and savings. In the circumstances here present, it requires no wild stretch of the imagination to perceive a "meeting of the minds" without the form of express words, either spoken or written, to the effect that the property in question was not considered by the parties as exclusively in the husband, with the wife having absolutely no material right, title, or interest therein; but, to the contrary, that the property was "theirs," each of the parties enjoying therein equal rights and privileges, at least as far as the community funds contributed to the payment of the purchase price thereof. In effect it was somewhat in the

12. Modern Woodmen of America v. Gray, 113 Cal.App. 729, 299 P. 754 (1931).

13. Gettman v. City of Los Angeles, Department of Water and Power, reprinted in Section 6.

14. Waters v. Waters, 75 Cal.App.2d 265, 170 P.2d 494 (1946).

nature of a partnership relationship that existed between the parties—
the husband on the one side, and the community consisting of the
husband and the wife, on the other side.

For purposes affecting strangers, the acquisition, through an installment contract, of the right to purchase real property, may be considered
as ownership of such property, in that such holding may entitle the
intending purchaser to the possession and the use of the property to the
exclusion of others; but, as between husband and wife, where community funds are used to a considerable extent in the payment of the
purchase price, the meaning of the statute relating to the definition of
separate and community property of spouses cannot be so limited. The
confidential relationship existing between husband and wife forbids such
a strict construction to be placed upon the statute as will destroy the
probable intent of the husband and wife with reference to the manner in
which the ownership of the property is enjoyed. Any other construction
in these days of liberal terms, with reference to installment purchase
price contracts for the sale of real property, including the possible
provision of "a dollar down and a dollar per week," would permit a
husband or a prospective husband, to buy or to agree to buy any
reasonable quantity of lots or lands on the payment by him from his
separate funds of a comparatively insignificant sum and thereafter to
pay practically the entire purchase price from the community funds, and
yet successfully maintain that, because in its inception the naked right
to purchase, carrying with it the right of use and possession, was his
separate property, it so remained. It would seem improbable that,
through general definitions of terms, the intention of the law-makers
was to bring about a result which, in many if not a majority of instances,
would be of so disastrous and unjust a consequence. Rather should it be
assumed that, when the Legislature undertook to define separate property as that owned by the husband before marriage, even though in other
statutes the right of exclusive possession and use was specified as the
indicia of ownership, the "ownership" in the husband through and by
virtue of which the wife's interest would be entirely excluded, would
necessarily be an absolute ownership, as distinguished from a limited
ownership, and that, so far as community funds might participate in the
acquisition or protection of vested rights, to that extent proportionally
should the property be considered as "community."

* * *

In passing upon the meaning of the word "owner," as contained in a
provision of a city charter, the Supreme Court of this state has ruled
that "the term 'owner' includes any person having a claim or interest in
real property, though less than an absolute fee." Higgins v. City of San
Diego, 131 Cal. 294, 304, 63 P. 470, 476. That authority, however, can
be regarded as nothing more than a generality, so far as the facts in the
instant case are concerned. Cases from other jurisdictions, particularly
Guye v. Guye, 63 Wash. 340, 115 P. 731, 37 L.R.A., N.S., 186; Barrett v.
Franke, 46 Nev. 170, 208 P. 435, and Heintz v. Brown, 46 Wash. 387, 90

P. 211, 123 Am.St.Rep. 937, in effect hold that, in circumstances analogous to those indicated in the findings herein, to which reference has been had, a part of property involved may be regarded as community and a part as separate—depending upon conditions, not essentially on the manner in which the contract for the purchase of the property was entered into or ostensibly acquired, but rather upon the manner in which the payments were made; and, while the principle announced in such decisions has been subjected to some criticism, the administration of strict justice to the parties concerned, rather than the application to the facts of the hard rules of law, lends an appealing force to the conclusions reached in the cases to which reference has been had. The governing rule is indicated in 5 Ruling Case Law, p. 834, as follows:

> "Thus property purchased by one spouse before marriage is separate property, though the deed therefor is not executed and delivered until after marriage, and this is true though a part of the purchase price is not paid until after marriage, in the absence of a showing that any part of the balance was paid with community funds. In any event it would be community property only to the extent and in the proportion that the purchase price is contributed by the community." *Incomplete*

In the instant case, the husband having acquired an inchoate right, on compliance with certain conditions, to become an absolute owner of the property in question, and the facts showing that the required conditions were met with funds furnished by the community, aided by other funds issuing directly from the property agreed to be purchased, justice demands that the rights of the parties should be measured by the direct contributions made by the respective parties to the purchase price of the property. Accordingly, the judgment of the trial court herein should have indicated that the community interest was entitled to share in the title to the property in the same proportion as the amount contributed to the purchase price by the community, to wit, $553.68, bore to the sum of $833.86—the total amount paid by the respective parties therefor.

It is ordered that that part of the judgment from which the appeal herein is taken be and the same is reversed; and the trial court be and it is directed to enter a new judgment on its findings of fact in accordance with the law as indicated by the opinion herein.

Notes

1. The reasoning of the court in Vieux v. Vieux was subsequently applied to the acquisition of real property financed by a purchase-money mortgage, where the husband acquired title subject to the mortgage before marriage and paid off the balance of the purchase-money loan with community funds during marriage. "[T]he rule developed through the decisions in California gives to the community a pro tanto community property interest in such property in the ratio that the payments on the purchase price with community funds bear to the payments made with separate funds." Forbes v. Forbes, 118 Cal.App.2d 324, 325, 257 P.2d 721, 722 (1953).

2. To the extent that the court in *Vieux* included the payment of interest and taxes by the community in formulating the apportionment, the decision has been disapproved by the California Supreme Court in *In re Marriage of Moore*, reprinted in Subsection B of this Section.

B. Borrowed Funds and Credit Acquisitions

Property acquired during marriage through a credit or loan transaction comes within the general presumption of community property.[15] The general presumption can be rebutted by using the tracing principle, establishing that separate property produced the acquisition.[16] The general presumption may also be overcome by showing that a contract controls the classification,[17] or that a gift to the spouse was intended.[18] The case may be taken out of the general presumption by raising one of the special statutory presumptions, or by showing that the acquisition was made while the spouses were living separate and apart.[19] The same classification principles that we examined in Chapter 2 thus apply to loan or credit acquisitions.

We have seen that when an item of separate property is sold, the sales proceeds are classified as separate property. This is simply a transmutation in form, and is a common example of the tracing principle. Similarly, when an item of separate property is used as the primary security for a loan, the money so produced—the loan proceeds—may be classified as separate property.[20] Other factors, however, frequently contribute to the production of the loan proceeds: lenders in such transactions may not rely solely on the underlying property as security, but may also consider the personal integrity of the borrower, even in cases where anti-deficiency legislation is applicable.[21] The personal integrity of the borrower has reference to the individual's earning ability and reputation for paying debts and may be considered a community asset during marriage. In addition, some time, energy and skill may be involved in procuring the loan and executing the necessary documents. To what extent should these other factors be taken into consideration when classifying the proceeds of a loan secured by separate property? Should they be the basis for apportionment, or should they be viewed as too speculative or insignificant? Should the testimony of the lender that he was motivated primarily by one factor or another be the basis for

---

15. Estate of Ellis, 203 Cal. 414, 264 P. 743 (1928); Gudelj v. Gudelj, 41 Cal.2d 202, 259 P.2d 656 (1953); Elliott v. Elliott, 162 Cal.App.2d 350, 328 P.2d 291 (1958).

16. Schuyler v. Broughton, 70 Cal. 282, 11 P. 719 (1886).

17. Vandervort v. Godfrey, 58 Cal.App. 578, 208 P. 1017 (1922); see Heney v. Pesoli, 109 Cal. 53, 41 P. 819 (1895).

18. Williams v. Tam, 131 Cal. 64, 63 P. 133 (1900); Vandervort v. Godfrey, 58 Cal. App. 578, 208 P. 1017 (1922).

19. Tagus Ranch Co. v. First Nat. Bank of Clovis, 7 Cal.App.2d 457, 46 P.2d 809

(1935). Hogevoll v. Hogevoll, 59 Cal. App.2d 188, 138 P.2d 693 (1943), apparently was such a case but the decision was on other grounds.

20. Schuyler v. Broughton, 70 Cal. 282, 11 P. 719 (1886); Estate of Abdale, 28 Cal.2d 587, 170 P.2d 918 (1946).

21. California's anti deficiency legislation is contained in part at West's Ann.Cal. Code of Civil Procedure § 580b, which prohibits deficiency judgments under various types of financing arrangements in cases involving certain types of residential real property. See also West's Ann.Cal.Code of Civil Procedure § 580a, § 580d and § 726.

classification of the loan proceeds? Perhaps these other factors could be considered incidental and minimal in the absence of evidence that they had a measurable effect in producing the loan.[22]

GUDELJ v. GUDELJ

Supreme Court of California, 1953.
41 Cal.2d 202, 259 P.2d 656.

EDMONDS, JUSTICE. Catherine Gudelj was awarded an interlocutory decree of divorce from John Gudelj on the ground of extreme cruelty.

The parties were married in 1938. Prior to that time, John was owner and operator of the Pacific Avenue Cleaners. He continued this business until 1943. In 1946, after his discharge from military service, he operated the Owl Cleaners in partnership with one Grinton. They dissolved the partnership in the following year, and John purchased a one-fourth interest in the Helene French Cleaners where he began to work as a "benzine man".

* * *

The court found that an undivided one-fourth interest in the Helene French Cleaners was the separate property of John. * * *

According to the record, the undivided one-fourth interest in the Helene French Cleaners was purchased by John for $11,500. John paid $1,500 of that amount in cash and executed a note for $10,000. No specific finding was made concerning the status of the note, but the trial court found that the cash payment was made from John's separate funds and concluded that the entire partnership interest is his separate property. Catherine contends that the evidence does not support these findings.

The evidence concerning the source of the $1,500, although confused and conflicting, is sufficient to support a finding that it was derived from John's separate property. John testified that the money came from the Owl Cleaners and, although he further stated that the equipment and fixtures of the business had been sold at a loss, apparently at least $1,500 was obtained from that source. Catherine claims that the Owl Cleaners must be presumed to have been community property because the business was acquired during the existence of the marriage. Civ. Code, Sec. 164. But that presumption is controlling only when it is impossible to trace the source of specific property. Falk v. Falk, 48 Cal.App.2d 762, 768, 120 P.2d 714. Here the presumption is rebutted by the testimony of John that the Owl Cleaners was purchased with funds acquired from the sale of the equipment of the Pacific Avenue Cleaners, admittedly his separate property, and from a bank account held jointly by John with his mother in which was deposited the proceeds from the sale of real property owned by them prior to John's marriage.

22. For a critical analysis of the California law regarding classification of credit acquisitions, see Young, Community Property Classification of Credit Acquisitions in California: Law Without Logic? 17 Cal. W.L.Rev. 173 (1981).

However, the record does not support the conclusion that the balance of the purchase price of the partnership interest was made from John's separate property. That part of the payment was represented by a note signed by John. There is a rebuttable presumption that property acquired on credit during marriage is community property. Civ.Code, Sec. 164; Hogevoll v. Hogevoll, 59 Cal.App.2d 188, 193–194, 138 P.2d 693. But "funds procured by the hypothecation of separate property of a spouse are separate property of that spouse". In re Estate of Abdale, 28 Cal.2d 587, 592, 170 P.2d 918, 922. The proceeds of a loan made on the credit of separate property are governed by the same rule. In re Estate of Ellis, 203 Cal. 414, 416–417, 264 P. 743. In accordance with this general principle, the character of property acquired by a sale upon credit is determined according to the intent of the seller to rely upon the separate property of the purchaser or upon a community asset. In re Estate of Ellis, supra, 203 Cal. 414, 416, 264 P. 743; Hogevoll v. Hogevoll, supra, 59 Cal.App.2d 188, 193–194, 138 P.2d 693; and see Schuyler v. Broughton, 70 Cal. 282, 285, 11 P. 719; Vandervort v. Godfrey, 58 Cal.App. 578, 582, 208 P. 1017. In the absence of evidence tending to prove that the seller primarily relied upon the purchaser's separate property in extending credit, the trial court must find in accordance with the presumption. See Falk v. Falk, supra, 48 Cal. App.2d 762, 767, 120 P.2d 714.

No testimony was offered concerning the intent of the seller in extending credit to John. John asserts, however, that shortly before the credit transaction, he and his mother sold real property for some $30,000, and the seller must have relied upon John's interest in the proceeds. Furthermore, he contends, his previous failures in attempts to operate cleaning businesses demonstrate that the basis for credit could not have been his personal ability and capacity. However, even if these facts be accepted as true, there is no evidence that the seller had knowledge of their existence. There being no satisfactory evidence to contradict the presumption, it must prevail.

Between the date of purchase of the partnership interest and the commencement of the present action, John withdrew from the profits of the business $3,600 per year. In addition, during that period a sum of $4,000 was withdrawn from the profits and credited upon his note. The trial court found $3,600 per year to be a reasonable wage for John's services to the partnership and that $4,000 was a reasonable return for two years on the $11,500 investment. These findings are supported by substantial evidence.

The trial court having concluded that the entire one-fourth interest in the partnership was John's separate property, no problem concerning an apportionment between the community and the separate property of John was presented. However, the $4,000 received by John as profit must be apportioned between the parties.

The husband has the management of the community personal property, Civ.Code, Sec. 172, and therefore, John properly could apply the community's share of the profits as well as his own toward the reduction of the debt incurred in purchasing the interest in the business. There being no evidence as to the present value of the one-fourth interest, it must be presumed that at the commencement of the suit it was worth $11,500, the amount he paid for it. John, having contributed $1,500 or ⅔ of the purchase price, is entitled to the same proportion of the $4,000, or $521.74. The community must be credited with the balance.

* * *

Insofar as the interlocutory decree disposes of the real property and concerns the rights and obligations of the parties with respect thereto, and disposes of the partnership interest in Helene Cleaners, it is reversed and the cause is remanded for a new trial upon the issues relating thereto; in all other respects the decree is affirmed, appellant to recover her costs on appeal.

BANK OF CALIFORNIA v. CONNOLLY
California District Court of Appeal, 1974.
36 Cal.App.3d 350, 111 Cal.Rptr. 468.

[In 1964 Kelber and Latimer acquired a 10 acre parcel of land called the 7th and Mountain property with borrowed funds obtained on their unsecured note, and also acquired a 67.744 acre parcel with borrowed funds obtained on their note secured by a mortgage of separate property. About that time Latimer, Connolly and Seward with the consent of Kelber entered into an agreement to split the profits from the subdivision and sale of the parcels of land title to which remained in Latimer and Kelber. The court rejected Mrs. Latimer's claim that the agreement was a transfer of community property land without her consent, but held it was necessary to determine whether the titles were community property in which Mrs. Latimer had an interest.]

TAMURA, ASSOCIATE JUSTICE. * * * We next consider the question whether the trial court properly determined that Latimer's interest in the properties in question was community property. Although Connolly and Seward did not raise this issue in their opening brief, they raise it in their reply brief in response to the Bank's and daughter's contention that the judgment properly restricted enforceability of the profit sharing agreement as to Mrs. Latimer's community interest to the reasonable value of services rendered by Connolly and Seward to the community and in response to the wife's contention that the agreement was wholly unenforceable as to her community interest.

The properties having been acquired by purchase during Latimer's marriage, his interest was presumed to be community, and the burden of overcoming the presumption by clear and convincing evidence rested with Connolly and Seward. (See v. See, 64 Cal.2d 778, 783, 51 Cal.Rptr. 88, 415 P.2d 776.)

Insofar as the 7th and Mountain property was concerned, the evidence supported the trial court's finding that Latimer's interest was community property. The property was acquired with proceeds of an unsecured loan from the United California Bank evidenced by a promissory note signed by Latimer and Kelber. The Bank's loan officer testified the loan was made solely in reliance upon the personal credit of Kelber and Latimer. The proceeds of the loan so made on the personal credit of either spouse are regarded as community property, particularly where the husband is the borrower. (Ford v. Ford, 276 Cal.App.2d 913, 80 Cal.Rptr. 435; 4 Witkin, Summary of Cal.Law (7th ed.) pp. 2727–2728, and cases there cited.)

As to the airport property, its acquisition was financed by a $420,000 loan secured by the property itself and a $360,000 loan secured by the Alta Loma property. The loan proceeds secured by the airport property were obviously community in nature. As to the $360,000 loan, it was conceded that Latimer's interest in the Alta Loma property was his separate property. Ordinarily funds borrowed by hypothecation of a spouse's separate property are also separate property. (Estate of Abdale, 28 Cal.2d 587, 592, 170 P.2d 918.) In the case at bench, however, the court found that although the Bank took trust deeds on both the airport property and the Alta Loma property, the loans were made "primarily" on the general credit of Kelber and Latimer. The Bank's loan officer testified the additional security on the Alta Loma property was taken only to comply with banking regulations restricting banks to a loan of up to 60 percent of the appraised value of property given as security. He also testified that in making the loans the Bank relied primarily on the general credit of Kelber and Latimer and not on the additional security of the Alta Loma property.

The foregoing evidence was sufficient to support the trial court's finding that Latimer's interest in the airport property was community. There is a rebuttable presumption that property acquired on credit during marriage is community so that "[i]n the absence of evidence tending to prove that the seller [in this case the lender] primarily relied upon the purchaser's separate property in extending credit, the trial court must find in accordance with the presumption." (Gudelj v. Gudelj, 41 Cal.2d 202, 210, 259 P.2d 656, 661.)

* * *

IN RE MARRIAGE OF GRINIUS
California District Court of Appeal, 1985.
166 Cal.App.3d 1179, 212 Cal.Rptr. 803.

WORK, ASSOCIATE JUSTICE.

* * *

FACTUAL AND PROCEDURAL BACKGROUND

Victor and Joyce Grinius were married the same day they signed an antenuptial agreement which listed their separate assets and stated "all property owned by [either spouse] at the time of the marriage and all property coming to [either spouse] from whatever source during the effective term of this Agreement shall be the separate property of [the respective spouse.]'' Victor listed common stock in two companies, $2,500 in a profit sharing plan, improved San Diego real property, and unimproved real properties in Florida. Joyce listed only her car and miscellaneous household furnishings.

The antenuptial agreement also provided:

"This Agreement shall be binding upon the parties during the first six years of marriage only. Thereafter, the terms of this Agreement may be renegotiated by the mutual agreement of both parties or, in the alternative, the parties may choose not to renegotiate its terms and to allow it to entirely lapse. In such latter event, each party shall immediately have, upon expiration of said first six years of marriage, all rights and obligations with respect to each other and with respect to property which are provided by law. Such rights and obligations shall be retroactive to the date of marriage without regard to the provisions otherwise contained in this paragraph."

However, even after a lapse, the parties' premarital separate property was to retain its separate character.

Shortly after marriage Victor resigned his job so he and Joyce could open a restaurant. Joyce apparently had worked in a restaurant for a number of years before marriage. They located a suitable building, costing $60,000. The purchase money was obtained from two sources: (1) a $20,000 downpayment from an $80,000 Small Business Administration (SBA) loan guaranty lent by California First Bank (hereafter referred to as SBA loan) and (2) $40,000 loaned by Home Federal Savings and Loan. Although only Victor signed the SBA loan guaranty, both Victor and Joyce signed the promissory note from California First Bank. Victor alone signed the Home Federal Savings and Loan promissory note. The SBA loan was secured by both community and separate property. Both Victor and Joyce negotiated the original purchase offer. However, without Joyce's knowledge, Victor placed title to the property in his name alone.

Victor and Joyce used the remaining $60,000 of the SBA loan to remodel the building, buy equipment, and pay their living and restaurant expenses. These funds were disbursed through the restaurant's checking account on which Victor and Joyce were the signators. Indeed, during the course of the marriage all personal and restaurant expenses were paid from this joint account.

Victor and Joyce both worked in the restaurant in several different capacities and continued to do so during the course of their marriage. Their community earnings were placed in the restaurant checking account; however, from time to time Victor also deposited funds received from his separate property into the account to prevent overdrafts.

Monthly payments on the purchase money loans were made from the joint restaurant checking account. In 1975 Victor also used $30,098.00 and $39,821.93 of his separate property funds to pay on the SBA and Home Federal loans, respectively. Again, in 1978 Victor paid $33,818 of separate property funds to retire the SBA loan. That same year, Victor and Joyce signed a $63,000 installment note in favor of San Diego Trust and Savings, secured by a trust deed on the restaurant property. From these proceeds, $42,000 was used to pay the outstanding balance on the Home Federal promissory note.

Victor and Joyce separated in April of 1980. Before trial, Victor stipulated the restaurant business was community property and the business was sold. Victor and Joyce and their respective counsels were each granted $5,000 from the sale proceeds. The trial court found all of the contested assets, except the restaurant real property, to be community property. The restaurant real property, worth $340,000, was determined to be Victor's separate property.

THE SEPARATE PROPERTY CHARACTERIZATION OF THE RESTAURANT REAL
PROPERTY IS NOT SUPPORTED BY SUBSTANTIAL EVIDENCE

I

A trial court's findings regarding a property's separate or community character is binding and conclusive on review when supported by substantial evidence (*Beam v. Bank of America,* 6 Cal.3d 12, 25, 98 Cal.Rptr. 137, 490 P.2d 257; *Hicks v. Hicks,* 211 Cal.App.2d 144, 149, 27 Cal.Rptr. 307), even though evidence conflicts or supports contrary inferences. (*Beam v. Bank of America, supra,* 6 Cal.3d at p. 25, 98 Cal.Rptr. 137, 490 P.2d 257; *Mears v. Mears,* 180 Cal.App.2d 484, 500–501, 4 Cal.Rptr. 618, disapproved on other grounds in *See v. See,* 64 Cal.2d 778, 785–786, 51 Cal.Rptr. 888, 415 P.2d 776.) However, substantial evidence is not synonymous with "any" evidence. (*Hall v. Department of Adoptions,* 47 Cal.App.3d 898, 906, 121 Cal.Rptr. 223.) It must have ponderable legal significance and " 'must be reasonable in nature, credible, and of solid value; it must actually be "substantial" proof of the essentials which the law requires in a particular case.' [Citation.] " (*Ibid.*)

We review the evidence supporting the trial court's characterization of the restaurant property as Victor's separate property.

Property bought during marriage by either spouse is rebuttably presumed to be community property (Civ.Code, § 5110; *See v. See, supra,* 64 Cal.2d 778, 783, 51 Cal.Rptr. 888, 415 P.2d 776; *In re Marriage of Aufmuth,* 89 Cal.App.3d 446, 455, 152 Cal.Rptr. 668, disapproved on other grounds in *In re Marriage of Lucas,* 27 Cal.3d 808, 815, 166 Cal.Rptr. 853, 614 P.2d 285), and typically the spouse asserting its separate character must overcome this presumption. Victor relies on the antenuptial agreement to support his separate property claim. Such agreements can control the character of marital property and do prevail when Family Law Act presumptions are to the contrary. (Civ.Code, § 5133; *In re Marriage of Dawley,* 17 Cal.3d 342, 357, 131 Cal.Rptr. 3,

551 P.2d 323; *Tompkins v. Bishop,* 94 Cal.App.2d 546, 549–550, 211 P.2d 14.)

Here, the antenuptial agreement is a comprehensive attempt to maintain the separate property character of assets acquired both before and during marriage, but it is time-limited. It lapsed six years after the date of marriage and reinvested the spouses with all communal rights retroactive to the date of marriage. Therefore, at trial the agreement had no effect on the presumption of community acquisition.

Victor next traces the source of payments for the restaurant property to overcome the fundamental community presumption. Specifically, he argues the purchase money loans were separate property and the restaurant real property, thus acquired, maintains the same character. (*In re Marriage of Mix,* 14 Cal.3d 604, 610, 122 Cal.Rptr. 79, 536 P.2d 479.)

"The character of property as separate or community is determined at the time of its acquisition. [Citations.]" (*See v. See, supra,* 64 Cal.2d 778, 783, 51 Cal.Rptr. 888, 415 P.2d 776; accord *Giacomazzi v. Rowe,* 109 Cal.App.2d 498, 500–501, 240 P.2d 1020.) Here, the restaurant property was acquired shortly after marriage and is presumed to be community property. (§ 5110.) However, the character of credit acquisitions during marriage is "determined according to the intent of the lender to rely upon the separate property of the purchaser or upon a community asset. [Citations.]" (*In re Marriage of Aufmuth, supra,* 89 Cal.App.3d 446, 455, 152 Cal.Rptr. 668.)

While the California courts have consistently and uncritically applied the intent-of-the-lender rule, they have inconsistently espoused the applicable test. (See generally Young, *Community Property Classification of Credit Acquisitions in California: Law without Logic?* (1981) 17 Cal.Western L.Rev. 173 (hereafter cited as *Classification of Credit Acquisitions*).) In early cases, the Supreme Court required a showing the lender relied *entirely* on the existing separate property of a spouse in extending the loan to characterize the loan proceeds as separate property. (*Estate of Holbert,* 57 Cal. 257, 259; *Estate of Ellis,* 203 Cal. 414, 416, 264 P. 743.) The more modern and oft-cited formulation found in *Gudelj v. Gudelj,* 41 Cal.2d 202, 259 P.2d 656, apparently relaxes the standard: "In the absence of evidence tending to prove that the seller *primarily* relied upon the purchaser's separate property in extending credit, the trial court must find in accordance with the [section 5110] presumption." (*Id.,* at p. 210, 259 P.2d 656; italics added.) The *Gudelj* opinion cited no authority for this apparent change and had no opportunity to apply the standard since no evidence of lender reliance on separate property was proffered. Later cases have been decided on seemingly different standards. Courts have found evidence of lender's intent in: (1) reliance on or hypothecation of separate property (*Bank of California v. Connolly,* 36 Cal.App.3d 350, 375, 111 Cal.Rptr. 468; *Ford v. Ford,* 276 Cal.App.2d 9, 13–14, 80 Cal.Rptr. 435; *Somps v. Somps,* 250 Cal.App.2d 328, 336–337, 58 Cal.Rptr. 304; *Hicks v. Hicks, supra,* 211

Cal.App.2d 144, 153, 27 Cal.Rptr. 307), (2) sole reliance on separate property (*Howard v. Howard,* 128 Cal.App.2d 180, 186, 275 P.2d 88); and (3) extension of the loan on the faith of existing property belonging to the acquiring spouse (*In re Marriage of Aufmuth, supra,* 89 Cal. App.3d 446, 455–456, 152 Cal.Rptr. 668; *In re Marriage of Stoner,* 147 Cal.App.3d 858, 863–864, 195 Cal.Rptr. 351.) Nonetheless, in all of the above cases, loan proceeds were characterized as a spouse's separate property *only* when direct or circumstantial evidence indicated the lender relied solely on separate property in offering the loan.

With the above review in mind, we restate the applicable standard: Loan proceeds acquired during marriage are presumptively community property; however, this presumption may be overcome by showing the lender intended to rely solely upon a spouse's separate property and did in fact do so. Without satisfactory evidence of the lender's intent, the general presumption prevails.

Victor presented no direct evidence of lender intent and instead offered circumstantial evidence to prove lender reliance on his separate property. (*Estate of Updegraph,* 199 Cal.App.2d 419, 422, 18 Cal.Rptr. 591.) He argues the "SBA loan guaranty was premised solely on [his] posting of collateral consisting of his entire separate property." However, a review of the SBA loan conditions outlined on the loan guaranty authorization refutes this contention. The SBA required nine separate conditions, only two of which necessitated hypothecation of Victor's separate property. Specifically, loan approval required: (1) a second deed of trust on the restaurant property and improvements, (2) Joyce's signature on the promissory note and all instruments of hypothecation, (3) a first lien on the restaurant machinery, equipment, furniture and fixtures presently owned and later acquired with the loan proceeds, (4) acquisition and assignment of an $80,000 life insurance policy on Victor, (5) purchase of hazard insurance on the restaurant property, (6) a third deed of trust on Victor's improved real property in San Diego, already subject to prior liens totalling $107,000, (7) assignment of 3100 shares of Victor's separate property stock, (8) the furnishing of the restaurant's quarterly balance sheets and profit and loss statements, and (9) the use of the SBA's management assistant services "as deemed necessary by SBA or Bank."

The primary collateral for the loan was the restaurant property. Alone, this hypothecation provides no inference of lender intent; to argue otherwise is to rely on circular reasoning. The requiring of Joyce's signature on the note and instruments of hypothecation does suggest the lender did look toward community assets for security. However, Joyce's signing of the documents, without more, does not compel a finding in favor of the community. (*Ford v. Ford, supra,* 276 Cal.App.2d 9, 13–14, 80 Cal.Rptr. 435; *Kenney v. Kenney,* 128 Cal.App.2d 128, 138, 274 P.2d 951, disapproved on other grounds in *See v. See, supra,* 64 Cal.2d 778, 785–786, 51 Cal.Rptr. 888, 415 P.2d 776.) Moreover, given the effect of the antenuptial agreement at the time of the loan, Joyce arguably had few, if any, existing community interests to pledge. Conditions three through five clearly suggest reliance on community interests. Both insurance policies and the restaurant equipment were purchased from the joint restaurant account and were presumptively community property. Indeed, Victor stipulated to the community nature of the restaurant business. Yet, some of the same loan proceeds challenged here were used for operating capital for the restaurant and were specifically earmarked for the purchase of trade fixtures and the liquor license, assets unquestioningly found to belong to the community. This inconsistency clearly contradicts Victor's contention.

Victor nonetheless relies on *Hicks v. Hicks, supra,* 211 Cal.App.2d 144, 27 Cal.Rptr. 307, to bolster his argument. In *Hicks,* the trial court made an "implied finding that the proceeds from the loans * * * were the separate property of [husband]." (*Id.,* at p. 153, 27 Cal.Rptr. 307.) Affirming, the Court of Appeal stated: "The trial court was entitled to conclude that the original bank loans were made to the [husband] on the credit of his separate property as, at the time they were obtained, he had been married less than a year and his community earnings were not then of paramount significance, whereas his separate property approximated $500,000 in value." (*Id.,* at p. 155, 27 Cal.Rptr. 307.) However, the court in *Hicks* did not point to any evidence of the lender's actual intent and, indeed, *specifically refrained* from detailing the basis for its conclusion. (*Id.,* at p. 153, 27 Cal.Rptr. 307.) Thus, *Hicks* provides no guidance in determining lender intent in a mixed collateral situation. As one commentator has noted, "Although the *Hicks* case may seem to have been reasonably and correctly decided, in truth it stands as an unfortunate example of an improper assumption regarding a critical factual issue which the *Gudelj* Rule addressed: Whether the lender (or credit seller) *in fact primarily relied* upon separate property of a spouse or upon the general credit of the spouse when credit was extended to that spouse." (*Classifications of Credit Acquisitions, supra,* at p. 216.)

Loan conditions eight and nine demonstrate the SBA's concern about the operation and management of the restaurant business. This interest is wholly consistent with the stated purpose of the SBA:

> "For the purpose of preserving and promoting a competitive free enterprise economic system, Congress hereby declares that it is the continuing policy and responsibility of the Federal Government to use all practical means and to take such actions as are necessary, consistent with its needs and obligations and other essential considerations of national policy, to implement and coordinate all Federal department, agency, and instrumentality policies, programs, and activities in order to: foster the economic interests of small businesses; insure a competitive economic climate conducive to the development, growth and expansion of small businesses; establish incentives to assure that adequate capital and other resources at competitive prices are available to small businesses; reduce the concentration of economic resources and expand competition; and provide an opportunity for entrepreneurship, inventiveness, and the creation and growth of small businesses." (15 U.S.C.A. § 631a,

subd. (a); see also Financing California Business (Cont.Ed.Bar 1976) §§ 1.8–1.9, pp. 6–8.)

In granting these small business loans, the SBA is constrained by statute and policy considerations. Many of these loan guidelines are outlined in Chapter 1 of Title 13 of the Code Federal Regulations. Section 120.2, subdivision (c)(1), of Chapter 1 specifically provides: "No financial assistance shall be extended unless there exists reasonable assurance the loan can and will be repaid pursuant to its terms. Reasonable assurance of repayment will exist *only* where the past earnings record and *future prospects indicate ability to repay the loan and other obligations.* It will be deemed not to exist when the proposed loan is to accomplish an expansion which is unwarranted in light of the applicant's past experience and management ability, or when the effect of making the loan is to subsidize inferior management." (Italics added.) Accordingly, in the absence of evidence the SBA acted contrary to their official duties in this instance (Evid.Code, § 664), we find the loan was extended on both the ability of the community to repay the note and to manage the restaurant. Therefore, the SBA loan funds are a community asset, not Victor's separate property.

The second purchase money loan from Home Federal Savings and Loan was secured by a first deed of trust on the restaurant property. Victor presents no evidence to rebut the community presumption and, indeed, concedes the Home Federal Loan was likely extended in reliance on the interest in the restaurant property already acquired with the SBA loan funds. Thus, this loan must also be seen as an asset of the community.

Finally, Victor asserts he solely owns the restaurant property by reason of record title. While our courts presume an ownership interest in property is as stated in title (*Gudelj v. Gudelj, supra,* 41 Cal.2d 202, 212, 259 P.2d 656; *Socol v. King,* 36 Cal.2d 342, 345, 223 P.2d 627), this presumption may be dispelled by an agreement between the parties that the respective interests should be otherwise. (*Machado v. Machado,* 58 Cal.2d 501, 506, 25 Cal.Rptr. 87, 375 P.2d 55; *Gudelj v. Gudelj, supra,* 41 Cal.2d at p. 212, 259 P.2d 656.) Here, Victor took title in his name alone, believing he was entitled to do so under the antenuptial agreement.[3] However, whatever authority the agreement may have granted Victor to take title separately,[4] that authority expired before the dissolu-

3. Victor's testimony on this point conflicts. However, we are compelled to review the evidence in a light most favorable to the judgment.

4. On appeal, Joyce argues for the first time Victor breached his fiduciary duties to her in not telling her the restaurant property was recorded in his name alone. (§§ 2228–2234; *Haseltine v. Haseltine,* 203 Cal.App.2d 48, 56–57, 21 Cal.Rptr. 238.) She further argues Victor should not now be allowed to profit from his wrongdoing by asserting a presumption based on title. While we need not reach this issue in light of the above reasoning, we do note, under the antenuptial agreement, it was reasonable, though in retrospect incorrect, for Victor to believe the restaurant property was his alone and to record title accordingly.

tion action, and retroactively reinstated the community presumption. Therefore, the community presumption prevails and the presumption arising from the form of title is without force.

In sum, Victor has failed to present sufficient evidence to rebut the presumption that property acquired during marriage is community property. Therefore, the restaurant property and all rents, issues and profits thereof are properly characterized as community property.

* * *

Note

Historically California courts took a variety of approaches to the classification of borrowed funds and credit acquisitions, including the mutual understanding or agreement of the parties, the intent of the borrower, and the intent of the lender. Why the intent of the lender came to be the dominant factor is unclear, but it has become the established rule. For a criticism of the intent of the lender test as applied in *Grinius,* see Perlman, *A Reappraisal of California's Intent of the Lender Rule,* 37 UCLA L.R. 389 (1989). Perlman conducted a survey of the lending practices of institutional lenders in Southern California. She found that the lenders rarely, if ever, rely solely on separate property in extending credit to a married person, and that even if a lender in fact did so, it would be unlikely to admit that fact because such an admission would work to its detriment. Thus, under the *Grinius* standard, it is practically impossible for a spouse to rebut the presumption that loan funds acquired during marriage are community property. Id. at 407–408.

––––––––––

The preceding materials involving borrowed funds and credit acquisition indicate that where existing property is hypothecated to secure a loan, the underlying classification of the property as separate or community remains unchanged, and repayment of the debt does not result in any change in classification. Where, however, the property being acquired is used to secure the payment of the purchase price, as in the typical purchase money mortgage or deed of trust situation, California courts have generally treated the transaction as an installment acquisition. The repayment of the loan is deemed to create new equities in the title, and apportionment is required.[23] Where classification of the asset must be made before the loan has been fully repaid and where substantial appreciation has occurred in the value of the property, complex apportionment problems can arise. Following a rash of conflicting appellate court decisions, the California Supreme Court undertook to clarify the apportionment rules in the cases of *In re Marriage of Lucas* [24]

23. See Forbes v. Forbes, 118 Cal. App.2d 324, 257 P.2d 721 (1953); In re Ball's Estate, 92 Cal.App.2d 93, 206 P.2d 1111 (1949); Ford v. Ford, 276 Cal.App.2d 9, 80 Cal.Rptr. 435 (1969).

24. In re Marriage of Lucas, reprinted in Chapter 2.

and *In re Marriage of Moore*.[25] These cases indicate that the method of apportionment should reflect not only the classification of the down payment and payments made on the purchase price, but should also recognize the effect of the security device in producing wealth in the underlying real property.

IN RE MARRIAGE OF LUCAS
Supreme Court of California, 1980.
27 Cal.3d 808, 166 Cal.Rptr. 853, 614 P.2d 285.

[This case is reprinted supra at p. 110.]

IN RE MARRIAGE OF MOORE
Supreme Court of California, 1980.
28 Cal.3d 366, 168 Cal.Rptr. 662, 618 P.2d 208.

MANUEL, JUSTICE.

David E. Moore appeals from an interlocutory judgment dissolving his marriage to Lydie D. Moore. He contests only the trial court's determination of the community property interest in the residence located at 121 Mira Way, Menlo Park and the finding that he deliberately misappropriated community property.

The principal issue to be decided in this case is the proper method of calculating the interest obtained by the community as a result of payments made during marriage on the indebtedness secured by a deed of trust on a residence which had been purchased by one of the parties before marriage.

Lydie purchased the house at 121 Mira Way in Menlo Park in April 1966, about eight months before the parties' marriage. The purchase price was $56,640.57. Lydie made a down payment of $16,640.57 and secured a loan for the balance of the purchase price. She took title in her name alone as "Lydie S. Doak, a single woman." Prior to the marriage she made seven monthly payments and reduced the principal loan balance by $245.18.

The parties lived in the house during their marriage and until their separation in June 1977. They made payment during this time with community funds and reduced the loan principal by $5,986.20. Lydie remained in the house and continued to make payments, reducing the principal by an additional $581.07 up to the time of trial. At that time the total principal paid on the purchase price was $23,453.02, the balance owing was $33,187.55, the market value of the house was $160,000, and the equity therein $126,812.45.

The trial court concluded that the residence was Lydie's separate property but that the community had an interest in it by virtue of the community property payments made during the course of the parties'

25. In re Marriage of Moore, reprinted below.

marriage. The trial court further concluded that the community interest was to be determined according to the ratio that the reduction of principal resulting from community funds bears to the reduction of principal from separate funds. No credit was given for the amount paid for interest, taxes and insurance.

Formula

The community interest was calculated by multiplying the equity value of the house by the ratio of the community's reduction of principal to the total amount of principal reduction by both community and separate property ($5,986.20 divided by $23,453.02 equals 25.5242 percent). The amount of the community interest was thus determined to be $32,367.86. Lydie's separate property interest was calculated by multiplying the equity value of the house by the ratio of the separate property reduction of principal to the total amount of principal reduction ($17,466.82 divided by $23,453.02 equals 74.4758 percent). Lydie's separate property interest was thus determined to be $94,444.59.

The parties agree that the community has acquired an interest in the house by virtue of the community funds used to make the payments.[1] They disagree, however, as to how the interest is to be determined. Appellant contends that the community property interest should be based upon the full amount of the payments made, which includes interest, taxes and insurance, rather than only on the amount by which the payments reduce the principal. He relies on Vieux v. Vieux (1926) 80 Cal.App. 222, 251 P. 640.

In *Vieux,* the husband contracted before marriage to buy certain property and paid $280 on account of the purchase price. After the parties' marriage they spent $553.68 of community funds for payment of principal, interest and taxes. The Court of Appeal held that the trial court erred in finding the property to be solely the husband's separate property and stated the rule as follows: "Thus property purchased by one spouse before marriage is separate property * * *, and this is true though a part of the purchase price is not paid until after marriage, in the absence of a showing that any part of the balance was paid with community funds. In any event it would be community property only to the extent and in the proportion that the purchase price is contributed by the community." (80 Cal.App. at p. 229, 251 P. 640.) The court concluded that "the community interest was entitled to share in the title to the property in the same proportion as the amount contributed to the purchase price by the community, to wit, $553.68 bore to the sum of $833.86 [sic]—the total amount paid by the respective parties therefor." (Ibid.)

Although the *Vieux* court included interest and taxes in its calculation, there is no indication that the issue of the propriety of doing so was presented to the court. The concern in that case was with the question

1. Although the trial court designated the community's interest as an "equitable charge or right," it is clear under California law that the interest is properly characterized as a community property interest in the house. (See Forbes v. Forbes (1953) 118 Cal.App.2d 324, 325, 257 P.2d 721; Estate of Neilson (1962) 57 Cal.2d 733, 744, 22 Cal.Rptr. 1, 371 P.2d 745.)

of whether there should be any community interest at all. Since the *Vieux* court did not expressly consider the question of including interest and taxes in the community's interest in the property, we do not consider it to be persuasive authority on that issue.

Where community funds are used to make payments on property purchased by one of the spouses before marriage "the rule developed through decisions in California gives to the community a pro tanto community property interest in such property in the ratio that the payments on the purchase price with community funds bear to the payments made with separate funds." (Forbes v. Forbes, supra, 118 Cal.App.2d 324, 325, 257 P.2d 721; see also Bare v. Bare (1967) 256 Cal.App.2d 684, 690, 64 Cal.Rptr. 335; In re Marriage of Jafeman (1972) 29 Cal.App.3d 244, 257, 105 Cal.Rptr. 483; Estate of Neilson (1962) 57 Cal.2d 733, 744, 22 Cal.Rptr. 1, 371 P.2d 745.) This rule has been commonly understood as excluding payments for interest and taxes. For example in Bare v. Bare, the Court of Appeal directed the trial court to determine the increase in equity in the house during marriage and the fair market value of it before and after the marriage, stating: "the community is entitled to a minimum interest in the property represented by the ratio of the community investment to the total separate and community investment in the property. In the event the fair market value has increased disproportionately to the increase in equity the wife is entitled to participate in that increment in a similar proportion." (256 Cal.App.2d at p. 690, 64 Cal.Rptr. 335; accord In re Marriage of Jafeman, supra, 29 Cal.App.3d at pp. 256–257, 105 Cal.Rptr. 483.) Decisions of other community property jurisdictions are in accord (see, e.g., Hanrahan v. Sims (1973) 20 Ariz.App. 313, 512 P.2d 617, 621; Gapsch v. Gapsch (1954), 76 Idaho 44, 277 P.2d 278, 283; Merkel v. Merkel (1951) 39 Wash.2d 102, 234 P.2d 857, 864), and *Vieux* apparently stands alone in suggesting a contrary rule.

Appellant argues, however, that interest and taxes should be included in the computation because they often represent a substantial part of current home purchase payments. We do not agree. Since such expenditures do not increase the equity value of the property, they should not be considered in its division upon dissolution of marriage. The value of real property is generally represented by the owners' equity in it, and the equity value does not include finance charges or other expenses incurred to maintain the investment. Amounts paid for interest, taxes and insurance do not contribute to the capital investment and are not considered part of it. A variety of expenses may be incurred in the maintenance of investment property, but such expenses are not considered in the valuation of the property except to the extent they may be relevant in determining its market value from which in turn the owners' equity is derived by subtracting the outstanding obligation. Upon dissolution, it is the court's duty to account for and divide the assets and the debts of the community. Payments previously made for interest, taxes and insurance are neither. Moreover, if these items were considered to be part of the community's interest, fairness would also require that the community be charged for its use of the property.

In summary, we find no basis for departing from the present rule which excludes amounts paid for interest, taxes, and insurance from the calculation of the respective separate and community interests. We turn to that calculation in this case.

Although many formulae have been suggested, we are not persuaded that any of them would be an improvement over a formula based on the reasoning of In re Marriage of Aufmuth (1979) 89 Cal.App.3d 446, 152 Cal.Rptr. 668, which was approved in In re Marriage of Lucas (1980) 27 Cal.3d 808, 166 Cal.Rptr. 853, 614 P.2d 283. We were there concerned with determining the respective community and separate interests in a residence purchased during marriage with a combination of community and separate funds where the community contributed the loan and subsequent payments on it and there was an agreement or understanding that the party contributing the separate property down payment was to retain a pro rata separate property interest. (Id., at pp. 816–817, 166 Cal.Rptr. 853, 614 P.2d 283.) The formula we used there recognized the economic value of the loan taken to purchase the property. In the formula postulated in *Lucas* the proceeds of the loan were treated as a community property contribution on the assumption that the loan was made on the strength of the community assets. (Id., at pp. 816–817, fn. 3, 166 Cal.Rptr. 853, 614 P.2d 283.)

In the present situation, the loan was based on separate assets and was thus a separate property contribution; the down payment was also a separate property contribution. Therefore under the *Lucas/Aufmuth* formula the proceeds of the loan must be treated as a separate property contribution. Accordingly, the formula would be applied as follows: The separate property percentage interest is determined by crediting the separate property with the down payment and the full amount of the loan less the amount by which the community property payments reduced the principal balance of the loan ($16,640.57 plus ($40,000 minus $5,986.20) equals $50,654.37). This sum is divided by the purchase price for the separate property percentage share ($50,654.37 divided by $56,640.57 equals 89.43 percent). The separate property interest would be $109,901.16, which represents the amount of capital appreciation attributable to the separate funds (89.43 percent of $103,-359.43) added to the amount of equity paid by separate funds ($17,-466.82). The community property percentage interest is found by dividing the amount by which community property payments reduced the principal by the purchase price ($5,986.20 divided by $56,640.57 equals 10.57 percent). The community property share would be $16,911.29, which represents the amount of capital appreciation attributable to community funds (10.57 percent of $103,359.43) added to the amount of equity paid by community funds ($5,986.20).

In this case the trial court used a different formula which appears to have been based upon a statement in In re Marriage of Jafeman, supra,

29 Cal.App.3d 244, 256, 105 Cal.Rptr. 483, that might be interpreted to mean that the interests are to be determined according to the proportionate equity contributions only, with no credit given for the loan contribution. This formula might be appropriate when the obligation on the property has been fully paid. To apply it in the present situation, however, when the purchase price of the amount owing on the loan has not been fully paid ignores the role of the loan and produces inconsistencies with the principles of the *Lucas/Aufmuth* formula.

Although the trial court erred in determining the parties' interests in the residence, the error was in David's favor. Since he was not prejudiced by the error and Lydie did not appeal, reversal of this portion of the judgment is unwarranted. (Cal. Const. art. VI, § 13; Walker v. Etcheverry (1941) 42 Cal.App.2d 472, 476, 109 P.2d 385; Johnson v. Schilling & Co. (1961) 194 Cal.App.2d 123, 134, 14 Cal.Rptr. 684; 6 Witkin, Cal.Procedure 2d, Appeal, §§ 212–214, pp. 4203–4204.)

* * *

BIRD, C.J., and TOBRINER, MOSK, CLARK, RICHARDSON and NEWMAN, JJ., concur.

IN RE MARRIAGE OF FRICK

California District Court of Appeal, 1986.
181 Cal.App.3d 997, 226 Cal.Rptr. 766.

JOHNSON J. * * *

Jerome owned certain real property prior to his marriage to Hiroko which he used to operate the Mikado Hotel and Restaurant. During the marriage he used community property funds to reduce the principal balance of the encumbrance on the real property. "Where community funds are used to make payments on property purchased by one of the spouses before marriage 'the rule developed through decisions in California gives to the community a pro tanto community property interest in such property in the ratio that the payments on the purchase price with community funds bear to the payments made with separate funds.' " (Cites omitted.) (*In re Marriage of Moore* (1980) 28 Cal.3d 366, 371, 372, 168 Cal.Rptr. 662, 618 P.2d 208; accord *In re Marriage of Marsden* (1982) 130 Cal.App.3d 426, 436–437, 181 Cal.Rptr. 910.) Under this formula, one first determines the separate property and community property percentage interest in the property. The separate property percentage interest is determined by crediting the separate property with the down payment and the full amount of the loan on the property less the amount by which the community property payments reduced the principal balance of the loan. This sum is divided by the purchase price. The resulting figure is the separate property percentage share. The community property percentage share is determined by dividing the amount in which community property payments reduced the principal by the purchase price. (*In re Marriage of Moore, supra,* 28 Cal.3d at pp. 373–374, 168 Cal.Rptr. 662, 618 P.2d 910.) The separate property interest in the property as valued at the end of marriage is determined by adding all the prenuptial appreciation, the amount of capital appreciation during marriage attributable to the separate funds (determined by multiplying the capital appreciation during marriage by the separate property percentage interest), and the amount of equity paid by separate funds. (*In re Marriage of Marsden, supra,* 130 Cal.App.3d at pp. 437–439, 181 Cal.Rptr. 910.) The community property share in the value of the property is determined by adding the amount of capital appreciation during marriage attributable to community funds to the equity paid by community funds. (*Id.,* 28 Cal.3d at p. 374, 168 Cal.Rptr. 662, 618 P.2d 910.)

The trial court applied the above formula in determining the parties' respective interests in the real property.[3] Jerome contends, however, the trial court erred by calculating the separate and community property percentage interest based on the purchase price of the property rather than on the fair market value of the property at the time of marriage. Jerome, in essence, seeks not only to be awarded all the premarriage appreciation, but wants that appreciation to be factored in when determining the respective percentage interest in the property. We do not believe this is proper.

Under the formula described above, Jerome indisputably was entitled to all the capital appreciation which accrued prior to marriage. The community until marriage had absolutely no interest in the property and, as such, should not and did not reap any of the benefits of the prenuptial appreciation. The issue is how to divide the appreciation accruing during marriage, i.e., what percentage goes to the separate property interest and what percentage goes to the community property interest. We believe fairness dictates that the separate and community property's respective interest should be based on the ratio of capital contribution to the purchase price. It is this ratio (percentage) which best reflects the parties' respective interests in the property at the time the appreciation at issue is accruing. The community should share in the appreciation that accrues during marriage in the same proportion that its capital contribution bears to the total capital contribution required to own the property outright. This is the method of computa-

---

3. In particular, the trial court found the purchase price of the property was $708,220. Jerome made a down payment of $118,958. He made loan payments before marriage totaling $162,762 and the property had increased in value to $1,150,000 by the time of marriage, i.e., it appreciated $441,780. The community contributed loan payments during marriage of $308,341. The property interest credited to separate property was $399,879 (down payment plus full amount of the loan minus the community loan payments). The community property percentage interest in the property was 43.54 percent ($308,341 divided by $708,-220). The separate property interest was 56.46 percent ($399,879 divided by $708,-220). The property increased in value by $700,000 during marriage. The community was entitled to 43.54 percent of that increase or $304,779. Jerome was entitled to 56.46 percent of that increase or $395,220. As such, the community's monetary share in the property at the end of marriage was $613,120 ($308,341 [loan payments] plus $304,779 [appreciation]). Jerome's share in the property was $1,118,720 ($441,780 [premarriage appreciation] plus $395,220 [marriage appreciation] plus $118,958 [down payment] plus $162,762 [premarriage loan payments]).

tion that has historically been followed in this state and we believe it is the appropriate one. To do as Jerome asks would give him *double* credit for premarital appreciation in the value of this property. We see no justification for this approach. Indeed it appears to fail the test of fundamental fairness.[4]

* * *

Notes

1. The preceding principal cases approve the so-called *Aufmuth* method of calculating the community and separate property interests in a real property acquisition involving a purchase-money mortgage. Essentially this approach involves classification of the down payment, characterization of the loan proceeds, and classification of principal payments made on the loan. Whether the purchase and loan transaction occurred before or after marriage is of major importance in classifying the loan proceeds, and in many cases, classification of the loan proceeds will be the critical factor in determining which estate will receive the lion's share of the appreciation. Should such an "apportionment formula" be applied literally and mechanically to every purchase-money mortgage transaction? Should it be used in apportioning rents and profits as well as increased values? The underlying problem is whether we should treat the typical real property purchase as a single integrated transaction or as three separate transactions—a purchase, a loan, and an encumbrance. Realistically, it is one complex transaction, and indeed, is so treated by the court in *Lucas* and *Moore* but for the classification of the loan.

2. The *Aufmuth* approach to apportionment was also followed by the court in In re Marriage of Marsden, 130 Cal.App.3d 426, 181 Cal.Rptr. 910 (1982). Prior to marriage, the husband paid $6,300 for an 80–year lease of a parcel of real property. He constructed a house on the property, which was financed by $2,000 cash payment and a $30,000 loan. Payments totalling $7,000 were made on the loan prior to marriage. During marriage, payments totalling $9,200 were paid from community funds. The house and leasehold interest were valued at $65,000 at the time of the marriage and $182,500 at the time of trial. The court credited the husband's separate property estate with the down payments and the full amount of the loan, less the amount by which the community property payments reduced the principal balance. The court also gave the husband the benefit of the appreciation occurring prior to marriage. The result was to give the husband a separate property percentage interest of approximately 85%.

3. Other approaches have been suggested by the commentators. One proposal involves averaging the total capital appreciation over the period from the time of purchase to the time of separation. Capital appreciation

---

4. Jerome cites *Garten v. Garten* (1956) 140 Cal.App.2d 489, 295 P.2d 23 and *Estate of Murphy* (1976) 15 Cal.3d 907, 126 Cal. Rptr. 820, 544 P.2d 956 to support his position. However, we do not believe these cases compel us to reach a counter result. As *Garten* provides " 'the rule developed through the decisions in California gives to the community a *pro tanto* community property interest in such property in the ratio that the payments *on the purchase price* with community funds bear to the payments made with separate funds.' " (Cites omitted; italics added.) *Garten v. Garten, supra,* 140 Cal.App.2d at p. 494, 295 P.2d 23.)

attributable to the loan proceeds, as well as equity from reduction of loan principal, is divided between separate property and community property in proportion to the number of monthly payments made by the respective interests to the total number of monthly payments made. The author states that this method "accounts for both the compound nature of home appreciation, and for the accelerating reduction of the loan principal." Wagner, *Apportionment of Home Equity In Marital Dissolutions Under California Community Property Law: Is the Current Approach Equitable?* 9 Community Property Journal 31, 39 (Winter 1982).

Professor Bruch advocates a return to the original definition of community property, under which the fruits of separate property were allocated to the community. The fruits of separate property should be deemed to include not only rents and profits, but also natural appreciation, according to Professor Bruch. Under this approach, a home purchased before marriage would be divided equally, except to the extent of separate property actually invested in the property. Bruch, *The Definition and Division of Marital Property in California: Towards Parity and Simplicity,* 33 Hastings L.J. 769, 789–798 (1982).

SECTION 4.   THE CLASSIFICATION OF IMPROVEMENTS

In the preceding sections of this Chapter, we were concerned with the classification of acquisitions which were produced by both separate and community property contributions. The cases concerning the classification of business profits, credit acquisitions and installment acquisitions essentially involved the acquisition of new titles or equities. The classification process in those cases was based primarily upon application of the tracing principle. In this section we are concerned with the classification of the increased value of an item of property due to improvement of the subject matter. In the improvement cases the tracing principle can be used to show that either community or separate property produced the increased values. However the improvement doctrine as it has developed in California denies the estate supplying the improvement funds any ownership interest in the improved property. At best reimbursement may be in order, and even reimbursement may be denied absent a contract calling for it.

The cases may be broadly grouped into two types, based upon the nature of the estate used in making the improvements and the nature of the estate improved.

A. Improvements to Separate Property

SHAW v. BERNAL
Supreme Court of California, 1912.
163 Cal. 262, 124 P. 1012.

[Lot 6 was purchased in the name of Mrs. Shaw at the instance of her husband. This was found to be her separate property. During the marriage Mr. Shaw improved this lot and thereafter sold it and purchased another tract of land with the entire proceeds. The classification of this lot, as separate property of Mrs. Shaw or as community property was raised after the death of Mrs. Shaw. This is an appeal from a judgment holding it to be her separate property.]

ANGELLOTTI, J. * * * Mr. Shaw thereafter built a house on said lot 6, block 250, using therefor $700 of "the money that came from France," and, he claimed, about $700 more of his own earnings. If we assume that all the money expended in constructing the house on this land was community property, it still remains that both the land and the building constructed thereon constituted separate property of the wife. A similar question was early decided by this court. The conveyance of land purchased with community funds had been by express direction of the husband, made to the wife with the intent on his part to make to her a gift of the property. Subsequently the husband from community funds constructed a dwelling house thereon. The court said: "The question is, who was the owner of the house when it was built under those circumstances. It admits of only one answer—the owner of the lot was also the owner of the house. It formed a part of the real estate, and the title to the home is necessarily included in the title to the lot on which it is erected, in the absence of an agreement sufficient to pass the title to the house alone. Peck v. Brummagim, 31 Cal. 441, 448, 89 Am.Dec. 195. This holding is in accord with the general rule stated in 21 Cyc. 1648, as follows: "Improvements made during marriage on the separate property of either husband or wife, although with community funds, will as a general rule belong to the spouse owning the separate property." An agreement between the parties may produce a different result as is implied in the above quotation from Peck v. Brummagim, supra, creditors of the husband may perhaps establish a claim to improvements so constructed where they can show that the expenditure therefor was a fraud upon them (see Maddox v. Summerlin, 92 Tex. 483, 49 S.W. 1033, 50 S.W. 567), the wife might reach as community property a building erected by the husband from community funds on his separate property, for the very purpose of fraudulently depriving her of her interest therein (see Smith v. Smith, 12 Cal. 216, 73 Am.Dec. 533), but it is clearly the rule that where a husband deliberately constructs from community funds a building upon the separate property of his wife, in the absence of any sufficient agreement or undertaking to the contrary, as between him and her, the title to the building follows the title to the land and is separate property of the wife, and neither he nor the marital partnership has any title to any portion of the property, either land or building. The authorities hold that the most that the marital partnership may acquire under such circumstances, if anything, is a right to reimbursement to the extent of the value added to the property by the improvements. Whether the right to reimbursement exists in such cases is a question not at all involved in this proceeding and we express no opinion thereon. In support of the views we have expressed are the following authorities, in addition to those already cited: McKay on Community Property, § 249; Ballinger on Community Property, note to section 19; 6 American and English Encyclopedia of Law (2d Ed.) 324; Rice v. Rice, 21 Tex.

58; Maddox v. Summerlin, 92 Tex. 483, 49 S.W. 1033, 50 S.W. 567; Humphreys v. Newman, 51 Me. 40. The only expression of opinion that we have found that may be claimed to be in any way opposed to the views we have stated is in Collins v. Bryan, 40 Tex.Civ.App. 88, 88 S.W. 432, a case decided by the Civil Court of Appeals of Texas. There was absolutely nothing in the evidence relative to this property to take the case from the effect of the rule we have discussed. The disposition of the rents received from the house constructed on said lot, viz., their collection by Mr. Shaw and the placing of the same by him in the bank to his credit, is immaterial in the determination of the question we have been discussing.

* * *

The judgment is affirmed.

Notes

1. In Shaw v. Bernal and other cases decided prior to the institution of equal management and control, the husband had sole management and control of the community property. If he used community funds to improve his wife's separate property, he could be presumed to have intended a gift and the community would not be entitled to reimbursement. This principle was reiterated in a number of cases, including Dunn v. Mullan, 211 Cal. 583, 296 P. 604, 77 A.L.R. 1015 (1931), and Marriage of Jafeman, 29 Cal.App.3d 244, 105 Cal.Rptr. 483 (1972). Should this presumption be continued in light of the equal management and control provisions of Civil Code §§ 5125 and 5127? See In re Marriage of Camire, 105 Cal.App.3d 859, 164 Cal.Rptr. 667 (1980).

2. The court in Shaw v. Bernal uses the law of fixtures in concluding that the improvements to real property take on the underlying character of the land. A similar approach was taken in the case of Lewis v. Johns, 24 Cal. 98, 85 Am.Dec. 49 (1864), where the husband used his time and skill to make his wife's separate property land produce crops. The court held that the community had no interest in the land or crops, and at most could be reimbursed if there was a contract to that effect. The common law accession doctrines have been modified in California by Civil Code Section 1013.5 and Code of Civil Procedure Sections 741 and 871.1. There is no case law concerning the possible effects of these modifications on the community property improvement doctrine.

3. At the end of the opinion in Shaw v. Bernal, the court states that "[t]he disposition of the rents received from the house constructed on said lot, viz., their collection by Mr. Shaw and the placing of the same by him in the bank to his credit, is immaterial" to the issue of classification of the improvement. On what issue might such evidence have a bearing?

4. It is not always easy to distinguish between an improvement and a new acquisition, and yet that distinction may be crucial to classification. In Estate of Bernatas, 162 Cal.App.2d 693, 328 P.2d 539 (1958), the facts showed that during the marriage community funds were used to renovate the wife's separate property house, including the addition of a new roof and furnace. Community funds were also used to pay a F.H.A. mortgage on the

house. The mortgage had been contracted prior to marriage. The court discussed some improvement cases, noting that where a husband uses community funds to improve his wife's separate property, he is presumed to make a gift to her. The court also considered some installment purchase cases involving apportionment based on the community and separate property contributions. The court failed to recognize however that the expenditures for renovation, including the new roof and the new furnace, were of the type generally characterized as improvements, and that expenditures made on payment of a mortgage were of the type usually characterized as installment payments permitting apportionment of the title.

PROVOST v. PROVOST
California District Court of Appeal, 1929.
102 Cal.App. 775, 283 P. 842.

CRAIG, ACTING P.J. Appellant Anthony Provost and the respondent Maria Provost intermarried on October 20, 1904, and lived together until January 8, 1925, when they separated. Prior to this marriage said appellant acquired a small parcel of real property of the value of about $300, described as lot 33, block 2, of subdivision No. 1 of Dolgeville, in the city of Alhambra, known and designated for the purposes of this case as the "Alhambra property." Thereafter the spouses improved the same with community funds, and enhanced its value to about $12,000. * * * On August, 26, 1924, Anthony Provost conveyed to appellant Edna L. Gomes, his daughter by a former marriage, all of his right, title, and interest in and to the Alhambra property together with the improvements thereon.

* * *

After a trial before the court without a jury, it was found that all of the allegations of grounds for divorce were untrue, and it was adjudged that neither the plaintiff nor the defendant Anthony Provost be granted a divorce. The findings of fact further recite that the Alhambra property was conveyed by Provost to his daughter for valuable consideration and without the plaintiff's knowledge; that it was the separate property of the husband and that he had a legal right to convey the same, but that Mrs. Gomes had given nothing of value therefor; that both of the spouses were entitled to their support from its income, and that they had no other means of support, but that said conveyance had been made for the purpose of depriving the plaintiff of her interest therein, and that Mrs. Gomes had collected all income therefrom since the date of conveyance. The trial court directed that each of the spouses receive one-half the income, if any, derived from the ranch property, or that, in the event of sale, the proceeds be equally divided between them; that Mrs. Gomes retain title to the Alhambra property, but that Anthony Provost receive the income therefrom and pay to the plaintiff $40 per month, the balance, if any, to be devoted to his own use; that, if said income be insufficient for the support and maintenance of both spouses, this property be sold under execution, and the proceeds applied in a manner best suited to their necessities. Liens in favor of the plaintiff and her husband were created and imposed thereon to secure the payment of said amounts.

The defendants appealed, and here contend that the Alhambra property was at all times separate, that Anthony Provost had a legal right to convey it, and conveyed the same for a valuable consideration, and that the trial court erred in imposing a lien thereon or directing that it be sold, as heretofore mentioned.

* * *

A more serious problem is presented as to the legal status and propriety of the trial court's ruling as to the Alhambra realty and improvements placed upon a parcel of the husband's land by community endeavors.

That improvements made during the marriage on separate property of either husband or wife with community funds will as a general rule belong to the spouse owning the property is stated in 21 Cyc. 1648, and the language is quoted with approval in Peck v. Brummagim, 31 Cal. 440, 89 Am.Dec. 195. However, it is significant that in this and every other California case, except in Estate of Barreiro, 86 Cal.App. 764, 261 P. 509, where the principle has been applied, it has been a fact that the property improved by the expenditure of community money was realty belonging to the wife. In each such instance the husband exercising his legal authority has used funds of the community to annex valuable structures to the wife's separate property. In Shaw v. Bernal, 163 Cal. 262, 124 P. 1012, 1014, it is stated: " * * * But it is clearly the rule that where a husband deliberately constructs from community funds a building upon the separate property of his wife, in the absence of any sufficient agreement or undertaking to the contrary, as between him and her, the title to the building follows the title to the land and is separate property of the wife, and neither he nor the marital partnership has any title to any portion of the property, either land or building." Upon that phase of the decision the court concludes: "In view of what we have said as to the rule applicable where a husband voluntarily constructs with community funds buildings upon the separate property of the wife, there is nothing in the foregoing testimony to compel a conclusion that any part of the property here involved, land or improvements, was community property at the date of death of Mrs. Shaw."

In Smith v. Smith, 47 Cal.App. 650, 191 P. 60, 62, it is said: "The expenditure by a husband of either his separate funds or the community funds of himself and wife in improving his wife's separate property does not operate to change the title. As between them, in the absence of any specific agreement to the contrary, the title to the improvements follows the land." And from Carlson v. Carlson, 10 Cal.App. 300, 101 P. 923, 925, we quote: "In the absence of any specific agreement, no lien would be created on account of money expended by a husband upon the separate property of the wife. Peck v. Brummagim, 31 Cal. 450, 89 Am.Dec. 195. The law will not infer from such expenditures alone an agreement either to change the character of the property or an intent to charge the same with a lien. It must rather be presumed that it was the intention of the husband to advance the money paid for the benefit of the wife's estate, and that it was intended to accrue to her interest. Flournoy v. Flournoy, 86 Cal. 294, 21 Am.St.Rep. 39, 24 P. 1012."

It is apparent that the reason back of each of these decisions stressed in the opinion on the subject, except in Estate of Barreiro, supra, which will be considered separately, is that a husband had authority to control the disposition of the community funds, and that he voluntarily annexed them to the separate property of the wife, who exercised no such power. From these facts the intention of the husband is presumed to have been that the improvements made with the community money should become a part of the separate property of the wife. To merely state a case where the facts are reversed and the husband has spent community funds in improving his own separate estate is to make manifest the palpable impropriety of applying these decided cases as precedents for holding that, simply because community property is annexed to the separate property of one of the spouses, the whole is thereby for all purposes, the separate property of that spouse. Since the facts are reversed, logic compels the conclusion that the community funds do not merge in the separate property where the husband has, without consent of the wife, improved his own separate property with that belonging to the community. To hold otherwise would be to permit the authority of the husband in controlling the community property, given him in the interest of greater freedom in its use and for its transfer for the benefit of both himself and his wife, to become a weapon to be used by him to rob her of every vestige of interest in the community property with which the law has expressly invested her. Such a conclusion would violate every sense of justice, and outrage every principle of fair dealing, known to the law. The provisions of our Code do not require us to so hold, nor do the prior decisions of this jurisdiction compel or warrant a ruling which would thus uphold the marital marauding of the wife's estate. If it be true that, in order for the community property to remain such, there must be an agreement to that effect, where, under the direction of the husband, it is annexed to the separate property of the wife, then, where as in the instant case the husband has used his legal authority in the handling of the community funds to enhance the value of his own separate lands in order that it should become a part thereof, and be changed in its character to separate property, an agreement to that effect should be shown. Such consent cannot be presumed from the wife's mere silence, for the law has given her no right to say "No." It would be a novelty to hold that one who has no right to speak is presumed to have waived property rights by silence alone.

There is authority in other jurisdictions upholding the demands of justice in cases of this character and protecting the rights of the wife in community funds. In Sims v. Billington, 50 La.Ann. 968, 24 So. 637, it was held that, although buildings and improvements placed upon separate property of the husband during marriage and paid for with community funds belonged to the husband, the community has an interest therein which will be sustained, and the separate estate will be charged with the amount that such improvements have enhanced the value of the property. In Legg v. Legg, 34 Wash. 132, 75 P. 130, 132, it was said: "In equity and fairness to Malena Legg, as the survivor of the community, she should be reimbursed for betterments placed on the land by the community." A lien was there impressed upon the property for the amount allowed, but only to secure its payment to the widow after sale, which had been ordered by the trial court. And in Furrh v. Winston, 66 Tex. 521, 1 S.W. 527, 529, it is said: "It is well settled that separate estate of one member of the community must reimburse the community for any proper improvements made in good faith upon the separate estate with community funds." Our Supreme Court long since recognized the universal application of these principles, and announced upon the authority of New York, Louisiana, and Texas decisions that the beneficent purposes of the statute cannot be frustrated by voluntary transfer by a husband for the purpose of defeating any rights which the wife may have. Smith v. Smith, 12 Cal. 216, 73 Am.Dec. 533; Estate of Barreiro, supra. Text writers also have perceived that the common law and civil law authorities are in accord that, while no lien is imposed, yet compensation may be claimed, in the event of improvement of separate property by community investment. McKay on Community Property (2d Ed.) p. 659, § 1013; Freeman on Cotenancy and Partition (2d Ed.) § 138.

In Estate of Barreiro, supra, the opinion asserts: "We therefore have but one question to settle: Were the improvements presumptively community property?" This follows the statement: "We do not mean to say that a fund might not be traced through this medium to its destination, and the character of the property finally acquired be determined according to the facts, because such is not the case before us, but only that in the instant case no character is given to the property by proof other than that the land was separate property." And so it is evident that this authority makes no pretense of holding that, where it is an established fact that valuable improvements paid for with community funds have been placed upon the husband's separate property, the entire estate is to be held as his without compensation or redress of any character to the wife. Later in the same case it is said: "The authorities hold that the most that the marital partnership may acquire under such circumstances, if anything, is a right to reimbursement to the extent of the value added to the property by the improvements."

We conclude that, while the Alhambra property must be regarded as being the separate estate of the defendant Provost, the plaintiff through proper proceedings and pleadings has a right to compensation in the amount of her share in the community, measured by the improvement that such property has effected in his separate property. This situation is not affected by the fact that defendant Provost deeded the entire estate at Alhambra to his daughter, for it was expressly found that this transaction was for the fraudulent purpose of depriving the wife of her right to separate maintenance from her husband, and that the daughter gave nothing of value for the property transferred to her.

Other arguments are advanced and discussed in the briefs which we do not regard necessary to consider in this decision. The judgment is reversed and the cause remanded for a new trial in accordance with the views herein expressed. Of course, the trial court may in the ends of justice even permit an amendment to the pleadings before another trial is had, but the rights of the parties can and should be determined in this action.

Judgment reversed.

Notes

1. Where community property is used to improve the separate property of the spouse making the improvement, the community estate acquires no interest in the improved property. To deny reimbursement in this situation would permit a married person to manage and control community property in fraud of his spouse. In re Marriage of Jafeman, 29 Cal.App.3d 244, 105 Cal.Rptr. 483 (1972). If, however, the other spouse consents to the transaction, no fraud is possible, and reimbursement would not be in order. See Estate of La Belle, 93 Cal.App.2d 538, 209 P.2d 432 (1949).

2. If reimbursement is appropriate, what should be the measure of recovery by the community? In Marriage of Warren, 28 Cal.App.3d 777, 104 Cal.Rptr. 860 (1972), the court drew a distinction between the case of a spouse improving his own separate property with community funds and that of a spouse using community funds to improve the other's separate property. In the former situation, the community is entitled to reimbursement in either the amount expended or the value added, whichever is greater, so that there will be no benefit from the breach of trust. In the latter case, any right of reimbursement arises solely on the basis of an agreement to reimburse. The court concluded that "[i]t is clear that the amount of reimbursement in the case of an agreement must be the amount expended."

3. Should the distinction between the *Shaw* and *Provost* cases continue to obtain in light of the equal management and control provisions now in effect? This issue was resolved by the court in Marriage of Frick, 181 Cal.App.3d 997, 1019, 226 Cal.Rptr. 766, 779 (1986), as follows:

Prior to 1975, when the husband used community funds to improve his own separate property, the community was entitled to be reimbursed for this expenditure unless the wife consented to the use of the funds. (In re Marriage of Jafeman (1972) 29 Cal.App.3d 244, 256, 105 Cal.Rptr. 483.) This rule was premised on the fact the husband was the manager of the community funds. (Ibid.) To permit the husband to improve his separate property with community funds operated as a constructive fraud upon his wife. (In re Marriage of Warren (1972) 28 Cal.App.3d 777, 781–782, 104 Cal.Rptr. 860.) The community's right to reimbursement was measured either by the increased value of the property or the amount expended, whichever is greater. (Id., at pp. 782–783, 104 Cal.Rptr. 860.) Beginning in 1975, both spouses were granted equal management and control of the community real and personal property, with limited exceptions. (Civ.Code, §§ 5125 and 5127.) However, we do not believe this change in the law should alter the basic principles discussed above. Indeed, we believe the effect of this change should be to place each spouse in the same position as the husband was before 1975. If either spouse appropriates community funds for his or her own benefit, *without the consent of the other spouse,* the community should be reimbursed. Even if in theory both spouses have an equal right to management and control, if one spouse acts in his or her self-interest to the detriment of the community interest, the community should be entitled to restitution.

4. The principles developed by the courts in the improvements cases have been applied by analogy to the payment of property taxes, assessments, and encumbrances. See, e.g., Estate of Turner, 35 Cal.App.2d 576, 96 P.2d 363 (1939); In re Marriage of Walter, 57 Cal.App.3d 802, 129 Cal.Rptr. 351 (1976).

B. Improvements to Community Property

IN RE MARRIAGE OF SMITH

California District Court of Appeal, 1978.
79 Cal.App.3d 725, 145 Cal.Rptr. 205.

OPINION

KAUFMAN, ACTING PRESIDING JUSTICE.

Sieglinde A. Smith (wife) appeals from portions of an interlocutory judgment of dissolution of marriage entered September 2, 1976. Wayde W. Smith, petitioner below and respondent on appeal, will be referred to as husband.

When they separated on April 1, 1975, the parties had been married 19 years and approximately 2 months. Wife was then 43 years old; husband was 44. The parties had two sons who were 19 and 20 years of age at the time of trial.

During the last 10 years of their marriage, the parties owned and operated a custom sign-making business. Basically, husband handled the technical work, production and sales. Wife performed primarily bookkeeping and clerical duties. Net income from this business averaged $17,000 per year from 1972 to 1974. For 1975 it was $9,818.

In addition to the family business and the residence, the parties owned two automobiles and several small rental properties.

As the result of an order to show cause heard August 19, an order was made on September 2, 1975, giving husband exclusive use, occupancy and control of the family business and excluding wife therefrom. The order also provided for joint occupancy of the family residence. Husband was ordered to pay during his occupancy the trust deed payments and charges for electricity, water and trash pickup. Wife was ordered to pay charges for gas. In addition, husband was ordered to pay to wife

$200 per month spousal support. The parties were permitted to continue to collect rents from the properties under their respective control and ordered to pay therefrom any trust deed payments, taxes, insurance premiums, assessments and utility bills that should become due. The property known as the Kingman property under the control of wife produced a net income of approximately $90 per month.

Trial was had April 22, 1976. The interlocutory judgment entered September 2, 1976, awarded the family business to husband. The family residence was awarded to wife. In accordance with a stipulation of the parties, one of the rental properties in which the parties had a gross equity of $9,382 was ordered sold with the proceeds of sale to be used primarily for the payment of community debts and attorney fees of both parties. The other rental properties were distributed to the parties in accordance with their wishes, wife receiving the Kingman property. Husband was ordered reimbursed from the community $2,678.77 paid by him after the separation of the parties on preexisting community obligations. Properties purchased in whole or in part or improved with wife's separate funds were found to be community property and wife was denied any reimbursement therefor. Husband was ordered to pay wife $1,476.50 to equalize the property division.

* * *

Use of Wife's Funds to Purchase or Improve Property

During the marriage wife inherited some $14,000 from an uncle. Wife deposited these funds in a checking account owned by the parties jointly. Thereafter, from the funds so deposited, wife paid $1,500 as a down payment on real property referred to as the Costa Mesa property and $7,556 in payment of the costs of construction of a swimming pool added to the family residence. While wife was in Germany on personal business, an opportunity to purchase a cutter for use in the family business materialized, and husband purchased the cutter with $1,925 from these funds. The court found these properties were community property and denied wife reimbursement for any of her separate funds used in the acquisition or improvement of them. The pertinent part of the interlocutory judgment reads: "The Court finds * * * that any contributions heretofore made by [wife] toward the acquisition of any of the assets of the parties were merged with the community estate and were a gift to the 'community' and awards nothing to [wife] by reason thereof."

Wife contends the finding and order are erroneous, but it is not entirely clear whether she contends that the court should have determined these properties or some interest therein to be her separate property or that it should have ordered reimbursement to her from the community. For example, it is urged that the court's use of the expression "merged with the community estate" indicates the court erroneously applied the commingling doctrine, which doctrine, of course, is germane to determining whether property is community or separate, not to the propriety of reimbursement.

Wife is correct that no problem of commingling was presented, for the testimony of both parties established the moneys paid in the acquisition and improvement of these properties came from the funds wife inherited. However, we are not persuaded the court's use of the quoted language indicates it applied the commingling doctrine. More likely, all it meant was that the funds used had become community property by virtue of a gift thereof to the community by wife. In any event, the quoted language clearly includes a finding that the funds used constituted a gift to the community, and this finding is conclusive as to the character of the property. "[E]ven in the absence of an explicit agreement, * * * a court may find a transmutation of property if the circumstances clearly demonstrate that one spouse intended to effect a change in the status of his separate property." (Beam v. Bank of America, 6 Cal.3d 12, 25, 98 Cal.Rptr. 137, 146, 490 P.2d 257, 266; see also In re Marriage of Wall, 30 Cal.App.3d 1042, 1050, 106 Cal.Rptr. 690). The finding of a trial court that the property is either separate or community in character is binding on the appellate court if supported by substantial evidence. (Beam v. Bank of America, supra; In re Marriage of Wall, supra, 30 Cal.App.3d at p. 1048, 106 Cal.Rptr. 690.) Here, the finding of the trial court that wife's separate funds used in the purchase and improvement of these properties was intended by wife to be a gift to the community and that the properties constitute community property is amply supported by the evidence.

In the first place, the record indicates it was never seriously contended at trial these properties were separate property. In wife's response to the petition for dissolution all properties are listed as subject to disposition by the court and there is no request to confirm any property as the separate property of wife. As we read the record, at trial wife's position was that she was entitled to reimbursement. Moreover, wife testified she considered the swimming pool, the Costa Mesa property and the business equipment to be part of the community property. She further testified she never requested reimbursement or return of the moneys expended in the purchase and improvement of these properties. Husband testified there was never any discussion between the parties about the funds thus expended retaining their separate character or about the property purchased with these funds becoming wife's separate property. Wife's testimony that no gift was intended by her only created a conflict in the evidence for resolution by the trial court.

Neither was wife entitled to reimbursement. With respect to transactions prior to separation, it is well settled that a spouse who uses his or her separate property for community purposes is entitled to reimbursement from the community or separate property of the other spouse only if there is an agreement between the parties to that effect. (E.g., Weinberg v. Weinberg, 67 Cal.2d 557, 570, 63 Cal.Rptr. 13, 432 P.2d 709; See v. See, 64 Cal.2d 778, 784–785, 51 Cal.Rptr. 888, 415 P.2d 776; In re Marriage of Cosgrove, 27 Cal.App.3d 424, 430–431, 103 Cal.Rptr. 733.)

There is no evidence whatever of any agreement for wife's reimbursement, and the court's finding that wife intended these expenditures of her separate funds to be gifts to the community is entirely inconsistent with the existence of such an agreement.

* * *

Note

The cases involving the use of separate funds to improve community property are similar in some ways to cases involving the use of separate property to pay a community obligation or expense, in which the owner of the separate property is presumed to have made a gift to the community. See, e.g., In re Marriage of Lucas, 27 Cal.3d 808, 166 Cal.Rptr. 853, 614 P.2d 285 (1980); In re Marriage of Epstein, 24 Cal.3d 76, 154 Cal.Rptr. 413, 592 P.2d 1165 (1979); Weinberg v. Weinberg, 67 Cal.2d 557, 63 Cal.Rptr. 13, 432 P.2d 709 (1967); See v. See, 64 Cal.2d 778, 51 Cal.Rptr. 888, 415 P.2d 776 (1966). This presumption is rebuttable. If the presumption of a gift is rebutted, then the separate property estate would not be entitled to any ownership interest in the improved property, but would have a right to reimbursement under the traditional California improvement principles. However, the law respecting the use of separate funds to make improvements to community property has been changed by statute. West's Ann.Cal.Family Code § 2640 provides as follows:

(a) "Contributions to the acquisition of the property," as used in this action, include downpayments, payments for improvements, and payments that reduce the principal of a loan used to finance the purchase or improvement of the property but do not include payments of interest on the loan or payments made for maintenance, insurance, or taxation of the property.

(b) In the division of the community estate under this division, unless a party has made written waiver of the right to reimbursement or signed a writing that has the effect of a waiver, the party shall be reimbursed for the party's contributions to the acquisition of the property to the extent the party traces the contributions to a separate property source. The amount reimbursed shall be without interest or adjustment for change in monetary values and shall not exceed the net value of the property at the time of the division.

Note that the constitutionality of the retroactive application of Section 2640 is open to question. See In re Marriage of Fabian, 41 Cal.3d 440, 224 Cal.Rptr. 333, 715 P.2d 253 (1986). Therefore, the judicial rule of non-reimbursement applied in *Smith* may continue to have some application.

SECTION 5. PERSONAL INJURY DAMAGE AWARDS

The approach taken by the California legislature and courts to the classification of personal injury damages recovered by a spouse during marriage has varied greatly over the years. Theoretically at least it would be possible to apportion an award of personal injury damages on the basis of the nature of the compensation; e.g., to the extent that the award compensated for lost wages or lost earning ability, it could be classified as community property, while damages for pain and suffering could be deemed separate property.[26] California however has never adopted an apportionment theory for the classification of personal injury damages. At times such awards have been classified as wholly community, and at other times as wholly separate property.

A cause of action for personal injury arising during marriage would fall within the general presumption of community property and, prior to 1957, this was the California rule.[27] The cause of action was viewed as a property right and classifiable as community property;[28] and if the action was community property, the damages flowing from it were likewise community property.[29] A cause of action arising prior to marriage was deemed separate property, and under the tracing principle, any damages recovered were classified as separate property.[30] These classification principles were applied by the courts to cases of negligent personal injury,[31] assault and battery,[32] false imprisonment[33] and injury to or wrongful death of a relative.[34]

The classification of personal injury and related damages as community property gave rise to problems, most notably the imputed negligence doctrine. Where the wife was injured by the negligence of a third person, any contributory negligence on the part of the husband was imputed to the wife.[35] The rationale for imputing the husband's conduct to the wife was to preclude his benefitting from his own wrongful conduct via his community property interest in any damages recovered by the wife.[36] Attempts to avoid the doctrine of imputed negligence took

26. Akers, Separate or Community Character of Personal Injury Recovery, 5 Community Property J. 107 (1978). Other relevant considerations include when the cause of action arose and when the award was received. Nakamura, The Classification of Personal Injury Damages Under Community Property Law: Proposals for Application and Reform, 14 Pacific Law Journal 973 (1983).

27. See: McFadden v. Santa Ana, Orange & Tustin St. Ry. Co., 87 Cal. 464, 25 P. 681, 11 L.R.A. 252 (1891); Flores v. Brown, 39 Cal.2d 622, 248 P.2d 922 (1952).

28. See: Moody v. Southern Pacific Co., 167 Cal. 786, 141 P. 388 (1914); Zaragosa v. Craven, 33 Cal.2d 315, 202 P.2d 73, 6 A.L.R.2d 461 (1949); Franklin v. Franklin, 67 Cal.App.2d 717, 155 P.2d 637 (1945); Finley v. Winkler, 99 Cal.App.2d (Supp.) 887, 222 P.2d 345 (1950).

29. See Zaragosa v. Craven, 33 Cal.2d 315, 202 P.2d 73, 6 A.L.R.2d 461 (1949).

30. Finley v. Winkler, 99 Cal.App.2d (Supp.) 887, 222 P.2d 345 (1950); Morris-

sey v. Kirkelie, 5 Cal.App.2d 183, 42 P.2d 361 (1935).

31. McFadden v. Santa Ana, Orange & Tustin St. Ry. Co., 87 Cal. 464, 25 P. 681, 11 L.R.A. 252 (1891); Basler v. Sacramento Gas & Electric Co., 158 Cal. 514, 111 P. 530, Ann.Cas. 1912A, 642 (1910); Zaragosa v. Craven, 33 Cal.2d 315, 202 P.2d 73, 6 A.L.R.2d 461 (1949); Kesler v. Pabst, 43 Cal.2d 254, 273 P.2d 257 (1954).

32. Martin v. Costa, 140 Cal.App. 494, 35 P.2d 362 (1934).

33. Gomez v. Scanlan, 155 Cal. 528, 102 P. 12 (1909).

34. Christiana v. Rose, 100 Cal.App.2d 46, 222 P.2d 891 (1950); Flores v. Brown, 39 Cal.2d 622, 248 P.2d 922 (1952).

35. Flores v. Brown, 39 Cal.2d 622, 248 P.2d 922 (1952).

36. The cases have involved negligent husbands but the doctrine is equally applicable in cases involving negligent wives. The court in Flores v. Brown, 39 Cal.2d 622, 630, 248 P.2d 922, 926 (1952), uses the

the form of contracts between spouses changing the classification of the cause of action.[37]

In 1957 the legislature intervened and amended the statutes to classify the damages recovered in personal injury actions as the separate property of the injured spouse.[38] The amendment did not classify the underlying cause of action or amounts received in compromise of such right of action, but it would seem that the legislative intent to abrogate the doctrine of inter-spousal imputed contributory negligence would have resulted in a separate property classification.[39] The classification of personal injury awards as the separate property of the injured spouse did ameliorate the unfairness of the imputed negligence doctrine, but created other serious problems, including unfavorable gift and inheritance tax consequences.[40] In 1966 the California Law Revision Commission, after studying the propriety of the separate property classification, made a report pointing out the undesirable effects of the 1957 legislation, and recommending that personal injury damages again be classified as community property, with additional legislation to eliminate the interspousal imputed contributory negligence doctrine.[41] Following the recommendations of the commission, new legislation was enacted in 1968 and was carried over into the Family Law Act of 1969.

Under the current statutory scheme, the classification of personal damage awards and settlements depends largely upon when the underlying cause of action arose. If the cause of action arose after dissolution or while the parties were living separate and apart, the award will be classified as separate property.[42] By implication, if the cause of action arose during marriage, the personal injury damages or settlement will be classified as community property.[43] However, on termination of the marriage by dissolution, community property damages are not subject to the usual equal division requirement, but rather, are generally assigned to the injured party unless the court determines that "the interests of justice require another disposition."[44]

words "negligent spouse" in stating the doctrine.

37. Such agreements were effective if they were made before the cause of action arose. An agreement made after the cause of action arose, however, was deemed ineffective to avoid the imputed negligence doctrine. Kesler v. Pabst, 43 Cal.2d 254, 273 P.2d 257 (1954).

38. Former West's Ann.Cal.Civil Code, § 163.5 added by Cal.Stats.1957, c. 2334, p. 4065.

39. See Estate of Simoni, 220 Cal. App.2d 339, 33 Cal.Rptr. 845 (1963).

40. 1 Markey, California Family Law Practice and Procedure, § 5.38 (1982).

41. Cal.L.Rev.Com.Rpts., Recom. & Stud. 1966–67, pp. 1389–1402.

42. West's Ann.Cal.Family Code § 781 (a). Personal injury damages paid by one spouse to the other are also classified as the separate property of the injured spouse. West's Ann.Cal.Civ.Code § 5126(c).

43. West's Ann.Cal.Family Code § 780.

44. West's Ann.Cal.Family Code § 2603. Disability pensions and workers compensation benefits are in some ways analogous to personal injury awards but present certain additional classification problems. These matters are considered in the next section of this chapter, which deals with various employment related benefits.

WEST'S ANNOTATED FAMILY CODE OF CALIFORNIA

§ 780. Community property

Except as provided in Section 781 and subject to the rules of allocation set forth in Section 2603, money and other property received or to be received by a married person in satisfaction of a judgment for damages for personal injuries, or pursuant to an agreement for the settlement or compromise of a claim for such damages, is community property if the cause of action for the damages arose during the marriage.

(Stats.1992, c. 162 (A.B. 2650), § 10, operative Jan. 1, 1994.)

§ 781. Separate property

(a) Money or other property received or to be received by a married person in satisfaction of a judgment for damages for personal injuries, or pursuant to an agreement for the settlement or compromise of a claim for those damages, is the separate property of the injured person if the cause of action for the damages arose as follows:

(1) After the entry of a judgment of dissolution of a marriage or legal separation of the parties.

(2) While either spouse, if he or she is the injured person, is living separate from the other spouse.

(b) Notwithstanding subdivision (a), if the spouse of the injured person has paid expenses by reason of the personal injuries from separate property or from the community property, the spouse is entitled to reimbursement of the separate property or the community property for those expenses from the separate property received by the injured person under subdivision (a).

(c) Notwithstanding subdivision (a), if one spouse has a cause of action against the other spouse which arose during the marriage of the parties, money or property paid or to be paid by or on behalf of a party to the party's spouse of that marriage in satisfaction of a judgment for damages for personal injuries to that spouse, or pursuant to an agreement for the settlement or compromise of a claim for the damages, is the separate property of the injured spouse.

(Stats.1992, c. 162 (A.B. 2650), § 10, operative Jan. 1, 1994.)

§ 782. Injuries to married person by spouse; primary resort to separate property; consent of injured spouse to use of community property; indemnity

(a) Where an injury to a married person is caused in whole or in part by the negligent or wrongful act or omission of the person's spouse, the community property may not be used to discharge the liability of the tortfeasor spouse to the injured spouse or the liability to make contribution to a joint tortfeasor until the separate property of the tortfeasor spouse, not exempt from enforcement of a money judgment, is exhausted.

(b) This section does not prevent the use of community property to discharge a liability referred to in subdivision (a) if the injured spouse gives written consent thereto after the occurrence of the injury.

(c) This section does not affect the right to indemnity provided by an insurance or other contract to discharge the tortfeasor spouse's liability, whether or not the consideration given for the contract consisted of community property.

(Stats.1992, c. 162 (A.B. 2650), § 10, operative Jan. 1, 1994.)

§ 783. Injuries to married person by third party; extent concurring negligence of spouse allowable as defense

If a married person is injured by the negligent or wrongful act or omission of a person other than the married person's spouse, the fact that the negligent or wrongful act or omission of the spouse of the injured person was a concurring cause of the injury is not a defense in an action brought by the injured person to recover damages for the injury except in cases where the concurring negligent or wrongful act or omission would be a defense if the marriage did not exist.

(Stats.1992, c. 162 (A.B. 2650), § 10, operative Jan. 1, 1994.)

§ 2603. Community estate personal injury damages; assignment

(a) "Community estate personal injury damages" as used in this section means all money or other property received or to be received by a person in satisfaction of a judgment for damages for the person's personal injuries or pursuant to an agreement for the settlement or compromise of a claim for the damages, if the cause of action for the damages arose during the marriage but is not separate property as described in Section 781, unless the money or other property has been commingled with other assets of the community estate.

(b) Community estate personal injury damages shall be assigned to the party who suffered the injuries unless the court, after taking into account the economic condition and needs of each party, the time that has elapsed since the recovery of the damages or the accrual of the cause of action, and all other facts of the case, determines that the interests of justice require another disposition. In such a case, the community estate personal injury damages shall be assigned to the respective parties in such proportions as the court determines to be just, except that at least one-half of the damages shall be assigned to the party who suffered the injuries.

(Stats.1992, c. 162 (A.B. 2650), § 10, operative Jan. 1, 1994.)

IN RE MARRIAGE OF DEVLIN
California District Court of Appeal, 1982.
138 Cal.App.3d 804, 189 Cal.Rptr. 1.

EVANS, ASSOCIATE JUSTICE.

The question presented is whether the trial court erred in awarding the bulk of the parties' community property to husband on the basis that the property was acquired with husband's personal injury proceeds.

The parties were married in July 1975, and separated in May 1977. At that time, wife initiated proceedings to dissolve the marriage, but the parties reconciled prior to the entry of a final judgment of dissolution. The couple remained together until May 1981, and wife later filed the instant action to dissolve the marriage.

Prior to the time the parties first separated, husband was severely injured in an automobile accident, rendering him a paraplegic. The personal injury damages, totaling at least $175,000, were received by husband sometime after the parties reconciled.

At trial, the evidence demonstrated that all of the personal injury damages had been spent, and that all of the property of the community at the time of separation was purchased with the personal injury proceeds. Most of this property consists of equity in real property and a mobile home placed thereon and used as the family residence. The mobile home has been specially equipped and adapted for husband's benefit.

The trial court determined that all of the community property was traceable to husband's personal injury proceeds and awarded the bulk of the property (i.e., the realty and the mobile home) to husband. Wife was awarded some miscellaneous personal property "needed for her to get a new start." Wife appeals.

DISCUSSION

Personal injury damages received or to be received from a cause of action arising during marriage are community property. (Civ.Code, § 4800, subd. (c) [now Family Code § 2603] see Hand v. Superior Court (1982) 134 Cal.App.3d 436, 440–442, 184 Cal.Rptr. 588.) Upon dissolution or separation, however, section 4800, subdivision (c), provides that these proceeds, labeled "community property personal injury damages," are to be assigned to the injured spouse unless the court, considering the facts of the case, determines the interests of justice require another disposition. In such case, the community property personal injury damages are assigned to the respective parties in such proportions as the court determines to be fair, except that at least one-half of such damages must be assigned to the spouse who suffered the injuries. (§ 4800, subd. (c).) "Community property personal injury damages" are thus a species unique to the Family Law Act; they are held as community property during marriage, but upon dissolution such damages are subject to special assignment rules. (In re Marriage of Mason (1979) 93 Cal. App.3d 215, 222–223, 155 Cal.Rptr. 350; see Hand v. Superior Court, supra, 134 Cal.App.3d at pp. 441–442, 184 Cal.Rptr. 588; 2 Markey, Cal.Family Law (1978) Division of Property, § 24.11[2], p. 24–17.)

Section 4800, subdivision (c), specifies that "community property personal injury damages shall be assigned to the party who suffered the injuries unless the court, after taking into account the economic condition and needs of each party, the time that has elapsed since the recovery of the damages or the accrual of the cause of action, and all other facts of the case, determines that the interests of justice require another disposition. In such case, the community property personal injury damages shall be assigned to the respective parties in such proportions as the court determines to be just, except that at least one-half of such damages shall be assigned to the party who suffered the injuries * * *." Thus, section 4800, subdivision (c), not only recognizes the special nature of community property personal injury damages, but also vests discretion in the trial court in distributing these damages upon dissolution of the marriage. (See 8 Cal.Law Revision Commission (1967) pp. 1392–1393, 1396–1397 (hereafter Law Revision Report).)

Wife does not take issue with the foregoing discussion. It is her position, however, that community property personal injury damages encompass only that money or other property which is *received* from a cause of action arising during marriage. She contends that as the property divided herein was *purchased* with community property personal injury damages, such property is not subject to division pursuant to provisions of section 4800, subdivision (c). We disagree.

Such a narrow interpretation of subdivision (c) defeats the purpose of the statute. To accept this interpretation would require that community property personal injury damages be placed in a bank account and never utilized, lest all, or at least that part of the damages spent and converted in form (i.e., into a house, car, iron lung) be treated upon dissolution as ordinary community property. The fallacy in such reasoning is that often at least some portion, and possibly all, of the community property personal injury damages must be spent, both on the needs of the community and on needs unique to the injured spouse. Using community property personal injury damages to purchase an artificial limb, iron lung, specially adapted home or car, etc., may be essential to alleviate the pain and suffering of the injured spouse and to allow the injured spouse to function as normally as possible. Under wife's analysis, because the iron lung and artificial limb do not constitute money or property received, but are instead products purchased with community property personal injury damages, these assistive devices are subject to division just as any ordinary community property. Obviously, the Legislature did not intend such an unjust and absurd result. It is clear the mere conversion of community property personal injury damages from money into a different form does not, standing alone, remove the items purchased from the purview of section 4800, subdivision (c). (See Law Revision Report, supra, at p. 1397 ("Subdivision (c) applies even though money recovered for personal injury damages has been invested in securities or other property"); Reppy, Community Property in California (1980) pp. 145–148.)[3] Ordinarily, "community property personal injury damages" lose their character only if irretrievably "*commingled* with *other* community property." (§ 4800, subd. (c); emphasis added.)

Wife contends however that the fact that the parties took title to both of these items in joint tenancy requires they be treated as ordinary community property. She seeks to transmute community property personal injury damages into ordinary community property. Wife notes that when a spouse uses separate property to purchase a family residence and title is taken in joint tenancy or by community property, the residence will be deemed to be community property in the absence of a showing of any agreement to the contrary. (§ 5110; In re Marriage of

---

3. In this case, the specially adapted mobile home is to husband what an artificial limb is to a spouse who had lost use of that limb. Just as the artificial limb is not subject to division as ordinary community property, neither should the specially adapted mobile home. As we view section 4800, subdivision (c), however, it is not essential that any item purchased with community property personal injury damages be specially adapted for the injured spouse to avoid treatment upon dissolution as ordinary community property. To the contrary, using community property personal injury damages to purchase a home and/or car which are not specially adapted for the injured spouse does *not* remove these items from the scope of section 4800, subdivision (c).

Lucas (1980) 27 Cal.3d 808, 815, 166 Cal.Rptr. 853, 614 P.2d 285; In re Marriage of Hayden (1981) 124 Cal.App.3d 72, 76–77, 177 Cal.Rptr. 183; In re Marriage of Cademartori (1981) 119 Cal.App.3d 970, 975, 174 Cal.Rptr. 292.) There is no reason, wife argues, why a family residence purchased during marriage with community property personal injury damages should not be subject to these same principles of law. Because there was no evidence presented regarding any agreement or understanding between the parties concerning their respective interests in the residence and realty, wife asserts the trial court was required to treat these items as ordinary community property, irrespective of the source used to purchase them. Again, we disagree.

The point missed in wife's argument is that the rules regarding the transmutation of separate property to community property do not apply to community property personal injury damages. Separate property is subject to the complete control of the spouse owning that property. When that spouse voluntarily decides to use separate property for community purposes, it is logical to imply a gift of that property to the community in the absence of any agreement or understanding to the contrary. (See, e.g., In re Marriage of Lucas, supra, 27 Cal.3d at pp. 814–817, 166 Cal.Rptr. 853, 614 P.2d 285; Weinberg v. Weinberg (1967) 67 Cal.2d 557, 570, 63 Cal.Rptr. 13, 432 P.2d 709; 1 Markey, Cal.Family Law (1978) Community Property, § 5.21[6][b], p. 5–43.)

The inferences that can be drawn, however, when separate property is voluntarily used for community purposes cannot be applied to community property personal injury damages. These damages *are* community property and are subject to the management and control of *both* spouses. (§ 5125.) Aside from immediately dissolving the marriage, the injured spouse has no right to segregate community property personal injury damages from the other community property of the marriage. Because community property personal injury damages are community property, it is to be expected that when the parties buy a residence with such proceeds they will take title in joint tenancy or as community property. Thus, the form of title in which property is taken when purchased with community property personal injury damages is not determinative as to how such property should be divided upon dissolution. (See generally 1 Markey, op. cit. supra, at p. 5–29.) [4]

4. In this regard, we take issue with one part of the otherwise well-reasoned analysis contained in the Law Revision Report. Relying on Weinberg v. Weinberg, supra, 67 Cal.2d 557, 63 Cal.Rptr. 13, 432 P.2d 709, the Law Revision Report suggests that community property personal injury damages may, by implied agreement, be transmuted into ordinary community property, thus removing such damages from the scope of section 4800, subdivision (c). (Law Revision Report, supra, at p. 1397.) This assertion is manifestly incorrect. When *Weinberg* was decided, personal injury damages received from a cause of action accruing during marriage were the *separate property* of the injured spouse. (7 Witkin, Summary of Cal.Law (8th ed. 1974) Community Property, § 14, pp. 5106–5107; § 79, p. 5166.) Separate property, whether by agreement or by gift, may be transmuted into community property. (Id., at pp. 5159–5166.) Because community property personal injury damages *are* community property, however, it is nonsensical to suggest such damages may be removed from the scope of section 4800, subdivision (c), simply because of the manner in which the damages have been used.

In light of this analysis, the only time proceeds from a personal injury award lose their character as community property personal injury damages is, in the absence of an express agreement, when such proceeds have been "commingled" with other community property and it is impossible to trace the source of the property or funds. Generally, "commingling" is a word of art, used to connote the mixture of separate property or funds with community property or funds. (1 Markey, op. cit. supra, at p. 5–29.) As used in section 4800, subdivision (c), "commingling" clearly refers to the mixture of community property personal injury damages with *other* community property into one undistinguishable, amorphous mass.

In this case there is no issue of commingling. Although the community property personal injury damages were initially deposited in the couple's joint bank account, the property purchased with the community property personal injury damages was easily traced as the evidence demonstrated, and the parties agree, there was no *other* community property with which these damages could be commingled.[6]

We thus examine the award in this case. Having traced all of the parties' community property to the community property personal injury damages, the trial court was required to award this property to husband unless it determined the interests of justice mandated a different disposition. (§ 4800, subd. (c).) The court noted husband has suffered injuries from which in all likelihood he will never recover. The court also considered that the mobile home has been specially adapted for husband's benefit and that even with the award of the realty and mobile home, husband, for the rest of his life, will probably exist at or below the poverty level. In contrast, wife has both the education and ability with which to secure gainful employment and be self-supporting. Exercising its discretion, the court determined the bulk of the community property (the mobile home and realty) should be awarded to husband, and awarded the remaining community property (some miscellaneous personal property) to wife. This award was a proper exercise of the court's discretion and will not be disturbed on appeal.

* * *

Wife's other assertions have been considered and are without merit.

The judgment is affirmed.

Note

In the case of In re Marriage of Morris, 139 Cal.App.3d 823, 189 Cal.Rptr. 80 (1983), the trial court divided the community property equally

---

6. It is obvious the mere mixing of community property personal injury damages with other community property is not sufficient to remove the community property personal injury damages from the scope of section 4800, subdivision (c). Because community property personal injury damages are subject to the management and control of both spouses, it is a natural consequence that the damages might be mixed with other community property. It is only when community property personal injury damages are so mixed with other community property that the damages can no longer be traced and identified that they become "commingled" and section 4800, subdivision (c), is inapplicable.

with the exception of certain funds which had been received by the wife during marriage as a personal injury settlement. The court awarded the personal injury settlement funds entirely to the wife. On appeal it was argued that the trial court had erred in failing to award the husband offsetting community property to equalize the division. The appellate court rejected the argument, noting that although the statutory language was not entirely clear, "the statutory provision that community property personal injury damages 'shall be assigned to the party who suffered the injuries' was intended to be an exception to the equal division mandate * * *." See also In re Marriage of Mason, 93 Cal.App.3d 215, 155 Cal.Rptr. 350 (1979).

SECTION 6.   EMPLOYMENT RELATED BENEFITS

The employment relationship can give rise to a wide variety of benefits in addition to basic salary or wages. Examples include various types of retirement and pension plans, disability benefits for an injured or incapacitated employee, termination benefits, and survivors' death benefits. The threshold question that arises in many cases is whether a particular type of benefit is susceptible of classification as community property. The answer to this question depends primarily on the underlying nature of the benefit. To the extent that a particular benefit represents deferred compensation for services rendered during marriage by the employee spouse, it is likely that the benefit will be classified as community property.[45] Similarly, where the benefit is designed to replace lost wages that would otherwise have arisen during marriage, it will generally be classified as community property.[46] On the other hand, where the benefit represents compensation for post separation or post dissolution services rendered by the employee, it should be denominated as the separate property of the employee spouse.[47]

Once it has been determined that the benefit at issue is capable of being classified as community property, various other concerns may arise, including valuation of the right or benefit, the proper method of apportionment where the benefit represents compensation for services rendered prior to marriage as well as during marriage, and the most appropriate method of structuring the division of the benefit between the employee and the non-employee spouse. These and related issues are explored in the cases in this section; for organizational purposes, the cases have been grouped into the categories of retirement benefits, disability benefits and termination benefits, but it should be recognized that there are many areas of overlap, and some cases do not fit neatly into any particular category.

45.   See, e.g., In re Marriage of Brown, 15 Cal.3d 838, 126 Cal.Rptr. 633, 544 P.2d 561 (1976), reprinted in Chapter 3, Section 1.

46.   See, e.g., In re Marriage of Saslow, 40 Cal.3d 848, 221 Cal.Rptr. 546, 710 P.2d 346 (1985), reprinted in this Section.

47.   See, e.g., In re Marriage of Hug, 154 Cal.App.3d 780, 201 Cal.Rptr. 676 (1984), reprinted in this Section.

A. *Retirement Benefits*

Although courts in some jurisdictions view retirement pensions as gratuities, it has long been held under California law that such benefits "do not derive from the beneficence of the employer, but are properly part of the consideration earned by the employee."[48] To the extent that pension benefits represent deferred compensation for services rendered by the employee spouse during marriage, they will be classified as community property.[49] In the *Brown* decision, previously considered, this principle was extended to include even "non-vested" pension rights.[50]

It should be noted the commonly used terms "pensions" and "retirement benefits" actually encompass a wide variety of different types of plans, benefits, funds and accounts, but their common distinguishing characteristic is that they are all forms of deferred compensation, and it is this feature that admits of their classification as community property.

There are some useful distinctions that may be drawn between different types of retirement plans and pension rights. One such distinction is between the "defined contribution" plan and the "defined benefit" type of plan. Under a defined contribution plan (also referred to as an "individual account" plan), the employer and employee contributions are allocated to an account on behalf of each individual participating employee. The participant's account is increased each year with his or her allocable share contributions and earnings. Because each participating employee in effect has a separate account, it is relatively easy to ascertain the value of the employee's interest in the plan.[51] A defined contribution plan always has an ascertainable cash value, even though under the terms of the plan, the employee may not currently be able to reach it.[52]

By contrast, a defined benefit plan does not contemplate keeping an individual account for each employee because the amount of the employee's pension is not dependent on the actual employer or employee contributions. The defined benefit type of plan essentially promises the employee that upon a stated retirement age, the plan will have sufficient funds to pay the employee a specified monthly pension for life. For example, upon the completion of a specific term of employment, the employee may be entitled to a certain percentage of his average annual income for a specific period preceding retirement.[53] If the employee spouse has not yet reached retirement age, valuation of the community

48. In re Marriage of Fithian, 10 Cal.3d 592, 596, 111 Cal.Rptr. 369, 371, 517 P.2d 449, 451 (1974).

49. See, e.g., In re Marriage of Brown, 15 Cal.3d 838, 126 Cal.Rptr. 633, 544 P.2d 561 (1976), reprinted in Chapter 3, Section 1.

50. Id.

51. In re Marriage of Bergman, 168 Cal. App.3d 742, 748 n. 4, 214 Cal.Rptr. 661, 664 n. 4 (1985), reprinted in this Section; Wish-

ard, Deferred Compensation: Pensions and Benefits, 1 California Family Law Service § 13:18, p. 607 (1986).

52. Blumberg, Marital Property Treatment of Pensions, Disability Pay, Workers' Compensation, and Other Wage Substitutes: An Insurance, or Replacement, Analysis, 33 UCLA Law Rev. 1250, 1258 (1986).

53. Id.

property interest in the plan may be somewhat speculative because the present value is dependent on a wide range of unknown variables.[54]

Another distinction that should be drawn is between "vested" and "matured" pension rights. The term "vested" as used in the marital property context means that the pension right will survive the discharge or voluntary termination of the employee.[55] A matured pension right, by contrast, is one in which all conditions precedent have taken place or are within the control of the employee. An employee's right to a pension may vest after a prescribed term of employment but may not mature until the employee reaches the specified retirement age and elects to retire.[56]

The apportionment principles previously considered in other contexts (e.g., apportionment of business profits) are also applicable to retirement benefits in cases where the employee spouse rendered services to the employer prior to marriage or during separation as well as during the marriage. In these situations, to the extent that the retirement benefits represent deferred compensation for the services rendered prior to marriage or while the spouses were living separate and apart, they should be classified as the separate property of the employee spouse; while the portion of the benefit attributable to services performed during marriage should be classified as community property. The method of apportionment used will depend in part on the nature of the plan. For example, in the *Gettman* case, reprinted in this Section, the court apportioned the benefits on the basis of the relative contributions made prior to and during marriage; however, this type of apportionment would not be possible under a defined benefit type of plan.

Once the classification of the retirement benefits has been resolved, questions of valuation and division between the parties may still remain. If the benefits have matured and are currently being paid to the retired spouse at the time of dissolution, the court can order that one half of the community property benefit payments be paid to the other spouse as such payments are received. If the pension plan has been joined, the court may order the plan to pay the applicable portion of each payment directly to the non-employee spouse.[57] The *Gillmore* case, reprinted in

54. Blumberg, Marital Property Treatment of Pensions, Disability Pay, Workers' Compensation, and Other Wage Substitutes: An Insurance, or Replacement, Analysis, 33 UCLA L.Rev. 1250, 1258–59 (1986).

55. In re Marriage of Brown, 15 Cal.3d 838, 126 Cal.Rptr. 633, 544 P.2d 561 (1976), reprinted in Chapter 3, Section 1.

56. Aloy v. Mash, 38 Cal.3d 413, 212 Cal.Rptr. 162, 696 P.2d 656 (1985), reprinted in Chapter 7.

57. West's Ann.Cal.Civ.Code § 4351. The federal Retirement Equity Act of 1984 (10 U.S.C.A. § 1056) authorizes qualified

pension plans subject to the Employees Retirement Income Security Act (29 U.S.C. § 1056) to pay benefits to a former spouse under a qualified domestic relations order ("QDRO"). The Retirement Equity Act does not prescribe the method of division, but allows the court or parties to divide the asset in any manner so long as the order meets the Act's requirements. For discussion of the Retirement Equity Act, see Wishard, Deferred Compensation; Pensions and Benefits, California Family Law Service §§ 13.24–13.29 (1986).

this Section, involves the issues raised where the pension rights have matured, but the employee spouse has elected not to retire.[58]

If the benefits have not yet matured, valuation and division at dissolution may be more problematic. In this situation the court may place a present value on the pension benefits, award the benefits to the employee spouse, and award the non-employee spouse other community assets of equal value. However, in valuing non-vested and/or non-matured benefits, the court must take into account the possibility that the employee spouse may die or terminate his employment prior to maturity. The problem is particularly acute if a defined benefits type of plan is at issue. Alternatively, if the court concludes that it should not attempt to place a present value on the benefits due to uncertainties affecting the vesting or maturation of the pension, the court may continue jurisdiction and award each spouse a share in future payments when they are made.[59] The *Bergman* case, reprinted in this Section, addresses the valuation and division problems inherent in a non-matured defined benefit type of plan.

Retirement pensions are not the only type of deferred compensation subject to the community property system. Profit sharing plans and stock option plans have been viewed as closely analogous to pension rights, and have been accorded similar treatment by the courts. The *Hug* case, reprinted in this Section, is illustrative.

§ 2610. Retirement plans; orders to assure benefits

* * * (a) Except as provided in subdivision (b), the court shall make whatever orders are necessary or appropriate to ensure that each party receives the party's full community property share in any retirement plan, whether public or private, including all survivor and death benefits, including, but not limited to, any of the following:

(1) Order the division of any retirement benefits payable upon or after the death of either party in a manner consistent with this division.

(2) Order a party to elect a survivor benefit annuity or other similar election for the benefit of the other party, as specified by the court, in any case in which a retirement plan provides for such an election, provided that no court shall order a retirement plan to provide increased benefits determined on the basis of actuarial value.

(3) Order the division of accumulated community property contributions and service credit as provided in Article 1.2 (commencing with Section 21215) of Chapter 9 of Part 3 of Division 5 of Title 2 of, or Article 2.5 (commencing with Section 75050) of Chapter 11 of Title 8 of, the Government Code.

(4) Order the division of community property rights in accounts with the State Teachers' Retirement System pursuant to Chapter 7.5 (commencing with Section 22650) of Part 13 of the Education Code.

---

58. In re Marriage of Gillmore, 29 Cal.3d 418, 174 Cal.Rptr. 493, 629 P.2d 1 (1981), reprinted in this Section.

59. In re Marriage of Brown, 15 Cal.3d 838, 544 P.2d 561, 126 Cal.Rptr. 633 (1976), reprinted in Chapter 3, Section 1.

(5) Order a retirement plan to make payments directly to a nonmember party of his or her community property interest in retirement benefits.

(b) A court shall not make any order that requires a retirement plan to do either of the following:

(1) Make payments in any manner that will result in an increase in the amount of benefits provided by the plan.

(2) Make the payment of benefits to any party at any time before the member retires, except as provided in paragraphs (3) and (4) of subdivision (a), unless the plan so provides.

(c) This section shall not be applied retroactively to payments made by a retirement plan to any person who retired or died prior to January 1, 1987, or to payments made to any person who retired or died prior to June 1, 1988, for plans subject to paragraphs (3) and (4) of subdivision (a).

Stats.1993, c. 219, § 112.

GETTMAN v. CITY OF LOS ANGELES, DEPARTMENT OF WATER & POWER

California District Court of Appeal, 1948.
87 Cal.App.2d 862, 197 P.2d 817.

DORAN, JUSTICE. This appeal involves certain proceeds payable upon the death of Ernest L. Gettman, an employee of the Los Angeles Department of Water and Power, under the provisions of what is referred to as the Water and Power Employees' Retirement Plan. * * * The trial court rendered judgment giving to the named beneficiary, Wallace A. Gettman, the entire proceeds of these funds. Appellant's motions for a new trial and to set aside the judgment and enter a new and different judgment were denied.

The following statement of facts is based upon the pleadings and stipulations. On August 10, 1938, Ernest L. Gettman "became a member of the Water and Power Employees' Retirement Plan, naming Eunice S. Gettman, his then wife, as beneficiary. Eunice S. Gettman died prior to March 8, 1939." On March 8, 1939, Mr. Gettman changed the named beneficiary to Wallace A. Gettman, decedent's son, respondent herein. On March 11, 1944, Ernest L. Gettman married a second wife, Lois Gettman, appellant; and on May 30, 1946, Gettman died intestate, leaving the widow Lois Gettman, Wallace A. Gettman, adult son by the first marriage, and Wendla Gettman, a two-year old daughter by the decedent's second marriage. Lois Gettman was duly appointed administratrix, and both the widow and the son filed claims to the proceeds due under the above mentioned retirement plan.

It was further stipulated that the Death Benefit involved herein amounts to $2,750; that the total amount paid by decedent into the Death Benefit Fund was $71.55, of which amount 72.83% was paid previous to decedent's marriage to appellant Lois Gettman, and 27.17% was paid after said marriage. According to the stipulation, "payments into the Retirement Fund are separate and distinct from the payments into the Death Benefit Fund and are payable to the member upon either his retirement or his leaving the employ of the Department of Water & Power of the City of Los Angeles. That the payments into the Retirement Fund in the event of death prior to retirement, in effect, represent an account of the member and that interest is paid thereon.''

The trial court found that the total amount paid into the Retirement Fund, including interest, to the date of Gettman's death was $914.10; 57.46% of Gettman's contributions thereto were made prior to the second marriage of March 11, 1944, and 42.54% after said marriage. As hereinbefore indicated, the trial court concluded that the son and named beneficiary, "is entitled to the sum of $3,664.10 (the total amount) due from the Department", and gave judgment accordingly.

It is argued in appellant's brief that, (1) "The Conclusions of Law and Judgment are not supported by the evidence and the Findings of Fact"; (2) that Lois Gettman, as administratrix, is entitled to that portion of the Retirement Fund which was contributed to out of Gettman's earnings, with interest, namely $525.29, "which was the separate property of Ernest L. Gettman prior to his marriage to Lois Gettman * * *"; (3) "That the widow, Lois Gettman, is entitled to that portion of the Retirement Fund which was contributed to out of (Gettman's) salary or earnings", with interest, namely $388.51, "which was the community property of Ernest L. Gettman and Lois Gettman during their marriage"; and (4) that the widow is entitled to the entire Death Benefit Fund of $2,750 "inasmuch as the last contribution for said Death Benefit was paid out of the salary or earnings of Ernest L. Gettman" during said marriage, "and which contribution paid for a specified period of future protection and the amount collectible under said Death Benefit was fixed and determined by the rate of earnings of Ernest L. Gettman immediately prior to his death".

The respondent Wallace A. Gettman, decedent's son and named beneficiary, contends that if the court "awarded Lois Gettman any of the funds due * * * under the Retirement Fund, the court would be making a new contract for the deceased", and that such holding "would overrule the provisions of the Retirement system * * * that the employee may designate his beneficiary", which designation was made in this case.

Still another view is presented in a brief filed by the respondent Los Angeles Department of Water & Power. After a discussion of the provisions and purposes of the Retirement Plan, and the law in reference to community property, the Department brief attacks the trial court's finding that the entire sum payable "was and is the separate property of the deceased, Ernest L. Gettman". It is there pointed out that "the record shows without conflict that the contributions with which the death benefits were purchased were deducted from the earnings of the decedent and paid into the Retirement Fund and Death Benefit Fund both before and after his marriage to Lois Gettman. Therefore the payment of all such contributions prior to said marriage constituted an investment of separate property, and the payment of all such contributions subsequent to said marriage represented an investment of community assets". On this theory the widow, Lois Gettman, as survivor of the community, would be entitled to one-half of that portion of the benefits which were purchased with community funds, the balance being payable to Wallace A. Gettman, decedent's named beneficiary. The exact result of this computation is that the widow should receive $373.59 from the Death Benefit Fund, and $194.43 from the Retirement Fund, or a total of $568.02, with the balance payable to Wallace A. Gettman. The Department's theory is, of course, unacceptable to either the widow, appellant herein, or to the son, Wallace A. Gettman, respondent.

Under the existing law of community property and the decisions concerning proceeds from insurance purchased with community and separate money, the judgment of the trial court giving the entire death and retirement funds to the named beneficiary must be reversed. The stipulated facts concerning contributions to these funds require an equitable division thereof in accordance with the theory set forth in the brief of the Department of Water and Power to which reference has heretofore been made. In this connection it may be mentioned that the Department has no possible interest in the disposition of the amount payable other than securing the protection resulting from a judicial determination in respect to rights of the rival claimants.

The appellant's contention that since the last month of protection was purchased with community money the entire amount payable from the Death Benefit Fund constitutes community assets which would pass to the widow, is clearly untenable. In Modern Woodmen of America v. Gray, 113 Cal.App. 729, 733, 299 P. 754, 755, the insured had paid premiums from 1898 to 1923, naming a first wife as beneficiary. Later there was a change of beneficiary as in the instant case, and a second marriage during which four quarterly premiums were paid from community funds. Upon the insured's death, the second wife, as in the present case, claimed the entire proceeds upon theories similar to those here advanced. The court there said: "Where, as here, the life insurance is paid for partly with community and partly with separate funds, the proceeds of the policy should in our judgment be apportioned in the same ratio that the amount of such community funds paid for premiums bears to the amount of separate funds paid for such purpose. This is the rule applied to tangible property purchased partly with community and partly with separate funds", citing Vieux v. Vieux, 80 Cal.App. 222, 229, 251 P. 640, and other cases. And in McBride v. McBride, 11 Cal.App.2d 521, 524, 54 P.2d 480, 481, the additional observation was made: "It is also argued that because the insurer was a so-called assessment company, each new premium payment initiated a new policy of insurance. There is no merit in these contentions."

The appellant's brief seeks to escape the consequence of the above holdings by the claim that "The Death Benefit * * * is not an insurance policy in that Ernest L. Gettman had no control over his contributions into said fund; he had no control over the amount payable upon his death inasmuch as such amount was based upon the compensation received by him immediately prior to his death; he had no loan value or privileges connected therewith." But, by whatever name the benefit in question may be called, the analogy is clear and unassailable. Since both community and separate funds went into the creation of the benefit, no equitable division is possible other than that sanctioned in the decisions mentioned.

The case of Cheney v. City and County of San Francisco, 7 Cal.2d 565, 569, 61 P.2d 754, 756, has been cited by all parties to this appeal in support of the several arguments. The Cheney case, however, involved factual elements not here present, namely a prenuptial agreement, and an interlocutory decree of divorce. But the retirement fund with which that case was concerned was not dissimilar to the one here under discussion, and the reviewing court there said: "We are perforce committed to the view that the amount payable from the employees retirement system upon the husband's death represented earnings. As such it was community property unless the agreement executed by the husband and wife providing otherwise was still in force." Since the agreement providing that "earnings" of each party should be deemed separate property of that party, was still in force, the husband's nominated beneficiary was held entitled to the entire fund,—the husband's separate property by virtue of the agreement. There is nothing in the Cheney case nor in any other decision cited, contrary to the view hereinbefore expressed.

The judgment of trial court is reversed with directions to enter a judgment in favor of the appellant Lois Gettman in the total sum of $568.02, representing $373.59 from the Death Benefit Fund and $194.43 from the Retirement Fund; and in favor of respondent Wallace A. Gettman in the total sum of $3,096.08, representing $2,376.41 as the balance from said Death Benefit Fund, and $719.67 as the balance from said Retirement Fund.

Notes

1. The method of apportionment used in pensions and retirement plans depends partly on the structure and operation of the particular plan. In *Gettman,* the court worked out an apportionment based on the actual contributions under the plan. A simpler approach involves proration on the basis of time: the length of employment during the period of marriage divided by the overall length of employment will determine the community's share of the pension or retirement benefits. For example, if the spouse has been employed for twenty years, and was married for five of those years, the community interest in the plan would be twenty-five percent. The "time rule" is the method most frequently used, but is certainly not the only acceptable method. See In re Marriage of Judd, 68 Cal.App.3d 515, 522–23, 137 Cal.Rptr. 318, 321 (1977); In re Marriage of Poppe, 97 Cal.App.3d 1, 158 Cal.Rptr. 500 (1979); In re Marriage of Adams, 64 Cal.App.3d 181, 134 Cal.Rptr. 298 (1976). For a discussion of the problems inherent in the "time rule," see W. Reppy, Community Property in California (1980) 90–91.

One problem associated with use of the time rule is that it does not take into account the fact that the majority of pensions accrue at a disproportionate rate over the employee's career span. The employee spouse is treated as though he had earned the same amount of pension benefits each year of his employment, when in fact his salary and concomitant benefits were probably significantly higher in the later years. The justification most frequently given for use of the time rule is that an employee's contributions during the early years of employment, even though based on a smaller salary, may be substantially equivalent to or even worth more than contributions during later years, due to the longer period of accumulated interest and investment income prior to the commencement of benefit payments. See In re Marriage of Judd, 68 Cal.App.3d 515, 523, 137 Cal.Rptr. 318, 322 (1977); Note, *Distribution of Pension Benefits in Marital Dissolutions: Determining the Time of Valuation of the Community Interest*, 24 Santa Clara L.Rev. 999, 1009–1010 (1984); W. Reppy, Community Property in California (1980) 90–91.

2. Suppose that under the particular retirement plan, employees earn the maximum amount of retirement benefits possible after twenty years of service, but that the employee spouse actually worked for the employer for thirty years, twenty-five years during marriage and five years prior to marriage. How should the benefits be apportioned as between the community and separate interests, assuming that this is a defined benefit type of plan? This issue arose in Marriage of Henkle, 189 Cal.App.3d 97, 234 Cal.Rptr. 351 (1987), where the court held that once maximum retirement benefits have been earned, further employment thereafter during marriage does not count as service during marriage for the purpose of applying the time rule to determine the community interest in an employee spouse's retirement plan.

IN RE MARRIAGE OF BERGMAN

California District Court of Appeal, 1985.
168 Cal.App.3d 742, 214 Cal.Rptr. 661.

KING, ASSOCIATE JUSTICE.

* * *

I. FACTS

Joan and Elmer were married August 22, 1959, and separated April 19, 1980. They had five children, two of whom were minors at the time of trial.

Elmer was employed in federal civil service from 1961 until 1976. Prior to marriage he had performed almost two years of military service which counts as service towards his federal longevity retirement. In 1976, as a result of developing severe hypertension, Elmer became permanently and totally disabled. He has been receiving a disability pension since that time. Pursuant to his pension plan Elmer becomes eligible for longevity retirement when he reaches age 62 in 1997 at which time his benefits will be recomputed as longevity retirement.[2]

2. Applying *In re Marriage of Samuels* (1979) 96 Cal.App.3d 122, 158 Cal.Rptr. 38, the trial court correctly ruled that Elmer's disability benefits are separate rather than

During the marriage Joan worked at several jobs. She was a school teacher at the time of the separation, but sometime thereafter she started working for a tax planning service. As a teacher for eight years she made contributions to the California State Teachers' Retirement System. After separation Joan and the minor children moved out of the family residence.

* * *

II. THE PENSION PLANS

a. *Method of division*

Elmer's primary contention is that the court abused its discretion by failing to divide the community interest in his defined benefit pension plan on an in kind basis; instead the court used the cash out method.[4] It determined the present value of the community property interest in Elmer's pension plan, awarded it to him, and gave an offsetting award of other community property to Joan. Elmer also contends, even if this was not an abuse of discretion, that the court erred in fixing the present value of the community interest in his pension plan at $86,000.

We first address the claimed abuse of discretion by the court's choosing to cash out Joan's interest and award the entire community interest in Elmer's plan to him. Upon dissolution of a marriage, the trial court has broad discretion in the division of the community proper-

community property; however, upon becoming eligible for longevity retirement, there is a community interest in those benefits. (See also *In re Marriage of Stenquist* (1978) 21 Cal.3d 779, 148 Cal.Rptr. 9, 582 P.2d 96.)

4. For purposes of our discussion of pension plans, it is appropriate to define terms we will be using. Both Elmer's and Joan's pension plans were defined benefit plans which, in their particular cases, required contributions by the employee. The benefit each will receive, however, does not depend on the dollars contributed by them or their employer, but is based on a combination of factors, including highest income level achieved, years of service at retirement and age at retirement. To determine the present value of such a plan, it is necessary that expert testimony, normally from actuaries, be presented. This testimony includes not only the expert's opinion as to present value, but what factors, economic, health and otherwise, the expert considered in reaching his opinion.

Pension rights may be vested (a right which survives the discharge or voluntary termination of the employee), or nonvested (a right which requires additional service to become vested). The right may also be matured (employee has an unconditional

right to retire and obtain immediate payment of benefits) even though the employee has not chosen to retire. (See *In re Marriage of Brown* (1976) 15 Cal.3d 838, 842, 126 Cal.Rptr. 633, 544 P.2d 561.)

Community interests in defined benefit pension plans, as we shall discuss, may be disposed of in dissolution actions by a cash out (the entire community interest at its present value is awarded to the employee spouse with offsetting assets awarded to the other spouse to accomplish an equal division) or by a division in kind (the community interest is divided between the parties, and the plan, when benefits become payable, usually makes separate payments to each according to their proportionate interest).

As contrasted to a defined benefit plan, the other kind of retirement plan is a defined contribution plan where the employer's obligation is related to its annual contribution. The benefit for the employee upon retirement depends upon the value of the employee's account at that time. There is no need for expert testimony to determine the present value of a defined contribution plan at dissolution because its value is the amount of contributions made between the marriage and separation, plus accruals thereon, and all accruals thereon

ty interest in a spouse's pension rights and can exercise its discretion in either of two ways. The trial court may either determine the present value of community property rights and award them to one spouse with offsetting community or other assets to the other (commonly called the cash out method), or it may divide the community interest in kind between the spouses, reserving jurisdiction to supervise future payments to each spouse. (*In re Marriage of Brown, supra,* 15 Cal.3d at p. 848, 126 Cal.Rptr. 633, 544 P.2d 561.) Prior to its decision in *Brown,* our Supreme Court had indicated a preference, when feasible, for the trial court to award the employee spouse all of the community interest in his or her pension rights and to compensate the other spouse with other property of equal value. (*Phillipson v. Board of Administration* (1970) 3 Cal.3d 32, 46, 89 Cal.Rptr. 61, 473 P.2d 765, disapproved on other grounds by *In re Marriage of Brown, supra,* 15 Cal.3d at p. 851 fn. 14, 126 Cal.Rptr. 633, 544 P.2d 561.) However, in deciding *Brown,* the Supreme Court referred to its statement in *Phillipson* and expressly stated it had not intended to specify a preference; thus the trial "court retains the discretion to divide the community assets in any fashion which complies with the provisions of Civil Code section 4800." (*In re Marriage of Brown, supra,* 15 Cal.3d at p. 848 fn. 10, 126 Cal.Rptr. 633, 544 P.2d 561; see also *In re Marriage of Skaden* (1977) 19 Cal.3d 679, 688, 139 Cal.Rptr. 615, 566 P.2d 249; *In re Marriage of Freiberg* (1976) 57 Cal.App.3d 304, 312, 127 Cal.Rptr. 792, disapproved on other grounds in *In re Marriage of Gillmore* (1981) 29 Cal.3d 418, 425, 174 Cal.Rptr. 493, 629 P.2d 1.)

Here, both parties presented evidence from experts on the present value of Elmer's pension benefits and his probability of receipt of them. The court exercised its discretion in favor of awarding the community interest in those benefits solely to Elmer, awarding offsetting assets to Joan to accomplish an equal division. It is clear the court did in fact exercise its discretion, since it utilized the cash out method to dispose of Elmer's pension while, as we shall discuss later, it divided the community interest in Joan's pension benefits in kind.

Elmer's chief criticism of the court's exercise of discretion is based on his contention that due to his poor health the actual receipt of his longevity retirement benefits is too uncertain and speculative for the trial court to choose the alternative of a cash out to him, since it places all of the risks of future receipt of benefits on him. We know of no case which holds that one spouse's health condition deprives the court of its discretion to cash out the other spouse's interest in the former's pension plan and compels instead a division in kind. We decline to so hold. Health is only one of many factors to be considered by the trial judge. The value of Elmer's longevity retirement benefits is less speculative than would usually be true. The parties stipulated that 89.1 percent of his years of service were during marriage and additionally stipulated there should be a 25 percent reduction in the present value of his pension rights to take into account his poor health and the increased risk of his early death. Additionally, because of his disability, there is no need to speculate about what advances he would make up the career ladder or how many years he would work after separation. Thus, as to fixing a value, it can be done with greater certainty than would normally be true.

It is true that Elmer's reduced life expectancy is a factor to be used not only in determining present value, but also in deciding how the trial court should exercise discretion in awarding the community property interest in pension benefits.[5] All other things being equal, where the employee spouse has significant health problems, the trial court could very well find that an in kind distribution is the method which is most fair to both parties.[6] However, depending upon the evidence presented and the arguments of counsel, there are numerous factors the court may consider in determining how to exercise its discretion to divide community property interest in pension rights, and the weight to be given to each is peculiarly within the purview of the trier of fact.

The other alternative method of awarding the community share of pension rights or benefits is to divide that share between the parties in kind. The court will usually use the time rule to allocate separate and community interests (*In re Marriage of Judd* (1977) 68 Cal.App.3d 515, 522, 137 Cal.Rptr. 318; *In re Marriage of Freiberg, supra,* 57 Cal.App.3d at p. 310, 127 Cal.Rptr. 792), but is not required to do so. (See *In re Marriage of Poppe* (1979) 97 Cal.App.3d 1, 158 Cal.Rptr. 500 [court utilized a point system rather than a strict time rule because of the factual circumstances].)

Elmer exercised his right pursuant to Code of Civil Procedure section 632 to request a statement of decision on the issue of "distribution of respondent's retirement rather than reservation of benefits until received by respondent." The court in its statement of decision indicated it chose to cash out Joan because: (1) there were sufficient assets to award Joan property of equal value, (2) the economic circumstances justified the division, and (3) the court felt this was the preferable mode of division since it resulted in pension rights going to the employee spouse. Thereafter, in a request for clarification of statement of decision, Elmer indicated it was unclear what economic circumstances the court relied upon to justify the distribution of his retirement plan to

between the date of separation and trial of the issue.

5. One of the more comprehensive lists of factors that might be considered is set forth in 1979 California Family Law Report 1050–1051 (reproduced as Chart 5 in Cal. Fam.Law Prac.), which we attach as an exhibit to this opinion for the benefit of the bench and bar. Changes in the law since the publication of this chart should be considered, including the enactment by Congress of the Domestic Relations Tax Reform Act of 1984 (PL 98–369) and the Retirement Equity Act of 1984 (29 U.S.C. § 1001 et seq.) which now requires that private as

opposed to public plans provide a survivorship benefit for spouses and former spouses.

6. One respected domestic relations actuarial expert has expressed the view that the fairest disposition of community interests in pension plans is the cash out method, not a division in kind. See "A Fair Value is a Fair Value," Projector, Family Law News and Review, No. 2, Los Angeles County Bar Association. Of course the actuary is looking at the interest in the pension plan isolated from all other factors which the trial court may consider in exercising its discretion between a cash out and a division in kind.

him. The court issued a clarification which stated that the court had considered the issue relative to the uncertainty of Elmer's receiving his retirement rights but had decided in light of the nature and extent of community property and the need to have an equitable, workable and practical division of property, to exercise its discretion to award the community interest in the pension rights to Elmer based upon its present value.

Because it is not possible to develop comprehensive guidelines for trial courts to follow in deciding whether to cash out or divide in kind community interests in pensions, and because this decision is reached primarily by the weighing of equitable and factual considerations, appellate courts should not second guess the exercise of the broad discretion of trial courts in the absence of a clear showing of an abuse of that discretion. (See *In re Marriage of Emmett* (1980) 109 Cal.App.3d 753, 169 Cal.Rptr. 473; *In re Marriage of Adams* (1976) 64 Cal.App.3d 181, 134 Cal.Rptr. 298.) Elmer has not sustained his burden of demonstrating an abuse of discretion by the trial court; the award to Elmer of the community property interest in his pension plan must therefore stand.

* * *

Elmer contends the trial court abused its discretion in ordering an open ended reservation of jurisdiction over the community property interest in Joan's pension plan, especially since the court cashed Joan out of his pension plan and awarded it to him, making an offsetting award to her to accomplish an equal division of community property. Joan replies that the trial court has broad discretion to reserve jurisdiction over the community interest in pension plans and to divide that interest when benefits become payable.

Thus the parties disagree as to whether the trial court made the best disposition of Joan's pension. They do agree, however, both in their briefs and at oral argument, that the court did not divide the community interest in Joan's pension; it simply retained jurisdiction to do so when Joan becomes eligible to obtain benefits under the plan.[10] If the parties' description of the trial court's disposition (or nondisposition) of the community property interest in Joan's pension plan is accurate, we would agree that the trial court abused its discretion.

Pursuant to Civil Code section 4800, subdivision (a), in a dissolution action "the court shall * * * in its judgment of dissolution of marriage * * * or at a later time if it expressly reserves jurisdiction to make such a property division, divide the community property and the quasi-community property of the parties equally." By this direction the Legislature requires that community property be divided at the time of the litigation of the dissolution action, although it has recognized the

---

10. A distinction should be drawn between an open ended reservation of jurisdiction to divide community interests in a pension in the future, and one which presently divides those interests and reserves or retains jurisdiction to supervise their payment when benefits are received in the future. As we shall discuss the court has no authority to do the former, but does have authority to do the latter.

trial court's power to bifurcate and try one or more issues in the case, including termination of marital status, reserving jurisdiction for a later time to try other issues, including support and the division of any remaining community property. Neither the legislative history of section 4800 nor any case analysis but one, provides authority for the proposition that a court may reserve jurisdiction indefinitely to divide a community asset. It is not uncommon, and is often of assistance to the parties in reaching a settlement of other issues, for the court to bifurcate and try one or more issues before or after the termination of the marital status of the parties. Quite often there are cases with a pivotal issue which, once it is decided, will enable the parties to settle all other issues. This may be an issue of value, the character of property as separate or community, which party is to be awarded a specific community asset, or whether an asset such as goodwill even exists. In such cases the court is encouraged to separately try and decide the pivotal issue in the hope the parties will then be able to settle all other issues. The best resolution in any case, especially dissolution actions, is one reached by agreement of the parties themselves.

The trial court possesses broad discretion to consider the manner in which issues should be tried, including the bifurcation and separate trial of pivotal issues. However, nothing in Civil Code section 4800, including the language "shall * * * at a later time if it expressly reserves jurisdiction to make such a property division, divide the community property * * *," authorizes the court to wait for years until a pension plan begins paying benefits in the future before dividing the community interest therein.

Any research of California law with regard to the disposition of community interests in pension plans, whether or not vested, should begin with *In re Marriage of Brown, supra,* 15 Cal.3d 838, 126 Cal.Rptr. 633, 544 P.2d 561. In adopting a new rule that vested and "nonvested pension rights are not an expectancy, but a contingent interest in property" the court not only changed existing law, it also provided guidance to the trial courts as to the two methods of disposition which trial judges have available to them in dividing community interests in pension plans. (*Id.,* at p. 841, 126 Cal.Rptr. 633, 544 P.2d 561.) Our Supreme Court clearly specified *only* two methods of dividing community pension rights. The trial court can determine the present value of the community interest in the pension right and cash out the other spouse by awarding it to the employee spouse, or, if "it should not attempt to divide the present value of pension rights, it can instead award each spouse an appropriate portion of each pension payment as it is paid." (15 Cal.3d at p. 848, 126 Cal.Rptr. 633, 544 P.2d 561.) Nowhere in *Brown* does the Supreme Court authorize or suggest that there is statutory or case authority for a trial court to retain open ended jurisdiction to divide community interests in a pension plan after the conclusion of litigation of the dissolution action.

The only case to authorize a reservation of jurisdiction over the division of community interests in a pension plan until benefits could be received is *In re Marriage of Carl* (1977) 67 Cal.App.3d 542, 136 Cal.Rptr. 703. We respectfully disagree with the decision in *Carl* and believe a discussion of the reasoning in that case will demonstrate its erroneous result. In *Carl* the trial court had failed to consider the husband's community interest in the nonvested pension plan of the wife because the trial had occurred prior to the complete change in the law announced in *Brown.* The court in *Carl* stated that the husband "is entitled to share in [wife's] pension, if and when she receives it" but, since it is nonvested, "There is still nothing for the court to divide." Because of this analysis, the court determined that instead of reversing and remanding the cause to the trial court, it would simply modify the judgment by adding "the court reserves jurisdiction regarding [husband's] claim to an interest in [wife's] nonvested pension plan." (67 Cal.App.3d at p. 546, 136 Cal.Rptr. 703.) As a result of *Carl,* several later cases, without analysis, added this method of disposition of interests in pension plans to the two alternatives authorized in *Brown.*

We disagree strongly with this ruling in *Carl* because "Pension rights, whether or not vested, represent a property interest; to the extent such rights derive from employment during coverture, they comprise a community asset subject to division in a dissolution proceeding." (*In re Marriage of Brown, supra,* 15 Cal.3d at p. 842, 126 Cal.Rptr. 633, 544 P.2d 561.) Thus, pursuant to *Brown,* there is something for the trial court to divide, that is, the community property interest of the parties in the pension. It is a property right, whether vested or nonvested, not an expectancy. In keeping with the intent of the Legislature providing for the division of community assets during the dissolution litigation, trial courts have only the two alternatives stated in *Brown,* i.e., to cash out the nonemployee spouse at the present value of the community interest in the pension and award it to the employee spouse, or to divide the community interest in the pension in kind. Additionally, we conceive of no good reason to perpetuate family law litigation indefinitely when such property interests can and should be divided as part of the litigation process of dividing all other community property of the parties.

After a thorough search of the record, we are unable to find any evidence presented to the trial court of the present value of Joan's pension plan, the amount of her contributions to it, or, indeed, even its existence. Apparently the disposition of the community interest in her pension plan was agreed to during an in-chambers conference, probably immediately prior to the commencement of trial. Although we only surmise that is what has occurred here, it is appropriate to remind the trial bench and bar that our review is limited to the record before us. Despite the informality which often accompanies the litigation of family law cases, it is crucial that statements be placed on the record memorializing stipulations reached in off the record conferences between counsel, or counsel and the court.

Despite the absence of anything in the record about the existence of Joan's pension plan, the parties nonetheless agree there is such a plan with the State Teachers' Retirement System. Joan testified she had been a teacher for eight years. A review of her property declaration filed prior to trial does list such a pension and values it at $10,700. We suspect, however, that this represents the amount of her contributions to the plan, not the plan's present value at the time of the filing of her declaration.

Nevertheless, although no evidence was presented to the court as to the amount of the contributions, the terms of the plan, the date at which Joan would be eligible for payment of retirement benefits, or any facts upon which her retirement benefits could be presently valued, the court still had the ability to make an in kind division of the community interest in the plan by applying the time rule. "This method of dividing the community interest in the pension renders it unnecessary for the court to compute the present value of the pension rights, and divides equally the risk that the pension will fail to vest." (*In re Marriage of Brown, supra,* 15 Cal.3d at p. 848, 126 Cal.Rptr. 633, 544 P.2d 561.) Thus, even though there is neither expert testimony nor any other information except for the fact that a pension plan exists, and regardless of whether the interest in the plan is vested, the court can divide the community interest between the parties.[11] Thus the court had the discretion to divide the community interest in Joan's pension by a cash out of Elmer's interest or an in kind division, but it did not have authority to retain an open ended jurisdiction over the division of the community interest.

However, our review of the trial court's order in the interlocutory judgment reveals, contrary to the posture of the parties on appeal, that the court did not simply retain an open ended jurisdiction to divide the community interest in the pension plan; it did indeed divide it. As to each party the court made the following award in the interlocutory judgment of dissolution: "One-half of the community interest in the California State Teachers' Retirement Benefits in [Joan's] name. The court reserves jurisdiction to divide said benefits which shall be distributed at the earliest date when [Joan] is eligible to draw her pension."

This language accomplishes a present division of the community interest in Joan's pension plan. Indeed, since the plan itself was joined as a claimant and appeared in the action, if the wording of the order is modified to reflect the dates of marriage and separation, it is unlikely any supervision by the court will ever be necessary.[12]

To accomplish this, it is necessary that the wording more carefully allocate community and separate interests by the time rule, that is, by a consideration of the ratio of the time Joan was employed as a teacher between the dates of marriage and separation, and the total amount of

11. Thus in a case like *In re Marriage of Hargrave, supra,* 163 Cal.App.3d 346, 209 Cal.Rptr. 764, when no evidence is before the court as to the interest in the plan, in addition to that court's suggestions that the trial court can require additional evidence or appoint its own expert, it can also divide the community interest in kind.

12. For a discussion on joinder of pension plans see California Practice Guide Family Law, Hogoboom & King (TRG 1985) at 8–131 through 8–133.

time she was so employed. Again the record is incomplete. It appears that Joan was still teaching at the date of separation but soon thereafter terminated that employment. It is unknown whether Joan has returned to teaching or will do so in the future.

Under these circumstances, since we uphold the trial court's exercise of discretion to award the community interest in Joan's retirement plan to the parties in kind, we modify the provisions of the interlocutory judgment as to the community interest in Joan's retirement plan with the California Teachers' Retirement System. Said interest shall be that fraction of the total benefits, the numerator of which represents the number of months of Joan's employment between the dates of marriage and separation, and the denominator of which is the total number of months of Joan's service. (See *In re Marriage of Judd, supra,* 68 Cal.App.3d at p. 523, 137 Cal.Rptr. 318.) This fraction, multiplied by the benefit paid under the plan, is the community property interest in benefits under the plan and it is awarded one-half to each party. Any remaining benefit paid under the plan is confirmed to Joan as her separate property.

In making this decision, we acknowledge that the amount which Joan will receive from her pension plan upon achieving eligibility for retirement is less certain than is true with Elmer's plan. It is not known if Joan will return to teaching or what salary level she may ultimately achieve if she does so. By using the formula set forth above, it makes no difference whether or not Joan returns to teaching. This formula still determines that portion of benefits which are community.

The decision how to award the community interest in future pension plan payments is one within the trial court's broad discretion and Elmer has made no showing of any abuse of that discretion as to Joan's retirement plan. (See *In re Marriage of Skaden, supra,* 19 Cal.3d at p. 688, 139 Cal.Rptr. 615, 566 P.2d 249; *In re Marriage of Brown, supra,* 15 Cal.3d at p. 848, 126 Cal.Rptr. 633, 544 P.2d 561.) Considering all of the circumstances, it appears that the court's reservation of jurisdiction was reasonable. The fact the trial court present valued Elmer's pension plan and awarded it to him (with offsetting assets to Joan), does not require the community interest in Joan's plan to be treated identically.

* * *

Low, P.J., concurs.

Haning, Associate Justice, concurring.

I concur in the result, based on my view that trial courts should have broad discretion in dissolution cases. The Family Law Act has created as many problems as it was intended to solve in the area of property distribution. Unfortunately, the appellate courts have added to the problem and created further confusion. We have also contributed mightily to the growth of the expert witness industry. Actuaries and other appraisers have never had it so good. This has, of course, only served to drive up the cost of obtaining a divorce, which is a regrettable consequence, since at the time the family is disintegrating the parties need to preserve, rather than dissipate, their assets.

When actuaries, such as those who testified as experts in the instant case, render their opinions on the present value of a pension plan, they necessarily make certain assumptions as to future economic conditions. As we know from various painful historical examples, economic forecasting is less than an exact science. Predictions of future human behavior are even less exact. Thus, when we accept testimony as to what the interest rate will be ten or twenty years down the road, we are engaging in (to borrow a phrase from the Vice–President) "voodoo economics." Trying to guess whether an individual will remain with a particular employer long enough to ever collect a nickel by way of pension is hazardous at best, and sheer tomfoolery when we start awarding large sums of present cash based upon such guesswork.

In short, in those situations where the pension is unvested, or where certain conditions remain to be fulfilled before the employee can collect anything, I think the better practice is to defer the division of that asset until such time as we know what we have.

EXHIBIT
PRESENT VALUATION OR RESERVATION OF

EMPLOYEE–SPOUSE

Present Valuation	Reservation of Jurisdiction
1. Ability to control all of benefits when pension matures.	Pension may never mature (due to death, cessation of employment, or termination of business).
2. Avoids potentially-protracted litigation over pension.	Avoids potentially complex and lengthy trial concerning present valuation of pension.
3. Permits employee-spouse to take full advantage of future salary increases (avoids "time rule").	Plan benefits may become less generous in the future.
4. Full freedom to elect among alternative benefit packages when pension matures.	Law may become less liberal toward non-employee spouse (e.g., courts may expand pre-emption doctrine).
5. Avoids joinder of pension.	Avoids expense of actuary's valuation.
6. May simplify drafting of divorce decree.	Non-employee spouse may die and never collect community share.
7. Avoids possibility that pension payments may be converted to spousal support, under *In re Marriage of Verner* (1978) 77 CA3d 718, 143 CR 826, 1978 CFLR 1079.	Prevents non-employee spouse from devising community interest in pension. (*Waite v. Waite* (1972) 6 C3d 461, 99 CR 325, 492 P2d 13).
8. If pension division is taxable, permits employee-spouse possibly to claim a "stepped-up" basis.	Employee-spouse may not have to pay tax on community share of pension benefits paid to non-employee spouse.
9. Permits employee-spouse to take full advantage of future liberalized pension rules or conditions (e.g., earlier vesting).	May reduce—or obviate—future spousal support obligation when both spouses receive pension payments. (See *In re Marriage of Stenquist* (1978) 21 C3d 779, 148 CR 9, 582 P2d 96, 1978 CFLR 1198).
10. May be more acceptable to employer (who will not have to be concerned with possible enforcement problems).	May escape garnishment (especially if the pension is a federal non-civil service benefit).
11. May permit employee-spouse to have increased ability to provide for second spouse and children.	Provides employee-spouse with more liquid assets at the time of trial (when he or she may most need them).

JURISDICTION: PRACTICAL CONSIDERATIONS

NON–EMPLOYEE–SPOUSE

Present Valuation	Reservation of Jurisdiction
Avoids possibility that pension may never mature.	Ability to exercise control over half of community share of benefit, upon maturity.
Avoids potentially-protracted litigation over pension.	Avoids potentially complex and lengthy trial concerning present valuation of pension.
Plan benefits may become less generous in the future.	Permits non-employee spouse to share in future salary increases, under "time rule" (See 1977 CFLR 1138).
Law may become less liberal toward non-employee spouse.	Possible ability to have "veto power" in electing among alternative benefit packages. (See 1978 CFLR 1011).
Avoids joinder problems.	Avoids expense of actuary's valuation.
Non-employee spouse may die and never collect share.	May simplify drafting of divorce decree.
Non-employee spouse can devise lump-sum "cash-out", but not future pension payments.	Pension payments may possibly be converted to spousal support, under *Verner*.
Avoids income tax liability on future payments (if "assignment of income doctrine" does not apply).	Better to receive community share of future payments, since non-employee spouse may have future "assignment of income" tax liability even without receiving payments. (See 1978 CFLR 1181).
Without monthly pension income, may facilitate future claim for support.	Permits non-employee spouse to share in future liberalized pension rules.
Avoids enforcement problems.	
Provides non-employee spouse with more liquid assets at the time of trial.	May permit non-employee spouse to have increased ability in the future to provide for second spouse and children.

*

Notes

1. Valuation of retirement benefits can be an exceedingly complex question due to the number of variables involved. Every plan contains different elements or features which can substantially affect valuation. These elements include (1) the terms of vesting determining the benefits to the employee who voluntarily or involuntarily terminates his employment prior to retirement; (2) the amount of benefits to be paid at retirement; (3) the possible loss of retirement benefits if the employee becomes disabled and receives disability benefits; (4) the rights of the employee spouse to select alternative plans; (5) the possibility of a lump sum award rather than continuing payments; (6) provisions regarding early and late retirement; (7) the options available to the non-employee spouse if the employee spouse dies after retirement; and (8) death benefits in lieu of retirement. B. Clemens and D. Jaffe, Division and Taxation of Retirement Benefits in Dissolution Proceedings, Employment Retirement and Deferred Compensation Plans on Dissolution of Marriage: Valuation, Distribution and Tax Aspects, C.E.B. 1986, at 27; Note, Distribution of Pension Benefits in Marital Dissolutions: Determining the Time of Valuation of the Community Interest, 24 Santa Clara L.Rev. 999, 1001 (1984). Other relevant valuation factors include the age, length of service and health of the employee spouse.

Due to the complexity of valuation problems, experts are frequently consulted for guidance and assistance. For example, with respect to a defined contribution type of plan, an accountant may be employed to identify and trace the contributions made by or on behalf of the employee spouse to the current value of the account. If the plan is a defined benefit plan, as in *Bergman*, actuarial testimony may be necessary. *Id.*

2. In *Bergman* the court reiterated the point that the method of division of deferred compensation rights is left to the discretion of the trial court. Attacks on the exercise of this discretion have generally been unavailing. For example, in Marriage of Ramer, 187 Cal.App.3d 263, 231 Cal.Rptr. 647 (1986), the wife contended that the trial court improperly refused to effect a present division of the community property interest in the husband's pension and that the trial court should have awarded the pension to the husband and the family residence to the wife with an equalizing payment from the husband to offset the value of the pension. The appellate court rejected these contentions:

> Evidence adduced at the first trial placed the value of the retirement rights at between $78,000 and $84,000. The equity in the family residence, on the other hand, amounted to about $53,000. In view of the substantial demands on husband's current income, the fact that husband is not yet eligible to retire and the fact that no other substantial community assets were available from which to provide an equalizing payment, we cannot say the court's refusal to make an immediate division and its reserving jurisdiction over the pension rights was an abuse of discretion.

3. The present division approach was followed by the appellate court in Marriage of Verlinde, 189 Cal.App.3d 918, 234 Cal.Rptr. 694 (1987). In *Verlinde* the husband requested the trial court to assign a present actuarial value to each party's community retirement benefits and to award the

benefits to each respective spouse, "cashing out" one against the other. The wife requested the court to reserve jurisdiction over the division and payment of each party's retirement benefits until payments actually commenced. The trial court's choice of the former division method was held to be an appropriate exercise of discretion. The reviewing court also held that the use of actuarial valuation based upon male-female mortality tables was constitutionally permissible.

IN RE MARRIAGE OF GILLMORE

Supreme Court of California, 1981.
29 Cal.3d 418, 174 Cal.Rptr. 493, 699 P.2d 1.

BIRD, CHIEF JUSTICE.

Did the trial court abuse its discretion in a dissolution action when it refused to order the immediate payment of a nonemployee spouse's interest in a retirement benefit, where the employee spouse was eligible to retire and receive the benefit but had chosen not to do so?

I.

Vera and Earl Gillmore separated in 1978 after a marriage of 14 years. The trial court issued an interlocutory decree dissolving their marriage on November 27, 1978, and entered a final judgment of dissolution on January 19, 1979. The decree awarded Vera physical custody of their minor child as well as $225 per month child support and $100 per month spousal support.

The community property was divided evenly, with the exception of Earl's interest in a retirement plan managed by his employer, Pacific Telephone Company. The court found that Earl would become eligible to retire on April 11, 1979, at which time he would be entitled to a monthly benefit of $717.18. Vera's interest in that benefit was found to be approximately $177.14 per month. The court specifically reserved jurisdiction over the retirement plan.

Earl continued to work after he became eligible to retire in April 1979. He represented that he was a "healthy, active man" in his early 50's, and he intended to work for some time to come. He was not required to retire until he reached the age of 70.

In July 1979, Vera requested an order directing Earl to pay to Vera her share of the pension benefits immediately, retroactive to the date he became eligible to collect them. Earl responded with a request to modify child and spousal support. The trial court denied both requests, retained jurisdiction over the retirement benefits, and held that it had discretion to delay distribution of the benefits until Earl actually retired.

II.

Under California law, retirement benefits earned by a spouse during a marriage are community property, subject to equal division upon the dissolution of that marriage. (*In re Marriage of Brown* (1976) 15 Cal.3d

838, 842, 126 Cal.Rptr. 633, 544 P.2d 561, Civ.Code, § 4800.) [1] This is true whether the benefits are vested or nonvested, matured or immature. (*Brown, supra,* at p. 842, 126 Cal.Rptr. 633, 544 P.2d 561.) [2] Vera and Earl agree that Earl's retirement benefits are community property to the extent they were earned during their marriage. The sole disagreement concerns the *timing* of the distribution of those benefits. Vera contends that the trial court abused its discretion when it refused to order Earl to begin immediate payments to her of her share. Earl claims that the trial court had discretion to postpone distribution of the benefits until he actually retired and began to receive payments from the pension plan.

Trial courts have considerable discretion to determine the value of community property and to formulate a practical way in which to divide property equally. (*In re Marriage of Connolly* (1979) 23 Cal.3d 590, 603, 153 Cal.Rptr. 423, 591 P.2d 911.) However, that discretion has been strictly circumscribed by the statutory requirement that *all* community property be divided *equally* between the parties. (Civ.Code, § 4800.) [3] A trial court has been held to abuse its discretion when it improperly classifies community property as the separate property of one of the spouses or fails to arrive at an equal division of the community property. (*In re Marriage of Olson* (1980) 27 Cal.3d 414, 422, 165 Cal.Rptr. 820, 612 P.2d 910; *In re Marriage of Brown, supra,* 15 Cal.3d at p. 847, 126 Cal.Rptr. 633, 544 P.2d 561.)

Under the cases and statutory law, Earl cannot time his retirement to deprive Vera of an equal share of the community's interest in his pension. It is a "settled principle that one spouse cannot, by invoking a condition wholly within his control, defeat the community interest of the

---

1. *Brown, supra,* 15 Cal.3d at page 851, footnote 14, 126 Cal.Rptr. 633, 544 P.2d 561, disapproved the following cases, cited hereinafter, only so far as they declared nonvested pensions did not constitute a divisible community property interest: *Smith v. Lewis* (1975) 13 Cal.3d 349, 118 Cal.Rptr. 621, 530 P.2d 589; *In re Marriage of Fithian* (1974) 10 Cal.3d 592, 111 Cal.Rptr. 369, 517 P.2d 449; *Waite v. Waite* (1972) 6 Cal.3d 461, 99 Cal.Rptr. 325, 492 P.2d 13; *Phillipson v. Board of Administration* (1970) 3 Cal.3d 32, 89 Cal.Rptr. 61, 473 P.2d 765; *In re Marriage of Martin* (1975) 50 Cal.App.3d 581, 123 Cal.Rptr. 634; *In re Marriage of Peterson* (1974) 41 Cal.App.3d 642, 115 Cal.Rptr. 184; *Bensing v. Bensing* (1972) 25 Cal.App.3d 889, 102 Cal.Rptr. 255.

2. A "vested" benefit cannot be forfeited if employment ends. Rather, it "survives the discharge or voluntary termination of the employee." (*In re Marriage of Brown, supra,* 15 Cal.3d at p. 842, 126 Cal.Rptr. 633, 544 P.2d 561.) A retirement benefit "matures" when the employee has

an unconditional right to payment, i.e., all the "conditions precedent to the payment of the benefits have taken place or are within the control of the employee. [Citations.]" (*In re Marriage of Fithian, supra,* 10 Cal.3d at p. 596, 111 Cal.Rptr. 369, 517 P.2d 449; *Brown, supra,* 15 Cal.3d at p. 842, 126 Cal.Rptr. 633, 544 P.2d 561; *Smith v. Lewis, supra,* 13 Cal.3d at p. 355, fn. 4, 118 Cal.Rptr. 621, 530 P.2d 589; *In re Marriage of Peterson, supra,* 41 Cal.App.3d at pp. 649–650, 115 Cal.Rptr. 184.) Earl's benefits have vested in that if he retires or loses his job for any reason he will be entitled to immediate benefits. They have matured in that the sole condition on his enjoyment of the benefits, his retirement, is within his control.

3. Section 4800 provides in pertinent part that except in certain narrow circumstances (see § 4800, subds. (b) and (c)), "the court shall * * * divide the community property and the quasi-community property of the parties * * * equally." (Civ. Code, § 4800, subd. (a).)

other spouse." (*In re Marriage of Stenquist* (1978) 21 Cal.3d 779, 786, 148 Cal.Rptr. 9, 582 P.2d 96. See also *Waite v. Waite, supra,* 6 Cal.3d at p. 472, 99 Cal.Rptr. 325, 492 P.2d 13; *In re Marriage of Peterson, supra,* 41 Cal.App.3d at pp. 650–651, 115 Cal.Rptr. 184.)

Earl's retirement benefits are both vested and matured. (See *ante,* fn. 2.) He will not forfeit his benefits if he leaves his employment voluntarily, is terminated or retires. The only condition precedent to payment of the benefits is his retirement, a condition totally within his control. A unilateral choice to postpone retirement cannot be manipulated so as to impair a spouse's interest in those retirement benefits.

In re Marriage of Stenquist, supra, 21 Cal.3d 779, 148 Cal.Rptr. 9, 582 P.2d 96, involved a husband's election to receive disability benefits (usually separate property), rather than retirement pay (usually community property). This court held that the husband could not use this election to deprive his wife of her interest in his retirement benefits. "[T]o permit the husband, by unilateral election of a 'disability' pension, to 'transmute community property into his own separate property' (*In re Marriage of Fithian, supra,* 10 Cal.3d 592, 602 [111 Cal.Rptr. 369, 517 P.2d 449]), is to negate the protective philosophy of the community property law as set out in previous decisions of this court." (*Stenquist, supra,* 21 Cal. at p. 782, 148 Cal.Rptr. 9, 582 P.2d 96.)

The result of the husband's unilateral decision in *Stenquist* would have been to deprive the wife of any interest in his retirement benefits. In the present case, Vera is no less entitled to protection. The fact that the deprivation she faces is less than total is not decisive. Earl would deprive Vera of the immediate enjoyment of an asset earned by the community during the marriage. In so doing, he would subject Vera to the risk of losing the asset completely if Earl were to die while he was still employed. Although Earl has every right to choose to postpone the receipt of his pension and to run that risk, he should not be able to force Vera to do so as well.[4]

---

4. Earl claims that the trial court's decision resulted in an equal division of the retirement benefits since he and Vera will receive their shares of the benefits at the same time—the time that he chooses to retire. However, he overlooks the fact that both the timing of receipt and the control of an asset are important aspects of its value. "Postponement, especially late in life, is often the equivalent of complete defeat. Not only are the employee spouse's chances of dying on the job increasing with each passing year (in which case the pension rights would vanish under most plans), the present value of money is much more valuable as a person enters the last years of his life." (Note, *In re Marriage of Stenquist: Tracing the Community Interest in Pension Rights Altered by Spousal Election* (1979) 67 Cal.L.Rev. 856, 879, fn. 76.) A benefit which may be received at some unknown time in the future is of less value than one received immediately. (*In re Marriage of Tammen* (1976) 63 Cal.App.3d 927, 931, 134 Cal.Rptr. 161; see Projector, *Valuation of Retirement Benefits in Marriage Dissolutions* (1975) 50 L.A.Bar Bull. 229.) Further, a benefit over which an individual has no control is of less value than a benefit that can be managed personally. Thus, Earl's decision to wait to receive his pension when it will be most profitable and most convenient for him deprives Vera of both the immediate enjoyment of her benefits and the power to manage them to her own advantage. Her financial situation may involve factors significantly different from his. Both the husband and the wife should be able to make their independent decisions about how to handle their shares of the community property.

The case of *In re Marriage of Luciano* (1980) 104 Cal.App.3d 956, 164 Cal.Rptr. 93, is directly on point. In *Luciano,* the trial court ordered that a nonemployee spouse must wait until the employee spouse actually retires before receiving his or her share of the retirement benefits. The Court of Appeal held that "[t]o uphold the trial court's ruling as to the *time* Dorothy is to commence receiving her portion of this community asset would give Ferdinand the option of determining the receipt by Dorothy of her own property which would be basically unfair. The employee spouse cannot by election defeat the nonemployee spouse's interest in the community property by relying on a condition solely within the employee spouse's control. [Citations.] * * * [¶] A proper order for a trial court to make in these circumstances is that the nonemployee spouse is the one who has the choice as to when his or her share of the pension shall begin." (*Id.,* at p. 960, 164 Cal.Rptr. 93.)

Similar results were reached in two earlier cases. In *In re Marriage of Martin, supra,* 50 Cal.App.3d 581, 123 Cal.Rptr. 634, the appellate court held that where the only condition to receipt of the benefits by one spouse was the employee spouse's decision to retire and apply for them, the benefits should be divided as community property. The language of the court is instructive. "The only condition to the payment of the pension benefits is a condition entirely within [the husband's] control, and that is not an uncertainty precluding division of the asset upon dissolution of marriage." (*Martin, supra,* 50 Cal.App.3d at p. 584, 123 Cal.Rptr. 634.) Similarly a trial court decision to order the immediate payment of a share of a husband's vested, matured pension benefits to his wife, where the husband was eligible to retire but had not yet done so, was upheld in *Bensing v. Bensing, supra,* 25 Cal.App.3d at pages 892–893, 102 Cal.Rptr. 255.[5]

These cases, however, do not preclude the employee spouse from choosing among alternative retirement plans. The employee spouse retains the right (1) to change or terminate employment; (2) to agree to a modification of the retirement benefits; or (3) to elect between alternative benefits. (*In re Marriage of Brown, supra,* 15 Cal.3d at p. 849, 126 Cal.Rptr. 633, 544 P.2d 561.) "[T]he employee spouse retains the right to determine the nature of the benefits to be received." (*In re Marriage of Stenquist, supra,* 21 Cal.3d at p. 786, 148 Cal.Rptr. 9, 582 P.2d 96, fn. omitted.)

The right of the employee spouse is nonetheless limited by the fact that the nonemployee spouse owns an interest in the retirement benefits. Thus, *Brown* notes that the employee spouse has a right to agree to

---

5. See also *In re Marriage of Adams* (1976) 64 Cal.App.3d 181, 185–186, 134 Cal. Rptr. 298, finding that a nonemployee spouse had the option of taking her share of the benefits either at the time of dissolution or at the time the employee spouse retired.

To the extent that it conflicts with this court's present holding, dictum in *In re Marriage of Freiberg* (1976) 57 Cal.App.3d 304, 311, 127 Cal.Rptr. 792, which suggests that the employee spouse can control the time at which the retirement payments to the nonemployee will commence, is disapproved. The nonemployee spouse in that case apparently did not request immediate distribution of the benefits. Further, the timing of the distribution was not before the court.

"a reasonable * * * *nondetrimental* modification of the pension system" (*In re Marriage of Brown, supra,* 15 Cal.3d at p. 849, fn. 11, 126 Cal.Rptr. 633, 544 P.2d 561, emphasis added), and *Stenquist* finds that the employee spouse retains the right to elect "*higher than ordinary* retirement benefits." (*In re Marriage of Stenquist, supra,* 21 Cal.3d at p. 786, fn. 6, 148 Cal.Rptr. 9, 582 P.2d 96, emphasis added.) If the right to choose among alternative retirement plans is exercised in a way which impairs the nonemployee's interest in the benefits, the nonemployee spouse must be compensated.[6]

Thus, although the husband in *Stenquist* had every right to choose a disability pension rather than retirement pay, his choice did not prevent the court from ordering him to pay to the wife an amount equivalent to what her interest would have been had he chosen retirement pay. Similarly, Earl retains the right to determine what retirement benefits he will receive. He can retire now or at some time in the future. He also retains the option of choosing between the alternative pension plans offered by his employer. However, if he opts for an alternative that deprives Vera of her full share of the retirement benefits, he must compensate her for the interest she loses as a result of his decision.

Compensation is possible here because the value of Vera's interest is known to the court. Also, the only condition to the payment of the benefits, Earl's retirement, is entirely within his control. However, "if the court concludes that because of uncertainties affecting the vesting or maturation of the pension that it should not attempt to divide the present value of pension rights, it can instead award each spouse an appropriate portion of each pension payment as it is paid." (*In re Marriage of Brown, supra,* 15 Cal.3d at p. 848, 126 Cal.Rptr. 633, 544 P.2d 561, fn. omitted.) In this case, the pension benefits have already vested and matured. There are no "uncertainties affecting * * * vesting or maturation" that could lead the trial court to conclude that distribution of the pension must be delayed. Therefore, the trial court abused its discretion when it refused to order the immediate distribution of this vested and mature retirement benefit.

Earl's claim that he is being forced to retire misses the point. He is free to continue working. However, if he does so, he must reimburse Vera for the share of the community property that she loses as a result of that decision. His claim that the court lacks jurisdiction to order him to make payments to Vera because it lacks jurisdiction over his separate property also lacks merit. Earl alone will make the decision to use

---

6. Trial courts can limit the employee spouse's freedom to choose to the extent necessary to protect the interests of the nonemployee spouse. For instance, *In re Marriage of Lionberger* (1979) 97 Cal. App.3d 56, 67–70, 158 Cal.Rptr. 535, affirmed a trial court order precluding the husband from choosing a pension plan option that would have decreased the size of his wife's interest. In *Phillipson v. Board of Administration, supra,* 3 Cal.3d 32, 48, 89 Cal.Rptr. 61, 473 P.2d 765, the court ordered the husband to choose a particular retirement benefit because such an order was the only way to protect the wife's interest. See also *Ball v. McDonnell Douglas Corp.* (1973) 30 Cal.App.3d 624, 630–631, 106 Cal.Rptr. 662, in which the appellate court noted that the trial court could have made an order limiting the employee's freedom to choose among alternative plans if the nonemployee spouse had requested it.

separate property to reimburse Vera, when and if he decides not to retire. His situation is not unlike that faced by a couple ordered to divide a house that they own as community property. If one of the spouses chooses to keep the house, he or she is free to use separate property to purchase the other's interest. Here, Earl must divide his retirement benefits with Vera. If he does not wish to retire, he must pay her an amount equivalent to her interest.[7]

Earl's suggestion that Vera can be adequately compensated through spousal support is contrary to current law. "As we have affirmed many times, adjustments in the amount of alimony awarded will not mitigate the hardship caused the wife by the denial of her community interest in the pension payments. Alimony lies within the discretion of the trial court and may be modified with changing circumstances: 'the spouse "should not be dependent on the discretion of the court * * * to provide her with the equivalent of what should be hers as a matter of absolute right."' (*In re Marriage of Brown, supra,* 15 Cal.3d 838, 848, 126 Cal.Rptr. 633, 544 P.2d 561.)" (*In re Marriage of Stenquist, supra,* 21 Cal.3d at p. 787, fn. 8, 148 Cal.Rptr. 9, 582 P.2d 96.)

Earl asserts that Vera should be required to demonstrate a financial need to justify the immediate distribution of the retirement benefits. However, financial status is not relevant when dividing community property. The courts are statutorily required to divide community property equally. (Civ.Code, § 4800.) A court may consider the equities of the parties' financial situations in determining *spousal support,* but only after the community property has been equitably divided. The retirement benefit must first be divided equally. Earl may then renew his motion for a modification of spousal support in light of this new distribution of the community property.[8]

In the past, this court has encouraged trial courts, if feasible, to award all pension rights to an employee spouse, compensating the nonemployee spouse with other community property of equal value. (*In*

---

7. One commentator argues that when an employee who is eligible to retire chooses to continue working, part of his or her salary is actually attributable to community effort. "[F]rom an economist's perspective, the employee spouse's compensation for continued employment is not the full amount of his paycheck. Rather, his compensation is only that amount above the pension benefits that he will not receive while he continues working. For example, in the matured pension situation, if the employee can receive retirement pay in the amount of X dollars without working, then his actual compensation for services rendered is not the amount of his paycheck, Y dollars, but Y minus X dollars. This is nothing more than a reapplication of the 'benefits foregone' formula of *Stenquist* [21 Cal.3d 779, 148 Cal.Rptr. 9, 582 P.2d 96]. [Fn. omitted.] Therefore, rather than pe-

nalizing the spouse for not retiring, the contrary is true—the community is being penalized because it is forced to subsidize the employee spouse's salary, which becomes his separate property." (Note, *In re Marriage of Stenquist: Tracing the Community Interest in Pension Rights Altered by Spousal Election, supra,* 67 Cal.L.Rev. 856, 879.)

Since this court does not find any taking of separate property, it is not necessary to discuss Earl's constitutional claim.

8. "Of course, the [respondent] spouse may seek a prospective modification of his or her support payments in light of any new partition of an asset not previously adjudicated." (*Henn v. Henn* (1980) 26 Cal.3d 323, 332, fn. 8, 161 Cal.Rptr. 502, 605 P.2d 10.)

re Marriage of Skaden (1977) 19 Cal.3d 679, 688–689, 139 Cal.Rptr. 615, 566 P.2d 249; *In re Marriage of Brown, supra,* 15 Cal.3d at p. 848, fn. 10, 126 Cal.Rptr. 633, 544 P.2d 561; *Phillipson v. Board of Administration, supra,* 3 Cal.3d at p. 46, 89 Cal.Rptr. 61, 473 P.2d 765.) This type of a division was not possible here since the trial court severed the issue of retirement benefits from the division of the remainder of the community property. At the time the retirement benefits were to be divided, the community property had already been distributed. As a result, there was no longer any community property which could be offset against the retirement benefits.

Frequently, parties are able to arrive at a reasonable settlement of these issues. (*In re Marriage of Skaden, supra,* 19 Cal.3d at pp. 688–689, 139 Cal.Rptr. 615, 566 P.2d 249.) For example, the nonemployee spouse may choose to wait, preferring to receive the retirement benefits when the employee spouse actually retires. The nonemployee may thereby ensure some protection for the future and may be able to share in the increased value of the pension plan. (See *In re Marriage of Adams, supra,* 64 Cal.App.3d at p. 186, 134 Cal.Rptr. 298.) [9] However, if the nonemployee spouse chooses to receive immediate payments, as Vera does, he or she has a right to do so. Any inequities caused by the immediate distribution of retirement benefits can be resolved through adjustments in spousal support.

There are various ways in which Earl could compensate Vera. He could "buy out" her share of the retirement benefits, paying her the present value of her share of the pension plan. (See Projector, *supra,* 50 L.A.Bar Bull. 229; Hardie, *Pay Now or Later: Alternatives in the Disposition of Retirement Benefits on Divorce* (1978) 53 State Bar J. 106). Or, he could begin to pay her a share of the retirement payments on a monthly basis. (E.g., *In re Marriage of Martin, supra,* 50 Cal.App.3d at p. 585, 123 Cal.Rptr. 634; *Bensing v. Bensing, supra,* 25 Cal.App.3d at pp. 893–894, 102 Cal.Rptr. 255.) Both of these methods of payment constitute an equal distribution of the benefits. However, the parties may have preferences based on numerous factors not presently before this court, including the tax consequences of the alternative plans. Therefore, the exact method of distribution must be left to the discretion of the trial court on remand.

III.

That portion of the trial court's order denying Vera's request for the immediate distribution of her share of Earl's retirement benefits is

---

9. The nonemployee spouse, of course, cannot have it both ways. The decision to ask for distribution of the retirement benefits before the employee spouse actually retires "constitutes an irrevocable election to give up increased payments in the future which might accrue due to increased age, longer service and a higher salary." (*In re* *Marriage of Luciano, supra,* 104 Cal.App.3d at p. 961, 164 Cal.Rptr. 93, citation omitted.) Thus, if Vera chooses to receive her share of the retirement benefits immediately, she will forfeit her right to share in the increased value of those benefits in the future.

reversed. The cause is remanded to the trial court for further proceedings consistent with the views expressed in this opinion.

TOBRINER, MOSK, RICHARDSON, NEWMAN, BARRY DEAL and KONGSGAARD, JJ., concur.

Notes

1. The Retirement Equity Act of 1984, which amended certain aspects of the Employees Retirement Income Security Act (ERISA), in accordance with the *Gillmore* decision recognizes the right of the non-employee spouse to receive his or her share of the community property portion of the benefits payable to the employee spouse as of the date the latter is eligible for retirement even though the employee spouse elects to continue working. This right may be secured by direct attachment of the plan. 29 U.S.C.A. § 206(d)(3)(E)(i)(II); see Wishard, *Deferred Compensation; Pensions and Benefits,* California Family Law Service § 13:26 at 612 (1986); J. Stein and J. Zuckerman, California Community Property § 5.24[5] (1986).

2. Assume that at the time of dissolution, the pension benefits of the employee spouse have not yet matured, and the court reserves jurisdiction to divide the benefits when the employee spouse becomes eligible for retirement rather than attempting a present valuation and division of the community property portion of the benefits. This "reserved jurisdiction" approach is consonant with the *Brown* decision; it also avoids the difficulties inherent in present valuation and allows the spouses to share both in the sums subsequently paid under the plan and in the risk of termination. Reppy, Community and Separate Interests in Pensions and Social Security Benefits After Marriage of Brown and ERISA, 25 UCLA L.Rev. 417, 428 (1978).

3. Suppose that the non-employee spouse dies before the benefits mature. What happens to his or her share of the unpaid benefits? In Waite v. Waite, 6 Cal.3d 461, 99 Cal.Rptr. 325, 492 P.2d 13 (1972), the California Supreme Court held that the non-employee spouse's rights terminate at death; hence the payments would go entirely to the employee spouse rather than to the heirs of the deceased spouse. The rationale for this rule, which came to be known as the "terminable interest" rule, was that retirement benefits are intended to support the parties during retirement and a deceased spouse no longer needs support. The terminable interest rule was widely criticized and was largely eroded by later cases. See, e.g., Bowman v. Bowman, 171 Cal.App.3d 148, 217 Cal.Rptr. 174 (1985); Chirmside v. Board of Admin., Pub. Employees Retirement Sys., 143 Cal.App.3d 205, 191 Cal. Rptr. 605 (1983); Culhane, Toward Pension Equality: A Reexamination of California's Terminable Interest Doctrine, 14 Sw.L.Rev. 613 (1984). Legislation subsequently abolished the terminable interest rule. West's Ann.Cal. Family Code § 2610 [formerly Civil Code § 4800.8] requires that the court, in dividing community property interests in any retirement plan, make whatever orders are necessary or appropriate to assure that each party receives a full community property share of any retirement plan. In an uncodified section, the legislature expressed its intent "to abolish the terminable interest rule * * * in order that retirement benefits shall be divided in accordance with Section 4800." Cal.Stats.1986, ch. 686, § 2. The statute does not require, however, that a retirement system be directed to designate

a divorcing nonemployee spouse as a 'surviving spouse' for the purposes of receiving survivor and death benefits on the later death of the employee spouse. In re Marriage of Carnall, 216 Cal.App.3d 1010, 265 Cal.Rptr. 271 (1989).

4. Note that not all retirement systems allow for direct payment to a nonemployee spouse before the employee spouse actually retires. Must such a system be required to make direct payment under *Gillmore?* This question was addressed in Marriage of Jensen, 235 Cal.App.3d 1137, 286 Cal. Rptr. 911 (1991). The husband had been employed by the Orange County District Attorney's office during the course of the marriage. At the time the couple separated, he was eligible to retire, but had elected not to. His spouse wanted immediate distribution of her interest in the Orange County Employees Retirement System plan (OCERS). OCERS objected, arguing that it was not required to disburse any funds until the employee spouse actually retired. The appellate court agreed with OCERS:

> The question presented is whether a public pension plan, such as OCERS, may be required, in the absence of specific provision in the plan, to disburse vested and matured community property retirement funds to a *nonemployee* spouse before the *employee* spouse actually retires. A similar issue was addressed recently in *In re Marriage of Nice* (1991) 230 Cal.App.3d 444, 281 Cal.Rptr. 415.

> The husband in *Nice* was employed by the City of Los Angeles. Like Melvin, he had opted to continue working after separating from his wife, although he was eligible for retirement. His wife, however, wished to begin receiving her share of the community pension immediately. Citing Civil Code section 4800.8 and *In re Marriage of Gillmore* (1981) 29 Cal.3d 418, 174 Cal.Rptr. 493, 629 P.2d 1, the court ordered the Board of Pension Commissioners to commence making payments.

> The appellate court reversed. It noted *Gillmore* "nowhere requires the pension plan to pay instead of the employee spouse. Instead, *Gillmore's* sketch of the possibilities seems to make clear that the employee spouse—not the pension plan—must compensate the nonemployee spouse. The trial court retains discretion over the exact method of distribution. That discretion, however, does not appear to include shifting the responsibility for compensating the nonemployee spouse to a third party. While continuing employment, the employee spouse retains responsibility for compensating the nonemployee spouse whose community property interest has been impaired by the employee spouse's decision to continue employment. [Citation.]" (*Id.* at p. 450, 174 Cal.Rptr. 493, 629 P.2d 1.) In essence, said the appellate court, "the trial court's order required the pension plan to pay benefits earlier than it would otherwise have had to do so, and to pay benefits while the employee spouse was still working, something it was not contractually obligated to do." (*Ibid.*)

> We agree with *Nice's* holding. *Gillmore* permits a nonemployee spouse to begin receiving his or her share of retirement benefits as soon as the employee spouse becomes *eligible* to retire. The rationale for that holding was that "[a] unilateral choice to postpone retirement cannot be manipulated so as to impair a spouse's interest in those

retirement benefits.'' (*In re Marriage of Gillmore, supra,* 29 Cal.3d at p. 423, 174 Cal.Rptr. 493, 629 P.2d 1.) However, *Gillmore* does not identify the person or entity from whom the nonemployee spouse is to receive payment. Rather, noting there were various ways in which the employee spouse could "buy out" the nonemployee spouse's share and recognizing the parties may have preferences based on numerous factors not presently before the court, including tax consequences, the court left to the discretion of the trial court on remand the exact method of distribution. (*Id.* at p. 429, 174 Cal.Rptr. 493, 629 P.2d 1.) One possible scenario depicted payment by the employee spouse of an amount equivalent to the nonemployee spouse's interest. (*Id.* at p. 427, 174 Cal.Rptr. 493, 629 P.2d 1.) But the *Gillmore* court said nothing which, in our view, could be construed as placing the onus on the retirement plan.

Moreover, the terms and conditions of OCERS, as set forth in sections 31450 et seq. of the Government Code, do not permit the payment of benefits before the employee spouse retires. Pursuant to Government Code section 31673, a member of OCERS is eligible to receive a retirement allowance only "upon retirement." Government Code section 31672 provides that a member who meets the qualifications for retirement "may be retired upon filing with the board a written application, setting forth the date upon which he [or she] desires his [or her] retirement to become effective...." And, Government Code section 31680 suggests that an employee must actually stop working in order to receive retirement benefits.

Respondents acknowledge that the county retirement plan, unlike PERS and STRS, does not specifically provide for payment of benefits to a nonmember spouse. They also recognize it is impermissible for a court to make orders which enlarge the liability of the retirement plan beyond that which is required by contract. Nonetheless, they insist Civil Code section 4800.8 mandates the action taken by the trial court. They are wrong.

As OCERS points out, the legislative intent behind this statute was to abolish the terminable interest rule "in order that retirement benefits shall be divided in accordance with [Civil Code] Section 4800." (Stats. 1986, ch. 686, § 2.) As we explained in *In re Marriage of Carnall, supra,* 216 Cal.App.3d 1010, 265 Cal.Rptr. 271, the objective of section 4800.8 "is to ensure that [wife] and others similarly situated receive their full and fair community share of a spouse's retirement plan." (*Id.* at p. 1023, 265 Cal.Rptr. 271.) The statute does not, however, permit the court to alter the terms of a contract.

Civil Code section 4800.8, as amended in 1988 (Stats.1988, ch. 542, eff. June 1, 1988), requires and empowers the trial court to do whatever is "necessary or appropriate" to ascertain that each spouse receives his or her full share of the community retirement plan, whether public or private, including but not limited to ordering the division of accumulated contributions pursuant to Government Code section 21215 et seq. and Education Code section 22650 et seq. (Civ.Code, § 4800, subds. (c) & (d).) In other words, the statute merely safeguards the spouses' respective interests by ordering the division of the community retirement plan *in accordance with the plan;* it does not circumscribe the manner in which the division of retirement benefits will be accomplished.

Rather, it is the retirement plans themselves, as spelled out in Government Code section 21215 (PERS) and Education Code section 22650 (STRS), which authorize the distribution of accumulated contributions to nonemployee spouses. A trial court has no authority to require disbursement of retirement benefits *other than as set forth in the plan.*

We are sympathetic to respondents' position. Indeed, as stated in Statutes 1988, chapter 542, section 8, "It is the intent of the Legislature that this act apply to *all public retirement benefits* in which there is an undivided community property interest and in all dissolution of marriage or legal separation cases which are pending on the effective date of this act or in which the court has reserved jurisdiction over the benefit or not yet awarded the benefit." (Italics added.) However, our hands are tied.

The county retirement plan does not provide for distribution of benefits to a nonemployee spouse before the employee spouse actually retires. Accordingly, OCERS did not anticipate making such payments. Until such time as the plan is amended by the Legislature, neither Civil Code section 4800.8 nor *In re Marriage of Gillmore, supra,* 29 Cal.3d 418, 174 Cal.Rptr. 493, 629 P.2d 1, authorizes the action taken by the trial court.

The judgment is reversed and the matter is remanded to the trial court with directions to revise the judgment to provide that until such time as Melvin elects to retire, OCERS is not required to distribute to Jeanne her interest in Melvin's retirement benefits.

IN RE MARRIAGE OF HUG

California District Court of Appeal, 1984.
154 Cal.App.3d 780, 201 Cal.Rptr. 676.

KING, ASSOCIATE JUSTICE.

* * *

Maria and Paul were married on April 31, 1956, and separated on June 9, 1976. On November 6, 1972, Paul left a position with International Business Machines, Inc. (IBM) to begin employment at Amdahl. While employed at Amdahl, he was granted options to purchase 3,100 shares of Amdahl's stock. The trial court found that the stock option plan was adopted "for the purpose of attracting and retaining the services of selected directors, executives and other key employees and for the purpose of providing an incentive to encourage and stimulate increased efforts by them."

Amdahl granted the first of the disputed options on August 9, 1974, an option to purchase 1,000 shares at $1.00 per share. The trial court found that this option "replaced" an earlier option to purchase 1,000 shares at $20.00 per share which had been awarded on November 22, 1972, just two weeks after Paul commenced employment at Amdahl. Paul and Amdahl mutually rescinded the 1972 agreement in August of 1974. Amdahl also granted the second option on August 9, 1974, for 1,300 shares at $1.00 per share. Amdahl granted a third option for 800 shares on September 15, 1975, at $5.00 per share. Each of the options was exercisable over four years each in yearly increments of 30%, 25%, 25%, and 20%.

Since portions of the options were exercisable only after the parties' separation, the court sought to allocate the options to reflect the relationship between periods of Paul's community contribution in comparison to his overall contribution to earning the option rights. In other words, the trial court attempted to fairly allocate the stock options between compensation for services prior to and after the date of separation.[1]

Thus, the court found that "[t]he community property portion of the unexercised shares is the product of a fraction whose numerator is the length of service expressed in months by respondent [Paul] with Amdahl from the date of commencement of service to the date of separation of the parties and the denominator is the length of service expressed in months from the date of commencement of service to the date when an option could be first exercised, multiplied by the number of shares that could be purchased on the date of exercise." Application of this formula to the disputed 1,835 shares of Amdahl stock yielded the division noted above.

Paul agrees that an apportionment should be accomplished according to a time rule, but contends the trial court utilized an erroneous formula.[2] Paul contends that the proper time rule should begin as of the date of granting the option, not the date of commencement of employment, since the options were not granted an incentive to become employed by Amdahl. In addition, he argues that each annual option is a separate and distinct option which is compensation for services during that year, thus it accrues after the date of separation and should be totally his separate property.

Our research leads us to conclude that the issue before us, that of determining community and separate property interests in employee stock options granted to the employee's spouse prior to the date of separation but only exercisable thereafter, is an issue of first impression.

1. Post separation earnings of a spouse are the separate property of that spouse. (Civ.Code, § 5118.)

2. The term "time rule" has heretofore been primarily utilized to describe a formula for determining the community interest in retirement benefits according to the ratio of the length of employment between the date of marriage (or date of commencement of employment, if later) and the date of separation to the total length of employment. (*In re Marriage of Judd* (1977) 68 Cal.App.3d 515, 137 Cal.Rptr. 318; *In re Marriage of Adams* (1976) 64 Cal.App.3d 181, 134 Cal.Rptr. 298.)

Treatises which describe employee stock options in the context of general corporations law strongly suggest that contractual rights to such benefits vary so widely as to preclude the accuracy of any but the most general characterization of them. Thus, there is no compelling reason to require that employee stock options must always be classified as compensation exclusively for past, present, or future services. Rather, since the purposes underlying stock options differ, reference to the facts of each particular case must be made to reveal the features and implications of a particular employee stock option.

At the most general level, employment benefits such as stock options may be classified as an alternative to fixed salaries to secure optimal tax treatment.[3] (5 Fletcher, Cyclopedia Corporations (rev. ed. 1976) § 2136, p. 514.) In this sense, stock options fall into the same category as, for example, fringe benefits, health and welfare benefits, incentive compensation based on company profits, deferred compensation plans, and pension and profit-sharing arrangements. (1 Washington and Rothschild, Compensating the Corporate Executive (3d ed. 1962) pp. 29–30. See also Steadman, Increasing Management's Real Income Through Deferral and Stock Options (1960) 15 Bus.Law 764.)

Along with the general goal of structuring compensation favorably, other purposes accompany various benefit plans. "Bonus and profit-sharing arrangements may take various forms such as a stock-purchase option for a certain period, a management stock-purchase plan, or an employees' stock-purchase plan. The primary purpose of a company stock-option plan is the attraction and retention of executive, key or qualified personnel, and the granting of such option is considered a form of compensation * * *. The purchase of shares by the executive officers in connection with an employee stock-purchase plan which may give the privilege of obtaining shares on a large scale at less than the market price often amounts to a lucrative bonus." (5 Fletcher, *supra,* § 2143.1, at p. 551.) A number of factors may prompt companies to use such alternatives, among them management's wish for a direct share in company profits, the possibility of increasing management's incentive and efforts, cutting taxes and providing security for the executive. (1 Washington and Rothschild, *supra,* at p. 30.)

If any of the various purposes of stock option plans can be said to bear emphasis, it is probably that of providing incentive. "One of the most widespread programs for providing employees with additional incentive and creating an identification of interest between the company and the key employees is a stock option plan." (The Lawyer's Basic

---

3. The tax benefits to an employee of qualified stock option plans can be substantial, if the employer is a company with a high potential which is achieved by the time the options are exercisable. In Paul's case, for example, if Amdahl stock is selling for $20.00 when his options are exercisable he will pay only $1.00 or $5.00 (his option price), yet he will receive stock worth $20.00 a share, with no recognizable taxable gain. Presumably he will refrain from selling the stock until the gain qualifies for capital gains treatment. Thus, Paul will not only receive a substantial gain, but it will be taxed at the highly favorable capital gains rate, rather than the higher rate charged if the same sum were paid to him as salary taxable as ordinary income.

Corporate Practice Manual (ALI 2d ed. 1978) § 8.06, p. 130.) "Share options are a form of incentive compensation based on the idea that good management results in higher prices which render the share option valuable." (Henne, Corporations (2d ed. 1970) § 248, p. 492. See also Steadman, Stock Options and Other Executive Incentive Arrangements (1959) 13 Vand.L.Rev. 311, 314–315.)

Consistent with the emphasis on incentive is the supposition that options are granted for future services, either primarily or exclusively. This proposition appears bolstered by the general rule that option agreements must ordinarily be supported by consideration, and that "[i]n practice, consideration will usually be supplied by the executive in the form of continued services." (2 Washington and Rothschild, Compensating the Corporate Executive (3d ed. 1962) p. 575.)

Nevertheless, the temptation to conclude that options are earned exclusively by future services lessens somewhat in light of the flexibility and variety of option plans, as well as the size and circumstances of the offering company. "For the smaller company, for the company without substantial cash resources, for the company in distressed circumstances, stock options may provide a means of attracting strong management willing to render its services for modest current compensation in return for substantial future rewards on a tax-favored basis." (2 Washington and Rothschild, *supra,* at p. 571.) Although the purpose of providing incentive remains in the latter situation (and such an arrangement may be geared to future services as well) the primary goal appears to be *deferring compensation for present services.* At the least, such a use of stock options seems consistent with providing compensation for *either* present or future services, just as would its use as a bonus, noted in the description above. Further, the incentive and future service emphasis of stock options diminishes somewhat in view of their ready susceptibility to modification, which frequently dissolves the distinctions among them. (*Ibid.*)

Finally, stock options may be used as additional compensation, *even for past services,* so long as to meet reasonable expectations as to such compensation which existed while the employee rendered the services. (2 Washington and Rothschild, *supra,* at p. 578.) Also, although out of keeping with common business practice, companies frequently provide rewards or bonuses for past services. (5 Fletcher, *supra,* § 2143, at p. 538.)

Thus, no single characterization can be given to employee stock options. Whether they can be characterized as compensation for future services, for past services, or for both, depends upon the circumstances involved in the grant of the employee stock option.

In the instant case, the trial court found that the stock option agreement arose from the standard corporate purpose of "attracting and retaining the services of selected directors, executives and other key employees and for the purpose of providing an incentive to encourage and stimulate increased efforts by them." Since the options are keyed to periods of employment after the date of each grant, Paul argues that the options constitute compensation exclusively for future services rather than past or present services. For that reason, he says the period of employment prior to the granting of the option to him contributed nothing to earning the options and should be excluded from the time frame by which the court calculated its "time rule" allocation formula.

Treatment of the other types of deferred compensation suggest that Paul's contention relies too heavily on a single feature of the option agreement: the periods of time set as a prerequisite to exercising the options. Decisions applying the type of time rule in question have been willing to adjust the rule to the requirements of particular cases.

* * *

These cases amplify the message * * * that in the context of marital property settlement the rights to benefits of various kinds derive from any number of sources. Benefits may be a function of longevity or time, or of the nature or frequency of services rendered. The receipt of benefits may be perceived entirely apart from any period of service and turn instead on the purpose for which they were created.

* * *

By including the two years prior to the granting of the options in question, the trial court impliedly found that period of service contributed to earning the option rights in issue. (See *Elliot v. Jensen* (1960) 187 Cal.App.2d 389, 393, 9 Cal.Rptr. 642 [subsidiary findings necessary to support the judgment are implied].) Substantial evidence supports this finding. Prior to becoming employed by Amdahl, Paul had worked for IBM Corporation for nearly seven years, at which point his retirement benefits, according to Maria's testimony, would have vested. In this context, the timing of such a critical career move apparently led the court to infer that inducements offered by Amdahl to some extent replaced the benefits left behind at IBM. Additionally, as noted above, Amdahl's option plan was designed to attract as well as to retain key employees. The parties discussed the implications of Paul's jump to Amdahl, and the offer of stock in some form seems to have been a key inducement to making the move. These facts support an implied finding that the options were earned from the commencement of Paul's employment at Amdahl.

The evidence further shows that providing incentive was far from Amdahl's only purpose in granting the options. The record shows that Paul anticipated the options from the outset and that Amdahl, in part, likely granted them in lieu of present compensation during the initial period of Paul's employment, a time when Amdahl's success was limited. Assuming the evidence demonstrated to the court's satisfaction that option rights represented deferred compensation for present services, the court was justified in finding that the option rights were earned in part during the first two years.

* * *

In sum, the evidence supports a finding that the options were earned from the outset of Paul's service with Amdahl. The trial court impliedly arrived at this determination by considering the compensation scheme as a whole, including the implications of Paul's move from IBM and the place option rights occupied in the entire context of his service. Additionally, another option agreement took the place of the first, indicating that options were a critical feature in the total scheme of compensation. Paul's emphasis on the fact that the options, as is usually the case, became exercisable after specific periods of service subsequent to their granting diminishes in relation to the details of the entire employment circumstance.

Nothing in the makeup of the Amdahl stock option plan requires that they be construed as compensation exclusively for future services. Further, case law suggests that the time provisions of a compensation plan not be too literally construed, at least in the context of marital property, lest courts overlook the realities of when and how compensation is earned, as well as the purposes behind it. (E.g., *In re Marriage of Poppe, supra,* 97 Cal.App.3d at p. 1, 158 Cal.Rptr. 500.)

* * *

Considering the frequency with which employee stock options are provided as part of key employee compensation packages, it is surprising that the allocation of community and separate property interests therein has not previously been addressed by California's appellate courts. Although we approve the use of the time rule fashioned by the trial court under the facts of this case, we stress that no single rule or formula is applicable to every dissolution case involving employee stock options. Trial courts should be vested with broad discretion to fashion approaches which will achieve the most equitable results under the facts of each case.

Undoubtedly there are other factual circumstances where the application of the time rule approved here would also achieve an equitable result. * * * [I]t is possible that equity could require a determination that stock options are solely the separate property of the employee spouse. An employee spouse can be expected to make this argument as to options granted after the date of separation and certainly for any granted after the dissolution of the marriage. Since the community interest in the employee options under the time rule we approve, commences with the date of employment, four years before the granting of the options, it could be argued by a nonemployee spouse that options granted to the employee spouse four years after the dissolution has occurred would contain a community interest therein. We want to make clear that by approving the time rule fixing the community interest in Paul's options beginning at a point in time four years before he and Maria separated, when his employment commenced with Amdahl, we do not mean to imply that stock options Paul may be granted after the divorce will be subject to a similar time rule and therefore possess a community interest. That issue is not before us.[4]

We mention the foregoing alternatives to emphasize that the trial court should exercise its discretion to fashion an equitable allocation of separate and community interests in employee stock options exercisable by the employee spouse after the date of separation of the parties. We recognize that were we to adopt an inflexible rule, it might help litigating spouses and their counsel settle option disputes and, at the same time, provide an easy measure to be applied by trial courts. However, to do so would be to follow the recent tendency of appellate courts and the Legislature, which we decry, to adopt rules which on the surface are easy to apply and foster consistency yet, as applied, too often achieve inequitable results.[5]

In the 200 years since the formation of our country, its incredible population growth and the increasing complexity of both our society and our government have virtually eliminated the ability of the executive and legislative branches of our state and federal governments to be responsive to the problems and concerns of the individual citizen. The beauty of our system of justice is that the individual citizen still enjoys the opportunity to have the judicial branch of government, at both trial and appellate court levels, focus exclusively on his or her litigation. A special benefit of a system which allows for equitable considerations, especially in the family law field, is to afford the judge before whom the litigants appear, subject to applicable legal principles, the opportunity to fashion a remedy which achieves a just result. While critics may claim this results in inconsistency, we believe the strength of the judicial system is enhanced when the judiciary possesses the ability in family law cases to tailor a remedy to fit the circumstances of the individual litigants before the court.

---

4. Claims of a community interest in employee stock options granted to the employee spouse after the dissolution of the marriage would appear too speculative and would lack the immediacy and specificity necessary for exercise of jurisdiction over them. (See *In re Marriage of Fonstein* (1976) 17 Cal.3d 738, 131 Cal.Rptr. 873, 552 P.2d 1169; see also *Weinberg v. Weinberg* (1967) 67 Cal.2d 557, 63 Cal.Rptr. 13, 432 P.2d 709.)

5. A recent example of appellate courts limiting trial court discretion by developing a simple and inflexible rule is *In re Marriage of Lucas* (1980) 27 Cal.3d 808, 166 Cal.Rptr. 853, 614 P.2d 285, which held that the separate property of one spouse placed in joint tenancy with the other becomes their community property, absent an agreement or understanding to the contrary. This is a simple rule, easy to apply, and inflexible. The difficulty with it is that it ignores normal human conduct in marriages and the fact that the transferring party usually acts without legal advice and with no understanding of the legal consequences while, at the same time, assuming that the marriage is going to last forever.

The apparently unforeseen inequities which resulted from this simple, inflexible rule caused the Legislature to enact anti-*Lucas* legislation only three years later. (See Civ.Code, § 4800.2.) At the present session of the Legislature efforts are being undertaken in the name of consistency to narrow and limit the discretion of trial courts in fixing child support. (See Assem.Bill No. 1527.) Such efforts, if successful, are just as certain to lead to inequitable results. The lesson to appellate courts and the Legislature should be that, subject to the application of proper legal principles, because of the variety and complexity of factual circumstances which occur in marital relationships, trial courts should have broad discretion to achieve equity for the litigants who appear before them.

Finally, by approving a time rule allocating community and separate property interests in employee stock options in this case, we reach a result which continues Paul and Maria's joint ownership interests in the community options. We do not suggest that this will always be the proper method of distribution of employee stock options. For example, some stock options are publicly traded or can otherwise be valued, even though exercisable in the future. In either case, it would appear to be most equitable to fix the value of the community interests as of the date of separation and distribute the community interests to the employee spouse, awarding other community property of equivalent value to the nonemployee spouse in order to achieve the equal division of community property required by Civil Code section 4800, subdivision (a). Employee stock options are normally exercisable on the condition that the employee remain with the employer and, as between the spouses, that is obviously within the control of the employee spouse. Additionally, to whatever extent an increase in the value of the company stock results from the employee's performance, or a decrease in the value of the stock occurs because of the company's poor performance or the economy, or because the employee terminates his employment, the risk of such rewards or losses is best borne by the employee spouse.

The trial court properly exercised its discretion in fashioning the time rule it utilized to equitably allocate the separate and community property interests in the Amdahl employee stock options. Paul's arguments to the contrary overlook the community interests in contractual rights earned during the marriage as a factor of employee compensation.

The judgment is affirmed.

Low, P.J., and Haning, J., concur.

Notes

1. The employer's reasons for granting the stock options may be an important factor in their classification as community or separate property and in the apportionment method to be utilized. For example, in Marriage of Nelson, 177 Cal.App.3d 150, 157–58, 222 Cal.Rptr. 790, 795 (1986), the court noted that the employer's intent was to compensate the employee for future as opposed to past efforts, and indicated that this factor could properly be taken into account in devising an apportionment formula. Similarly, in Marriage of Harrison, 179 Cal.App.3d 1216, 225 Cal.Rptr. 234 (1986), the fact that the option represented "golden handcuffs" to assure that the employee spouse would stay with the company rather than deferred compensation for past services was viewed as a significant factor supporting the trial court's method of apportionment. For a discussion of the *Hug*, *Nelson* and *Harrison* cases, see 2 California Family Law Monthly 399 (1986).

2. In addition to receiving stock options, the employee spouse in the *Nelson* case noted above also received a year end bonus of $9000 after the parties had separated. The trial court's finding that the bonus was entirely separate property was affirmed on appeal. The employee spouse had testified that although he had received similar bonuses in the past, there was no contract associated with the bonuses, that some employees had received

lesser amounts or none at all, and that the company made the decision at the end of each year. The appellate court held that on the basis of this testimony, the trial court could properly conclude that at the time of separation, the employee spouse had only "an expectancy" of a year end bonus. In re Marriage of Nelson, 177 Cal.App.3d 150, 158, 222 Cal.Rptr. 790, 795 (1986).

B. Disability Benefits

The California courts traditionally viewed workers' compensation and disability benefits as being analogous to personal injury damages and classified them accordingly. In support of this analogy, the courts reasoned that disability pay does not represent deferred compensation for past services but rather serves as compensation for the personal anguish, pain and suffering caused by permanent disability as well as for the loss of earnings resulting from premature retirement and from the diminished ability to compete in the job market.[60] Thus disability pay was deemed to be more comparable to personal injury damages than to retirement benefits.[61] The statutes then in effect classified personal injury damages received during marriage as community property; amounts received after dissolution were classified as separate property.[62] Therefore only disability payments received during marriage were classified as community property. The right to payments subsequent to dissolution was deemed the "separate and personal right" of the disabled spouse.[63] In the Stenquist[64] decision and in the Saslow[65] case reprinted in this Section, the California Supreme Court reassessed the classification of disability payments, and concluded that under certain circumstances post-dissolution disability payments may be subject to classification as community property.

IN RE MARRIAGE OF SASLOW
Supreme Court of California, 1985.
40 Cal.3d 848, 221 Cal.Rptr. 546, 710 P.2d 346.

BIRD, CHIEF JUSTICE.

Where disability insurance policies are purchased during marriage with community funds, but the benefits are received after the parties have separated, are the benefits the separate property of the disabled spouse?

---

60. In re Marriage of Jones, 13 Cal.3d 457, 462, 119 Cal.Rptr. 108, 111–112, 531 P.2d 420, 423–424 (1975).

61. Id. Workers' compensation awards received similar treatment, although the courts recognized that pain and suffering were not generally elements of a workers' compensation award. In re Marriage of McDonald, 52 Cal.App.3d 509, 125 Cal.Rptr. 160 (1975).

62. In 1980 California Civil Code section 5126 was amended to make the classification dependent on when the cause of ac-

tion arose rather than on when the damages were received.

63. In re Marriage of Jones, 13 Cal.3d 457, 464, 119 Cal.Rptr. 108, 113, 531 P.2d 420, 425 (1975).

64. In re Marriage of Stenquist, 21 Cal.3d 779, 148 Cal.Rptr. 9, 582 P.2d 96 (1978).

65. In re Marriage of Saslow, 40 Cal.3d 848, 221 Cal.Rptr. 546, 710 P.2d 346 (1985), reprinted in this Section.

I.

After 18 years of marriage, Eileen and Ernest Saslow (hereafter wife and husband respectively) separated in 1975.

During the marriage, the husband purchased several disability insurance policies payable upon his disability. He paid the premiums with community funds. Although the couple owned several orange groves, a residence, some stocks, and eight life insurance policies, the husband did not invest in a retirement or pension plan.

Prior to 1972, the husband had an active private medical practice as an allergist. He was forced to close his office in 1972 because of long-standing psychological problems. The deposition testimony of his psychiatrist indicated that the husband, who was 59 years old at the time of trial in 1978, was likely to remain disabled for the rest of his life. The wife suffers from Hodgkin's disease.

When he was unable to continue his practice and while the parties were still married, the husband began to receive benefits payable under the disability policies. The benefits totaled $2,181 per month until the husband reached the age of 60, when one of the policies expired and the benefits were reduced to $1,881 per month. A second policy will expire and the benefits from another policy will decrease when the husband reaches age 70, reducing the monthly payments to $631. When the husband reaches age 75, a third policy will expire and the benefits will be reduced to $506 per month. That amount will be payable each month until the husband's death.

The trial court entered an interlocutory decree of dissolution on May 15, 1978, but reserved jurisdiction to determine the division of property. After an eight-day trial, the court found the bulk of the couple's substantial assets to belong to the community and divided them equally. The future benefits to be paid to the husband from the disability policies were found to be his separate property. He was ordered to pay half of the benefits as spousal support.

The wife's primary argument on appeal is that the benefits from the disability policies, which were purchased with community funds, are community property and must be divided equally between the parties upon dissolution. She notes, correctly, that although she is receiving spousal support equivalent to half of the disability payments, "[spousal support] lies within the discretion of the trial court and may be modified with changing circumstances: 'the spouse "should not be dependent on the discretion of the court * * * to provide her with the equivalent of what should be hers as a matter of absolute right."'" (*In re Marriage of Stenquist* (1978) 21 Cal.3d 779, 787, fn. 8, 148 Cal.Rptr. 9, 582 P.2d 96, hereafter *Stenquist;* accord *In re Marriage of Brown* (1976) 15 Cal.3d 838, 848, 126 Cal.Rptr. 633, 544 P.2d 561.)

* * *

II.

Although this court has twice addressed the status of a disability *pension* in the context of a marital dissolution, the court has never directly addressed the status of benefits from private disability insurance policies purchased with community funds.[1]

In *In re Marriage of Jones* (1975) 13 Cal.3d 457, 119 Cal.Rptr. 108, 531 P.2d 420 (hereafter *Jones*), the issue was whether a military disability pension received by an ex-serviceman, who had not acquired a vested right to retirement pension benefits, was his separate property or the property of the community. This court held that the disability pension was his separate property. (*Id.*, at p. 461, 119 Cal.Rptr. 108, 531 P.2d 420.)

However, the rationale underlying the *Jones* decision has been substantially eroded, leaving it with little continued validity. In *Jones*, this court held that a serviceman's right to disability pay acquired *before* he had a vested right to a retirement pension was not a community asset. (*Jones, supra,* 13 Cal.3d at p. 461, 119 Cal.Rptr. 108, 531 P.2d 420.) At the time *Jones* was decided, only vested rights to retirement benefits were considered to be community assets. (*French v. French* (1941) 17 Cal.2d 775, 778, 112 P.2d 235.) The *French* case was overruled in *In re Marriage of Brown, supra,* 15 Cal.3d at p. 851, 126 Cal.Rptr. 633, 544 P.2d 561. The holding in *Brown* "undermine[d] the fundamental premise of *Jones:* that the award of a serviceman's 'disability' pension to the serviceman as his separate property would not impair any community interest of his spouse." (*Stenquist, supra,* 21 Cal.3d at p. 785, 148 Cal.Rptr. 9, 582 P.2d 96.)

The *Jones* court also characterized disability payments as more analogous to personal injury damages than to retirement pay. (*Jones, supra,* 13 Cal.3d at pp. 462–464, 119 Cal.Rptr. 108, 531 P.2d 420.) At the time *Jones* was decided, personal injury damages received after the

---

1. Other community property jurisdictions are not uniform in their characterization of disability benefits as community or separate property. (See generally Annot. (1979) 94 A.L.R.3d 176, 222–229.) In Idaho, New Mexico and Texas, disability benefits of several types have been treated as community property. (*Guy v. Guy* (1977), 98 Idaho 205, 560 P.2d 876 [group term disability policy]; *Hughes v. Hughes* (1981) 96 N.M. 719, 634 P.2d 1271 [civil service disability policy]; *Busby v. Busby* (Tex. 1970) 457 S.W.2d 551 [disability retirement benefits]; *Grost v. Grost* (Tex.App.1978) 561 S.W.2d 223 [same]; *Anthony v. Anthony* (Tex.App.1981) 624 S.W.2d 388 [federal workers' compensation benefits, to the extent that they replaced civil service disability benefits].) In other states, the status of disability benefits is less clear. For example, Washington has cases going both ways. (See *Chase v. Chase* (1968), 74 Wash.2d 253, 444 P.2d 145 [lump sum disability payment community property]; *Marriage of Huteson* (1980) 27 Wash.App. 539, 619 P.2d 991 [state-mandated disability retirement benefits separate property]; *Ross v. Pearson* (1982) 31 Wash.App. 609, 643 P.2d 928 [privately purchased disability policy community property]; *In re Marriage of Kittleson* (1978) 21 Wash.App. 344, 585 P.2d 167 [refusal to adopt "inflexible rule"].) The law in Arizona also seems unsettled. (See, e.g., *Flowers v. Flowers* (1978) 118 Ariz. 577, 578 P.2d 1006 [federal civil service disability policy and privately purchased disability policy both community property]; *Rickman v. Rickman* (1980), 124 Ariz. 507, 605 P.2d 909 [veteran's disability benefits separate property]; *Villasenor v. Villasenor* (1982) 134 Ariz. 476, 657 P.2d 889 [disability retirement pension divided into community and separate property components].)

couple separated were the separate property of the injured spouse. (*Id.,* at pp. 462–463, 119 Cal.Rptr. 108, 531 P.2d 420; *Washington v. Washington* (1956) 47 Cal.2d 249, 254, 302 P.2d 569; former Civ.Code, § 5126.)[2] Here, too, the law has changed.

Civil Code section 5126, which governs the treatment of personal injury damages in dissolution proceedings, was amended in 1979. (Stats.1979, ch. 638, § 3, p. 1971.) As a result, personal injury damages from a cause of action which arises during the marriage are now classified as a community asset, even if they are received after separation.[3] Hence, another fundamental premise of the *Jones* decision is no longer valid.[4]

This court most recently addressed the status of a disability retirement pension in *In re Marriage of Stenquist, supra,* 21 Cal.3d 779, 148 Cal.Rptr. 9, 582 P.2d 96. In *Stenquist,* the husband lost a limb, but remained in military service for 17 more years. At retirement, the husband, whose right to a retirement pension had vested, was entitled to take regular "retirement" pay at the rate of 65 percent of his basic pay or "disability" pay at the higher rate of 75 percent. Assuming that he would prefer the higher rate, the Army began to pay him disability benefits.

2. Prior to 1979, Civil Code section 5126 provided that "(a) All money or other property received by a married person in satisfaction of a judgment for damages for personal injuries * * * is the separate property of the injured person *if such money or other property is received* * * * [¶] (1) After the rendition of a decree of legal separation or a final judgment of dissolution of a marriage. [¶] (2) While either spouse, if he or she is the injured person, is living separate from the other spouse. [¶] (3) After the rendition of an interlocutory decree of dissolution of a marriage. * * *" (Stats.1969, ch. 1608, § 8, p. 3342, amended by Stats.1970, ch. 1575, § 5, p. 3286 and Stats.1972, ch. 905, § 1, p. 1609, emphasis added.)

3. After the 1979 amendment, the pertinent part of section 5126 reads: "(a) All money or other property received or to be received by a person in satisfaction of a judgment for damages for personal injuries * * * is the separate property of the injured person *if the cause of action for such damages arose* as follows: [¶] (1) After the rendition of a decree of legal separation or a final judgment of dissolution of a marriage. [¶] (2) While either spouse * * * is living separately from the other spouse. [¶] (3) After the rendition of an interlocutory decree of dissolution of a marriage." (Stats. 1979, ch. 638, § 3, p. 1971; emphasis added.)

4. While personal injury damages from a cause of action which arises during the marriage are now community property (Civ. Code, § 5126), the method for assignment of those damages upon dissolution of the marriage is different than the assignment of other types of community property. Subdivision (a) of Civil Code section 4800 provides that community property shall be divided equally. However, subdivision (c) creates an exception. "Notwithstanding subdivision (a), community property personal injury damages shall be assigned to the party who suffered the injuries unless the court, after taking into account the economic condition and needs of each party, the time that has elapsed since the recovery of the damages or the accrual of the cause of action, and all other facts of the case, determines that the interests of justice require another disposition. In such a case, the community property personal injury damages shall be assigned to the respective parties in such proportions as the court determines to be just, except that at least one-half of the damages shall be assigned to the party who suffered the injuries * * *." (Civ.Code, § 4800, subd. (c).) This provision represents an exception to the otherwise strict rule in California that community property must be divided equally. (See Civ.Code, § 4800, subd. (a); *In re Marriage of Juick* (1971) 21 Cal.App.3d 421, 427, 98 Cal.Rptr. 324.)

In the dissolution proceeding which was commenced after the husband's retirement, the trial court ruled that the portion of his disability pension benefits that was equivalent to what he would have been entitled to under the ordinary retirement pension constituted a community asset. (*Id.,* at p. 783, 148 Cal.Rptr. 9, 582 P.2d 96.) Only that portion of the disability payments which could be attributed to military service prior to the marriage and the portion of the payments which *exceeded* the regular retirement pension were held to be his separate property. (*Id.,* at p. 788, 148 Cal.Rptr. 9, 582 P.2d 96.)

In affirming the trial court's disposition, this court articulated two rationales. First, it held that it could not "permit the serviceman's election of a 'disability' pension to defeat the community interest in his right to a pension based on longevity." (*Stenquist, supra,* 21 Cal.3d at p. 786, 148 Cal.Rptr. 9, 582 P.2d 96.) Such a result would "violate the settled principle that one spouse cannot, by invoking a condition wholly within his control, defeat the community interest of the other spouse." (*Ibid.*) It would unjustly deprive the wife of a valuable property right " 'simply because a misleading label has been affixed to [the] husband's pension fund benefits.' " (*Id.,* at pp. 786–787, 148 Cal.Rptr. 9, 582 P.2d 96.)

Second, the *Stenquist* court discussed the purposes of a military disability pension. Such pensions were said to function in part to compensate the veteran for lost earnings and personal suffering caused by the disability. To that extent they were held to constitute separate property. (*Stenquist, supra,* 21 Cal.3d at pp. 787–788, 148 Cal.Rptr. 9, 582 P.2d 96.)

However, the court recognized that a "disability" pension received later in life might function principally as a retirement pension. (*Ibid.*) Indeed, the court found that the "primary objective" of the disability pension in *Stenquist* was to provide retirement support. Therefore, it held that the portion of the disability pension that was equivalent to the regular retirement pension was community property. (*Id.,* at pp. 788–789, 148 Cal.Rptr. 9, 582 P.2d 96.)

Following the *Stenquist* decision, several Courts of Appeal have held that the portion of employer-provided disability benefits that functions as retirement pay must be treated as community property. (*In re Marriage of Justice* (1984) 157 Cal.App.3d 82, 204 Cal.Rptr. 6; *In re Marriage of Pace* (1982) 132 Cal.App.3d 548, 183 Cal.Rptr. 314; *In re Marriage of Samuels* (1979) 96 Cal.App.3d 122, 158 Cal.Rptr. 38; *In re Marriage of Webb* (1979) 94 Cal.App.3d 335, 156 Cal.Rptr. 334.) These courts reasoned that when the employee-spouse reaches the age at which he would be eligible for a retirement pension, "the predominate purpose of his [disability] benefits [ ] shift[s] to retirement support." (*In re Marriage of Pace, supra,* 132 Cal.App.3d at p. 553, 183 Cal.Rptr. 314.)

Accordingly, disability benefits have been denominated community property to the extent that they equal the benefits foregone under a retirement pension. (*Ibid.*) Courts have determined the age at which the "shift" in purpose to retirement support takes place by looking to the age of retirement eligibility specified in the employment contract. (See, e.g., *id.,* at pp. 550–551, 183 Cal.Rptr. 314 [age 55]; *In re Marriage of Justice, supra,* 157 Cal.App.3d at p. 89, 204 Cal.Rptr. 6; *In re Marriage of Samuels, supra,* 96 Cal.App.3d at p. 128, 158 Cal.Rptr. 38 [age 62]; *In re Marriage of Webb, supra,* 94 Cal.App.3d at pp. 339–340, 156 Cal.Rptr. 334 [age 50].)

The purpose analysis utilized in *Stenquist* and its progeny is more difficult to apply in the context of this case. The husband's disability payments may serve all of the purposes discussed in those cases. However, it is difficult to determine what portion of the benefits serves each purpose, since there is no alternative retirement pension with which to compare the disability payments. Similarly, it is difficult to determine the *age* at which the benefits cease to compensate for the husband's lost wages and begin to provide retirement support. Were it not for his disability, the husband, as a self-employed physician, might have chosen to retire at 55 or he might have worked until he was 80.

There are two possible rules for apportionment of the disability benefits which would avoid the difficult factual determinations presented by this case. However, adoption of either of these rules would frequently result in inequitable distribution of property, contrary to "the protective philosophy of the community property law as set out in previous decisions of this court." (*Stenquist, supra,* 21 Cal.3d at p. 782, 148 Cal.Rptr. 9, 582 P.2d 96.)

First, this court could hold that "disability" benefits provided by private disability insurance policies are always the separate property of the disabled spouse. However, since all or a portion of such disability payments may serve a retirement function, their characterization as the separate property of the disabled spouse would often " 'deprive [the nondisabled spouse] of a valuable property right simply because a misleading label has been affixed to [the disabled spouse's] *pension* fund benefits.' " (*Stenquist, supra,* 21 Cal.3d at pp. 786–787, 148 Cal.Rptr. 9, 582 P.2d 96, quoting *In re Marriage of Cavnar* (1976) 62 Cal.App.3d 660, 665, 133 Cal.Rptr. 267, emphasis added.)

This court has already held that in the context of military disability pensions such an inequitable result is unwarranted. (*Stenquist, supra,* 21 Cal.3d 779, 148 Cal.Rptr. 9, 582 P.2d 96.) No reason exists to allow such a result when the disability benefits are paid pursuant to policies purchased with community funds from private insurance companies.

The other possible rule would be to characterize all disability policies which are purchased with community funds as community property. Such a rule would provide for easy apportionment of the benefits, and would be consistent with basic community property principles since the source of the benefits is community property. (See 7 Witkin, Summary of Cal.Law (8th ed.1974) Community Property, § 3, p. 5096.) But such a rule would also often lead to inequitable results.

The primary purpose of disability benefits is to compensate the disabled spouse for lost earnings—earnings which would normally be separate property after dissolution. (*Stenquist, supra,* 21 Cal.3d at p. 787, 148 Cal.Rptr. 9, 582 P.2d 96.) If post-dissolution disability benefits are held to be community property, a young ablebodied ex-spouse will be able to work and retain all his or her earnings, and will in addition be entitled to half the disability benefits of the disabled ex-spouse. This might impose a grave hardship on the disabled individual, who not only may not be able to work, but who may also require special equipment or extraordinary care.

In short, although application of the *Stenquist* purpose analysis may be difficult in this and other disability benefit cases, "[i]t does not impose a burden so heavy that for reasons of expediency [this court] must settle for the less equitable, all-or-nothing rule[s] [outlined above]." (*Stenquist, supra,* 21 Cal.3d at p. 785, fn. 4, 148 Cal.Rptr. 9, 582 P.2d 96.)

The approach taken by this court in *Stenquist* provides for the most equitable distribution of disability insurance benefits. This approach requires that the trial court treat disability benefits as separate property insofar as they are intended to replace postdissolution earnings that would have been the separate-property income of the disabled spouse, and treat the benefits as community property insofar as they are intended to provide retirement income.[5]

As indicated, especially in cases like the instant one, the determination of the intent of the parties regarding the purpose of the benefits will not always be easy. However, trial court judges have extensive experience in making such difficult factual determinations. The task is not so formidable that a simple, but inequitable, rule would be preferable.

Apportionment of the benefits need not be arbitrary or speculative. The court may consider testimony of the spouses' intent, both at the time the disability insurance was originally purchased and at the times that decisions were made to continue the insurance in force rather than let it lapse. Absent evidence of actual intent, the court may ascertain a normal retirement age at which the disabled spouse would have been most likely to retire had no disability occurred.

In fixing that age, the court may take into account any circumstances relevant to the normal expectations in the disabled spouse's

---

5. To the extent that it is inconsistent with the views expressed in this opinion, *In re Marriage of Donnelly* (1983) 142 Cal. App.3d 135, 190 Cal.Rptr. 756 is disapproved. The *Donnelly* court reasoned that the "income protection policy" at issue in that case was analogous to a life insurance policy purchased by the community during marriage, which is a community asset. (*Donnelly, supra,* 142 Cal.App.3d at p. 137, 190 Cal.Rptr. 756; *New York L. Ins. Co. v. Bank of Italy* (1923) 60 Cal.App. 602, 606, 214 P.2d 61.) However, life insurance proceeds, unlike disability insurance benefits, can never be considered a substitute for subsequent earnings that would be separate property if accrued after separation of the spouses. By its very nature, life insurance purchased during the marriage with community funds is designed to make resources available to the surviving spouse after all possibility of gainful employment has been terminated by death.

community or former workplace about the age at which a person having the spouse's occupation, qualifications, and vocational history would retire. There may be evidence of the ages at which similarly situated workers have retired. A range of expected retirement ages may be derived from such sources as the federal schemes for social security and for individual retirement accounts, or from the provisions in governmental or institutional retirement systems for retirement of particular classes of employees. The nature of the disability policies at issue may provide evidence of the parties' intent or expectations.

Although the end result may be inexact in many cases, this solution is likely to produce far less harm than a rigid holding that all proceeds from disability insurance policies are the separate property of the disabled spouse or, alternatively, that all proceeds are community property.

On remand, the trial court must determine the extent to which the disability policies at issue were intended to provide retirement protection to both parties in their later years. The evidence indicates that rather than investing in a retirement plan, the husband chose to utilize community funds to purchase extensive disability coverage. With his long history of psychological problems, he may have been aware that he might not be able to continue the practice of medicine due to his disability.

There is no evidence that at the time the policies were purchased the parties contemplated dissolution. The husband may have chosen to protect the community's financial future through disability insurance rather than a retirement pension. Thus, the trial court may determine that the disability benefits in this case are entirely community property.

Alternatively, the court may determine that at least some portion of the benefits was intended as a substitute for the husband's future preretirement earnings. This portion of the benefits, if received after the parties' separation, must be denominated the husband's separate property.[6]

* * *

The community property interest in benefits from a disability insurance policy purchased during marriage with community funds must be determined according to the analysis used by this court in *In re Marriage of Stenquist, supra,* 21 Cal.3d 779, 148 Cal.Rptr. 9, 582 P.2d 96. That portion of the benefits intended by the parties to provide retirement support must be denominated community property. The portion of the benefits, if any, which was intended by the parties to replace the husband's lost earnings in the event of his disability must be considered his separate property. In this case, the trial court erroneously found that the benefits were the separate property of the disabled spouse.

---

6. As previously noted, the trial court ordered the husband to pay the wife half of the disability payments as spousal support. On remand, the trial court is directed to redetermine spousal support in light of any recharacterization of the disability benefits as community property.

Accordingly, the judgment is reversed. The cause is remanded for further proceedings to determine (1) the extent of the community interest in the disability policies, (2) the proper distribution of the benefits from the policies, (3) the proper amount of spousal support, (4) additional findings regarding the character of the other property at issue, and (5) proper distribution of that property as directed herein.

MOSK, KAUS, BROUSSARD, REYNOSO, GRODIN and LUCAS, JJ., concur.

C. Termination Benefits

In addition to retirement and disability benefits, the employment relationship may give rise to a variety of other "fringe benefits," including severance pay and other types of termination benefits. If these benefits were received during marriage, the classification issues are fairly easy to resolve. But cases involving post-separation or post-dissolution benefits are more problematic. A major determinative factor is whether payment of the benefits stems from an earned absolute right pursuant to the employment contract or is fashioned at the time of termination to alleviate the difficulties accompanying unemployment.

IN RE MARRIAGE OF LAWSON

Court of Appeals, First District, 1989.
208 Cal.App.3d 446, 256 Cal.Rptr. 283.

MERRILL, ASSOCIATE JUSTICE.

In this case we decide whether the post-dissolution employment separation allowance paid to a former spouse should be characterized as community or separate property.

I

Neil and Priscilla Lawson (Husband and Wife) were married on July 1, 1960, and separated June 11, 1985. Judgment of dissolution was entered on July 29, 1986. Husband's employment with Shell Oil Company commenced in 1958, two years before his marriage, and continued until January 1, 1987. Pursuant to a stipulated order, Wife's proportional community property interest in Husband's pension benefits was awarded to her.

In November 1986, Husband received notice from his employer of the merger of two Shell divisions and the resulting elimination of two account sales manager positions, including his own. Shell initiated the merger in order to reduce or consolidate the work force or improve the efficiency of the work force. Shell offered Husband the option of participating in a severance program specifically designed for those employees affected by the merger.[1] In opting to accept the offer, Husband considered the fact that his employment in the newly merged division was likely to continue only for another two to three years at

1. The plan was titled "Shell Oil Company's Special Severance Program for Certain Fuel Sales Account Managers or Certain Jobber Territory Managers Located in California or Washington."

which time there was no assurance of a similar program. Husband also determined he would have less difficulty in seeking new employment if he left Shell at the age of 52, rather than at the age of 55. This was the first time Husband had been offered or been made aware of Shell's severance program for excess employees.

The following plan provisions are pertinent to our analysis. The purpose of the severance plan offered to Husband was "to provide a separation allowance for certain employees" affected by the work force reduction following the merger. The release and settlement agreement provided that the separation allowance was not a part of the employee's "regular or normal salary or benefit program as an employee." The plan did not affect his pension benefits in which Wife shared pursuant to the stipulated order. In order to participate and be eligible for the severance allowance, the employee was required to execute a release in favor of Shell for any claim arising from his or her employment termination. The termination had to have occurred sometime between November 1, 1986, and January 31, 1987. Yet the employee was required to continue to work until Shell decided his or her services were no longer needed. The amount of the severance allowance was computed on a basis of two weeks' salary for each year of service, but in no event to exceed one year's basic pay. Voluntary termination, death, disability, or discharge prior to the termination date scheduled by Shell disqualified the employee from participation and receipt of any separation pay. However, if a former employee died after termination but before receipt of the entire separation allowance, it would be paid to the surviving spouse, children or estate. The allowance would not be paid to the beneficiaries if the employee died before the effective date of termination. Finally, Shell reserved the right to revoke or alter the plan and the right to accept or reject an employee's participation in the plan. The plan was signed by Shell on October 17, 1986.

Wife successfully petitioned the superior court for a division of the separation allowance. In its order the court stated Husband's " 'separation allowance' is subject to division between the parties (time line rule division) as are his pension benefits, that allowance being part of an 'early retirement package' being calculated on a longevity formula, and being structured more as a retirement benefit rather than a severance benefit (it does not seem to be fashioned to assist him during a temporary period of unemployment)...." Husband was ordered to pay Wife a 43.75 percent community interest in the separation allowance. He appeals.

II

Husband argues that the separation allowance must be characterized as his separate property for several reasons. He submits that the right to participate in the plan was not absolute, and it did not arise from any employment contract with Shell, and was for the purpose of compensating him for his future loss of earnings and living expenses while seeking new employment. Our analysis of the characteristics of the separation allowance leads us to agree with Husband and reverse the judgment.

It is axiomatic that "property attributable to community earnings must be divided equally when the community is dissolved" (*In re Marriage of Brown* (1976) 15 Cal.3d 838, 847–848, 126 Cal.Rptr. 633, 544 P.2d 561), while the earnings and accumulations of a spouse after separation are separate property. (Civ.Code, § 5118.)

California courts have reasoned that pension benefits must be considered a part of the consideration earned by the employee. (*In re Marriage of Fithian* (1974) 10 Cal.3d 592, 596, 111 Cal.Rptr. 369, 517 P.2d 449, cert. den. *sub nom. Fithian v. Fithian* (1974) 419 U.S. 825, 95 S.Ct. 41, 42 L.Ed.2d 48 disapproved on other grounds in *In re Marriage of Brown, supra,* 15 Cal.3d at p. 851, fn. 14, 126 Cal.Rptr. 633, 544 P.2d 561.) Accordingly, the right to receive pension benefits arises out of the employment agreement and is a form of deferred compensation for services rendered. (*In re Marriage of Brown, supra,* 15 Cal.3d at p. 845, 126 Cal.Rptr. 633, 544 P.2d 561.) The contractual right to future pension benefits, though nonvested and unmatured, are thus a divisible community interest to the extent they are earned by the time, skill and effort of a spouse during marriage. (*Id.,* at pp. 844, 846, 126 Cal.Rptr. 633, 544 P.2d 561.)

Similarly, vested termination benefits which arise in an employment agreement represent a divisible community property interest, to the extent they are community in nature. (*In re Marriage of Skaden* (1977) 19 Cal.3d 679, 682, 139 Cal.Rptr. 615, 566 P.2d 249.) The insurance agency agreement in *Skaden* provided that the benefits, a percentage of the premiums, were payable in the event of "termination" two or more years after its effective date and that termination occurred upon the written notice of either party or the death of the agent. The high court based its analysis on whether the compensation represented a form of deferred compensation for services rendered. The court reasoned that there was no distinction between vested rights to contractual pension benefits and contractual termination benefits. Both were paid because of the employment contract. More importantly, the *Skaden* court found it significant that nothing in the agency agreement suggested such benefits were " 'consideration for termination' " as the payments would be made even if the termination was involuntary, e.g., upon the agent's death. Finally, the court rejected the argument that the benefits should be characterized as consideration for the agent's post-termination compliance with certain conditions. Noting that the agreement provided for payment directly related to the number and character of the policies credited to him upon termination, the court determined payment was truly deferred compensation for services rendered. (*Id.,* at pp. 685–687, 139 Cal.Rptr. 615, 566 P.2d 249.)

In contrast, our courts have consistently held disability payments to be the separate property of the spouse who receives them, except for that portion payable as pension benefits. (*In re Marriage of Flockhart* (1981)

119 Cal.App.3d 240, 243, 173 Cal.Rptr. 818; *In re Marriage of Robinson* (1976) 54 Cal.App.3d 682, 684–686, 126 Cal.Rptr. 779; see *In re Marriage of Stenquist* (1978) 21 Cal.3d 779, 782, 148 Cal.Rptr. 9, 582 P.2d 96.) An employee receives disability payments because of his or her status as a disabled person. Likewise, workers' compensation awards after separation have been characterized as the separate property of the recipient spouse. Courts have analyzed that "[t]he purpose underlying both is to presently compensate an individual for the loss of earnings compelled by the disability, not to pay him compensation for services previously rendered." (*In re Marriage of Flockhart, supra,* 119 Cal. App.3d at p. 243, 173 Cal.Rptr. 818, citing *In re Marriage of McDonald* (1975) 52 Cal.App.3d 509, 512, 125 Cal.Rptr. 160.)

Analysis according to the function of the particular payment has been a consistent factor in the severance or termination benefit cases. *Flockhart* concerned termination benefits paid by the federal government to an employee adversely affected by the expansion of a national park. The "weekly layoff benefits" were paid in accordance with a federal statute. It was evident that the purpose of the statute was to replace lost income as the recipient's payments were reduced by present earnings. The Court of Appeal equated the benefits there to disability payments and workers' compensation as they were not made pursuant to an agreement but because of the former spouse's status as an "affected employee." (*In re Marriage of Flockhart, supra,* 119 Cal.App.3d at pp. 242–243, 173 Cal.Rptr. 818.) The court distinguished *Skaden* on the ground that the employment termination payments in that case involved a contractual right for deferred compensation. (*Id.,* at p. 243, fn. 2, 173 Cal.Rptr. 818.)

In *In re Marriage of Wright* (1983) 140 Cal.App.3d 342, 189 Cal. Rptr. 336, the court held that the one-time voluntary payment of employee termination pay by the employer hospital constituted the separate property of the recipient. In *Wright,* husband's employment was terminated because of harassment by wife and her father, a chaplain at the hospital. The payment equaled almost one year's pay, was not part of an employment contract, and was paid to the employee in anticipation of the difficulties he was likely to encounter in finding new employment. The court distinguished *Skaden* because the contractual payments there continued "*irrespective of continued employment.*" (*Id.,* at pp. 345–346, 189 Cal.Rptr. 336.) Instead *Wright* found the voluntary termination payments to be analogous to the disability benefit and workers' compensation cases. "Such [disability] payments serve the principal purpose of compensating the disabled employee for his/her injury, including prospective loss of earnings and diminished earning capacity. [Citation.]" (*Id.,* at pp. 344–345, 189 Cal.Rptr. 336.)

Similarly, in *In re Marriage of Kuzmiak* (1986) 176 Cal.App.3d 1152, 222 Cal.Rptr. 644, cert. den. *sub nom. Kuzmiak v. Kuzmiak* (1986) 479 U.S. 885, 107 S.Ct. 276, 93 L.Ed.2d 252, the appellate court held military separation pay for an officer's involuntary discharge was the separate property of the service member. The primary inquiry made by the

Kuzmiak court was whether the purpose of the statutory separation pay was to compensate for past services or to ease the adjustment into civilian life. (*Id.,* at pp. 1157–1158, 222 Cal.Rptr. 644.) The statute's legislative history indicated that the payment was intended to assist the service member during the transition period to private employment. Further, if the service member reenlisted and later became eligible for retirement pension, he or she was required to reimburse the separation pay from the retirement payments as the purpose of the statute would not be served. Because of this reimbursement feature and the fact that husband reenlisted in the service, *Kuzmiak* concluded that wife had a community interest in the separation pay to the extent it constituted an unmatured right to husband's retirement pension. (*Id.,* at pp. 1158–1159, 222 Cal.Rptr. 644.) However, the court made it clear that without reenlistment and reimbursement from his longevity retirement pension, the separation pay is the separate property of husband.

In contrast, contractual severance pay to a retiring National Football League player based on the number of seasons worked was held to be deferred compensation for services rendered and thus community property in *In re Marriage of Horn* (1986) 181 Cal.App.3d 540, 547–548, 226 Cal.Rptr. 666. The Court of Appeal compared the particular characteristics of the severance pay at issue there with the *Flockhart–Wright–Kuzmiak* line of cases and concluded the absolute nature of the right to receive such payment was determinative of its community property characterization. Certain features of the severance pay contract provision emphasized its deferred compensation status, e.g., that the right to receive the payment was contractual and arose after a certain number of years of employment, that the lump sum payment would definitely be paid in the future upon his permanent retirement, that the player would receive the severance pay in addition to his retirement, that his beneficiaries or estate would receive the monies upon the player's death, and that even though reimbursement was required if the player returned to professional football within 12 months, he would ultimately receive the payment. *Horn* distinguished the disability cases and the *Flockhart–Wright–Kuzmiak* line of cases on the basis that they involved no absolute contractual rights to the severance pay. As *Horn* was married during the time that he was accruing the right to receive the severance pay, it was found to be a divisible community interest. (*Id.,* at pp. 544–548, 226 Cal.Rptr. 666.)

The question presented here is whether Husband had accrued an absolute right to receive the separation allowance or whether it is more analogous to the disability cases and the *Flockhart–Wright–Kuzmiak* line of cases. We turn to the particular characteristics of the severance plan.

In contrast to the absolute contractual right to the pay in *Horn,* the pay here was wholly conditional on the employee signing the release and agreeing to leave when Shell determined the time was right. If Husband was reemployed by Shell, the plan required repayment of that portion in excess of the normal salary he would have received had he stayed on the job. It does not appear that the separation allowance would then be repaid upon his final retirement.

While Husband did not qualify as a recipient because of some involuntary circumstance, such as a disability, work-related injury or layoff, neither was his participation in the plan wholly in his control. Because of the feature denying payment upon voluntary or involuntary termination prior to the date set by Shell, the plan was more in the character of a true severance benefit for employer-determined termination.

The indefinite character of the right to receive the payment is also demonstrated by the various qualifying conditions. Termination had to occur during a three-month period in order for the employee to qualify. Voluntary termination or involuntary termination, i.e., by death or disability, prior to Shell's predetermined termination date disqualified the employee from the plan. The employee's beneficiaries would not receive the separation allowance if the employee died before Shell's termination date. Finally, the plan was subject to Shell's revision or revocation.

These factors convince us that the right to receive the separation pay did not accrue during the marriage and that the plan was more in the nature of the voluntary noncontractual payment made by the employer in *Wright*. This is emphasized by the provision reserving to Shell the right to accept or reject employees as participants and the fact that the plan was not presented to employees until late October 1987.

Moreover, that the pay was intended as future replacement compensation for long-term employees pursuing new jobs or professions is evidenced by two plan provisions. First, the plan itself states its purpose is "to provide a separation allowance for certain employees" affected by the work force reduction following the merger. Additionally, the repayment provision upon reemployment demonstrates that the pay was for transition purposes only.

It is clear that Husband's separation pay should have been confirmed to him as his separate property and that the trial court erred in granting Wife's petition. Unlike *Skaden* and *Horn*, the instant case does not involve a contractual right for deferred compensation. The characteristics of the plan indicate to us that it was intended as future compensation during the employee's transition period. Further, like *Flockhart*, *Wright* and *Kuzmiak*, the separation allowance here was dependent upon Husband's status during a very limited time period.

We find no significance in the fact that the payment was made at two times over a one-year period. Furthermore, undue emphasis should not be placed on the fact that one of the bases for determining the amount of the allowance is the employee's years of service. In fashioning a severance allowance, fair play may dictate that longevity of employment be factored into the formula for arriving at a monetary figure, even though the right to participate in the plan does not accrue from past services. Finally, the plan features are highly analogous to the payments of disability benefits or workers' compensation as the payment is designed to replace present lost wages. (See Blumberg, *Marital Property Treatment of Pensions, Disability Pay, Workers' Compensation, and other Wage Substitutes: An Insurance, or Replacement, Analysis* (1986) 33 UCLA L.Rev. 1250, 1266.)

* * *

The judgment is reversed. The trial court is directed to vacate its judgment awarding Wife 43.75 percent share in Husband's separation allowance and to enter a new judgment declaring the separation allowance to be the separate property of Husband.

WHITE, P.J., and STRANKMAN, J., concur.

Note

In addition to the common employment related benefits considered in this Section, an employee may be entitled to a wide range of other fringe benefits, such as payment for accrued sick leave and/or vacation time when the employment relationship terminates. It has been held outside the dissolution context that vacation pay is similar to retirement benefits in that it is another form of deferred compensation: "[V]acation pay is not an inducement for future services, but is compensation for past services * * *." Suastez v. Plastic Dress–Up Co., 31 Cal.3d 774, 783, 183 Cal.Rptr. 846, 851, 647 P.2d 122, 127 (1982). In *Suastez* the California Supreme Court concluded that a proportionate right to a paid vacation "vests" as the labor is rendered, and therefore on termination of employment, the employee must be paid in wages for a pro rata share of his vacation pay.

In Marriage of Lorenz, 146 Cal.App.3d 464, 194 Cal.Rptr. 237 (1983), the wife argued that the husband's accrued vacation pay was a community asset subject to division at dissolution. The husband testified that he had accumulated 120 hours of vacation time, but that if it was not used, he would not be paid for it. The appellate court stated:

> No such monetary value can be placed upon the assets claimed here by wife. The mere fact that these assets are of benefit to husband does not compel the conclusion that that benefit must, or can, be divided. We imagine that there are many "assets" held by a spouse at the time of marriage, particularly those arising out of employment, which are not subject to division. For example, an employee may be entitled to use the facilities of a health club owned by his employer, to purchase meals at an employer-owned cafeteria at reduced prices, or to receive a discount for purchases made at an employer-owned retail establishment. An employee may be given the privilege of choosing to work four ten-hour days per week rather than five eight-hour days per week, thus entitling him or her to a three-day weekend. All of these benefits, although of value to the employee spouse, are not convertible into cash. They are, therefore, not divisible on dissolution of the marriage.

The court upheld the trial court's conclusion that the husband's accrued vacation time was not an item of community property subject to division. The reasoning of the court in *Lorenz* was sharply criticized by the court in Marriage of Gonzales, 168 Cal.App.3d 1021, 214 Cal.Rptr. 634 (1985): "If ease of valuation has something to do with the definition of divisible community property, as *Lorenz* suggests, the Mona Lisa could not qualify because it is literally priceless. Yet it would be ludicrous to suggest such property should be awarded to one spouse without corresponding credit to the other, however arbitrarily determined." The *Gonzales* court concluded that the right to a paid vacation constitutes deferred compensation for services rendered, and "[t]here is no reason deferred wages cannot be commuted to present value and divided."

Chapter 5

MANAGEMENT AND CONTROL

SECTION 1. GENERAL PRINCIPLES

The California community property system as originally established in 1850, in keeping with the social values and attitudes of the time, treated the wife as someone unsophisticated in business matters and primarily involved with household concerns.[1] The early statutes placed management and control of community property in the husband, giving him the same disposition powers over community property as he had over his own separate property.[2] The wife was eventually accorded sole control over her separate property.[3]

The husband retained the exclusive right to management and control of all community property until 1951, when the wife's earnings and personal injury recoveries were placed in her control so long as they were kept separate and distinct from other community property,[4] and were not invested in real property.[5] If either of these events occurred, control was shifted to the husband. The 1951 legislation started a period of dual control, as contrasted with the preceding era of single control. There is no reason to doubt that the wife's control was subject to the same restrictions and limitations as the courts had imposed on that of the husband.

The period of dual control came to an end on January 1, 1975, when the legislature instituted the concept of "equal management," giving either spouse the right to manage the community property. The legisla-

---

1. In the constitutional convention one delegate said: "Sir, the God of nature made woman frail, lovely, and dependent * * *." Browne, Debates in the Convention of California, p. 259 (1850).

2. Cal.Stats.1849–50, c. 103, secs. 6 and 8.

3. The Act of 1850 initially placed the control of the wife's separate property in the husband; however, the adoption of the Field Code in 1872 accorded the wife exclusive management and control rights over her separate property. Prager, The Persis-

tence of Separate Property Concepts in California's Community Property System, 1849–1875, 24 U.C.L.A.L.Rev. 1, 26 (1976).

4. The language of the statute was: "until it is commingled with community property subject to the management and control of the husband." See old section 171C of West's Ann.Cal.Civil Code, later renumbered section 5124.

5. Section 5127 of West's Ann.Cal.Civil Code, prior to January 1, 1975.

tion declared that the new form of management and control was to extend to community property already in existence as well as to new acquisitions.[6]

The area of control and management of community property gives rise to three basic questions: First, what are the permissible acts of use and management? Second, what remedies are available between the spouses for the protection of their interests in the community property? Third, what remedies are available to a married person for the protection of his or her interest in community property that has been wrongfully transferred to a third person?

The right to control and manage community property has never been unqualified. It is supposed to be exercised for the benefit of the family, and acts in fraud of the rights of the other spouse[7] or acts of gross mismanagement amounting to constructive fraud,[8] have never been within its scope. Although the statute states that the power of control and management now exercisable by either spouse confers an "absolute power of disposition," it also requires that each spouse act as a fiduciary with respect to the other spouse in managing and controlling community property.[9] In addition to these general limitations on the exercise of management and control rights, specific restrictions have been added by the legislature over the years. For example, even when the husband had exclusive management and control, he was statutorily precluded from making a gift of community property or transferring community real property without his wife's consent. These restrictions now apply to both spouses under the current equal management legislation.[10]

Essentially a legitimate act of management is one for the benefit of the family. There may be disagreement between the spouses, however, as to whether a particular act was in fact undertaken for the benefit of the community. Even where a particular act is within the sphere of legitimate management and control, its effects may be to give one spouse special benefits while impairing the other spouse's share in the commu-

6. Cal.Stats.1974, c. 1206, p. 2609. Retroactive application of the 1975 legislation was upheld in Robertson v. Willis, 77 Cal. App.3d 358, 143 Cal.Rptr. 523 (1978).

7. "She has * * * rights therein which have been always safeguarded against the fraudulent or inconsiderate acts of her husband with relation thereto and for the assertion and safeguarding of which she has been given access to appropriate judicial remedies both before and after the time when her said rights and interests would ripen and become vested * * * whenever such rights and ultimate interests were affected by or threatened with such forms of invasion." Stewart v. Stewart, 199 Cal. 318, 342, 249 P. 197, 207 (1926).

8. Kirby v. San Francisco Savings & Loan Society, 95 Cal.App. 757, 273 P. 609 (1928). If the act is deliberate, penalties may be imposed under West's Ann.Cal.Family Code § 2602.

9. West's Ann.Cal.Family Code § 1100. Prior case law indicated that although the spouse exercising management and control over community property may "act like an owner," he was an owner with quasi-fiduciary obligations. See, e.g., Vai v. Bank of America, 56 Cal.2d 329, 15 Cal.Rptr. 71, 364 P.2d 247 (1961); Fields v. Michael, 91 Cal.App.2d 443, 205 P.2d 402 (1949).

10. West's Ann.Cal.Family Code §§ 1100, 1102.

nity estate.[11] Resolution of this type of problem requires some sort of accounting by the benefitted party. Normally this occurs as part of the general accounting required in dissolution proceedings or in the administration of a decedent's estate. But suppose the marriage is not terminated by death or dissolution. Can one spouse require the other to account for the misuse of community property while the marriage continues? It is clear that a transfer of community property in violation of a statutory restriction gives rise to an immediate action by the injured spouse.[12] Should the same rule apply where no statutory restriction is involved, but the act is inequitable because it benefits the actor at the expense of the other spouse?[13]

Not all community property is within the ambit of the equal management and control provisions. Under Family Code Section 1100(d), a spouse "who is operating or managing a business or an interest in a business which is community personal property has the primary management and control of the business or interest." Does this mean that one spouse can use community funds to establish a business and then refuse the other spouse any voice in the management of the business? If the business itself is personal property, but consists of real property assets, does the sole management provision extend to such assets? These questions and others raised by the community property business management provision have not yet been judicially resolved.[14] There are other limitations on the scope of the equal management provisions. In addition to the above exemptions for community property businesses, the legislature also enacted Financial Code Sections 851, 6750, 6751 and 11200, relating to the ownership incidents of bank and savings and loan accounts. These sections are primarily aimed at the protection of financial institutions, but in fact may operate to restrict the management and control powers of the spouse of an account holder. Thus,

---

11. The use of community funds to pay one spouse's debts is not considered improper, see Grolemund v. Cafferata, 17 Cal.2d 679, 111 P.2d 641 (1941), but gives the other spouse a right to an accounting. Somps v. Somps, 250 Cal.App.2d 328, 58 Cal.Rptr. 304 (1967).

12. Britton v. Hammell, 4 Cal.2d 690, 52 P.2d 221 (1935).

13. The statute expressly provides that a court may order an accounting of the property and obligations of the parties to a marriage and may determine the rights of ownership in or access to the community property; such relief may be sought without filing an action for dissolution. West's Ann.Cal.Family.Code § 1101. See Fields v. Michael, and Wilcox v. Wilcox, reprinted in this Section; see generally Bruch, Management Powers and Duties Under California's Community Property Laws, 34 Hastings L.J. 227 (1982).

14. Family Code § 1100(d) states that primary management and control means that the managing spouse may act alone in all transactions, but shall give written notice to the other spouse of any sale, lease, encumbrance or other disposition of all or substantially all of the personal property used in the operation of the business. However, a failure to give written notice will not adversely affect the validity of the transaction, but merely gives the spouse the accounting remedies specified in Section 5125.1. The statute does not specify what happens if the non-managing spouse objects to the transaction after receiving such written notice. For a general discussion of the equal management legislation and its attendant problems, see Reppy, Retroactivity of the 1975 California Community Property Reforms, 48 S.Cal.L.Rev. 977 (1975).

significant community assets of a family may well be outside the scope of common control.

WEST'S ANNOTATED FAMILY CODE OF CALIFORNIA

§ 721. Contracts with each other and third parties; fiduciary relationship

(a) Subject to subdivision (b), either husband or wife may enter into any transaction with the other, or with any other person, respecting property, which either might if unmarried.

(b) Except as provided in Sections 143, 144, 146, and 16040 of the Probate Code, in transactions between themselves, a husband and wife are subject to the general rules governing fiduciary relationships which control the actions of persons occupying confidential relations with each other. This confidential relationship imposes a duty of the highest good faith and fair dealing on each spouse, and neither shall take any unfair advantage of the other. This confidential relationship is a fiduciary relationship subject to the same rights and duties of nonmarital business partners, as provided in Sections 15019, 15020, 15021, and 15022 of the Corporation Code, including the following:

(1) Providing each spouse access at all times to any books kept regarding a transaction for the purposes of inspection and copying.

(2) Rendering upon request, true and full information of all things affecting any transaction which concerns the community property. Nothing in this section is intended to impose a duty for either spouse to keep detailed books and records of community property transactions.

(3) Accounting to the spouse, and holding as a trust any benefit or profit derived from any transaction by one spouse without the consent of the other spouse which concerns the community property.

(Stats.1992, c. 162 (A.B.2650), § 10, operative Jan. 1, 1994.)

§ 1100. Community personal property; management and control; restrictions on disposition

(a) Except as provided in subdivisions (b), (c), and (d) and Sections 761 and 1103, either spouse has the management and control of the community personal property, whether acquired prior to or on or after January 1, 1975, with like absolute power of disposition, other than testamentary, as the spouse has of the separate estate of the spouse.

(b) A spouse may not make a gift of community personal property, or dispose of community personal property for less than fair and reasonable value, without the written consent of the other spouse. This subdivision does not apply to gifts mutually given by both spouses to third parties and to gifts given by one spouse to the other spouse.

(c) A spouse may not sell, convey, or encumber community personal property used as the family dwelling, or the furniture, furnishings, or fittings of the home, or the clothing or wearing apparel of the other spouse or minor children which is community personal property, without the written consent of the other spouse.

(d) Except as provided in subdivisions (b) and (c), and in Section 1102, a spouse who is operating or managing a business or an interest in a business that is all or substantially all community personal property has the primary management and control of the business or interest. Primary management and control means that the managing spouse may act alone in all transactions but shall give prior written notice to the other spouse of any sale, lease, exchange, encumbrance, or other disposition of all or substantially all of the personal property used in the operation of the business (including personal property used for agricultural purposes), whether or not title to that property is held in the name of only one spouse. Written notice is not, however, required when prohibited by the law otherwise applicable to the transaction.

Remedies for the failure by a managing spouse to give prior written notice as required by this subdivision are only as specified in Section 1101. A failure to give prior written notice shall not adversely affect the validity of a transaction nor of any interest transferred.

(e) Each spouse shall act with respect to the other spouse in the management and control of the community assets and liabilities in accordance with the general rules governing fiduciary relationships which control the actions of persons having relationships of personal confidence as specified in Section 721, until such time as the assets and liabilities have been divided by the parties or by a court. This duty includes the obligation to make full disclosure to the other spouse of all material facts and information regarding the existence, characterization, and valuation of all assets in which the community has or may have an interest and debts for which the community is or may be liable, and to provide equal access to all information, records, and books that pertain to the value and character of those assets and debts, upon request.

(Stats.1993, c. 219, § 100.8, operative Jan. 1, 1994.)

§ 1101. Claim for breach of fiduciary duty; court ordered accounting; addition of name of spouse to community property; limitation of action; consent of spouse not required; remedies

(a) A spouse has a claim against the other spouse for a breach of the fiduciary duty imposed by Section 1100 or 1102 that results in impairment to the claimant spouse's present undivided one-half interest in the community estate, including, but not limited to, a single transaction or a pattern or series of transactions, which transaction or transactions have caused or will cause a detrimental impact to the claimant spouse's undivided one-half interest in the community estate.

(b) A court may order an accounting of the property and obligations of the parties to a marriage and may determine the rights of ownership in, the beneficial enjoyment of, or access to, community property, and the classification of all property of the parties to a marriage.

(c) A court may order that the name of a spouse shall be added to community property held in the name of the other spouse alone or that the title of community property held in some other title form shall be reformed to reflect its community character, except with respect to any of the following:

(1) A partnership interest held by the other spouse as a general partner.

(2) An interest in a professional corporation or professional association.

(3) An asset of an unincorporated business if the other spouse is the only spouse involved in operating and managing the business.

(4) Any other property, if the revision would adversely affect the rights of a third person.

(d)(1) Except as provided in paragraph (2), any action under subdivision (a) shall be commenced within three years of the date a petitioning spouse had actual knowledge that the transaction or event for which the remedy is being sought occurred.

(2) An action may be commenced under this section upon the death of a spouse or in conjunction with an action for legal separation, dissolution of marriage, or nullity without regard to the time limitations set forth in paragraph (1).

(3) The defense of laches may be raised in any action brought under this section.

(4) Except as to actions authorized by paragraph (2), remedies under subdivision (a) apply only to transactions or events occurring on or after July 1, 1987.

(e) In any transaction affecting community property in which the consent of both spouses is required, the court may, upon the motion of a spouse, dispense with the requirement of the other spouse's consent if both of the following requirements are met:

(1) The proposed transaction is in the best interest of the community.

(2) Consent has been arbitrarily refused or cannot be obtained due to the physical incapacity, mental incapacity, or prolonged absence of the nonconsenting spouse.

(f) Any action may be brought under this section without filing an action for dissolution of marriage, legal separation, or nullity, or may be brought in conjunction with the action or upon the death of a spouse.

(g) Remedies for breach of the fiduciary duty by one spouse as set out in Section 721 shall include, but not be limited to, an award to the other spouse of 50 percent, or an amount equal to 50 percent, of any asset undisclosed or transferred in breach of the fiduciary duty plus attorney's fees and court costs. However, in no event shall interest be assessed on the managing spouse.

(h) Remedies for the breach of the fiduciary duty by one spouse when the breach falls within the ambit of Section 3294 of the Civil Code shall include, but not be limited to, an award to the other spouse of 100 percent, or an amount equal to 100 percent, of any asset undisclosed or transferred in breach of the fiduciary duty.

(Stats.1992, c. 162 (A.B.2650), § 10, operative Jan. 1, 1994.)

§ 1102. Community real property; spouse's joinder in conveyances; application of section; limitation of actions

(a) Except as provided in Sections 761 and 1103, either spouse has the management and control of the community real property, whether acquired prior to or on or after January 1, 1975, but both spouses, either personally or by a duly authorized agent, must join in executing any instrument by which that community real property or any interest therein is leased for a longer period than one year, or is sold, conveyed, or encumbered.

(b) Nothing in this section shall be construed to apply to a lease, mortgage, conveyance, or transfer of real property or of any interest in real property between husband and wife.

(c) Notwithstanding subdivision (b):

(1) The sole lease, contract, mortgage, or deed of the husband, holding the record title to community real property, to a lessee, purchaser, or encumbrancer,

in good faith without knowledge of the marriage relation, shall be presumed to be valid if executed prior to January 1, 1975.

(2) The sole lease, contract, mortgage, or deed of either spouse, holding the record title to community real property to a lessee, purchaser, or encumbrancer, in good faith without knowledge of the marriage relation, shall be presumed to be valid if executed on or after January 1, 1975.

(d) No action to avoid any instrument mentioned in this section, affecting any property standing of record in the name of either spouse alone, executed by the spouse alone, shall be commenced after the expiration of one year from the filing for record of that instrument in the recorder's office in the county in which the land is situated.

(e) Nothing in this section precludes either spouse from encumbering his or her interest in community real property, as provided in Section 2033, to pay reasonable attorney's fees in order to retain or maintain legal counsel in a proceeding for dissolution of marriage, for nullity of marriage, or for legal separation of the parties.

(Stats.1993, c. 219, § 101, operative Jan. 1, 1994.)

§ 1103. Management and control of community property; one or both spouses having conservator of estate or lacking legal capacity; law governing

(a) Where one or both of the spouses either has a conservator of the estate or lacks legal capacity to manage and control community property, the procedure for management and control (which includes disposition) of the community property is that prescribed in Part 6 (commencing with Section 3000) of Division 4 of the Probate Code.

(b) Where one or both spouses either has a conservator of the estate or lacks legal capacity to give consent to a gift of community personal property or a disposition of community personal property without a valuable consideration as required by Section 1100 or to a sale, conveyance, or encumbrance of community personal property for which a consent is required by Section 1100, the procedure for that gift, disposition, sale, conveyance, or encumbrance is that prescribed in Part 6 (commencing with Section 3000) of Division 4 of the Probate Code.

(c) Where one or both spouses either has a conservator of the estate or lacks legal capacity to join in executing a lease, sale, conveyance, or encumbrance of community real property or any interest therein as required by Section 1102, the procedure for that lease, sale, conveyance, or encumbrance is that prescribed in Part 6 (commencing with Section 3000) of Division 4 of the Probate Code.

(Stats.1992, c. 162 (A.B.2650), § 10, operative Jan. 1, 1994.)

TYRE v. AETNA LIFE INSURANCE CO.

Supreme Court of California, 1960.

54 Cal.2d 399, 6 Cal.Rptr. 13, 353 P.2d 725.

TRAYNOR, JUSTICE. Plaintiffs, the widow and three adult daughters of the insured, appeal from a judgment for defendant in an action to recover the widow's community property interest in the proceeds of a life insurance policy.

The facts are not in dispute. Rebecca Tyre (hereafter called plaintiff) and Louis Tyre, the insured, were married in Los Angeles in 1917 and lived there as husband and wife until Mr. Tyre's death in 1957. Defendant issued its policy in the face amount of $20,000 upon the life of the insured in 1926. All the premiums were paid from community funds. The original beneficiary was the Tyre Brothers Glass Company. Upon the insured's retirement from the business in 1946, he changed the beneficiary of the policy to make it payable to plaintiff in a lump sum. In 1950 the insured exercised his option under the policy of selecting an alternate settlement. He directed that upon his death plaintiff receive an annuity based on her life expectancy at that time. If she failed to survive him by ten years, the monthly payments were to be divided among the three daughters for the balance of the ten-year period only. As so amended the policy continued in force for the remainder of the insured's life and was in effect at his death.

Plaintiff was 59 years and 8 months of age at the time her husband died. An average person of that age has a life expectancy, established by standard mortality tables, of 14 years. Under the terms of her husband's choice of settlement, plaintiff will receive $20,664 in installments of $123 per month if she lives out her full expectancy. If she fails to survive the ten-year period, defendant's total liability will be $14,760. To receive $10,000, plaintiff must survive 6.77 years. Plaintiff has suffered three heart attacks and the trial court found that her life expectancy may be less than that of an average person of her age.

The insured changed the method of payment without plaintiff's knowledge or approval. Since the policy had been in the possession of a bank as collateral security for a loan, plaintiff did not learn of the change until a few months after her husband's death. She promptly disavowed his choice and requested payment of the face amount of the original policy in cash. Defendant refused to alter the method of settlement. Plaintiff and her daughters thereupon brought this action praying for $10,000 in cash representing plaintiff's community interest and a declaration that the remaining $10,000 be paid according to the insured's selection at $61.50 per month. Defendant contends that it is not obligated to pay any sum under the policy except $123 per month for plaintiff's life or ten years, whichever is longer.

A policy of insurance on the husband's life is community property when the premiums have been paid with community funds. New York Life Ins. Co. v. Bank of Italy, 60 Cal.App. 602, 606, 214 P. 61; Blethen v. Pacific Mut. Life Ins. Co., 198 Cal. 91, 99, 243 P. 431; Grimm v. Grimm, 26 Cal.2d 173, 175, 157 P.2d 841. During the existence of the marriage the respective interests of the husband and wife in community property are present, existing, and equal (Civ.Code, § 161a), but "the husband has the management and control of the community personal property, with like absolute power of disposition, other than testamentary, as he has of his separate estate; provided, however, that he cannot make a gift of such community personal property, or dispose of the same without a valuable consideration, * * * without the written consent of the wife." Civ.Code, § 172. When the community is dissolved by death, "one-half of the community property belongs to the surviving spouse; the other half is subject to the testamentary disposition of the decedent." Prob. Code, § 201. Both parties rely on these sections. Plaintiff contends that she became entitled, immediately upon her husband's death, to one-half of each part of the community property. Defendant contends that the insured had power to enter into the supplemental contract by virtue of his general powers of management and control and that plaintiff cannot disavow his contract.

Plaintiff could not avoid a contract entered into for a valuable consideration by her husband in the course of his lifetime management of the community personalty even though it was made without her consent and temporarily affected her control immediately following his death. Thus, in Beemer v. Roher, 137 Cal.App. 293, 30 P.2d 547 (see also Beemer v. Roher, 137 Cal.App. 298, 30 P.2d 549), the husband invested community funds in a savings and loan "accumulative investment certificate." The wife sought immediate recovery of the entire sum and the trial court ordered payment "forthwith." On appeal the court awarded the wife her one-half community interest in the sums evidenced by the certificate, but held that she was not entitled to immediate payment because her right to recover possession was subject to the same statutory provisions and written agreements that would have governed the husband in withdrawing the funds. A relevant statute provided that holders of certificates in savings and loan institutions, including accumulative investment certificates, might not be permitted to withdraw moneys without first having given a notice of intention to withdraw not less than thirty days nor more than six months previously. Stats.1931, ch. 269, §§ 5.01(c), 6.01. The husband entered into the investment in the normal course of his lifetime management of the community personalty. Under the terms of his investment, the wife's management and control of her share of the community property at her husband's death could have been postponed at most for six months. Another type of lifetime investment that might temporarily impede distribution of the wife's community property interest is a partnership or family corporation arrangement providing for a winding up period or an option in the surviving members to buy out the community interest. See Wood v. Gunther, 89 Cal.App.2d 718, 201 P.2d 874.

In the present case, however, the husband's election to have the policy proceeds paid as an annuity instead of in a lump sum was not an exercise of his nontestamentary power of management during his lifetime, but an attempt to dispose of proceeds after his death. Until he died he could elect to have the proceeds paid as a lump sum or as an annuity actuarially worth that sum. Of course, as between the husband and defendant there was consideration for the change in method of payment. The right to an annuity was consideration for the surrender of the right to a lump sum payment. Similarly there is consideration between the insurance company and the insured when the insured changes the beneficiary from one person to another. Nevertheless, it is settled that even though the insurance contract provides that the insured husband has the right to change the beneficiary without the wife's consent when she is named as such, any such change of beneficiary without her consent and without a valuable consideration other than substitution of beneficiaries is voidable, and after the death of the husband the wife may maintain an action for her community share in the proceeds of the policy. Grimm v. Grimm, supra; Blethen v. Pacific Mut. Life Ins. Co., supra, 198 Cal. at page 101, 243 P. at page 435; New York Life Ins. Co. v. Bank of Italy, supra, 60 Cal.App. at page 607, 214 P. at page 63; Beemer v. Roher, 137 Cal.App. 293, 296–297, 30 P.2d 547; McBride v. McBride, 11 Cal.App.2d 521, 523–524, 54 P.2d 480; Mundt v. Connecticut General Life Ins. Co., 35 Cal.App.2d 416, 421, 95 P.2d 966; see Spreckels v. Spreckels, 172 Cal. 775, 784–785, 158 P. 537. These cases recognize that although the payment of insurance proceeds is a matter of contract between the insured and the insurer, the insured's exercise of his unilateral right under the contract to select the beneficiary is testamentary in character. Similarly, the insured's exercise of his unilateral right under the terms of the policy to determine whether the proceeds shall be paid as a lump sum or in the form of an annuity is testamentary in character. Section 201 of the Probate Code gives the husband testamentary control over only one-half of the community property, and the word "testamentary" as used in that section is not limited to formal testaments. Thus, although a wife can set aside a husband's unauthorized gift of community property in its entirety during his lifetime (Britton v. Hammell, 4 Cal.2d 690, 692, 52 P.2d 221), she is limited to the recovery of her one-half share after his death on the theory that his testamentary powers validate the gift of his half interest. Britton v. Hammell, supra; Lahaney v. Lahaney, 208 Cal. 323, concurring opinion at page 329, 281 P. 67; Note, 24 Cal.L.Rev. 306. Similarly, a wife's gift causa mortis of community property (Odone v. Marzocchi, 34 Cal.2d 431, 439, 211 P.2d 297, 212 P.2d 233, 17 A.L.R.2d 1109) and a husband's gift of a community life insurance policy (Mazman v. Brown, 12 Cal.App.2d 272, 274, 55 P.2d 539) have been upheld as to the spouse's community interest by reference to the testamentary power.

Just as the husband cannot deprive his wife of her community interest by exceeding his testamentary powers to make gifts of more than half the community property to third persons, so he cannot defeat her interest by making a testamentary gift to her under conditions that restrict her management and control of the property. Her remedy in both situations is to disavow the gift and stand on her community rights.

Defendant contends, however, that plaintiff has chosen to accept her husband's gift of his one-half interest in the policy according to its terms and that she has thereby lost the power to set the policy aside as to her community interest. Defendant has been permitted to raise this issue for the first time in this court because the facts are not disputed and the issue merely raises a new question of law. Burdette v. Rollefson Construction Co., 52 Cal.2d 720, 725–726, 344 P.2d 307 and cases cited.

When the husband attempts to dispose of his wife's share of the community property as well as his own, naming her as one of the takers, she must elect between her community rights and her husband's gift. In re Estate of Wolfe, 48 Cal.2d 570, 574–575, 311 P.2d 476; In re Estate of Moore, 62 Cal.App. 265, 270–272, 216 P. 981; In re Estate of Ettlinger, 73 Cal.App.2d 967, 970, 167 P.2d 738. If she accepts the gift, she must relinquish all inconsistent claims. Lauricella v. Lauricella, 161 Cal. 61, 69, 118 P. 430; Mazman v. Brown, 12 Cal.App.2d 272, 275–276, 55 P.2d 539. Under these cases an election is required here. Plaintiff has elected to stand on her community rights even though she prays for half the community assets used to purchase the annuity in cash and the other half according to her husband's plan. Plaintiff is the sole primary beneficiary under the policy. Only in the event that she fails to survive her husband by ten years will the alternate beneficiaries have any claim to the proceeds. Moreover, the alternate beneficiaries have joined in the prayer. In this situation, unlike the Lauricella and Mazman cases where the wife was only a partial beneficiary and the other beneficiaries asserted adverse interests, plaintiff sufficiently indicated her election by demanding her statutory share in cash and requesting her husband's share under his plan.

Although plaintiff has not lost her right to set aside her husband's unauthorized disposition of her community interest, she is nevertheless not entitled to receive his share under the terms of the policy. By electing to stand on her community rights, plaintiff has disqualified herself as the beneficiary of her husband's gift. If the primary beneficiary of a life insurance policy disqualifies himself, the proceeds are payable to the alternate beneficiary and not to the insured's estate even though the alternate beneficiary's interest was conditioned upon surviving the primary beneficiary as well as the insured. Beck v. West Coast Life Ins. Co., 38 Cal.2d 643, 646–647, 241 P.2d 544, 26 A.L.R.2d 979. The husband's share of the policy therefore became payable to the three daughters upon plaintiff's disqualification as primary beneficiary.

Defendant contends that even if plaintiff is entitled to her share in a lump sum, the daughters should receive the monthly payments only for the ten-year period that measures the company's minimum liability under the policy. Plaintiff's disqualification as the primary beneficiary, however, does not remove her life as the measurement for the annuity; otherwise, the husband's donees may be deprived of the benefit of his investment.

Plaintiff seeks statutory interest on her recovery commencing thirty days after the date of her husband's death. Civ.Code, § 3287. Until she notified the company of her election to stand on her community property rights, however, the company was authorized to make payments in accordance with the terms of the policy. Blethen v. Pacific Mut. Life Ins. Co., 198 Cal. 91, 101–102, 243 P. 431; Ins.Code, § 10172. The record does not disclose the date upon which plaintiff first demanded the payment of her community property interest in cash. That date properly marks the commencement of interest.

The judgment is reversed and the trial court is ordered to enter judgment in accordance with the views expressed herein.

GIBSON, C.J., and PETERS, WHITE and DOOLING, JJ., concur. SCHAUER and McCOMB, JJ., dissent.

Note

In Tyre v. Aetna Life Insurance Co., reprinted above, the court indicates that authorized control and management does not include acts directed toward controlling community property after the termination of the marriage. The investment of community funds in a partnership or in bank certificates of deposit might well produce effects after termination of the marriage, and yet the court suggests that these would be legitimate acts of management. What is the basis for this distinction?

LISTER v. LISTER

California District Court of Appeal, 1984.
152 Cal.App.3d 411, 199 Cal.Rptr. 321.

GILBERT, ASSOCIATE JUSTICE.

We here affirm an interlocutory judgment dissolving the marriage of Lloyd Lister (husband) and Melanie Lister (wife), and ordering husband to reimburse the community for property used to satisfy his premarital and post-separation debts and to pay a portion of his wife's attorneys' fees.

FACTS

Husband and wife married on August 24, 1974. They separated in December 1979, reconciled in April 1981, and again separated in July of 1981. The interlocutory judgment of dissolution, entered March 1, 1982, gave wife custody of the two minor children of the parties and provided for child support but no spousal support. In the equal division of community property and debts, husband received the interest in the Central Plaza Union Station, which he operated in equal partnership with his cousin Jerald Riefkohl, and wife was awarded the family residence and furnishings.

When husband and wife were married, they purchased a single family home on Mammoth Street in Camarillo. They lived there until March 1976 when they purchased another home on Corte Aquacalte. The Riefkohls then moved into the Mammoth residence and made the mortgage payments. Title was transferred to the Riefkohls in March 1978 by a quitclaim deed executed by husband and wife. No cash changed hands but Jerald Riefkohl cancelled husband's premarital debts in the amount of $20,330.73. No documentary evidence was introduced regarding these alleged loans other than ledger entries showing cash advances Jerald Riefkohl made to husband between May 1972 and June 1974.

Wife and her father, William Thompson, testified that husband told them he sold the house to the Riefkohls for $48,000 with a $23,000 gain.

Wife signed the quitclaim deed to complete the sale, but she testified that had she known the house was to be traded to the Riefkohls solely in exchange for cancellation of husband's premarital debts, she would not have agreed to the transaction. She also testified that she executed the quitclaim deed to the Riefkohls in 1976 without the presence of a notary, thinking it was an escrow document. The court noted that the quitclaim deed was notarized and dated in 1978. At about the time husband delivered the quitclaim deed to them, the Riefkohls entered into an agreement to sell the property to others for $58,000 for a net gain of $28,000.

Husband's testimony was inconsistent with respect to his disclosures to his wife. He testified at his deposition that he told her nothing at the time the house was transferred. At trial he said he explained to her that his cousin had agreed to cancel a substantial amount of debts in exchange for the equity in the house, that he reviewed these amounts with her, and that she agreed to those terms. He admitted that he did not identify the debts as his premarital obligations, but denied that he had told her the house was sold.

* * *

The trial judge found that wife did not know about or consent to the transfer of the house to the Riefkohls solely in cancellation of her husband's premarital debts. The judge thus concluded the transfer was a breach of husband's fiduciary obligation to his wife and an abuse of his power of management and control. (Civ.Code, § 5125.) He also found that husband had transferred this community asset to a creditor to satisfy a debt that was not as great as the value of the asset. He therefore ordered husband to reimburse the community $20,330.73.
* * *

DISCUSSION

Husband argues that the consent of his wife was not required for the transfer of the Mammoth residence because the community received consideration for that transfer. (*Gunn v. United Air Lines, Inc.*, (1982) 138 Cal.App.3d 765, 188 Cal.Rptr. 302; *In re Marriage of Smaltz* (1978) 82 Cal.App.3d 568, 147 Cal.Rptr. 154.) This ignores the court's finding that he misrepresented the transaction to his wife, who signed the quitclaim deed believing a sale of the property had been made.

The trial court's finding that husband misappropriated a community asset " 'is binding upon an appellate court if it is supported by sufficient evidence or if it is drawn from evidence which is conflicting or subject to differing inferences.' [Citations.]" (*In re Marriage of Walter* (1976) 57 Cal.App.3d 802, 129 Cal.Rptr. 351.) This finding is supported by the testimony of both wife and her father concerning her husband's misrepresentations and Jerald Riefkohl's testimony that the sole consideration for the transfer was the cancellation of husband's premarital debts.

The community property, with the exception of wife's earnings, traditionally is liable for all debts of the husband, however and wherever contracted. (*Weinberg v. Weinberg* (1967) 67 Cal.2d 557, 563, 63 Cal. Rptr. 13, 432 P.2d 709.) Nonetheless, the community may be entitled to reimbursement if the husband uses community property funds to discharge his separate indebtedness. (*In re Marriage of Walter, supra,* 57 Cal.App.3d at 806, 129 Cal.Rptr. 351; see also 7 Witkin, Summary of Cal.Law (8th ed. 1974) Community Property, § 84, pp. 5173–5174.)

Currently spousal obligations are viewed first from the creditors' standpoint and for this purpose the community property is liable. On dissolution of the marriage where equal division of the community property and liabilities are in issue, transactions of the spouses *inter se* are subject to review and the separate debts of one spouse may be excluded from the shared community obligations. (See *In re Marriage of Epstein* (1979) 24 Cal.3d 76, 89, 154 Cal.Rptr. 413, 592 P.2d 1165.) "Between the spouses, certain obligations which are properly characterized as separate may be assigned to the responsible person if unpaid, or reimbursement may be ordered in favor of the community if the debt was paid from community assets." (*In re Marriage of Stitt* (1983) 147 Cal.App.3d 579, 587, 195 Cal.Rptr. 172.) Although the community property may be at risk where one spouse has separate debts, this does not preclude the court from ordering reimbursement to the community following a nonconsensual transfer of community real property. (See, e.g. *Mitchell v. American Reserve Ins. Co.* (1980) 110 Cal.App.3d 220, 167 Cal.Rptr. 760.)

In the case of *In re Marriage of Stitt, supra,* 147 Cal.App.3d 579, 195 Cal.Rptr. 172, wife incurred an obligation for attorneys' fees for her defense on charges of embezzlement. Husband transferred to wife his community interest in the family residence in reliance on her representation that it would be prudent to do this because of her embezzlement trial. She told him that the property would be conveyed back to him after completion of the trial. Wife's attorneys took a note for their fees secured by a trust deed on the family residence. The court, applying equitable principles, held that husband should receive his community interest free of this debt because of "the separate nature of the obligation" of the wife. (*Id.,* at p. 588, 195 Cal.Rptr. 172.) The court also recognized that her conduct which gave rise to the obligation to pay attorney's fees was tortious or criminal. (Civ.Code, § 5122.)

Here, although the conduct giving rise to husband's obligation was not tortious, and was not as egregious as wife's conduct in *Stitt,* the same equitable principles should nevertheless apply. Husband's actions in mismanaging the community property constituted a violation of Civil Code section 5125. It is questionable whether husband's debt was collectible. Other than some journal entries showing advances made between May 6, 1972 and June 3, 1974, there was no documentary evidence of this debt. There were no checks written for the money, no promissory notes, and no agreements indicating when the money should be repaid. Although the statute of limitations operates on the remedy and does not extinguish the debtor's obligation (*Mitchell v. County Sanitation Dist.* (1957) 150 Cal.App.2d 366, 370, 309 P.2d 930), the statute of limitations defense still may have been available to wife. (See Code Civ.Proc., § 339, subd. (1); *Dorland v. Dorland* (1884) 66 Cal. 189, 190, 5 P. 77.)

The circumstances of this case are distinguishable from *Gunn* and *Smaltz* upon which Mr. Lister heavily relies. The sole question in *Gunn* was whether a surviving second wife was entitled to share after her husband's death in that portion of his retirement fund attributable to the increase in its value during their marriage. Under the terms of a property settlement agreement with his first wife, husband had received the retirement fund subject to a proviso that he designate the four sons of his first marriage as beneficiaries. The court held that his contributions to the fund during his second marriage were not gifts of community property which would entitle his second wife to claim a share of the proceeds. Instead, these were contractual obligations under a property settlement agreement for which the community property of the second marriage was liable.

Similarly, in *Smaltz,* the community was not entitled to reimbursement for payments of spousal support which husband had made to a former wife from community property pursuant to court order. *Smaltz* noted by contrast that the community has a right to reimbursement if a spouse has abused the right of management and control. (Civ.Code, § 5125.) Neither *Gunn* nor *Smaltz* involved bad faith dealings between the spouses. Here, husband acted in bad faith in managing the community. The court therefore properly ordered him to reimburse the community for the amount of his premarital obligation.

* * *

The judgment is affirmed. Wife to receive costs on appeal.

STONE, P.J., and ABBE, J., concur.

Notes

1. Where the husband used community property to pay income taxes on his separate property, it was held in the final accounting on dissolution that the husband must reimburse the community estate. In re Marriage of Epstein, 24 Cal.3d 76, 154 Cal.Rptr. 413, 592 P.2d 1165 (1979). Similarly, where taxes on the husband's separate property were paid out of community funds, the community estate was entitled to reimbursement in the final accounting in probate. Estate of Turner, 35 Cal.App.2d 576, 96 P.2d 363 (1939); In re Marriage of Walter, 57 Cal.App.3d 802, 129 Cal.Rptr. 351 (1976).

2. Even the involuntary forfeiture of a community property asset may give rise to a right of reimbursement. In the case of Marriage of Beltran, 183 Cal.App.3d 292, 227 Cal.Rptr. 924 (1986), the husband was an Army colonel when the couple separated. While their dissolution action was pending, the husband was convicted of child molestation; as a result, he was dismissed from the Army and stripped of all military benefits, including his pension and accrued leave. As part of the dissolution judgment, the trial court charged the husband with receipt of the forfeited pension and leave

and ordered that the wife be reimbursed for one-half of the benefits ($59,230.50). The award to the wife was upheld on appeal:

> In our view, wife should not be made in effect to share in a penalty imposed upon husband for his criminal conduct. We accordingly conclude as a matter of equity that criminal conduct on the part of husband which directly caused forfeiture of pension benefits justified the trial court's conclusion that wife was entitled to reimbursement for her share of such lost community property.

3. When spouses begin to live "separate and apart" within the meaning of West's Ann.Cal. Family Code § 771, one spouse may well have de facto exclusive physical possession of all or part of the community property. Does this necessarily mean that he or she has exclusive management and control over such community assets? It has been held that when "one spouse has the exclusive use of a community asset during the period between separation and trial, that spouse may be required to compensate the community for the reasonable value of that use." In re Marriage of Garcia, 224 Cal.App.3d 885, 274 Cal.Rptr. 194, 197 (1990). For a case involving a spouse's duty to account for community property in his possession when the parties began to live separate and apart, see In re Marriage of Valle, 53 Cal.App.3d 837, 126 Cal.Rptr. 38 (1975).

4. In Weinberg v. Weinberg, 67 Cal.2d 557, 63 Cal.Rptr. 13, 432 P.2d 709 (1967), the husband paid alimony to his first wife out of the community property. At the time, he had a separate property estate. The Supreme Court, in holding that these payments should be charged ratably to community and separate property stated:

> "The policy of protecting the husband's creditors outweighs the policy of protecting family income even from premarital creditors of the husband. Community property is therefore available to such creditors. (Grolemund v. Cafferata, supra, 17 Cal.2d 679, 689, 111 P.2d 641; Nichols v. Mitchell (1948) 32 Cal.2d 598, 610, 197 P.2d 550; Odone v. Marzocchi (1949) 34 Cal.2d 431, 440, 211 P.2d 297, 212 P.2d 233, 17 A.L.R.2d 1109.) As such a creditor, a husband's first wife can levy against the community property of his second marriage for alimony payments due. (Bruton v. Tearle (1936) 7 Cal.2d 48, 57, 59 P.2d 953, 106 A.L.R. 580; Yager v. Yager (1936) 7 Cal.2d 213, 220, 60 P.2d 422, 106 A.L.R. 664.) As manager of the community property 'with like absolute power of disposition, other than testamentary, as he has of his separate estate' (Civ. Code, § 172), the husband may also voluntarily discharge such obligations from community property. In California, there are ordinarily no separate as distinguished from community debts of the husband. With exceptions not relevant here, 'our community system is based upon the principle that all debts which are not specifically made the obligation of the wife are grouped together as the obligations of the husband and the community property.' (Grolemund v. Cafferata, supra, 17 Cal.2d 679, 688, 111 P.2d 641, 645.) It does not follow, however, that the community can never claim reimbursement from the husband's separate estate when community property has been used to discharge a husband's obligation. The husband's legal right of management and control has long been recognized to imply correlative

duties to his wife. His duties are analogous to those of a partner; he cannot obtain an unfair advantage from the trust placed in him as a result of the marital relationship. (Vai v. Bank of America (1961) 56 Cal.2d 329, 337–339, 15 Cal.Rptr. 71, 364 P.2d 247; Fields v. Michael (1949) 91 Cal.App.2d 443, 447–448, 205 P.2d 402.)''

In the case of In re Marriage of Smaltz, 82 Cal.App.3d 568, 147 Cal.Rptr. 154 (1978), the husband paid alimony to his first wife out of community property of the second marriage. Because he had no separate funds at the time, he could not be said to be taking an unfair advantage at the expense of his spouse, and reimbursement to the community was not required. In neither case did the court really consider whether the payments were of benefit to the community.

West's Ann.Cal. Family Code § 915 currently provides that if community property is used to pay spouse or child support obligations arising from a prior marriage, the community will be reimbursed if separate income was available at the time of the payments. This provision essentially represents a codification of the holding in *Smaltz*.

WILLIAMS v. WILLIAMS

California District Court of Appeal, 1971.
14 Cal.App.3d 560, 92 Cal.Rptr. 385.

GUSTAFSON, ASSOCIATE JUSTICE. Plaintiff wife and defendant husband were married May 8, 1955. Almost 13 years later the marriage had deteriorated to the point where divorce was imminent. The husband thereupon withdrew $39,251.50 from a savings and loan association account and received $73,237.76 from the dissolution of a stock account at the office of a stock broker. The failure of the trial court to make any findings with respect to this total sum of $110,489.26 is the principal point giving rise to this appeal.

The first question is whether, assuming that some or all of the $110,489.26 available to the husband immediately prior to the filing of this action was community property, any of it still existed as such at the time of the dissolution of the marriage. The second question is whether, if the community property portion of the cash was not shown to have been disposed of for community purposes, the wife should have a right to a judgment against the husband in this action for her share of it.

The first of these two questions is a question of fact which should have been resolved by the trial court. The evidence with respect to the $110,489.26 was that the accountant appointed by the court was able to trace $22,126 as having been spent by the husband on mortgage payments, taxes and other expenses on real property. Whether any of this amount was spent on the real property which was found to be the separate property of the husband is not clear from the record. The accountant further found that $39,000 was paid by the husband to five persons. The husband claimed that the payments were made to discharge debts created by loans from those individuals to him. The court did not find that the debts actually existed and, if they did, that they were community debts. The accountant was unable to find what happened to the remaining $49,363.26. The husband testified that he spent this amount in the year preceding trial for ordinary living expenses and that he had no money left. The trial court made no finding with respect to the disposition of this $49,363.26.

The question of what if anything remained of such portion of the $110,489.26 as was community property was clearly raised by the pleadings and the evidence. By submitting proposed findings to the court, the wife satisfied section 632 of the Code of Civil Procedure placing upon the party desiring findings the burden of requesting them. Failure of the trial court to make findings with respect to the $110,489.26 was error and we therefore remand with instructions to the trial court to make findings on the issue under discussion.

It may well be that the findings which we have instructed the trial court to make will obviate the necessity of resolving the second of the two questions we have posed above. If the court finds that all of the community portion of the $110,489.26 was expended for proper community purposes, and that the remainder was the husband's separate property, then the second question need never be reached. If, on the other hand, the court determines that all of the community property was not used for authorized purposes, the second issue will be squarely raised. On the possibility that the second issue will be reached, we think it proper to indicate our views on it.

As to the second question, the extent of a husband's duty to his wife with respect to community property has not been uniformly or satisfactorily defined by the cases. In Fields v. Michael (1949) 91 Cal.App.2d 443, 205 P.2d 402 the wife was permitted to recover from the estate of her deceased husband half of the value of gifts of community personal property which the husband made without the consent of the wife while he was living. The community property was treated as though it were the corpus of a trust of which the husband was the trustee. In Vai v. Bank of America (1961) 56 Cal.2d 329, 15 Cal.Rptr. 71, 364 P.2d 247, the husband was said to have the "duties of a fiduciary" with respect to community property. But the husband is the manager of the community property (Civ.Code, § 5105) and, except as specifically prohibited by statute, he may do with the community personal property what he could do with his separate estate. (Civ.Code, § 5125.) Although a trustee or a fiduciary might be personally liable for a loss sustained by virtue of an improvident investment in speculative stock, we question whether a husband is liable to his wife for a loss sustained under those circumstances.

In White v. White (1938) 26 Cal.App.2d 524, 79 P.2d 759, the court rejected the husband's argument that the trial court had no jurisdiction to render a personal judgment in favor of the wife for community income disposed of by the husband "regardless of the fact that no satisfactory account has been made by him of such funds." The court stated: "Where the handling of the community funds is entrusted by law to the husband, a certain amount of precaution devolves upon him to keep an approximately accurate account of their disbursements * * * or to take the legal consequences of being unable to satisfactorily account therefor." (Accord: Pope v. Pope (1951) 102 Cal.App.2d 353, 227 P.2d 867.) We suspect that it would be extremely rare to find a man who has been married for many years who can account for every cent of his income during the marriage. Again, we question the wisdom of requiring the husband at his peril to be a bookkeeper.

Easier to accept is the proposition that if the husband uses community property for the purpose of preserving or improving his own separate property, the wife is entitled to be reimbursed for her share. (Gelfand v. Gelfand (1934) 136 Cal.App. 488, 29 P.2d 271; Provost v. Provost (1929) 102 Cal.App. 775, 283 P. 842.)

The *Vai, Fields, Provost* and *White* cases were cited without disapproval in Weinberg v. Weinberg (1967) 67 Cal.2d 557, 63 Cal.Rptr. 13, 432 P.2d 709, where, however, the husband's duties were described as "analogous to those of a partner; he cannot obtain an unfair advantage from the trust placed in him as a result of the marital relationship." It would seem that a husband's duty not to obtain an unfair advantage over his wife by reason of his control of the community property does not require that the husband be as prudent as a trustee or that he keep complete and accurate records of income received and disbursed.

But here we are not concerned with the disposition of community property many years prior to a divorce action. The $110,489.26 in dispute here was intact immediately prior to the filing of the action. Under these circumstances, the husband would obtain "an unfair advantage" over his wife if he is not required to account for that portion of the money which was community property and to reimburse the wife for her share of any of the community property not shown to have been used for community purposes.

While we have referred only to the $110,489.26 available to the husband immediately prior to the filing of the divorce action, the wife points out that other sums of money thereafter became available to the husband from other sources. The husband on the other hand points out that the accountant appointed by the court to audit the parties' financial records did not purport to account for all disbursements made by the husband. Since we conclude that the portion of the judgment disposing of the community property must be reversed, as already indicated, retrial of the issue of community property will not be limited to the item of $110,489.26, but will include all sums of money received and disposed of by the husband after April 1, 1968, when the divorce action was imminent.

* * *

That portion of the judgment disposing of the community property is reversed and the cause is remanded for further proceedings in accordance with the views expressed herein. In all other respects, the judgment is affirmed.

Wood, P.J., concurs.

Thompson, Associate Justice. I concur in the result reached in the majority opinion. I disagree, however, with the reasoning of that portion of the opinion which discusses the issue of the wife's right to any part of the $110,489.26 not shown to have been expended for community purposes. In my view, the question is one of burden of proof and of producing evidence. In a dispute over disposition of property in a divorce action, the wife has the burden of proof of establishing the existence of community property, and except as she may be aided by presumptions must produce evidence which carries that burden. (Estate of Nelson, 104 Cal.App. 613, 286 P. 439; See v. See, 64 Cal.2d 778, 51 Cal.Rptr. 888, 415 P.2d 776.)

Where, as here, the wife has concededly established the existence of community assets, has established that certain of those assets are missing, and has presented evidence from which it may be inferred that the husband wrongfully disposed of them, she has, in my opinion, met her burden of proof. The issue then shifts to the validity of dispositions of community property by the husband. On that issue, whether dispositions of community property by the husband are proper on the one hand or fraudulent or illegal on the other, I think the better rule would place the burden of producing evidence of the nature of the dispositions upon the husband. It is appropriate to place the burden of producing evidence upon the party who has access to the facts where those facts are inaccessible to the other party to the litigation. (See Fowler v. Seaton, 61 Cal.2d 681, 687, 39 Cal.Rptr. 881, 394 P.2d 697.) In the situation here present for decision, the husband, as manager and controller of the community property, has access to the facts from which it may be determined whether a disposition of community assets by him was proper or improper. Conversely, the wife, as the passive beneficiary of the husband's management of community property, has little if any access to those facts.

The applicability of the principle of burden based upon superior knowledge of the facts to the situation of the case at bench is strongly indicated by the decision of our Supreme Court in See v. See, supra, 64 Cal.2d 778, 51 Cal.Rptr. 888, 415 P.2d 776. While *See* involves the problem of commingling of community property with separate property of the husband and not the question of unexplained disappearance of community funds, the court rationalizes its decision denying the husband the ability to rebut commingling by establishing an excess of community expenses over community income by reference to the consequences of the husband's right of management and control of the community property. (64 Cal.2d 778, 784, 51 Cal.Rptr. 888, 415 P.2d 776; see also Weinberg v. Weinberg, 67 Cal.2d 557, 563, 63 Cal.Rptr. 13, 432 P.2d 709; Vai v. Bank of America, 56 Cal.2d 329, 337, 15 Cal.Rptr.

71, 364 P.2d 247; White v. White, 26 Cal.App.2d 524, 529, 79 P.2d 759; Pope v. Pope, 102 Cal.App.2d 353, 359, 227 P.2d 867.)

I would instruct the court on retrial to proceed in accord with the principles of burden of proof and of producing evidence recited in this concurring opinion.

FIELDS v. MICHAEL

California District Court of Appeal, 1949.
91 Cal.App.2d 443, 205 P.2d 402.

[A widow filed a claim against the estate of her deceased husband for one half of the value of gifts he had made out of community property without her consent. When the claim was rejected she brought an action against the estate for the same sum and asked for an accounting to determine if additional gifts had been made. The trial court sustained a demurrer without leave to amend on the grounds that the widow had not stated a cause of action. This appeal followed.]

SHINN, PRESIDING JUSTICE. * * *

* * * The paramount issue presented is whether plaintiff may proceed directly against the estate of her husband to secure relief from his dissipation of the community funds through secret and unauthorized inter vivos gifts, or must seek recourse solely against the donees.

Section 574 of the Probate Code provides that "any person, or the personal representative of any person, may maintain an action against the executor or administrator of any testator or intestate who in his lifetime has wasted, destroyed, taken, or carried away, or converted to his own use, the property of any such person * * *."

The facts alleged in the complaint are in our opinion sufficient to bring the action within these provisions. Even before the husband was forbidden by statute to make a gift of community property without his wife's consent, his power of disposition had never been deemed to include the privilege of acting in fraud of the rights of the wife in the community property. Smith v. Smith, 12 Cal. 216, 225, 73 Am.Dec. 533; Lord v. Hough, 43 Cal. 581, 585. Where actual fraud is alleged, as it is here, it would seem clear that a husband who has made unauthorized gifts of a large share of the community property may be held accountable to the offended wife as in the case of any other person who has wrongfully disposed of the property of another.

The position of the husband, in whom the management and control of the entire community estate is vested by statute, (Civ.Code, secs. 161a, 172, 172a) has been frequently analogized to that of a partner, agent or fiduciary. In re Estate of McNutt, 36 Cal.App.2d 542, 552, 98 P.2d 253; Grolemund v. Cafferata, 17 Cal.2d 679, 684, 111 P.2d 641; Lyman v. Vorwerk, 13 Cal.App. 507, 509, 110 P. 355; 1 de Funiak, Principles of Community Property, sec. 95, p. 263. Section 2219 of the Civil Code provides: "Everyone who voluntarily assumes a relation of personal confidence with another is deemed a trustee * * * as to the person who reposes such confidence * * *." It is clear that, being a party to the confidential relationship of marriage, the husband must, for some purposes at least, be deemed a trustee for his wife in respect to their common property. Cf. Vanasek v. Pokorny, 73 Cal.App. 312, 320, 238 P. 798; Arnold v. Leonard, 114 Tex. 535, 273 S.W. 799, 804. * * * Disregarding the allegations of intent to defraud, it is abundantly clear from those remaining that Fields must be held to have consummated a fraud against plaintiff. Nine years prior to their marriage, section 172 of the Civil Code was amended to provide that the husband could not make a gift of community property without the written consent of his wife. Stats.1891, p. 425. Fields' disregard of this affirmative duty imposed upon him as manager of the community estate was a violation of his fiduciary obligations as defined in sections 2228 and 2229 of the Civil Code, supra. Even if good faith were to be shown, he would nevertheless be subject to personal liability for disposing of trust property in an unauthorized manner. Civ.Code, sec. 2238.

It is well settled, of course, that a gift made in violation of section 172 is, as against the donee, voidable by the wife in its entirety during the husband's lifetime, Matthews v. Hamburger, 36 Cal.App.2d 182, 97 P.2d 465; Lynn v. Herman, 72 Cal.App.2d 614, 165 P.2d 54, and to the extent of one-half after his death. Trimble v. Trimble, 219 Cal. 340, 26 P.2d 477; Ballinger v. Ballinger, 9 Cal.2d 330, 70 P.2d 629. The beneficiary of a trust, however, is not required to pursue the trust property, but may elect to hold the trustee (or after his death, his estate) personally liable, McElroy v. McElroy, 32 Cal.2d 828, 831, 198 P.2d 683; Lathrop v. Bampton, 31 Cal. 17, 23, 89 Am.Dec. 141; and the latter may not escape such liability by showing that the trust property has been dissipated. 54 Am.Jur., sec. 253, p. 196. Manifestly, a wife whose community property rights have been violated, as plaintiff alleges hers have been, is entitled to pursue whatever course is best calculated to give her effective relief. Where the amount of the gifts and identity of the donees are known, and the property can be readily reached, the former remedy may be decidedly more advantageous to the plaintiff than an action against the husband's estate, since the assets of the latter may be insufficient to satisfy a judgment. On the other hand, where recourse against the donees would be ineffective to give relief, as in the present instance, a denial of the alternative remedy would not only be in disregard of rudimentary principles applicable to persons acting in a fiduciary capacity, insofar as the husband stood in that relation, but would also amount to a concession that the law is powerless to accord to the wife's community interest the full protection which section 172 was evidently designed to ensure. We think the law is not so toothless. Whether the action is viewed as one based upon actual fraud, or as one based upon a violation of a statutory limitation upon the husband's power of control and management, is immaterial, for the dissipation of community assets by means of unauthorized gifts is in either view a conversion of the "property" of the wife such as would subject the husband's estate to suit under section 574 of the Probate Code. The statutory language is sufficiently comprehensive to include any wrongful conduct resulting in a loss of "property" to another.

It cannot be successfully contended that the assets given away were not, at least to the extent of one-half, "property" of the wife. Even prior to the enactment in 1927 of section 161a of the Civil Code, which defined the interests of the husband and wife in community property as "present, existing and equal," it was well recognized that the "mere expectancy" which the wife had was a considerably more definite and personal interest than that of an ordinary heir. Stewart v. Stewart, 199 Cal. 318, 342, 249 P. 197; Riley v. Gordon, 137 Cal.App. 311, 30 P.2d 617; Siberell v. Siberell, 214 Cal. 767, 7 P.2d 1003. Although not amounting to a vested interest, her property rights were so far recognized that equitable relief was available where necessary to safeguard against threatened wrongful dispositions of community assets by the husband. See Mahl v. E.A. Portal Co., Inc., 81 Cal.App. 494, 497–498, 254 P. 278; Greiner v. Greiner, 58 Cal. 115, 121. The extent to which the wife's interest may have been enlarged by section 161a need not be inquired into here (see Simmons, Interest of Wife in Community Property, 22 Cal.L.Rev. 404; 3 Cal.Jur. Ten. Year Supp., sec. 90, p. 597), for we think the plaintiff's right to relief extends to gifts out of community assets acquired prior to its enactment, and hence, a fortiori, out of assets acquired subsequent thereto.

* * *

Upon the basis of a suggestion by way of dictum in Hunt v. Authier, supra, that section 574 "assumes, for the purpose of its effective operation, the existence of a cause of action against the tort feasor during his lifetime on behalf of any person authorized by law then to sue him," it is contended that plaintiff may not maintain her suit since no cause of action existed in her as against Fields during his lifetime. Whether the wording of the section justifies such an assumption as a necessary limitation upon its meaning in the absence of express language similar to that contained in its companion section 573, need not be decided here, for we think that a cause of action in favor of plaintiff did exist prior to Fields' death. Because of his fraudulent concealment of the facts concerning his administration of the community estate, she did not know the such a cause of action existed, and accordingly is not barred by the statute of limitations, Pashley v. Pacific Electric R. Co., 25 Cal.2d 226, 153 P.2d 325; but a cause of action nevertheless arose at the time when plaintiff's primary rights were invaded by Fields' wrongful disposition of her property. See Wulfjen v. Dolton, 24 Cal.2d 891, 895–896, 151 P.2d 846, 849, citing Pomeroy, Code Remedies, 5th Ed., sec. 251, p. 536. As noted in the last cited case, the cause of action "may entitle the injured party to many forms of relief, and the relief is not to be confounded with the cause of action, one not being determinative of the other."

Accordingly, we need not consider what type of action plaintiff might have prosecuted, or whether she could have maintained any action against the husband during the existence of the marriage which would not have for one of its purposes a division of the community property, such as an action for separate maintenance. The question is not whether plaintiff, during the existence of the marriage could have prosecuted her cause of action against Fields and have obtained the relief which she now seeks against his estate. It is sufficient that he was guilty of wrongful acts for which she was entitled to redress. If she could not then have maintained an action against him for the value of her interest in the property which he had given away, it would have been due to the policy of the law to forbid vexatious and unnecessary litigation between spouses, and also upon the ground that during the existence of the marriage the husband has the control and management of the community property of which he cannot be divested except through procedure authorized by statute. A wife is not so restricted if she sues for separate maintenance; nor has it ever been questioned that in an action for divorce, or thereafter, she may seek enforcement of all her community property rights. See Gelfand v. Gelfand, 136 Cal.App. 448, 29 P.2d 271; Crossan v. Crossan, 35 Cal.App.2d 39, 94 P.2d 609; Stewart v. Stewart, 204 Cal. 546, 555, 269 P. 439; Dunn v. Mullan, 211 Cal. 583, 590, 296 P. 604, 77 A.L.R. 1015; Provost v. Provost, 102 Cal.App. 775, 283 P. 842; Wheeland v. Rodgers, 20 Cal.2d 218, 222, 124 P.2d 816; Falk v. Falk, 48 Cal.App.2d 762, 768, 120 P.2d 714. Many of the cited cases involved reimbursement to the wife where community funds had been expended in the improvement of the separate property of the husband. The reasons supporting reimbursement to the wife in such situations clearly support plaintiff's right to redress upon the facts pleaded in her complaint. Cf. Vragnizan v. Savings Union Bank & Trust Co., 31 Cal.App. 709, 713, 161 P. 507. There is, as far as we know, no recorded precedent for the maintenance of an action exactly like the present one, although, as we say, it is not distinguishable in principle from other actions based upon constructive frauds committed by the husband. Rights such as plaintiff asserts have invariably been respected and proper redress has been given. The instant case does not differ in substance, but only in the form of relief sought. It is not all important that the present action in that respect is novel. * * *

Defendant places much reliance upon the fact that the complaint does not contain an allegation that plaintiff disaffirmed the gifts during her husband's lifetime. Her contention is that the gifts were valid until they were disaffirmed by plaintiff and as they were not disaffirmed plaintiff had no cause of action for the recovery of the property. This appears to have been the theory upon which the demurrer was sustained. We think it is without merit. Disaffirmance was no part of the right to avoid the gifts. The right to avoid them had to be complete before plaintiff could have exercised her right of election to disaffirm them. Otherwise, repudiation of her husband's actions would have meant nothing. Disaffirmance would have only been one step in a procedure for enforcing the right.

* * *

The judgment is reversed with directions to overrule the demurrer and permit defendant to answer.

Note

In the principal case, the court likened the husband's management and control function to that of a trustee, with attendant fiduciary obligations and controls. This principle is now reflected in West's Ann. Cal. Family Code § 1100(e) which provides that in managing and controlling the community property, each spouse shall act "in accordance with the general rules governing fiduciary relationships of personal confidence as specified in Section 721." Section 721 states that the confidential relationship between spouses imposes a duty of the "highest good faith and fair dealing" and is a fiduciary relationship subject to the same rights and duties as nonmarital business partners.

WILCOX v. WILCOX

California District Court of Appeal, 1971.
21 Cal.App.3d 457, 98 Cal.Rptr. 319.

COUGHLIN, ASSOCIATE JUSTICE. Plaintiff appeals from a judgment of dismissal following an order sustaining defendant's demurrer without leave to amend.

Plaintiff's complaint alleges he and defendant are husband and wife; defendant has taken, is in exclusive possession of, and has secreted $30,000 of community funds; demand has been made upon her for this money; and she refuses to pay the same to plaintiff.

Defendant's demurrer to the complaint was upon the ground: "This Court does not have jurisdiction over the subject matter of this action, in that there is no statutory authority which allows a spouse to sue the other for mismanagement of community funds."

The court sustained the demurrer without leave to amend.

The cause of action alleged in plaintiff's complaint is not premised upon defendant's mismanagement of community funds, as stated in her demurrer, but upon defendant's violation of plaintiff's right to manage, control and dispose of community funds.

By statute a husband "has the management and control of the community personal property, with like absolute power of disposition, other than testamentary, as he has of his separate estate," subject to certain exceptions not material to the case at bench. (Civ.Code § 5125.) The right of the husband thus conferred to manage, control and dispose of community personal property is invaded by his wife when she deprives him thereof by taking, secreting and exercising exclusive control over community funds. A husband has a cause of action against his wife for such an invasion and violation of his right in the premises with attendant appropriate remedies. These conclusions are dictated by the principles stated and applied in Harris v. Harris, 57 Cal.2d 367, 370, 19 Cal.Rptr. 793, 369 P.2d 481; Odone v. Marzocchi, 34 Cal.2d 431, 437–

439, 211 P.2d 297; Fields v. Michael, 91 Cal.App.2d 443, 447–449, 205 P.2d 402; Lynn v. Herman, 72 Cal.App.2d 614, 617, 165 P.2d 54; Salveter v. Salveter, 135 Cal.App. 238, 240, 26 P.2d 836; Johnson v. National Surety Co., 118 Cal.App. 227, 230, 5 P.2d 39; McAlvay v. Consumers' Salt Co., 112 Cal.App. 383, 396, 297 P. 135; and Mitchell v. Moses, 16 Cal.App. 594, 599, 117 P. 685. (See also McKay v. Lauriston, 204 Cal. 557, 564, 269 P. 519; Greiner v. Greiner, 58 Cal. 115, 121.)

The right of the husband to maintain an action against his wife to protect his property rights in community funds, including the right to manage, control and dispose of such with the incident right to possession thereof for this purpose, is not dependent upon statutory authority to sue his wife, as claimed by defendant in her demurrer. In McAlvay v. Consumers' Salt Co., supra, 112 Cal.App. 383, 396, 297 P. 135, 141, the court said: "[T]he right of a husband to maintain an action to quiet his title to community property against the wife has been frequently upheld * * *." In Salveter v. Salveter, supra, 135 Cal.App. 238, 240, 26 P.2d 836, the court upheld the right of the husband to recover and required his wife to account for community funds which were the proceeds of community property. In neither of the foregoing cases was the right of the defendant to sue premised on statutory authority. Basic to the situation at bench is the provision of Civil Code section 3523 that: "For every wrong there is a remedy."

The order sustaining the demurrer was error.

The judgment is reversed.

Note

Wilcox v. Wilcox is one of the few reported decisions involving redress of management and control violations prior to termination of the marriage by death or dissolution proceedings. To what extent should the community property system permit interspousal litigation to be maintained outside of the dissolution context? Professor Bruch, in her article *Management Powers and Duties Under California's Community Property Law: Recommendations for Reform*, 34 Hastings L.J. 227 (1982), posited that there are certain basic spousal rights with regard to the management and control of community property, including the right to know, the right to sound management, the right to participate, and the right to be made whole. She indicated that filing for dissolution should not be the sole method of protection afforded to a spouse whose rights have been infringed. West's Ann.Cal. Family Code §§ 721, 1100 and 1101 now incorporate many of Professor Bruch's suggestions for reform, including the recognition of a spousal duty to make full disclosure of the existence of community assets and debts on request, the right to seek an accounting, and the right to petition the court for access to or beneficial enjoyment of community property. Professor Oldham on the other hand sees potential problems with the accounting remedy:

Although at first glance, the accounting remedy seems appropriate, it could present some problems. In an accounting, the spouse is asked to list all property, and specify whether it is separate or community. It is not clear that spouses will be represented by independent counsel in such matters. It does seem possible that a spouse contemplating divorce could utilize an accounting as a means to obtain advantageous admissions from the other spouse regarding the character of property. The other spouse might not be too vigilant in scrutinizing such an accounting, being unaware that a divorce filing was imminent. If the spouse initiated the accounting to trap the other into making admissions regarding the character of property before obtaining legal advice, such behavior probably violates the duties spouses have to one another.

Oldham, *Management of the Community Estate During an Intact Marriage,* 56 Law & Contemporary Problems 99, 119–120 (1993).

SECTION 2. RECAPTURE AND REIMBURSEMENT PROCEEDINGS

Under Family Code Sections 1100 and 1102, although either spouse has the right to manage and control community property, neither spouse may make a gift of community property without the consent of the other, and neither may convey community real property, even for consideration, unless the other spouse joins in the conveyance. When a married person transfers community property in violation of the statutory restrictions, two persons may be in need of protection. In the gift or gratuitous transfer situation, only the spouse needs protection, but where real property has been transferred for consideration, both the spouse and the transferee may be in need of protection.

The judicially developed rules governing the recapture of community property transferred in violation of Family Code Sections 1100 and 1102 are fairly well defined, although as recent case law indicates, they are not inflexible. During the marriage, the injured spouse can set aside the transfer in toto and bring the property back into the community estate.[15] After the termination of the marriage, the injured spouse can recapture only one half of the property, on the theory that the injured spouse can trace his or her half interest into the hands of the third person and recapture it as separate property.[16] The spouse who made the wrongful transfer is bound by the transaction,[17] and the third person transferee holds title until the recapture action is successfully prosecuted.[18] The transaction is thus not treated as void, but rather as voidable by the non-consenting spouse.[19]

Family Code Section 1102, which precludes all transfers of community real property, both gratuitous and non-gratuitous, unless both spouses join in the conveyance, is the successor to the 1917 legislation restricting the husband from making a transfer of community real property unless his wife joined in the conveyance. The present statute raises a rebuttable presumption that a transfer by the record title holder

---

15. Droeger v. Sloan, reprinted in this section.

16. See Mazman v. Brown, reprinted in this Section.

17. Dargie v. Patterson, 176 Cal. 714, 169 P. 360 (1917).

18. See Strong v. Strong, 22 Cal.2d 540, 140 P.2d 386 (1943).

19. Spreckels v. Spreckels, reprinted in this Section.

to a good faith purchaser without knowledge of the marriage relationship is valid. It also contains a special one-year statute of limitations. Implicit in the language of Section 1102 is the recognition that the injured spouse has an immediate action against the third person for recapture of the real property and against the other spouse for reimbursement. It would seem, however, that if the property was acquired prior to 1975 by the wife in her name alone and was transferred to a good faith purchaser for value, the husband would be unprotected due to the separate property presumption voiced in Family Code Section 803, which is made conclusive in this situation.

In proceedings to recapture real property transferred in violation of Family Code Section 1102, the courts have protected the purchaser of community real property in two different ways. Under certain circumstances, they may apply the equitable doctrines of estoppel and waiver to deny the recapture remedy to the complaining spouse.[20] Where the remedy is granted, they may make the judgment conditional on reimbursing the third person.[21]

SPRECKELS v. SPRECKELS

Supreme Court of California, 1916.
172 Cal. 775, 158 P. 537.

SHAW, J. This is an action by Claus A. Spreckels and Rudolph Spreckels as executors of the will of Anna C. Spreckels, and also in their capacity as executors of the will of Claus Spreckels, and by them and Emma C. Ferris, as individuals, to compel an accounting by the defendants respecting certain property received by them from the decedent Claus Spreckels in his lifetime, and for restitution thereof, so far as it exceeded one-half of the community property of Claus Spreckels and Anna C. Spreckels, his wife, and, if restitution cannot be made, then for judgment for the value thereof. The court below sustained a demurrer to the second amended complaint, and thereupon gave judgment for the defendants. From this judgment the plaintiffs appeal.

* * * In the eight years between 1896 and 1905, Claus Spreckels made gifts to John D. Spreckels and Adolph B. Spreckels of large amounts of this community property aggregating in value about $25,-000,000, according to the allegations of the complaint, leaving remaining in his possession and ownership, at the time of his death, other property not exceeding $10,000,000 in value. Anna C. Spreckels did not, in her husband's lifetime, consent to the making of any of these gifts, either in writing or otherwise. The plaintiffs, by this action, seek to recover, on behalf of the estate of Claus Spreckels and also on behalf of the estate of Anna C. Spreckels and also in their own right, as legatees and devisees of

---

20. Schelling v. Thomas, 96 Cal.App. 682, 274 P. 755 (1929); Vierra v. Pereira, 12 Cal.2d 629, 86 P.2d 816 (1939); Rice v. McCarthy, 73 Cal.App. 655, 239 P. 56 (1925).

21. Mark v. Title Guarantee & Trust Co., reprinted in this Section.

the entire estate of Anna C. Spreckels, a one-half interest in the specific property so given to the defendants, or an amount equal to one-half thereof, if such property cannot be identified.

* * * Section 9 of the act of 1850 remained in force until the enactment of the Civil Code in 1872, the subject being therein covered by section 172 thereof. * * *

This section remained without alteration until 1891 (St.1891, p. 425) when a proviso was added making the section read as follows:

> "The husband has the management and control of the community property, with the like absolute power of disposition, other than testamentary, as he has of his separate estate; provided, however, that he cannot make a gift of such community property, or convey the same without a valuable consideration, unless the wife, in writing, consent thereto." * * *

The appellants contend that the declaration of the proviso that the husband "cannot make a gift" of community property, unless the wife consent thereto in writing, limits his power in that respect absolutely, so that such a gift is absolutely void even in his own lifetime, and may be recovered by him or by the executors of his will after his death. They also contend that if not void as to the husband such gifts are absolutely void as to the wife, if she survives him, and that she, in her lifetime, or her representatives or heirs after her death, may recover the same. Upon these theories they seek to maintain the sufficiency of the complaint.

* * *

We are satisfied that the proviso of 1891 does not render a gift of community property by the husband without the consent of the wife void as to him, nor confer upon him, in his lifetime, or upon his personal representatives after his death, any right or power to revoke the gift or recover the property. There is nothing in the language to express the idea that the title does not, as before, remain wholly in him. The provision is merely for a limitation upon his power to dispose of it. He is bound by his own gift as fully as if it was of his separate estate. The demurrer was properly sustained so far as the executors of the will of Claus Spreckels are concerned.

Neither does the proviso purport to vest in the wife, during the marriage, any present interest or estate in the community property given away by the husband without her written consent. In view of the long-settled doctrine that the entire estate therein is in the husband during the marriage relation, a doctrine that had become a fixed and well-understood rule of property, it is not to be supposed that the Legislature would have made a change of so radical a character without plain language to that effect. We do not find in the proviso such language, nor anything that can reasonably be so construed. If it confers upon her, during the marriage, any right respecting such gifts, it is nothing more than a right to revoke the gift and, if necessary, sue to recover the property, not as her separate estate, but to reinstate it as a part of the community property, with the title vested in the husband and subject to sale by him, as before.

We do not find it necessary to determine whether this right accrues to her at once when the gift is made, or whether it remains in abeyance until her expectancy in the community property becomes vested by the dissolution of the marriage by death or divorce. In either case, upon the facts alleged, the present action must fail, as we will now proceed to show.

If the right accrues to her upon the making of the gift, a cause of action would exist in her favor at that moment to set aside the gifts. The statute of limitations would immediately begin to run against that cause of action, if she had knowledge of the gift, or was put on inquiry concerning it. If she was ignorant thereof at the time, it would begin to run as soon as she discovered the fact, or in the exercise of reasonable diligence should have discovered it. The alleged gifts of real property were made not later than 1897, and the latest gifts of personal property were made in 1904. One ground of demurrer is that the cause of action is barred by the statute of limitations. * * * There is no claim here that Mrs. Spreckels did not know of these gifts when they were made, nor any allegations excusing her ignorance thereof and failure to make discovery, as is required in such cases. Lady Washington v. Wood, 113 Cal. 486, 45 P. 809; Del Campo v. Camarillo, 154 Cal. 657, 98 P. 1049; People v. San Joaquin, etc., Ass'n, 151 Cal. 807, 91 P. 740. In the absence of averment, it must be presumed that she knew of them. Consequently, assuming that she had such right during the marriage, the statute of limitations immediately thereupon began to run against her, and any action by her of that character would have been barred, as to the real property, in 1902, and as to the personal property in 1907 or 1908. Code Civ.Proc., secs. 318, 338, 343. In this aspect of the case it is immaterial whether the gifts are regarded as absolutely void, with respect to her right, or only voidable. In either case the action would be barred. If barred as to her, it would, of course, be barred as to her representatives and heirs after her death.

If we assume the other alternative, that the right of the wife to attack these gifts did not accrue in this case until the dissolution of the marriage by the death of the husband, the case presents a somewhat different aspect. The action, in that event, would not be barred by the statute of limitations. The right of her heirs and personal representatives to avoid the gifts and to recover what would have been her share thereof if the husband died seised of this property leaving her surviving would be complete. It is claimed on the part of the respondents that the provisions of her will show a ratification and confirmation of these gifts. In the consideration of this question it is, therefore, material to determine whether such gifts, as to the wife, became absolutely void upon the death of the husband, or only voidable at her option. If absolutely void, the result would be that the title to the property would have vested in her at his death, and the gifts would perhaps be incapable of confirmation except by a transfer from her.

We are of the opinion that the gifts did not become void at the death of the husband, but were only voidable by the wife at her option. The limitation upon his power to give is not greater in its prohibitive effect than the preceding limitation upon his testamentary power. One is as absolute as the other. Both, in terms, include all the community property, and appear to withhold power to dispose of all or any of it in the proscribed manner. Yet, as above stated, it is well settled that a husband's testamentary disposition of more than one-half of the community property is not absolutely void as to the wife, but only voidable. The limitation upon the husband's power to make a gift is even less positive than that upon the testamentary power, for it depends upon two questions of fact; the absence of a valuable consideration, and the absence of her written consent, both of which may have to be proven by collateral evidence. The gift, when made, immediately vests the property in the donee subject to her right of revocation. She may give her consent at any time during her life, and if she does, the gift becomes absolute with respect to her. The provision was manifestly intended solely for the benefit of the wife. If she seeks to assert such right, it is incumbent upon her to show that the facts exist upon which it depends. The conclusion seems inevitable that the gift is not absolutely void with respect to her, but only voidable by her upon proof of the facts necessary to that end. * * *

* * * It is not alleged that she did not also have full knowledge of all of the alleged gifts by her husband to the defendants. The allegations show that she did have full knowledge of a large part of them. The fourth clause of his will, above quoted, certainly put her on inquiry as to all of them. It is alleged that she caused an inquiry to be made concerning them. In this condition of her affairs she proceeded, on August 16, 1909, seven months after the probate of her deceased husband's will, to make and execute her own will. The second clause declares: "I hereby give, devise, and bequeath all of my estate, of every kind and description" to the three children, Claus A., Rudolph and Emma C., plaintiffs herein. * * *

The words "I hereby give all *my* estate, of every kind and description" to the three other children, excluded John and Adolph from participation in her estate. At that time, and up to her death, they held the property given to them by their father out of the community property. He had declared in his will that because of these gifts he gave them none of the remaining property. He thereby, in effect, declared, as a part of his last will, that they were to keep and hold all of the property he had given to them. Knowing this, and because of this disposition by him of a part of the community property, in effect because they already had the whole of that part, not a half interest only, she declared that she intentionally omitted to give them any share in the remainder disposable by her. The declaration is entirely inconsistent with the existence of a purpose, desire, or intention on her part that her executors or the beneficiaries under her will should have the right to recover a half of that which she says had been "given and advanced" to them. The provision, in connection with the circumstances under which it was made, precludes all idea that she regarded the property so given to the two defendants, or any part thereof or right in regard thereto, as any part of her descendible estate, or that the other three children were to receive, by her will or otherwise, any claim to that property or right to an accounting thereof. It was equivalent to an express ratification and confirmation of said gifts, and it was a consent thereto, by her, in writing, advisedly made. This will she retained unrevoked until her death, showing that notwithstanding her alleged direction to the plaintiff, Claus A. Spreckels, soon after the death of her husband, to begin an action to recover the property so given to John and Adolph, her last and final wish and will was that they should retain it all, but should receive nothing from her.

The plaintiffs have endeavored to avoid these consequences, and prevent consideration of her testamentary confirmation of the gifts, by alleging that Anna C. Spreckels "did not, at any time during her life, consent in writing or otherwise to said gifts." The respective wills of Claus Spreckels and Anna C. Spreckels, both of which are alleged to have been duly probated, are, however, incorporated into the complaint as parts thereof. This renders the aforesaid allegation inoperative, so far as it is inconsistent with the terms of her will. When applied to the will which it is alleged she made, the allegation amounts to no more than the conclusion of the pleader that the provision of the will did not constitute a consent to the gifts, or a confirmation thereof. In our opinion they were both a consent in writing and a ratification and confirmation, and they effectually contradict and nullify the above allegation.

Upon this view of the case it is immaterial whether the gifts to John and Adolph were or were not made to prevent the wife from receiving one-half of the community property of said marriage, or with the design of excluding the other children from ultimate participation, by will or inheritance from her, in any part thereof. It is also unnecessary to consider the question whether or not the right of the widow to attack or avoid those gifts survived her death, and passed to the executors of her will, or to those to whom she devised and bequeathed her estate. During her lifetime she was the only person who had the right to gainsay these gifts. Her power in that respect was complete, so far as others were concerned, and her ratification and confirmation thereof by her will concluded all other persons, regardless of the motive that prompted the gifts or of the nature of her right to avoid them.

The judgment is affirmed.

Notes

1. The court in *Spreckels* left open the question of whether the cause of action to attack or avoid the gift survives the non-consenting spouse. Initially such a cause of action was held to be personal, but in Harris v. *Harris*, 57 Cal.2d 367, 19 Cal.Rptr. 793, 369 P.2d 481 (1962), the Supreme

Court held that the right to set aside the gift survives the death of the non-consenting spouse, and may be exercised by the personal representative of the deceased spouse.

2. In *Spreckels*, the court reiterated the statutory rule that the husband could not make a gift of community property unless the wife consented thereto in writing, but concluded that such consent may be established by later acts of "ratification." Does knowledge of the gifts coupled with a failure to object amount to ratification? In Marriage of Stephenson, 162 Cal.App.3d 1057, 209 Cal.Rptr. 383 (1984), the husband opened several custodial savings accounts pursuant to the Uniform Gifts to Minors Act (UGMA) for the benefit of the couple's minor children. Community funds were deposited in the accounts. Under the UGMA, such deposits constitute irrevocable transfers indefeasibly vesting the funds in the minor child. The trial court found that the wife had knowledge of and participated in opening these savings accounts for their children, and concluded that she was not entitled to have the transfers set aside. The appellate court reversed:

> Since 1978, section 5125, subdivision (b) has provided: "A spouse may not make a gift of community personal property, or dispose of community personal property without a valuable consideration, without the written consent of the other spouse."

> A gift made by one spouse in violation of this section is voidable by the other spouse in its entirety during the donor spouse's lifetime if the community has not yet been dissolved but if action is taken after the donor spouse's death or after the community has been dissolved, it is voidable only to the extent of one-half. (*Bank of California v. Connolly* (1973) 36 Cal.App.3d 350, 377, 111 Cal.Rptr. 468; *Harris v. Harris* (1962) 57 Cal.2d 367, 369, 19 Cal.Rptr. 793, 369 P.2d 481.)

> We deal first with those UGMA accounts opened by Roy. The record is devoid of evidence that Beth gave her written consent to the opening of those accounts with community property funds.

> The referee concluded, however, that Beth "will not now be heard to allege that the UGMA Accounts were opened without her written consent and said gifts, made with the consent and approval of both Petitioner and Respondent, are irrevocable and, when made, conveyed to the minor children indefeasibly vested legal title."

> In urging the correctness of this conclusion, Roy relies on the provisions of section 1157, subdivision (b) which states that a gift made pursuant to the UGMA is "irrevocable and conveys to the minor indefeasibly vested legal title to the custodial property * * *." We conclude that this subdivision does not preclude a spouse from voiding a gift of community property that is otherwise voidable. (See *In re Marriage of Hopkins* (1977) 74 Cal.App.3d 591, 602, fn. 7, 141 Cal.Rptr. 597; cf. *Estate of Bray* (1964) 230 Cal.App.2d 136, 40 Cal.Rptr. 750.)

> In *Bray*, the husband purchased savings bonds with community funds without the knowledge or consent of his wife. He registered those bonds jointly in the names of himself and his son. Husband subsequently died and the son contended that pursuant to statutory and case authority he was entitled to full ownership of the bonds, regardless of

the community property laws. The court rejected this contention, concluding that this would result in an impermissible conversion of the wife's assets. Accordingly, the court held that the purchase of the savings bonds by husband could not defeat the community property interest of the wife.

We, too, conclude that one spouse cannot defeat the interest of the other spouse in the community property by unilaterally purporting to make a gift of it pursuant to the UGMA. Consequently, absent written consent, written ratification, waiver or estoppel, the non-donor spouse is not precluded from voiding the gift.

The referee apparently concluded that Beth is estopped or has waived her right to void the subject gifts. "Questions of waiver and estoppel involve issues of fact for the trial court." (*Los Angeles Fire & Police Protective League v. City of Los Angeles* (1972) 23 Cal.App.3d 67, 75, 99 Cal.Rptr. 908.) "Estoppel applies to prevent a person from asserting a right where his conduct or silence makes it unconscionable for him to assert it." (*In re Marriage of Recknor* (1982) 138 Cal.App.3d 539, 546, 187 Cal.Rptr. 887.) Either unjust enrichment or a change in position may be the basis of an unconscionable injury which will estop a person from asserting the requirement of a writing. (*Mintz v. Rowitz* (1970) 13 Cal.App.3d 216, 224–225, 91 Cal.Rptr. 435.)

"Waiver requires a voluntary act, knowingly done, with sufficient awareness of the relevant circumstances and likely consequences. [Citation.] There must be actual or constructive knowledge of the existence of the right to which the person is entitled. [Citation.] The burden is on the party claiming a waiver to prove it by evidence that does not leave the matter doubtful or uncertain and the burden must be satisfied by clear and convincing evidence that does not leave the matter to speculation. [Citation.] This rule particularly applies to cases involving a right favored in law such as * * * the right to retain lawful property entitlement * * *." (*In re Marriage of Moore* (1980) 113 Cal.App.3d 22, 27, 169 Cal.Rptr. 619.)

In support of the trial court's conclusion, claimants refer to evidence demonstrating that Beth had knowledge and participated in the couple's program of opening up savings accounts for their children pursuant to the UGMA.

This evidence is insufficient to support a finding of either estoppel or waiver. With regard to estoppel, the record contains neither evidence that the claimant children changed their position in a manner that will cause them to suffer an unconscionable injury should Beth void the gifts, nor evidence that Beth will be unjustly enriched in such an event. Accordingly, there is insufficient evidence to support a finding that Beth is estopped to void the subject gifts.

With regard to waiver, the evidence to which Roy refers is insufficient to demonstrate that Beth knowingly and voluntarily waived her property interest in the UGMA accounts set up by Roy or that she knowingly and voluntarily waived her right to veto such transactions by withholding her written consent.

The cases to which claimants refer in support of their assertion are distinguishable. Those cases involve situations in which a wife's participation or acquiescence in the disposition of community property to third parties induced those parties to deal with the property as if she had consented to that disposition, to the detriment of the third parties. (See *MacKay v. Darusmont* (1941) 46 Cal.App.2d 21, 26, 115 P.2d 221; *Bush v. Rogers* (1941) 42 Cal.App.2d 477, 479–480, 109 P.2d 379.) The record contains no such evidence of detrimental reliance in this case.

The amendments to section 5125, subdivision (b) clearly demonstrate the Legislature's desire to strictly regulate one spouse's ability to give away community property. This is evidenced by the 1975–1978 version of that subdivision under which a spouse was precluded from making any gift of community personal property. The re-enactment of the provision allowing for gifts of community personal property with the *written* consent of the other spouse in 1978 must be interpreted to require something more than the tacit approval of the gift by the non-donor spouse. A different interpretation would entirely vitiate the writing requirement. We decline to engage in such "doctrinal machinations." (See Bruch, *Management Powers and Duties Under California's Community Property Law: Recommendations For Reform* (1982–1983) 34 Hastings L.J. 227, 239–240.) While the application of this rule may be harsh in the case at bench, any change in this scheme is for the Legislature and not this court to make.

See also Marriage of Stallworth, 192 Cal.App.3d 742, 237 Cal.Rptr. 829 (1987), holding that in the absence of written consent, written ratification, waiver or estoppel, the nondonor spouse is not precluded from avoiding the gift.

MAZMAN v. BROWN

California District Court of Appeal, 1936.
12 Cal.App.2d 272, 55 P.2d 539.

Roth, Justice Pro Tem. Samuel Mazman, in his lifetime while married to Thelma Mazman, plaintiff and appellant herein, took out a policy of insurance in the State Life Company of Indianapolis, Ind., on his life in the sum of $5,000, and up to the time of his accidental death paid all premiums thereon with community funds. The policy contained a provision for payment of double benefits in case of death by accident, by reason of which $10,000 was distributed by the insurance company to the beneficiaries named in the policy, to wit, one-third to Thelma, his wife, and two-thirds to one E.A. Brown, as trustee for the parents of the insured. * * *

While Brown, as trustee of the insurance proceeds, was in the possession of the same, the instant action was instituted by plaintiff wife to enforce her demand for one-half of the trust estate. Said action, by reason of the facts outlined, has resolved itself into a claim against Logian, as administrator, for one-half of the $6,708.26, which became part of the estate of the insured's mother. Plaintiff predicates her demand on the theory that the insurance was bought and paid for with community funds, and that her husband, the insured, could give away no more than one-half of the proceeds thereof. This is undoubtedly the law. * * * Logian, the administrator, conceded the soundness of the legal principle urged by appellant, but differed as to its application, and contended in the trial court, as he does here, that appellant was entitled to one-half of the face of the policy, to wit, $5,000 in the aggregate, and not to one-third of the policy, pursuant to its terms, and one-half of the remaining two-thirds. The trial court decreed that the administrator's position was the correct one, and, since by stipulation of counsel it appeared that Logian had already paid to plaintiff $1,650, which, added to the one-third of the face of the policy already received by her, to wit $3,333.34, aggregated $4,983.34, the trial court gave judgment for $16.66 in favor of plaintiff, from which judgment she takes this appeal.

If the insured in this case had made his parents the sole beneficiaries of the policy in question, then, upon the facts as here outlined and under the law as settled by the authorities cited, appellant would be entitled to no more than one-half of the proceeds of the policy. The difficulty which is created by the facts of this case is caused by the solicitude which the deceased showed for his wife by making her even a partial beneficiary. A husband undoubtedly has a right to give away his one-half of the community property. (Civ.Code, § 1401, now § 201, Probate Code); and he may do it by valid gift to take effect upon his death as by way of an insurance policy, as well as by a will. Blethen v. Pacific Mutual Life Ins. Co., 198 Cal. 91, 100, 243 P. 431; Travelers' Ins. Co. v. Fancher, 219 Cal. 351, 355, 26 P.2d 482. It has been determined that "the designation of a beneficiary in a policy of life insurance initiates in favor of the beneficiary an inchoate gift of the proceeds of the policy, which, if not revoked by the insured prior to his death, vests in the beneficiary at the time of his death." Fancher Case, supra, 219 Cal. 351, at page 353, 26 P.2d 482, 483; Blethen v. Pacific Mutual Life Ins. Co., supra. The failure of plaintiff to distinguish between an inchoate gift and a completed gift is, we believe, the source of confusion in this case. To illustrate, if, during the lifetime of a husband and wife, the spouses have $10,000 in a bank and the husband by agreement makes a completed gift of one-third of that amount to his wife, the one-third thus given becomes the separate property of the wife, and the two-thirds remaining continues to be community property to the extent of 100 per cent. thereof. 3 Cal.Jur.Supp. 649; In re Estate of Fingland, 129 Cal.App. 395, 18 P.2d 747. If, prior to such gift, or after the consummation of such a gift, the husband by will disposed of the whole of said bank account and bequeathed one-third to his spouse and the remaining two-thirds to his parents, there is no doubt that all that would be disposed of by the will would be the remaining two-thirds in the bank account and not the original whole. This remaining two-thirds, being community property, would unquestionably be subject to the claim of the surviving wife for 50 per cent. thereof, if she elected to enforce her community rights instead of taking under the will. If the facts of the instant case were analogous to those of the illustration given, appellant would undoubtedly be correct in her contention in the case at bar. Here, however, there is no completed gift, and there could be none under the circumstances and facts of this case until the death of the insured. At the time of the insured's death, the dispositions made by the insured of the insurance proceeds vested simultaneously to the extent and in the amounts that such gifts could be validly made. Under the law as it has been settled in this state, the insured could not make a valid gift of the proceeds of insurance purchased with community funds in excess of 50 per cent. thereof, without the written consent of the wife. Civ.Code, § 172; Travelers' Ins. Co. v. Fancher, 219 Cal. 351, 354, 26 P.2d 482; Blethen v. Pacific Mutual Life Ins. Co., 198 Cal. 91, 99, 243 P. 431. If a gift of insurance proceeds in excess of 50 per cent. is made to someone other than the wife, and the wife herself is named as a partial beneficiary in the insurance policy, the wife is confronted with the same election which she is bound to make if community property were similarly disposed of by will; that is to say, she must decide to take under the policy, or to stand on her community rights as to the proceeds of such policy. If she takes under the policy, she thereby makes an election and waives her right to exercise her power of revocation as to that portion of the gift in excess of 50 per cent. Fancher Case, supra, 219 Cal. 351, 26 P.2d 482; Blethen v. Pacific Mutual Life Ins. Co., 198 Cal. 91, 100, 243 P. 431; Jenkins v. Jenkins, 112 Cal.App. 402, 297 P. 56. If however, she elects to stand on her community rights, then she is entitled to her 50 per cent. in lieu of the one-third given, and the remaining 50 per cent. would go to the other beneficiaries named, since it is settled that the gift by the husband of community property in excess of 50 per cent, does not invalidate the entire disposition, but is invalid only as to the excess on complaint of the wife. Travelers' Ins. Co. v. Fancher, 219 Cal. 351, 352, 26 P.2d 482; Spreckels v. Spreckels, 172 Cal. 775, 158 P. 537; Dargie v. Patterson, 176 Cal. 714, 169 P. 360; Trimble v. Trimble, 219 Cal. 340, 343, 26 P.2d 477. "If, after the gift is made, the wife gives her consent, the requirements of the statute are fulfilled, and no further action is required to make it a valid and effective gift." Blethen v. Pacific Mutual Life Ins. Co., 198 Cal. 91, 99, 243 P. 431, 434.

* * *

* * * We are satisfied that the logic and justice of the situation here presented impel the conclusion that the surviving wife is bound to make the election suggested. In the instant case, so far as the record shows the wife did elect to take under the policy; subsequently, and after her election had been completed, she made a demand for one-half of the two-thirds which was earmarked for her parents-in-law. Her demand was conceded to the extent that she was entitled to one-half of the face of the policy, and by virtue of the judgment entered she received the difference between what she took under the policy, the amount she received from the executor of her deceased mother-in-law in partial compliance with her demand, and one-half of the policy.

The executor, who is the defendant and respondent here, does not complain of the judgment and does not appeal therefrom. As we view the situation, appellant received all and more than she was legally entitled to.

The judgment is affirmed.

ESTATE OF WILSON

California District Court of Appeal, 1986.
183 Cal.App.3d 67, 227 Cal.Rptr.3d 67.

KING, ASSOCIATE JUSTICE.

In this case we hold that when a spouse deposits community property funds in a bank account in his name as trustee for a third person, upon that spouse's death only one-half of the community property in the account is transmitted to the third person. The other one-half, being the surviving spouse's share of community property, goes to the survivor even though he or she is already receiving more than one-half of the total community property of the parties.

Billy W. Bowens, a son of the decedent, and Mildred Tolliver, mother of two minor children of decedent, appeal from an order which awarded Ruth Wilson (Wilson) half the funds in three separate "Totten trusts"[1] created by Milburn Warren Wilson (decedent) in favor of three of his children. Bowens and Tolliver contend Wilson is not entitled to any part of the disputed trust accounts because decedent had the right to make a testamentary disposition of one-half of the entire community property taken as a whole, rather than merely one-half of each community property asset.[2] We affirm the judgment.

Decedent died intestate on June 12, 1983, leaving a surviving spouse, Wilson, and nine children. Decedent opened ten Totten trust bank accounts for his children and four bank trust accounts for his wife prior to his death. At his death the children's accounts totalled approximately $131,500 and Wilson's accounts totalled approximately $38,500.

---

1. The Totten trust basically allows a decedent to make a testamentary disposition of cash assets without going through the formalities of drawing up a will. "Under a rule established in the New York case of *Matter of Totten*, [179 N.Y. 112, 71 N.E. 748], if a depositor merely opens a bank account *in his own name as trustee* for another person, intending to reserve the power to withdraw funds during his lifetime, a *tentative trust* is created, *revocable* during the trustor's lifetime or by his will, and at his death presumptively an absolute trust. *Partial revocation* takes place whenever the depositor withdraws money from the account, and the beneficiary is entitled only to the balance on deposit at death. But if the *beneficiary dies first,* the tentative trust is terminated." (7 Witkin, Sum-

mary of Cal.Law (8th ed. 1974) Trusts, § 17, p. 5379, emphasis in original.) California has recognized the legitimacy of Totten trusts for a long time (*Kosloskye v. Cis* (1945) 70 Cal.App.2d 174, 160 P.2d 565; *Estate of Collins* (1978) 84 Cal.App.3d 928, 932, 149 Cal.Rptr. 65, stating the Totten trust doctrine "is accepted law in this state"), and recently the Legislature authorized this form of testamentary disposition by enacting the Multiple–Party Accounts Law. (Prob.Code, § 5100 et seq.)

2. Bowens and Tolliver do not dispute on appeal the court's implicit finding that the funds for these accounts came from community property nor that the accounts themselves were community property during decedent's lifetime.

Wilson claims she had no knowledge of these accounts prior to decedent's death. She first discovered the trust accounts when she opened his safety deposit box and found the bank books.

Wilson filed a community property petition under Probate Code section 650[3] claiming all of decedent's community property as her own, including the children's trust accounts. Bowens and Tolliver objected to the requested distribution of any of the money in the children's accounts because it constituted less than half of the total value of the Wilsons' community property.

The trial court awarded Wilson all community property land, vehicles and household furnishings. In addition, the court awarded her 100 percent of all the trust accounts not subject to dispute and 50 percent of the three accounts held by decedent as trustee for the children.

Bowens and Tolliver argue former section 201[4] required the court to deny Wilson's request for one-half of each of the trust accounts because the statute specifically allowed decedent to dispose of his one-half of the community property at his death. Section 201 stated prior to its repeal: "Upon the death of either husband or wife, one-half of the community property belongs to the surviving spouse; the other half is subject to the testamentary disposition of the decedent, and in the absence thereof goes to the surviving spouse, subject to the provisions of sections 202 and 203 of this code."

Contrary to the assertion of Bowens and Tolliver, the statutory language of section 201 does not clearly indicate the meaning of "community property" in this context. The phrase "one-half of the community property" is, on its face, capable of meaning either one-half of the "total value" of all community property or one-half of "each item" of community property.

All cases cited by the parties as well as those found by our independent research treat the testamentary right articulated in section 201 as meaning the decedent has a right to dispose of only one-half of *each community property asset* to someone other than a spouse, although none of the cases directly hold the decedent's right of disposition is so limited.

Bowens and Tolliver rely on *Odone v. Marzocchi* (1949) 34 Cal.2d 431, 212 P.2d 233, to support their argument that the term "community property" as used in section 201 means the "total value of the communi-

---

3. Probate Code section 650, subdivision (a), provides in pertinent part: "A surviving spouse * * * may file a petition in the superior court in the county in which the estate of the deceased spouse may be administered alleging that administration of all or a part of the estate is not necessary for the reason that all or a part of the estate is property passing or belonging to the surviving spouse."

Unless otherwise indicated, all further statutory references are to the Probate Code.

4. Decedent opened all the trust accounts at issue and died before 1985, therefore section 201 governs his testamentary disposition of assets despite its repeal as of January 1, 1985. (See Stats.1983, ch. 842, p. 3024, § 19.) The relevant language of section 201, however, continues in substance in the new sections 100, 6101 and 6401. (See Cal.Law Revision Committee com., 52 West's Ann.Prob.Code (1986 Supp.) § 100, pp. 28–29.)

ty property." In *Odone,* a wife gave $5,400 to a friend just before the wife went into the hospital. She asked him to pay her bills with the money, and to return the balance to her if she lived, but to keep the balance if she died. She died eight days after making this request. Decedent's husband brought suit to recover this personal property from his wife's friend. The court held this gift *causa mortis* "upon [the wife's] death may be avoided by [the husband] as to one-half only." (*Odone v. Marzocchi, supra,* 34 Cal.2d at p. 439, 212 P.2d 233.)

Bowens and Tolliver argue this holding is consistent with their view of section 201 because the $5,400 constituted *all* of the community property of both spouses. However, they are unable to point out where such a finding appears in the opinion. An independent review of *Odone* reveals the court made no such finding. In fact, the court held the husband could avoid his wife's gift only as to "one-half thereof," without any consideration whatsoever of the total amount of the parties' community property or the percentage of the community which the $5,400 gift constituted. In reaching its conclusion, the court relied on the rule that "a gift made *inter vivos* by the husband to a third person of community property without the wife's consent is valid as to *one-half thereof* at his death, although the wife, during her husband's lifetime may set it aside *in toto.*" (*Id.,* at p. 438, 212 P.2d 233, emphasis added.)

In *Trimble v. Trimble* (1933) 219 Cal. 340, 26 P.2d 477, the court allowed the wife to set aside a one-half interest in each of two parcels of property that her husband had given to their children, without her consent, shortly before he died. The court gave the wife a one-half interest in each parcel of land without any consideration of the total value of community property left to her or of the total value of each piece of property. The *Trimble* court unequivocally held "the deeds executed by the deceased without consideration and without the consent of his wife are valid conveyances as to *one-half of the property sought to be conveyed,* but may be avoided by his wife as to her half of said community property." (*Id.,* at p. 347, 26 P.2d 477, emphasis added.)

The California Supreme Court examined a closely related issue when, under the then existing law of intestacy, a decedent's spouse was entitled to one-half of the community property and surviving children were entitled to the other half. The court held that at the time of decedent's death the children acquired a present vested interest in an undivided one-half of the community property and the surviving spouse acquired an identical interest in the other one-half of the community property. (*Estate of Sweitzer* (1932) 215 Cal. 489, 11 P.2d 633.)

In *Tyre v. Aetna Life Ins. Co.* (1960) 54 Cal.2d 399, 403, 6 Cal.Rptr. 13, 353 P.2d 725, the California Supreme Court implied that a surviving spouse "became entitled, immediately upon her husband's death, to one-half of each part of the community property." The *Tyre* court held a "husband cannot deprive his wife of her community interest by exceeding his testamentary powers to make gifts of more than half the community property to third persons * * * "　(*Id.*, at p. 405, 6 Cal.Rptr. 13, 353 P.2d 725.)

While these cases did not involve Totten trusts, they dealt with analogous situations. Each concerned an inter vivos gift to someone other than the surviving spouse of community property which became a testamentary disposition upon the donor's death. Similarly, a Totten trust is created during the decedent's life and is a gift to the same extent that any revocable trust is a gift.[5] At the donor's death the Totten trust becomes a testamentary disposition of the assets contained within it. Because a Totten trust is indistinguishable from the cases examined above, the same treatment should apply.

A general rule emerges from these cases. If a spouse, after the death of the decedent, proves a lack of consent to a gift, it will be avoided to the extent of the nonconsenting spouse's one-half interest in community property transferred. (*In re Marriage of Stephenson* (1984) 162 Cal.App.3d 1057, 1070–1071, 209 Cal.Rptr. 383; see also *Trimble v. Trimble, supra,* 219 Cal. at p. 347, 26 P.2d 477.)

The rationale of this rule is founded in the nature of community property. "The respective interests of the husband and wife in community property during continuance of the marriage relation are present, existing and equal interests." (Civ.Code, § 5105.) In other words, each spouse has a vested undivided one-half interest in the community property.[6] Death of a spouse only dissolves the community; it does not affect the character of the property acquired or rights vested before the spouse's death. (*Solko v. Jones* (1931) 117 Cal.App. 372, 376, 3 P.2d 1028, disapproved on other grounds in *Flores v. Brown* (1952) 39 Cal.2d 622, 632, 248 P.2d 922.)

Because each asset is only half his or hers to give, a spouse cannot make a testamentary disposition to a third party of any specific item of community property except by a "forced election" requiring the surviving spouse to elect either to take under the testamentary scheme or to take his or her community property share.[7] To give an example, one

5. In both *Odone* and *Tyre* the gifts were revocable. In *Odone,* the gift of $5,400 was conditional on the wife's death and also on the amount of money she would need during her illness. In *Tyre,* the insured husband could have changed the named insurance beneficiary from his wife to a third party at any time before he died.

6. The vested nature of the surviving spouse's claim to one-half of the community property upon the death of the other spouse is consistent with, but not dependent on, the vested nature of the surviving spouse's community property rights during marriage. (*Estate of Murphy* (1976) 15 Cal.3d 907, 916, 126 Cal.Rptr. 820, 544 P.2d 956.) "[T]he surviving spouse's rightful claim to half of the community property on the other spouse's death stems not from the rights held during the marriage but from the survivor's vested interest existent immediately upon death unless and until voluntarily relinquished." (*Ibid.*)

7. The doctrine of election provides that when a testator spouse disposes of property, by will, which belongs in part or in whole to the surviving spouse, and in the same will devises other property to the surviving spouse, an election is forced. (*Tassi v. Tassi* (1958) 160 Cal.App.2d 680, 685, 325 P.2d 872.) The surviving spouse cannot at the same time take the benefits offered by the will and repudiate the losses, but must either accept the terms of the will completely or reject them completely. (*Ibid.*) Although the doctrine of election has been most frequently applied to wills, it has also been held to apply to any instrument creat-

spouse cannot devise the family residence to a third party even if there are sufficient other community assets to counterbalance the gift's value, because each spouse only owns an undivided one-half interest in the residence. Obviously, the decedent cannot give away more than he or she owns. Indeed, it would be quite unfair to allow either spouse to give away an asset that both spouses treasure based merely on the contingency of who dies first. The mere existence of a Totten trust at the time of the death of one spouse does not put the surviving spouse to a forced election.

Although this rule makes less practical sense in the context of fungible assets like money, as we have here, the same rule applies. (See *Odone v. Marzocchi, supra,* 34 Cal.2d 431, 212 P.2d 233.) Thus while the decedent cannot leave a third party the entire balance of an account which has $10,000 of community property in it and is held as trustee for the third party, the decedent can, by will, leave a legacy of $10,000 to the third party from his one-half share of the community property.

In sum, since each Totten trust is an individual community property asset in which the decedent had only a one-half undivided interest at the time he died, he could pass on to third parties only his one-half of that asset—in this case one-half of the funds in each account. Although the practical effect of this rule limits the ability to make testamentary dispositions of community property through Totten trusts, individuals possess virtually unlimited ability to dispose of their share of the community assets at death by will.

The judgment is affirmed.

Low, P.J., and HANING, J., concur.

Note

West's Ann. California Probate Code § 5020 now expressly provides that a nonprobate transfer of community property on death that is executed without a spouse's written consent is not effective as to the nonconsenting spouse's interest in the property. However, the clarifying legislation does not address the "entity" versus "aggregate" issues addressed in *Wilson.*

DROEGER v. FRIEDMAN, SLOAN & ROSS

Supreme Court of California, 1991.
54 Cal.3d 26, 283 Cal.Rptr. 584, 812 P.2d 931.

PANELLI, JUSTICE.

We granted review to determine whether a security interest in community real property given by one spouse to secure attorney fees during a pending marital dissolution proceeding is valid under Civil Code

ing property rights. (*Estate of Waters* 775; see also 7 Witkin, Summary of Cal. (1972) 24 Cal.App.3d 81, 85, 100 Cal.Rptr.

section 5127 [now Family Code section 1102].[1] Resolution of this question requires that we clarify the general rules governing transfers[2] by one spouse in violation of section 5127.[3]

* * *

I. FACTS AND PROCEEDINGS

In 1982, Joanna Droeger (Wife) commenced a marital dissolution proceeding against appellant John Droeger (Husband). Wife retained Friedman, Sloan & Ross (Friedman) as her counsel in the proceeding. * * *

On November 3, 1986, Wife executed a promissory note in the amount of $31,158.66 in favor of Friedman for attorney fees and costs. On the same day, Wife executed a deed of trust on two parcels of the community's real property securing the note. Husband did not join in the execution of the note or the deed of trust.

Husband commenced action in superior court to quiet title to the community realty that is encumbered by the deed of trust. Relying on *Mitchell v. American Reserve Ins. Co.* (1980) 110 Cal.App.3d 220, 167 Cal.Rptr. 760 (*Mitchell*), Friedman demurred to Husband's second amended complaint, claiming that the deed of trust was enforceable against Wife's one-half interest in the property. The court sustained the demurrer without leave to amend and entered a judgment of dismissal. Husband's motion for reconsideration was denied.

Concluding that the intent of section 5127 was to prevent division of community real property except by agreement of both spouses, or by the death of one spouse, or by dissolution of the marriage, the Court of Appeal reversed. The Court of Appeal held that Husband was entitled to void the encumbrance in its entirety. We affirm.

II. SECTION 5127

Section 5127, [now Family Code section 1102], which applies to the management and control of community real property, states in part, "either spouse has the management and control of the community real property ..., but both spouses either personally or by duly authorized agent, must join in executing any instrument by which such community real property or any interest therein is leased for a longer period than one year, or is sold, conveyed, or encumbered ...."

Law (8th ed. 1974) Wills and Probate, § 21, p. 5542.)

1. Hereafter, all statutory references are to the California Civil Code unless otherwise indicated.

2. Section 5127 applies to leases for a longer period than one year, sales, conveyances, and encumbrances of community real property. For convenience, these actions will collectively be referred to as "transfers."

3. The precise order we issued to the parties stated: "The issues to be argued before this court shall be limited to (1) whether Civil Code section 5127 permits one spouse to encumber his/her interest in community property without the consent of the other spouse, and (2) if so, whether a security interest in community property given by one spouse for attorney fees during a pending dissolution is valid."

Since 1975, when reforms of the community property laws (discussed *post*) became effective, the appellate courts have reached inconsistent results in determining the effect of violations of section 5127 where one spouse has made a transfer without obtaining the other spouse's signature or authorization. Both lines of cases agree that a deed of trust, signed by only one spouse, cannot create a valid lien on the entire community real property; the nonconsenting spouse has authority to void the lien on his or her one-half interest in the property. The cases differ, however, on whether the nonconsenting spouse has the authority to void the lien entirely. (See *Mitchell, supra,* 110 Cal.App.3d 220, 167 Cal.Rptr. 760; *Andrade Development Co. v. Martin* (1982) 138 Cal.App.3d 330, 187 Cal.Rptr. 863 (*Andrade*).)

The conflict in the Court of Appeal cases cannot be understood or resolved without examining the history of section 5127. The language of section 5127 is substantially derived from that found in former section 172a, which dates back to 1917. The history of former section 172a and section 5127 reveals the evolution of the recognition of the wife's equal status in California community property law. As will be seen, however, the evolving recognition of the wife's equality has not always been reflected in the case law.

At the beginning of the California community property system in 1849, the husband was regarded as the full and complete owner of the community property and had the exclusive management and control of the community property. The wife's interest was an expectancy which was limited to the rights she would accrue only if she survived the termination of the marriage. (See Prager, *The Persistence of Separate Property Concepts in California's Community Property System* (1977) 24 UCLA L.Rev. 1, 35.) The first provision of our statutory law on the subject of the rights of the husband and wife in community property was section 9 of the Community Property Act of April 17, 1850 (Stats. 1850, ch. 103, § 9, p. 254). Under section 9 of the Act "[t]he husband shall have the entire management and control of the common property, with the like absolute power of disposition as of his own separate estate."

Construing the Community Property Act, early cases held that, during the marriage, the estate of the husband in the community property was absolute, while that of the wife was a mere expectancy, as that of an heir. (See *Spreckels v. Spreckels* (1916) 172 Cal. 775, 158 P. 537 (*Spreckels*).) Section 9 of the Community Property Act of 1850 remained in force until the enactment of the Civil Code in 1872. The substance of section 9 of the act was covered by section 172 of the Civil Code. In 1891, section 172 was amended to read, "[t]he husband has the management and control of the community property, with the like absolute power of disposition, other than testamentary, as he has of his separate estate; *provided, however,* that he cannot make a gift of such community property, or convey the same without a valuable consideration, unless the wife, in writing, consent [sic] thereto."

Interpreting the 1891 proviso, the *Spreckels* court upheld the concept of the husband's almost absolute power over the community property. According to the court, the proviso did not "vest in the wife, during the marriage, any present interest or estate in the community property given away by the husband without her written consent.... If [the proviso] confers upon her, during the marriage, any right respecting such gifts, it is nothing more than a right to revoke the gift and, if necessary, sue to recover the property, not as her separate estate, but to reinstate it as a part of the community property, with the title vested in the husband and subject to sale by him, as before." (*Spreckels, supra,* 172 Cal. at p. 782, 158 P. 537.)

Dargie v. Patterson (1917) 176 Cal. 714, 169 P. 360 (*Dargie*) addressed the question left unanswered by *Spreckels,* i.e., whether the wife could avoid a deed in its entirety, or "only so far as is necessary to protect her rights." (*Id.* at p. 718, 169 P. 360.) In *Dargie* the husband had made a gift of community real property during the marriage without the knowledge or consent of the wife. After the husband died, the wife filed an action to set aside the transfer. We held that "the only logical conclusion is that the wife's right to assail the conveyance where, as here, the action is brought after the husband's death, is limited to an undivided half of the property." (*Ibid.*) The rationale for the decision was that because the husband had died, his testamentary power existed and the widow need not be given greater rights than she would have enjoyed if the gift had never been made. Consequently, we invalidated the transfer only as to the wife's portion of the community property.

In 1917 former section 172a was added to the Civil Code. (Stats. 1917, ch. 583, § 2, p. 829.) Former section 172a continued to uphold the husband's sole management and control of the community real property, but, significantly, provided that "the wife must join with him in executing any instrument by which such community real property or any interest therein is leased for a longer period than one year, or is sold, conveyed, or encumbered. ..."

The concept of a wife's interest in community property as being no more than a mere expectancy was abrogated in 1927. Legislation enacted in 1927 (Stats.1927, ch. 265, § 1, p. 484) gave the wife a "present, existing, and equal interest" in the community property. (See *Byrd v. Blanton* (1983) 149 Cal.App.3d 987, 992, 210 Cal.Rptr. 458.) This enactment, however, was motivated by the desire to obtain federal income tax benefits for California taxpayers (i.e., to allow income splitting based on community co-ownership, before joint returns were allowed for all married couples) and did not increase the wife's power to manage the community property. (See Reppy, *Retroactivity of the 1975 Community Property Reforms* (1978) 48 So.Cal.L.Rev. 977, 1089.)

In *Lahaney v. Lahaney* (1929) 208 Cal. 323, 281 P. 67 we addressed a case under former section 172a where the husband had died prior to the wife instituting an action to set aside his inter vivos gift of community real property. We held that the deed executed by the husband was valid, subject only to the wife's right to institute, seasonably, an action in equity to revoke the deed and reinstate the property as community property with the title vested in the husband. (208 Cal. at p. 326, 281 P. 67.) As the wife brought the action after the husband's death, we concluded that the community was already divided and she could only recover her one-half interest in the property.

In *Pretzer v. Pretzer* (1932) 215 Cal. 659, 12 P.2d 429, *Trimble v. Trimble* (1933) 219 Cal. 340, 26 P.2d 477, and *Heuer v. Heuer* (1949) 33 Cal.2d 268, 201 P.2d 385, we considered similar questions of the effect of a husband's disposition of community real property without the wife's consent. In all three cases the community had been dissolved, either by death or divorce, prior to the wife's action, and in all three we held that the transfer was invalid only as to the wife's remaining one-half interest in the property.[4]

In *Britton v. Hammell* (1935) 4 Cal.2d 690, 52 P.2d 221 (*Britton*), we discussed for the first time an action brought by a nonconsenting spouse while the marriage, and hence the community, was still in existence. John Britton procured a decree of divorce from his first wife, Sophie Britton, in 1891. He acquired property in 1916, and in 1923 and 1924 he conveyed title to the property to Rose Britton, supposedly his second wife. She later conveyed it back to him as his separate property. Rose died in 1926 and John deeded the property away. Sophie brought action to declare the deeds void and to compel the return of the property to the community. In a separate action, John's divorce decree from Sophie was annulled because it had been procured by fraud. Because the first marriage was determined to be still in existence when the deeds were made, we concluded that Sophie was entitled to set aside the gift of community real property in its entirety.

We gave four reasons for our decision in *Britton* allowing a complete set aside of the gift: If the wife "were only permitted to recover a one-half interest, and that one-half interest recovered were to remain community property, it would still be subject to the husband's control, with the result that the protection given the wife by the statute would be substantially nullified. If, on the other hand, the one-half interest recovered were regarded as her separate property, there would be a resulting division or partition of the community property during the marriage by the husband's arbitrary act, without consent of the wife. Our law does not contemplate this means of dividing the community property. It provides only for division after dissolution of the community by death or divorce, [or during marriage with the consent of both spouses]." (*Britton, supra*, 4 Cal.2d at p. 692, 52 P.2d 221.) As mentioned, we also noted that the cases allowing the wife to recover only

4. *Heuer v. Heuer, supra*, 33 Cal.2d 268, 201 P.2d 385, involved somewhat unique facts in that the wife, suing after she was validly divorced, agreed during appeal that she would be satisfied if her one-half community interest in the property was restored to her. We noted that "[t]his would be proper since the conveyances by the husband may be deemed valid as to his community interest [citations] in the property...." (*Id.* at p. 271, 201 P.2d 385.)

one-half are based on the right of the husband to testamentary disposition of one-half of the property. Hence, gifts before death are will substitutes. We noted that this reasoning does not apply in an ongoing marriage. Finally, under the laws in effect at the time the case was decided, if the wife could not recover the whole property during the marriage, the husband could impair the wife's right to receive a larger share of the community property at dissolution where the grounds for divorce were adultery or extreme cruelty of the husband. (*Id.* at pp. 692–693, 52 P.2d 221.)

In *Britton,* we distinguished *Trimble v. Trimble, supra,* 219 Cal. 340, 26 P.2d 477, and *Lahaney v. Lahaney, supra,* 208 Cal. 323, 281 P. 67, as cases that were concerned with an action by the wife after her husband's death and premised on the theory that at his death, the husband had a right to dispose of his one-half interest in the property.[5]

In 1969, former section 172a became part of the Family Law Act as section 5127 (Stats.1969, ch. 1608, § 8, p. 3342, operative Jan. 1, 1970). In 1975, reforms of the community property laws became effective, including legislation giving either spouse the management and control of the community property (§ 5125) and making section 5127 gender neutral. (Stats.1974, ch. 1206, § 5, p. 2610.) The 1975 reforms, therefore, changed the context in which section 5127 must be interpreted. As can be seen from the cases discussed, the concept of equal management was a radical and significant change in community property law and was a landmark step toward recognizing equality of the spouses. Accordingly, the 1975 reform legislation marked a significant dividing line between the husband-dominated community property law of the past and the equal managerial rights of the present day.

Before the 1975 reforms, the law was clear as to the extent of relief allowed to a spouse who disapproved of a transfer made in violation of section 5127. If the action was brought after the transferor-spouse's death or after dissolution of the marriage, the set-aside was limited to the nonconsenting spouse's one-half community property interest. (See *Trimble v. Trimble, supra,* 219 Cal. 340, 26 P.2d 477; *Pretzer v. Pretzer, supra,* 215 Cal. 659, 12 P.2d 429.) If the action was brought during the ongoing marriage, however, the nonconsenting spouse was permitted to set aside the transfer in its entirety. (See *Britton, supra,* 4 Cal.2d 690, 52 P.2d 221; *Vaughan v. Roberts, supra,* 45 Cal.App.2d 246, 113 P.2d 884.)

---

5. The *Britton* rule was approved in *Vaughan v. Roberts* (1941) 45 Cal.App.2d 246, 113 P.2d 884. In *Vaughan,* the husband signed a promissory note and also executed a deed of trust on community real property to secure the note. The Court of Appeal stated: "The [trial] court also found that the note and trust deed were neither signed nor authorized to be signed by Mrs. Vaughan, and that the instruments which affect the title to real property were therefore void. We are of the opinion that is a correct conclusion of law.... [¶] It has been held that a conveyance of community real property by the husband, without the authorization of his wife, contrary to the provisions of section 172a of the Civil Code, is at least voidable in a suit by the wife during the marriage. (*Britton v. Hammell,* 4 Cal.(2d) 690 [52 P.2d 221] ...)" (*Vaughan v. Roberts, supra,* 45 Cal.App.2d at p. 259, 113 P.2d 884.)

After the 1975 reforms, however, a split of authority developed in the appellate courts concerning the extent of relief available when the nonconsenting spouse brought an action during the marriage. One line of decisions holds that transfers are voidable only as to the nonconsenting spouse's one-half interest, regardless of when the action is brought. (See *Wolfe v. Lipsy* (1985) 163 Cal.App.3d 633, 209 Cal.Rptr. 801; *Head v. Crawford* (1984) 156 Cal.App.3d 11, 202 Cal.Rptr. 534; *Mitchell, supra,* 110 Cal.App.3d 220, 167 Cal.Rptr. 760.) Equally recent decisions, including the Court of Appeal decision in this case, expressly disapprove of the *Mitchell* line of authority, and hold that if relief is sought during marriage, the entire transfer should be set aside. (See *Harper v. Raya* (1984) 154 Cal.App.3d 908, 201 Cal.Rptr. 563; *Andrade, supra,* 138 Cal.App.3d 330, 187 Cal.Rptr. 863; *In re Jones* (C.D.Cal.1985) 51 B.R. 834. See also, Hogoboom & King: Cal.Practice Guide: Family Law 1 (Rutter 1990) §§ 8:163–8:163.3 rev. # 1, 1991.)

As indicated, the leading and most frequently cited cases on each side of the issue are *Mitchell, supra,* 110 Cal.App.3d 220, 167 Cal.Rptr. 760, and *Andrade, supra,* 138 Cal.App.3d 330, 187 Cal.Rptr. 863. *Mitchell* holds that a transfer by one spouse is valid as to the transferring spouse's one-half interest in the property, but may be invalidated by the nonconsenting spouse as to his or her one-half interest in the property. *Andrade,* on the other hand, allows the nonconsenting spouse to invalidate the transfer entirely. Both cases are similar in that the applicable law was the same, the transfer was deemed by the court not to be a gift, title to the property was held in the names of both spouses, and the marriage was continuing at the time that the nonconsenting spouse moved to set aside the transfer. (*In re Jones, supra,* 51 B.R. 834, 837.[6])

Since the confusion in this area of the law appears to have developed after enactment of the 1975 amendments to the community property laws, we must determine whether the amendments are such that the reasoning of the *Britton (supra,* 4 Cal.2d 690, 52 P.2d 221) court is no longer controlling when the nonconsenting spouse brings an action while the community is still in existence. We shall conclude that our reasoning supporting *Britton* is still valid, and hence the *Andrade, supra,* 138 Cal.App.3d 330, 187 Cal.Rptr. 863 line of cases is correct.

In our view, *Mitchell* did not completely analyze section 5127 and the relevant case law. The *Mitchell* court reasoned that because the community is liable for the contracts of either spouse which are made after marriage (§ 5116), the community realty is subject to execution for

---

6. In *Jones,* the husband, during the ongoing marriage, executed a deed of trust on community real property without his wife's consent to secure a bail bond. The court held that under section 5127, during the existence of the community, the nonconsenting spouse can set aside a unilateral transfer of real property by the other spouse in its entirety and can restore the real property to its status as undivided community property. (51 B.R. at p. 839.) While we note that "federal decisions are in no event controlling in matters of state law" (see *Estate of D'India* (1976) 63 Cal. App.3d 942, 948, 134 Cal.Rptr. 165; accord, *Ware v. Heller* (1944) 63 Cal.App.2d 817, 821, 148 P.2d 410), the *Jones* opinion is instructive and helpful as it is interpreting similar issues as those in this case and discusses the same California cases.

the debts contracted during the marriage. Hence, the *Mitchell* court concluded, it follows that the deed of trust must also be valid. (*Mitchell, supra,* 110 Cal.App.3d at p. 223, 167 Cal.Rptr. 760.)

This analysis ignores section 5127's plain language requiring the signature of both spouses for a valid transfer of community realty. Furthermore, *Mitchell* makes no mention of *Britton* but instead relies on *Gantner v. Johnson* (1969) 274 Cal.App.2d 869, 79 Cal.Rptr. 381 (*Gantner*). Yet, *Gantner* specifically notes that its discussion concerned the "rules applying to transfers of community property by the husband *as manager of the community property.*" (*Id.* at p. 876, 79 Cal.Rptr. 381, emphasis added.[7])

In its disapproval of *Mitchell* and related cases, the *Andrade* court pointed out that since *Gantner, supra,* 274 Cal.App.2d 869, 79 Cal.Rptr. 381, section 5127 has been amended to provide both spouses with equal management and control of community real property. "It is highly questionable whether the rules espoused in *Gantner* survive after the amendments to section 5127 which have significantly altered former concepts of the spouses' respective rights and responsibilities concerning their community property." (*Andrade, supra,* 138 Cal.App.3d at p. 337, 187 Cal.Rptr. 863.) Like the *Andrade* court, we conclude that the correct rule is the one that protects each spouse from the unauthorized acts of the other that may defeat the community interests in the real property. (*Andrade, supra,* 138 Cal.App.3d at p. 337, 187 Cal.Rptr. 863.)

Of the four reasons (see, *ante,* p. 588 of 283 Cal.Rptr., p. 935 of 812 P.2d) for our opinion in *Britton,* only one is called into question by the 1975 amendments. In *Britton* we said that allowing the husband's gift of community real property to stand might defeat the power of the court to award more than half of the community property to an "innocent" wife at the time of dissolution. (*Britton, supra,* 4 Cal.2d at p. 692, 52 P.2d 221.) The 1975 Family Law Act amendments also removed the concept of fault in divorce, and courts are now generally required to make an equal division of the community property. (§ 4800, subd. (a).) However, in making an equal division, each individual piece of community property does not have to be equally divided. (§ 4800, subd. (b).) Although the court may not award a greater part of the community property to one spouse, it can determine to which spouse a particular piece of community property shall be awarded. Since the court retains power to award a specific asset to a spouse, the change in the law is not so significant as to undermine our holding in *Britton.* The other reasons

---

7. *Gantner* relies on two cases, *Heuer v. Heuer, supra,* 33 Cal.2d 268, 201 P.2d 385, and *Woods v. Bradford* (1967) 254 Cal. App.2d 501, 62 Cal.Rptr. 391, which are dissimilar to the facts in *Mitchell.* In *Heuer,* the transfer was made by the husband before divorce, and the former spouse, suing after the divorce, agreed during an appeal that she would be satisfied "if her one-half community interest in the property involved [was] restored to her." (*Heuer, supra,* 33 Cal.2d at pp. 270–271, 201 P.2d 385.) *Woods* involved a transfer of only an undivided one-half interest made after divorce pursuant to court order. The court found that section 5127 (then former section 172a) had no application to the case. (*Woods, supra,* 254 Cal.App.2d at p. 505, 62 Cal.Rptr. 391.)

underlying our decision in *Britton* are still valid and support the right of the nonconsenting spouse during the marriage to invalidate the transfer in its entirety.

More importantly, the *Britton, supra,* 4 Cal.2d 690, 52 P.2d 221 and *Andrade, supra,* 138 Cal.App.3d 330, 187 Cal.Rptr. 863 line of cases is consistent with the plain language of section 5127. "It is axiomatic that in the interpretation of a statute where the language is clear, its plain meaning should be followed." (*Great Lakes Properties, Inc. v. City of El Segundo* (1977) 19 Cal.3d 152, 155, 137 Cal.Rptr. 154, 561 P.2d 244.) The statute requires that both spouses join in executing "*any* instrument" conveying "*any* interest" in the community's real property. (Emphasis added.) The term "any" (particularly in a statute) means "all" or "every." (*California State Auto. Assn. Inter–Ins. Bureau v. Warwick* (1976) 17 Cal.3d 190, 195, 130 Cal.Rptr. 520, 550 P.2d 1056 ["From the earliest days of statehood we have interpreted 'any' to be broad, general and all embracing."]; *Estate of Wyman* (1962) 208 Cal. App.2d 489, 492, 25 Cal.Rptr. 280; *Emmolo v. Southern Pacific Co.* (1949) 91 Cal.App.2d 87, 92, 204 P.2d 427.) The language, "any interest," would include the consenting spouse's one-half undivided interest. Therefore, under the plain language of section 5127, both spouses "must join in executing any instrument" encumbering such interest.[8]

Friedman argues that encumbrances under section 5127 should be treated differently than leases, sales, and conveyances. We disagree. As the United States Supreme Court has stated, "[i]t is a familiar principle of statutory construction that words grouped in a list should be given related meaning." (*Third National Bank v. Impac, Limited, Inc.* (1974) 432 U.S. 312, 322, 97 S.Ct. 2307, 2313, 53 L.Ed.2d 368; see also, *Schreiber v. Burlington Northern, Inc.* (1985) 472 U.S. 1, 8, 105 S.Ct. 2458, 2462, 86 L.Ed.2d 1; *Securities Industries Ass'n v. Board of Governors* (1984) 468 U.S. 207, 218, 104 S.Ct. 3003, 3009, 82 L.Ed.2d 158.) In each of these cases the high court rejected an argument that one word in a list should be construed to have a substantially different effect than others. Furthermore, the *Mitchell* analysis, which Friedman urges us to adopt, does not support the argument that encumbrances should be treated differently. *Mitchell* noted that *Gantner, supra,* 274 Cal.App.2d 869, 876–877, 79 Cal.Rptr. 381, involved a conveyance, and then applied *Gantner's* analysis, by analogy, to cases involving encumbrances. The *Mitchell* court did not indicate that encumbrances should in any way be treated differently. (*Mitchell, supra,* 110 Cal.App.3d at p. 223, 167 Cal.Rptr. 760.)

Amicus Curiae Mortgage Institute of California argues that after the 1975 reforms, the power of either spouse to transfer community property is greater than before the reforms. In effect, it argues that equal

8. A spouse wishing to transfer community real property during the marriage who is unable to obtain the consent of the other spouse is not completely without recourse. Section 5125.1, subdivision (e) permits the courts to "dispense with the requirement of the other spouse's [arbitrarily refused] consent ... if the proposed transaction is in the best interests of the community."

management concepts lead to the conclusion that both spouses should now be able to transfer community property during the marriage, and that the transfer should be valid as to the consenting spouse's one-half interest. However, the earlier cases upholding a husband's ability to transfer his one-half community property interest during the marriage were based on the husband's power as *sole* manager of the community property. (See, e.g., *Gantner, supra,* 274 Cal.App.2d at p. 876, 79 Cal.Rptr. 381.) The 1975 reforms, and the advent of concepts of equal management and *shared* responsibility for the community property, support our interpretation of section 5127 as requiring both spouses' consent for the effective transfer of community real property.

Amicus Curiae Mortgage Institute of California also contends that the Legislature has expressed its approval of *Mitchell* by failing to enact legislation proposed by the California Law Revision Commission that would have expressly overruled that case. We disagree. In our view, the Law Revision Commission did not believe that its recommended legislation would change California law. The commission stated that enactment of its recommendations would "[codify] general California law and overrule[ ] the contrary case of Mitchell...." (Recommendations Relating to Disposition of Community Property (Sept. 1983) 17 Cal.Law Revision Com.Rep. (1984) p. 279, fn. 33.)[9] It is apparent that the commission viewed the recommended statutes as codifying the general law as it existed, and saw *Mitchell* as an aberrant case, inconsistent with general California law. Given the deficiencies in the *Mitchell* analysis, the soundness of the *Britton* and *Andrade* line of cases, and our own interpretation of section 5127, the fact that *Mitchell* has not specifically been legislatively abrogated is not sufficient evidence that the Legislature approves of the decision.[10]

* * *

V. CONCLUSION

In summary, we conclude that during the existence of the community, the nonconsenting spouse should be fully protected against efforts by the other spouse to transfer community real property in contravention of

9. The commission further noted that its proposed new section would codify "general California law that a disposition avoided during marriage must be set aside as to the interest of both spouses, not just the interest of the non-joining or non-consenting spouse. See, e.g., *Britton v. Hammell,* 4 Cal.2d 690 [52 P.2d 221] (1935) ...; *Andrade Development Co. v. Martin,* 138 Cal. App.3d 330 [187 Cal.Rptr. 863].... This overrules Mitchell...." (*Id.* 110 Cal. App.3d at p. 291, 167 Cal.Rptr. 760.)

10. The Mortgage Institute of California also argues that the enactment of section 5125.1, operative July 1, 1987, is further evidence of the Legislature's approval of *Mitchell* and establishes the remedies for a

transfer in violation of section 5127. Section 5125.1 states in part that "[a] spouse has a claim against the other spouse for a breach of the duty imposed by Section 5125 or 5127 that results in substantial impairment to the claimant spouse's present undivided one-half interest in the community estate."

Our review of the legislative history of section 5125.1 does not support amicus curiae's contention that enactment of section 5125.1 signals legislative approval of *Mitchell* or the view that section 5125.1 amended section 5127 to provide the exclusive remedy to a spouse who objects to the unilateral transfer of community property.

section 5127. In such cases, the attempted transfer is subject to a timely action during the marriage to avoid it. A transfer of the community real property without both spouses consent adversely affects the nonconsenting spouse's interests and the dissolution court's ability to make an equitable division of the community property. Allowing the transfer to stand against a challenge by the nonconsenting spouse could have the effect of partitioning the community property during the marriage, an event the Legislature has expressly sought to avoid. (See Code Civ. Proc., § 872.210, subd. (b).) The effect of enforcing one-spouse transfers would be to make community property more like property held as tenants in common and could result in the nonconsenting spouse being forced to become a tenant-in-common with a stranger.

We believe the *Britton, supra,* 4 Cal.2d 690, 52 P.2d 221 and *Andrade, supra,* 138 Cal.App.3d 330, 187 Cal.Rptr. 863 line of cases to be consistent with the nature of community property in California today. Both spouses hold equal undivided one-half interests in the property. Joint ownership of the property requires that during an ongoing marriage *both* spouses must consent before such property is leased for a period longer than one year, sold, conveyed, or encumbered. (§ 5127.) Community property principles of equal management and shared responsibility mandate that the nonconsenting spouse is entitled to invalidate in its entirety the other spouse's transfer of community real property.

The judgment of the Court of Appeal that section 5127 prevents one spouse from encumbering the community's real property without the other spouse's consent is affirmed.[17]

LUCAS, C.J., and MOSK, BROUSSARD, ARABIAN and BAXTER, JJ., CONCUR.

KENNARD, JUSTICE, dissenting.

I respectfully dissent.

The issue in this case is whether, after the parties to a marriage have separated, a spouse has the right to encumber his or her one-half interest in community real property without the consent of the other spouse to secure the payment of attorney fees incurred in a marital dissolution proceeding. Construed under well-established rules, the controlling statutes disclose a legislative intent to grant spouses that right. Today's decision not only contravenes that intent, but will make it virtually impossible for many economically weaker spouses to obtain adequate legal representation in contested divorce proceedings.

I

In 1982, Joanna Droeger (Wife) commenced a marital dissolution action against her husband, John Droeger (Husband), a partner in a San Francisco law firm. She retained the law firm of Friedman, Sloan &

---

17. Friedman argues that if we affirm the judgment of the Court of Appeal, Friedman should be given an opportunity to meet the requirements of section 5125.1, subdivision (e). We disagree. Section 5125.1, subdivision (e) is intended for the benefit of a party to the marital community, not a party's lawyers. Section 5125.1, subdivision (e) specifically states that a court may dispense with the requirement of the other spouse's consent "upon the motion of a spouse" (emphasis added).

Ross to represent her in this action, and entered into a written fee agreement with the law firm.

The litigation was lengthy, as dissolution proceedings sometimes are; Wife was unable to pay her attorney fees on a current basis, and by November 1986 had fallen seriously in arrears. Rather than withdraw as counsel, Friedman, Sloan & Ross accepted a promissory note for its attorney fees from Wife; the promissory note was secured by a deed of trust on her interest in certain community real property. Wife executed the promissory note after being advised by the law firm that she had the right to consult independent counsel concerning this transaction.

In December 1986, the parties reached a settlement, which was never implemented. The attorneys for both Wife and Husband successfully moved to withdraw from the case. Wife and Husband apparently remain married, and Wife has never paid her attorney fees.

Friedman, Sloan & Ross did not seek to enforce its deed of trust. But Husband then filed this lawsuit against Friedman, Sloan & Ross, seeking to quiet title and void the deed of trust not only as to his interest in the property but also as to Wife's interest.

Wife's financial arrangement with her attorneys is representative of a practice commonly utilized in family law cases. As one manual on California family law observes: "[T]he right to place a lien on the client's property [in dissolution actions] is often created in the fee agreement to provide security for the payment of fees. Typically, such a lien may be in the form of a second deed of trust on the client's real property, such as a residence." (Cal.Family Law Service (1986) *Termination of Marital Relationship* § 21:18, p. 330.)[1] Another legal text advises: "If the money [to pay the attorney a retainer in a dissolution proceeding] cannot be obtained from community bank accounts, the spouse should consider borrowing the money using community property as security...." (3 Markey, Cal.Family Law Practice and Procedure (rev. ed. 1991) § 40.32[4], p. 40–80.)

The common practice of retaining counsel whose fees are secured by a deed of trust is, by its nature, not one that an economically stronger spouse will frequently wish to utilize. Rather, retaining counsel by executing a promissory note secured by a deed of trust on the spouse's

---

1. Under the Rules of Professional Conduct and the decisions of this court, an attorney may ensure payment of fees by acquiring a promissory note secured by a deed of trust on the client's real property so long as (1) the attorney fully discloses the terms of the transaction to the client in an understandable fashion, (2) the terms are fair and reasonable, and (3) the client consents in writing after having had an opportunity to consult independent counsel. (Rules Prof. Conduct, rule 3–300; *Hawk v. State Bar* (1988) 45 Cal.3d 589, 593, 247 Cal.Rptr. 599, 754 P.2d 1096.)

Of course, even when an attorney holds a promissory note secured by a deed of trust, the attorney is not necessarily entitled to fees in any given amount. In this context, as well as others, clients are protected from overreaching by rule 4–200 of the Rules of Professional Conduct, the general law of contract (see Civ.Code, §§ 1670.5, 1770, subd. (s)), and the inherent powers of the courts to review attorney-fee contracts to prevent unfairness (see *Roa v. Lodi Medical Group, Inc.* (1985) 37 Cal.3d 920, 933, 211 Cal.Rptr. 77, 695 P.2d 164).

interest in community real property is desirable primarily for those spouses who do not have access to substantial sums of money. For such spouses, the alternative may simply be that they will not be represented by a lawyer in dissolution proceedings.

Legal representation in dissolution cases is particularly important when child custody is contested or there are complex property issues, such as determining the value of the other spouse's business or professional practice. To effectively litigate such issues, an attorney must engage in extensive factual and legal investigations, and must charge correspondingly high attorney fees. Economically weaker spouses who cannot secure payment of attorney fees may be unable to conduct adequate discovery or to sufficiently prepare for motions that may be critical to the outcome of the case. Economically stronger spouses, on the other hand, can afford to protect their interests by funding legal efforts through current earnings or separate property. Thus, spouses who cannot secure their fee obligations through liens on community real property, and are thereby denied the ability to utilize their property to protect their interests, may be unable to meaningfully contest the demands of economically stronger spouses in family law actions.

* * *

II

Husband contends that the deed of trust given by Wife is void even as to her share of the community property under Civil Code section 5127 (hereafter section 5127). That statute provides in pertinent part: "[B]oth spouses either personally or by duly authorized agent, must join in executing any instrument by which such community real property or any interest therein is leased for a longer period than one year, or is sold, conveyed, or encumbered...."

* * *

One "elementary rule" of statutory construction is that statutes in pari materia—that is, statutes relating to the same subject matter—should be construed together. (*Hunstock v. Estate Development Corp.* (1943) 22 Cal.2d 205, 210, 138 P.2d 1.) We have long recognized the principle that even though a statute may appear to be unambiguous on its face, when it is considered in light of closely related statutes a legislative purpose may emerge that is inconsistent with, and controlling over, the language read without reference to the entire scheme of the law. (E.g., *Great Lakes Properties, Inc. v. City of El Segundo, supra,* 19 Cal.3d at pp. 155–156, 137 Cal.Rptr. 154, 561 P.2d 244; *Leroy T. v. Workmen's Comp. Appeals Bd.* (1974) 12 Cal.3d 434, 438, 115 Cal.Rptr. 761, 525 P.2d 665.) The rule of in pari materia is a corollary of the principle that the goal of statutory interpretation is to determine legislative intent.

In this case, the surest guide to the intent of the Legislature is a statute that deals with the same subject matter as section 5127 and expresses the Legislature's approval of the long-standing practice of relying on community real property to secure attorney fees in dissolution cases.

In 1989, the Legislature enacted Code of Civil Procedure section 412.21. Subdivision (a) of Code of Civil Procedure section 412.21. (hereafter section 412.21(a)) provides in relevant part:

"[I]n an action for dissolution of marriage, ... the summons shall ... contain temporary restraining orders set forth in this section. Upon the filing of a petition for dissolution ... and issuance of the summons and upon personal service of the petition and summons on the respondent ... a temporary restraining order shall be in effect against both parties until the final decree is entered or the petition is dismissed, or until further order of the court:

" . . . .

"(2) Restraining both parties from transferring, encumbering, hypothecating, concealing, or in any way disposing of any property, *real or personal,* whether community, quasi-community, or separate, without the written consent of the other party or an order of the court, except in the usual course of business or for the necessities of life and requiring each party to notify the other party of any proposed extraordinary expenditures.... However, *nothing in the restraining order shall preclude the parties from using community property to pay reasonable attorney's fees in order to retain legal counsel in the action.*" (Italics added.)

There can be no explanation of the last sentence of section 412.21(a)(2) except that the Legislature specifically intended that spouses have the power to use community property to pay attorney fees in dissolution actions. The Legislature, though not mandating that community property be used to pay attorney fees, clearly contemplated the practice and approved it. If the Legislature had been of the view that section 5127 precluded resort to community property to pay attorney fees, there would have been no reason to include the statement in question.

Moreover, section 412.21(a)(2) does not limit the community property that may be used to pay attorney fees to readily accessible or "liquid" community personal property, as the majority suggests. Rather, the first sentence of the section expressly refers to both real and personal community property; the second sentence refers generally to community property, and does not state that only one type of community property may be used to pay attorney fees. The obvious conclusion is that when the Legislature in the last sentence of section 412.21(a)(2) used the phrase "community property" without limitation, it meant both types of community property. Because community real property is ordinarily not "liquid," the only practical means to use it to pay attorney fees is through an encumbrance.

It is the duty of this court to harmonize statutes on the same subject (e.g., *Dyna–Med, Inc. v. Fair Employment & Housing Com., supra,* 43

Cal.3d at p. 1387, 241 Cal.Rptr. 67, 743 P.2d 1323; *Long Beach Police Officers Assn. v. City of Long Beach* (1988) 46 Cal.3d 736, 746, 250 Cal.Rptr. 869, 759 P.2d 504), giving effect to all parts of all statutes if possible (e.g., *Select Base Materials v. Board of Equal., supra,* 51 Cal.2d at p. 645, 335 P.2d 672). In applying that duty to the issue presented here, this court must give preference to a reasonable construction of section 5127 that harmonizes it with section 412.21(a).

* * *

Harmonizing the two provisions in this manner serves the purpose of section 412.21(a) by allowing what the Legislature expressly intended to permit. And, as I will show, it comports fully with the legislative purpose underlying section 5127, which is to protect one spouse from fraudulent or improvident expenditures by the other spouse during the continued existence of the marriage.

Giving full effect to the legislative intent reflected in section 412.-21(a) does not at all impair the purpose of section 5127, which is to protect nonconsenting spouses in ongoing marriages from fraudulent or ill-advised transfers of community real property. Accordingly, I would hold that under sections 412.21(a) and 5127 the parties to a dissolution action may encumber community real property to the extent of their interests to secure reasonable attorney fees in the dissolution action.[3]

In this case, Wife unilaterally encumbered her undivided one-half interest in community real property to secure attorney fees in her dissolution action against Husband. Since then, the parties have apparently decided to remain married, and Husband now contends that the encumbrance must be held entirely void. In accordance with the analysis set forth above, I would hold the encumbrance valid as to Wife's interest.

* * *

3. The majority contends that section 412.21(a) does not "create an exception" to section 5127, or impliedly repeal that section. These contentions miss the dissent's point. The dissent has shown that when section 5127 is interpreted in light of the legislative purpose to protect spouses in continuing marriages, and construed with a view toward harmonizing it with section 412.21(a), the conclusion is inescapable that the Legislature did not intend to bar spouses from using their interests in community real property to secure attorney fees in a dissolution action. No discussion of exceptions or implied repeal is necessary to resolve this issue.

The majority claims that harm could result under the dissent's approach if an economically stronger spouse encumbered his or her interest in the community residence to secure attorney fees, the spouse defaulted, the mortgage lender foreclosed, and the mortgage lender then brought an action for partition against the other spouse. (Maj. opn., *ante,* at p. 595, fn. 15 of 283 Cal.Rptr., at p. 942, fn. 15 of 812 P.2d.) Although harm according to this scenario might occur in isolated cases, this possibility should be contrasted with the certainty that, under the majority's approach, injustice and hardship for economically weaker spouses will result in an entire class of cases when the spouses' inability to use their property to secure attorney fees deprives them of effective legal representation.

Finally, the majority contends that under the dissent's approach the trial court's role might be made more difficult in some cases. Although the trial court's duty of equal division of community assets under Civil Code section 4800 might be made more complicated after an encumbrance, this factor is no reason to deprive spouses of their rights.

BYRD v. BLANTON

California District Court of Appeal, 1983.
149 Cal.App.3d 987, 197 Cal.Rptr. 190.

OPINION

SONENSHINE, ASSOCIATE JUSTICE.

Jewell Blanton, claiming a community property interest in property in the name of her mother-in-law, Lillie Mae Byrd, filed a complaint alleging constructive fraud and civil conspiracy and asking the court to quiet title and to restore it to her. Byrd cross-complained for forcible detainer, possession of the premises (ejectment) and money damages. The summary proceeding was heard first and the court found against Byrd on the action for forcible detainer but granted judgment for ejectment. The damage award of $9,350 was stayed pending resolution of Jewell's complaint.

Jewell appeals, arguing the court erred in finding the statute of limitations contained in Civil Code section 5127 [now Family Code Section 1102] barred an assertion of her community property interest in the real property.

FACTS

In 1960, Byrd and her son Joseph Blanton purchased a residence in Laguna Beach, California. Each contributed to the down payment, but title was taken in Joseph's name alone. They resided in the property together and each made payments toward the mortgage until 1964 when Joseph married Jewell and he and his bride moved to New York. Byrd continued living in the property and made the payments from 1964 to 1968 when Joseph and Jewell returned to California and took up residence with Byrd. Payments on the mortgage (including several refinances) were thereafter made by the Blantons.

In March of 1978 Joseph executed a deed changing title from his name alone to joint tenancy with his mother who recorded the deed. Joseph succumbed to cancer in May and died intestate. In June, Jewell retained a lawyer who failed to file an action to recover the community property interest. She then hired other counsel who filed the present action from which this cross-complaint was severed.

The court did not make a finding as to the exact amount of the community interest in the property but did conclude, "it would appear to the court that those payments during the marriage would have created some kind of a community property interest in the property." The court, applying the one year limitation period of section 5127, refused to allow Jewell to assert this interest as a defense to the ejectment action.

DISCUSSION

Is the statute of limitations contained in section 5127 applicable to this transaction?

Examination of the applicable authorities, including section 172a, a logical construction of section 5127 and public policy underlying the family law statutes dictate our conclusion: The one year statute of limitations contained in section 5127 is not a bar when as here the transfer takes place without the knowledge or consent of the non-signing spouse and the transferee has knowledge of the marital relationship.[7] Any other interpretation would place bad faith and bona fide transferees on the same footing.

Jewell urges the one year statute of limitations applies only to *lessees, purchasers or encumbrancers in good faith without knowledge of the marriage relation,* and because Byrd had knowledge of the marriage relation and was a donee,[8] the statute is inapplicable to this transaction. Byrd simply relies on the language of the statute, citing *Strong v. Strong* (1943) 22 Cal.2d 540, 140 P.2d 386 and *Horton v. Horton* (1953) 115 Cal.App.2d 360, 252 P.2d 397. However, the latter authorities are distinguishable either on their facts or in light of the code sections applicable at the time they were decided.

* * *

The purpose of the limitation contained in section 5127 is "to protect third parties who might rely on the recorded instruments." (*Schindler v. Schindler* (1954) 126 Cal.App.2d 597, 604, 272 P.2d 566.) Statutes of limitation "are designed to promote justice by preventing the revival of hoary claims that have been *allowed* to slumber until evidence has been lost, memories have faded and witnesses have disappeared." (*Liberty Mutual Ins. Co. v. Fales* (1973) 8 Cal.3d 712, 718, 106 Cal.Rptr. 21, 505 P.2d 213, emphasis added.) This places "an opposing party on notice within a reasonable time that a claim is pending against him * * *." (*Id.,* at p. 718, 106 Cal.Rptr. 21, 505 P.2d 213.) These statutes were enacted to *prevent* fraud, not to provide a protective shield for its perpetration.

To extend the shortened limitation period to all gift conveyances executed by the spouse holding record title would be patently unfair. A spouse could conspire with a donee, convey community property standing of record in the spouse's name and quietly await the passage of one year before the donee asserts ownership. We find it unlikely the Legislature intended to provide a nonsignatory spouse merely with the protection of an annual perusal of the county recorder's files for a possible transfer by the record holding spouse. "[A] construction that would create a wholly unreasonable effect or an absurd result should not be given." (*Barnes v. Chamberlain* (1983) 147 Cal.App.3d 762 at p. 766, 195 Cal.Rptr. 417.)

7. We do not reach the issue of a bad faith donee transfer to a bona fide purchaser. See *Mark v. Title Guarantee & Trust Co.* (1932) 122 Cal.App. 301, 9 P.2d 839 (requiring wife to restore innocent purchasers to their original position).

8. At least as to the Blantons' community interest in the property.

Lastly, we must construe the application of the limitation section of 5127 "with reference to the whole body of law of which it is a part so as all may be harmonized and have effect." (*Barnes v. Chamberlain, supra,* 147 Cal.App.3d 762, 767, 195 Cal.Rptr. 417.) Throughout the evolution of our present day family law statutes, the trend has been toward achieving greater equality between spouses. Wife was given a "present, existing, and equal" interest in community property by the adoption of section 161a in 1927 and, in 1975, was granted equal management and control. There can no longer be the inference of dominion by husband prevalent in the era of *Strong* and *Horton*. While property standing of record in one spouse's name *appears* validly alienable by that spouse alone, section 5127 *requires* the other spouse's signature. The one year limitation period only protects bona fide transferees with no knowledge of the marriage relation who have no reason to suspect another signature is necessary.

We find the limitation in section 5127 is not a bar to Jewell's community property claim. The property stood in the name of her husband alone and was conveyed by him alone without her knowledge or consent to a donee who knew of the marriage relation and the nonsigning spouse's lack of knowledge or consent.

The judgment for possession of the premises (ejectment) and damages is reversed. Jewell to recover her costs on appeal.

CROSBY, ACTING P.J., and WALLIN, J., concur.

Hearing denied; MOSK, J., dissenting.

Note

In Waldeck v. Hedden, 89 Cal.App. 485, 265 P. 340 (1928), the husband entered into an agreement to exchange certain community real property for plaintiff's stock ranch. The agreement was not signed by the wife, but she together with her husband gave possession of the real property to the plaintiff. No deeds were ever executed, and the plaintiff sued for specific performance. The appellate court concluded that such facts were not sufficient to raise an estoppel, and that the wife's defense was not barred by the one year statute of limitations.

MARK v. TITLE GUARANTEE & TRUST CO.

California District Court of Appeal, 1932.
122 Cal.App. 301, 9 P.2d 839.

JENNINGS, J.   * * * The trial court found that plaintiff was the wife of defendant William Mark; that all payments made by defendant William Mark under the contract of purchase entered into between him and the defendant Title Guarantee & Trust Company were made from earnings of said William Mark during coverture, and that the money so paid had not been acquired by William Mark by gift, bequest, devise, or descent, and that William Mark, without the knowledge or consent of plaintiff, his wife, and without her joining in the sale, transfer, or assignment, did assign, transfer, and sell to defendants Carl Siegrist and Caroline Siegrist all of his right, title, and interest in and to the contract to purchase the real property made by him with the Title Guarantee & Trust Company; that defendants Siegrist paid to William Mark a specified sum of money in consideration of the sale and assignment of the property to them, and that William Mark retained the whole of the money thus received for his own use and benefit, and that no portion thereof entered into the community of plaintiff and defendant William Mark; that, at the time of the sale to defendants Siegrist, William Mark represented to them that he was unmarried, and the Siegrists accepted the transfer believing that William Mark was unmarried; that William Mark so represented himself to be unmarried for the purpose of inducing the Siegrists to accept the transfer without the necessity of having his wife join therein and for the further purpose of transferring the property without his wife knowing of the same and with the intention of obtaining the money paid to him by the Siegrists and of applying such money to his own use, and that he then had in mind the filing of an action for divorce against his wife, which action he did institute on December 4, 1926, and in his complaint in such divorce suit he did not include the contract or the proceeds obtained by him from its sale and assignment as community property; that plaintiff did not learn of the sale and transfer of the contract until after the institution of the divorce suit; that the plaintiff did not know of the assignment and transfer to the Siegrists at the time it was made, nor did she consent to or approve of it; that the issues involved herein were not adjudicated adversely to plaintiff in the divorce action, and that the moneys received by defendant William Mark from the sale of the contract were not adjudicated in said divorce suit. From the findings thus made the court drew the following conclusions: First, that defendants Siegrist were purchasers in good faith and for value and without notice that defendant William Mark was married; second, that plaintiff was not estopped or precluded from questioning the validity of the sale of the contract; third, that, by reason of defendants Siegrist being purchasers in good faith and for value, they acquired good and legal title to the contract under the provisions of section 172a of the Civil Code, and that the sale and transfer to them is conclusively presumed to be valid, and that they thereby acquired all right, title, and interest of plaintiff and defendant William Mark in and to said contract. In accordance with the findings thus made and the conclusions of law drawn therefrom, judgment was rendered denying to plaintiff the relief which she sought.

* * *

The conclusion of the court that the purchase of community property by a third person in good faith without knowledge of the marriage relation from a husband who, without the knowledge or consent of his wife, alone executes the instrument by which the property is conveyed is conclusively presumed to be valid, is based upon the provisions of section 172a of the Civil Code. Upon the interpretation which is to be placed upon the language of this section, therefore, the correctness of the trial court's conclusion depends. * * *

It is to be observed that the section states that the sole lease, contract, mortgage, or deed of the husband to a lessee, etc., in good faith without knowledge of the marriage relation, shall be presumed to be valid. The section does not say that such conveyance shall be conclusively presumed to be valid. Nevertheless, in Rice v. McCarthy, 73 Cal.App. 655, 662, 239 P. 56, 58, Presiding Justice Finlayson of the District Court of Appeal for the Second Appellate District, Division 2, in discussing the language of the proviso which is here under consideration, used the following language: "The word 'presumed,' as used in the declaration of the proviso that every lease, contract, mortgage or deed which is under its protecting aegis 'shall be presumed to be valid,' is doubtless used in the sense that it is conclusively presumed that every such lease, contract mortgage, or deed is valid. We have, then, in this part of the section, what is tantamount to an express statutory recognition of the passing of the title to the lessee, grantee, vendee, or mortgagee whenever those conditions exist which are defined in the proviso."

The learned author of the opinion then proceeded to analyze the concluding clause of the section which provides that "no action to avoid such instrument shall be commenced after the expiration of one year from the filing for record of such instrument in the recorder's office in the county in which the land is situate," and arrived at the conclusion that the language of this clause is to be interpreted as referring back to and modifying the language in the first part of the section, wherein it is said: "The husband has the management and control of the community real property, but the wife must join with him in executing any instrument by which such community real property or any interest therein is leased for a longer period than one year, or is sold, conveyed, or encumbered." The interpretation thus placed upon the language of the concluding clause of section 172a of the Civil Code as this clause read until it was recast by the amendment in 1927 (St.1927, p. 827), differs from the interpretation given by the Supreme Court in McKay v. Lauriston, 204 Cal. 557, 564, 269 P. 519, 522, wherein Justice Curtis, in discussing the 1917 amendments to sections 172 and 172a of the Civil Code, uses the following language: "All that the Legislature by these amendments did do or attempt to do was to cast about the interest of the wife in both the real and personal property of the community during the continued existence of the marriage relation added safeguards and protection against the fraudulent or inconsiderate acts of the husband in the exercise of his control and dominion over these properties of the nature of those already provided for in earlier statutes and especially in and by the 1891 amendment to section 172 of the Civil Code. It follows, to our minds, irresistibly that the same reasoning which was applied to the earlier amendment of section 172 of the Civil Code equally applies to those changes in and revision thereof accomplished by the Legislature in 1917. Additional force, is, if needed, given to this conclusion when the particular provisions of section 172a as added to the Code in that year are subjected to careful consideration; for it is made to therein appear that the sole lease, contract, mortgage or deed of the husband holding the record title to community real property to a lessee, purchaser or incumbrancer in good faith, without knowledge of the marriage relation, shall be presumed to be valid *and shall be so unless an action to avoid such instrument shall be commenced within one year from the recordation thereof.* [Italics ours.]   This provision renders the conveyance of the whole of the community real estate to a purchaser or incumbrancer thereof in good faith voidable but not void. * * * "

However, careful reading of the decision in Rice v. McCarthy, supra, leads to the conclusion that the language stating that the presumption of validity declared by the proviso in section 172a, Civil Code, to attach to the sole transfer of community real estate by the husband to a purchaser in good faith without knowledge of the marriage relation is a conclusive presumption is dictum, and that the language interpreting the concluding clause of the section relative to the institution of an action to avoid the instrument whereby the husband alone has transferred real property of the community is likewise dictum. The question which was presented to the court for decision was whether or not the trial court had erred in failing to make findings upon the facts which were pleaded by the defendant in the action as constituting estoppel upon the plaintiff wife. It was urged that the doctrine of estoppel was not invocable by the husband's transferee. The decision was that the doctrine of estoppel was invocable and that the trial court had erred in failing to make findings upon the facts pleaded by the defendant which it was claimed raised an estoppel in his favor. It was not necessary to the decision to consider whether the presumption of validity declared by the proviso is a conclusive presumption or a disputable presumption. Furthermore, it may be noted that, if the presumption of validity is conclusive, there was no point in considering the doctrine of estoppel, since there is no possibility of the wife in any manner avoiding the sole transfer of community property by her husband to a purchaser in good faith without knowledge of the marital relation. Once these facts are established, any attempt on her part to avoid her husband's sole conveyance must fail, if the presumption is conclusive. It may likewise be conceded that the above-quoted language of Justice Curtis in McKay v. Lauriston, supra, is dictum. Under these circumstances, therefore, it is proper to consider whether the language of the proviso declaring that the sole lease, contract, mortgage, or deed of the husband to a lessee, purchaser, or incumbrancer, in good faith, without knowledge of the marriage relation, shall be presumed to be valid, is a conclusive presumption or merely a disputable presumption. A presumption is defined in section 1959 of the Code of Civil Procedure as a deduction which the law expressly directs to be made from particular facts. Section 1957 of the same Code classifies presumptions as indirect evidence. Section 1962, Code of Civil Procedure, specifies certain presumptions which are exclusively deemed to be conclusive. This section contains seven subdivisions. The first six specify certain presumptions, none of which directly or by implication relates to the presumption mentioned in the proviso of section 172a, Civil Code, here under consideration. Subdivision 7 is in the following language: "Any other presumption which, by statute, is expressly made conclusive." Section 1963, Code of Civil Procedure, is entitled "All other presumptions may be controverted." The language of the first part of this section is as follows: "All other presumptions are satisfactory if uncontradicted. They are denominated disputable presumptions, and may be controverted by other evidence." Then follow forty specifications of presumptions which are described as being of the character of disputable presumptions. Since section 172a of the Civil Code does not expressly declare that the presumption of validity which attaches to the sole lease, contract, or deed of a husband holding record title to community property to a lessee or purchaser in good faith without knowledge of the marriage relation is a conclusive presumption, it logically follows that, under the language of the above-mentioned sections of the Code of Civil Procedure, the presumption is one that may be controverted.

Section 164 of the Civil Code provides that "whenever any real or personal property, or any interest therein or encumbrance thereon, is acquired by a married woman by an instrument in writing the presumption is that the same is her separate property. * * *" If the statute contained no further reference to the presumption, it would undoubtedly be held to be not a conclusive presumption, but a disputable presumption capable of being controverted by evidence showing that, although the written instrument conveying the property ran to the wife alone, nevertheless, in fact, the property was community property. This was the holding of the court in Pabst v. Shearer, 172 Cal. 239, 242, 156 P. 466. To the same effect are the decisions in Stafford v. Martinoni, 192 Cal. 724, 221 P. 919, and Goucher v. Goucher, 82 Cal.App. 449, 255 P. 892. But there is further reference in the section to the presumption, and it is expressly declared that as to a purchaser, incumbrancer, payor, or any other person dealing with a married woman, in good faith and for a valuable consideration, the presumption is conclusive. In view of such express legislative declaration, there can be no doubt that, in favor of one dealing with a married woman in good faith and for a valuable consideration, it would be held that the presumption that she was the sole owner of property conveyed to her by written instrument was incapable of being controverted. Section 172a, Civil Code, does not, however, contain such express declaration evidencing legislative intent that the presumption of validity shall be incapable of being controverted. The question which naturally suggests itself is: "How may the presumption be controverted?" Not, of course, by a showing that the husband who had held himself out to the innocent purchaser as being unmarried was in fact married, since the existence of the marital relation is a fact essential to the creation of the presumption; not by a showing of knowledge of the marital relation by the innocent purchaser or lack of consideration for the language of the proviso presupposes the existence of consideration and lack of knowledge of the marital relation in order that the presumption of validity shall apply. By a process of elimination it may be reasonably deduced that the only escape from the presumption of validity lies in a showing by the wife that she was uninformed of the execution of the instrument conveying title to or an interest in the community property, and that she did not consent to, or acquiesce in, its execution. In other words, she must be able to avoid the working of the doctrine of estoppel. This is expressly recognized in Rice v. McCarthy, supra, where the decision was that the trial court had erred in failing to find upon the facts claimed by the innocent purchaser to have raised an estoppel against the wife who sought to avoid her husband's sole contract for sale of the community real property. But in the instant case the trial court has specifically found that the wife "did not at the time of making said sale of said contract know of the same, nor did she ever consent thereto or approve the same." By this finding, which we must assume is not lacking in evidentiary support, the possibility of an estoppel being claimed against the wife is removed, and the court rightly concluded that the wife was not estopped from questioning the validity of the sale of the contract. Inasmuch, therefore, as we are of the opinion that the presumption of validity established by the proviso of section 172a, Civil Code, is a disputable presumption, it necessarily follows that we entertain the view that the trial court's conclusion that the presumption of validity is conclusive against appellant was incorrect.

In view of the determination thus reached it is apparent that the judgment in favor of respondents should be reversed. Since the findings as herein noted successfully negative the existence of facts that would constitute an estoppel against appellant, and it further appears from the findings that the action was instituted within a period of one year from the date of the assignment by the respondent William Mark to respondents Siegrist, no good reason appears why judgment should not be directed to be entered in accordance with the prayer of appellant's complaint. The prayer of the complaint seeks cancellation of the transfer by respondent William Mark to respondents Siegrist and that the property which was the subject of the transfer be declared to be community property of appellant and respondent William Mark. The ultimate effect of a decree setting aside the transfer by the respondent William Mark to respondents Siegrist will be to restore the property to the status that it occupied prior to the transfer, i.e., community property of appellant and her husband, William Mark. The effect cannot be to vest title to the property in appellant. Since the property was community property, the interest of appellant therein was a mere expectancy, possessing none of the attributes of an estate either at law or in equity. Stewart v. Stewart, 199 Cal. 318, 335, 249 P. 197; McKay v. Lauriston, supra. The conveyance by appellant's husband, respondent William Mark, was not, under the decisions, a void conveyance, but a valid transfer, subject only to the right in appellant to institute, seasonably, in equity, an action to revoke the transfer and reinstate the property as community property with the title vested in the husband. Lahaney v.

Lahaney, 208 Cal. 323, 281 P. 67. But equity in its zeal to protect the inchoate expectancy of the wife against injurious invasion on her husband's part is not blind to the obvious equity that exists in favor of innocent purchasers in good faith from the husband without knowledge of the marriage relation. If an unconditional decree is rendered herein in conformity with the prayer of appellant's complaint restoring the property to the status of community property, the necessary effect will be to restore to the husband, respondent William Mark, the legal title to the property at the expense of those who have been deceived by his false representation that he was unmarried. The opportunity is thus afforded to him to deal again with the property as though it were his sole and separate property and to mulct other innocent purchasers who may be induced to part with money on the faith of his representation that he is unmarried. That a court of equity should lend its aid to the production of such a result is incredible, but the difficulty of protecting the expectancy of the innocent wife and at the same time of safeguarding the rights of innocent purchasers is apparent. The trial court has found that the money received by the husband was retained by him for his own use and benefit, and that no part of it entered into the community of appellant and her husband, William Mark. As to that part of the court's finding that the husband retained the whole of the money received by him from the sale of the property for his own use and benefit, it must be assumed that it has evidentiary support, and its correctness may not therefore be questioned. It is, however, doubtful whether the remainder of the finding, declaring that no part of the proceeds of the sale entered into the community of appellant and her husband, is in reality a finding of fact.

Sections 162 and 163, Civil Code, define the separate property of wife and husband, respectively, as property which either spouse owned before marriage or which was afterwards acquired by gift, bequest, devise, or descent. Section 164, Civil Code, declares that all other property acquired after marriage by either spouse or by both is community property. The court's findings leave no doubt that the property which was the subject of transfer by the husband was community property. The proceeds of the sale of this property must have been of the same character. A conclusion that, because the husband retained for his own use money received by him from the sale of community property, therefore the money thus received did not enter into the community property of the spouses, is not warranted. The fact that the wife derived no benefit from the transaction and that the husband expended the whole of the proceeds for his own sole benefit did not change the complexion of the property. Its character was not altered because the husband, instead of conserving the money, used it for his own purposes. That portion of the finding wherein the court found that no part of the proceeds of the sale by the husband "entered into the community" would seem, therefore, not to be a finding of fact but a legal conclusion which the court drew from the fact that the husband retained the proceeds for his own use, and, as suggested, the conclusion was incorrect. Since the proceeds of the sale were community property, and did enter into the community estate of appellant and her husband, it is apparent that the community estate, having once profited through the husband's act in selling the property without the wife's knowledge and consent, will again profit if the property is unconditionally restored to its former status and that it will profit at the expense of innocent purchasers. Appellant has sought the aid of equity to protect her expectancy. She is an actor appealing for equitable relief. The relief sought is only indirectly for her benefit. It is directly for the benefit of an estate in which she has an expectancy. The effect of unconditionally granting the relief sought by appellant will be to work a manifest injustice upon innocent persons who possess equitable rights growing out of the subject in controversy. The situation thus presented warrants the application of the equitable maxim that he who seeks equity must do equity. If, therefore, appellant's prayer, is to be granted, and the property restored to its former status of community property, it should be accomplished only upon condition that the innocent purchasers shall be restored to the position which they occupied when, without knowledge of the marriage relation, and relying upon the husband's representation that he was unmarried, they parted with their money in return for his sole transfer. The trial court has found that the amount paid by the innocent purchasers, respondents Siegrist, was $2,076.88, and that it was paid on December 1, 1926.

The judgment is reversed.

Note

Where one spouse knows that the other has transferred community real property and thereafter accepts some of the payments made by the purchaser, an estoppel can be raised. See Rice v. McCarthy, 73 Cal.App. 655, 239 P. 56 (1925). Similarly, where the spouse knows her husband has made such a transfer and she is in a position to speak up and voice her disapproval and to sue to set aside the transaction, but she remains silent and inactive while the purchaser changes his position, an estoppel can be raised. See Berniker v. Berniker, 30 Cal.2d 439, 182 P.2d 557 (1947). On estoppel see also Vierra v. Pereira, 12 Cal.2d 629, 86 P.2d 816 (1939); Bush v. Rogers, 42 Cal.App.2d 477, 109 P.2d 379 (1941); MacKay v. Darusmont, 46 Cal.App.2d 21, 115 P.2d 221 (1941).

Chapter 6

CREDITORS' RIGHTS

Throughout the history of the California community property system, the rights of creditors have been co-extensive with spousal management and control rights. In Grolemund v. Cafferata,[1] decided during the era of sole control of community property by the husband, the court reasoned that the husband, by virtue of his management and control of community property, could use it to pay his debts and therefore his creditors could reach such assets in the absence of some statutory exemption;[2] conversely, since the wife had no management and control rights, her creditors could not reach any community property assets unless some statute specifically so provided.[3] When the wife was given management and control rights over her earnings and personal injury recoveries, the same reasoning gave her creditors the right to reach such assets.[4] When the equal management legislation was enacted, the legis-

---

1. Grolemund v. Cafferata is reprinted in this Section.

2. During the nineteenth century, the absence of husbands because of some land rush, gold rush, or military service, made it necessary for married women to earn a living for their families. In many cases even after the husband's return the wife had to continue to work. By 1870 statutes were being enacted to protect families by removing the earnings of wives from assets available to satisfy the creditors of husbands. See Madden, Handbook of the Law of Persons and Domestic Relations, § 53, p. 152 (1931); 3 Vernier, Am.Fam.Laws, § 167, p. 166 (1935). In 1870 California enacted such a statute, Civil Code Section 168, which remained in effect until repealed in 1975. Under this statute creditors of the husband could not reach the community property earnings of the wife so long as they were kept separate and distinct from other assets, Street v. Bertolone, 193 Cal. 751, 226 P. 913 (1924); Finnigan v. Hibernia Savings and Loan Society, 63 Cal. 390, 11 P.C.L.J. 362 (1883), and so long as the wife did not waive the exemption. Pfunder

v. Goodwin, 83 Cal.App. 551, 257 P. 119 (1927); Tinsley v. Bauer, 125 Cal.App.2d 724, 271 P.2d 116 (1954).

3. Cal.Stats.1937, c. 508, p. 1497.

4. A similar step was taken in Texas in 1913. In his Commentary on the Community Property Law of Texas, 13 Vernon's Annotated Revised Civil Statutes of the State of Texas, 39 (1960), Huie stated the matter as follows: "By the Act of 1913 the wife was given the management of her separate property and at the same time the management of the community property was divided between the husband and the wife. The purpose seems to have been to divide the management along natural lines—along the same lines that ownership is divided when community property rules are not applicable. The wife was to manage her separate property, the revenue from her property, and her personal earnings; the husband was to manage his separate property, the revenue from his property, and his personal earnings. The same natural lines were to control in determining the rights of creditors. The wife's creditors

lature made it clear that this approach to creditors' rights would continue; the preamble to the 1975 reform legislation contains a declaration that "the liability of community property for the debts of the spouses has been co-extensive with the right to manage and control community property and should remain so * * *." [5]

An important corollary of the axiom that creditors' rights are co-extensive with management and control rights is that a creditor in a transaction undertaken by a married person for community benefit is a creditor of the contracting spouse and not of both spouses; a creditor who seeks to reach community assets under the management and control of a married person normally has to establish the personal liability of that person.[6] It should also be noted that the rights of creditors may be substantially affected by interspousal agreements altering the classification of property.[7]

Because both spouses have equal management and control rights over the community property, California's managerial approach to creditors' rights generally means that all community property is liable for debts incurred by either spouse during marriage. However, as we saw in the preceding chapter, there are certain limited situations where one spouse may exercise exclusive management and control rights over certain community assets. For example, a spouse who is operating a community property business has the "primary management" of the business.[8] A community property bank account in the name of one spouse is free from the control of the other spouse.[9] If one spouse is placed under a conservatorship, the other spouse will have exclusive management and control rights over the community property.[10] The current creditors' rights legislation makes it clear that the community

were to look to the estate committed to the wife's management for satisfaction of their claims; the husband's creditors were to look to the estate committed to his management. As to the administration of the two estates during the marriage and the rights of third persons dealing with either of the spouses, the law was to be comparable to that in the modern modified common-law jurisdictions. There was to be no need, in determining powers of management and rights of creditors to distinguish between income and principal or between income produced by property and income produced by personal efforts. At the same time there was to be no change in beneficial ownership; at the dissolution of the marriage the property was to be divided in the same way that it had been before; the basic principle that the husband and wife share equally in revenue derived from both individual capital and individual efforts was to be retained. The partnership idea of the civil law was to be retained, but instead of one partnership, one might say, there were to be two, one managed by the husband and one managed by the wife. Each partnership was to have its own manager, its own physical assets, and its own creditors. The managing partner was to have unlimited personal liability for partnership debts; the other partner's liability was to be limited to the partnership assets."

5. Cal.Stats.1974, c. 1206, p. 2609, § 1.

6. See Robertson v. Willis, 77 Cal. App.3d 358, 143 Cal.Rptr. 523 (1978); Marriage of Barnes, 83 Cal.App.3d 143, 147 Cal.Rptr. 710 (1978).

7. For example, in Leasefirst v. Borrelli, 13 Cal.App. 4th Supp. 28, 17 Cal.Rptr.2d 114 (1993), the spouses had executed a premarital agreement whereby the earnings of each spouse would be the separate property of the acquiring spouse. The earnings of the wife were thereby characterized as her separate property, and hence not liable for a debt contracted by her husband.

8. West's Ann.Cal.Family.Code § 1100.

9. West's Ann.Cal.Fin.Code § 851.

10. West's Ann.Cal.Prob.Code § 3051.

property will be liable for the debts of either spouse in these situations, notwithstanding the principle that liability follows management and control.[11]

There are other qualifications to the basic principle that creditors' rights are co-extensive with spousal management and control rights. In some situations, the creditor of a spouse can reach property not subject to the contracting spouse's management. For example, both husband and wife may enter into a principal-agent relationship; if that occurs (and courts have found it easy to establish an agency relationship between husband and wife), then the obligations incurred by the agent become the debts of the principal, subjecting property under the principal's management and control to liability.[12]

A major statutory qualification of the basic creditors' rights principle is seen in the tort judgment situation. California originally followed the common law rule that a husband was liable for the torts of his wife.[13] This rule was abrogated by statute in California in 1913,[14] and the rules governing tort obligations are now contained in Family Code Section 1000. This statute varies in two significant respects from the basic principle concerning creditors' rights. The statute calls for the classification of tort debts as community or separate, and provides for preferential access depending on such classification. It should be noted that the classification of a tort debt as separate or community does not substantively affect the rights of a creditor; it cannot increase or decrease the amount of property a creditor can ultimately reach. It primarily regulates the rights of the spouses vis-a-vis each other.[15] Furthermore, the preferential treatment of assets does not necessarily limit the married debtor's use of assets within his or her control and management to discharge tort obligations. Any resultant inequities can be resolved in appropriate accounting proceedings between the spouses.

Inter-spousal torts are governed by Family Code Section 782, which exempts community property (except for indemnity insurance proceeds) from satisfaction of a personal injury claim by one spouse against the other until the tort-feasor's separate property is exhausted. This section makes no distinction between cases where the tort was connected with a community activity and cases where it was not.

Another exception to the basic creditors' rights principle involves obligations incurred for "necessaries." Family Code Section 914 provides that a spouse is personally liable for debts incurred for "necessaries of life" by the other spouse, and that the separate property of the nondebtor spouse may be applied to the satisfaction of such obligations.

11. Liability of Marital Property for Debts, 17 Cal.L.Revision Comm'n. Reports 1, 10–11 (1984).

12. See Hulsman v. Ireland, reprinted in this Section.

13. Henley v. Wilson, 137 Cal. 273, 70 P. 21, 92 Am.St.Rep. 160, 58 L.R.A. 941 (1902).

14. West's Ann.Civil Code § 171a added in 1913; now West's Ann.Cal. Family Code § 1000.

15. Bruch, Management Powers and Duties Under California's Community Property Laws, 34 Hastings L.J. 227 (1982).

The definition of "necessaries" may well depend on the accustomed standard of living of the spouses.[16]

A final exception to the principle making creditors' rights co-extensive with management and control involves debts incurred by a spouse prior to marriage. California courts initially adopted the common law rule that when a man married, he took on liability for the premarital debts of his wife: "When a man takes to himself a wife, he takes her for better or for worse and with her debts and encumberances."[17] By statute in California, this liability extended only to the community property in the husband's management and control, and not to his separate property.[18] Current legislation provides that neither the separate property of a spouse nor the earnings of the spouse after marriage is liable for the debts of the other spouse contracted before marriage. After the earnings are paid, they will remain protected so long as they are in an account over which the debtor spouse has no withdrawal rights and are uncommingled with other community property.[19]

WEST'S ANNOTATED FAMILY CODE OF CALIFORNIA

§ 900. Construction of part

Unless the provision or context otherwise requires, the definitions in this chapter govern the construction of this part.

(Stats.1992, c. 162 (A.B.2650), § 10, operative Jan. 1, 1994.)

§ 902. Debt

"Debt" means an obligation incurred by a married person before or during marriage, whether based on contract, tort, or otherwise.

(Stats.1992, c. 162 (A.B.2650), § 10, operative Jan. 1, 1994.)

§ 903. Time debt is incurred

A debt is "incurred" at the following time:

(a) In the case of a contract, at the time the contract is made.

(b) In the case of a tort, at the time the tort occurs.

(c) In other cases, at the time the obligation arises.

(Stats.1992, c. 162 (A.B.2650), § 10, operative Jan. 1, 1994.)

§ 910. Community estate; liability for debts

(a) Except as otherwise expressly provided by statute, the community estate is liable for a debt incurred by either spouse before or during marriage, regardless of which spouse has the management and control of the property and regardless of whether one or both spouses are parties to the debt or to a judgment for the debt.

16. In Wisnom v. McCarthy, 48 Cal.App. 697, 192 P. 337 (1920), a maid employed by the wife was held to be a "necessity of life."

17. Johnson v. Taylor, 120 Cal.App. Supp. 771, 4 P.2d 999 (1931).

18. Id.

19. West's Ann.Cal.Family Code § 910.

(b) "During marriage" for purposes of this section does not include the period during which the spouses are living separate and apart before a judgment of dissolution of marriage or legal separation of the parties.

(Stats.1992, c. 162 (A.B.2650), § 10, operative Jan. 1, 1994.)

§ 911. Earnings of married persons; liability for premarital debts; earnings held in deposit accounts

(a) The earnings of a married person during marriage are not liable for a debt incurred by the person's spouse before marriage. After the earnings of the married person are paid, they remain not liable so long as they are held in a deposit account in which the person's spouse has no right of withdrawal and are uncommingled with other property in the community estate, except property insignificant in amount.

(b) As used in this section:

(1) "Deposit account" has the meaning prescribed in Section 9105 of the Commercial Code.

(2) "Earnings" means compensation for personal services performed, whether as an employee or otherwise.

(Stats.1992, c. 162 (A.B.2650), § 10, operative Jan. 1, 1994.)

§ 912. Quasi-community property; treatment

For the purposes of this part, quasi-community property is liable to the same extent, and shall be treated the same in all other respects, as community property.

(Stats.1992, c. 162 (A.B.2650), § 10, operative Jan. 1, 1994.)

§ 913. Separate property of married person; liability for debt of spouse

(a) The separate property of a married person is liable for a debt incurred by the person before or during marriage.

(b) Except as otherwise provided by statute:

(1) The separate property of a married person is not liable for a debt incurred by the person's spouse before or during marriage.

(2) The joinder or consent of a married person to an encumbrance of community estate property to secure payment of a debt incurred by the person's spouse does not subject the person's separate property to liability for the debt unless the person also incurred the debt.

(Stats.1992, c. 162 (A.B.2650), § 10, operative Jan. 1, 1994.)

§ 914. Personal liability for debts incurred by spouse; separate property applied to satisfaction of debt

(a) Notwithstanding Section 913, a married person is personally liable for the following debts incurred by the person's spouse during marriage:

(1) A debt incurred for necessaries of life of the person's spouse while the spouses are living together.

(2) Except as provided in Section 4302, a debt incurred for common necessaries of life of the person's spouse while the spouses are living separately.

(b) The separate property of a married person may be applied to the satisfaction of a debt for which the person is personally liable pursuant to this section. If separate property is so applied at a time when nonexempt property in the community estate or separate property of the person's spouse is available but is not applied to the satisfaction of the debt, the married person is entitled to reimbursement to the extent such property was available.

(Stats.1993, c. 219, § 100.4, operative Jan. 1, 1994.)

§ 915. Child or spousal support obligation not arising out of marriage; reimbursement of community

(a) For the purpose of this part, a child or spousal support obligation of a married person that does not arise out of the marriage shall be treated as a debt incurred before marriage, regardless of whether a court order for support is made or modified before or during marriage and regardless of whether any installment payment on the obligation accrues before or during marriage.

(b) If property in the community estate is applied to the satisfaction of a child or spousal support obligation of a married person that does not arise out of the marriage, at a time when nonexempt separate income of the person is available but is not applied to the satisfaction of the obligation, the community estate is entitled to reimbursement from the person in the amount of the separate income, not exceeding the property in the community estate so applied.

(c) Nothing in this section limits the matters a court may take into consideration in determining or modifying the amount of a support order, including, but not limited to, the earnings of the spouses of the parties.

(Stats.1993, c. 219, § 100.5, operative Jan. 1, 1994.)

§ 916. Division of property; subsequent liability, right of reimbursement; interest and attorney's fees

(a) Notwithstanding any other provision of this chapter, after division of community and quasi-community property pursuant to Division 7 (commencing with Section 2500):

(1) The separate property owned by a married person at the time of the division and the property received by the person in the division is liable for a debt incurred by the person before or during marriage and the person is personally liable for the debt, whether or not the debt was assigned for payment by the person's spouse in the division.

(2) The separate property owned by a married person at the time of the division and the property received by the person in the division is not liable for a debt incurred by the person's spouse before or during marriage, and the person is not personally liable for the debt, unless the debt was assigned for payment by the person in the division of the property. Nothing in this paragraph affects the liability of property for the satisfaction of a lien on the property.

(3) The separate property owned by a married person at the time of the division and the property received by the person in the division is liable for a debt incurred by the person's spouse before or during marriage, and the person is personally liable for the debt, if the debt was assigned for payment by the person in the division of the property. If a money judgment for the debt is entered after the division, the property is not subject to enforcement of the judgment and the judgment may not be enforced against the married person, unless the person is made a party to the judgment for the purpose of this paragraph.

(b) If property of a married person is applied to the satisfaction of a money judgment pursuant to subdivision (a) for a debt incurred by the person that is assigned for payment by the person's spouse, the person has a right of reimbursement from the person's spouse to the extent of the property applied, with interest at the legal rate, and may recover reasonable attorney's fees incurred in enforcing the right of reimbursement.

(Stats.1992, c. 162 (A.B. 2650), § 10, operative Jan. 1, 1994.)

§ 920. Conditions governing right of reimbursement

A right of reimbursement provided by this part is subject to the following provisions:

(a) The right arises regardless of which spouse applies the property to the satisfaction of the debt, regardless of whether the property is applied to the satisfaction of the debt voluntarily or involuntarily, and regardless of whether the debt to which the property is applied is satisfied in whole or in part. The right is subject to an express written waiver of the right by the spouse in whose favor the right arises.

(b) The measure of reimbursement is the value of the property or interest in property at the time the right arises.

(c) The right shall be exercised not later than the earlier of the following times:

(1) Within three years after the spouse in whose favor the right arises has actual knowledge of the application of the property to the satisfaction of the debt.

(2) In proceedings for division of community and quasi-community property pursuant to Division 7 (commencing with Section 2500) or in proceedings upon the death of a spouse.

(Stats.1992, c. 162 (A.B. 2650), § 10, operative Jan. 1, 1994.)

§ 930. Liability for debts enforced on or after Jan. 1, 1985   *[replaced old law]*

Except as otherwise provided by statute, this part governs the liability of separate property and property in the community estate and the personal liability of a married person for a debt enforced on or after January 1, 1985, regardless of whether the debt was incurred before, on, or after that date.   *1984 Civil Code*

(Stats.1993, c. 219, § 100.6, operative Jan. 1, 1994.)

§ 1000. Liability for injury or damage caused by spouse; property subject to satisfaction of liability; satisfaction out of insurance proceeds; limitation on exercise of reimbursement right

(a) A married person is not liable for any injury or damage caused by the other spouse except in cases where the married person would be liable therefor if the marriage did not exist.   *co-N/o of vehicle.*

(b) The liability of a married person for death or injury to person or property shall be satisfied as follows:

(1) If the liability of the married person is based upon an act or omission which occurred while the married person was performing an activity for the benefit of the community, the liability shall first be satisfied from the community estate * * * and second from the separate property of the married person.

(2) If the liability of the married person is not based upon an act or omission which occurred while the married person was performing an activity for the benefit

of the community, the liability shall first be satisfied from the separate property of the married person and second from the community estate * * *.

(c) This section does not apply to the extent the liability is satisfied out of proceeds of insurance for the liability, whether the proceeds are from property in the community estate or from separate property. Notwithstanding Section 920, no right of reimbursement under this section shall be exercised more than seven years after the spouse in whose favor the right arises has actual knowledge of the application of the property to the satisfaction of the debt.

(Stats.1993, c. 219, § 100.7, operative Jan. 1, 1994.)

GROLEMUND v. CAFFERATA

Supreme Court of California, 1941.
17 Cal.2d 679, 111 P.2d 641.

[A judgment for damages arising out of an automobile accident was obtained against Caesaer Grolemund and executions issued. Caesaer Grolemund and his wife, Lena, sued to enjoin the sale of community property under these executions. The community property included some personal property acquired prior to 1927 and some real and personal property acquired after 1927. From a judgment against plaintiffs, Lena Grolemund appealed.]

CURTIS, JUSTICE. * * * The principal question to be decided on this appeal is whether community property may be subjected to the satisfaction of a judgment against the husband for his tort. Fundamental to our determination of this basic issue is consideration of the change wrought in our community system by enactment in 1927 of section 161a of the Civil Code. The general rule that community property in California acquired prior to 1927 has always been held liable for the husband's debts (Cal.Jur.Supp., vol. 3, p. 663, sec. 146) was given unqualified recognition by this court in the celebrated case of Spreckels v. Spreckels, 116 Cal. 339, 343, 48 P. 228, 36 L.R.A. 497, 58 Am.St.Rep. 170, wherein it is stated that the creditor of the husband could, at his option, sell under execution either the husband's separate property or the community property. The rule announced in that case has never been departed from by any decision of this court to which our attention has been called. Appellant claims, however, that by virtue of the enactment in 1927 of section 161a of the Civil Code, the wife now has a vested interest in the community property, of which she cannot be deprived because of the debt of the husband alone. Respondents resist this contention as contrary to the statutes and prior decisions of the courts of this state. Because of the emphasis placed by the parties on this enactment as it reflects on the instant issue, we shall consider first its effect upon the property of the Grolemunds acquired subsequent to the enactment of said section 161a.

* * * Since our analysis of the respective rights of the Grolemunds in this community real property must be governed by the law enforced at the time of the acquisition in 1930, we shall refer briefly to relevant

statutory provisions enacted prior to 1927, with which section 161a must be correlated.

Section 172 of the Civil Code, while it does not specifically create a liability or an exemption for any particular type of community property, gives to the husband "the management and control of the community personal property, with like absolute power of disposition, other than testamentary, as he has of his separate estate". It reasonably follows from the express language above quoted that this section in effect subjects the entire community personalty (with the exception of the wife's earnings, Civ.Code, sec. 168) to any and all contracts of the husband, as well as to judgments arising out of his tort. Furthermore, since the only limitation upon the husband is to refrain from making a gift of such property without consideration, he is not limited from paying it out in compromise or satisfaction of a tort claim, for payment of a tort claim is not payment without consideration.

Section 172a of the Civil Code gives the husband "the management and control of the community real property", subject to the proviso that in regard to conveyances the wife must join with him in executing the necessary instruments. Since this restriction concerns only voluntary transfers, it has no application to the instant case involving the satisfaction of a judgment by levy of execution, so that for all practical purposes herein the husband's power of management and control of the community real property involved here is as absolute and complete as it is with respect to community personal property, as outlined in section 172. * * * That the addition in 1927 of section 161a, defining the interests of the spouses in community property, did not change the rule vesting in the husband the entire management and control of the community property is manifest by the express recognition accorded sections 172 and 172a in the later statute. Cal.Jur.Supp., vol. 3, p. 608, sec. 98; Beemer v. Roher, 1934, 137 Cal.App. 293, 30 P.2d 547; Hannah v. Swift, 9 Cir., 1932, 61 F.2d 307, 310.

With reference to California legislation on the question of liability or exemption of property of the spouses for payment of obligations arising out of the husband's tort, the sole enactments are section 168, which exempts the wife's earnings (community property) from liability for debts of the husband, and section 171, which extends the same exemption in respect to the wife's separate property. It is significant to note that nothing is said in regard to the liability of the husband's separate property, the husband's earnings, or the balance of the community property (the wife's earnings excepted by Civ.Code, sec. 168) in regard to an obligation created by the husband's tort. From this silence of the legislature it logically can be inferred that it was thereby intended that the husband, as agent of the community, should retain the power to divest the parties of their community property by his own act in the same manner that he might divest himself of his separate property, so long as he did not make a gift of the former without consideration. To hold that the husband could not subject the community property to liability for his tort would be to hold that he could not manage and control the same. To illustrate, suppose that the tort action had never been instituted by Emilio Cafferata and his co-plaintiffs, but that Caesaer Grolemund, after injuring these parties, had made a voluntary settlement of his liability. It cannot be said that the husband would be without power to use common funds to pay for the damages sustained by the injured persons because of his negligent act. Or let us suppose that the damage suit was brought and judgment had gone against Caesaer Grolemund, as here but that no execution had been levied, it is obvious that the husband could satisfy such judgment voluntarily from a bank account under his control but which consisted of community funds. The foregoing analysis compels us to conclude that there is no logical distinction to be drawn between satisfaction of a judgment against the husband by levy of execution against the community property and satisfaction of a like judgment by the husband's voluntary payment from community funds. To hold otherwise would be to deny in toto the operation of sections 172 and 172a of the Civil Code, which would be contrary to the express terms of section 161a.

* * *

Appellant advances the argument that the statutes of Washington and the statutes of California regarding community property are the same, and, therefore, the rules announced in decisions of the Washington courts interpreting their code sections should be followed here. This contention is singularly devoid of merit in view of the fact that the underlying theories of the community system in the two states are entirely distinct. The Washington statutes are based on the theory of tenancy by entireties, with its fundamental concept of "community debts", and in that state the community property is not liable for the separate debts of the husband, much less of the wife, but is liable only for so-called "community debts". Cal.Jur.Supp., vol. 3, p. 665, sec. 147, and cases there cited. For example, in Sun Life Assur. Co. v. Outler, 172 Wash. 540, at page 544, 20 P.2d 1110, at page 1112, the Washington court said: "The test of a community obligation is: 'Was the transaction carried on for the benefit of the community?'" Thus, in Washington where the system makes the community property responsible only for "community debts" or "community liabilities", the community property cannot be reached for the individual tort of either the husband or wife. But in California there is no like concept of "community debts", though occasionally the courts in this state refer to such, overlooking the fact that the phrase is not appropriate to the California system. Cal.Jur. Supp., vol. 3, p. 666, sec. 147. A complete reading of all our code sections on community property clearly demonstrates that our community system is based upon the principle that all debts which are not specifically made the obligation of the wife are grouped together as the obligations of the husband and the community property (with the single exception of the wife's earnings, which are exempted from certain types of debt, Civ.Code, sec. 168). This proposition was confirmed in Street v. Bertolone, 193 Cal. 751, 753, 226 P. 913: "The term 'the debts of the husband,' unless otherwise qualified, includes debts incurred by the husband for the benefit of the community as well as his own separate debts." Since in this state there is strictly no such thing as "community debts" in the sense in which they exist in Washington, the decisions of the latter state lose force as a precedent here.

* * *

Since it is our opinion that the enactment of section 161a of the Civil Code, defining the interests of the spouses in community property, has not altered the situation with respect to the wife's interest remaining subject to the husband's power of management and control, all community property, whether acquired prior to or subsequent to July 29, 1927 (the effective date of this statute), is liable for satisfaction of the husband's debts. As the date of acquisition is immaterial here, the preceding discussion applies with equal force to the personal property in San Francisco purchased by the Grolemunds in 1926 and eliminates any necessity for separate treatment of that phase of this proceeding.

Our conclusion in the instant case is not only in conformity with legal principles, but is consonant with practical considerations and public policy as well, for otherwise a person injured by the separate act of the husband would fail to gain redress for his damage in such case where the only property of the spouses is community. This obviously unfair and unjust result would have a disastrous effect on the very foundation of our community system and would be entirely out of harmony with the general rule that the community property is liable for the husband's debts. The trial court properly held that respondents may proceed to levy execution upon both the community real and personal property of the Grolemunds, and sell the same in satisfaction of the tort judgment obtained against the husband alone.

The judgment appealed from is accordingly affirmed.

Note

Under Family Code Section 1000 which governs tort obligations, if the tort arose out of an activity performed for the benefit of the community, the liability will be satisfied first from community property and then from the tortfeasor's separate property. Conversely, if the tort did not arise out of a community benefit activity, the tortfeasor's separate property will be primarily liable, with the community property having secondary liability. With this qualification, the principles voiced in Grolemund v. Cafferata still obtain. The following case discusses the scope of community benefit activities.

IN RE MARRIAGE OF HIRSCH

Court of Appeal, Fourth District, 1989.
211 Cal.App.3d 104, 259 Cal.Rptr. 39.

OPINION

WALLIN, ACTING PRESIDING JUSTICE.

Husband appeals from an order denying his motion to classify certain debts satisfied with his post-dissolution separate property as community obligations.

* * *

Claudia Mirken and Clement Hirsch were married in 1963 and separated in 1970. Prior to and during the marriage, Clement owned shares of stock in the Bank of Los Angeles and served on its board of directors. In 1966, the bank merged with United States National Bank (USNB) and Clement's shares were converted into USNB stock. Clement sat on the new board of directors from January 1966 until March 1971, six months after the parties had separated.

In November 1973, the trial court entered an interlocutory decree dividing the community property. The decree contained an express reservation of jurisdiction to divide community property or pay community debts not then known or established.

Shortly thereafter, USNB collapsed and Clement learned he had been named as a defendant in two federal court actions alleging various statutory and contractual causes of action, plus negligence and intentional misconduct as a director of USNB. Clement promptly moved to establish a community reserve from which any ultimate liability arising out of the actions could be satisfied. The court denied the motion on the basis that Clement's liability, if any, was too uncertain at that time. It stated Clement could seek reimbursement from Claudia for her contributive share at a later date.

Thereafter, a third lawsuit was filed against Clement arising out of his tenure on the USNB board. Clement then sent an accounting to Claudia's counsel of the funds expended by him in defense of the USNB litigation and requested reimbursement for one-half that amount. The letter also stated, "[s]ettlement negotiations are on-going, and if a reasonable settlement of the law suits [sic] and claims are made, Mr. Hirsch will look to [Claudia] for a contribution of one-half of any amounts payable pursuant to such settlement." Claudia responded by disclaiming any financial responsibility for the USNB lawsuits and making clear she did not wish to participate in any settlement negotiations.

Upon the advice of counsel, Clement settled all three lawsuits and moved for a postjudgment order declaring the settlement amounts and expenses of defense community debts. He sought reimbursement for $423,130.19, one-half the amount he expended in settling the lawsuits, including attorney's fees and costs.

Believing Civil Code section 5122 to be the applicable statute[1] for determining the character of the settlement obligations, Clement pre-

---

1. Civil Code section 5122 provides, "(a) A married person is not liable for any injury or damage caused by the other spouse except in cases where he or she would be liable therefor if the marriage did not exist. [¶] (b) The liability of a married person for death or injury to person or property shall be satisfied as follows: [¶] (1) If the liabil-

sented testimony that his reason for serving on the board of USNB was to benefit the community. He said he agreed to sit on the USNB board and various other boards because the positions were prestigious, challenging and offered the potential to develop contacts in the business community. The parties stipulated Clement's USNB director's salary constituted community income.[2]

Jacob Shearer, the attorney who represented Clement in the USNB lawsuits, testified he believed Clement's exposure to liability was limited to the negligence causes of action. Apparently there had been an article in the Wall Street Journal which Shearer believed should have put the board on notice of the problems which eventually led to USNB's collapse. In Shearer's opinion, Clement's failure to heed the warnings constituted "gross negligence." However, he did not feel Clement was exposed to any liability for the alleged intentional torts. At the most, he felt Clement's exposure amounted to continued malfeasance in ignoring instances of self-dealing by C. Arnholt Smith, the owner of USNB, and ignoring the Journal article. Shearer testified one of the lawsuits was nothing more than a "strike suit"[3] and that he recommended settlement of all three lawsuits because defense costs alone would exceed $1 million.

Claudia presented little evidence in support of her contention the settlement obligations should be characterized as Clement's separate debt. Her attorney testified the causes of action in the USNB lawsuits were based primarily on intentional conduct by Clement.[4] In addition, the court had before it Claudia's earlier declaration stating she urged Clement to resign from the board but he refused.

After the hearing, the court made the following findings in its memorandum of intended decision: "[T]he liabilities incurred by [Clement] in the settlement of the three lawsuits and the attendant attorneys fees arising out of his service as a member of the board of directors of the United States National Bank during and after the marriage of the parties are not community obligations. [Clement's] motion to have these liabilities declared to be community obligations and requesting

ity of the married person is based upon an act or omission which occurred while the married person was performing an activity for the benefit of the community, the liability shall first be satisfied from the community property and second from the separate property of the married person. [¶] (2) If the liability of the married person is not based upon an act or omission which occurred while the married person was performing an activity for the benefit of the community, the liability shall first be satisfied from the separate property of the married person and second from the community property...." [Now see Family Code § 1000.]

2. However, Clement testified the salary was not a factor in his decision to serve on the board. Clement's director's salary was $10,000 annually, hardly motivation for an individual whose net worth at the time was over $10 million dollars; nor apparently was his separate property stock in USNB a motivating factor. The value of his stock was approximately $20,000. He held only 5 percent of that stock personally and the remaining 95 percent was held in trust.

3. It appears Clement was well-advised. The complaint in this lawsuit set forth 194 causes of action and sought hundreds of millions of dollars in damages. Clement settled it for $5,000.

4. This was presumably to establish that the conduct fell within the rule of *In re Marriage of Stitt* (1983) 147 Cal.App.3d 579, 195 Cal.Rptr. 172, discussed *post*.

reimbursement from the community is denied. [¶] The basis for this intended decision is that the settlement obligations and the attorneys fees in connection therewith were incurred by [Clement] as a result of his tortious conduct and pursuant to the holding of *In re Marriage of Stitt* should therefore not be charged against the community."

The proposed order submitted by Claudia's counsel and ultimately signed by the court was in substantial conformity with the memorandum of intended decision except it deleted any reference to the *Stitt* decision.[5] Clement appeals, contending the trial court erred in failing to apply the "benefit of the community" test of Civil Code section 5122[6] to the allegedly tortious conduct which formed the basis of the lawsuits against him. Had the court properly applied this test, Clement argues, it would have found the amounts paid to settle those lawsuits were community obligations.

* * *

Since the passage of the Family Law Act in 1970 there has been a surprising absence of guidelines for classifying debts arising out of allegedly tortious conduct. Although the trial court's role is obvious once a debt has been properly characterized as a community obligation, the appropriate method for reaching that determination has not been made clear.

We begin with the fundamental principle applicable to the division of property in a dissolution proceeding: " 'In dividing the community property equally under the mandate of Civil Code section 4800, subdivision (a), the court must distribute both the assets and the obligations of the community so that the residual assets awarded to each party after the deduction of the obligations are *equal*.' (*In re Marriage of Fonstein* (1976) 17 Cal.3d 738, 748 [131 Cal.Rptr. 873, 552 P.2d 1169].)" (*In re Marriage of Schultz* (1980) 105 Cal.App.3d 846, 853, 164 Cal.Rptr. 653.)[7] "[T]ransactions of the spouses *inter se* are subject to review and the separate debts of one spouse may be excluded from the shared community obligations. [Citation.] 'Between the spouses, certain obligations which are properly characterized as separate may be assigned to the responsible person if unpaid, or reimbursement may be ordered in favor of the community if the debt was paid from community assets.' [Cita-

5. The order signed by the court states, "the liabilities incurred by [Clement] for settlements, attorneys fees and costs regarding lawsuits against [Clement] which arose from his service as a member of the Board of Directors of the United States National Bank of San Diego do not constitute community obligations. The court further determines that [Clement] is not entitled to reimbursement from the community, or otherwise from [Claudia], regarding such liabilities."

6. All statutory references are to the Civil Code unless otherwise specified.

7. There are statutory exceptions to the equal division rule of section 4800, subdivision (a) which are inapplicable here. For example, in a bankrupt estate in which the community's liabilities exceed its assets, the court is not required to assign the obligations equally to each spouse; instead, it may effect an equitable division, taking into consideration the respective earning capacities of the spouses as well as other factors it deems relevant. (§ 4800, subd. (c)(2).)

tion.]'' (*In re Marriage of Lister* (1984) 152 Cal.App.3d 411, 417, 199 Cal.Rptr. 321.) Although a creditor may be able to reach a community asset to satisfy a debt incurred by one spouse alone, in a dissolution action the court may properly require the debtor spouse to bear the entire burden of the obligation if it finds that debt to be a separate obligation.

Relying on *In re Marriage of Stitt, supra*, 147 Cal.App.3d 579, 195 Cal.Rptr. 172, the court below found the settlement obligations incurred by Clement to be his separate debt because the underlying lawsuits alleged tortious conduct committed by him. In *Stitt*, wife incurred attorney's fees in defending against civil and criminal charges of embezzlement from her employer. Wife settled the civil action and was convicted in the criminal action. In a subsequent dissolution proceeding, wife argued the attorney's fees should be regarded as a community obligation because they were incurred during marriage. Husband conceded the community was responsible to the attorneys for the obligation, but contended that as part of the dissolution action, the court could properly assign that obligation to wife as her separate debt. Husband relied on section 5122, which states that a married person is generally not liable for damages caused by a tortfeasor spouse. The trial court agreed with husband, finding wife was required to satisfy the attorney's fee obligation from her share of the community assets.

On appeal, the court was similarly persuaded that section 5122 was applicable and operated to shield the community from liability for the tortious acts of wife: "We use the term 'community obligation' for convenience. It has been said that there are no separate debts as distinguished from community debts. [Citations.] However, for practical purposes the spousal obligations are to be viewed first from the creditor's standpoint, which may encompass both community and separate property, then from the standpoint of the spouses who are interested not only in the equal division of the community property and liabilities but also in preventing a 'separate debt' of one spouse from being included in the shared community obligations. [Citation.]

"........................

"Because husband did not participate in wife's embezzlement and no benefit to the community was shown, ... [¶] ... in the settlement of marital rights the court could seek an equitable result because of the separate nature of the obligation. In this instance the court found it appropriate to assign the full financial responsibility for the wife's embezzlement to the wife, preventing her assertion of 'community debt' from diminishing the husband's share of the community property. This was consistent with the general principle found in section 1714 that the actor is solely responsible for wilful and negligent acts unless shared, mitigated or excused because of other principles of law." (*Id.*, at pp. 587–588, 195 Cal.Rptr. 172.)

In a remarkable leap, the court then states, "[r]eturning to section 5122, we find a legislative direction that between the spouses the mere fact of marriage should not change the usual rules of personal responsibility for the consequences of criminal or tortious activity. Although the section spells out the order in which creditors may satisfy tort claims from the property of the spouses, it does not forbid one spouse from later disclaiming responsibility for the tort liability of the other in a dissolution proceeding. . . ." (*Id.,* at p. 588, 195 Cal.Rptr. 172.)

We are mystified as to where the *Stitt* court found this so-called legislative direction to apply section 5122 in a dissolution proceeding and effect an "equitable" division of property where *any* tortious conduct is involved, be it negligent or intentional. The proper statutory focus in the assignment of spousal obligations is section 4800. And although the "benefit of the community" language of subdivision (b) of section 5122 is useful in characterizing an obligation as separate or community in nature, the section itself is a creditors' statute, designed for their protection; it is not a legislative return to the pre–1970 "fault" concept of division of marital property.

Confined to its facts, *Stitt* is correct. An innocent spouse is not required to share in losses incurred by the intentionally tortious or criminal conduct of a spouse where there is no benefit to the community. But the holding in *Stitt* is overbroad because it includes negligent as well as intentional torts.[8] Thus, to the extent *Stitt* holds the negligent conduct of a spouse engaged in an activity benefiting the community provides sufficient justification to characterize a debt as a separate obligation, it is incorrect.

A few examples illustrate the point. Assume a spouse who is an attorney commits malpractice and is held liable for a substantial judgment. Since the law practice was an activity intended to produce income for the community, the malpractice judgment would be a shared community debt, even though it results from one spouse's negligence. But the same result should also follow when the negligence occurs while driving the family car on a personal errand. Neither spouse should bear the entire financial burden of such a loss. Finally even criminal or intentionally tortious conduct which results in obtaining substantial ill-gotten assets for the community creates a shared community debt. A spouse who temporarily doubles the value of the community through a fraudulent scheme should not forfeit all of his or her rights to the honestly obtained assets when restitution is made.

Turning to the facts before us, it is impossible to know whether the tortious conduct which gave rise to the resulting obligation was negligent or intentional since Clement settled those lawsuits before trial. However, as stated *ante,* the characterization of the conduct alone does not resolve the question. Even if Clement's conduct was intentionally tortious, he presented evidence his activities benefited the community.

---

8. Although intentional torts and crimes rarely benefit the community, we can envision situations in which the community would be enriched by such conduct. For example, had wife put the embezzled funds into a community account or other community property, it would have been appropriate for the community to bear the corresponding loss.

Clement's exposure to liability arose out of his actions while serving on the board of USNB, which took place for the most part during his marriage to Claudia. The remuneration he received for serving on the board was undisputedly community property.

Claudia presented no evidence that Clement's service on the board was to protect his separate property stock or further any of his separate property businesses. There was therefore no legitimate basis to characterize the settlement obligations as Clement's separate debt.

The order is reversed and the matter remanded to the trial court to determine the reasonableness of the attorney's fees incurred by Clement in defending the lawsuits.

SMALLWOOD, J.*, concur.

CROSBY, J., concurs in the result.

AMERICAN OLEAN TILE CO. INC. v. SCHULTZE

California District Court of Appeal, 1985.
169 Cal.App.3d 359; 215 Cal.Rptr. 184.

KING, ASSOCIATE JUSTICE.

In this case we hold that after the execution of a valid marital settlement agreement, negotiated at arms length and providing a community business is transferred to the spouse who had been exclusively operating it as his separate property, all obligations of the business incurred thereafter are the sole obligation of the recipient spouse, even though incurred before entry of an interlocutory judgment of dissolution of the marriage incorporating the marital settlement agreement. We further hold that amendments to the Family Law Act providing for the personal liability of a spouse and the liability of separate or community property for debt, which are expressly declared by the Legislature to be applicable to all debts enforced on or after a given date, do not violate due process, even as to debts incurred before the operative date of the amendments.

American Olean Tile Company (American) sued Horst and Irmgard Schultze, whose marriage had been dissolved, for nonpayment of a promissory note executed by Horst on May 6, 1981. The Schultzes had separated on April 1, 1980. On May 1, 1981, they executed a marital settlement agreement dividing their community property; it was incorporated by reference into the interlocutory judgment of dissolution of marriage filed June 19, 1981.

Pursuant to the marital settlement agreement Horst received H & S Tile, a community business, as his separate property. Irmgard received other property. There is no dispute that the marital settlement agreement was an arms length, negotiated agreement in which the interests of

* Judge, Orange County Superior Court,   Council.
assigned by the Chairperson of the Judicial

the spouses were adverse and each was represented by counsel. After the separation Irmgard received no support from Horst and no benefits from the operation of his business. She also had no knowledge of any debts Horst incurred after the separation or of his execution of the promissory note. The family home was to be sold and, after payment of community bills, the balance was to be divided between Horst and Irmgard.

After separation, Horst continued to operate the tile business. On May 6, 1981, he signed a promissory note in favor of American for $13,747.80 for unpaid invoices which were merged into the promissory note. Horst failed to make any payments on the note. In August 1981 American filed a complaint against Horst for the debt incurred for the goods received and for the promissory note. A default judgment against Horst was entered on November 25, 1981. When it became apparent to American that Horst could not be located for satisfaction of the judgment, American obtained an order vacating the original judgment and permitting filing of an amended complaint which claimed former community property held by Irmgard was liable for the unpaid account and the promissory note since both were incurred and executed during her marriage to Horst.

American applied for and was granted a prejudgment attachment of a promissory note, secured by a deed of trust on real property, which was originally payable to Irmgard and Horst. The promissory note was converted to cash and remained subject to the prejudgment attachment order. The sheriff of San Mateo County was ordered to hold the proceeds of the note pursuant to the order.

The case was tried May 13, 1983. Horst did not appear. In its decision filed August 10, 1983, the court stated: "The defendants Schultzes entered into a marital settlement agreement May 1, 1981. Defendant Horst Schultze received by the agreement as his separate property the family business known as H & S Tile. On May 6, 1981, defendant Horst Schultze executed a promissory note in favor of plaintiff, the subject of this lawsuit, for purchases he had made prior to that date. The defendant Horst Schultze was dealing with the obligations of his separate property and not community property when he executed the promissory note to plaintiff. Further, any account stated or book account that existed prior to May 6, 1981, was merged into the promissory note executed by defendant Horst Schultze. [¶] Therefore, let judgment as prayed be entered as to Horst Schultze plus costs and attorney fees. [¶] The pre-judgment attachment as to Irmgard Helen Schultze is discharged." A judgment was entered for Irmgard pursuant to the court's decision, and against Horst for $13,932.59 plus interest, attorney fees and costs.

American contends the trial court erred in finding that the community property held by Irmgard was not liable for debts incurred by Horst after separation. This argument fails because income earned and obligations incurred after separation in the operation of a separate property business are not community in nature. (See Civ.Code, § 5118; *In re Marriage of Bouquet* (1976) 16 Cal.3d 583, 128 Cal.Rptr. 427, 546 P.2d 1371.) Here the note was a separate obligation of Horst, having been incurred after the date of separation at a time when the business had become his separate property.

When, by execution of a marital settlement agreement, a community property business of the spouses becomes the separate property of one of them, a creditor seeking to enforce a business debt incurred thereafter "will be restricted to satisfaction from the separate property of the debtor spouse, provided: (1) The transmutation agreement was not entered into to defraud an existing creditor of either spouse;[28] and (2) The creditor was not misled to its detriment by the failure of the spouses to inform it that by virtue of an agreement between them the supposed community assets on which the creditor relied were in fact separate assets.[29] [¶] A third-party contract-creditor will not be entitled to recover against former community assets transmuted into the separate property of the noncontracting spouse, since the creditor can easily avoid the risk of unknown interspousal transfers by obtaining both spouses' signatures on contracts or notes.[30] " (Markey, Cal.Family Law Prac. & Proc., § 5.72[4][c].)

"**28.** *See Robertson v. Willis* (1978) 77 Cal.App.3d 358, 363, 143 Cal.Rptr. 523; *Gould v. Fuller* (1967) 249 Cal.App.2d 18, 24, 57 Cal.Rptr. 23."

"**29.** *In re Marriage of Dawley* (1976) 17 Cal.3d 342, 357 fn. 11, 131 Cal.Rptr. 3, 551 P.2d 323."

"**30.** *See Kennedy v. Taylor* (1984) 155 Cal.App.3d 126, 130, 201 Cal.Rptr. 779."

American's argument also fails under new statutes governing spouses' liability for debts upon dissolution of a marriage, which were enacted in 1984 and are applicable to this case.

Under the new legislation, separate and community property held by the nondebtor spouse *will not be liable* for debts incurred by the other spouse *unless the nondebtor spouse was assigned the debt* in the division of the property. (Civ.Code, § 5120.160.)[1] This legislation applies to all debts *enforced* on or after the operative date of the amendments (January 1, 1985). (Civ.Code, § 5120.320.)[2]

1. Civil Code section 5120.160, subdivision (a), provides in part: "(2) The separate property owned by a married person at the time of the division and the property received by the person in the division is *not liable* for a debt incurred by the person's spouse before or during marriage, and the person is not personally liable for the debt, *unless the debt was assigned for payment by the person in the division of the property.* Nothing in this paragraph affects the liability of property for the satisfaction of a lien on the property. (3) The separate property owned by a married person at the time of the division and the property received by the person in the division *is liable* for a

debt incurred by the person's spouse before or during marriage, and the person is personally liable for the debt, *if the debt was assigned for payment by the person in the division of the property.* If a money judgment for the debt is entered after the division, the property is not subject to enforcement of the judgment and the judgment may not be enforced against the married person, unless the person is made a party to the judgment for the purpose of this paragraph." (Emphasis added.)

2. Civil Code section 5120.320 states: "Except as otherwise provided by statute, the provisions of this chapter govern the liability of separate and community proper-

Therefore, pursuant to Civil Code section 5120.320, the new rule contained in Civil Code section 5120.160 will be effective in cases such as this in which the debtor had not yet satisfied the debt at the time that the amendments became operative. Since Irmgard was not assigned the debt in the interlocutory judgment of dissolution of marriage, she is *not* personally liable for Horst's debt, *nor* is the former community property now held by Irmgard liable for the debt. The trial court's decision was correct both under former law and under the new amendments to the Family Law Act.

The Legislature may amend the Civil Code retroactively when "expressly so declared" pursuant to Civil Code section 3. American argues, however, that it would violate due process to apply the amendments concerning liability of marital property to debts incurred before the operative date of the statutory change.

Rather than applying retroactively, these amendments have the effect of prospectively defining, as between spouses and creditors, how enforcement of debts is to be carried out. Even assuming arguendo that the statutory changes constitute a retroactive change, under the circumstances here there is no unconstitutional deprivation of any vested property rights of American.

Even if vested rights are impaired, the impairment of vested property rights may be carried out with due process of law under many circumstances. "The state's inherent sovereign power includes the so-called 'police power' right to interfere with vested property rights whenever reasonably necessary to the protection of the health, safety, morals, and general well being of the people. * * * The constitutional question, on principle, therefore, would seem to be, not whether a vested right is impaired by a marital property law change, but whether such a change reasonably could be believed to be sufficiently necessary to the public welfare as to justify the impairment." (*Addison v. Addison* [1965] 62 Cal.2d 558 at p. 566 [43 Cal.Rptr. 97, 399 P.2d 897, 14 A.L.R.3d 391], quoting Armstrong, *"Prospective" Application of Changes in Community Property Control—Rule of Property or Constitutional Necessity?* (1945) 33 Cal.L.Rev. 476, 495.) In determining whether a retroactive law contravenes the due process clause, we consider such factors as the significance of the state interest served by the law, the importance of the retroactive application of the law to the effectuation of that interest, the extent of reliance upon the former law, the legitimacy of that reliance, the extent of actions taken on the basis of that reliance, and the extent to which the retroactive application of the new law would disrupt those actions. (See generally Reppy, *Retroactivity of the 1975 California Community Property Reforms* (1975) 48 So.Cal.L.Rev. 977, 1048–1049; Note, *Retroactive Application of California's Community Property Statutes* (1966) 18 Stan.L.Rev. 514, 518–519, 521–522; Hoch-

ty and the personal liability of a married person for a debt enforced on or after the operative date of this chapter, regardless whether the debt was incurred before, on, or after the operative date."

man, *The Supreme Court and the Constitutionality of Retroactive Legislation* [1960] 73 Harv.L.Rev. 692; Greenblatt, *Judicial Limitations on Retroactive Civil Legislation* (1956) 51 Nw.U.L.Rev. 540, 559.) (*In re Marriage of Bouquet, supra,* 16 Cal.3d at pp. 592–593, 128 Cal.Rptr. 427, 546 P.2d 1371.)

Referring to its opinion in *Addison,* the Supreme Court in *Bouquet* stated: "Nevertheless, we deemed the retroactive application of the legislation a proper exercise of the police power. The state's paramount interest in the equitable distribution of marital property upon dissolution of the marriage, we concluded, justified the impairment of the husband's vested property rights. (See generally *Williams v. North Carolina* (1942) 317 U.S. 287, 298 [87 L.Ed. 279, 285–286, 63 S.Ct. 207, 213, 143 A.L.R. 1273].)" (*Id.,* at p. 593, 128 Cal.Rptr. 427, 546 P.2d 1371.)

In the context of marital dissolutions, which are equitable proceedings, courts should give great deference to expressed legislative intent for retroactivity of statutory amendments because of "The state's paramount interest in the equitable distribution of marital property upon dissolution of the marriage. * * *" (*Id.*)

American also claims that the trial court erred in failing to award a specific sum for attorney fees against Horst as part of its decision and judgment, although the judgment did award American "costs of suit and attorney fees." This is incorrect, since the attorney fees are an element of costs of suit pursuant to Civil Code section 1717. Thus, American should recover attorney fees against Horst as part of its costs of suit. The judgment is affirmed.

Low, P.J., and Haning, J., concur.

Notes

1. At dissolution, the community property and quasi-community property must be divided equally between the spouses under West's Ann.Cal. Family Code Section 2550. Prior case law permitted a creditor to satisfy a debt out of any property that would have been liable for the debt prior to the division at dissolution. Thus a creditor could reach former community property that had been awarded to the nondebtor spouse. See, e.g., Frankel v. Boyd, 106 Cal. 608, 39 P. 939 (1895); Vest v. Superior Court, 140 Cal.App.2d 91, 294 P.2d 988 (1956). This rule was criticized as unsound:

> It creates procedural burdens of tracing former community property in the hands of the nondebtor spouse and raises problems whether any increase in value of the property, due to improvements, inflation, or otherwise, is also liable and whether the property should be traceable through changes in form after it has lost its community identity. These practical difficulties also demonstrate that the principles supporting liability of community property during marriage are not applicable after division of the property upon dissolution.

Liability of Marital Property for Debts, 17 Cal.L.Revision Comm'n Reports, 1, 23 (1984). West's Ann.Cal. Family Code § 916 reverses the case law rule allowing a creditor to enforce a money judgment against former community property in the hands of a nondebtor spouse after dissolution. Under § 916, the former community property received by the nondebtor spouse at dissolution will be liable only if the nondebtor spouse was assigned the debt in the division proceedings. The rules governing the assignment of debts at dissolution are treated in Chapter 7.

2. Suppose that the spouses begin to live separate and apart and during the period of separation, one of them enters into one or more contractual obligations. Assume that one of the obligations is unpaid, and that the creditor obtains a personal judgement against the debtor spouse. Is the entire community property estate liable for the satisfaction of the judgment? See West's Ann.Cal. Family Code § 910(6); c.f., In re McCoy, 90 B.R. 448 (Bkrtcy.D.Cal.1988).

Chapter 7

DIVISION OF COMMUNITY PROPERTY AT DISSOLUTION

When a marriage is terminated by the death of one spouse or by dissolution proceedings, it is necessary to make a determination of the property rights of the interested parties and to achieve an appropriate division of the various property interests. This chapter focuses on the division of marital property on dissolution or judicial separation. There are basically two ways to achieve a division of property on dissolution. The most common is a property settlement agreement negotiated by the parties.[1] The other method involves litigation in the context of the dissolution proceeding. The first section of this chapter examines some of the major problems involved in the negotiated property settlement agreement. The second section treats issues associated with judicially mandated property divisions, including jurisdiction, valuation, and the equal division requirement. The final section deals with post-dissolution remedies for fraud or mistake.

The statutory provisions dealing with the division of property, child and spousal support, and property settlement agreements on judicial separation or dissolution are contained in the Family Law Act, enacted in 1969 and effective January 1, 1970.[2] The Act made a number of significant changes in the prior law, most notably the elimination of "fault" as a basis for the termination of marriage. Under the prior law, the person seeking a divorce was required to submit evidence establishing that at least one of the several grounds for divorce existed. These grounds included adultery, extreme cruelty, wilful desertion, wilful ne-

1. "Both in the United States and England, the overwhelming majority of divorcing couples resolve distributional questions concerning marital property, alimony, child support, and custody without bringing any contested issue to court for adjudication." Mnookin & Kornhauser, Bargaining in the Shadow of the Law: The Case of Divorce, 88 Yale L.J. 950, 951 (1979).

2. Cal.Stats.1969, c. 1608, p. 3314. The Family Law Act has been recodified in the West's Ann. California Family Code, operative January 1, 1994.

glect, habitual intemperance, and conviction of a felony.[3] Proof of "fault" also had economic consequences: The "innocent" spouse was entitled to more than half of the community property. The greater the fault, the larger the share of community property that was awarded to the non-offending spouse:

> The rule drawn from the cases * * * is that the greater the offense the larger the proportion of the community property that must be awarded to the innocent spouse;—where the acts of cruelty are of a flagrant character and have extended over a long period of time the portion of the community property awarded to the nonoffending party should be greater than if the acts were more trivial yet sufficient to warrant the granting of a divorce. It obviously follows that where the divorce is granted on the more heinous ground of adultery as well as for extreme cruelty the amount awarded to the innocent party should be greater than if granted on the ground of cruelty alone.[4]

Because of the linkage of fault with property awards, the former law provided a financial incentive for exaggerating the transgressions of the offending spouse.[5] It also led to increased acrimony and occasional perjury. Criticism of this system and proposals for reform eventually led to the adoption of what is commonly referred to as "no-fault divorce" in California. The legislators recognized that the fault requirement coupled with the potential for economic advantage promoted additional bitterness between the parties and had a deleterious impact on their children.[6] Consequently, the Family Law Act eliminated fault both as a legal basis for divorce and as a financial incentive in property divisions. Under the Family Code, there are only two grounds for dissolution: incurable insanity and irreconcilable differences. Moreover, the community property must be divided equally without regard to the reasons for the dissolution.

WEST'S ANNOTATED FAMILY CODE OF CALIFORNIA

§ 2300. Effect of dissolution

The effect of a judgment of dissolution of marriage when it becomes final is to restore the parties to the state of unmarried persons.

(Stats.1992, c. 162 (A.B. 2650), § 10, operative Jan. 1, 1994.)

3. Assembly Comm. Report on Assembly Bill No. 530 and Senate Bill No. 252, 1969 Journal of the California Assembly 8053, 8054–55. Proof of fault was required in all divorce proceedings except those involving allegations of incurable insanity.

4. Arnold v. Arnold, 76 Cal.App.2d 877, 881–882, 174 P.2d 674 (1946).

5. L. Weitzman, The Divorce Revolution 12 (1985).

6. For a discussion of the background of the no-fault legislation, see L. Weitzman, The Divorce Revolution 16–19 (1985); Comment, The End of Innocence: Elimination of Fault in California Divorce Law, 17 UCLA L.Rev. 1306 (1970); Comment, Irreconcilable Differences: California Courts Respond to No–Fault Dissolutions, 7 Loy. L.A.L.Rev. 453 (1974).

§ 2310. Grounds for dissolution or legal separation

Dissolution of the marriage or legal separation of the parties may be based on either of the following grounds, which shall be pleaded generally:

(a) Irreconcilable differences, which have caused the irremediable breakdown of the marriage.

(b) Incurable insanity.

(Stats.1992, c. 162 (A.B. 2650), § 10, operative Jan. 1, 1994.)

§ 2311. Irreconcilable differences defined

Irreconcilable differences are those grounds which are determined by the court to be substantial reasons for not continuing the marriage and which make it appear that the marriage should be dissolved.

(Stats.1992, c. 162 (A.B. 2650), § 10, operative Jan. 1, 1994.)

§ 2312. Incurable insanity

A marriage may be dissolved on the grounds of incurable insanity only upon proof, including competent medical or psychiatric testimony, that the insane spouse was at the time the petition was filed, and remains, incurably insane.

(Stats.1992, c. 162 (A.B. 2650), § 10, operative Jan. 1, 1994.)

§ 2313. Support of incurably insane spouse; order for support or bond

No dissolution of marriage granted on the ground of incurable insanity relieves a spouse from any obligation imposed by law as a result of the marriage for the support of the spouse who is incurably insane, and the court may make such order for support, or require a bond therefor, as the circumstances require.

(Stats.1992, c. 162 (A.B. 2650), § 10, operative Jan. 1, 1994.)

§ 2320. Entry of judgment of dissolution

A judgment of dissolution of marriage may not be entered unless one of the parties to the marriage has been a resident of this state for six months and of the county in which the proceeding is filed for three months next preceding the filing of the petition.

(Stats.1992, c. 162 (A.B. 2650), § 10, operative Jan. 1, 1994.)

§ 2322. Separate domicile or residence

For the purpose of a proceeding for dissolution of marriage, the husband and wife each may have a separate domicile or residence depending upon proof of the fact and not upon legal presumptions.

(Stats.1992, c. 162 (A.B.2650), § 10, operative Jan. 1, 1994.)

§ 2330. Petition

(a) A proceeding for dissolution of marriage or for legal separation of the parties is commenced by filing a petition entitled "In re the marriage of _____ and _____" which shall state whether it is a petition for dissolution of the marriage or for legal separation of the parties.

(b) In a proceeding for dissolution of marriage or for legal separation of the parties, the petition shall set forth among other matters, as nearly as can be ascertained, the following facts:

(1) The state or country in which the parties were married.

(2) The date of marriage.

(3) The date of separation.

(4) The number of years from marriage to separation.

(5) The number of children of the marriage, if any, and if none a statement of that fact.

(6) The age and birth date of each minor child of the marriage.

(7) The social security numbers of the husband and wife, if available, and if not available, a statement to that effect.

(Stats.1992, c. 162 (A.B. 2650), § 10, operative Jan. 1, 1994.)

§ 2333. Irreconcilable differences; order for dissolution

Subject to Section 2334, if from the evidence at the hearing the court finds that there are irreconcilable differences which have caused the irremediable breakdown of the marriage, the court shall order the dissolution of the marriage or a legal separation of the parties.

(Stats.1992, c. 162 (A.B. 2650), § 10, operative Jan. 1, 1994.)

§ 2334. Grounds for continuance; powers of court

(a) If it appears that there is a reasonable possibility of reconciliation, the court shall continue the proceeding for the dissolution of the marriage or for a legal separation of the parties for a period not to exceed 30 days.

(b) During the period of the continuance, the court may make orders for the support and maintenance of the parties, the custody, and support of the minor children of the marriage, attorney's fees, and for the preservation of the property of the parties.

(c) At any time after the termination of the period of the continuance, either party may move for the dissolution of the marriage or a legal separation of the parties, and the court may enter a judgment of dissolution of the marriage or legal separation of the parties.

(Stats.1992, c. 162 (A.B. 2650), § 10, operative Jan. 1, 1994.)

§ 2335. Evidence of specific acts of misconduct; admissibility

In a pleading or proceeding for dissolution of marriage or legal separation of the parties, including depositions and discovery proceedings, evidence of specific acts of misconduct is improper and inadmissible, except in any of the following cases:

(a) Where child custody is in issue and the evidence is relevant to that issue.

(b) Where a domestic violence prevention order is sought or has been obtained and the evidence is relevant in connection with the order.

(Stats.1992, c. 162 (A.B. 2650), § 10, operative Jan. 1, 1994.)

§ 2336. Default; proof required

(a) No judgment of dissolution or of legal separation of the parties may be granted upon the default of one of the parties or upon a statement or finding of fact made by a referee; but the court shall, in addition to the statement or finding of the referee, require proof of the grounds alleged, and the proof, if not taken before the court, shall be by affidavit.

(b) If the proof is by affidavit, the personal appearance of the affiant is required only when it appears to the court that any of the following circumstances exist:

(1) Reconciliation of the parties is reasonably possible.

(2) A proposed child custody order is not in the best interest of the child.

(3) A proposed child support order is less than a noncustodial parent is capable of paying.

(4) A personal appearance of a party or interested person would be in the best interests of justice.

(c) An affidavit submitted pursuant to this section shall contain a stipulation by the affiant that the affiant understands that proof will be by affidavit and that the affiant will not appear before the court unless so ordered by the court.

(Stats.1992, c. 162 (A.B.2650), § 10, operative Jan. 1, 1994.)

§ 2337. Severance and grant of early and separate trial on issue of dissolution status; conditions imposed; jurisdiction reserved

(a) In a proceeding for dissolution of marriage, the court, upon noticed motion, may sever and grant an early and separate trial on the issue of the dissolution of the status of the marriage apart from other issues.

(b) The court may impose upon a party any of the following conditions on granting a severance of the issue of the dissolution of the status of the marriage, and in case of that party's death, an order of any of the following conditions continues to be binding upon that party's estate:

(1) The party shall indemnify and hold the other party harmless from any taxes, reassessments, interest, and penalties payable by the other party if the dissolution of the marriage before the division of the parties' community estate results in a taxable event to either of the parties by reason of the ultimate division of their community estate, which taxes would not have been payable if the parties were still married at the time the division was made.

(2) Until judgment has been entered on all remaining issues and has become final, the party shall maintain all existing health and medical insurance coverage for the other party and the minor children as named dependents, so long as the party is legally able to do so. At the time the party is no longer legally eligible to maintain the other party as a named dependent under the existing health and medical policies, the party or the party's estate shall, at the party's sole expense, purchase and maintain health and medical insurance coverage that is comparable to the existing health and medical insurance coverage. If comparable insurance coverage is not obtained, the party or the party's estate is responsible for the health and medical expenses incurred by the other party which would have been covered by the insurance coverage, and shall indemnify and hold the other party harmless from any adverse consequences resulting from the lack of insurance.

(3) Until judgment has been entered on all remaining issues and has become final, the party shall indemnify and hold the other party harmless from any adverse consequences resulting to the other party if the bifurcation results in a termination of the other party's right to a probate homestead in the residence in which the other party resides at the time the severance is granted.

(4) Until judgment has been entered on all remaining issues and has become final, the party shall indemnify and hold the other party harmless from any adverse consequences resulting to the other party if the bifurcation results in the loss of the rights of the other party to a probate family allowance as the surviving spouse of the party.

(5) Until judgment has been entered on all remaining issues and has become final, the party shall indemnify and hold the other party harmless from any adverse consequences resulting to the other party if the bifurcation results in the loss of the other party's rights to pension benefits, elections, or survivors' benefits under the party's pension or retirement plan to the extent that the other party would have been entitled to those benefits or elections as the surviving spouse of the party.

(6) The party shall cause the party's retirement or pension plan to be joined as a party to the proceeding for dissolution, and if the party has a private pension plan covered by ERISA, then the party shall cause a qualified domestic relations order, as defined in Section 1056 of Title 29 of the United States Code, to be served upon the party's pension plan.

(7) The party shall indemnify and hold the other party harmless from any adverse consequences if the bifurcation results in the loss of rights to social security benefits or elections to the extent the other party would have been entitled to those benefits or elections as the surviving spouse of the party.

(8) Any other condition the court determines is just and equitable.

(c) A judgment granting a dissolution of the status of the marriage shall expressly reserve jurisdiction for later determination of all other pending issues.

(Stats.1992, c. 162 (A.B. 2650), § 10, operative Jan. 1, 1994.)

§ 2338. Decisions; judgments

(a) In a proceeding for dissolution of the marriage or legal separation of the parties, the court shall file its decision and any statement of decision as in other cases.

(b) If the court determines that no dissolution should be granted, a judgment to that effect only shall be entered.

(c) If the court determines that a dissolution should be granted, a judgment of dissolution of marriage shall be entered. After the entry of the judgment and before it becomes final, neither party has the right to dismiss the proceeding without the consent of the other.

(Stats.1992, c. 162 (A.B. 2650), § 10, operative Jan. 1, 1994.)

§ 2339. Finality of judgment; waiting period

(a) Subject to subdivision (b) and to Sections 2340 to 2344, inclusive, no judgment of dissolution is final for the purpose of terminating the marriage relationship of the parties until six months have expired from the date of service of a copy of summons and petition or the date of appearance of the respondent, whichever occurs first.

(b) The court may extend the six-month period described in subdivision (a) for good cause shown.

(Stats.1992, c. 162 (A.B. 2650), § 10, operative Jan. 1, 1994.)

§ 2344. Death of party after entry of judgment

(a) The death of either party after entry of the judgment does not prevent the judgment from becoming a final judgment under Sections 2339 to 2343, inclusive.

(b) Subdivision (a) does not validate a marriage by either party before the judgment becomes final, nor does it constitute a defense in a criminal prosecution against either party.

(Stats.1992, c. 162 (A.B. 2650), § 10, operative Jan. 1, 1994.)

Notes

1. The most common ground for dissolution in California is that of irreconcilable differences. Suppose that one spouse believes that the marriage has irretrievably broken down and desires a divorce, but the other spouse believes that their differences can be resolved, and wants the marriage to continue. Should the court grant a dissolution under these circumstances? See Marriage of Walton, 28 Cal.App.3d 108, 104 Cal.Rptr. 472 (1972). As a practical matter, the issue of irreconcilable differences is rarely contested. The refusal of one spouse to live with the other is generally viewed as sufficient justification for ending the marriage. J. Major, *Termination of Marital Relationship,* California Family Law Service §§ 20:15–20:16 (1986).

2. It should be noted that a dissolution proceeding may have several different components, including termination of the marriage itself, division of property, spousal support, child support, and child custody. In many cases the proceedings are "bifurcated," i.e., the court may grant a dissolution order, terminating the marriage relationship, leaving resolution of the property, support and custody issues for a later date. See West's Ann.Code Family Code Section § 2337.

3. With the adoption of the Family Law Act in 1969, California became the first state to enact no-fault dissolution procedures. In the intervening years, more jurisdictions followed California's lead, and now all American jurisdictions have some form of no-fault divorce. Freed & Walker, *Family Law in the Fifty States: An Overview,* 19 Family Law Quarterly 331, 341 (1985). The impetus underlying the widespread adoption of no-fault legislation was the desire to reduce acrimony, hostility and perjury in divorce proceedings by eliminating proof of "guilt." In her book *The Divorce Revolution,* sociologist Lenore Weitzman states that the divorce law reforms have "revolutionized the divorce process and have substantially altered the pattern of property, alimony and custody awards. However, these laws have also had unanticipated, unintended, and unfortunate consequences." On the basis of a ten year empirical study of the effects of no-fault divorce, Professor Weitzman concludes that women have lost the bargaining leverage that they once had in divorce proceedings. She attributes this loss to a number of factors, including the fact that neither spouse needs the consent of the other, that there is no innocent or guilty party, and that there will be an equal division of the marital property without reference to need or fault.

The result, according to Professor Weitzman, has been the creation of a new impoverished class of divorced women and their children. L. Weitzman, The Divorce Revolution (1985); see also Stein, When D–I–V–O–R–C–E Spells P–O–V–E–R–T–Y, San Francisco Chronicle, October 30, 1985 at 39.

Weitzman's conclusions have been subject to some criticism. For example, in her book *Backlash,* Susan Faludi points to discrepancies between Weitzman's empirical data and the report of the U.S. Census Bureau, which issued a study on the economic effects of divorce in 1991. Faludi argues that "the real source of divorced women's woes can be found not in the fine print of [no fault] divorce legislation but in the behavior of husbands and judges. * * * In the end, the most effective way to correct the post-divorce inequities between the spouses is simple: correct pay inequality in the work force." S. Faludi, Backlash (1991) at 21–25.

4. From an economic standpoint, it has been posited that "a no-fault regime is inefficient compared to a fault regime—on efficiency grounds too many divorces occur under no-fault, but the right number occur under fault," and therefore no-fault divorce should be eliminated "so that marriage will be preserved when it is economically efficient to do so." Zelder, *The Economic Analysis of the Effect of No–Fault Divorce Law on the Divorce Rate,* 16 Harvard Journal of Law & Public Policy 241, 259–262 (1993).

5. "Domestic tort" actions brought in conjunction with a dissolution proceeding may provide a means of introducing evidence of spousal misconduct in order to obtain a larger portion of the marital property. For example, in Twyman v. Twyman, 790 S.W.2d 819 (Tex.App.1990), the wife filed a cause of action for negligent infliction of emotional distress in addition to her petition for divorce. The trial court rendered a judgement dissolving the marriage and dividing the estate, and in addition, awarded the wife $15,000 for her tort claim. The decision was sustained on appeal, but is currently under review by the Texas Supreme Court. Twyman v. Twyman, 790 S.W.2d 819 (Tex.App.1990); compare Chiles v. Chiles, 779 S.W.2d 127 (Tex.App.1989). It is uncertain how widespread the field of domestic torts may become, but family law experts warn that "any lawyer who takes on even an occasional divorce case should be aware of the list of potential torts that could arise." National Law Journal, September 23, 1991 at 30.

SECTION 1. DIVISION BY PROPERTY SETTLEMENT AGREEMENT

A. Scope and Validity

When a marriage breaks down, three general types of economic problems may arise: the division of property, the provision of spousal support, and the provision of child support. These problems may be resolved through litigation, but are most commonly the subject matter of a negotiated agreement; such agreements are variously referred to as property settlement agreements, divorce settlements and marital termination agreements.

California has a strong public policy favoring marriage, and a contract which directly promotes family breakdown and dissolution would be contrary to public policy and void. Where, however, the marriage has broken down and the spouses are contemplating dissolution, the settlement of the spouses' property interests made in recognition of these facts, even where made conditional on a final dissolution decree, is not contrary to that public policy.

HILL v. HILL

Supreme Court of California, 1943.
23 Cal.2d 82, 142 P.2d 417.

GIBSON, C.J. This action was brought by a divorced wife to recover payments under a property settlement agreement executed on August 14, 1928, while the parties thereto were still husband and wife, but living separate and apart. The trial court found and concluded that the execution and delivery of the agreement "was at the time and date conditioned upon and in contemplation of, and for the purpose of promoting an immediate and forthwith dissolution of the marriage," and that the agreement was therefore void as against public policy and good morals. Judgment was entered for defendant from which plaintiff appeals.

Plaintiff and defendant were married in 1906 and separated in 1926 and it appears from the evidence that they had no intention or expectation of ever living together again. In 1926, defendant husband commenced an action for divorce in which plaintiff wife filed a cross-complaint for separate maintenance. It was stipulated here "that the judge who tried the case decided the case in favor of Mrs. Hill, but before signing the findings and judgment the judge passed away." Negotiations leading to the execution of the agreement in controversy were commenced two years later when plaintiff called upon Mr. Horton, defendant's attorney, at his request. In response to questions by Mr. Horton plaintiff stated she had grounds for divorce but she did not want to commence an action therefor; that she would however think the matter over and if she decided to get one it would have to be on her terms. On the same day defendant informed plaintiff that if she did not give him a divorce he would quit the practice of medicine, in which event he would not have enough to pay her anything. A few weeks later a second interview took place between plaintiff and Mr. Horton in which questions relating to support of plaintiff and the minor children of the parties, in the event of a divorce, were discussed, but no agreement was reached. At the time of these conversations plaintiff was not represented by counsel, but shortly thereafter plaintiff notified Mr. Horton that she had employed Mr. Haas to represent her in future negotiations. After some discussion between the attorneys, Mr. Horton prepared and forwarded to Mr. Haas a property settlement agreement which recited that "in the event the party of the second part [plaintiff] does obtain an interlocutory decree of divorce, and thereafter obtains a final decree of divorce, that the following agreement is made as a full and complete property settlement between said parties, and full and complete settlement for the support and maintenance of the said party of the second part and the said two minor children" and "this agreement shall not become effective * * * until or unless the party of the second part may have obtained * * * a divorce." Mr. Haas returned the contract unsigned together with a draft prepared by him which omitted the provision just quoted. Following further discussions between the attorneys, the agreement prepared by Mr. Haas was signed by the defendant and mailed to Mr. Haas together with a letter from Mr. Horton reading as follows: "I am sending you these contracts * * * the same to be held by you and not delivered or used except in the event of an action being filed by Mrs. Hill for divorce against Dr. Hill and the obtaining of the decree of divorce by one or the other of the parties. I will appreciate your getting the complaint prepared, signed, filed and served as soon as possible, and I will then put in an appearance and advise you." A complaint charging defendant with desertion and seeking court approval of the property settlement agreement was filed on August 17, 1928, and within a few days thereafter the defendant filed an answer in which he also requested the court to approve the agreement. On September 7, 1928, an interlocutory decree was entered for plaintiff which provided that "it appearing that a full and complete property settlement has been entered into * * * said property settlement is hereby approved." Mr. Horton was present at the hearing of the case but it does not appear that he took any part in the proceedings. A final decree of divorce was entered on September 17, 1929, which contained the following provision: "The disposition of property and the payment of alimony is covered by the property settlement agreement heretofore entered into * * * the said agreement having been approved at the time of the trial of this cause."

The evidence clearly shows that the agreement was made in contemplation of divorce and conditioned thereon to the extent that it was not to become effective except upon "the obtaining of a decree of divorce by one or the other of the parties." In support of the findings it also may be inferred that plaintiff was unwilling to proceed with an action for the dissolution of the marriage unless a satisfactory agreement was entered into providing for a settlement of her property rights and for the support of herself and the minor children of the parties. Defendant was unwilling that the property settlement agreement should become effective until and unless a divorce was obtained by one of the parties, and his answer in the divorce action shows that he was desirous that all of the property rights of the parties including his obligations to support plaintiff be finally disposed of by the approval of such agreement in the judgment of divorce. It appears, however, that the parties had been separated for more than two years when this agreement was entered into and that they had no intention of ever living together as husband and wife again. Although plaintiff had a meritorious cause of divorce she did not tell defendant that she would get one, and there is no evidence whatsoever of collusion. No evidence was offered tending to show that defendant agreed not to defend an action or to do anything to facilitate the granting of a divorce. Defendant contends, however, that since the agreement was to become effective only in the event of divorce (a condition which he himself imposed), it is void as against public policy and he should not be bound thereby. Under the agreement plaintiff relinquished her right of inheritance and agreed to a division of property and the amount to be contributed by defendant for the support of herself and the minor children. Defendant asked the court to approve the agreement and limit his obligations according to it terms after plaintiff, in reliance thereon, refrained from asking the court for alimony and for a division of the community property. Certainly, as between the parties, every principle of justice and equity demands that defendant be compelled to stand by his contract and we do not believe in the circumstances here presented, that any rule of public policy requires that he be relieved of his obligations under this agreement.

Because preservation of the marriage relationship is considered essential to the maintenance of organized society, it has been stated generally that the law will not countenance any contract having for its object the dissolution of a marriage. * * * Agreements not to defend or to abandon a defense in a divorce action, to destroy or conceal evidence in proceedings for divorce, and to procure or furnish testimony of certain facts which will successfully support or defeat a divorce action, or which provide that payment to the party procuring evidence to be used in such an action is contingent upon the result of the action have been held void as parts of collusive arrangements to facilitate divorce. * * * Even in the absence of such a collusive arrangement certain agreements have been held void as *contra bonos mores* upon the theory they had a direct tendency to promote dissolution of the marriage relationship. Thus, the courts have refused to enforce an agreement by a husband to pay his wife a fixed sum in full satisfaction of her claims for alimony if he should thereafter give the wife cause for divorce. * * * An agreement by the husband to pay the wife's counsel fees in the event of a divorce, and an agreement between a plaintiff in a divorce action and her attorney for a contingent fee have also been held void. * * *

Property settlement agreements between husband and wife have in like manner been held invalid when regarded as inseparable parts of agreements for divorce which are contrary to the public policy favoring preservation of marriage. Under the early common law, this policy was so inflexible as to be considered a barrier to agreements for separation and for the adjustment of property rights upon separation. * * *

It is now well settled, however, that a husband and wife may agree to an immediate separation, and having so agreed or having actually separated, may enter into contracts adjusting their property rights. * * * As said in Brown v. Brown, 83 Cal.App. 74, at 82, 256 P. 595, "The whole theory of the law has been to prevent * * * agreements which have for their purpose the severance of the marriage relation in the future and not to invalidate agreements where the separation has already taken place or is an instant fact." * * *

Accordingly, by the great weight of modern authority, property settlement agreements, are upheld even though made in contemplation of divorce.   * * *   The rule is stated in 17 Am.Jur., section 499, as follows: "The validity of such agreements depends on whether there is an attempt to obtain a divorce not justified by the real facts and thus to practice a fraud upon the court.   * * *   Under this rule, where a separation has been induced by the vicious conduct or disability of one of the parties, without inducement or fault of the other, a contract looking to a settlement of property rights and the proper maintenance of the one not in fault is in no sense repugnant to public policy." The California decisions are in accord with this view * * *. It has also been said in this state that property settlements are "highly favored in the law."   * * *

Such contracts made in contemplation of divorce are entered into upon the assumption that divorce will follow.   * * *   It would therefore seem proper for the parties to provide for any possible failure of this assumption in their contract. And it has accordingly been held that agreements conditioned upon divorce, in the sense that they are to become effective upon dissolution of the marriage do not contravene public policy.   * * *

Recent California cases have upheld property settlement agreements thus conditioned upon divorce. In Cookinham v. Cookinham, 219 Cal. 723, 28 P.2d 1045, this court approved a property settlement agreement under which a husband agreed to pay his wife $200 per month for the support of herself and minor child during the pendency of the wife's action for divorce, and thereafter, if the court determined that the wife was entitled to a divorce, the sum of $150 per month for her support until her death or remarriage and $50 per month for the support of the minor child until the latter attained her majority. In rejecting the contention that the agreement was *contra bonos mores* the court remarked: " * * * it is to be observed that the parties were living separate and apart and the agreement conclusively establishes their intent to amicably settle and adjust all of their property rights. This they were competent to do and were authorized by law to do." In Ettlinger v. Ettlinger, 3 Cal.2d 172, 44 P.2d 540, during the pendency of the wife's action for separate maintenance, the parties entered into a property settlement agreement under which the husband agreed to pay the wife $250 per month "in the event of a divorce between the parties." Subsequently, and, as the wife contended, in consideration of the execution of the agreement, she changed the form of her action from one for separate maintenance to one for absolute divorce. The validity of the agreement was in issue in the divorce proceedings where the agreement was approved and adopted in interlocutory and final decrees. On appeal from an order reducing the amount of payments, this court held the agreement was immune from judicial modification. The validity of the same agreement was again challenged in Ettlinger v. Ettlinger, 46 Cal.App.2d 628, 116 P.2d 482. It was there held the previous decision of the Supreme Court was res judicata upon the issue of the legality of the agreement, and that in the state of the record, a finding that the agreement was *contra bonos mores* would have been entirely wanting in evidentiary support. The court pointed out that it was not claimed that the divorce was obtained by collusion or that the wife did not have a meritorious cause of action for divorce. In Howard v. Adams, 16 Cal.2d 253, 105 P.2d 971, 130 A.L.R. 1003, this court held an agreement by which defendant undertook to support her niece, if the niece would procure the divorce she contemplated in another state in order to avoid publicity damaging to defendant's social and business connections, was not against public policy. The fact that the husband admitted his marital relations were discordant and that the wife had a good cause of action for divorce was, in the opinion of the court, a complete answer to any contention that the contract was invalid because it might have a tendency to induce, or did in fact, induce, the wife to proceed to obtain a divorce and the husband to permit her to prosecute the action without opposition. In Queen v. Queen, 44 Cal.App.2d 475, 112 P.2d 755, a property settlement agreement presented to the court for enforcement contained the following provision: "This agreement shall be and become effective if, as, and when within a period of six (6) months from the date hereof a decree of divorce is entered granting to the party of the second part a divorce from the party of the first part. * * * If a divorce shall not be so granted * * * then this agreement shall be and become forthwith null and void and of no effect. * * *" In holding the agreement was enforceable, the court answered the contention that the wife was persuaded to obtain a divorce as a result of the execution of the agreement by pointing to the recitals therein that the parties had separated, that the wife was about to institute an action for divorce, and that the parties were desirous of arriving at an agreement respecting the settlement of their property rights and providing for the support of the wife in the event a divorce was obtained. In Morrow v. Morrow, 40 Cal.App.2d 474, 105 P.2d 129, the signing of a stipulation by the wife in a divorce action to the effect that she should be awarded $75 a month as alimony was not against public policy, the court stating that the stipulation did not tend to interfere with the real and substantial status of the marriage contract as the parties were already separated. * * *

Respondent relies upon certain decisions in this state to support his contention that a property settlement agreement conditioned upon divorce is invalid, but, with one exception hereafter noted, we find nothing in those decisions inconsistent with the principles expressed in the foregoing cases. In the leading case of Pereira v. Pereira, 156 Cal. 1, 103 P. 488, 134 Am.St.Rep. 107, 23 L.R.A., N.S. 880, the parties had separated and the wife commenced an action for divorce. During its pendency the parties became reconciled and the action was dismissed. The parties then executed an agreement providing among other things that if the husband should thereafter give the wife cause for divorce and if she should establish a right thereto in an action against him, the husband would pay the wife $10,000 in full settlement of alimony and property rights. After concluding that the agreement therein "could not but encourage him [the husband] to yield to his baser inclinations, and inflict the injury" which would compel the wife to obtain a divorce, the court stated: "It shows by its terms that it is not an agreement to settle property rights accruing by reason of a marital offense already perpetrated and complete as a cause of action for divorce. There is therefore no force in the claim, as applied to this case, that it is * * * valid as a settlement of such rights, even if it were conceded that such an agreement might under some circumstances be permitted to stand." Whiting v. Whiting, 62 Cal.App. 157, 216 P. 92, involved an antenuptial contract similar to the contract in the Pereira case. Newman v. Freitas, 129 Cal. 283, 61 P. 907, 50 L.R.A. 548, involved a contingent fee contract between the wife and an attorney which the court considered tended directly to bring about alienation of husband and wife by offering a stranger a premium to advise dissolution of the marriage ties. The court pointed out, moreover, that the power of the court to compel the husband to pay his wife's counsel fees in a divorce action removed the necessity and reason for the rule permitting contingent fee contracts. (See 21 Va. L.Rev. 446.) In Moss v. Moss, 20 Cal.2d 640, 128 P.2d 526, 141 A.L.R. 1422, the plaintiff husband sought a declaration of his obligations under a property settlement, the sole consideration for which, he alleged, was a promise by the defendant wife to procure a divorce. The trial court sustained a demurrer to the complaint and this court affirmed the judgment. Since it was admitted by demurrer that the *sole consideration* for the agreement was the promise of the wife to procure a divorce, we assumed for the purposes of the decision that the agreement was invalid and held that the trial court had discretion in a declaratory action to refuse relief where it appeared the plaintiff was a party of equal fault to the illegal transaction. We expressly refrained, however, from passing upon the validity of the agreement.

Respondent also cites Brown v. Brown, 8 Cal.App.2d 364, 47 P.2d 352 as holding that if it is the essence of the agreement that one of the parties obtain a divorce and if the promises made in contemplation thereof are conditioned upon a dissolution of the marriage, the contract is unenforceable. Although it does not appear in the Brown case that the parties had separated at the time the agreement was entered into, and for that reason the case may be factually distinguishable from the situation here presented, the language of that opinion is hereby disapproved insofar as it is inconsistent with anything said by us here.

It thus appears that with the one exception none of the foregoing cases relied upon by defendant is authority for his position that a property settlement agreement entered into after separation, without collusion, is invalid solely because it is not to become effective unless a divorce is obtained by one of the parties. Defendant contends, however, that the judgment declaring the agreement invalid must be affirmed because the trial court determined not only that the agreement in question was "conditioned upon and in contemplation of" divorce, but also that it was "for the purpose of promoting an immediate and forthwith dissolution of the marriage." While it is true that contracts condemned by the courts usually have been termed "promotive of divorce" as distinguished from those "incidental to divorce" or "conditioned upon divorce," this terminology is not always accurate or descriptive. The validity of such contracts must be determined in the light of the factual background of each case and considerations of public policy appropriate thereto. Most property settlement agreements are incidental to or conditioned upon divorce, since they are means employed in the disposition of property upon divorce, and they are also promotive of divorce in the sense that an amicable adjustment of property rights facilitates the completion of contemplated divorce proceedings.

Public policy seeks to foster and protect marriage, to encourage parties to live together, and to prevent separation. * * * But public policy does not discourage divorce where the relations between husband and wife are such that the legitimate objects of matrimony have been utterly destroyed. * * * In the absence of fraud, collusion or imposition upon the court, public policy does not prevent parties who have separated from entering into a contract disposing of their property rights which shall become effective only in the event one of the parties obtains a divorce, even though such a contract may be a factor in persuading a party who has a good cause for divorce to proceed to establish it.

Applying these principles to the facts of the present case we conclude that the agreement is valid and enforceable. Prior to the execution of the contract the parties were living separate and apart as a result of a marital offense committed by the husband which constituted good grounds for divorce. They had no intention or expectation of resuming marital relations. At the time of the commencement of the negotiations which led to the execution of this agreement the domestic status of the parties was unsettled and their relations unsatisfactory. The husband had sued for divorce and the wife had countered with a suit for separate maintenance and the case had been tried. As appears from the stipulation, the court announced its intention to deny the husband a divorce and to award the wife separate maintenance. The wife did not at any time agree to obtain a divorce and the husband did not agree to aid her in procuring a divorce by refraining from defending against an action or concealing evidence from the court. There is no intimation that the subsequent divorce was collusive. In language of the court in Morrow v. Morrow, 40 Cal.App.2d 474, 482–483, 105 P.2d 129, the agreement "did not tend to interfere with the real substantial status of their marriage contract as the parties were already separated. They occupied the position of husband and wife in name only. It did not facilitate the divorce any more than the numerous valid property settlements which the courts of this state have recognized and approved."

The judgment is reversed and the cause remanded with directions to enter judgment in accordance with the views expressed herein.

Notes

1. It is advantageous for the spouses to come to an agreement for the division of their property rather than litigating these issues in a dissolution proceeding. In addition to saving time and reducing costs and attorneys'

fees, the parties can tailor their property division and support provisions to meet their particular needs and circumstances. For example, one spouse might be willing to accept less than half of the community property in exchange for higher spousal or child support payments. Conversely, one party might agree to accept less than half of the community property in exchange for a waiver of spousal support. The parties to a property settlement agreement are free to enter into whatever type of property division they desire, including an unequal division. This cannot be done in a litigated property division. The dissolution court is statutorily mandated to make an equal division of the community and quasi-community property. In arriving at an equal division, the court is not required to take the parties' preferences and desires into account. J. Stein & J. Zuckerman, California Community Property § 10.97 (1986).

2. During marriage a husband and wife stand in a fiduciary relationship with respect to the management and control of the community property. This requirement continues until the property has been divided by the parties or by the court, and includes the obligation to make a full disclosure to the assets. West's Ann.Cal. Family Code § 1100. The limits of this duty and remedies for its breach in the context of property settlement agreements are explored in section 3 of this Chapter.

B. Enforcement and Modification

A fair and equitable property settlement agreement, once executed by the parties, is a binding contract and may be enforced under general principles of contract law. It is common, however, for parties to such an agreement to seek judicial sanction of the agreement in connection with the dissolution proceedings. Two types of judicial action are available: the court can simply approve the agreement, or the agreement can be merged in the dissolution judgment.

Frequently agreements are "incorporated" in the dissolution judgment. Incorporation can be accomplished by setting forth the agreement provisions in the judgment, or by reference to and clear identification of the agreement in the judgment. The fact of incorporation in and of itself has no legal significance. The legal effect turns on the intention of the parties; i.e., whether the parties intended merely to seek court approval of the agreement, or whether they intended the contract to become part of the judgment. If the agreement is deemed to be simply approved by the court, enforcement of the agreement lies in a cause of action for breach of contract. If a merger was intended, however, the agreement becomes part of the court order. In effect, the agreement is superseded by the judgment, and the obligation is no longer contractual. The agreement must be enforced as a judgment, not as a contract.[7]

The issue of the modifiability of a property settlement agreement usually pertains only to spousal and child support provisions, inasmuch as property division provisions are not generally modifiable. Under

7. 2 Markey, California Family Law Practice and Procedure (1982) § 26.13, and cases there cited.

prior law, if spousal support provisions were integrated into the property division, the spousal support provisions were non-modifiable. The court had to review the agreement to determine whether or not it was "integrated." [8] The modifiability of support provisions is now governed by Family Code Section 3585, which provides that child support provisions are separate and severable and subject to modification or revocation at any time at the discretion of the court. Spousal support provisions are modifiable unless the agreement specifically provides to the contrary.

WEST'S ANNOTATED CALIFORNIA FAMILY CODE

§ 3585. Severability of child support provisions; orders based on agreements

The provisions of an agreement between the parents for child support shall be deemed to be separate and severable from all other provisions of the agreement relating to property and support of the wife or husband. An order for child support based on the agreement shall be law-imposed and shall be made under the power of the court to order child support.

(Stats.1992, c. 162 (A.B. 2650), § 10, operative Jan. 1, 1994.)

§ 3590. Severability of support provisions; orders based on agreements

The provisions of an agreement for support of either party shall be deemed to be separate and severable from the provisions of the agreement relating to property. An order for support of either party based on the agreement shall be law-imposed and shall be made under the power of the court to order spousal support.

(Stats.1992, c. 162 (A.B.2650), § 10, operative Jan. 1, 1994.)

§ 3591. Modification or termination of agreements

(a) Except as provided in subdivisions (b) and (c), the provisions of an agreement for the support of either party are subject to subsequent modification or termination by court order.

(b) An agreement may not be modified or terminated as to an amount that accrued before the date of the filing of the notice of motion or order to show cause to modify or terminate.

(c) An agreement for spousal support may not be modified or revoked to the extent that a written agreement, or, if there is no written agreement, an oral agreement entered into in open court between the parties, specifically provides that the spousal support is not subject to modification or termination.

(Stats.1992, c. 162 (A.B.2650), § 10, operative Jan. 1, 1994.)

§ 3650. Support order

"Support order" as used in this chapter means a child, family, or spousal support order.

(Stats.1992, c. 162 (A.B.2650), § 10, operative Jan. 1, 1994.)

---

8. See, e.g., Flynn v. Flynn, 42 Cal.2d 55, 265 P.2d 865 (1954).

§ 3651. Powers of court; application of section

(a) Except as provided in subdivisions (b) and (c) and subject to Article 3 (commencing with Section 3680) and Sections 3552, 3587, and 4004, a support order may be modified or terminated at any time as the court determines to be necessary.

(b) A support order may not be modified or terminated as to an amount that accrued before the date of the filing of the notice of motion or order to show cause to modify or terminate.

(c) An order for spousal support may not be modified or terminated to the extent that a written agreement, or, if there is no written agreement, an oral agreement entered into in open court between the parties, specifically provides that the spousal support is not subject to modification or termination.

(d) This section applies whether or not the support order is based upon an agreement between the parties.

(e) This section is effective only with respect to a property settlement agreement entered into on or after January 1, 1970, and does not affect an agreement entered into before January 1, 1970, as to which Chapter 1308 of the Statutes of 1967 shall apply.

(Stats.1992, c. 162 (A.B.2650), § 10, operative Jan. 1, 1994.)

IN RE MARRIAGE OF HUFFORD

California District Court of Appeal, 1984.
152 Cal.App.3d 825, 199 Cal.Rptr. 726.

Thompson, Associate Justice.

In this appeal we are called upon to determine whether judicial modification of spousal support is precluded by a boiler plate provision in a marital settlement agreement which merely provides that the agreement is entire and cannot be amended, altered or modified by the parties except by a writing signed by both parties. For the reasons to follow, we have concluded that such a provision does not fulfill the exception of Civil Code section 4811, subdivision (b), to exclude judicial modification.

Guy Hufford (husband) appeals from the denial of his order to show cause for modification of spousal support of his ex-wife, Dorothy Hufford (wife).

On March 1, 1978, husband and wife filed in court a signed written "stipulation" and waiver of rights prepared by wife's counsel, covering among other things spousal support, division of property, attorney's fees and waivers. Paragraph 2 of the agreement provided for husband to pay wife spousal support of $1,200 per month for the first two years after entry of an interlocutory judgment of dissolution, and thereafter $600 per month until wife remarried or died.

Paragraph 6 recited the parties' agreement that "this court shall retain jurisdiction, after rendering the Final Judgment of Dissolution in the subject action, to determine all issues raised by this agreement and not specifically excluded from this reservation of jurisdiction."

Paragraph 10 provided: "This agreement is entire. We may not alter, amend or modify it, except by an instrument in writing executed by both of us. It includes all representations of every kind and nature made by each of us to the other. This agreement shall be binding upon and inure to the benefit of both of us, and of our heirs, administrators, executors, successors, and assigns."

On March 15, 1978, the Ventura Superior Court entered an interlocutory decree of dissolution of marriage ordering spousal support, property division, attorney's fees and execution of further documents in substantially identical language with the provisions of the stipulation. The decree did not in any way refer to the prior stipulation; nor did it contain the provisions of paragraphs 6 or 10.

On July 14, 1982, husband filed an order to show cause for modification of spousal support on grounds of alleged reduced ability to pay because of lesser income and increased obligations for a new wife and five children, coupled with ex-wife's reduced need. The wife opposed the motion on the ground that paragraph 10 of the stipulation rendered the spousal support provision nonmodifiable.

The superior court denied husband's request for modification. The court found that the order for spousal support contained in the judgment of dissolution was not modifiable because the provision in paragraph 10 of the stipulation constituted compliance with Civil Code section 4811, subdivision (b), as to nonmodifiability of spousal support, and the provision of paragraph 6 of the stipulation did not constitute a reservation of jurisdiction to modify spousal support.

This appeal followed.

DISCUSSION

Civil Code [1] section 4811, subdivision (b), provides in pertinent part:

"(b) The provisions of any agreement for the support of either party shall be deemed to be separate and severable from the provisions of the agreement relating to property. All orders for the support of either party based on such agreement shall be deemed law-imposed and shall be deemed made under the power of the court to make such orders. *The provisions of any agreement or order for the support of either party shall be subject to subsequent modification or revocation by court order, * * * except to the extent that any*

---

1. Unless otherwise indicated, all statutory references are to the Civil Code. Section 4811, subdivision (b), applies to all property settlement agreements entered into on or after January 1, 1970. (See § 4811, subd. (c).)

For a discussion of contractual foreclosure of judicial modification under 1967 amendments to former section 139, the predecessor of section 4811, see *Knodel v. Knodel* (1975) 14 Cal.3d 752, 764–766, 122 Cal. Rptr. 521, 537 P.2d 353.

Also, for a thorough discussion of statutory and case law on pre–1967 agreements, see II The Cal. Family Lawyer, ch. 26 (Cal. Cont.Ed.Bar 1963); Propper, *The Judgment of Dissolution and the Agreement—Incorporation, Merger, Integration and Approval* (1975) 51 L.A.Bar J. 177; Annot. Modification of Divorce Decree—Alimony (1975) 61 A.L.R.3d 520, 595–602.

*written agreement * * * specifically provides to the contrary."* (Italics added.)

Thus, there is a general rule in favor of modifiability by the court of spousal support provisions.

> *"The evident purposes of Civil Code section 4811 were to* dispose of the abstruse and unprofitable jurisprudence which had grown up around the concepts of integration and severability [citations] and *establish a legislatively declared social policy that contractual provisions for the support of a spouse be subject to modification by the court in the light of changed circumstances unless the parties explicitly agree to preclude such modification.* The utility of this policy is obvious. Even in the absence of inflationary distortions, the parties to a marital settlement agreement can hardly anticipate and provide for unexpected changes of circumstance which may invalidate the expectations reflected in the agreement. Despite the public interest in reserving for judicial redetermination on the basis of changed circumstances contractual provisions for support, the Legislature left it open to marital partners to preclude judicial modification by inserting in the agreement a specific provision to that effect." *(In re Marriage of Nielsen* (1980) 100 Cal.App.3d 874, 877–878, 161 Cal.Rptr. 272.) (Italics added.)

Although an agreement making spousal support nonmodifiable by the court is not contrary to public policy (*In re Marriage of Hawkins* (1975) 48 Cal.App.3d 208, 212–213, 121 Cal.Rptr. 681), "[u]nderlying section 4811 is the policy determination that the public interest is best served when support awards reflect changes in need or ability to pay" (*Esserman v. Esserman* (1982) 136 Cal.App.3d 572, 577, 186 Cal.Rptr. 329).

In determining whether the trial court properly found that the language in the agreement herein was legally sufficient to preclude judicial modification of spousal support under section 4811, subdivision (b), we first view, from an historical perspective, cases considering that issue.

In re Marriage of Smiley (1975) 53 Cal.App.3d 228, 125 Cal.Rptr. 717, held that a general provision of an agreement incorporated into the dissolution decree containing language "that this agreement is entire, indivisible, and shall constitute an integrated agreement, which is not subject to modification [and] [t]his agreement may not be amended except by an instrument in writing signed by both parties" *(id.,* at p. 231, 125 Cal.Rptr. 717) rendered spousal support nonmodifiable under section 4811, subdivision (b), notwithstanding the language in the spousal support provision of the agreement that "the support of Wife is subject to any order, Decree or Judgment of any Court based thereon" *(id.,* at pp. 230, 233). The court held the latter language simply made it clear that contempt was a permissible method of enforcement and the former language was sufficient to satisfy the statutory requirement that written agreements specifically provide against modifiability by the court.[2]

Forgy v. Forgy (1976) 63 Cal.App.3d 767, 134 Cal.Rptr. 75, held under former section 139 (the predecessor of section 4811) that the following language precluded later judicial modification of spousal support: " '[i]n the event that either the Husband or the Wife shall hereafter obtain a decree of absolute or limited divorce, such decree shall incorporate the provisions of this Agreement to the extent acceptable to the Court, but such decree shall in no way affect this Agreement or any of the terms, covenants, or conditions thereof, it being understood that this Agreement is absolute, unconditional and irrevocable.' " (*Id.,* at p. 770, 134 Cal.Rptr. 75.)

The *Forgy* court explained: "The word 'decree' used therein impliedly includes the orders embodied in the decree and any modification of those orders. Any other interpretation would permit the court to comply with the agreement in its 'decree' but forthwith effect noncompliance therewith by a subsequent decree or order. As thus interpreted the agreement provides, a court decree incorporating its provisions and any modification thereof shall in no way affect the spousal support provisions thereof as to which the agreement 'is absolute, unconditional and irrevocable.' A modification of those provisions certainly would 'affect' them and render nugatory the understanding of the parties the agreement was absolute and irrevocable. [¶] To comply with the nonmodifiable provisions of section 139 it is not necessary the parties to a separation agreement state categorically: 'The provisions of this agreement for support are not subject to modification or revocation by court order.' To the contrary, 'no particular magic words are needed' to provide the exception to modifiability contemplated by the statute. [Citations.]" (*Id.,* at pp. 770–771.)[3]

---

2. The full text of the general provision in *Smiley* was as follows:

" '3. The parties hereto acknowledge that this agreement constitutes their entire understanding and that neither has made any promise, covenant, representation, or warranty, except as herein expressly set forth, and that this document contains all of the negotiations and agreements having been merged herein. The parties further covenant and agree that each and every promise, covenant, and undertaking herein set forth has been made as consideration for each and all of the remaining promises, covenants, and undertakings herein, and that this agreement is entire, indivisible, and shall constitute an integrated agreement, which is not subject to modification. This agreement may not be amended except by an instrument in writing signed by both par-

ties.' " (53 Cal.App.3d at pp. 230–231, 125 Cal.Rptr. 717.)

The spousal support provision provided: " '1. Husband shall pay to Wife, as alimony for her support and maintenance, the sum of $850.00 per month commencing September 1, 1970 and continuing monthly thereafter for five years, thence at the rate of $700.00 per month for the succeeding five years, thereafter $600.00 per month until the death or marriage of Wife. This provision for the support of Wife is subject to any order, Decree or Judgment of any Court based thereon.' " (*Id.,* at p. 230, 125 Cal.Rptr. 717.)

3. However, parol evidence is inadmissible to prove nonmodifiability of an agreement which contains no provision on the issue of modifiability. (*In re Marriage of Wright* (1976) 54 Cal.App.3d 1115, 1121, 126 Cal.Rptr. 894.)

In re Marriage of Kilkenny (1979) 96 Cal.App.3d 617, 158 Cal.Rptr. 158, relying on *Forgy, supra,* held that the terms "absolute, unconditional and irrevocable" as intended in the agreement prohibited modification of spousal support by court decree. The *Kilkenny* court pointed out that the provision in its agreement that " '[i]t is the intention of the parties that this agreement, whether or not incorporated in any decree of divorce, shall be binding upon the parties, and shall be absolute, unconditional and irrevocable' " presented an even stronger showing of nonmodifiability than did *Forgy* because the parties more clearly stated their intent. (96 Cal.App.3d at p. 620, 158 Cal.Rptr. 158.)

Subsequently, *In re Marriage of Nielsen, supra,* 100 Cal.App.3d 874, 161 Cal.Rptr. 272, addressed the issue of what general boiler plate language in agreements, if any, was sufficient to preclude judicial modification of spousal support. The court, relying upon *Forgy, supra,* held that a provision in the final paragraph that the agreement shall not depend for its effectiveness on court approval nor be affected thereby was a specific provision rendering spousal support nonmodifiable. (*Id.,* at p. 878, 161 Cal.Rptr. 272.)[4]

However, the *Nielsen* court also held that neither the paragraph establishing spousal support of $214 per month "continuing for the remainder of wife's life" nor the general release of rights paragraph was sufficient to prohibit judicial modification. The court explained:

"The paragraph of the agreement dealing with spousal support is silent on the question of modification. The general release of rights[5] * * * refers, among other items, to 'all claims of either party upon the other for support and maintenance * * * it being understood that this present agreement is intended to settle the rights of the parties hereto in all respects.' *So far as the contractual relations of the parties are concerned, the general release of rights would be held to express an intention that the obligation of support would be governed by agreement. [Citation.] But the release of rights provision is entirely silent with respect to the power of modification vested in the court by Civil Code section 4811. Therefore, * * * there was no specific provision* in the release language *precluding modification by judicial action.* Just as parol evidence may not be received to supply a missing provision against modification [citation], the statute cannot be avoided by drawing inferences as to the intention of

4. That provision provided in full: " '* * * EFFECTIVE DATE: This Agreement is executed on and shall be effective from and after the 9th day of February 1972. This Agreement may, if desired, be submitted to the Court for its approval, but this Agreement shall not depend for its effectiveness on such approval, nor be affected thereby.' " (*Ibid.*)

5. " 'RELEASE OF RIGHTS: 1. Except as otherwise provided in this Agreement, each party to this Agreement does hereby release the other from any and all liabilities, debts, or obligations, of every kind and character, heretofore or hereafter incurred, and from any and all claims and demands, including all claims of either party upon the other for support and maintenance as Wife or as Husband, it being understood that this present agreement is intended to settle the rights of the parties hereto in all respects.' " (*Id.,* at p. 877, fn. 2, 161 Cal.Rptr. 272.)

the parties from a general 'release of rights' *paragraph which contains no 'specific' provision concerning judicial modification.*" (*Id.,* at p. 878, 161 Cal.Rptr. 272.) (Italics added.)

Soon thereafter, *In re Marriage of Aylesworth* (1980) 106 Cal.App.3d 869, 165 Cal.Rptr. 389, held that prefatory language in a marital settlement agreement, providing that " '[w]ith the exception of provisions relating to child custody and child support, this Agreement is intended to be a final, binding, and nonmodifiable agreement between said parties' " (*id.,* at p. 873, 165 Cal.Rptr. 389), fulfilled the exception requirement of section 4811, subdivision (b) (*id.,* at p. 874, 165 Cal.Rptr. 389).

More recently, *Fukuzaki v. Superior Court* (1981) 120 Cal.App.3d 454, 174 Cal.Rptr. 536, discussed what language in an agreement was sufficiently specific to preclude judicial modification of spousal support. The *Fukuzaki* agreement contained boiler plate provisions that (1) the purpose of the agreement was to make a final and complete settlement of all rights and obligations concerning the wife's support; (2) the agreement contained the entire agreement of the parties; (3) the agreement was to be submitted to the court for incorporation into the interlocutory judgment, and (4) mutual release of rights by both parties.[6]

Fukuzaki held that these provisions, individually and collectively, were not sufficiently specific to avoid the power of the court to modify a spousal support agreement where the paragraph reciting the agreement for spousal support was silent on the question of modification.

6. The pertinent provisions of the settlement agreement in *Fukuzaki* provided:

" '4. PURPOSE OF AGREEMENT. The purpose of this agreement is to make a final and complete settlement of all rights and obligations concerning the support of wife and minor child and the custody of our minor child.

" '8. AGREEMENT IS ENTIRE. This agreement contains the entire agreement of the parties on the matters it covers, and supersedes any previous agreement between us. No other agreement, statement or promise made by or to either of us or the agent or representative of either of us shall be binding on us unless it is in writing and signed by both of us or unless contained in an order of a court of competent jurisdiction. This agreement shall inure to the benefit of and be binding on each of us and the heirs, personal representatives, assigns and other successors in interest of each of us.

" '10. INCORPORATION AND MERGER INTO JUDGMENT. This agreement shall be submitted to the court for incorporation and merger into the interlocutory judgment of dissolution of marriage in the pending proceeding between us.

" '17. RELEASE OF RIGHTS. We agree that the following clauses shall apply to this instrument:

" '(a) Except as otherwise provided for in this instrument, each of us releases the other from any and all liabilities, debts, or obligations on our marital property that have been or will be incurred, and from any and all claims and demands, it being understood that by this present agreement we intend to settle all aspects of our marital property rights.

" '(b) We agree that any and all property acquired by either one of us from and after the effective date of this instrument shall be the sole and separate property of the one so acquiring it; and each of us waives any and all property rights in or to such future acquisitions and hereby grants to the other all such future acquisitions of property as the sole and separate property of the one so acquiring the same from the effective date of this instrument * * *.' " (*Fukuzaki v. Superior Court, supra,* 120 Cal.App.3d at p. 457, 174 Cal.Rptr. 536.)

The *Fukuzaki* court explained:

"The provisions for a 'final and complete' settlement coupled with a release of all obligations and a provision that the agreement is entire and binding on the parties and their heirs do not equate with the requirement of a 'specific' provision for nonmodification such as 'nonmodifiable' [citation], or 'irrevocable' [citation]. Although no particular magic words are needed to provide the exception to nonmodifiability contemplated by section 4811, subdivision (b), some specific unequivocal language directly on the question of modification is required. The subject agreement is entirely silent with respect to the power of modification placed on the court by Civil Code section 4811. *The import of the statute may not be 'avoided by drawing inferences as to the intention of the parties' from general provisions of the agreement which do not contain a specific provision concerning judicial modification.* [Citation.]" (*Fukuzaki, supra,* 120 Cal.App.3d at p. 458, 174 Cal.Rptr. 576.) (Italics added.)

Subsequently, in 1982, in *Esserman v. Esserman, supra,* 136 Cal. App.3d 572, 186 Cal.Rptr. 329, the court held that section 4811, subdivision (b), applies to private agreements made after entry of a final judgment of dissolution. The court pointed out that, regardless of whether support provisions in the earlier agreement and judgment were nonmodifiable, the court had authority to modify the spousal support arrangement in the later private agreement. The *Esserman* court found, citing *Fukuzaki v. Superior Court, supra,* that there was no language in the later private agreement which would meet the "test of 'specific unequivocal language directly on the question of [judicial] modification.'" (*Id.,* at p. 577, 186 Cal.Rptr. 329.)

Finally, *In re Marriage of Forcum* (1983) 145 Cal.App.3d 599, 193 Cal.Rptr. 596, is the most recent case to consider in detail what language in an agreement or order is legally sufficient to bring into play the provisions of section 4811, subdivision (b), that orders for spousal support are modifiable except to the extent that a written agreement of the parties "specifically provides to the contrary." (*Id.,* at p. 604, 193 Cal.Rptr. 596.) There, as in *Nielsen,* a general provision that the agreement was effective upon execution and did not depend upon court approval for effectiveness was involved. The court held that a specific provision for a dollar-a-year spousal support payments had the legal effect of retaining the court's jurisdiction to modify spousal support. The court reasoned that a specific provision would prevail over the more general *Nielsen*-type provision to permit future judicial modification (145 Cal.App.3d at pp. 601, 605, 193 Cal.Rptr. 596.)

In addition to the *Nielsen*-type provision, the *Forcum* agreement *also* provided that (1) the agreement was entire and could not be altered, amended or modified except in a writing executed by both parties, and (2) each party, except for provisions contained in the agreement, released the other from any and all liabilities, obligations and claims, including all claims of either party upon the other for support. *Forcum* pointed out that "these provisions are insufficient to cause spousal support to be nonmodifiable." (145 Cal.App.3d at p. 604, 193 Cal.Rptr. 596.)

Moreover, in an instructive observation, the *Forcum* court stressed:

> "A dispute on the issue of nonmodifiability of spousal support would not arise if the provision for spousal support within the marital settlement agreement stated 'spousal support is nonmodifiable.' Section 4811, subdivision (b), provides that spousal support is always modifiable unless the agreement of the parties specifically provides to the contrary. Careful draftsmen preparing marital settlement agreements providing for spousal support should specifically state that spousal support is nonmodifiable, if that is the agreement of the parties." (*Ibid.*)

With this historical perspective in mind, we now turn to the agreement in this case. Paragraph 10 of the agreement is a classic example of general boiler plate language which is routinely inserted in most contracts. Such a provision is obviously intended to prohibit those kinds of oral modifications of a written contract which would otherwise be permitted under section 1698. (See 14 Cal.Jur.3d, Contracts, § 222, pp. 501–503; Timbie, *Modification of Written Contracts in California* (1972) 23 Hast.L.J. 1549, 1554–1564; see, e.g., *Mitchell v. Mitchell* (Me.1980) 418 A.2d 1140, 1142.)

Wife argues that under decisional law this paragraph precludes judicial modification of spousal support. Wife points to the "strikingly similar" language in *Smiley, supra,* 53 Cal.App.3d 228, 125 Cal.Rptr. 717, which was held sufficient to cause spousal support to be nonmodifiable. However, the provision herein more closely parallels the provision in *Forcum, supra,* 145 Cal.App.3d 599, which was deemed insufficient. Thus, insofar as *Smiley* and *Forcum* can be distinguished, *Forcum* is more on point.

Furthermore, insofar as there is a conflict between the 1975 *Smiley* decision and the 1983 *Forcum* decision, we find the rationale of the latter authority more persuasive. We agree with *Forcum* that general language that an agreement is entire and may not be altered, amended or modified is insufficient to invoke the exception to the statutory rule.

Whereas the earlier cases stressed the fact that no magic words were necessary and appeared willing to infer intent to make spousal support nonmodifiable from general language, the most recent cases have emphasized the need for specific unequivocal language directly on the issue of judicial modification. We are concerned about judicial erosion of the statutory policy in favor of modifiability of spousal support and the danger of inferring a contrary intent of the parties from seemingly-innocuous boiler plate provisions. (See Cal.Family L.Rep. (1980) p. 1304.) Since, under section 4811, subdivision (b), the court is vested with the power to modify spousal support unless the parties specifically agree to preclude judicial modification, draftsmen should specifically state that "spousal support is nonmodifiable" in the provision for spousal support if that is the intended agreement of the parties.

Moreover, insufficiency of this boiler plate language to specifically preclude modification by the court is even more obvious in this case than in *Forcum* because here the language merely states that "we"—that is, the parties—may not modify the document. Nowhere in the paragraph is there a limitation, even by implication, on the court's power to do so. Thus, although the paragraph expresses an intention regarding the contractual relations of the parties, it does not comply with the requirement enunciated in *Fukuzaki* and *Nielsen* that in order to foreclose the power vested in the court by section 4811, there must be a specific provision concerning judicial modification. (*Fukuzaki, supra,* 120 Cal. App.3d at p. 458, 174 Cal.Rptr. 536; *Nielsen, supra,* 100 Cal.App.3d at p. 878, 161 Cal.Rptr. 272.)

In addition, a contract must be read as a whole with each part helping to interpret the other. (§ 1641.) Here, paragraph 6 of the agreement expressly retains the jurisdiction of the court to determine all issues which are not specifically excluded from the reservation. Thus, this paragraph reinforces our unwillingness to infer an intent to prohibit judicial modification of spousal support from the boiler plate language in paragraph 10. We are not persuaded by wife's argument, relying on *Smiley,* that this paragraph merely makes the agreement subject to enforcement by contempt. All such orders already are. (See §§ 4811, subd. (b); 4380.) Nor do we find any language in paragraph 10 that can reasonably be construed as a specific exclusion of the court's jurisdiction.

In any event, the agreement does not unequivocally exclude judicial modification and, therefore, is ambiguous on that issue. But any ambiguity must be resolved in favor of the general statutory rule of modifiability, rather than the exception (*Moyer v. Workmen's Comp. Appeals Bd.* (1973) 10 Cal.3d 222, 232, 110 Cal.Rptr. 144, 514 P.2d 1224) and against the wife whose counsel drafted the agreement (§ 1654).[7] Accordingly, the judgment (order) denying the motion to show cause re modification is reversed, and the cause is remanded to the superior court to hold a hearing on the merits.

SCHAUER, P.J., and JOHNSON, J., concur.

SECTION 2. DIVISION BY COURT ORDER

In a proceeding under the Family Code for the dissolution of marriage or legal separation, the trial court has the jurisdiction to inquire into and make appropriate orders for the settlement of the property rights of the parties.[9] Consequently, if the parties are unable to agree to a division of their property, the community property and quasi-community property of the parties will be subject to disposition by

---

7. Our interpretation of the agreement is not affected by the fact that paragraph 10 was not incorporated in the interlocutory decree. Section 4811 makes the question of whether the parties and the court intended to or did merge a settlement agreement into an interlocutory decree irrelevant to determine whether a court may modify spousal support payments. (*In re Marriage of Nielsen, supra,* 100 Cal.App.3d at pp. 876–877, 161 Cal.Rptr. 272; *In re Marriage of Harris* (1976) 65 Cal.App.3d 143, 149–150, 134 Cal. Rptr. 891.)

9. West's Ann.Cal.Family Code § 2010.

the court in the dissolution proceedings. If the court believes that the total value of the community property does not exceed $50,000, it may submit the issues of classification, valuation and division to arbitration for resolution.[10] The Family Code controls the disposition of property by the court in a dissolution proceeding. The relevant provisions are set forth below. Succeeding subdivisions of this section will treat the various issues which may be encountered in a litigated division, including jurisdictional problems, the equal division requirement, valuation problems, and tax consequences.

WEST'S ANNOTATED CALIFORNIA FAMILY CODE

§ 2500. Construction of division

Unless the provision or context otherwise requires, the definitions in this part govern the construction of this division.

(Stats.1992, c. 162 (A.B.2650), § 10, operative Jan. 1, 1994.)

§ 2501. Community estate

"Community estate" includes both the community and quasi-community assets and liabilities of the parties.

(Stats.1992, c. 162 (A.B. 2650), § 10, operative Jan. 1, 1994.)

§ 2502. Separate property

"Separate property" does not include quasi-community property.

(Stats.1992, c. 162 (A.B. 2650), § 10, operative Jan. 1, 1994.)

§ 2550. Manner of division of community estate

Except upon the written agreement of the parties, or on oral stipulation of the parties in open court, or as otherwise provided in this division, in a proceeding for dissolution of marriage or for legal separation of the parties, the court shall, either in its judgment of dissolution of the marriage, in its judgment of legal separation of the parties, or at a later time if it expressly reserves jurisdiction to make such a property division, divide the community estate of the parties equally.

(Stats.1992, c. 162 (A.B. 2650), § 10, operative Jan. 1, 1994.)

§ 2551. Characterization of liabilities; confirmation or assignment

For the purposes of division and in confirming or assigning the liabilities of the parties for which the community estate is liable, the court shall characterize liabilities as separate or community and confirm or assign them to the parties in accordance with Part 6 (commencing with Section 2620).

(Stats.1992, c. 162 (A.B.2650), § 10, operative Jan. 1, 1994.)

§ 2552. Valuation of assets and liabilities

(a) For the purpose of division of the community estate upon dissolution of marriage or legal separation of the parties, except as provided in subdivision (b),

---

10. West's Ann.Cal.Family Code § 2554.

the court shall value the assets and liabilities as near as practicable to the time of trial.

(b) Upon 30 days' notice by the moving party to the other party, the court for good cause shown may value all or any portion of the assets and liabilities at a date after separation and before trial to accomplish an equal division of the community estate of the parties in an equitable manner.

(Stats.1992, c. 162 (A.B.2650), § 10, operative Jan. 1, 1994.)

§ 2553. Powers of court

The court may make any orders the court considers necessary to carry out the purposes of this division.

(Stats.1992, c. 162 (A.B.2650), § 10, operative Jan. 1, 1994.)

§ 2554. Failure to agree to voluntary division of property; submission to arbitration

(a) Notwithstanding any other provision of this division, in any case in which the parties do not agree in writing to a voluntary division of the community estate of the parties, the issue of the character, the value, and the division of the community estate may be submitted by the court to arbitration for resolution pursuant to Chapter 2.5 (commencing with Section 1141.10) of Title 3 of Part 3 of the Code of Civil Procedure, if the total value of the community and quasi-community property in controversy in the opinion of the court does not exceed fifty thousand dollars ($50,000). The decision of the court regarding the value of the community and quasi-community property for purposes of this section is not appealable.

(b) The court may submit the matter to arbitration at any time it believes the parties are unable to agree upon a division of the property.

(Stats.1992, c. 162 (A.B.2650), § 10, operative Jan. 1, 1994.)

§ 2555. Disposition of community estate; revision on appeal

The disposition of the community estate, as provided in this division, is subject to revision on appeal in all particulars, including those which are stated to be in the discretion of the court.

(Stats.1992, c. 162 (A.B.2650), § 10, operative Jan. 1, 1994.)

§ 2556. Community property or debts; continuing jurisdiction

In a proceeding for dissolution of marriage, for nullity of marriage, or for legal separation of the parties, the court has continuing jurisdiction to award community estate assets or community estate liabilities to the parties that have not been previously adjudicated by a judgment in the proceeding. A party may file a postjudgment motion or order to show cause in the proceeding in order to obtain adjudication of any community estate asset or liability omitted or not adjudicated by the judgment. In these cases, the court shall equally divide the omitted or unadjudicated community estate asset or liability, unless the court finds upon good cause shown that the interests of justice require an unequal division of the asset or liability.

(Stats.1992, c. 162 (A.B.2650), § 10, operative Jan. 1, 1994.)

§ 2580. Division of property; presumptions

(a) For the purpose of division of property upon dissolution of marriage or legal separation of the parties:

(1) Property acquired by the parties during marriage on or after January 1, 1984, and before January 1, 1987, in joint tenancy form is presumed to be community property.

(2) Property acquired by the parties during marriage on or after January 1, 1987, in joint form, including property held in tenancy in common, joint tenancy, tenancy by the entirety, or as community property is presumed to be community property.

(b) The presumptions under subdivision (a) are presumptions affecting the burden of proof and may be rebutted by either of the following:

(1) A clear statement in the deed or other documentary evidence of title by which the property is acquired that the property is separate property and not community property.

(2) Proof that the parties have made a written agreement that the property is separate property.

(c) Nothing in this section affects the character of property acquired by married persons that is not described in subdivision (a).

(Stats.1992, c. 162 (A.B.2650), § 10, operative Jan. 1, 1994.)

§ 2600. Powers of court

Notwithstanding Sections 2550 to 2552, inclusive, the court may divide the community estate as provided in this part.

(Stats.1992, c. 162 (A.B.2650), § 10, operative Jan. 1, 1994.)

§ 2601. Conditional award of an asset of the community estate to one party

Where economic circumstances warrant, the court may award an asset of the community estate to one party on such conditions as the court deems proper to effect a substantially equal division of the community estate.

(Stats.1992, c. 162 (A.B.2650), § 10, operative Jan. 1, 1994.)

§ 2602. Additional award or offset against existing property; award of amount determined to have been misappropriated

As an additional award or offset against existing property, the court may award, from a party's share, the amount the court determines to have been deliberately misappropriated by the party to the exclusion of the interest of the other party in the community estate.

(Stats.1992, c. 162 (A.B.2650), § 10, operative Jan. 1, 1994.)

§ 2603. Community estate personal injury damages; assignment

(a) "Community estate personal injury damages" as used in this section means all money or other property received or to be received by a person in satisfaction of a judgment for damages for the person's personal injuries or pursuant to an agreement for the settlement or compromise of a claim for the damages, if the cause of action for the damages arose during the marriage but is not separate property as described in Section 781, unless the money or other property has been commingled with other assets of the community estate.

(b) Community estate personal injury damages shall be assigned to the party who suffered the injuries unless the court, after taking into account the economic condition and needs of each party, the time that has elapsed since the recovery of the damages or the accrual of the cause of action, and all other facts of the case, determines that the interests of justice require another disposition. In such a case, the community estate personal injury damages shall be assigned to the respective parties in such proportions as the court determines to be just, except that at least one-half of the damages shall be assigned to the party who suffered the injuries.

(Stats.1992, c. 162 (A.B.2650), § 10, operative Jan. 1, 1994.)

§ 2604. Community estates of less than $5,000; award of entire estate

If the net value of the community estate is less than five thousand dollars ($5,000) and one party cannot be located through the exercise of reasonable diligence, the court may award all the community estate to the other party on conditions the court deems proper in its judgment of dissolution of marriage or legal separation of the parties.

(Stats.1992, c. 162 (A.B.2650), § 10, operative Jan. 1, 1994.)

§ 2610. Retirement plans; orders to assure benefits

The court shall make whatever orders are necessary or appropriate to ensure that each party receives the party's full community property share in any retirement plan, whether public or private, including all survivor and death benefits, including, but not limited to, any of the following:

(a) Order the division of any retirement benefits payable upon or after the death of either party in a manner consistent with this division.

(b) Order a party to elect a survivor benefit annuity or other similar election for the benefit of the other party, as specified by the court, in any case in which a retirement plan provides for such an election.

(c) Order the division of accumulated community property contributions and service credit as provided in Article 1.2 (commencing with Section 21215) of Chapter 9 of Part 3 of Division 5 of Title 2 of the Government Code.

(d) Order the division of community property rights in accounts with the State Teachers' Retirement System pursuant to Chapter 7.5 (commencing with Section 22650) of Part 13 of the Education Code.

(Stats.1992, c. 162 (A.B.2650), § 10, operative Jan. 1, 1994.)

§ 2620. Community estate debts; confirmation or division

The debts for which the community estate is liable which are unpaid at the time of trial, or for which the community estate becomes liable after trial, shall be confirmed or divided as provided in this part.

(Stats.1992, c. 162 (A.B.2650), § 10, operative Jan. 1, 1994.)

§ 2621. Premarital debts; confirmation

Debts incurred by either spouse before the date of marriage shall be confirmed without offset to the spouse who incurred the debt.

(Stats.1992, c. 162 (A.B.2650), § 10, operative Jan. 1, 1994.)

§ 2622. Marital debts incurred before the date of separation; division

(a) Except as provided in subdivision (b), debts incurred by either spouse after the date of marriage but before the date of separation shall be divided as set forth in Sections 2550 to 2552, inclusive, and Sections 2601 to 2604, inclusive.

(b) To the extent that community debts exceed total community and quasi-community assets, the excess of debt shall be assigned as the court deems just and equitable, taking into account factors such as the parties' relative ability to pay.

(Stats.1992, c. 162 (A.B.2650), § 10, operative Jan. 1, 1994.)

§ 2623. Marital debts incurred after the date of separation; confirmation

Debts incurred by either spouse after the date of separation but before entry of a judgment of dissolution of marriage or legal separation of the parties shall be confirmed as follows:

(a) Debts incurred by either spouse for the common necessaries of life of either spouse or the necessaries of life of the children of the marriage for whom support may be ordered, in the absence of a court order or written agreement for support or for the payment of these debts, shall be confirmed to either spouse according to the parties' respective needs and abilities to pay at the time the debt was incurred.

(b) Debts incurred by either spouse for nonnecessaries of that spouse or children of the marriage for whom support may be ordered shall be confirmed without offset to the spouse who incurred the debt.

(Stats.1993, c. 219, § 113, operative Jan. 1, 1994.)

§ 2624. Marital debts incurred after entry of judgment of dissolution or after entry of judgment of legal separation; confirmation

Debts incurred by either spouse after entry of a judgment of dissolution of marriage but before termination of the parties' marital status or after entry of a judgment of legal separation of the parties shall be confirmed without offset to the spouse who incurred the debt.

(Stats.1992, c. 162 (A.B.2650), § 10, operative Jan. 1, 1994.)

§ 2625. Separate debts incurred before date of separation; confirmation

Notwithstanding Sections 2620 to 2624, inclusive, all separate debts, including those debts incurred by a spouse during marriage and before the date of separation that were not incurred for the benefit of the community, shall be confirmed without offset to the spouse who incurred the debt.

(Stats.1992, c. 162 (A.B.2650), § 10, operative Jan. 1, 1994.)

§ 2626. Reimbursements

The court has jurisdiction to order reimbursement in cases it deems appropriate for debts paid after separation but before trial.

(Stats.1992, c. 162 (A.B.2650), § 10, operative Jan. 1, 1994.)

§ 2627. Educational loans; liabilities for death or injuries; assignment

Notwithstanding Sections 2550 to 2552, inclusive, and Sections 2620 to 2624, inclusive, educational loans shall be assigned pursuant to Section 2641 and liabilities subject to paragraph (2) of subdivision (b) of Section 1000 shall be assigned to the spouse whose act or omission provided the basis for the liability, without offset.

(Stats.1992, c. 162 (A.B.2650), § 10, operative Jan. 1, 1994.)

§ 2640. Contributions to the acquisition of the property; waivers; amount of reimbursement

(a) "Contributions to the acquisition of the property," as used in this section, include downpayments, payments for improvements, and payments that reduce the principal of a loan used to finance the purchase or improvement of the property but do not include payments of interest on the loan or payments made for maintenance, insurance, or taxation of the property.

(b) In the division of community estate property acquired on or after January 1, 1984, by the parties during marriage unless a party has made a written waiver of the right to reimbursement or signed a writing that has the effect of a waiver, the party shall be reimbursed for the party's contributions to the acquisition of the property to the extent the party traces the contributions to a separate property source. The amount reimbursed shall be without interest or adjustment for change in monetary values and shall not exceed the net value of the property at the time of the division.

(Stats.1992, c. 162 (A.B.2650), § 10, operative Jan. 1, 1994.)

§ 2641. Community contributions to education or training

(a) "Community contributions to education or training" as used in this section means payments made with community or quasi-community property for education or training or for the repayment of a loan incurred for education or training, whether the payments were made while the parties were resident in this state or resident outside this state.

(b) Subject to the limitations provided in this section, upon dissolution of marriage or legal separation of the parties:

(1) The community shall be reimbursed for community contributions to education or training of a party that substantially enhances the earning capacity of the party. The amount reimbursed shall be with interest at the legal rate, accruing from the end of the calendar year in which the contributions were made.

(2) A loan incurred during marriage for the education or training of a party shall not be included among the liabilities of the community for the purpose of division pursuant to this division but shall be assigned for payment by the party.

(c) The reimbursement and assignment required by this section shall be reduced or modified to the extent circumstances render such a disposition unjust, including, but not limited to, any of the following:

(1) The community has substantially benefited from the education, training, or loan incurred for the education or training of the party. There is a rebuttable presumption, affecting the burden of proof, that the community has not substantially benefited from community contributions to the education or training made less than 10 years before the commencement of the proceeding, and that the community has substantially benefited from community contributions to the education or training made more than 10 years before the commencement of the proceeding.

(2) The education or training received by the party is offset by the education or training received by the other party for which community contributions have been made.

(3) The education or training enables the party receiving the education or training to engage in gainful employment that substantially reduces the need of the party for support that would otherwise be required.

(d) Reimbursement for community contributions and assignment of loans pursuant to this section is the exclusive remedy of the community or a party for the education or training and any resulting enhancement of the earning capacity of a party. However, nothing in this subdivision limits consideration of the effect of the education, training, or enhancement, or the amount reimbursed pursuant to this section, on the circumstances of the parties for the purpose of an order for support pursuant to Section 4320.

(e) This section is subject to an express written agreement of the parties to the contrary.

(Stats.1992, c. 162 (A.B.2650), § 10, operative Jan. 1, 1994.)

§ 2650. Jurisdiction; division of real and personal property; applicability of section

In a proceeding for division of the community estate, the court has jurisdiction, at the request of either party, to divide the separate property interests of the parties in real and personal property, wherever situated and whenever acquired, held by the parties as joint tenants or tenants in common. The property shall be divided together with, and in accordance with the same procedure for and limitations on, division of community estate.

(Stats.1992, c. 162 (A.B.2650), § 10, operative Jan. 1, 1994.)

§ 2660. Division of real property situated in another state

(a) Except as provided in subdivision (b), if the property subject to division includes real property situated in another state, the court shall, if possible, divide the community property and quasi-community property as provided for in this division in such a manner that it is not necessary to change the nature of the interests held in the real property situated in the other state.

(b) If it is not possible to divide the property in the manner provided for in subdivision (a), the court may do any of the following in order to effect a division of the property as provided for in this division:

(1) Require the parties to execute conveyances or take other actions with respect to the real property situated in the other state as are necessary.

(2) Award to the party who would have been benefited by the conveyances or other actions the money value of the interest in the property that the party would have received if the conveyances had been executed or other actions taken.

(Stats.1992, c. 162 (A.B.2650), § 10, operative Jan. 1, 1994.)

§ 3800. Definitions

As used in this chapter:

(a) "Custodial parent" means a party awarded physical custody of a child.

(b) "Deferred sale of home order" means an order that temporarily delays the sale and awards the temporary exclusive use and possession of the family home to a custodial parent of a minor child or child for whom support is authorized under Sections 3900 and 3901 or under Section 3910, whether or not the custodial parent has sole or joint custody, in order to minimize the adverse impact of dissolution of marriage or legal separation of the parties on the welfare of the child.

(c) "Resident parent" means a party who has requested or who has already been awarded a deferred sale of home order.

(Stats.1992, c. 162 (A.B.2650), § 10, operative Jan. 1, 1994.)

§ 3801. Determination of economic feasibility of deferred sale

(a) If one of the parties has requested a deferred sale of home order pursuant to this chapter, the court shall first determine whether it is economically feasible to maintain the payments of any note secured by a deed of trust, property taxes, insurance for the home during the period the sale of the home is deferred, and the condition of the home comparable to that at the time of trial.

(b) In making this determination, the court shall consider all of the following:

(1) The resident parent's income.

(2) The availability of spousal support, child support, or both spousal and child support.

(3) Any other sources of funds available to make those payments.

(c) It is the intent of the Legislature, by requiring the determination under this section, to do all of the following:

(1) Avoid the likelihood of possible defaults on the payments of notes and resulting foreclosures.

(2) Avoid inadequate insurance coverage.

(3) Prevent deterioration of the condition of the family home.

(4) Prevent any other circumstance which would jeopardize both parents' equity in the home.

(Stats.1992, c. 162 (A.B.2650), § 10, operative Jan. 1, 1994.)

§ 3802. Grant or denial of order; discretion of court

(a) If the court determines pursuant to Section 3801 that it is economically feasible to consider ordering a deferred sale of the family home, the court may grant a deferred sale of home order to a custodial parent if the court determines that the order is necessary in order to minimize the adverse impact of dissolution of marriage or legal separation of the parties on the child.

(b) In exercising its discretion to grant or deny a deferred sale of home order, the court shall consider all of the following:

(1) The length of time the child has resided in the home.

(2) The child's placement or grade in school.

(3) The accessibility and convenience of the home to the child's school and other services or facilities used by and available to the child, including child care.

(4) Whether the home has been adapted or modified to accommodate any physical disabilities of a child or a resident parent in a manner that a change in residence may adversely affect the ability of the resident parent to meet the needs of the child.

(5) The emotional detriment to the child associated with a change in residence.

(6) The extent to which the location of the home permits the resident parent to continue employment.

(7) The financial ability of each parent to obtain suitable housing.

(8) The tax consequences to the parents.

(9) The economic detriment to the nonresident parent in the event of a deferred sale of home order.

(10) Any other factors the court deems just and equitable.

(Stats.1992, c. 162 (A.B.2650), § 10, operative Jan. 1, 1994.)

§ 3803. Contents of order

A deferred sale of home order shall state the duration of the order and may include the legal description and assessor's parcel number of the real property which is subject to the order.

(Stats.1992, c. 162 (A.B.2650), § 10, operative Jan. 1, 1994.)

§ 3804. Recordation of order

A deferred sale of home order may be recorded in the office of the county recorder of the county in which the real property is located.

(Stats.1992, c. 162 (A.B.2650), § 10, operative Jan. 1, 1994.)

§ 3805. Orders considered to constitute additional child support

A deferred sale of home order may be considered to constitute additional child support pursuant to subdivision (b) of Section 4055.

(Stats.1992, c. 162 (A.B.2650), § 10, operative Jan. 1, 1994.)

§ 3806. Payment of maintenance and capital improvement costs; order

The court may make an order specifying the parties' respective responsibilities for the payment of the costs of routine maintenance and capital improvements.

(Stats.1992, c. 162 (A.B.2650), § 10, operative Jan. 1, 1994.)

§ 3807. Time for modification or termination of orders; exceptions

Except as otherwise agreed to by the parties in writing, a deferred sale of home order may be modified or terminated at any time at the discretion of the court.

(Stats.1992, c. 162 (A.B.2650), § 10, operative Jan. 1, 1994.)

§ 3808. Remarriage or other change in circumstances; rebuttable presumption

Except as otherwise agreed to by the parties in writing, if the party awarded the deferred sale of home order remarries, or if there is otherwise a change in circumstances affecting the determinations made pursuant to Section 3801 or 3802 or affecting the economic status of the parties or the children on which the award is based, a rebuttable presumption, affecting the burden of proof, is created that further deferral of the sale is no longer an equitable method of minimizing the adverse impact of the dissolution of marriage or legal separation of the parties on the children.

(Stats.1992, c. 162 (A.B.2650), § 10, operative Jan. 1, 1994.)

A. *Jurisdiction to Divide Property*

Under Family Code Section 2010, the court has the power to divide the community property and quasi-community property of the parties in dissolution or legal separation proceedings.[11] This necessarily includes the power to classify property as separate or community,[12] but once such classification is made the court has no jurisdiction over the separate property of the spouses.[13] However, Civil Code Section 4800.4 allows the court to divide the separate property interests in jointly held property if either party requests such a division.[14]

Another jurisdictional issue involves the power of the court to determine property rights in a default proceeding. Prior to the Family Law Act, in order to invoke the jurisdiction of the court to divide community property it was necessary to plead the existence of such property and request a division. A general prayer would support a division if the issues of classification and division had actually been contested, but would not support a division in default proceedings.[15] Although terminology has changed (the divorce complaint is now a petition for dissolution), it appears that the rules regarding pleading the existence of property and request for division should continue to apply, and that a distinction between contested and default proceedings will continue to obtain.[16]

GIONIS v. SUPERIOR COURT
Court of Appeal Fourth District 1988.
202 Cal.App.3d 786, 248 Cal.Rptr. 741.

OPINION

WALLIN, ASSOCIATE JUSTICE.

Thomas A. Gionis seeks a writ of mandate compelling the superior court to vacate its order denying his motion to bifurcate the issue of his

---

11. Personal jurisdiction is required over a respondent in order to adjudicate his or her rights in the community or quasi-community property. A judgment affecting property rights entered without personal jurisdiction is not entitled to full faith and credit. In re Marriage of Leff, 25 Cal. App.3d 630, 102 Cal.Rptr. 195 (1972). There are a variety of bases for obtaining the requisite personal jurisdiction, including domicile, residence, and consent. See West's Ann.Cal.Code of Civil Procedure § 410.10.

12. Salveter v. Salveter, 206 Cal. 657, 275 P. 801 (1929).

13. In re Marriage of Buford, 155 Cal. App.3d 74, 202 Cal.Rptr. 20 (1984); Robinson v. Robinson, reprinted in this Section.

14. Prior to the enactment of Civil Code Section 4800.4, some courts held that because the interests of the spouses in property held as joint tenants or as tenants in common were a species of separate property, such property was not subject to division in dissolution proceedings and a separate partition action was required. See, e.g., Barba v. Barba, 103 Cal.App.2d 395, 229 P.2d 465 (1951); compare Crook v. Crook, 184 Cal.App.2d 745, 7 Cal.Rptr. 892 (1960).

15. Burtnett v. King, reprinted in this Section.

16. Cf. Irwin v. Irwin, 69 Cal.App.3d 317, 138 Cal.Rptr. 9 (1977), discussed infra at p. 571.

marital status from all other issues. He claims the trial court abused its discretion by denying his motion as untimely. We agree with petitioner and issue the writ.

* * *

Aissa and Thomas Gionis were married on February 14, 1986. In June 1987 Aissa filed a petition for legal separation and a separate petition for dissolution of marriage. Both petitions requested sole custody of the parties' infant daughter as well as child and spousal support.

Thomas responded and filed a motion to change venue. The declarations supporting and opposing the motion revealed deep bitterness between the parties over the issue of child custody. The parties then stipulated to proceed with the petition for dissolution of marriage, and agreed that the court acquired jurisdiction over both parties for that purpose in June 1987.

On January 29, 1988, Thomas moved to bifurcate the issue of marital status from the issues of custody, support and property division. His declaration stated the marriage had irrevocably failed, reconciliation was not possible and although the trial of the dissolution would be brief, the remaining issues would require discovery and a more lengthy trial. He further stated he wanted his marital status resolved so he could make investments and obtain credit without having to seek quitclaim deeds from Aissa or worry that a lender might rely on community rather than separate credit. Aissa's opposition to the motion raised procedural objections; she set forth no substantive reasons why bifurcation would be against her interests.

The court denied the motion, stating there was no compelling reason to bifurcate since the petition had been on file less than a year. "I don't really find a good cause stated for proceeding after only about seven months since the filing.... [¶] I'll tell you one I granted. They had been separated for a couple of years, and the wife had two babies, on her husband's health insurance policy; and he was not the father of either one of them. And I thought that was good cause. And I granted that." Additionally, the judge apparently felt the parties should be required to undergo a period of sexual restraint before being permitted to dissolve their marriage. He stated twice: "Tell them to take a cold shower." Thomas filed this petition for a writ of mandate, contending the trial court abused its discretion by refusing to bifurcate the action.

Separating the termination of a marriage from controversies over spousal support, child custody and division of marital property is not a new idea. In *Hull v. Superior Court* (1960) 54 Cal.2d 139, 5 Cal.Rptr. 1, 352 P.2d 161, the Supreme Court explained the concept of "divisible divorce" as follows: "Severance of a personal relationship which the law has found to be unworkable and, as a result, injurious to the public welfare is not dependent upon final settlement of property disputes. Society will be little concerned if the parties engage in property litigation of however long duration; it will be much concerned if two people are forced to remain legally bound to one another when this status can do nothing but engender additional bitterness and unhappiness." (*Id.,* at pp. 147–148, 5 Cal.Rptr. 1, 352 P.2d 161.)

This philosophy was incorporated into the Family Law Act * * * which removed the issue of marital fault from domestic relations litigation. (*In re Marriage of Fink* (1976) 54 Cal.App.3d 357, 126 Cal.Rptr. 626.) "[T]he new Family Law Act embodied a legislative intent that the dissolution of marriage should not be postponed merely because issues relating to property, support, attorney fees or child custody were unready for decision." (*Id.,* at p. 363, 126 Cal.Rptr. 626.) Complying with that legislative intent, courts have encouraged bifurcation of marital status from other issues. (*In re Marriage of Wolfe* (1985) 173 Cal.App.3d 889, 219 Cal.Rptr. 337; *In re Marriage of Lusk* (1978) 86 Cal.App.3d 228, 150 Cal.Rptr. 63; *In re Marriage of Van Sickle* (1977) 68 Cal.App.3d 728, 137 Cal.Rptr. 568; *In re Marriage of Fink, supra,* 54 Cal.App.3d 357, 126 Cal.Rptr. 626.)

In light of the policies favoring bifurcation, the trial court was mistaken in its apparent belief that Thomas was required to justify his request with a compelling showing of need. Two previous cases in which the granting of a bifurcation motion was contested upheld the order based on declarations strikingly similar to Thomas'. In *In re Marriage of Fink, supra,* 54 Cal.App.3d 357, 126 Cal.Rptr. 626, the husband's declaration stated "that reconciliation was not possible, that the dissolution hearing would be brief, and that the other issues (ascertainment and division of community property, spousal support and attorney fees) would require a long trial preceded by extensive discovery." (*Id.,* at pp. 359–360, 126 Cal.Rptr. 626.) And in *In re Marriage of Lusk, supra,* 86 Cal.App.3d 228, 150 Cal.Rptr. 63, the husband's declaration "averred that he had no intention of reconciling with wife, that he believed it was in the best interest of all parties that the marriage be dissolved without further delay 'so that all parties may develop a new life with a reasonable degree of stability and certainty' and with the hope that 'immediate dissolution of the marriage will remove a great deal of emotional strain and pressure' from both husband and wife and 'may help facilitate a settlement regarding the other reserved issues.'" (*Id.,* at p. 231, 150 Cal.Rptr. 63.)

In his declaration Thomas maintained reconciliation was impossible and the issues other than status would require a lengthy trial. He continued with extensive personal reasons why he wanted his brief marriage to Aissa dissolved quickly.[1] Absent a showing by Aissa why

---

1. Thomas' declaration states in part: "I do not want the status of my marriage to effect [sic] any investments I wish to make. As examples, I should not be required to seek a quitclaim deed from Petitioner if I decide to invest in real property or other business ventures, nor should I be required to obtain Petitioner's consent to make application for and sign any loan documents regarding my finances. I should not have to run the risk that any business deals I decide to make are construed to be community property because community credit rather than my own separate credit was utilized. With a bifurcation, I can receive more favorable tax treatment (lower tax

bifurcation should not be granted, Thomas' declaration provided a proper basis for the motion.

* * *

Thomas' declaration contained sufficient reasons supporting his motion to bifurcate, and the trial court abused its discretion by refusing to grant it. Consistent with the legislative policy favoring no fault dissolution of marriage, only slight evidence is necessary to obtain bifurcation and resolution of marital status. On the other hand, a spouse opposing bifurcation must present compelling reasons for denial.

* * *

SCOVILLE, P.J. and CROSBY, J., concur.

ROBINSON v. ROBINSON
California District Court of Appeal, 1944.
65 Cal.App.2d 118, 150 P.2d 7.

W.J. WOOD, JUSTICE. In this action to quiet title plaintiff has appealed from a judgment awarding to defendant a life interest in the real property which is the subject of the litigation.

An interlocutory decree was awarded to Theresa Robinson, defendant herein, on June 10, 1942, she having theretofore commenced an action against plaintiff for separate maintenance in which she later changed her prayer to ask for a divorce. In the divorce action she listed various properties of the parties, some of which she alleged to be community property. She specifically alleged that the real estate which is the subject of the present litigation was the separate property of the plaintiff herein, Lewis Robinson. A cross-complaint was filed in the divorce action and the court in its interlocutory decree of divorce ordered the plaintiff herein to pay to defendant herein the sum of $12.50 per month until the further order of the court and also gave her "the right to remain in and to continue to reside and enjoy possession of the premises she now occupies at 1609 East 110th Street, Los Angeles." A part of the community property was awarded to each of the parties. In the final decree of divorce, which was entered on June 17, 1943, no reference was made to the real property involved in this action.

The present action was commenced on January 12, 1943. By its judgment entered on October 5, 1943, the court decreed that plaintiff is the owner in fee of the land described in the complaint, "subject however, to a life estate therein of defendant Theresa Robinson during

rates) in the filing of a separate return as an unmarried person as distinguished from filing a separate return as a married person. The greater the net cash flow I have after taxes, the greater my ability will be to support my family. [¶] I should not be constrained in my financial or social endeavors by the fact that Petitioner and I were married for only approximately a year. [¶] In addition to the foregoing, the dissolution of my marriage to Petitioner is a condition precedent to my obtaining clearance from the archdiocese to remarry, should I chose [sic] to do so.

her natural life to use the improvement thereon consisting of a dwelling known as 1609 East 110th Street, Los Angeles, California."

The power of the court in disposing of the property of the parties in a divorce action is limited to their community property. In such a proceeding the court has no power to dispose of the separate property of one of the parties, nor to carve out a life estate therein. Roy v. Roy, 29 Cal.App.2d 596, 85 P.2d 223. In the divorce action of the parties to the present litigation no issue was made concerning the ownership of the real estate in question, for it was specifically alleged by the wife that the realty was the separate property of the husband. The court therefore was without jurisdiction to award to the wife a life estate therein.

The judgment is reversed. The purported appeal from the order denying a motion for a new trial is dismissed.

Notes

1. Although the court in a dissolution proceeding has no jurisdiction over the parties' separate property, it has been held that the parties may stipulate to a determination and disposition of all their property rights, and that their consent confers authority to dispose of separate property. Spahn v. Spahn, 70 Cal.App.2d 791, 162 P.2d 53 (1945); In re Marriage of Dorris, 160 Cal.App.3d 1208, 207 Cal.Rptr. 160 (1984); see also Family Code § 2650.

2. Suppose that one of the parties to the dissolution proceeding dies before the entry of the final judgment. What is the effect of death on the court's jurisdiction in a dissolution proceeding? If the court is deemed to retain jurisdiction to determine and divide the parties' community interests, is the judgment binding on the deceased spouse's successors in interest? See McClenny v. Superior Court, 62 Cal.2d 140, 41 Cal.Rptr. 460, 396 P.2d 916 (1964); Stevenson v. Superior Court, 62 Cal.2d 150, 41 Cal.Rptr. 466, 396 P.2d 922 (1964); Kinsler v. Superior Court, 121 Cal.App.3d 808, 175 Cal. Rptr. 564 (1981); In re Marriage of Shayman, 35 Cal.App.3d 648, 111 Cal.Rptr. 11 (1973).

3. Can a dissolution judgment affect the property rights of third persons? In the case of In re Marriage of Davis, 68 Cal.App.3d 294, 137 Cal.Rptr. 265 (1977), the wife filed a petition for dissolution, joining her husband's mother as a party. The wife alleged that the mother held legal title to community real property for convenience only. The mother appeared and argued that the dissolution court had limited jurisdiction and could not try title to the property in her name. The appellate court held that the trial court had jurisdiction, and that its determination of the issue and its order that the mother convey title to the husband and wife were proper.

B. The Equal Division Requirement

With certain limited exceptions, the dissolution court is required to divide the community and quasi-community property of the parties equally. Family Code Section 2501 defines the divisible "community estate" to include both the community and quasi-community assets and liabilities of the parties.[17]

Various methods of division may be used to divide the community and quasi-community property between the spouses. For example, the court could make a division in kind, awarding one-half to each spouse. Or the court could award each spouse an undivided one-half interest in the particular asset. It would also be possible to award one spouse certain items, and give the other spouse other items of equal value. Finally, the court could order a particular asset sold, and the proceeds divided equally between the spouses.[18] No one method of division is appropriate to all cases or even to all assets in a single case, and the trial court generally has a great deal of flexibility in selecting the most suitable method of division.[19] Certain kinds of assets have given rise to more division problems than others; these include pension and retirement benefits [20] and out of state real property.[21] The situation where there is only one significant community property asset can create problems, particularly where that asset is the family home and there are minor children. Finally, the division of the community estate where the liabilities exceed the value of the assets may be problematic.[22]

There are certain statutory exceptions to the basic rule requiring an equal division of community and quasi-community property. Under Family Code Section 2602 the trial court may award, from one spouse's share of the property, any sums deliberately misappropriated by that spouse to the exclusion of the community property interest of the other spouse. This is not so much an exception to the equal division rule as it is a way of ensuring an equal division in the face of misappropriation.[23] The following exceptions, however, are true limitations on the equal division rule.

One such exception involves the small community property estate. If the net value of the community property estate is less than $5,000 and one party cannot be located through the exercise of reasonable diligence, the dissolution court may award all of the property to the other spouse.[24]

The other major statutory exception to the equal division rule involves the treatment of personal injury damage awards. Personal

17. For purposes of dividing and assigning liabilities, the court must characterize the obligations as either separate or community and assign them to the appropriate party under West's Ann.Cal. Family Code § 2551.

18. In re Marriage of Rives, 130 Cal. App.3d 138, 181 Cal.Rptr. 572 (1982).

19. See In re Marriage of Connolly, 23 Cal.3d 590, 153 Cal.Rptr. 423, 591 P.2d 911 (1979); In re Marriage of Gillmore, 29 Cal.3d 418, 174 Cal.Rptr. 493, 629 P.2d 1 (1981).

20. Problems involved in the division of employment benefits were previously considered in Chapter 4, Section 6.

21. See, e.g., In re Marriage of Fink, 25 Cal.3d 877, 160 Cal.Rptr. 516, 603 P.2d 881 (1979).

22. See Marriage of Eastis, 47 Cal. App.3d 459, 120 Cal.Rptr. 861 (1975), reprinted in this section.

23. It has been held that negligent conduct resulting in a loss of assets to the community does not constitute misappropriation under this provision. Intentional misconduct appears to be the standard. See In re Marriage of Partridge, 226 Cal. App.3d 120, 276 Cal.Rptr. 8 (1990).

24. West's Ann.Cal.Family Code § 2604.

injury damages recovered by a spouse during marriage are classified as community property.[25]   On dissolution, however, Family Code Section 2603 mandates that such personal injury damages are to be assigned to the injured spouse, unless the court determines that the interests of justice require another disposition. Factors to be considered include the economic needs and circumstances of each party and the time that has elapsed since the recovery of the damages or the accrual of the cause of action.[26]

IN RE MARRIAGE OF STALLWORTH

California District Court of Appeal, 1987.

192 Cal.App.3d 742, 237 Cal.Rptr. 829.

KING, ASSOCIATE JUSTICE.

William Stallworth appeals from a judgment of dissolution of marriage. He asserts multiple errors in the classification and distribution of certain assets * * *.

William and Carol Stallworth were married 14½ years and had one son, Robert, born November 30, 1976. They separated in October 1983, and William filed for dissolution in February 1984. The matter came to trial in April 1985. Although William filed objections to the trial court's proposed statement of decision, they were rejected.

THE FAMILY HOME

It was undisputed that the Stallworth family home, the parties' major asset, was community property. The court found it had a fair market value of $138,250 with a loan balance of $16,000, for an equity of $122,250. In making its disposition of the home the court found "that the mental condition of the minor child of the parties and the financial condition of the parties require that [Carol] and the minor child be allowed to live in the family residence until the said child shall reach the age of 18 years, dies, marries, becomes otherwise emancipated, or until [Carol] remarries, discontinues her residence at said residence, or resides therein with a male with whom she is cohabiting who also resides at said residence. Upon the happening of any of the above circumstances, the residence shall be placed on the market for sale and the proceeds of said sale divided equally between the parties. [Carol] shall pay all mortgage payments, taxes, upkeep, and homeowners association payments on the said residence while she resides there."[1]   The court left title to the

---

25. See Chapter 4, Section 5.

26. Id.

1. In reaching the decision to defer sale of the family home the trial court stated it took into consideration that William "is also receiving a reduction in spousal support payments." We know of no authority to defer the sale of the family home over the objection of the supporting spouse, because the supporting spouse will then be able to pay less spousal support. Of course, to the extent Carol's house payments are low, her needs are less and less spousal support should be ordered. The determination to defer sale of the family home to permit the custodial parent and the child to remain in the home, as we will discuss, violates the requirement for equal division of community property under Civil Code section 4800, unless ordered as a factor of child support. If the sale of the family

home in the names of the parties as joint tenants.[2]

The testimony was uncontroverted that Robert was under a psychiatrist's care, was in a special education program at school, and attended a private reading program at the school's recommendation. These facts, standing alone, are insufficient to support an inference that a move from the family home would have an adverse social or emotional impact on Robert. There was no evidence that Robert's circumstances would be adversely affected by a move from the family home or, if so, that the effect would offset the economic detriment to William of deferring his receipt of his community share of the equity in the home for a 10–year period.

Carol testified she could not obtain equivalent housing in the same district for a comparable price ($238 a month for mortgage, taxes and insurance). The court reduced William's family support obligation by $150 in light of the low house payments on the family residence.[3] There was no evidence as to whether and at what cost Carol could obtain comparable housing in the same neighborhood or school district, although she believed the cost would be greater. If a sale causes Carol's housing cost to increase, this increased need should result in higher support. (See fn. 1, *supra*.) Finally, Carol presented no evidence to justify continuing the family home award, if any, for 10 years, until Robert reached the age of 18.[4] Since Civil Code section 4800.7 provides that a "family home award" means "an order that awards *temporary* use of the home," the evidence would have to justify a family home award for a 10–year period. (Emphasis added.) Even if the evidence justifies a family home award, the trial court must exercise its discretion in setting the duration of the award in accordance with the evidence on that issue.

"The trial court's authority to award the family residence to the parties as tenants-in-common and award the custodial parent exclusive possession as additional child support was first approved in *In re Marriage of Boseman* (1973) 31 Cal.App.3d 372 [107 Cal.Rptr. 232]. *Boseman* was followed in *In re Marriage of Herrmann* (1978) 84 Cal. App.3d 361 [148 Cal.Rptr. 550] [award of note reversed; house should be awarded to parties as tenants-in-common, with exclusive possession to

home would cause the custodial spouse to incur higher housing costs, the remedy is to order higher child and spousal support, not to defer sale of the home. (See *Burchard v. Garay* (1986) 42 Cal.3d 531, 539, 229 Cal. Rptr. 800, 724 P.2d 486.)

2. The trial court's failure to change title to the family home to tenancy-in-common is error since, upon the death of one party, that party's share should pass through his or her estate, not go to the former spouse as the surviving joint tenant.

3. William cites no authority for his proposal to extend the principal of reimbursement for exclusive use of a community asset between separation and trial (*In re Mar-*

riage of Watts (1985) 171 Cal.App.3d 366, 374, 217 Cal.Rptr. 301) to orders after trial, nor was evidence presented establishing the rental value of the community residence. Whether pretrial or post-trial, the court, in fixing support, must consider the needs of the supported person. To the extent those needs are less because of lower housing costs, the support ordered, as here, should reflect this fact.

4. The court did retain jurisdiction to modify the order deferring sale in the event of a change of circumstances. (See Civil Code section 4800.7, which has been enacted since the trial in this case.)

custodial parent, when award to either party is economically unfeasible]. The third part of the trilogy, *In re Marriage of Duke* (1980) 101 Cal.App.3d 152 [161 Cal.Rptr. 444], requires that the sale of the house be deferred and that a *Boseman/Herrmann* order be made under certain designated circumstances." (Adams & Sevitch, Cal.Family Law Practice (Seventh Ed.) § E.56.0.1, parallel citations omitted, emphasis in original.) We have previously noted our disagreement with *Duke's* limitation on the trial court's discretion by stating "*Duke* has been described as holding that deferring the sale of the family home until the youngest child of the parties reaches the age of majority must always be ordered where adverse economic, emotional and social impacts on the minor result from an immediate loss of a long-established family home and are not outweighed by the economic detriment to the out-spouse by the delay in receiving his or her share of the proceeds in the equity of the family home. We believe the better rule is that of *In re Marriage of Herrmann, supra,* 84 Cal.App.3d 361 [148 Cal.Rptr. 550], and *In re Marriage of Boseman, supra,* 31 Cal.App.3d 372 [107 Cal.Rptr. 232], that the trial judge should weigh these factors, as well as others, and be vested with broad discretion in making a disposition of the family home." [¶] * * * As a practical matter, it should be noted that the emotional attachment of a child to a home may be minimal if the child is very young and of questionable significance if the child is an older teenager. However, in the event the court exercises its discretion to order a deferral of sale of the family home, we do not agree that sale of the family home must always be deferred until the youngest child of the parties reaches the age of 18. Where such deferral would delay sale for many years the trial court has the discretion to determine an appropriate earlier time at which a sale might take place, such as when the child would naturally be changing schools to one outside of the immediate neighborhood. [¶] Additionally, we believe that the factor of economic detriment to the noncustodial parent should be broadly construed in today's economic circumstances. Given the extremely high cost of housing in urban areas in California, only the very wealthy are in a position to purchase a new home without receiving their share of a sizeable equity in an existing home. Thus, deferral of the sale of the family home would not only interfere and perhaps preclude the out-spouse from obtaining suitable housing accommodations to be able to enjoy the frequent and continuing contact with his or her children which is the public policy of California as set forth in [Civil Code] section 4600, subdivision (a), but may well preclude obtaining adequate housing for themselves and any later family they may acquire, and limit their ability to be able to get on with living their own life in their postdivorce world. If considerable appreciation has taken place, tax factors should also be considered in reaching the decision whether or not to defer a sale, even if they are not clearly immediate and specific as would be required for accomplishing an equal division of the property. * * * If deferral of the sale would deprive the out-spouse of a deferral of tax on the gain by precluding the tax-free 24-month roll-over of equity into a new residence under Internal Revenue Code section 1034, or of the one time exclusion of gain up to $125,000 under Internal Revenue Code section 121 and Revenue and Taxation Code section 17155, it is certainly equitable to consider these factors in determining the disposition of the family home. It could be argued that the loss of the tax benefits of Internal Revenue Code sections 1034 and 121, and their California counterparts, provide sufficient economic detriment to the out-spouse so as to require, as a matter of law, an immediate, rather than a deferred, sale of the family home." (*In re Marriage of Horowitz* (1984) 159 Cal.App.3d 368, 374, fn. 6, 205 Cal. Rptr. 874.)

The trial judge has broad discretion to defer the sale of the family home after weighing the factors outlined above. The problem in the instant case is that the record discloses no evidence was presented on these factors; thus the trial court could not have weighed them. For this reason we must reverse the trial court's determination to defer the sale of the family home and remand this issue for retrial. We express no opinion as to how the trial court should exercise its discretion on this issue because of the lack of evidence in the record.

For the guidance of the trial court upon retrial, in the event a determination is again made to defer the sale of the family home, we note that William's request for an order requiring Carol to maintain insurance on the home naming him as coinsured was not granted. "If such an order is made, the in-spouse should be given the right to sole use and possession of the property and would normally be given the responsibility to pay all mortgage payments, taxes, insurance and expenses of reasonable maintenance. If these costs would be less than the reasonable rental value of the property, it would appear equitable to offset any child or spousal support payments by one-half of the difference. It is appropriate for the court to reserve jurisdiction for the purposes of modification of the order in the event of any change of circumstances. As indicated above, there should be a provision in the order giving the in-spouse an opportunity to purchase the interest of the out-spouse at the end of the deferral period, or upon further order of the court. At that time, the court should also retain jurisdiction to reimburse the in-spouse for capital improvements made by that spouse. Finally, such an order should require the in-spouse to maintain the property in a condition comparable to that at the time of trial and to maintain all appropriate insurance coverage with the out-spouse as a coinsured. A variant of this order is to require the parties to share the monthly payments in order to assure each receives one-half of the tax benefits flowing from them. Such an arrangement must be utilized with caution because it may become a source of continuing friction between the former spouses." (*In re Marriage of Horowitz, supra,* 159 Cal.App.3d at p. 373, fn. 5, 205 Cal.Rptr. 874.) Although we stated in *Horowitz* that it would be equitable to provide an offset against support to the extent of one-half the difference between the reasonable rental value and the housing expense attributable to the family home, in retrospect, this will usually be unnecessary and may result in inequity. In fact, as here, there usually is insufficient income available to allow all members of the postdivorce family to enjoy the same standard of living enjoyed when living together prior to separation. In fixing the amount of child or spousal support the needs of the supported party must be considered; the lower the housing expense, the lower the needs of the supported party and therefore the lower the amount of support which will be ordered. (See fns. 1 & 3, *supra*.)

* * *

Low, P.J., concurs.

HANING, ASSOCIATE JUSTICE, concurring in part and dissenting in part.

* * *

Numerous decisions of the Courts of Appeal have upheld the trial court's discretion, under appropriate circumstances, to defer the sale of the family residence. (*In re Marriage of Duke* (1980) 101 Cal.App.3d 152, 161 Cal.Rptr. 444; *In re Marriage of Herrmann* (1978) 84 Cal. App.3d 361, 148 Cal.Rptr. 550; *In re Marriage of Boseman* (1973) 31 Cal.App.3d 372, 107 Cal.Rptr. 232.) I conclude that the present circumstances are appropriate for such an order.

The parties were married for nearly 15 years. The husband is a journeyman plumber earning in excess of $50,000 annually. The wife has not been employed outside the home and has no demonstrable earning capacity save for nominal income obtained through sales of Tupperware products. She has only a high school education, but has enrolled in college and is pursuing a course of study leading to a baccalaureate degree.

The minor son of the parties is suffering from psychiatric problems. He is unable to handle ordinary classroom work at school without additional help, and is attending a special educational program. The wife's assumption of her formal education is laudable, and should be encouraged. Achievement of her degree will promote her ability to become self-supporting and relieve the husband of much, if not all of his spousal support obligation. The wife's education will also enure to the child's benefit. If remaining in the family residence temporarily will accelerate or advance the wife's educational program, the trial court is acting well within its discretion to permit her to remain.

I think the child's situation speaks for itself. His circumstances and the need for continued treatment are not disputed, and the current low house payments greatly facilitate the continuation of his medical and educational needs. The trial court found that the mental condition of the child and the financial condition of the parties require that the wife and child be permitted to reside in the family residence temporarily. It reserved jurisdiction to modify their occupancy of the residence upon a sufficient change of circumstances. If the wife maintains her present educational progress she will complete school long before the child reaches 18. By that time, if not before, the child's circumstances may also have changed, and the trial court can reassess the situation.

The *possible* adverse tax consequences of the deferred sale of the residence were *not* presented to the trial court by the husband. Although he urges us to do so, we cannot speculate on appeal that such consequences exist. (See, e.g., 9 Witkin, Cal.Procedure (3d ed. 1985) Appeal, § 250.) The trial court found that the child's mental condition and the financial circumstances of the parties required that the wife and child remain in the family residence until the circumstances changed. I think its finding is supported by substantial evidence, and should be affirmed.

* * *

Notes

1. What factors should the trial court consider in determining whether to defer sale of the family residence? In the case of In re Marriage of Duke, 101 Cal.App.3d 152, 161 Cal.Rptr. 444 (1980), the appellate court indicated that considerations in addition to economic circumstances may play a significant role:

> The value of a family home to its occupants cannot be measured solely by its value in the marketplace. The longer the occupancy, the more important these noneconomic factors become and the more traumatic and disruptive a move to a new environment is to children whose roots have become firmly entwined in the school and social milieu of their neighborhood. * * * [R]ecognition should be given to the emotional attachments of a custodial parent and children in weighing respective interests to determine the benefits to be attained in delaying the sale of the family home.

The current statute lists additional considerations, including the child's grade in school, the convenience of the house to the school, the continued employment of the resident parent, the tax consequences, and the economic detriment to the nonresident parent, together with "any other factors the court deems just and reasonable." West's Ann.California Family Code § 3802.

2. In addition to providing express statutory recognition of the "family home award," West's Ann.Cal. Family Code § 3807 provides a standard for the modification of such awards. Under prior law, unless the award was designated as additional child support (in which case it could be modified at any time by a showing of changed circumstances), the award would be modified only upon the occurrence of a specific contingency.

3. Prior case law and the original version of West's Ann.Cal. Family Code § 3800 authorized the use of the family home award only where there was a duty to support minor children, with sale of the family residence typically deferred until the youngest child reached majority. The family home award was not applied in cases involving adult disabled children. In re Marriage of Cooper, 170 Cal.App.3d 883, 216 Cal.Rptr. 611 (1985). The statute has since been broadened to include disabled adult children to whom a duty of support is owed because of their inability to maintain themselves by work. One question arising under the amendment is how long the sale should be deferred in such a case. The court in *Cooper* noted that there is a

substantial difference between the duty of support owed minor children and the support of a permanently disabled child. In the latter case, the parents may never be relieved of their support obligations. Does this mean that sale of the family residence should be deferred until the death of the adult child, who may well outlive his parents?

4. The rules concerning the deferment of sale of the family home generally developed in cases where the spouse seeking deferral was the custodial parent of minor children. Temporary use of the home was viewed as additional child support. Does the equal division requirement preclude this remedy as additional spousal support? In re Marriage of Horowitz, 159 Cal.App.3d 368, 205 Cal.Rptr. 874 (1984) suggests that the only justification for the family home award is child support, but compare In re Marriage of Hurtienne, 126 Cal.App.3d 374, 178 Cal.Rptr. 748 (1981). In *Hurtienne*, the trial court placed the family residence in tenancy in common, and granted the wife an option to purchase the husband's interest "payable in full without interest on or before September 1, 1981. The forebearance of immediate receipt of said sum by petitioner [husband], and the denial of interest on the deferred payment thereof, is ordered by way of additional spousal support payable by petitioner to respondent." On appeal, the husband argued that the delayed option given to the wife failed to take into account possible appreciation of the asset during the option period, and hence resulted in an unequal division of the community property. The appellate court disagreed, concluding that there was a sufficient economic interest involved (i.e., the husband's inability to pay spousal support because of his unemployment) to support this form of partial spousal support. See also, In re Marriage of Garcia, 224 Cal.App.3d 885, 274 Cal.Rptr. 194 (1990). By contrast, child support may not be utilized to work out an equal division of the community property. In re Marriage of Juick, 21 Cal.App.3d 421, 98 Cal.Rptr. 324 (1971).

5. Prior to the enactment of West's Ann.Cal. Family Code § 3800 et seq. the courts relied on the "single asset" proviso of Civil Code Section 4800 in making family home awards. See, e.g., In re Marriage of Boseman, 31 Cal.App.3d 372, 107 Cal.Rptr. 232 (1973). The "single asset" proviso has had other applications. The following excerpt is illustrative:

In re Marriage of Warren, 28 Cal.App.3d 777, 104 Cal.Rptr. 860 (1972)— "Appellant asserts that a certain community asset created by his loan of community funds to his brother '[b]ecause of its highly questionable * * * nature, * * * should be divided equally between the parties or entirely disregarded as an asset in the division of the community property by the court.' He contends the court's decision to award the debt to him constituted a violation of the equal division mandate * * *.

"Appellant loaned $34,000 of community funds to his brother and took a promissory note from him in that amount dated March 15, 1962. By December 20, 1963, the note was paid down to the sum of $14,761, and a new promissory note in the amount of the balance due was drawn, dated March 23, 1964, with no interest payable for one year and a due date of March 23, 1972. The notes contain no schedule for installment payments of principal or a standard default paragraph.

"Appellant contends that this debt should not be regarded as an asset because his brother has 'disappeared.' However, there is no indication in the record that appellant has made any effort whatever to collect the debt. Since the statute of limitations has not yet run, this debt is still an asset under the law.

"Civil Code section 4800, subdivision (b), subsection (1) [now Family Code Section 2601] provides:

'Where economic circumstances warrant, the court may award any asset to one party on such conditions as it deems proper to effect a substantially equal division of the property.'

In view of the nature of the loan transaction, and the appellant's relationship to the debtor, the assignment made of this asset was clearly within the court's statutory discretion. There is no requirement that each asset be divided but merely that there be a mathematical equality in which the court, in its discretion, may utilize the single asset provision under the Family Law Act. (In re Marriage of Juick, 21 Cal.App.3d 421, 428, 98 Cal.Rptr. 324.)"

IN RE MARRIAGE OF TAMMEN
California District Court of Appeal, 1976.
63 Cal.App.3d 927, 134 Cal.Rptr. 161.

ELKINGTON, ASSOCIATE JUSTICE.

The instant appeal is taken by Richard W. Tammen (hereafter for convenience, "Richard") from an interlocutory judgment of dissolution of his marriage to Elizabeth L. Tammen (hereafter for convenience, "Elizabeth"). The issues relate only to the division of the parties' community property.

The community property awarded Elizabeth approximated 79 percent of the whole. To equalize the division the judgment ordered Elizabeth to execute and deliver to Richard a promissory note for $19,820.80 bearing simple interest at 7 percent, secured by a second trust deed on the major item of community property, the family residence which had been awarded to her. The note's principal, and all interest to accrue thereon, were to be payable "upon the expiration of ten years from the date thereof, upon the wife's remarriage, the sale of said real property, voluntarily refinancing by her, upon her ceasing to use or occupy the same as a family residence, or upon her death, whichever event shall first occur."

Richard contends that this arrangement is inequitable and unfair, and that the value of the promissory note is far less than that of the offsetting $19,820.80 of community property taken by Elizabeth.

We find ourselves in agreement, and for the reasons we now state.

Civil Code section 4800, subdivision (a), provides that upon dissolution of a marriage, the court shall *"divide the community property * * * of the parties * * * equally."* (Emphasis added.) Under this statute "clearly the ideal is a mathematically equal division." (In re Marriage of Juick, 21 Cal.App.3d 421, 427, 98 Cal.Rptr. 324, 329.) And to assure such an equal division the trial court must make findings of fact as to the nature and value of the specific items of community property of the parties. (In re Marriage of Lopez, 38 Cal.App.3d 93, 107, 113 Cal.Rptr. 58.)

Civil Code section 4800, subdivision (b)(1), provides that:

"(b) Notwithstanding subdivision (a), the court may divide the community property and quasi-community property of the parties as follows: (1) Where economic circumstances warrant, the court may award any asset to one party on such conditions as it deems proper to effect a substantially equal division of the property."

Under this provision it is contemplated that where a major item of community property not reasonably subject to division is awarded one party, the other shall be compensated in some manner so as to maintain the required equal division.

In the case at bench Elizabeth was awarded community property, including the family home, as a result of which she received $19,820.80 more than an equal division. In order that the division be equalized according to Civil Code section 4800, it became necessary that the court attach a condition to that award in order "to effect a substantially equal division of the [community] property." The condition decided upon was the above-mentioned promissory note.

The issue presented to us is whether, as a matter of law, the promissory note was worth substantially less than its face value of $19,820.80.

The note was a promise to pay money at a future time, which promise was secured by a deed of trust on real estate. It was "essentially a security" (Bk. of America, etc. v. Bk. of Amador Co., 135 Cal.App. 714, 719, 28 P.2d 86), and as with securities generally it had a value. That value was its "market value" (Bagdasarian v. Gragnon, 31 Cal.2d 744, 752–753, 192 P.2d 935; Bullock's, Inc. v. Security–First Nat. Bk., 160 Cal.App.2d 277, 281–282, 325 P.2d 185), which means "the price or value of the article as established or shown by sales in the way of ordinary business" (Sackett v. Spindler, 248 Cal.App.2d 220, 236, 56 Cal.Rptr. 435, 445; S.P. Mill Co. v. Billiwhack etc. Farm, 50 Cal.App.2d 79, 88, 122 P.2d 650).

It is a matter of common knowledge, subject to the judicial notice of the superior, and this, court that deeds of trust are bought and sold in the course of ordinary business. (See Evid.Code, § 451, subd. (f).)

It is observed that the promissory note of the case at bench was secured by a second deed of trust subject to a first such lien for $18,497.12. Realization of the money was long deferred. Neither its interest nor principal was payable for 10 years, except upon the uncertain contingencies that have been pointed out. There were attending considerations of probable inflation upon the value of the security, as well as the need for its owner to be alert, and able, to protect it against foreclosure of the senior deed of trust, and perhaps tax and other liens.

We have, and we are furnished with, no certain information concerning the market value of such a promissory note. But its face value would most certainly be discounted by the inferiority of its security, the long and uncertain deferment of its enjoyment, the probable effect of inflation upon it, and the concerns of its ownership. We share the common knowledge, and accordingly take judicial notice (see Evid.Code, § 451, subd. (f)), that it would at least be substantially less than its face value.

It follows that the community property of the parties was not divided equally, according to the mandate of Civil Code section 4800.

* * *

The judgment is reversed, and the superior court will take further proceedings not inconsistent with our opinion.

MOLINARI, P.J. and WEINBERGER, J., concur.

Notes

1. The use of a note as an offset was rejected in In re Marriage of Herrmann, 84 Cal.App.3d 361, 148 Cal.Rptr. 550 (1978). There the trial court awarded the house and custody of the child to the wife and awarded the husband a note for half the equity in the house. The appellate court indicated that discounting the note was not an effective solution, and instead ordered the trial court to place the house in tenancy in common with various contingencies for sale and later division of the proceeds.

2. If a note is used to equalize the property division, it should provide that the entire balance becomes due and payable on certain events such as the borrower's death, or the sale or refinancing of the asset. See In re Marriage of Hopkins, 74 Cal.App.3d 591, 141 Cal.Rptr. 597 (1977).

IN RE MARRIAGE OF EASTIS
California District Court of Appeal, 1975.
47 Cal.App.3d 459, 120 Cal.Rptr. 861.

GARDNER, PRESIDING JUSTICE. After a childless marriage of 3 years' duration, wife filed an action for dissolution of the marriage and, after a contested trial, the court entered a judgment of dissolution.

The court found that the wife had waived spousal support. It further found that the parties had community assets totalling $5,250 and community liabilities of $6,450. The wife was awarded community assets valued at $3,500 and ordered to pay $1,000 in community obligations. Thus, the net assets awarded to the wife amounted to $2,500. The husband was awarded community assets valued at $1,750 and ordered to pay $5,450 of community obligations. This left the husband with a net deficit of $3,700.

Husband appeals from that portion of the interlocutory judgment dividing the community assets and obligations.

Rather obviously the court was in error in its division of the community property of the parties. Civil Code, § 4800 provides that the court shall divide the community property equally. California Rules of Court define property as including "assets and obligations" (California Rules of Court, Rule 1201(d)) and further provide that the court "shall ascertain the nature and extent of all assets and obligations subject to disposition by the court * * * and shall divide such assets and obligations as provided in the Family Law Act." (California Rules of Court, Rule 1242; In re Marriage of Knickerbocker, 43 Cal.App.3d 1039, 118 Cal.Rptr. 232; In re Marriage of Carter, 19 Cal.App.3d 479, 97 Cal.Rptr. 274.) This was not done in the instant case. The matter must be returned to the trial court in order to effect an equal division of the meager assets. Just how that is to be done we leave to the ingenuity of the trial judge.

However, whatever the trial judge does the parties are going to be left with unpaid obligations after the division of the assets.

We thus turn to a consistent and perplexing problem facing trial judges—just what to do about the division of debts and obligations where there are either (1) no assets, only obligations, or (2) obligations remaining after the division of the assets. This is a very common situation facing the trial courts which the authors of the Family Law Act apparently did not contemplate.

It is true that the Rules of Court define property as including assets and obligations. But, realistically, in the division of property, obligations come into the picture only when there exist assets against which the obligations can be set off. This is recognized in California Marital Termination Settlements (CEB, 1971), p. 67, " * * * equal division of community * * * property under CC § 4800, requires an allocation of obligations as well as assets to each party. The obligations to be allocated are those that could be enforced against one or more assets included in the division, either because the obligation is secured by an encumbrance on the asset or because the asset could be reached on execution if the obligation were reduced to judgment."

However, when there are no assets, only obligations, an entirely different picture is presented.

Here, the husband contends that following the general philosophy of equality between the spouses contained in the Family Law Act, these obligations should be divided equally. He reaches this conclusion by arguing that such obligations are community property, referring to them as "negative property." We think that this is carrying principles of sexual egalitarianism too far. Whatever one may think of the social philosophy underlying the Family Law Act, at this point the need for absolute equality between husband and wife vanishes and certain pragmatic considerations take over.

Obligations, standing by themselves, are not property. It is not necessary to go back to Blackstone or Beowulf to observe that property is something of value. A debt is not. At this point, we are not dividing property in the usual sense of the word, we are attempting a just disposition of the responsibility for debts, liabilities and obligations which by their very nature are the complete antithesis of assets or property. Common sense would indicate that we should look to the respective abilities of the parties to pay these obligations. Thus, if one of the spouses has an earning capacity of $1,000 per month and the other has an earning capacity of $500 per month, it would be patently unjust to order the parties to pay the community debts equally. There is nothing in the Family Law Act to the contrary.

We construe the proper rule to be that if there are no assets to divide, only obligations, or after the equal division of the assets there remain obligations to be disposed of, the court has the discretion to order the payment of such obligations in a manner that is just and equitable, depending upon the respective earning capacities of the spouses and other relevant factors. When there are no assets, common sense would indicate that equal distribution of the obligations is not mandated either by Civil Code, § 4800, or California Rules of Court, Rule 1242. The definition of property as "assets and obligations" cannot be tortured to mean simply "obligations."

Judgment reversed as to that portion of the judgment purporting to divide the community property of the parties.

* * *

Notes

1. West's Ann.Cal. Family Code § 2620 et seq. now specifies the method for confirmation and division of debts at dissolution. Debts incurred by either spouse before marriage shall be confirmed without offset to the spouse who incurred the debt. Debts incurred during marriage and prior to separation must be divided equally, but "[t]o the extent the community debts exceed total community and quasi-community assets, the excess of debt shall be assigned as the court deems just and equitable, taking into account factors such as the parties' relative ability to pay." West's Ann.Cal. Family Code § 2622(b). This latter clause appears to represent a codification of the *Eastis* holding.

2. In addition to pre-marriage obligations, West's Ann.Cal. Family Code §§ 2623, 2624, 2625 and 2627 exclude certain other types of debts from the equal division mandate by requiring that they be confirmed without offset to the incurring party. These obligations include (1) debts incurred during marriage that were not incurred for the benefit of the community; (2) debts incurred after separation for "non-necessaries;" (3) debts incurred after a judgment of dissolution or legal separation. The statute does not define the terms "non-necessaries" or "benefit of the community."

3. Although a spouse is generally not entitled to reimbursement for separate funds expended to meet community obligations [See v. See, 64 Cal.2d 778, 51 Cal.Rptr. 888, 415 P.2d 776 (1966)], the California Supreme Court has held that reimbursement may be appropriate where one spouse uses his or her post-separation earnings to pay family expenses. In re Marriage of Epstein, 24 Cal.3d 76, 154 Cal.Rptr. 413, 592 P.2d 1165 (1979). West's Ann.Cal. Family Code § 2626 now expressly authorizes the trial court

to order reimbursement in cases it deems appropriate for debts paid after separation but prior to trial.

C. Valuation

Unless the court can simply divide the community property assets in kind, awarding one-half to each party, it must make a determination as to the value of the property. The statute requires that the valuation of the assets and liabilities of the parties be determined as near as practicable to the time of trial, unless one party shows good cause why a different date for valuation should be used.[27] Value is defined as the fair market value of the property, and is a question of fact for the trial court.[28]

Some assets present little difficulty in valuation. For example the value of community property bank or savings and loan accounts can be ascertained simply by checking the balances on deposit as of the date of trial.[29] The value of stocks and bonds listed on a stock exchange can be determined by checking the listed closing price for the particular security as of the date of trial.[30] Other types of assets present complex valuation questions. The *Micalizio* case, reprinted below, is illustrative.

IN RE MARRIAGE OF MICALIZIO

Court of Appeal Fourth District, 1988.
199 Cal.App.3d 662, 245 Cal.Rptr. 673.

OPINION

DABNEY, ASSOCIATE JUSTICE.

FACTS AND PROCEDURAL HISTORY

Robert Micalizio (Robert) has been employed since 1960 for the J.R. Norton Company (Norton), a closely-held agricultural corporation. In June 1963, Robert purchased stock in Norton for $100,000 and financed the purchase by executing two promissory notes which called for 19 annual principal payments of $2,500 with balloon payments in the 20th year. Each note stated: "This note is secured by a pledge of shares of stock." Robert, however, retained custody of the share certificates, which were issued in his name alone.

Norton pays dividends only on its preferred stock, all of which is owned by J.R. Norton. The remainder, totalling 25 percent of all stock, is owned by Robert (15 percent) and three other vice-presidents (collectively 10 percent). After a corporate merger, the 150,000 Norton shares were reissued to Robert in January 1971. In March 1971, Robert executed a corporate buy-sell agreement which specified that the minority shareholders could not sell or transfer their stock to any third person without first offering to sell it to the corporation for the lower of the

---

27. West's Ann.Cal. Family Code § 2552.

28. 2 Markey, California Family Law Practice and Procedure (1982) § 24.41.

29. Id. at § 24.45. This assumes that there has been no commingling of community and separate funds.

30. Id.

book value of the stock adjusted annually on the basis of standard accounting principles, or the amount offered by any third person.

Robert and Gerry Micalizio (Gerry) were married in June 1971. During their marriage, Robert and Gerry separated and maintained separate households at least four times for periods of six months to three years. Gerry wrote checks from a community account to make the principal payments on Robert's promissory notes. In 1974, the buy-sell agreement was modified to change the formula for determining the price of the stock in the event of a sale to the corporation.

Robert filed a petition for dissolution in May 1981. The judgment as to marital status became final in December 1981, and the court reserved jurisdiction on all other issues. A one-day court trial was held on August 16, 1984. The evidence showed that the value of the stock under the buy-sell agreements was approximately $13 per share. The 1971 buy-sell agreement and the 1974 modification were introduced as exhibits. Roger Stevenson, the secretary-treasurer of Norton, testified that if Norton were to liquidate all of its assets, its stock would be worth $25 per share. Stevenson further testified as to the history, activities, and operations of Norton.

On November 30, 1984, the court filed its "Ruling After Court Trial", which stated that the Norton stock had not been transmuted from Robert's separate property to community property. However, the court ruled that the stock should be valued "on the pro-tanto basis, allocating a portion of the value at the date of trial to the community." The court found that there was no evidence of pre-marriage appreciation in the value of the stock and found that nine annual principal installments of $2,500 on Robert's promissory notes to the Nortons had been made by the community, for a total contribution of 22.5 percent of the purchase price of the stock, or the equivalent of 33,750 shares. The court assigned a value of $13.667 per share to the stock, but directed division of the community shares in kind. The Ruling After Court Trial was never entered in the judgment book.

In June 1984, the buy-sell agreement was again amended to provide, among other things, that Norton must consent to all stock transfers, assignments, or conveyances. In addition, the amended agreement provided more favorable terms for payment to the shareholder from the corporation for shares redeemed or purchased. Robert did not advise the court or Gerry of the amendment during the trial. After learning of the amendment when she sought to have Norton issue shares in her name, Gerry filed a motion based on Code of Civil Procedure sections 657 and 473 for new trial or to set aside for fraud. Gerry claimed that the newly-discovered amendment was oppressive to her and made her shares of Norton stock unsalable. She therefore requested the court to order Robert to pay her the value of the shares of stock.

Gerry filed an "amended" motion for new trial or to set aside for fraud on April 12, 1985, in which she requested the court to order Robert to pay her the value of the shares of stock, and to fix the value at the "fair market price" rather than the contractual buy-out price. Robert submitted declarations of Norton officials stating that: (1) Norton would issue shares of stock to Gerry without the restrictions of the June 1984 agreement, and (2) as of September 30, 1984, the book value of the stock had declined to $12.04 per share because of losses incurred in the lettuce crop.

The court heard the amended motion, and on June 13, 1985, filed its ruling. The court noted that because no judgment had been entered on its earlier ruling, it would treat the amended motion as one to reopen, to reconsider, or for further argument. The court stated that the June 1984 amendment made the stock valueless to Gerry, but did not address Robert's contention that the stock would be issued to Gerry without the restrictions of that amendment. The court reconsidered its earlier valuation of the stock at the buy-back price of $13.67 per share, and concluded that its "real value" was $25 per share. The court entered judgment on April 29, 1986, incorporating its June 13, 1985 ruling. The court ordered Robert to execute a promissory note to Gerry in the amount of $421,875, amortized over 10 years, at 10 percent interest to compensate Gerry for her interest in the stock.

* * *

The Trial Court's Valuation of the Stock Was Not Supported by Substantial Evidence

Under Civil Code section 4800, subdivision (a), [now Family Code Sections 2550 et seq.] to divide community property equally, the court must make specific findings concerning the nature and value of all community assets of the parties unless property is divided in kind. (*In re Marriage of Hewitson* (1983) 142 Cal.App.3d 874, 884, 191 Cal.Rptr. 392.) The trial court's determination of the value of a particular asset is a factual one which will be upheld on appeal if supported by substantial evidence in the record. (*Id.*, at p. 885, 191 Cal.Rptr. 392.)

The court fixed the value of the Norton stock at $25 per share. The court stated that it had considered all of the evidence bearing on the value of the stock, including "the $13.67 figure established under the old agreements," and "the $25.00 figure per Mr. Stevenson."[3] The court also considered other testimony of Mr. Stevenson about the size, volume, and extent of Norton's operations.

Robert contends that Mr. Stevenson's testimony was not evidence of the value of Robert's minority stock holdings subject to transfer restric-

---

3. The only testimony by Mr. Stevenson on the value of the Norton stock came into evidence in response to a hypothetical question at the start of his cross-examination, as follows:

"BY MR. BROWN:

"Q. What do you think that the real value per share of this company is today? Not its book value, but real value. If you

were to liquidate all of the assets in a reasonable amount of time, if you were to take the appreciation in the real estate?

"A. Twenty-five million.

"Q. How much would that be per share?

"A. Approximately $25 a share."

tions.   Rather, Mr. Stevenson simply expressed an opinion on a hypothetical situation bearing no relation to the facts, and was not asked to
consider liquidation costs, contingent liabilities, or similar factors.
When a trial court accepts an expert's ultimate conclusion without
critical consideration of his reasoning, and it appears that the conclusion
was based upon improper or unwarranted matters, then the judgment
must be reversed for lack of substantial evidence.   (*Pacific Gas &
Electric Co. v. Zuckerman* (1987) 189 Cal.App.3d, 1113, 1136, 234 Cal.
Rptr. 630.)   For example, in *Hewitson, supra,* 142 Cal.App.3d at pp. 885–
887, 191 Cal.Rptr. 392, an expert attempted to determine the value of a
closely held corporation by using the selling price/book value ratio of
publicly traded companies.   The appellate court held that because of
differences between the two types of companies, the analogy was improper and the judgment based upon the expert's testimony was not supported by substantial evidence.   Similarly, in *In re Marriage of Rives*
(1982) 130 Cal.App.3d 138, 149–151, 181 Cal.Rptr. 572, the appellate
court reversed valuation of a queen bee business because the trial court
accepted the testimony of an expert who relied upon false assumptions
and improper factors and failed to consider all of the relevant factors
which established value.   Here, likewise, Mr. Stevenson's testimony
relied on a false assumption and did not include all of the relevant
factors which establish the value of minority shares in a closely held
corporation.

The basic question for the court was the value of the shares of stock
held by the community at the time of trial.   In *Hewitson, supra,* 142
Cal.App.3d at pp. 882–883, 191 Cal.Rptr. 392, the court recognized that
the determination of the value of closely-held stock is a difficult legal
problem, and urged the trial court to use the factors listed in the
Internal Revenue Service's Revenue Ruling 59–60 (1959)–1 Cum.Bull.
237 in such determination, unless there is some statutory or decisional
proscription against their use.[4]   In *Hewitson,* the court was faced with
the valuation of a closely-held corporation wholly owned by the parties.
Here, in contrast, Robert owned a mere minority interest in a closely-
held corporation dominated by members of the Norton family.[5]   In a
closely-held corporation, *in the absence of other influencing or determin-*

4.   Those factors include:

"(a) The nature of the business and the history of the enterprise from its inception.

"(b) The economic outlook in general and the condition and outlook of the specific industry in particular.

"(c) The book value of the stock and the financial condition of the business.

"(d) The earning capacity of the company.

"(e) The dividend-paying capacity.

"(f) Whether or not the enterprise has goodwill or other intangible value.

"(g) Sales of stock and the size of the block of stock to be valued.

"(h) The market price of stocks of corporations engaged in the same or a similar line of business having their stocks actively traded in a free and open market, either on an exchange or over-the-counter."   (Revenue Ruling 59–60 (1959)–1 Cum.Bull. 237.)

5.   There was *no* evidence in the record to suggest that the shareholder's buy-sell agreements were collusive or that they had been entered to deprive the shareholders' spouses of community property rights.

ing factors, one method for determining the value of a share of stock is by ascertaining the net market value of the property which those shares represent and by assigning to each share its proportionate worth. (*Estate of Rowell* (1955) 132 Cal.App.2d 421, 429, 282 P.2d 163.) However, as the court explained in *Hewitson,* it is incumbent on a court faced with a valuation problem to consider *each* factor which might have a bearing on the value of the shares. (*Hewitson, supra,* 142 Cal.App.3d at p. 888, 191 Cal.Rptr. 392.)

The court listed the factors which it considered in fixing the value of the stock, but did not consider either that Robert owned only a minority block of shares, or that Robert was restricted both as to the price he could obtain for his shares and as to his ability to sell them. Those restrictive agreements and the size of Robert's holdings were factors which have a bearing on the value of the shares. Section 8 of Revenue Ruling 59–60 directs consideration of agreements restricting the sale or transfer of stock. See, e.g. *Estate of Seltzer* (TC Memo 1985–519 (P–H Para. 85, 519) [When a shareholder died, her shares were sold to the corporation at the value specified in the shareholders' buy-sell agreement. The trial court held that the value under that agreement was controlling. The court explained that inasmuch as the estate was bound by the agreement, the estate's interest in the stock was by contract limited to the book value of the stock].) Moreover Revenue Ruling 59–60 directs consideration of the size of the block of stock. The comments in Revenue Ruling 59–60 state that a minority interest in an unlisted corporation's stock is more difficult to sell than a similar block of listed stock.

This court has also required consideration of restrictive agreements when valuing stock in a closely-held corporation. (*In re Marriage of Rosan* (1972) 24 Cal.App.3d 885, 101 Cal.Rptr. 295.) In *Rosan,* the husband owned 15 percent of the stock in Hudson Jewelers. An agreement between the husband and the majority shareholder provided that the husband's shares could not be sold or transferred to anyone other than the corporation or the other shareholder without prior written consent. The other shareholder could purchase such shares for the lower of their "computed value" or the price offered by a third party. "Computed value" was to be determined by a formula based primarily on the book asset value of the stock. Moreover, if the husband quit or was terminated for cause, the other shareholder could purchase the husband's stock for 70 percent of its "computed value." The trial court fixed the value of the stock for purposes of a community property division at 70 percent of its "computed value."

The wife argued that the trial court erred, first by failing to include goodwill, and second, by not valuing the stock at the entire "computed value." With respect to the first contention, this court stated that there was no evidence that the corporation planned a merger, and in the absence of such plan, the corporation or the other shareholder had the right to purchase the stock for the "computed value" if the husband offered it for sale, regardless of the existence of goodwill. (*Id.*, at p. 890, 101 Cal.Rptr. 295.)

With respect to the second contention, the court noted that for the husband to realize the full "computed value," he would have to die, become permanently disabled, be discharged from his employment without cause, or be offered at least that amount by a third person. The court stated: "An offer from a third person to purchase a minority interest in a closely held corporation paying no dividends for full 'computed value' would be an unlikely prospect," and the husband's death, disability or discharge without cause was also unlikely. (*Ibid.*)

The court concluded: "Under the circumstances disclosed by the evidence, and particularly in view of the restrictive conditions on the disposition of the stock and its resulting illiquidity, factors substantially affecting its value, the trial court was justified in assessing the value of the stock at 70 percent of its 'computed value.' Although that was its lowest value except in the event of a sale to a third person for less, it was the only value that was relatively certain." (*Id.*, at p. 891, 101 Cal.Rptr. 295.)

The Supreme Court in *In re Marriage of Fonstein* (1976) 17 Cal.3d 738, 131 Cal.Rptr. 873, 552 P.2d 1169 approved a similar approach in a valuation problem. The husband argued that his interest in a law partnership was valueless because it was contingent on his decision to withdraw and subject to modification by agreement of his partners. The court observed that the asset being divided was the interest in the partnership, not the contractual right to withdraw. However, the court explicitly approved the trial court's valuation based on the value of the right to withdraw from the firm as provided in the partnership agreement, and rejected the wife's argument that the value should be based on a percentage of partnership assets. (*Id.*, at pp. 745–747, 131 Cal. Rptr. 873, 552 P.2d 1169.)

Gerry's counsel ignores *Fonstein* and *Rosan*, and instead cites *In re Marriage of Fenton* (1982) 134 Cal.App.3d 451, 184 Cal.Rptr. 597 and *In re Marriage of Slater* (1979) 100 Cal.App.3d 241, 160 Cal.Rptr. 686, which involved the issue of evaluating the goodwill in professional practice, in light of the rule that "[W]here the issue is raised in a marital dissolution action, the trial court must make a specific finding as to the existence and value of the 'goodwill' of a professional business as a going concern whether related to that of a sole practitioner, a professional partnership or a professional corporation." (*In re Marriage of Lopez* (1974) 38 Cal.App.3d 93, 109, 113 Cal.Rptr. 58.) Although the courts in *Fenton* and *Slater* did not rely on the restrictive terms of partnership and stock purchase contracts when making required findings of the value of goodwill in professional practices, those decisions do not provide guidance on the issue of valuing a minority block of stock in a closely-held corporation.

We conclude that there was no substantial evidence to support the trial court's determination that the value of the Norton stock was $25 per share, and the judgment must be reversed.

* * *

DISPOSITION

The judgment is reversed. The trial court is directed to consider whether the community stock should be divided in kind under the principles set forth in *Connolly, supra,* 23 Cal.3d 590, 153 Cal.Rptr. 423, 591 P.2d 911 and *Lotz, supra,* 120 Cal.App.3d 379, 174 Cal.Rptr. 618. If the court determines that an in-kind division is not appropriate, the court is directed to determine the value of the stock in light of the principles set forth in *Hewitson, supra,* 142 Cal.App.3d 874, 191 Cal. Rptr. 392, 142 Cal.App.3d 874 and *Rosan, supra,* 24 Cal.App.3d 885, 101 Cal.Rptr. 295.

CAMPBELL, P.J., and McDANIEL, J., concur.

D. *Tax Consequences of Division*

The dissolution of a marriage and the attendant division of property are likely to trigger significant tax problems. For example, two items of community property may be of substantially equal value at the time of trial, but one may be a "high basis" asset and the other a "low basis" asset. The party receiving the low basis asset may incur substantial capital gains tax liability when and if that asset is sold. To what extent should the court consider such tax consequences in effecting an equal division of the community?

With regard to the property division itself, it has long been established that the equal division of community property between the spouses at dissolution is not a taxable event. As a practical matter, however, many community estates are not amenable to equal division without the addition of equalizing assets, such as a promissory note. Under prior law, if the equalizing assets involved separate property, a taxable transfer was deemed to have occurred.[31] This rule was changed by the Tax Reform Act of 1984. Under the current tax law, no gain or loss is recognized on a transfer of property between spouses (or between former spouses if the transfer was incident to the divorce).[32] For income tax purposes, the recipient is treated as if the property were acquired by gift, so that the basis of the transferee is the same as it was in the hands of the transferor.[33]

Finally, some mention should be made of the tax consequences of spousal and child support provisions. Spousal support payments should be carefully distinguished from payments made pursuant to a division of

31. See Carrieres v. Commissioner of Internal Revenue, 64 T.C. 959, affirmed 552 F.2d 1350 (9th Cir.1977).

32. Internal Revenue Code § 1041(a). A transfer is incident to the divorce if it

occurs within one year after the date of the divorce or is related to the cessation of the marriage.

33. Internal Revenue Code § 1041(b).

property. Periodic spousal support payments are generally deductible by the payor and taxable as income to the payee.[34] Payments made in discharge of property rights are not so treated. Child support payments should also be distinguished from spousal support. Child support payments are not deductible by the payor nor are they taxable to the person having custody of the child.[35]

IN RE MARRIAGE OF HARRINGTON

Court of Appeal, Second District, 1992.
6 Cal.App.4th 1847, 8 Cal.Rptr.2d 631.

GILBERT, ASSOCIATE JUSTICE.

Husband and wife dissolve their marriage. They sell their home at a profit and divide the proceeds. The capital gains taxes due from the profits are not the same for each party. Under the facts here we hold that each party alone is liable for his or her capital gains taxes.

Wife Judith W. Harrington appeals an order denying her motion that husband Ronald G. Harrington pay one-half of the capital gains taxes recognized upon her share of profits realized from the sale of the family residence. The trial court properly decided each party alone was liable for capital gains taxes due upon his or her share of the profits. We affirm.

FACTS

On January 5, 1988, Judith W. Harrington brought a petition to dissolve her nearly 25–year marriage to Ronald G. Harrington. Six months later, the Harringtons sold the family residence and realized a profit of $480,000. Husband and wife divided the $480,000 profit equally. Husband, a lawyer, then used part of his proceeds to purchase wife's community property interest in his law firm and to pay wife for her waiver of spousal support.[1]

In court proceedings husband declared he and wife orally agreed that each of them alone would be liable for any capital gains income taxes resulting from his or her equal share of the $480,000 profit. (Int.Rev.Code, §§ 1001, 1221; Rev. & Tax.Code, § 18031.) Husband stated he and wife discussed the subject often. Husband offered his legal expertise to suggest ways in which wife could defer recognition of capital gains taxes upon her share of the proceeds. The family accoun-

---

34. Internal Revenue Code §§ 71, 215. This rule obtains only if the spousal support payments come within the Internal Revenue Code's definition of "alimony or separate maintenance payment."

35. Internal Revenue Code § 71(c). Internal Revenue Code § 71(f) restricts the extent to which alimony can be concentrated in the first two years following the divorce. These provisions against "front loading" are intended to prevent the parties

in a dissolution proceeding from structuring a property settlement so that it will qualify as alimony.

1. For tax purposes, sale of the home yielded a "profit" of $480,000. Actual cash distributed to the Harringtons approximated $300,000. Apparently the remaining $180,000 was used to pay lenders, transactional costs or other debts.

tant also declared that wife acknowledged her capital gains tax obligation concerning one-half of the $480,000, or $240,000.

In contrast, wife declared she and husband had no oral agreement concerning responsibility for the capital gains taxes. Although she stated that she and husband frequently discussed methods to defer recognition of taxes, "[she] never made any agreement whatsoever [to] pay any particular portion of [the] taxes...."

The parties' written marital settlement agreement stated that "[t]he Court shall retain jurisdiction over the 1988 [tax] returns and all other jointly filed returns." It said nothing about liability for capital gains taxes.

Within two years of the sale of the family home, husband acquired a replacement residence in Ventura for $251,250. By so doing, he successfully deferred recognition of capital gains tax on the $240,000 profit he realized from sale of the family residence. (Int.Rev.Code, § 1034, subd. (a); Rev. & Tax.Code, § 18031.)

Within the same two years, wife purchased a condominium in Chicago for $120,000 and invested $5,000 in condominium improvements. She thus deferred recognition of capital gains tax on only $125,000 of the $240,000 profit she realized from sale of the family home. Wife incurred a capital gains tax of $52,000, reportable and due upon husband and wife's joint 1988 federal and state tax returns.

Wife sought an order in the trial court requiring husband to pay one-half of the $52,000 capital gains taxes then due. In support of her order, wife declared she had changed occupations and was not yet self-supporting. After moving to Chicago, she abandoned her profession as a schoolteacher due to her fears for her personal safety in the schools. Her current occupation, a personnel consultant, had not afforded her any commissions after 10 months' labors. Wife stated she used her share of the community property proceeds to support herself and could not pay the mortgage payments on a more expensive residence.

The trial court denied wife's motion and found husband and wife had an agreement that each alone would be liable for any capital gains income taxes recognized after division of the community property. The court also determined husband and wife should bear the tax burdens equally, any agreement aside. Wife's appeal followed.

On appeal wife argues 1) equal division of the community liabilities requires husband to pay one-half of the $52,000 capital gains taxes, and 2) enforcement of any oral agreement between them violates Civil Code section 4800, *In re Marriage of Maricle* (1990) 220 Cal.App.3d 55, 57–58, 269 Cal.Rptr. 204, and Code of Civil Procedure section 664.6.

DISCUSSION

I.

Wife contends an equal division of the assets and liabilities of the community property * * * compels equal liability for capital gains income taxes when those taxes are recognized. She argues the taxes arose because a community asset appreciated during marriage, and therefore tax liability must be shared equally. She claims burdening her with 100 percent of the $52,000 tax penalizes her for her inability to earn as much income as husband. Wife asserts she has acted responsibly and prudently in investing in a relatively inexpensive condominium to save the remainder of her separate property for her present support and future retirement.

Federal and state tax laws treat residential real property as a capital asset, yielding a taxable capital gain or profit upon sale. (Int.Rev.Code, §§ 1001, 1221; Rev. & Tax.Code, § 18031.) The tax laws also permit a postponement or deferral of income taxes upon the taxable gain if the selling taxpayer purchases, within two years of sale of the old residence, a new residence for an amount at least equal to the "adjusted sales price" of the old residence. (Int.Rev.Code, § 1034, subd. (a); Rev. & Tax.Code, § 18031.)

These deferral or postponement provisions of the federal and state tax laws obviously make it impossible to gauge what the ultimate tax gain liability will be. (*In re Marriage of Epstein* (1979) 24 Cal.3d 76, 88, 154 Cal.Rptr. 413, 592 P.2d 1165.) With successive purchase and sale of replacement residences by the taxpayer, the capital gains income taxes may be postponed for an indeterminate period of time. The trial court can not realistically apportion tax liability because of the uncertainty as to what the ultimate tax burden will be. (*Id.,* p. 88, fn. 10, 154 Cal.Rptr. 413, 592 P.2d 1165.)

Civil Code section 4800, subdivision (a) [now see Family Code Sections 2550 et seq.] requires the trial court, in dividing community assets and liabilities upon dissolution, to distribute the assets so that each party receives an equal share after deduction of community liabilities. (*In re Marriage of Fonstein* (1976) 17 Cal.3d 738, 748, 131 Cal.Rptr. 873, 552 P.2d 1169.) Once having divided the community property equally, the court is not required to speculate concerning what either party may do with his or her share, thereby incurring recognition of tax liability. (*Id.,* p. 749, 131 Cal.Rptr. 873, 552 P.2d 1169.) Whether either party could defer capital gains taxes depends upon factors unrelated to the equal division of community property. (*In re Marriage of Davies* (1983) 143 Cal.App.3d 851, 857–858, 192 Cal.Rptr. 212.) These factors include individual income two years later, individual savings, receipt of gifts or inheritance, ability to borrow money, and other circumstances not pertinent to the division of community property. (*Id.,* p. 858, 192 Cal.Rptr. 212.)

Here a taxable event—sale of residential real property—occurred during dissolution proceedings. Each party is equally liable for any income taxes incurred on his or her capital gain. The trial court was not required to account for the possibility that either spouse may or may not be able to postpone recognition of capital gains taxes by purchasing a replacement residence within two years. (*In re Marriage of Epstein, supra,* 24 Cal.3d 76, 88, fn. 10, 154 Cal.Rptr. 413, 592 P.2d 1165.) Neither is it appropriate for the trial court to retain jurisdiction to consider apportionment of tax liabilities when any capital gains taxes become recognized. (*In re Marriage of Davies, supra,* 143 Cal.App.3d 851, 858, 192 Cal.Rptr. 212.) The court's jurisdiction can not continue on and on into the indefinite future.

Wife mistakenly relies upon *In re Marriage of Epstein, supra,* 24 Cal.3d 76, 154 Cal.Rptr. 413, 592 P.2d 1165, *In re Marriage of Davies, supra,* 143 Cal.App.3d 851, 192 Cal.Rptr. 212, and *In re Marriage of Clark* (1978) 80 Cal.App.3d 417, 145 Cal.Rptr. 602. Those decisions concerned unequal distribution of proceeds from the sale of a community asset in order to equalize the uneven division of other community assets. Under those circumstances, each party is responsible for one-half of the capital gains taxes incurred by the sale, regardless of the party's share of the sale proceeds. (*In re Marriage of Davies, supra,* 143 Cal.App.3d at pp. 856–857, 192 Cal.Rptr. 212.) Although husband used some of the proceeds arising from sale of the family residence here to buy wife's community property interest in his law firm and her waiver of spousal support, husband has not requested apportionment of his tax liability, if any.

II.

Because the trial court's order imposing tax liability upon each party for his or her share of the capital gain was proper as a matter of law, we do not consider whether husband and wife had a valid oral agreement to apportion tax liability. If any applicable ground supports the trial court's order, the reviewing court will affirm the judgment. (*In re Marriage of Jacobs* (1982) 128 Cal.App.3d 273, 284, 180 Cal.Rptr. 234.)

Accordingly, the judgment is affirmed. Wife is to bear costs on appeal.

STEVEN J. STONE, P.J., and YEGAN, J., concur.

SECTION 3. POST DISSOLUTION REMEDIES

Suppose that after a judgment of dissolution has been entered and the time for appeal has expired, one of the parties discovers that a significant community asset had been concealed by the other party or had been inadvertently overlooked or omitted. This section explores the remedies available to the party in such a situation.

There is a strong public policy in favor of the finality of judgments and putting an end to litigation. There is also, however, a strong public policy against fraud. The courts have generally held that relief will be granted for extrinsic fraud, but not for intrinsic fraud.[36] The *Stevenot* case, reprinted in this section, illustrates the tension produced by these

36. See, e.g., Kulchar v. Kulchar, 1 Cal.3d 467, 82 Cal.Rptr. 489, 462 P.2d 17 (1969).

conflicting policies and the difficulties inherent in the extrinsic-intrinsic fraud distinction.

Another issue that has given rise to considerable litigation involves the omission of items of property due to inadvertence, negligence, or a misunderstanding of or uncertainty in the law. What is the effect of a dissolution judgment settling the parties' respective community property rights? Is it a conclusive determination of the identification of community property assets and the parties' interests therein, or is it only a determination of the parties' rights in property specifically before the court? California appellate courts took differing approaches to this problem. Some took a broad view of the property issue, holding that the trial court's judgment was a final determination of the extent of the community property estate, and could not be set aside in the absence of extrinsic fraud or mistake.[37] Others took a more restricted approach, finding that the judgment was binding only as to property before the court and was not a determination of the extent of the community property.[38] The Supreme Court undertook to resolve this conflict in the *Henn* case, reprinted in this section.

A. *Relief From Fraud*

IN RE MARRIAGE OF STEVENOT

California District Court of Appeal, 1984.
154 Cal.App.3d 1051, 202 Cal.Rptr. 116.

KING, ASSOCIATE JUSTICE:

In this case we explore the most repetitively troublesome issue in the family law field over the last 40 years, the issue of what constitutes extrinsic fraud justifying the setting aside of a judgment and marital settlement agreement in a family law action, and what constitutes intrinsic fraud and thus is insufficient to achieve this result. We analyze this issue mindful of changing times and the changing relationships between spouses, including overdue legislative recognition of such changes by eliminating the longstanding statutory mandate that the husband is the manager of the community property, and replacing it by providing effective January 1, 1975, that the parties have equal rights of management and control of the community.[1] Here, Richard G. Stevenot appeals from an order granting Pamela D. Stevenot's motion to set aside her default entered November 2, 1981, and the interlocutory judgment of dissolution of their marriage entered January 4, 1983, based upon the trial court's finding of extrinsic fraud. Pamela's motion did not seek to set aside the marital settlement agreement executed by the parties, which was incorporated into the interlocutory judgment, and the court specifically refrained from acting on this issue.

---

37. See, e.g., Kelley v. Kelley, 73 Cal. App.3d 672, 141 Cal.Rptr. 33 (1977).

38. See, e.g., Gorman v. Gorman, 90 Cal.App.3d 454, 153 Cal.Rptr. 479 (1979).

1. See Civil Code sections 5125, 5127.

Richard was a 49–year–old engineer. Pamela, 26 years old, had completed high school and was employed as a waitress. Richard filed his petition for dissolution of marriage in propria persona on August 10, 1981, alleging a five-year marriage [2] and no assets or obligations subject to disposition by the court as community or quasi community property.

Pamela was served with the summons and petition for dissolution on August 14, 1981, and executed a written acknowledgment of receipt thereof on the same date. Her default was entered November 2, 1981, after service upon her of a copy of the request to enter default. Richard obtained a default interlocutory judgment of dissolution of marriage by declaration on January 4, 1983, pursuant to Civil Code section 4511 and California Rules of Court, rules 1241 and 1286.5. The interlocutory judgment incorporated the marital settlement agreement of the parties dated July 8, 1981, as well as two one-page addenda executed September 18, 1982, and December 16, 1982. The marital settlement agreement provided Richard would make specified cash payments to Pamela, transferred specific property to each of the parties as their separate property, made provision for payment of specified debts, included a waiver by Pamela of any interest she had in Richard's pension plan with his employer, provided for the distribution of any tax refunds and contained the following statement: "Each party has made a full disclosure to the other of his current finances and assets [sic], and each enters into this agreement and relies thereon." The September addendum acknowledged Pamela's receipt of cash payments from Richard and an adjustment of the payments due under the marital settlement agreement, while the December addendum acknowledged that all payments to Pamela had been made.

On January 11, 1983, Pamela filed a motion to set aside her default and the interlocutory judgment. Attached to her motion was her supporting declaration stating that, with the exception of four months, she had lived with Richard since she was 19 years old, and "[d]uring the entire relationship, [Richard] had always been very intimidating, bossy, and had complete control of all aspects of [their] relationship, including the finances, running the property, and ownership of property." The declaration set forth the community assets of which Pamela was aware, and stated that in August 1981, when their relationship had deteriorated, Richard became very threatening: "He stated that he was going to go ahead and do the paperwork for the divorce, that he would give me $5,000 and some miscellaneous furniture and my vehicle, that I would not get anything more by going to court, and that there was no use going to a lawyer, since they would charge more than the value of the property I would get in any settlement." Pamela then described threats allegedly made by Richard, and stated "[b]ecause of these threats and the dominating relationship of [Richard] over me, I was intimidated, frightened, and afraid to discuss any of this with my family." She declared that

---

2. The parties were married three years. Richard's mathematical error apparently resulted from the fact that the parties had lived together for two years prior to their marriage.

Richard presented her with a separation agreement, which she signed and has not seen since, and a deed to their community property home. After signing the agreement and deed, she moved out. Four months later, when she was unable to "make it on her own financially," Richard allowed her to move back into the residence. "Although we did not continue our husband and wife relationship, the intimidation and overbearing attitude * * * continued. During this period, I asked him about the divorce proceedings, and he always gave me an evasive answer." She alleged that when she received the dissolution petition, she did not realize its legal significance as to property. She alleged she did not take action on the petition because she was in a state of fear from Richard's threats. In December 1982 she finally talked to her family about the divorce proceedings; they advised her to get a lawyer, she did, and the motion to set aside was filed. She requested in her motion that "the default be set aside so that the issues of spousal support, property division, and attorneys' fees could be determined."

In response to the motion, Richard filed a declaration denying Pamela's allegations with respect to his threatening conduct; he declared he suggested she speak to an attorney "regarding the divorce;" and he acknowledged that during the marriage he had control of the couple's "finances and property, the reason being not that I wanted to dominate that aspect of our marriage or dominate [Pamela], but rather, because [Pamela] was totally incapable and immature in handling such matters." He declared that he had never told Pamela not to seek the advice of an attorney; he had never prevented her from filing a response to the petition; and he did not "in any way hinder the exercise of her legal rights with respect to these proceedings or to be heard in court." He stated that the delay in obtaining the interlocutory judgment and final judgment resulted from his inexperience, since he appeared in propria persona, and from the clerk's office losing or otherwise misplacing his paperwork.

Pamela's motion was heard on February 1, 1983, with both parties present in court and represented by counsel. The parties were sworn and stated that their declarations filed with the court were true and correct. The remainder of the hearing consisted of offers of proof by counsel of matters not in the declarations, and of argument.[3] Pamela's

---

3. Judges assigned the hearing of domestic relations law and motion calendars in busy metropolitan courts must hear and decide a staggering number of cases while conducting the calendar in such a way that the parties and their counsel have a full and fair hearing. To accomplish this nearly impossible task, trial judges must adopt processes which expedite the hearing of motions and orders to show cause in domestic relations cases, one of the most important and sensitive tasks a judge faces. (See *In re Marriage of Brantner* (1977) 67 Cal.App.3d 416, 422, 136 Cal.Rptr. 635.)

Although trial judges, in the sound exercise of their discretion, may determine motions or orders to show cause (except for contempt) upon declarations alone and refuse to permit oral testimony pursuant to *Reifler v. Superior Court* (1974) 39 Cal. App.3d 479, 114 Cal.Rptr. 356, we believe a preferable procedure is that which the trial judge utilized here. Having fully reviewed the moving and responding papers prior to the hearing, Judge Edwards allowed counsel to make offers of proof of matters not in the declarations, made inquiries of the parties and counsel as necessary to gain infor-

counsel offered her testimony and that of her father and two sisters with respect to Richard's alleged threats, his answers in response to the status of the dissolution, his furnishing dissolution papers, and the status of the dissolution proceedings. Richard's counsel made offers of proof with respect to the status of property, its value, and discussions of the property by the parties and with respect to furnishing Pamela copies of divorce papers. The trial court, a particularly learned and knowledgeable family law judge, took a recess to carry out independent research on the legal issue of whether the facts constituted extrinsic or intrinsic fraud. Upon his return to the courtroom, the trial court gave the parties a very thoughtful and complete oral statement of decision in which he granted Pamela's motion.[4]

mation he needed to make his decision, and permitted counsel to argue their positions.

We fully approve this procedure because it expedites the hearing of a heavy domestic relations calendar, provides for a more pleasant, less formal, nonadversary atmosphere, and sets a tone much more likely to enable future settlement of litigation. Additionally, without expending the precious time which would be consumed by a more traditional question and answer type of heated adversary hearing, it permits the trial judge, the only one of the courtroom who knows what information in addition to the declarations is required to reach a decision, to quickly obtain information by inquiries to the parties and their counsel.

4. The court stated:

"I am going to grant the motion to set aside the default and the interlocutory decree. I am not ruling on the validity of the marital settlement agreement, but I think that the marital settlement agreement will be litigated at some point, and the result of that may be in fact what the current—that is, the state of affairs was before this proceeding started. * * * But what I am saying is that based on the facts before me, I think there should be a day in court to test that out. And so what I am doing is setting aside the default, setting aside the interlocutory decree, and I am giving you 15 days on behalf of your client to file a response in this case, and the matter will proceed thereafter as a normal dissolution. * * * I, however, have found that the way the proceedings went, it is sufficient evidence for me to believe that Mrs. Stevenot did not have full knowledge of the marital proceedings. Nothing I say has anything to do with her knowledge of what the content of the marital settlement agreement was because I really don't think that I am focusing upon that. I am focusing on the process of the dissolution, that she did not have full knowledge of

those proceedings and may well have been misled in understanding what those proceedings were, and I find she was misled to a sufficient extent for me to find that equitable relief will lie in this case.

"I find she did not take action in this proceeding to answer and to respond, that is, because she did not believe that there was anything that she could do, and that in fact she believed there were either no rights to protect or no assets she could gain by taking legal action. That is sufficient based on my reading of Adkins, Brennan, and the case of *In re Marriage of Coffee* [sic] at 63 Cal.App.3d 139 [133 Cal.Rptr. 583], just cited in Markey for the Court to support a finding of extrinsic fraud, grant the equitable relief, find that no laches existed because there was no reason for Mrs. Stevenot to take action until she learned that in fact she had rights and it is, to quote the language of the *Jorgenson case,* which is at 32 Cal.2d 13 [193 P.2d 728], 1948, 'One manner in which a court may test whether fraud or mistake may be characterized as intrinsic or extrinsic, if the party defrauded 'has received information or facts which should put him on inquiry and the inquiry, if made, would disclose the fraud.' I don't find that Mrs. Stevenot was put on inquiry until she in fact had talked to an attorney about this because she believed until that time that in fact there was no rights or no asset that she would have legal rights to."

Counsel for Richard asked the court whether it found that Pamela had no knowledge of the proceedings. The court replied: "No. No, I didn't say that she had no knowledge of her rights. She was deceived as to the fact that she had rights and that a legal proceeding would benefit her in any way based on the statement to her by her husband, not that she had no knowl-

As might be expected in this appeal, Richard denies any fraud and contends that if any fraud occurred, it was intrinsic fraud and the judgment should not have been set aside, while Pamela contends there was extrinsic fraud and the ruling of the trial court was correct.

For the past 40 years, no family law issue has so regularly captured the attention of the California Supreme Court as has the issue of what constitutes extrinsic and intrinsic fraud. The Courts of Appeal have regularly wrestled with this problem during the same period, and it is likely that hundreds, if not thousands, of such cases have been decided by trial courts during the same period with no appeals having been filed. In 1933, our Supreme Court noted, "The distinction between intrinsic and extrinsic fraud is quite nebulous * * *" (*Caldwell v. Taylor* (1933) 218 Cal. 471, 479, 23 P.2d 758.) More recently, one court correctly commented that, "the distinctions between extrinsic and intrinsic fraud are hopelessly blurred. Nonetheless, the California courts have remained married to the importance of the distinction whether or not and in fact it exists." (*In re Marriage of Guardino* (1979) 95 Cal.App.3d 77, 89, 156 Cal.Rptr. 883.) "The viability of the extrinsic-intrinsic distinction has been undermined further by its inconsistent application. While the courts purport to rely on the extrinsic-intrinsic distinction, an examination of California decisions indicates a strong emphasis on the presence or absence of equitable considerations in granting relief. While a party's entitlement to equitable relief depends upon the court's classification of the fraud involved, such inconsistency provides little indication of the likelihood of success under the particular factual circumstances." (Comment, *Seeking More Equitable Relief from Fraudulent Judgments: Abolishing the Extrinsic–Intrinsic Distinction* (1981) 12 Pacific L.J. 1013–1014.) It would appear to some that "the courts are more influenced by the presence or absence of equitable factors than by the type of fraud committed." (*Id.,* at p. 1029.)

Considering the attention this subject has been given by appellate court opinions in California, and the frequency with which it arises, the trial bench and the family law bar are entitled to be guided by more definitive rules in determining whether extrinsic fraud exists to set aside final judgments incorporating marital settlement agreements. In order to provide more guidance, and for the purpose of reaching a decision in the instant case, it is appropriate to first review the decisions of our Supreme Court on this subject.

The primary architect of California's law on the extrinsic-intrinsic fraud issue in family law cases has been one of its judicial superstars, Justice Roger Traynor. Over 40 years ago, Justice Traynor wrote, "The final judgment of a court having jurisdiction over persons and subject

edge of the legal proceedings. But, as I say, and I think my first statement is really the most important about this, while this will result in further legal action, I have not ruled on the marital settlement agreement. And the marital settlement agreement may be determinative on your client's part of all of the rights of the parties. I just find that given the process that has taken place up to now, the marital proceeding is one that I think should be set aside by my equitable powers."

matter can be attacked in equity after the time for appeal or other direct attack has expired only if the alleged fraud or mistake is extrinsic rather than intrinsic [citations]. Fraud or mistake is extrinsic when it deprives the unsuccessful party of an opportunity to present his case to the court [citations]. If an unsuccessful party to an action has been kept in ignorance thereof [citations] or has been prevented from fully participating therein [citation], there has been no true adversary proceeding, and the judgment is open to attack at any time. A party who has been given proper notice of an action, however, and who has not been prevented from full participation therein, has had an opportunity to present his case to the court and to protect himself from any fraud attempted by his adversary. [Citations] Fraud perpetrated under such circumstances is intrinsic, * * *'' (*Westphal v. Westphal* (1942) 20 Cal.2d 393, 397, 126 P.2d 105, citing in part to *United States v. Throckmorton* (1878) 98 U.S. 61, 25 L.Ed. 93 and *Caldwell v. Taylor* (1933) 218 Cal. 471, 23 P.2d 758.)

Six years later Justice Traynor pointed out, "[t]he terms 'intrinsic' and 'extrinsic' fraud or mistake * * * do not constitute, however, a simple and infallible formula * * * [Citations.] It is necessary to examine the facts in the light of the policy that a party who failed to assemble all his evidence at the trial should not be privileged to relitigate a case, as well as the policy permitting a party to seek relief from a judgment entered in a proceeding in which he was deprived of a fair opportunity fully to present his case. [¶] The latter policy applies when a party's adversary, in violation of a duty arising from a trust or confidential relation, has concealed from him facts essential to the protection of his rights, even though such facts concerned issues involved in the case in which the judgment was entered. * * * [¶] The same principle also applies in the cases concerning equitable relief from judgments approving and adopting property settlement agreements * * *.'' (*Jorgensen v. Jorgensen* (1948) 32 Cal.2d 13, 19–20, 193 P.2d 728.) In *Jorgensen*, Justice Traynor recognized that the public policy underlying the principle of res judicata, that there should be an end to litigation when a valid judgment has become final, must be balanced against the public policy that a party should not be deprived of a fair adversary proceeding in which to present fully his or her case. (*Id.*, at p. 18, 193 P.2d 728.)

In *Jorgensen*, the parties, each represented by counsel, entered into a marital settlement agreement. Mrs. Jorgensen later moved to set aside a default interlocutory judgment incorporating the marital settlement agreement, contending certain assets listed therein as her husband's separate property were in fact community property, and contending extrinsic fraud had occurred because she and her attorney had relied on the husband's representations. Justice Traynor explained that the husband, as the statutory manager of community property under then Civil Code sections 172, 173, and 158, occupied a position of trust and had a fiduciary duty to account to his wife for the community property when the parties were negotiating a property settlement agreement, and further pointed out that when the wife, in fact, exercises management or control over community assets, the same rule applies to her. A breach of the fiduciary duty occurs if one party deprives the other of the opportunity to protect his or her rights in concealed assets. (*Id.*, at p. 21, 193 P.2d 728.) The court in *Jorgensen* held that any fraud by virtue of husband's representation was intrinsic rather than extrinsic fraud, and therefore was insufficient to set aside the marital settlement agreement, since a husband, although statutorily the manager of the community property, is entitled at the time of divorce or separation to take a position favorable to his own interests by claiming as his separate property assets which a court might hold to be community property. Confronted with the assertion by one party that assets are separate property, the other party must ascertain her own position as to the character of the property and, if necessary, investigate the facts. A failure to carry out such an investigation results, at best, in intrinsic fraud which is insufficient to set aside the judgment and the marital settlement agreement.

Nine years later, our Supreme Court again examined factual circumstances to determine whether extrinsic fraud had occurred. A wife, prior to the execution of a marital settlement agreement and while represented by counsel, began an investigation of the property of the parties, but did not pursue it, being satisfied with the marital settlement agreement. The court, citing *Jorgensen,* held that the husband owed the wife no duty to force her to investigate property when she stated she was satisfied with the marital settlement agreement prepared by her own attorney. Because the parties dealt with each other at arms' length, or at least the husband gave the wife every opportunity to deal at arms' length when the marital settlement agreement was executed, the law recognized that the interests of the parties were adverse, and neither owed the duty of disclosure to the other which would have existed if the relationship had remained a confidential one. (*Collins v. Collins* (1957) 48 Cal.2d 325, 309 P.2d 420.)

Our Supreme Court's next venture into this field occurred four years later, when a wife sought rescission of a marital settlement agreement containing an inequitable property division on the basis of her deceased husband's alleged fraud prior to and at the time of its execution. Citing *Jorgensen,* a divided court ruled that the agreement must be set aside, holding that when the husband represented he would give her full information and enter into a fair and equitable property settlement agreement in return for her discontinuing adversary proceedings, this constituted extrinsic fraud, because the wife had not terminated the fiduciary relationship nor dealt with the husband at arms' length, and his duty as a trustee with management and control of the community imposed upon him a duty to account to his wife for community property. (*Vai v. Bank of America* (1961) 56 Cal.2d 329, 15 Cal.Rptr. 71, 364 P.2d 247.) The court distinguished the fiduciary relationship arising by virtue of a husband's management and control of community property from the confidential relationship which is presumed to exist between spouses. The latter, and obligations arising out of it, are dependent upon the existence of confidence and trust, but the fiduciary relationship as to the wife's interest in community property continues as long as the husband has control of that property, notwithstanding the absence of confidence and trust and the consequent termination of the confidential relationship. (*Id.*, at pp. 337–338, 15 Cal.Rptr. 71, 364 P.2d 247.)

The majority opinion in *Vai* has resulted in substantial confusion over the distinction between extrinsic and intrinsic fraud in family law cases. Perhaps the majority was influenced by the fact that Mrs. Vai's equitable proceeding was brought against the executor of her deceased husband's estate. In every other case, absent egregious conduct such as concealment of the existence of community assets or concealment of the existence of the proceedings, when a party requesting equitable relief has been represented by counsel in the proceedings, any fraud has been found to be intrinsic, rather than extrinsic, and insufficient to set aside a judgment and marital settlement agreement. It is arguable that the holding in *Vai* should be limited to its own facts and would appear to have been impliedly overruled by later Supreme Court decisions such as *In re Marriage of Connolly* (1979) 23 Cal.3d 590, 153 Cal.Rptr. 423, 591 P.2d 911, and *Miller v. Bechtel Corp.* (1983) 33 Cal.3d 868, 191 Cal.Rptr. 619, 663 P.2d 177.

It is highly significant that Justice Traynor, the author of the court's opinion in *Jorgensen,* and of the later landmark decision in *Kulchar v. Kulchar* (1969) 1 Cal.3d 467, 82 Cal.Rptr. 489, 462 P.2d 17, wrote a lengthy dissent in *Vai.* He would have upheld the trial judge's finding that the husband was not a fiduciary based upon substantial evidence. He pointed out that the wife was represented by counsel of her own choice at all times and her counsel had drafted the agreement which could be inferred to be fair and equitable. Thus, the spouses in negotiating the property settlement agreement could deal with each other at arms' length, with the *Jorgensen* exception that each must reveal information peculiarly within his or her own knowledge as to the existence of community property. (*Id.*, 56 Cal.2d at pp. 349–350, 15 Cal.Rptr. 71, 364 P.2d 247.) He also referred to the holding in *Collins* that "when the parties to a marriage are negotiating a property settlement agreement with recognition that their interests are adverse and are dealing at arms' length, neither spouse owes to the other the duty of disclosure which he or she would owe if their relation remained in fact a confidential one." (*Id.*, at p. 351, 15 Cal.Rptr. 71, 364 P.2d 247.) Furthermore, "[a] husband at the time of divorce or separation is entitled to take a position favorable to his own interest in claiming as his separate property assets that a court might hold to be community property. Confronted with the assertion by the husband that certain assets are his separate property the wife must take her own position and if necessary investigate the facts." (*Id.*)

Four years after *Vai,* the court held that a marital settlement agreement executed by a party represented by counsel which, unknown to them, differed from a stipulated settlement in open court, must be set aside as extrinsic rather than intrinsic fraud. (See *Lopez v. Lopez* (1965) 63 Cal.2d 735, 48 Cal.Rptr. 136, 408 P.2d 744.)

Without question, the landmark case in this area is Justice Traynor's opinion in *Kulchar v. Kulchar, supra,* 1 Cal.3d 467, 82 Cal.Rptr. 489, 462 P.2d 17, holding that the power to set aside or modify a valid final judgment can only be exercised when the circumstances are sufficient to overcome the strong policy favoring the finality of judgments; that is, only in exceptional circumstances should the consequences of res judicata be denied. (*Id.,* at p. 470, 82 Cal.Rptr. 489, 462 P.2d 17.)

The court defined extrinsic fraud as arising "when a party is denied a fair adversary hearing because he had been 'deliberately kept in ignorance of the action or proceeding, or in some other way fraudulently prevented from presenting his claim or defense.' [Citation]" The court also noted that the right to such relief has been extended to cases involving extrinsic mistake such as when a party becomes incompetent. (*Id.,* at p. 471, 82 Cal.Rptr. 489, 462 P.2d 17.) Justice Traynor went on to point out, "Relief is denied, however, if a party has been given notice of an action and has not been prevented from participating therein. He has had an opportunity to present his case to the court and to protect himself from mistake or from any fraud attempted by his adversary. [Citations.] Moreover, a mutual mistake that might be sufficient to set aside a contract is not sufficient to set aside a final judgment. The principles of res judicata demand that the parties present their entire case in one proceeding. * * * [Citation.] Courts deny relief, therefore, when the fraud or mistake is 'intrinsic'; that is, when it 'goes to the merits of the prior proceedings, which should have been guarded against by the plaintiff at that time.' [Citations.] [¶] Relief is also denied when the complaining party has contributed to the fraud or mistake giving rise to the judgment thus obtained [citation] 'If the complainant was guilty of negligence in permitting the fraud to be practiced or the mistake to occur equity will deny relief.' [Citation.]" (*Id.,* at pp. 472–473, 82 Cal.Rptr. 489, 462 P.2d 17.) Thus, in *Kulchar,* the court refused to set aside a stipulated judgment where a potential tax obligation had been overlooked, since any fraud or mistake was intrinsic because of a failure to fully investigate.

In the past ten years our Supreme Court has considered the issue of extrinsic and intrinsic fraud in four family law cases, all of which also involved settlement agreements or division of property prior to the 1975 statutory change giving the husband and wife equal management and control over community assets. Where the trial court found a husband had breached his fiduciary duty by failing to disclose facts as to the value, nature and extent of community property, the court, citing *Vai v. Bank of America, supra,* 56 Cal.2d at pp. 329, 337, 342–343, 15 Cal.Rptr. 71, 364 P.2d 247, reiterated that a spouse with management and control of community property has a fiduciary duty to disclose the existence of community assets and material facts affecting their value while negotiating a property settlement agreement, and this duty is not terminated by commencement of a dissolution proceeding or by the other party's retention of an attorney. However, the court also reiterated, under *Jorgensen,* that the managing spouse must be permitted to protect his own interests and assume a position adverse to the other, particularly when the other is represented by counsel. "Further, when a spouse, represented by independent counsel, determines to forego a suggested investigation and to accept a proposed settlement, that spouse may not later avoid the agreement unless there has been a misrepresentation or concealment of material facts. [Fn. omitted.] Under such circumstances, the spouse proposing the agreement is under no duty to compel the other to investigate, and the accepting spouse's decision, though ill-advised, is binding. [¶] Finally, during negotiation to settle marital property rights, fairness dictates the managing spouse be under no duty to *evaluate* the marital assets. And if the managing spouse does assert an opinion of value, he or she must be able to do so without warranty. Valuation, like designation of property as being either community or separate, is an issue on which reasonable views often differ, and in the absence of concealment of assets—or facts materially affecting their value—a property settlement agreement may not later be set aside solely on the basis of the managing spouse's inaccurate opinion of value or on his or her refusal to have rendered such opinion." (*Boeseke v. Boeseke* (1974) 10 Cal.3d 844, 850, 112 Cal.Rptr. 401, 519 P.2d 161.)

Five years ago, in *In re Marriage of Connolly, supra,* 23 Cal.3d 590, 153 Cal.Rptr. 423, 591 P.2d 911, our Supreme Court, in a decision which was a substantial departure from prior decisions, held a husband had no fiduciary obligation to inform the wife of facts affecting the value of community property stock in a company of which he was a director where the information would have been readily ascertainable by the wife or her attorney upon reasonable inquiry. The court found that the wife made a tactical decision, as in *Boeseke,* not to ascertain the complete status of the stock or to investigate it. The court rejected her claim that her husband owed her a fiduciary duty arising from the marital relationship, finding that from the filing of the petition for dissolution of marriage her relationship with her husband was an adversary one and any obligation or trust between them was terminated. The court further stated, citing *Boeseke, Collins,* and *Jorgensen,* "We have repeatedly held that parties may elect to deal with each other at arms' length and when they do so any fiduciary obligation otherwise owing is thereby terminated." (*Id.,* at p. 600, 153 Cal.Rptr. 423, 591 P.2d 911.) The court did not overrule its decision in *Vai v. Bank of America, supra,* 56 Cal.2d 329, 15 Cal.Rptr. 71, 364 P.2d 247, but distinguished it on the basis that the wife there had discontinued the adversary proceeding at the request of husband who had told her she would not have to pursue legal remedies in order to obtain a reasonable division of the property. *Connolly* casts considerable doubt upon Court of Appeal decisions reached prior to the 1975 statutory changes of Civil Code sections 5125 and 5127.

More recently one of the most clear cut examples of extrinsic fraud was reviewed by our Supreme Court in *In re Marriage of Park* (1980) 27

Cal.3d 337, 165 Cal.Rptr. 792, 612 P.2d 882. The court held the failure of the husband and his attorney to disclose to the trial court that his wife's failure to appear at trial was because she had been involuntarily deported during the course of the litigation, was extrinsic fraud requiring that the judgment be set aside. Unfortunately, in dictum, repeating extremely broad language in several Court of Appeal opinions involving pre–1975 property disputes, the opinion stated: "[t]he grounds for such equitable relief are commonly stated as being extrinsic fraud or mistake. However, those terms are given a broad meaning and tend to encompass almost any set of extrinsic circumstances which deprive a party of a fair adversary hearing. It does not seem to matter if the particular circumstances qualify as fraudulent or mistaken in the strict sense." [Citations.] (*Id.,* at p. 342, 165 Cal.Rptr. 792, 612 P.2d 882.) This language, which could be construed in a way which would permit every default judgment to be set aside, is only a dictum.

Finally, in a single month last year, our Supreme Court last dealt with this issue in two separate cases. In the first case, *Miller v. Bechtel Corp., supra,* 33 Cal.3d 868, 191 Cal.Rptr. 619, 663 P.2d 177, the wife filed an equitable action to set aside a marital settlement agreement, contending her former husband had misrepresented the value of community property stock in the corporation which employed him. She claimed that her husband had a fiduciary duty under *Vai* to provide her with full and correct information about the value of the stock. The court rejected this, but held that even if it were correct, when she became aware of facts to put a reasonably prudent person on inquiry as to the value of the stock, she had a duty to investigate and would be charged with the knowledge of what the investigation would have revealed. Given California's policy of liberal discovery, *Miller* would appear to provide that when the existence of an asset is disclosed, the other party has the duty to investigate to ascertain its true character and value, and any failure to do would obviate a finding of extrinsic fraud. The court further held that the fact the wife was mistaken as to the law and the facts was not enough to require relief if she could reasonably have discovered the mistakes, and thus, there was no extrinsic fraud.

In the second case, *In re Marriage of Modnick* (1983) 33 Cal.3d 897, 191 Cal.Rptr. 629, 663 P.2d 187, the court held that the fiduciary duty to disclose the existence of community assets doesn't terminate with the date of separation or the filing of a petition for dissolution, citing *Boeseke* and *Vai,* but continues until the community property is divided. In *Modnick* there was not only a nondisclosure but an active concealment of a community bank account, and this was clearly extrinsic fraud. The court addressed what equitable defenses might be available and, citing *Park,* said that whether laches should bar the moving party from obtaining equitable relief required a weighing of the reasonableness of the moving party in not filing the motion to vacate earlier as against the extent of prejudice to the opposing party, and that these two factors are interrelated in that the greater the prejudice, the more timely the relief must be sought. (*Id.,* at pp. 908–909, 191 Cal.Rptr. 629, 663 P.2d 187.)

Having reviewed our Supreme Court's decisions in family law cases involving extrinsic and intrinsic fraud over the past 20 years, we note that the instant case must be distinguished from them for several reasons. First and foremost, the duty between spouses arising from statutory authority to manage and control community property was significantly changed, effective January 1, 1975, by amendments to Civil Code sections 5125 and 5127. Prior to that date the statute placed upon the husband the authority to manage and control community property. The amendments conferred equal management and control rights on the husband and wife, and changed the fiduciary duty to one of good faith. The instant case, unlike any prior decision, is one where each party represented themselves in their dealings with each other. Finally, none of our Supreme Court's decisions involved a case where the moving party sought only to set aside a judgment of dissolution incorporating a marital settlement agreement, alleging extrinsic fraud, but did not seek to set aside the marital settlement agreement. This is significant, since setting aside of the judgment only nullifies the court's approval of the property settlement agreement, and does not vacate the agreement itself. (See *In re Marriage of Testa* (1983) 149 Cal.App.3d 319, 196 Cal.Rptr. 780; *Olson v. Olson* (1957) 148 Cal.App.2d 479, 306 P.2d 1036.)

Additionally, all of the foregoing Supreme Court cases involved property disputes arising when the husband, by statute, was the manager of the community property and was charged with a fiduciary duty to the wife. The Legislature, in amending Civil Code sections 5125 and 5127 to give each spouse equal right of management and control, imposed a lessor duty of good faith in the management and control of community property.

We now summarize our view of the present state of the law by which extrinsic fraud is an equitable basis for setting aside judgments and marital settlement agreements in family law cases, considering the foregoing holdings of our Supreme Court and the statutory amendments to Civil Code sections 5125 and 5127.

GENERAL RULE

After relief is no longer available under Code of Civil Procedure section 473 for mistake, inadvertence, surprise or excusable neglect, an otherwise valid and final judgment may only be set aside if it has been obtained through extrinsic, not intrinsic, fraud.

EXTRINSIC FRAUD

Fraud is extrinsic where the defrauded party was deprived of the opportunity to present their claim or defense to the court, that is, where they were kept in ignorance or in some other manner, other than from their own conduct, fraudulently prevented from fully participating in the proceeding. If a spouse discontinues adversary proceedings because of the specific representation of the other party and his or her counsel that the spouse will not have to pursue legal remedies to obtain an equal division of the community property, and an equal division does not take place, extrinsic fraud may be found to have occurred.

Extrinsic fraud is more likely to be found to exist where a party who is not represented by counsel is persuaded to enter into an inequitable agreement by the other party and their counsel.

The following acts constitute extrinsic fraud:

—Concealment by one party of the existence of a community asset, or prevention of participation in the proceeding by the other party, including a failure to disclose to the court the inability of the other party to participate.

—Failure to give notice of the action to the other party, or proceeding to obtain a judgment without the knowledge of the other party, while reconciled with him or her.

—Convincing the other party not to obtain counsel because the matter is not going to proceed.

—Completion of the dissolution after having represented to the other party that it would not proceed without further notice.

Fairness dictates that the managing spouse has no duty to evaluate assets and may take a position favorable to himself or herself as to the character of assets, and this is done without any warranty, either as to valuation or claims of separate property character, because these are issues on which reasonable minds may differ and an inaccurate opinion or a failure to give any opinion cannot be extrinsic fraud.

INTRINSIC FRAUD

Any fraud is intrinsic if a party has been given notice of the action and has not been prevented from participating therein, that is, if they had the opportunity to present their case and to protect themselves from any mistake or fraud of their adversary, but unreasonably neglected to do so.

When a claim of fraud goes to an issue involving the merits of the prior proceeding which the moving party should have guarded against at that time, or if the moving party was guilty of negligence in failing to prevent the fraud or mistake or in contributing thereto, or failed to take advantage of liberal discovery policies to fully investigate their claim, any fraud is intrinsic fraud. A mutual mistake which would be sufficient to otherwise set aside a contract is not sufficient to set aside a valid judgment incorporating a marital settlement agreement. Even though a party is mistaken as to the law and the facts, this is an insufficient basis to set aside a valid judgment incorporating a marital settlement agreement, if the party reasonably could have discovered the mistakes.

When a party was represented by counsel, absent concealment, any fraud will usually be intrinsic. After separation, each party can take a position favorable to themselves as to the character and valuation of assets, and any failure of the other party to investigate the facts constitutes intrinsic rather than extrinsic fraud.

DUTY

Spouses no longer have a fiduciary duty to each other, however, they do have a duty to deal with the other in good faith with regard to the management and control of community property. This requires the disclosure of all community assets, but not their valuation unless the valuation or factors affecting the valuation are peculiarly within the knowledge of one spouse, and reasonable inquiry and use of discovery proceedings by the other spouse would fail to disclose them. Prior to the date of separation or the filing of a petition for dissolution, whichever occurs first, there exists a confidential relationship which imposes trust and confidence between spouses. However, upon separation or the filing of a petition for dissolution, the confidential relationship ends and the parties deal with each other at arms' length. Thereafter, as to community property, except for concealment of a community asset or nondisclosure of information as to value peculiarly within the knowledge of one spouse, each spouse may take a position favorable to themselves as to separate or community character of property and its valuation, and representations to the other in this regard are made without warranty. Once spouses negotiate at arms' length, or in an adversary manner, neither owes the duty to the other which would be owed if the parties had a confidential relationship. The duty to disclose the existence of community assets continues until there has been a division of all such assets.

PUBLIC POLICY

Two conflicting public policies come into play, the policy of giving each litigant the opportunity to have their day in court, and the policy of finality of judgments and an end to litigation. The Legislature has determined that during the time frame provided by Code of Civil Procedure section 473 there is a strong public policy in favor of allowing litigants their day in court. Thus, by a lesser showing than extrinsic fraud (mistake, inadvertence, surprise, or excusable neglect) public policy favors setting aside judgments under section 473. Once relief is no longer available under section 473, the public policy in favor of finality of judgments predominates, and the power to set aside valid final judgments and marital settlement agreements incorporated therein should be only exercised when exceptional circumstances require that the consequences of res judicata be denied. Thus, during the period when relief under section 473 is available, there is a strong public policy in favor of granting relief and allowing the requesting party their day in court. Beyond this period there is a strong public policy in favor of the finality of judgments and only in exceptional circumstances should relief be granted.

MARITAL SETTLEMENT AGREEMENTS

Marital settlement agreements, once incorporated into a judgment, are no longer mere contracts and a showing of extrinsic fraud is required to set them aside. Thus, they become a hybrid, more like a judgment than a contract, and contract defenses such as mutual mistake are insufficient to set them aside. For the public policy reasons discussed above, a lesser showing of extrinsic fraud should be required to set aside a marital settlement agreement incorporated into a judgment being set aside pursuant to Code of Civil Procedure section 473, while a strong showing of extrinsic fraud is required to set aside a marital settlement agreement once relief is unavailable under section 473.

EQUITABLE CONSIDERATIONS

To set aside a judgment incorporating a marital settlement agreement on the ground of extrinsic fraud, the moving party must demonstrate that he or she has a meritorious case, that they have a satisfactory excuse for not presenting a defense to the original action and that they exercised diligence in seeking to set aside the default once the fraud had been discovered. Such a motion must not be granted if the moving party is guilty of laches or inexcusable neglect, and the court must weigh the reasonableness of the conduct of the moving party in light of the extent of the prejudice to the responding party. The burden is on the moving party, and the greater the prejudice to the responding party, the greater the burden on the moving party. The greater the prejudice to the responding party, the more likely it is that the court will determine that equitable defenses such as laches or estoppel apply to the request to vacate a valid judgment.

* * *

Having summarized the current status of California law on extrinsic fraud in family law cases, we turn again to the instant case. Pamela acknowledges she was validly served with a summons which include a warning her default would be entered if she failed to file a response within 30 days.[5]

Despite the receipt of this warning, and with no counterdeclaration disputing Richard's contention that he never did or said anything which would cause her to think he did not intend to proceed, Pamela did nothing. Six weeks later she received a copy of a request to the clerk of the court to enter her default. Again she did nothing. In September and December of 1982, she executed additional addenda to the marital settlement agreement acknowledging receipt of Richard's payments as called for by the agreement and acknowledging that he had fully complied with the agreement.

Once Pamela received notice that her default had been entered, she had six months to act to have the default set aside under the very liberal standards contained in Code of Civil Procedure section 473, which gives

---

5. That summons, in the form prescribed by California Rules of Court, rule 1283, contains the following warning: "TO THE RESPONDENT: The petitioner has filed a petition concerning your marriage. If you fail to file a response within 30 days of the date that this summons is served on you, your default may be entered and the court may enter a judgment containing injunctive or other orders concerning division of property, spousal support, child custody, child support, attorneys' fees, costs, and such other relief as may be granted by the court. The garnishment of wages, taking of money or property, or other court authorized proceedings may also result."

the trial court much broader power to vacate a valid judgment than the power to set aside a judgment thereafter under equitable powers of extrinsic fraud has occurred. (See *Karlslyst v. Frazier* (1931) 213 Cal. 377, 2 P.2d 362; *Weitz v. Yankosky* (1966) 63 Cal.2d 849, 48 Cal.Rptr. 620, 409 P.2d 700.)

Pamela did nothing until she had received all of the fruits of the agreement she had entered into with Richard, when, 16 months after service upon her of the summons and petition, she filed her motion. She contends that her failure to proceed was based upon Richard's intimidation, but she acknowledges that she lived separate and apart from him for four months immediately after service of process and did nothing to consult with her family or with an attorney about her rights during that time. Additionally, despite her allegations of intimidation, she returned to live in his home for financial reasons for over a year, although not in a husband-wife relationship. Her claim of intimidation, under these circumstances, is extremely doubtful.[6]

Under the circumstances of this case, having been served with a proper summons and petition for dissolution, not having been misled to believe the action would not proceed, and finally receiving notice of an entry of her default, Pamela has made no showing why she did not seek legal advice at a much earlier time than a year and a half after the entry of her default. Under these circumstances, as a matter of law, her conduct cannot be found to be reasonable. (See *Wilson v. Wilson* (1942) 55 Cal.App.2d 421, 130 P.2d 782.) She had a duty to exercise reasonable diligence to obtain legal advice and she totally failed to fulfill that duty. The basis of the trial court's ruling was that Pamela did not have full knowledge of the marital proceedings and may have been misled. From our summary of the law it is clear any misleading did not constitute extrinsic fraud. Any lack of knowledge of her rights in the proceeding resulted from her own lack of diligence in consulting an attorney. The parties here, both acting without representation by counsel, were representing themselves and dealing with each other at arms' length on an adversary basis, thus any fraud which occurred was intrinsic, rather than extrinsic, and not a basis for setting aside the default or the

---

6. It appears from Pamela's declaration in support of her motion that she is torn between whether to allege her failure to seek an attorney sooner was due to duress by Richard or because of extrinsic fraud committed by him. Duress is to be distinguished from extrinsic fraud, although, if proven, it is a valid ground to set aside a judgment and marital settlement agreement. Duress, however, is more than mere threats or puffing; a party must be shown to have intentionally used threats or pressure to induce action or nonaction to the other party's detriment. (See *In re Marriage of Gonzalez* (1976) 57 Cal.App.3d 736, 129 Cal.Rptr. 566.)

Here, the trial court made no finding of duress or that duress was a basis for the court's order setting aside the judgment. Since the law permits a spouse dealing at arms' length to give opinions about the character and value of property favorable to him without warranty or liability, statements between spouses to the effect that "getting a lawyer won't benefit you," being even more likely to occur, do not constitute extrinsic fraud. (See *Boeseke v. Boeseke, supra,* 10 Cal.3d at p. 844, 112 Cal.Rptr. 401, 519 P.2d 161.)

interlocutory judgment of dissolution.[7] Nothing, other than her own lack of diligence, prevented Pamela from participating in the action and any fraud was intrinsic. (4 Witkin, Cal.Proc., §§ 3752, 3754, 3756.) A party who seeks to set aside a default judgment pursuant to the court's equity power must make a substantially stronger showing of the excusable nature of his or her neglect than is necessary to obtain relief under Code of Civil Procedure section 473. (See *Carroll v. Abbott Laboratories, Inc.* (1982) 32 Cal.3d 892, 901 fn. 8, 187 Cal.Rptr. 592, 654 P.2d 775.)

Applying all the foregoing principles to the present case, Richard's conduct did not amount to extrinsic fraud. There is no evidence or claim that he concealed the existence of community assets. (See, e.g., *In re Marriage of Modnick, supra,* 33 Cal.3d at p. 907, 191 Cal.Rptr. 629, 663 P.2d 187; *Jorgensen v. Jorgensen, supra,* 32 Cal.2d at pp. 13, 21–22, 193 P.2d 728.) Should undisclosed assets be discovered, Pamela can bring an independent action to determine her community interest, if any. (*Henn v. Henn* (1980) 26 Cal.3d 323, 332, 161 Cal.Rptr. 502, 605 P.2d 10.) The trial court found she was not kept in ignorance of the proceedings. (Cf. *In re Marriage of Park* (1980) 27 Cal.3d 337, 340–342, 165 Cal.Rptr. 792, 612 P.2d 882.) Furthermore, as Richard pointed out in his declaration, Pamela made no contention in her declaration that he ever said or did anything "which would tend to mislead her into thinking that [he] did not intend to proceed." The declarations of the parties do not disclose any breach of Richard's duty to disclose the existence of assets or the legal proceedings. Rather, the record reveals that Richard and Pamela discussed the disposition of their property, spousal support, and the legal proceedings; that they signed a marital settlement agreement; that ten months after her default was entered, the marital settlement agreement was modified to acknowledge full payment of an obligation owned by Richard to her under the original agreement, partial payment of another, and modification of the support provision; that the marital settlement agreement was subsequently modified on December 16, 1982, acknowledging full payment of all obligations owned by Richard to Pamela under the agreement; that Pamela never consulted an attorney or attempted to defend the action because she felt intimidated

---

7. In this action the parties acted as thousands of other Californians have done in handling their own dissolution proceeding without consulting an attorney. Divorcing parties, of course, are free to represent themselves, but must be willing to accept the risks that arise by being their own lawyer, without any training or experience. There is an old adage that a lawyer who represents himself has a fool for a client. This adage should provide some indication of the risks that nonlawyers subject themselves to when they attempt to represent themselves.

Today, with the use of judicial council forms for family law proceedings which are specifically drafted to allow parties to represent themselves, it would be unfair to parties employing counsel for the law to treat persons deciding to represent themselves in a more favorable way. For this reason, the Stevenot's, having decided to represent themselves, are entitled to no better or different treatment than they would receive had they been represented by counsel. Mistake or inadvertence in failing to obtain counsel may be a ground for setting aside a judgment under Code of Civil Procedure section 473, but it is not extrinsic fraud and therefore not a basis for setting aside a final judgment on that ground. There was certainly no allegation by Pamela that any fraud had caused her not to obtain a lawyer at an earlier time and no allegations of any concealed facts which came to her attention which caused her to obtain counsel.

by Richard and did not believe she could gain anything by appearing; that she waited over 16 months from the time she acknowledged receipt of the summons and petition before she consulted an attorney; and that she sought no relief until over a year after her default had been entered.

A motion to vacate a judgment should not be granted where it is shown that the party requesting equitable relief has been guilty of inexcusable neglect. (*In re Marriage of Park, supra,* 27 Cal.3d at p. 345, 165 Cal.Rptr. 792, 612 P.2d 882.) While we must look to the extent of prejudice to the opposing party and to the reasonableness of the moving party in not filing the motion to vacate earlier, "[w]e have, however, found no case which permits the setting aside of a judgment in spite of inexcusable neglect, simply because the other side has not been prejudiced. [Citations.]" (*Carroll v. Abbott Laboratories, Inc., supra,* 32 Cal.3d at p. 900, 187 Cal.Rptr. 592, 654 P.2d 775.) In fact, since Richard fully complied with his obligations under the marital settlement agreement, setting aside the judgment would clearly prejudice him. "The greater the prejudice, the more timely must the relief be sought." (*McCreadie v. Arques* (1967) 248 Cal.App.2d 39, 47, 56 Cal.Rptr. 188.)

In sum, we conclude that the record does not disclose that Pamela was either deliberately kept in ignorance of the proceeding or fraudulently prevented by Richard from presenting her claims. (*In re Marriage of Modnick, supra,* 33 Cal.3d at p. 905, 191 Cal.Rptr. 629, 663 P.2d 187.) Any failure was due to her own failure to act diligently. Absent extrinsic fraud, it was error to set aside the default and interlocutory judgment of dissolution of marriage. As Justice Traynor stated, "Relief is denied, however, if a party has been given notice of an action and has not been prevented from participating therein. He has had an opportunity to present his case to the court and to protect himself from mistake or from any fraud attempted by his adversary." (*Kulchar v. Kulchar, supra,* 1 Cal.3d at p. 472, 82 Cal.Rptr. 489, 462 P.2d 17.) Pamela had her opportunity and failed to exercise diligence and take advantage of it.

The order after hearing is reversed.

LOW, P.J., and HANING, J., concur.

Hearing denied; BIRD, C.J., dissenting.

Notes

1. In *Marriage of Brennan,* 124 Cal.App.3d 598, 177 Cal.Rptr. 520 (1981), the wife appeared in the dissolution proceedings, but was not represented by counsel. Relying on the statements of her husband and his attorney that the property settlement agreement prepared by the husband's lawyer was fair and that she would not receive any more from the court, the wife agreed to an interlocutory judgment of dissolution containing the terms of the agreement. More than two years later, the wife filed a motion to vacate the judgment on the ground of fraud. The appellate court indicated that these facts gave rise to extrinsic fraud:

We are satisfied that Susan did not have a trial or "her day in court" * * *. It is true Susan appeared in court, but not to engage in battle.

Relief is denied for intrinsic fraud because the very object of the trial is to ascertain the truth from the conflict of evidence. [citation omitted.] Susan, because of the representations of Joseph and his attorney, believed no trial was necessary. She was in court merely to put her stamp of approval on an agreement she briefly thought was fair due to her reliance on the representations made to her. In addition to Joseph's statements that they were bankrupt, that the business Graphic Marking and Graphic Marketing Service was worthless and that he was proceeding with the dissolution to prevent her from losing the house until the youngest child became 18, are the representations of Joseph's attorney. He said: "I am going to be over fair with you * * *. I am going to talk your husband into letting you live in the house until the youngest child becomes eighteen. * * * I am the attorney for your husband's business and I can tell you that it's worthless." When Susan questioned the fairness of the offered spousal support, he stated: "That's all you would receive from the court." Clearly these statements by Joseph and his attorney to Susan were designed primarily to prevent a trial of the issues normally contested in a dissolution proceeding. Although Susan was obviously naive in accepting their representations, this does not preclude her from raising the issue of extrinsic fraud. There was no meaningful judicial time invested in trial of a cause or an issue; therefore, as stated in Los Angeles Airways, Inc. v. Hughes Tool Co., supra, 95 Cal.App.3d 1, 156 Cal.Rptr. 805, the equitable considerations for granting a hearing and penalizing fraud are quite compelling.

2. In Marriage of Jones, 195 Cal.App.3d 1097, 241 Cal.Rptr. 231 (1987), the appellate court held that the husband's statement to his wife that he was cancelling a previously executed marital settlement agreement when in fact he proceeded to obtain a default dissolution judgment constituted extrinsic fraud. The court indicated that when the husband told his wife he was cancelling the papers, he lulled her into believing that the dissolution would not proceed, deliberately keeping her in ignorance of the proceeding. Furthermore, the wife was not represented by counsel who could have apprised her of her rights.

3. The legislature has reinstated the fiduciary element as a component of the confidential relationship existing between husband and wife. West's Ann.Cal.Family Code § 721. Should this provision have a bearing on the extrinsic-intrinsic fraud distinction drawn by the courts?

MARRIAGE OF BROCKMAN
California District Court of Appeal, 1987.
194 Cal.App.3d 1035, 240 Cal.Rptr. 96.

KINGSLEY, ACTING PRESIDING JUSTICE.

Wife appeals the denial of her motion to vacate following a judgment of dissolution. We reverse.

The issue on appeal is whether wife can set aside a property and custody settlement agreement that she signed to end the parties' bitter custody dispute. The facts are as follows: In 1984, wife filed for divorce in Pasadena seeking to terminate her five-year marriage to respondent.

At the same time, she obtained an ex parte order restraining husband from approaching within 100 yards of herself, the couple's young son, and appellant's 14–year old daughter. This action was never served on respondent, however, and shortly thereafter he filed his own petition for dissolution in Burbank. In spite of the restraining order, appellant allowed respondent to take the children away for the weekend. Respondent flew the children from Sacramento, where they were staying with appellant, to Los Angeles, and refused to return them. He then applied for, and was granted, his own ex parte order in Burbank awarding him custody of the children.

After some six weeks with the children, however, respondent reconsidered and offered to return custody to appellant. Appellant stated that respondent promised to relinquish custody to her at an upcoming order to show cause. According to appellant, however, at the time of the hearing, respondent presented lengthy demands and threatened to keep custody of the children unless appellant agreed. Respondent's attorney wrote out a settlement agreement by hand, in a hallway of the courthouse, which appellant signed. Essentially, appellant gave up all claims to the couple's estimated $400,000 to $800,000 in community property in exchange for sole physical custody of the children. She was allowed to keep $10,000 and a Camaro automobile, and was awarded $500 a month in child support and $300 a month spousal support for ten years. Husband agreed to forfeit a $100,000 note if he should ever contest the custody or support order.

Eight months later, the judgment of dissolution was signed and entered by the court incorporating the above terms. Appellant moved to vacate the judgment, however, as it contained several provisions which were not a part of the agreement. Respondent indicated that he had no opposition to this motion.

In the meantime, however, appellant changed attorneys. Four months after the judgment was entered, she moved to vacate it in its entirety on the ground that the settlement agreement was coerced. The motion to vacate was denied and this appeal follows.

* * *

Having determined that appellant can appeal the denial of her motion to vacate, we now reach the merits of the case. As one would expect, the question of whether respondent coerced appellant into signing the settlement agreement by threatening to deprive her or her children is closely contested by the parties. On the one hand, the manifest inequality of the settlement agreement, the hurried circumstances of its drafting, and husband's history of violent behavior all contribute strongly to the conclusion that appellant was under duress. Moreover, as the court noted in *In re Marriage of Gonzalez* (1976) 57 Cal.App.3d 736, 747–748, 129 Cal.Rptr. 566:

"The involvement of the children that automatically raises the issue of their welfare places this type of litigation in an arena of its own. The emotions and fears of the parties are more intense and are not comparable to litigants in a normal civil action. If threatened use of a custody hearing can cause so much fear in the mind of the responding parent that contractual volition is destroyed, the court is not required to legally recognize the agreement when equity demands otherwise." On the other hand, supporting respondent's position is the fact that appellant waited more than a year to raise the issue of coercion and was undeniably represented by counsel throughout all the proceedings. No finding on the issue of duress, however, was made by the trial court.[4] Rather, the court relied on *In re Marriage of Stevenot* (1984) 154 Cal.App.3d 1051, 202 Cal.Rptr. 116, for the proposition that once a settlement agreement is incorporated into a judgment, it may only be set aside for extrinsic fraud.

Stevenot represents one of the latest and most able attempts to distinguish between intrinsic and extrinsic fraud. As *Stevenot* notes:

"The primary architect of California's laws on the extrinsic-intrinsic fraud issue in family law cases has been one of its judicial superstars, Justice Roger Traynor. Over 40 years ago, Justice Traynor wrote, "The final judgment of a court having jurisdiction over persons and subject matter can be attacked in equity after the time for appeal or other direct attack has expired only if the alleged fraud or mistake is extrinsic rather than intrinsic [citations]. Fraud or mistake is extrinsic when it deprives the unsuccessful party of an opportunity to present his case to the court [citations]. If an unsuccessful party to an action has been kept in ignorance thereof [citations] or has been prevented from fully participating therein [citation], there has been no true adversary proceeding, and the judgment is open to attack at any time. A party who has been given proper notice of an action, however, and who has not been prevented from full participation therein, has had an opportunity to present his case to the court and to protect himself from any fraud attempted by his adversary. [Citations.] Fraud perpetrated under such circumstances is intrinsic, * * *'" (*In re Marriage of Stevenot, supra,* 154 Cal.App.3d at 1061, 202 Cal.Rptr. 116.)

Stevenot then goes on to define extrinsic and intrinsic fraud:

"Fraud is extrinsic where the defrauded party was deprived of the opportunity to present his or her claim or defense to the court, that is, where he or she was kept in ignorance or in some manner, other than from his or her own conduct, fraudulently prevented from fully participating in the proceeding."

"* * *

"Any fraud is intrinsic if a party has been given notice of the action and has not been prevented from participating therein, that is, if he or she had the opportunity to present his or her case and to protect himself

---

4. The closest the court comes is saying that appellant "participated" in the settlement agreement. This does not reflect, however, whether her participation was or was not coerced.

or herself from any mistake or fraud of his or her adversary, but unreasonably neglected to do so." (*In re Marriage of Stevenot, supra,* 154 Cal.App.3d 1068, 1069, 202 Cal.Rptr. 116.)

The trial court evidently concluded that this encompassed the entire universe of grounds on which a judgment might be set aside. It does not. The briefest scrutiny demonstrates that there are many conditions that cannot be characterized as either extrinsic or intrinsic fraud, even with resort to the most procrustean measures. This is because the distinction between intrinsic and extrinsic fraud refers only to claims of fraud—that is mistake or misrepresentation by the opposing party. Grounds other than fraud have long been recognized as also permitting a judgment to be set aside. As the court observed in *Zastrow v. Zastrow* (1976) 61 Cal.App.3d 710, 716, 132 Cal.Rptr. 536:

"Fraud and mistake are the usual but not the only grounds for equitable relief from a judgment. The leading California case in this area (*Olivera v. Grace, supra,* [(1942) 19 Cal.2d 570, 122 P.2d 564]) involved an attack upon a judgment allegedly procured through the mental incompetence of the plaintiff's decedent. The decedent had suffered a head injury which resulted in unadjudicated mental incompetence, was served with papers in a deed reformation action and suffered a default at the hands of the plaintiff in that action. The Supreme Court sustained the claim as one justifying relief; spoke of equity's power 'to relieve incompetent defendants from judgments taken under circumstances of unfairness and injustice;' mentioned extrinsic fraud and extrinsic mistake as 'typical of the situations' in which equity interferes with final judgments; quoted from an authoritative text which posits accident (as well as fraud and mistake) as a ground of relief; finally voiced the following general rule: 'One who has been prevented by extrinsic factors from presenting his case to the court may bring an independent action in equity to secure relief from the judgment entered against him.' [Citation.] The quintessential basis for equitable relief from the judgment is not that the wife was defrauded or mistaken; rather, that some kind of disability deprived her of 'a fair opportunity fully to submit her case to the court.' [Citation.] *Olivera* demonstrates that fraud or mistake are not the exclusive grounds; that equity, indeed, does not limit the kinds of disability which justify relief."

Stevenot itself recognizes that duress is neither intrinsic or extrinsic fraud, but is still a ground for setting a judgment aside. *Stevenot* states:

"It appears from Pamela's declaration in support of her motion that she is torn between whether to allege her failure to seek an attorney sooner was due to duress by Richard or because of extrinsic fraud committed by him. Duress is to be distinguished from extrinsic fraud, although, if proven, it is a valid ground to set aside a judgment and marital settlement agreement." (*In re Marriage of Stevenot, supra,* 154 Cal.App.3d at 1973, footnote 6, 202 Cal.Rptr. 116.)

Accordingly we conclude that the trial court was in error by failing to determine whether appellant's consent to the settlement was coerced.

If the trial court should so decide, it must vacate the judgment and settlement agreement. The instant order denying the motion to vacate is therefore reversed and remanded to the trial court for further proceedings. Appellant to recover costs.

McCLOSKY and MUNOZ, JJ., concur.

Note

Duress as a ground for setting aside a judgement or invalidating a contract was further refined in Marriage of Baltins, 212 Cal.App.3d 66, 260 Cal.Rptr. 403, 413–416 (1989):

> The stringent definition of duress contained in Civil Code section 1569, codifying the early common law rule, has been relaxed. (*In re Marriage of Gonzalez, supra,* 57 Cal.App.3d at pp. 743–744, 129 Cal. Rptr. 566; *Rich & Whillock, Inc. v. Ashton Development, Inc.* (1984) 157 Cal.App.3d 1154, 1158–1159, 204 Cal.Rptr. 86 [economic compulsion].) Under the modern rule, " '[d]uress, which includes whatever destroys one's free agency and constrains [her] to do what is against [her] will, may be exercised by threats, importunity or any species of mental coercion [citation]. . . .' " (*Gonzalez, supra,* 57 Cal.App.3d at p. 744, 129 Cal.Rptr. 566.) It is shown where a party "intentionally used threats or pressure to induce action or nonaction to the other party's detriment. [Citing *Gonzalez.*]" (*In re Marriage of Stevenot, supra,* 154 Cal.App.3d at p. 1073, fn. 6, 202 Cal.Rptr. 116; see Rest.2d Contracts (1981) §§ 175, 176.) The coercion must induce the assent of the coerced party, who has no reasonable alternative to succumbing. (*Rich & Whillock, Inc. v. Ashton Development, Inc., supra,* 157 Cal.App.3d at pp. 1158–1159, 204 Cal.Rptr. 86.)

> To determine whether a contract (or a default judgment) was the product of duress, the courts look not so much to the nature of the threats, but to their effect on the state of the threatened person's mind. (*In re Marriage of Gonzalez, supra,* 57 Cal.App.3d at p. 744, 129 Cal.Rptr. 566; Rest.2d Contracts, § 175, com. c.) This the trial court did. In its ruling, it cited as particularly persuasive the "overwhelming" testimony of Dr. Deckoff, and of Attorneys Gaustad, Stephens, and Jordan, to the effect that Wife was "very emotional, upset and distraught to the point that . . . she was acting under her husband's will." To show lack of consent, it was unnecessary to establish that she lacked the capacity to contract, only that she was in such a mentally weakened condition due to anxiety and emotional anguish or exhaustion that she was unable to protect herself against Husband's demands. (*O'Neil v. Spillane, supra,* 45 Cal.App.3d at p. 155, 119 Cal.Rptr. 245; *Smalley v. Baker* (1968) 262 Cal.App.2d 824, 834–835, 69 Cal.Rptr. 521.)

> The testimony here graphically portrays an emotionally distraught wife who is unable to deal with her spouse on an arms-length basis and who is so intimidated by him that she is unable to take advantage of legal advice. It further reveals that her concerns about confronting Husband were well-founded. He actively interfered with her obtaining legal assistance and conducted himself in a manner calculated to deprive Wife of representation by counsel. He told Wife that he would not

discuss anything with a lawyer, but would only deal with her directly. Ultimately, when Wife signed the agreement from which the trial court granted her relief, she was not represented by counsel. Nor was she represented when she signed the earlier handwritten agreement and the documents required for the default hearing.

Lack of independent advice, standing alone, is not sufficient to support a finding that Wife's consent was obtained through coercion. (*Smith v. Lombard* (1927) 201 Cal. 518, 524, 258 P. 55 [undue influence]; *Marsiglia v. Marsiglia* (1947) 78 Cal.App.2d 701, 705, 178 P.2d 478 [undue influence].) But, it " '. . . is a fact to be weighed by the trial court in determining whether [that party] acted voluntarily and with a complete understanding of the transaction. [Citations.]' " (*Roeder v. Roeder* (1953) 118 Cal.App.2d 572, 581, 258 P.2d 581.) Here, the evidence shows Husband's active interference with Wife's attempts to obtain legal assistance. Under the circumstances of this case, lack of independent advice is persuasive evidence in support of the court's ruling.

Lack of independent advice is not the only indicia of duress present here. Perhaps the most significant mark is Wife's consent to a grossly unfair agreement by which she received only 10 to 15 percent of the community property and inadequate support for herself and the minor child. (See Rest.2d Contracts, § 208 [unconscionable contracts].) The evidence reveals no consideration for such an unequal agreement in the way of economic or psychological benefit to Wife or the child. Husband's assurance to Wife that his taking the bulk of the assets would save her the burden of debt financing has a hollow ring. He failed to consider that liquidation of assets or an adequate support award would have reduced or eliminated any such burden.

Husband made threats and misrepresentations. He threatened Wife with bankruptcy and urged her immediate action to prevent dissipation of her share of the property through credits to him of all payments for debts and support. He represented that she had no interest in his medical practice, telling her that she had not worked for it and that she was not an equal partner in the marriage. He aimed at her most vulnerable spot when he threatened not to see their child.

* * *

Upon dissolution of the marriage, the community property must be divided equally between the spouses, absent a contrary agreement. (Civ.Code, § 4800; *In re Marriage of Fonstein* (1976) 17 Cal.3d 738, 748, 131 Cal.Rptr. 873, 552 P.2d 1169.) Husband's medical practice, including goodwill, was a community asset; his representations were false. (*In re Marriage of Watts, supra,* 171 Cal.App.3d at p. 372, 217 Cal.Rptr. 301.) His statement that Wife had no interest in his medical practice was not mere opinion on character or value. Rather, it was couched in terms to reinforce her feeling of inadequacy and lack of equality.

After Wife's hope for reconciliation disappeared, she reasonably believed that she had no alternative to compliance with Husband's demands and that her only recourse was to salvage the assets assigned to her and to use the meager support to develop her self-sufficiency.

It is seldom possible to show intent by direct evidence; usually it must be shown by the totality of the circumstances. From the evidence we have set out, the court could infer that Husband intentionally used coercion to induce Wife's consent to an unconscionable contract and a default judgment dissolving the marriage. (*In re Cheryl E.* (1984) 161 Cal.App.3d 587, 601, 207 Cal.Rptr. 728; *Estate of Hannam* (1951) 106 Cal.App.2d 782, 786, 236 P.2d 208.)

In summary, the evidence shows that Wife's consent to the agreement and entry of a default judgment was procured by duress practiced on her by Husband and that his acts were intentional. She was effectively deprived of independent counsel; she was in a distraught and weakened condition emotionally and unable to confront Husband; he undermined her psychologically by repeatedly telling her she had not contributed as much as he to the marriage and was not an equal partner; he made threats and misrepresentations and pressured her into taking immediate action; she agreed to an unconscionable contract; and she had no reasonable alternative. Thus, through the "extrinsic" factor of duress, she was denied a fair adversary hearing.

* * *

B. *Omission of Assets*

HENN v. HENN

Supreme Court of California, 1980.
26 Cal.3d 323, 161 Cal.Rptr. 502, 605 P.2d 10.

BIRD, CHIEF JUSTICE.

This court must determine whether a former spouse may bring an action to establish her community property interest in her ex-husband's federal military pension which was not adjudicated or distributed in the final decree of dissolution.

I

Helen and Henry Henn were married in 1945. After 25 years, Henry petitioned for dissolution of their marriage in the Superior Court for the City and County of San Francisco. An interlocutory decree was granted on February 22, 1971, and a final judgment issued on May 19, 1971. The decree incorporated a property settlement which awarded the parties specific items of the marital community as their separate property. The decree also awarded Helen $500 monthly support payments until the death of either party or her remarriage.

Neither the pleadings nor the judgment made mention of the fully matured federal military retirement pension that Henry was receiving at the time of the interlocutory decree. The pension had been partially earned during the marriage, and its existence was known to Helen at the time of the dissolution proceedings. Henry concedes that the court made no determination with respect to the pension.

On October 17, 1973, in response to a motion by Henry in the San Francisco Superior Court to reduce the amount of Helen's spousal support, Helen moved for an order to show cause why Henry's retirement pension should not be divided as community property. In support of this motion, Helen filed a short declaration setting forth the nature of her interest in the pension and alleging that she had never relinquished her community property rights in that asset. Henry opposed Helen's motion. Admitting that at the time of the interlocutory decree his pension was in part community property, he argued that the court lacked jurisdiction to modify the property settlement incorporated in the judgment of dissolution since there was no showing of extrinsic fraud or mistake. Helen's motion was denied without opinion on March 5, 1974.

Approximately two and one half years later, Helen filed the underlying complaint in the Superior Court of San Mateo County. Helen sought (1) a determination that Henry's military pension was community property to the extent earned by Henry during their marriage; (2) a full accounting of all pension payments received by Henry since March 1, 1971; and (3) a division of the community property portion of the pension. In his answer to the complaint, Henry raised the defense of res judicata based on the original decree of dissolution and the 1974 denial of Helen's motion. He also contended that these proceedings, together with Helen's recovery in settlement of a malpractice action against her former attorneys, estopped her from maintaining the present action.[1] After a separate trial on these affirmative defenses, the trial court entered judgment on Henry's behalf. Helen appealed.

II

* * *

It is clear that Henry's entitlement to his federal military pension was fully vested and matured in 1971 at the time of the dissolution of the Henns' marriage. To the extent earned during the marriage, it was part of their community property. However, Henry argues that Helen is prevented from seeking a judicial division of her community property interest in this asset under the principles of res judicata and collateral estoppel. These defenses are grounded on the original decree of dissolution and property settlement and the subsequent denial of Helen's motion to modify the original decree to divide the military pension.

---

1. On November 8, 1974, Helen filed a malpractice action against the attorneys who represented her during the dissolution proceedings. She alleged that she had detrimentally relied upon their advice that Henry's pension was his separate property. That case was settled in April 1976. On appeal, Henry denied that he urged "the doctrine of election of remedies as an affir-mative defense," and conceded "that a litigant may pursue more than one remedy against different persons." Since Henry has not argued on appeal that Helen's recovery from her former attorneys prevents her from maintaining the present action, or otherwise limits her rights against him, that issue is not before this court.

The doctrine of res judicata has long been recognized to have a dual aspect. (See Teitelbaum Furs, Inc. v. Dominion Ins. Co., Ltd. (1962) 58 Cal.2d 601, 604, 25 Cal.Rptr. 559, 375 P.2d 439; Todhunter v. Smith (1934) 219 Cal. 690, 695, 28 P.2d 916. See also 4 Witkin, Cal.Procedure (2d ed. 1971) Judgment, § 148, p. 3293.) "In its primary aspect the doctrine of res judicata operates as a bar to the maintenance of a second suit between the same parties on the same cause of action." (Clark v. Lesher (1956) 46 Cal.2d 874, 880, 229 P.2d 865, 868.) Also, the doctrine comes into play in situations involving a second suit, not necessarily between the same parties, which is based upon a different cause of action. There "[t]he prior judgment is not a complete bar, but it 'operates [against the party against whom it was obtained] as an estoppel[4] or conclusive adjudication as to such issues in the second action as were actually litigated and determined in the first section.'" (Id., citations omitted.) Neither aspect is applicable to the original judgment of dissolution and property settlement in this case.

Under California law, a spouse's entitlement to a share of the community property arises at the time that the property is acquired. (Civ.Code, §§ 5107, 5108, 5110.) That interest is not altered except by judicial decree or an agreement between the parties. Hence "under settled principles of California community property law, 'property which is not mentioned in the pleadings as community property is left unadjudicated by decree of divorce, and is subject to future litigation, the parties being tenants in common meanwhile.'" (In re Marriage of Brown, supra, 15 Cal.3d at pp. 850–851, 126 Cal.Rptr. at p. 641, 544 P.2d at p. 569, quoting In re Marriage of Elkins (1972) 28 Cal.App.3d 899, 903, 105 Cal.Rptr. 59. Accord Estate of Williams (1950) 36 Cal.2d 289, 292–293, 223 P.2d 248; Lewis v. Superior Court (1978) 77 Cal.App.3d 844, 847–850, 144 Cal.Rptr. 1; Irwin v. Irwin (1977) 69 Cal.App.3d 317, 320–321, 138 Cal.Rptr. 9; Kelley v. Kelley (1977) 73 Cal.App.3d 672, 676, 141 Cal.Rptr. 33.) This rule applies to partial divisions of community property as well as divorces unaccompanied by any property adjudication whatsoever.

Helen's interest in Henry's military pension arose independent of and predates the original decree of dissolution and property settlement. This interest was separate and distinct from her interest in the items of community property which were divided at the time of the dissolution. Since it is conceded that the issue of Henry's military pension was not before the court which issued the final decree, the judgment of that court cannot be said to have extinguished Helen's putative interest in that asset.

Further, Helen cannot be collaterally estopped from litigating her community property right in that pension. Henry has not asserted that Helen is relying upon some factual or legal theory which was adjudicated in the prior litigation or which would have had to have been adjudicated

---

4. This second aspect is referred to as judgment by estoppel or, more commonly, collateral estoppel. (See Clark v. Lesher, supra, 46 Cal.2d at p. 880, 299 P.2d 865.)

if it had been raised at the time. (E.g., Sutphin v. Speik (1940) 15 Cal.2d 195, 202–205, 99 P.2d 652, 101 P.2d 497.) Rather, Henry argues that Helen's failure to assert her community property right in the pension, when there was an adjudication of her entitlement to other assets of the community, should preclude her from asserting her rights to the pension now.

The doctrine of collateral estoppel cannot be stretched to compel such a result. (Gorman v. Gorman, supra, 90 Cal.App.3d at pp. 464–465, 153 Cal.Rptr. 479; Lewis v. Superior Court, supra, 77 Cal.App.3d at p. 852, fn. 2, 144 Cal.Rptr. 1.)[5] As explained in Carroll v. Puritan Leasing Co. (1978) 77 Cal.App.3d 481, 490, 143 Cal.Rptr. 772, the rule prohibiting the raising of any factual or legal contentions which were not actually asserted but which were within the scope of a prior action, "does not mean that issues not litigated and determined are binding in a subsequent proceeding on a new cause of action. Rather, it means that once an issue is litigated and determined, it is binding in a subsequent action notwithstanding that a party may have omitted to raise matters for or against it which if asserted may have produced a different outcome." Hence, the doctrine of collateral estoppel is not applicable here because Henry failed to demonstrate that Helen is relying upon some specific factual or legal contention which could have been relevant to the adjudication of the parties' rights to the property distributed in the 1971 decree if it had been raised.[6]

Next, Henry argues that the denial of Helen's motion to modify the original decree in 1974 is a bar to the present action. The trial court summarily denied Helen's motion and Henry contends that this denial was a favorable ruling on the merit of his res judicata defense. Henry's position is that since Helen did not appeal the denial the ruling must stand although it is erroneous.

It is not clear from the record whether the denial of Helen's motion was based on the merit of her community property claim, the res judicata defense asserted by Henry, or some procedural defect such as lack of jurisdiction. There are no reported decisions that have held that a community property claim to an asset left unmentioned in a prior judicial division of community property may be adjudicated in a motion to modify the prior decree. The only reported decisions that address this issue correctly conclude that such claims may only be adjudicated in a

---

5. In re Marriage of Snyder (1979) 95 Cal.App.3d 636, 157 Cal.Rptr. 196; Fenn v. Harris (1979) 91 Cal.App.3d 772, 152 Cal. Rptr. 21; Sangiolo v. Sangiolo (1978) 87 Cal.App.3d 511, 151 Cal.Rptr. 27; Bridges v. Bridges (1978) 82 Cal.App.3d 976, 147 Cal.Rptr. 471. Contra, Kelley v. Kelley, supra, 73 Cal.App.3d at pages 677–678, 141 Cal.Rptr. 33, discussed post in footnote 6.

6. In support of his argument, Henry relies principally upon Kelley v. Kelley, supra, 73 Cal.App.3d 672, 141 Cal.Rptr. 33. That court, faced with a case similar to the instant one in all relevant considerations, ruled that the existence of a prior judicial division of community property precluded the plaintiff from litigating her entitlement to a pension which had not been adjudicated in the earlier proceeding. Kelley is disapproved to the extent that it stands for the proposition that any judicial division of community property necessarily precludes the subsequent litigation of community property rights in an asset known to exist at the time of the earlier proceedings, and which could have been adjudicated at that time.

separate action. (See Bodle v. Bodle (1978) 76 Cal.App.3d 758, 767, 143 Cal.Rptr. 115; In re Marriage of Cobb (1977) 68 Cal.App.3d 855, 860, fn. 1, 137 Cal.Rptr. 670.) Under these circumstances, Henry has not established that the motion was denied because Helen's claim lacked merit or was barred by the prior judicial division of community property.[7] Since it is not possible to ascertain from the record the trial court's basis for denying Helen's motion, that court's action cannot be used to bar the present action.

The enforcement of Helen's rights in the pension payments received by Henry since the 1971 adjudication and distribution of the community assets does not present any substantial danger of unjust enrichment. On remand, Henry may seek to limit retrospective enforcement of Helen's claim on an equitable estoppel theory by demonstrating that she in fact received additional support payments in lieu of a share in the pension.[8] (See Civ.Code, § 4800, subds. (a), (b).)

If Helen is allowed to recover her share of the pension payments received by Henry between 1971 and the initiation of the present action, a problem may arise. It may be substantially more burdensome for Henry to account for the pension payments he has received since the 1971 division of community assets than it would have been for him to have complied with a partition effected at that time. Henry is likely to have treated the asset as his separate property and disposed of it according to his needs. The court is confident that this problem may be adequately addressed under the defense of laches. The exercise of a court's authority to so limit equitable relief will provide litigants with an additional incentive to assert all tenable community property rights in assets known to exist at the time of the initial judicial distribution of the marital community.

The judgment is reversed.

TOBRINER, MOSK, CLARK, RICHARDSON, MANUEL and NEWMAN, JJ., concur.

Notes

1. The *Henn* rule is now partially codified at Family Code Section 2556, which provides as follows:

7. Since Henry did not deny the fact that the portion of the pension earned during marriage was community property, and given that his res judicata defense was fatally flawed, the procedural ground was the only valid basis for denial. "Jurisdiction, over a cause or parties after a final judgment, order or decree is exceptional and limited to special situations." (1 Witkin, Cal.Procedure (2d ed. 1971) Jurisdiction, § 286, p. 827.) The Legislature has not provided courts of dissolution with continuing jurisdiction to modify a judgment dividing community property after it has become final. Nor did the original judgment in this case reserve such power to the court. (E.g. In re Marriage of Borges (1978) 83 Cal. App.3d 771, 775, 148 Cal.Rptr. 118.) However, it is the ambiguity of the denial, not the court's lack of jurisdiction over the subject matter of the controversy, that prevents that action from barring the present litigation. If Henry had established that the denial constituted an adjudication of the merit of Helen's claim or his res judicata defense, it could have been entitled to res judicata effect as a valid exercise of the court's general equity jurisdiction. (Cf. Estate of Gilmaker (1962) 57 Cal.2d 627, 630, 21 Cal.Rptr. 585, 371 P.2d 321.)

8. Of course, the defendant spouse may seek a prospective modification of his or her support payments in light of any new partition of an asset not previously adjudicated.

In a proceeding for dissolution of marriage, for nullity of marriage, or for legal separation of the parties, the court has continuing jurisdiction to award community estate assets or community estate liabilities to the parties that have not been previously adjudicated by a judgment in the proceeding. A party may file a postjudgment motion or order to show cause in the proceeding in order to obtain adjudication of any community estate asset or liability omitted or not adjudicated by the judgment. In these cases, the court shall equally divide the omitted or unadjudicated community estate asset or liability, unless the court finds upon good cause shown that the interests of justice require an unequal division of the asset or liability.

2. In order to enter a valid judgment dividing an asset omitted from the original dissolution decree, the court must have personal jurisdiction over the defendant: The "lawsuit for division of community property is a wholly separate and independent action, not a subsequent proceeding within the original dissolution action [citations omitted]. Consequently, the trial court has no authority to render a personal judgment against defendant-husband unless jurisdiction again attaches." Tarvin v. Tarvin, 187 Cal. App.3d 56, 61, 232 Cal.Rptr. 13, 16 (1986).

3. In Simon v. Simon, 165 Cal.App.3d 1044, 212 Cal.Rptr. 87 (1985), the former wife filed an action seeking a division of the community property interest in two parcels of land purchased by the parties during marriage. The appellate court held that the wife's action, filed approximately nine years after the final dissolution judgment, was barred by the doctrine of laches. Nothing in the record explained the wife's delay in pursuing her rights, and the former husband had changed his position on the reasonable belief that all legal issues concerning the parcels had been resolved in the dissolution proceedings.

4. The omitted assets problem arose in the default context in Irwin v. Irwin, 69 Cal.App.3d 317, 138 Cal.Rptr. 9 (1977). There the wife filed a petition for dissolution on the prescribed printed form. She checked the box indicating "There is no property subject to disposition by the court in this proceeding," and left blank the box requesting that rights be determined as provided by law. The husband defaulted. Although the wife testified that the husband had a military retirement pension, neither the interlocutory decree nor the final judgment mentioned property rights. Some two years later, the wife filed an action to establish a community property interest in the pension, and the trial judge entered a judgment declaring that she had such an interest. The husband appealed. The appellate court noted that under the bifurcated divorce concept, where the property is not mentioned or distributed in the judgment of dissolution, the issue of property rights is not deemed adjudicated and may be the subject of a later independent action. The court also recognized that there was an exception established under case law prior to the Family Law Act: If the complaint alleged that there was no community property and a default judgment was entered, the decree constituted an adjudication to this effect. The husband contended that this case fell within the exception. The court disagreed, finding that by checking the box preceding the words "There is no property subject to disposition by the court in this proceeding," the wife was merely reserving the right to have this matter resolved in a later proceeding.

5. There are some limitations on the *Henn* rule. In Smith v. Smith, 127 Cal.App.3d 203, 179 Cal.Rptr. 492 (1981), the husband's state and federal retirement benefits were not included in the division of community property in the 1967 dissolution judgment. In 1968, the wife moved to amend the final decree under West's Ann.Cal.Code of Civil Procedure Section 473 on the grounds of mistake, inadvertence and excusable neglect. The motion was denied as untimely. Thereafter, the wife brought a new action, seeking either to have the dissolution decree set aside, or to partition the retirement benefits on the theory that she had not had an opportunity to litigate the issue in the dissolution proceedings as a result of her attorney's negligence. The husband's demurrer was sustained without leave to amend and the action was dismissed. The wife then sued her attorney for malpractice and recovered $100,000. In 1978 the wife again brought an action against her former spouse, demanding half of his retirement benefits. The trial court sustained the husband's res judicata defense. The appellate court affirmed, noting that the "plaintiff has manifestly received her day in court on the substance of her underlying claim, although not against her former husband." For a discussion of the liability of an attorney for omission of a potential community property asset, see Aloy v. Mash, 38 Cal.3d 413, 212 Cal.Rptr. 162, 696 P.2d 656 (1985), reprinted in this Section.

6. It has been held that a proceeding to modify child support is not an appropriate proceeding in which to raise the issue of division of community property omitted from a dissolution judgment. In re Marriage of Davis, 113 Cal.App.3d 485, 169 Cal.Rptr. 863 (1980).

7. To avoid the problems that can arise where an item of community property is omitted from a dissolution judgment, it has been suggested that a warranty provision be inserted in the judgment. For the nature and effect of such a provision, see In re Marriage of Smethurst, 102 Cal.App.3d 494, 162 Cal.Rptr. 300 (1980).

ALOY v. MASH

Supreme Court of California, 1985.
38 Cal.3d 413, 212 Cal.Rptr. 162, 696 P.2d 656.

KAUS, JUSTICE.

I

Marcella G. Aloy, plaintiff in a legal malpractice action, appeals from a summary judgment for defendant Eugene A. Mash, her former attorney in a 1971 dissolution action against her husband Richard. Marcella's claim of legal malpractice is based on defendant's failure to assert a community property interest in Richard's vested military retirement pension.[1]

---

1. The pension was vested because Richard had been in the service for over 20 years and thus had an unconditional right to it upon retirement.

It is unclear whether the pension could also be termed "matured." There is some inconsistency in the definition of a "ma-

tured" pension. Most cases define it as one in which all conditions precedent to the payment of the benefits have taken place or are within the control of the employee. (*In re Marriage of Gillmore* (1981) 29 Cal.3d 418, 422, fn. 2, 174 Cal.Rptr. 493, 629 P.2d 1; *In re Marriage of Fithian* (1974) 10

Marcella employed defendant Mash in January 1971 to represent her in the dissolution action. Richard was then on active military service and was therefore not receiving a pension although he had been in the service for over 20 years and was eligible to retire. (10 U.S.C. § 8911.) Defendant failed to claim any community property interest in Richard's pension and it was not put in issue in the dissolution action. The final decree of dissolution was entered in December 1971. Richard retired sometime between 1971 and 1980.

In 1971, the California view regarding the characterization of vested federal military retirement pensions as community or separate property was unsettled. In 1974, however, we held that federal preemption did not bar treating such federal military pensions as community property. (*In re Marriage of Fithian, supra,* 10 Cal.3d 592, 111 Cal.Rptr. 369, 517 P.2d 449.)

In 1980, Marcella filed a complaint against defendant alleging that he negligently failed to assert her community property interest in Richard's military retirement pension, which failure prevented her from receiving any share of his gross military retirement pension benefits "from either the date of separation and/or the date of [his] retirement."

Defendant moved for summary judgment on the ground that in 1971 the law regarding the character of federal military retirement pensions was unsettled, and that he had exercised informed judgment and was therefore immune from a claim of professional negligence. He submitted a declaration stating, among other things: "2. In 1971, it was my practice to read advance sheets, particularly in the dissolution area, an area in which I have regularly practiced. I would therefore have had knowledge of specific decisions at the time they were rendered or shortly thereafter. [¶] 3. In 1971, I relied on the case of *French v. French,* 17 Cal.2d 775, 112 P.2d 235 (1941) as authority that a non-matured military pension, that is, one owned by a person on active military duty, was not subject to division upon dissolution. I was also aware that in 1971 this case had not yet been overruled. I read the decision *In re Marriage of Fithian,* 10 Cal.3d 592, 111 Cal.Rptr. 369, 517 P.2d 449 (1974) shortly after it was issued in 1974. [¶] 4. I drafted the terms of the interlocutory decree based on my research, knowledge, and understanding of the law in 1971."

Marcella opposed the motion, asserting that it was a triable issue whether defendant had made an informed decision. She submitted excerpts from her deposition testimony in which she stated that the one time she asked defendant whether she was entitled to a portion of Richard's military retirement pension, he told her she had no such right

Cal.3d 592, 596, fn. 2, 111 Cal.Rptr. 369, 517 P.2d 449; *Smith v. Lewis* (1975) 13 Cal.3d 349, 355, fn. 4, 118 Cal.Rptr. 621, 530 P.2d 589.) Under this definition the pension was also matured. *In re Marriage of Brown* (1976) 15 Cal.3d 838, 842, 126 Cal.Rptr. 633, 544 P.2d 561, however, defined a "matured" benefit as one where there is an "unconditional right to immediate payment"—i.e., where the employee "reaches retirement age and elects to retire." Under the latter definition, Richard's pension had not matured since he was still on active duty.

because Richard was still on active duty. Marcella also submitted excerpts from defendant's deposition testimony where he discussed his knowledge and research as follows: "MR. WATTERS: Q. Are you a regular reader of the advance sheets, say from 1971 up until now? [¶] A. I read them. I get them in the office but I can't recall when I started getting them, frankly. Whether I got them in 1971, I don't know. I used to read the advance sheets all the time but I don't know when I got them. I still skim them, review them, when I can. [¶] Q. You review the cases in your particular area of practice? [¶] A. Yes, I do. [¶] Q. That would include the domestic area, up until you stopped doing domestic work, or slowed down? [¶] A. Right. [¶] Q. As of 1971, what was your case authority for your position that when someone in the military service was on active duty that their pension was not community property, what was your authority? [¶] A. I don't know what I checked with at that time. Probably the French case would be the authority. [¶] Q. A 1941 case? [¶] A. Whatever the date is. [¶] Q. Sir, any other authority that you can cite me other than the French case for that belief that you had? [¶] * * * [¶] A. I can't recall what else, what I might have looked up at that point. Might have been something else but I don't * * * [¶] A. Well, this is again going back to my thinking, what I might have thought back then, and I'd have to say probably the same thing, that if a person has been in the military, active military duty, was not drawing his pension, that it was not an item to be divided at that time. [¶] Q. This would be true when the person was in the service over twenty years, over twenty or under twenty years? [¶] MRS. MARRISON: Q. Do you understand the question? [¶] A. I presume he is asking what was in my mind at that time and I'm not sure in this case at that time what was in my mind. I'm not sure what I would have stated at that time. If you ask me the question in 1971, is that what you're asking?"

Marcella further submitted a declaration by James J. Simonelli, which stated that he was an attorney with an extensive practice in family law since 1970, and that in 1971 attorneys in the family law field in the San Joaquin Valley uniformly claimed a community property interest in vested military retirement pensions. Simonelli further stated that had he been representing Marcella in November 1971, he would have advised her that she had some community property interest in Richard's vested military retirement pension and that the only issue as to that interest was whether federal law preempted state enforcement of such an interest.

II

The criteria on appeals from summary judgments are too familiar to need restatement. In brief, if the record discloses triable issues with respect to negligence, causation and damages, the judgment must be reversed.

In *Smith v. Lewis* (1975) 13 Cal.3d 349, 118 Cal.Rptr. 621, 530 P.2d 589—a legal malpractice case based on an attorney's 1967 failure to claim a community property interest in the husband's vested retirement benefits—we affirmed a judgment for plaintiff and rejected the defendant attorney's contention that he should not be liable for mistaken advice when well-informed lawyers in the community had entertained reasonable doubt at the time as to the proper resolution of the legal issue. We found the situation in no way analogous to that in *Lucas v. Hamm* (1961) 56 Cal.2d 583, 15 Cal.Rptr. 821, 364 P.2d 685, involving the esoteric subject of the rule against perpetuities. We conceded that in 1967 the law regarding the community character of the husband's federal pension was unsettled. We said, however: "If the law on a particular subject is doubtful or debatable, an attorney will not be held responsible for failing to anticipate the manner in which the uncertainty will be resolved. [Citation.] But even with respect to an unsettled area of the law, we believe an attorney assumes an obligation to his client to undertake reasonable research in an effort to ascertain relevant legal principles and to make an informed decision as to a course of conduct based upon an intelligent assessment of the problem." (*Id.*, 13 Cal.3d, at pp. 358–359, 118 Cal.Rptr. 621, 530 P.2d 589.)

Smith v. Lewis, supra, is obviously of little help to defendant. His motion for summary judgment was, in fact, primarily based on *Davis v. Damrell* (1981) 119 Cal.App.3d 883, 174 Cal.Rptr. 257—a similar case in which Damrell, the wife's attorney, in 1970 failed to assert a community property interest in the husband's vested federal military retirement pension. The husband retired in 1973, and the wife filed suit against Damrell sometime thereafter. The Court of Appeal affirmed the summary judgment for Damrell on the ground that he had demonstrated compliance with the *Smith v. Lewis* standards by showing a thorough, contemporaneous research effort on an issue of unsettled law. He had submitted a declaration describing his detailed knowledge of legal developments and debate in the field. He traced his familiarity with the line of cases following the earlier *French* rule (*French v. French* (1941) 17 Cal.2d 775, 112 P.2d 235 [nonvested military pension was mere expectancy not subject to division as community property]), overruled in *In re Marriage of Brown* (1976) 15 Cal.3d 838, 126 Cal.Rptr. 633, 544 P.2d 561, and recounted his special interest in the *Wissner* case (*Wissner v. Wissner* (1950) 338 U.S. 655, 70 S.Ct. 398, 94 L.Ed. 424 [establishing the supremacy of a federal statute governing disposition of the proceeds of a military service life insurance policy]), which had motivated him to follow its progress from its inception.

Defendant's reliance on *Davis v. Damrell, supra,* is ill-advised, since the differences between his professional conduct and that of the defendant in that case inexorably point to potential liability on defendant's part. In brief, in *Davis* the defendant attorney was thoroughly familiar with all the pertinent authorities, state and federal, and had reached the conclusion, based primarily on *Wissner v. Wissner, supra,* 338 U.S. 655, 70 S.Ct. 398, 94 L.Ed. 424, that vested military pension benefits were not subject to California community property rules. His decision not to claim a community property interest in the husband's military pension was not actionable, as it represented "a reasoned exercise of an informed judgment grounded on a professional evaluation of applicable legal principles." (*Id.*, 119 Cal.App.3d, at p. 888, 174 Cal.Rptr. 257.) [2] Defendant, by contrast, relied on a single case—*French v. French* (1941) 17 Cal.2d 775, 112 P.2d 235 for the proposition that a nonmatured military pension was not subject to division on dissolution. At his deposition he never did answer the question whether he was aware that a military pension vests after 20 years of service, whether the serviceman retires or not. This would have been a vital point in his research, for in *French v. French* itself a dictum indicates that after retirement pay vests it becomes community property. (*Id.* at p. 778, 112 P.2d 235.) [3] He thus never even gave himself a chance to consider whether his client was entitled to a community share in monthly payments which, but for the husband's election not to retire, would have been vested pension payments. (See *In re Marriage of Gillmore, supra,* 29 Cal.3d 418, 423, 174 Cal.Rptr. 493, 629 P.2d 1; *Waite v. Waite* (1972) 6 Cal.3d 461, 472, 99 Cal.Rptr. 325, 492 P.2d 13.)

In sum, this is not a case where the defendant attorney, basing his judgment on all available data, made a rational professional judgment not to claim an interest in the husband's pension. Rather, he acted—more precisely, failed to act—on an incomplete reading of a single case, without appreciating the vital difference between a member of the armed forces who has not yet served long enough to be eligible to retire and one who has but chooses to stay in the service. As far as the issue of federal preemption is concerned, the record does not show that he ever considered it.

In sum, the record on which the motion for summary judgment was argued presented a triable issue of negligence.

III

The question whether the defendant's negligence caused damage in some amount need not detain us long. Footnote 9 to *Smith v. Lewis, supra,* 13 Cal.3d at pages 360–361, 118 Cal.Rptr. 621, 530 P.2d 589, makes this an a fortiori case. (See also *Martin v. Hall* (1971) 20 Cal.App.3d 414, at pp. 423–424, 97 Cal.Rptr. 730.) Nor—the arguments based on *McCarty v. McCarty* (1981) 453 U.S. 210, 101 S.Ct. 2728, 69 L.Ed.2d 589, aside—do we understand defendant to claim otherwise.

IV

McCarty v. McCarty, supra, decided on June 26, 1981, held that the application of community property principles impermissibly conflicts with the federal military retirement scheme. This, of course, happened

---

2. Amicus, appearing on behalf of defendant, argues that, were the rule otherwise, "[s]elf-defensive instincts would encourage lawyers to provide their clients with the most popular perception of the law rather than their own views. Candor and creativity would be replaced by consensus. Such a rule would be neither in the interest of clients nor lawyers." Brave words, but one suspects that a client whose interests coincide with the popular conception of the law would expect his attorney to advance them, particularly if the consensus is shared by the judiciary.

3. Presumably the same dictum was belatedly discovered by the defendant in *Smith v. Lewis.* (See *Smith v. Lewis, supra,* 13 Cal.3d at p. 358, fn. 7, 118 Cal.Rptr. 621, 530 P.2d 589.)

a decade after defendant had represented plaintiff. Nor, unlike the defendant attorney in *Davis v. Damrell, supra,* had defendant anticipated this development. Nevertheless he seeks to take advantage of *McCarty* in two ways: first, he argues that had he asserted a community property interest in Richard's pension, the United States Supreme Court case which invalidated any favorable ruling by a California court might have been *Aloy v. Aloy,* rather than *McCarty v. McCarty;* second, he argues that it simply cannot be actionable malpractice not to assert a claim which is eventually found to be invalid.

A

Defendant's first argument assumes, of course, that *McCarty v. McCarty* once and for all settled the question of Colonel McCarty's pension in his favor. Solely because we happen to know judicially that the *McCarty* controversy is far from over and do not wish to make any unnecessary statement which might affect its outcome, we shall assume defendant's hypothesis to be true.[4]

Assuming further that it is a legitimate subject of inquiry whether, at the critical time, the early '70's, the United States Supreme Court would have granted certiorari on the issue whether states could hold military pensions to be community property, all the available evidence is negative. After we first decided in favor of the nonmember spouse in *Fithian,* certiorari was denied (*Fithian v. Fithian* (1974) 419 U.S. 825, 95 S.Ct. 41, 42 L.Ed.2d 48), as was a petition for rehearing. (*Fithian v. Fithian, supra,* 419 U.S., at p. 1060, 95 S.Ct. at p. 644, 42 L.Ed.2d 657.) Shortly thereafter we reaffirmed *Fithian* in *In re Marriage of Milhan* (1974) 13 Cal.3d 129, 117 Cal.Rptr. 809, 528 P.2d 1145. Again certiorari was denied. (*Milhan v. Milhan* (1975) 421 U.S. 976, 95 S.Ct. 1976, 44 L.Ed.2d 467.) Nothing in the *Aloy v. Aloy* litigation suggests to us that it was more likely than *Fithian* or *Milhan* to persuade the high court that the military pension issue was one whose time had come.[5]

B

Finally we turn to the argument that the summary judgment was correct because the claim which defendant negligently failed to assert in

4. We know nothing about the details of the continuing *McCarty* litigation. It seems a fair guess, however, that it is somehow affected by the passage of the Federal Uniformed Services Former Spouses' Protection Act of 1982. (Pub.L. No. 97–252, tit. X.) It is, of course, 100 percent speculation whether the mythical *Aloy v. Aloy* (197_) —— U.S. ——, would have triggered similar federal legislation.

5. It is the repeated denial of certiorari which distinguishes this case from *Martin v. Hall, supra,* 20 Cal.App.3d 414, 423–424, 97 Cal.Rptr. 730. There an attorney retained to represent a client accused of crime, failed to assert the, under the circumstances, plausible bar of the multiple prosecution aspect of Penal Code section 654. His omission took place after we had hinted in *Neal v. State of California* (1960) 55 Cal.2d 11, 21, 9 Cal.Rptr. 607, 357 P.2d 839, that section 654 might preclude multiple prosecutions even in situations in which multiple punishment would be permissible. *Kellett v. Superior Court* (1966) 63 Cal.2d 822, 48 Cal.Rptr. 366, 409 P.2d 206, however, which eventually so held, was still some years down the road. On the issue of causation, the Court of Appeal held that it had "no reason to suppose that the result in a hypothetical *Martin v. Superior Court* would have been different." Here there is every reason to suppose that *Aloy v. Aloy* would not have escaped the confines of California.

1971 luckily turned out to be worthless in 1981—the serendipity defense. This argument is not based on any theory that in point of fact Marcella would not have benefited financially had a community property claim to Richard's pension rights been asserted in 1971. (See pt. III, *ante.*) Rather, defendant simply asserts that he was under no "duty to secure for plaintiff benefits to which she was not legally entitled." [6]

It is evident from the way defendant makes his point—"benefits to which she *was* not legally entitled"—that he assumes as a premise of his argument that *McCarty* has been retroactively applied and that, therefore, in a real sense *McCarty* "was" the law 10 years before it was decided, when defendant acted for Marcella.

Whatever may be said in favor of defendant's theory were this premise correct, the fact is that no case within our memory has received less retroactive application than *McCarty*. Starting with the last paragraph of the *McCarty* opinion itself, the judicial and legislative branches, state and federal, cooperated in a massive and largely successful drive to make *McCarty* disappear—prospectively, presently and retroactively. Some highlights of that effort are noted below.[7] The result is that, for

---

6. Amicus for defendant makes the same point more subtly by distinguishing between "fault"—conceded—and "error"—disputed.

7. 1. The United States Supreme Court itself did not think too highly of the result it felt compelled to reach: "We recognize that the plight of an ex-spouse of a retired service member is often a serious one. * * * That plight may be mitigated to some extent by the ex-spouse's right to claim Social Security benefits, cf. *Hisquierdo [v. Hisquierdo],* 439 U.S. [572], at 590 [99 S.Ct. 802, 812, 59 L.Ed.2d 1], and to garnish military retired pay for the purposes of support. Nonetheless, Congress may well decide, as it has in the Civil Service and Foreign Service contexts, that more protection should be afforded a former spouse of a retired service member. This decision, however, is for Congress alone." (*McCarty v. McCarty, supra,* 453 U.S. at pp. 235–236, 101 S.Ct. at 2742–2743.)

2. Congress, as part of the fiscal 1983 defense bill passed title X of Public Law No. 97–252, the Federal Uniformed Services Former Spouses' Protection Act (FUSFS-PA) which, in effect, nullified *McCarty* prospectively and, in part, retroactively. (See 10 U.S.C. § 1408 et seq.; § 1006 of the act allows enforcement of pre-*McCarty* judgments.)

3. Even without the benefit of or reliance on FUSFSPA, our cases uniformly held that pre-*McCarty* judgments treating military pensions as community property were not affected by *McCarty*. (*In re Mar-*

riage of Camp (1983) 142 Cal.App.3d 217, 219–221, 191 Cal.Rptr. 45; *In re Marriage of Parks* (1982) 138 Cal.App.3d 346, 348–349, 188 Cal.Rptr. 26; *In re Marriage of McGhee* (1982) 131 Cal.App.3d 408, 411, 182 Cal.Rptr. 456; *In re Marriage of Fellers* (1981) 125 Cal.App.3d 254, 256–258, 178 Cal.Rptr. 35; *In re Marriage of Sheldon* (1981) 124 Cal.App.3d 371, 377–380, 177 Cal.Rptr. 380.) This was declared to be the law even if the case was still pending on appeal at the time of the *McCarty* decision (*In re Marriage of Sheldon, supra,* 124 Cal. App.3d at pp. 380–384, 177 Cal.Rptr. 380), unless the member had preserved the preemption issue. (*In re Marriage of Jacanin* (1981) 124 Cal.App.3d 67, 70–71, 177 Cal. Rptr. 86.) Federal courts agreed. (*Wilson v. Wilson* (5th Cir.1982) 667 F.2d 497 [cert. den. 458 U.S. 1107, 102 S.Ct. 3485, 73 L.Ed.2d 1368]; *Erspan v. Badgett* (5th Cir. 1981) 659 F.2d 26, 28 [cert. den. 455 U.S. 945, 102 S.Ct. 1443, 71 L.Ed.2d 658]; *Marriage of Smith* (1982) 549 F.Supp. 761, 767.)

4. Courts of Appeal, with rare unanimity, seized on FUSFSPA to obliterate all traces of *McCarty*. (*In re Marriage of Sarles* (1983) 143 Cal.App.3d 24, 26–30, 191 Cal.Rptr. 514; *In re Marriage of Ankenman* (1983) 142 Cal.App.3d 833, 836–838, 191 Cal.Rptr. 292; *In re Marriage of Fransen* (1983) 142 Cal.App.3d 419, 427, 190 Cal. Rptr. 885; *In re Marriage of Hopkins* (1983) 142 Cal.App.3d 350, 353–361, 191 Cal.Rptr. 70; *In re Marriage of Frederick* (1983) 141 Cal.App.3d 876, 879–880, 190 Cal.Rptr. 588; *In re Marriage of Buikema*

most purposes, *McCarty* not only is not the law but never really was. As one Court of Appeal put it: "[T]here is no longer any *McCarty* rule to be retroactively applied." (*In re Marriage of Frederick* (1983) 141 Cal. App.3d 876, 880, 190 Cal.Rptr. 588.) It would be ironic if the chief legacy of *McCarty* were the immunization of legal malpractice by an attorney who never even pondered the issues which fathered *McCarty*'s brief life.

The judgment is reversed.

Mosk and Grodin, JJ., and Ramsey, J., concur.

Reynoso, Justice, dissenting.

I respectfully dissent. With the exception of the majority opinion, I know of no case which suggests that an attorney whose advice is correct may be held liable for malpractice.

Relying on the standard developed in *Smith v. Lewis* (1975) 13 Cal.3d 349, 118 Cal.Rptr. 621, 530 P.2d 589 and its progeny,[1] the majority concludes that an attorney may face malpractice liability despite the fact that the law is ultimately resolved in accordance with the advice given. Although this application of the *Smith* standard follows logically from its emphasis on the duty of care owed a client, it nonetheless raises a troubling anomaly: where the law is unsettled, the attorney who gives advice later determined to be correct may well have committed malpractice, while the attorney whose advice turns out to be erroneous may avoid liability entirely.

The law cannot tolerate such incongruous results. As Justice Holmes so aptly observed long ago, "[t]he life of the law has not been logic: it has been experience." (Holmes, Common Law (1881) 1.) Experience now tells us that the *Smith* standard, however rational and well-suited to its original purpose, no longer makes sense. We must therefore formulate a new standard that draws a fair and reasonable distinction between culpable and nonculpable practitioners.

The defect inherent in the *Smith* standard, made ever clearer by today's majority opinion, is that the concept of legal error is confused

---

(1983) 139 Cal.App.3d 689, 691, 188 Cal. Rptr. 856.)

5. This pretty much reduced the impact of *McCarty* to judgments which became final between June 25, 1981, the date of that decision, and February 1, 1983, the effective date of FUSFSPA. The few unfortunate nonmember spouses whose judgments did became final between those dates, were given special permission by the California Legislature to ask that the judgments be modified "to include a division of military retirement benefits payable on or after February 1, 1983, * * *" (Civ.Code, § 5124, added by Stats.1983, ch. 775, § 1, p. ___.)

It is noted that this court has yet to speak on the matters covered in this footnote. Our purpose in referring to the vari-

ous authorities is not to present them as immutably correct, but as indicative of general dissatisfaction with *McCarty*.

1. Prior to *Smith* attorneys in California were not liable "for lack of knowledge as to the true state of the law where a doubtful or debatable point [was] involved." (*Sprague v. Morgan* (1960) 185 Cal.App.2d 519, 523, 8 Cal.Rptr. 347.) *Smith* modified that rule so that even with regard to an unsettled area of the law an attorney is obligated to "undertake reasonable research in an effort to ascertain relevant legal principles and to make an informed decision * * *" (*Smith,* supra, 13 Cal.3d at p. 359, 118 Cal.Rptr. 621, 530 P.2d 589.)

with that of fault, converting a question of law into one of fact. Malpractice consists of four elements: duty arising out of the attorney-client relationship, breach of that duty, causation and damages. The second element breaks down further into two components: legal error and failure to use "such skill, prudence and diligence as lawyers of ordinary skill and capacity commonly possess and exercise in the performance of the tasks which they undertake." (*Lucas v. Hamm* (1961) 56 Cal.2d 583, 591, 15 Cal.Rptr. 821, 364 P.2d 685.) The first is a question of law, the second a question of fact.

The question of whether an attorney erred necessarily must be resolved before any issue of negligence arises. An attorney who renders erroneous advice may not be negligent in doing so. (See *Davis v. Damrell* (1981) 119 Cal.App.3d 883, 174 Cal.Rptr. 257.) A second attorney may fail to perform adequate research but somehow give his client accurate advice. Neither of these attorneys has committed malpractice. (See Mallen & Levit, Legal Malpractice (2d ed. 1981) § 250, p. 317.)

Where the law is settled, it is relatively easy to determine whether the attorney's advice was erroneous. Problems arise only with respect to issues of law that are unresolved or in a state of flux at the time the advice is given. In either instance, however, the question of whether the advice was wrong is a question of law.

Ironically, *Smith* itself reflects this basic approach. At the outset of the analysis the court stressed: "the crucial inquiry is whether his advice was *so legally deficient* when it was given that he may be found to have failed to use 'such skill, prudence, and diligence as lawyers of ordinary skill and capacity commonly possess and exercise in the performance of the tasks which they undertake.' [Citation.] We must, therefore, examine the indicia of the law which were readily available to defendant at the time he performed the legal services in question." (Id., 13 Cal.3d, at p. 356, 118 Cal.Rptr. 621, 530 P.2d 589.) (Emphasis added.)

Thus, *Smith* initially proposed a two-step test for determining whether an attorney has been negligent. As noted, the threshold inquiry is a legal one, whether adequate legal authority existed at the time to support the advice given. Only when this question is answered in the negative is it necessary to move to the second part of the test, the factual inquiry as to whether the attorney breached the standard of care in rendering the erroneous advice.

Applying this test to the case at bar reveals that Attorney Mash did not err in advising his client in 1971 that her husband's federal military pension was not community property. As the majority notes, "[i]n 1971, the California view regarding the characterization of vested federal military retirement pensions as community or separate property was unsettled." Ante, p. 163 of 212 Cal.Rptr., at p. 657 of 696 P.2d. In fact, Mash relied on an opinion of this court, *French v. French* (1941) 17 Cal.2d 775, 112 P.2d 235, in concluding that the pension was not divisible. As *French* remained good law, this reliance was neither unreasonable nor erroneous. Because Mash committed no error, the malpractice claim must fail.

It is imperative that a lawyer remain free to choose one of a number of reasonable and legally supportable solutions to an otherwise unsettled legal question and advise the client accordingly without facing a malpractice suit.

BIRD, C.J., and TABER, J., concur.

Chapter 8

DISTRIBUTION OF COMMUNITY PROPERTY AT DEATH

On the death of a married person, various problems may arise involving succession rights to the decedent's property and the use of community property to pay debts and expenses. These issues are generally covered in courses dealing with decedent estate administration. The purpose of this chapter is simply to give an overview of some of the community property problems involved in the administration process.

Under California law, a married person has the power of testamentary disposition over one-half of the community property and quasi-community property and all of his or her separate property.[1] If a married person dies without a will, the disposition of his or her property is controlled by the laws of intestate succession. Under Probate Code Section 6401, one-half of the community property already belongs to the surviving spouse; the decedent's one-half passes to the surviving spouse by intestate succession. The disposition of quasi-community property is substantially similar to community property; that is, if the decedent dies intestate, all of the quasi-community property passes to the surviving spouse.[2]

The disposition of the decedent's separate property depends upon which relatives in addition to the spouse survived the decedent.[3] For example, if the decedent left one child, the spouse and the child each receive one-half of the separate property. If the decedent left two or more children, the spouse receives one-third and the children split the remaining two-thirds of the separate property. If the decedent left no children or issue of children, but was survived by parents, or brothers, or sisters, those relatives will receive one-half of the separate property, and the spouse receives the other one-half. Only if the decedent left no issue, no parent, no brother or sister and no nieces or nephews will the surviving spouse receive all of the separate property. Because of the

---

1. West's Ann.Cal.Probate Code §§ 28, 100, 101, 6401.

2. West's Ann.Cal.Probate Code §§ 66, 101, 6101, 6401.

3. See West's Ann.Cal.Probate Code § 6402.

substantial difference in succession rights to community property and separate property, the various classification problems considered earlier are frequently at issue in probate proceedings.

Probate administration is essentially a three-fold process: it encompasses the collection and inventory of the decedent's assets, the payment of debts and taxes, and the distribution of the property to the beneficiaries under the decedent's will or to the decedent's heirs in case of intestacy. Not all property in which the decedent had an interest is subject to probate administration. For example, property held by the decedent and another in joint tenancy is not in the probate estate. Proceeds of life insurance policies are normally not included in the probate estate. With some limited exceptions, a decedent's separate property is subject to probate administration. If the deceased spouse died intestate leaving property passing to the surviving spouse under the intestate succession laws, or if the decedent died testate and by will bequeathed all or part of his property to the surviving spouse, the surviving spouse may use an abbreviated "set aside" procedure in lieu of the regular probate process. This set aside procedure is now available with respect to both community and separate property owned by the decedent.[4] Even though probate administration is not required, death taxes, if any, must be paid and title to the property must be cleared. To resolve these problems, there is now a special statutory procedure for the determination and confirmation of the property to the surviving spouse.[5] This procedure is faster and less costly than regular probate administration. It should be noted that the surviving spouse need not avail himself or herself of the set-aside procedure, and may elect to have the property administered in the decedent's probate estate.[6] It should also be noted that the set aside procedure is available only to the surviving spouse. If the decedent left his separate property or his interest in the community property to someone other than the surviving spouse, probate administration will probably be required.

One problem which may arise in connection with probate or property set-aside proceedings involves the payment of the decedent's debts. Where the decedent's estate consists of both community and separate property, should the debts simply be apportioned between the two estates ratably according to their relative sizes, or should the debts be classified, with community debts chargeable against the community property and separate debts payable out of separate property? In *Estate of Coffee*,[7] the court stated the administrator should pay the debts and charges ratably out of the two estates according to their respective values. Does this mean that the reimbursement principles developed by

---

4. Prior to 1985, the set aside procedure was available only for community property passing to the surviving spouse. The set aside statutes were amended in 1985 to encompass all property owned by a decedent that passes to the surviving spouse by will or intestacy. See West's Ann.Cal.Probate Code § 13500 et seq.

5. West's Ann.Cal.Probate Code § 13500 et seq.

6. West's Ann.Cal.Probate Code § 13502.

7. Estate of Coffee is reprinted in this chapter.

the courts in conjunction with dissolution proceedings have no place in probate or summary administration proceedings?[8]

Another problem which may arise in connection with the death of a married person involves the extent of the power of testamentary disposition. It is clear that a married person has the right to make a testamentary disposition of only one-half of the community property. Suppose, however, that the decedent's will provides for the disposition of all of the community property, and that the will also makes provision for the surviving spouse. May the surviving spouse keep his or her one-half of the community property and take the benefits provided for in the will, or must an election be made? The case of *Estate of Prager,* reprinted in this chapter, considers this and related problems.

WEST'S ANNOTATED PROBATE CODE OF CALIFORNIA

§ 28. Community Property

As used in this code, "community property" means:

(a) Community property heretofore or hereafter acquired during marriage by a married person while domiciled in this state.

(b) All personal property wherever situated, and all real property situated in this state, heretofore or hereafter acquired during the marriage by a married person while domiciled elsewhere, that is community property, or a substantially equivalent type of marital property, under the laws of the place where the acquiring spouse was domiciled at the time of its acquisition.

(c) All personal property wherever situated, and all real property situated in this state, heretofore or hereafter acquired during the marriage by a married person in exchange for real or personal property, wherever situated, that is community property, or a substantially equivalent type of marital property, under the laws of the place where the acquiring spouse was domiciled at the time the property so exchanged was acquired.

(Added by Stats.1983, c. 842, § 21.)

§ 66. Quasi-Community Property

As used in this code, "quasi-community property" means the following property, other than community property as defined in Section 28:

(a) All personal property wherever situated, and all real property situated in this state, heretofore or hereafter acquired by a decedent while domiciled elsewhere that would have been the community property of the decedent and the surviving spouse if the decedent had been domiciled in this state at the time of its acquisition.

(b) All personal property wherever situated, and all real property situated in this state, heretofore or hereafter acquired in exchange for real or personal property, wherever situated, that would have been the community property of the decedent and the surviving spouse if the decedent had been domiciled in this state at the time the property so exchanged was acquired.

(Added by Stats.1983, c. 842, § 21.)

8. See West's Ann.Cal.Probate Code § 11444; see also §§ 13550–54.

§ 100. Community Property

Applicable to estates of decedents who died on or after Jan. 1, 1985.

Upon the death of a married person, one-half of the community property belongs to the surviving spouse and the other half belongs to the decedent.

(Added by Stats.1983, c. 842, § 22.)

§ 101. Quasi-Community Property

Applicable to estates of decedents who died on or after Jan. 1, 1985.

Upon the death of a married person domiciled in this state, one-half of the decedent's quasi-community property belongs to the surviving spouse and the other half belongs to the decedent.

(Added by Stats.1983, c. 842, § 22.)

§ 102. Transfer of Quasi-Community Property; Restoration to Decedent's Estate; Requirements

Applicable to estates of decedents who died on or after Jan. 1, 1985.

(a) The decedent's surviving spouse may require the transferee of property in which the surviving spouse had an expectancy under Section 101 at the time of the transfer to restore to the decedent's estate one-half of the property if the transferee retains the property or, if not, one-half of its proceeds or, if none, one-half of its value at the time of transfer, if all of the following requirements are satisfied:

(1) The decedent died domiciled in this state.

(2) The decedent made a transfer of the property to a person other than the surviving spouse without receiving in exchange a consideration of substantial value and without the written consent or joinder of the surviving spouse.

(3) The transfer is any of the following types:

(A) A transfer under which the decedent retained at the time of death the possession or enjoyment of, or the right to income from, the property.

(B) A transfer to the extent that the decedent retained at the time of death a power, either alone or in conjunction with any other person, to revoke or to consume, invade, or dispose of the principal for the decedent's own benefit.

(C) A transfer whereby property is held at the time of the decedent's death by the decedent and another with right of survivorship.

(b) Nothing in this section requires a transferee to restore to the decedent's estate any life insurance, accident insurance, joint annuity, or pension payable to a person other than the surviving spouse.

(c) All property restored to the decedent's estate under this section belongs to the surviving spouse pursuant to Section 101 as though the transfer had not been made.

(Added by Stats.1983, c. 842, § 22.)

§ 103. Simultaneous Death; Community or Quasi-Community Property

Applicable to estates of decedents who died on or after Jan. 1, 1985.

Except as provided by Section 224, if a husband and wife die leaving community or quasi-community property and it cannot be established by clear and convincing evidence that one spouse survived the other:

(a) One-half of the community property and one-half of the quasi-community property shall be administered upon or distributed, or otherwise dealt with, as if one spouse had survived and as if that half belonged to that spouse.

(b) The other half of the community property and the other half of the quasi-community property shall be administered upon or distributed, or otherwise dealt with, as if the other spouse had survived and as if that half belonged to that spouse.

(Added by Stats.1983, c. 842, § 22.)

§ 6101. Property Which May Be Disposed of by Will

Applicable to estates of decedents who died on or after Jan. 1, 1985.

A will may dispose of the following property:

(a) The testator's separate property.

(b) The one-half of the community property that belongs to the testator under Section 100.

(c) The one-half of the testator's quasi-community property that belongs to the testator under Section 101.

(Added by Stats.1983, c. 842, § 55.)

§ 6400. Property Subject to Intestacy Provisions

Applicable to estates of decedents who died on or after Jan. 1, 1985.

Any part of the estate of a decedent not effectively disposed of by will passes to the decedent's heirs as prescribed in this part.

(Added by Stats.1983, c. 842, § 55.)

§ 6401. Surviving Spouse; Intestate Share; Community or Quasi-Community Property; Separate Property

Applicable to estates of decedents who died on or after Jan. 1, 1985.

(a) As to community property, the intestate share of the surviving spouse is the one-half of the community property that belongs to the decedent under Section 100.

(b) As to quasi-community property, the intestate share of the surviving spouse is the one-half of the quasi-community property that belongs to the decedent under Section 101.

(c) As to separate property, the intestate share of the surviving spouse is as follows:

(1) The entire intestate estate if the decedent did not leave any surviving issue, parent, brother, sister, or issue of a deceased brother or sister.

(2) One-half of the intestate estate in the following cases:

(A) Where the decedent leaves only one child or the issue of a deceased child.

(B) Where the decedent leaves no issue but leaves a parent or parents or their issue or the issue of either of them.

(3) One-third of the intestate estate in the following cases:

(A) Where the decedent leaves more than one child living.

(B) Where the decedent leaves one child living and the issue of one or more deceased children.

(C) Where the decedent leaves issue of two or more deceased children.

(Added by Stats.1983, c. 842, § 55.   Amended by Stats.1984, c. 892, § 40.)

§ 6402. Intestate Estate Not Passing to Surviving Spouse

Applicable to estates of decedents who died on or after Jan. 1, 1985.

Except as provided in Section 6402.5, the part of the intestate estate not passing to the surviving spouse under Section 6401, or the entire intestate estate if there is no surviving spouse, passes as follows:

(a) To the issue of the decedent; if they are all of the same degree of kinship to the decedent they take equally, but if of unequal degree, then those of more remote degree take in the manner provided in Section 240.

(b) If there is no surviving issue, to the decedent's parent or parents equally.

(c) If there is no surviving issue or parent, to the issue of the parents of either of them, the issue taking equally if they are all of the same degree of kinship to the decedent, but if of unequal degree those of more remote degree take in the manner provided in Section 240.

(d) If there is no surviving issue, parent or issue of a parent, but the decedent is survived by one or more grandparents or issue of grandparents, to the grandparent or grandparents equally, or to the issue of such grandparents if there is no surviving grandparent, the issue taking equally if they are all of the same degree of kinship to the decedent, but if of unequal degree those of more remote degree take in the manner provided in Section 240.

(e) If there is no surviving issue, parent or issue of a parent, grandparent or issue of a grandparent, but the decedent is survived by the issue of a predeceased spouse, to such issue, the issue taking equally if they are all of the same degree of kinship to the predeceased spouse, but if of unequal degree those of more remote degree take in the manner provided in Section 240.

(f) If there is no surviving issue, parent or issue of a parent, grandparent or issue of a grandparent, or issue of a predeceased spouse, but the decedent is survived by next of kin, to the next of kin in equal degree, but when there are two or more collateral kindred in equal degree, but claiming through different ancestors, those who claim through the nearest ancestor shall be preferred to those claiming through an ancestor more remote.

(g) If there is no surviving next of kin of the decedent and no surviving issue of a predeceased spouse of the decedent, but the decedent is survived by the parents of a predeceased spouse or the issue of such parents, to the parent or parents equally, or to the issue of such parents if both are deceased, the issue taking equally if they are all of the same degree of kinship to the predeceased spouse, but if of unequal degree those of more remote degree take in the manner provided in Section 240.

(Added by Stats.1983, c. 842, § 55. Amended by Stats.1984, c. 892, § 41; Stats.1985, c. 982, § 19.)

§ 6402.5 Predeceased Spouse; Portion of Decedent's Estate Attributable to Decedent's Predeceased Spouse

Applicable to estates of decedents who died on or after Jan. 1, 1985.

(a) For purposes of distributing real property under this section if the decedent had a predeceased spouse who died not more than 15 years before the decedent and there is no surviving spouse or issue of the decedent, the portion of the decedent's estate attributable to the decedent's predeceased spouse passes as follows:

(1) If the decedent is survived by issue of the predeceased spouse, to the surviving issue of the predeceased spouse; if they are all of the same degree of kinship to the predeceased spouse they take equally, but if of unequal degree those of more remote degree take in the manner provided in Section 240.

(2) If there is no surviving issue of the predeceased spouse but the decedent is survived by a parent or parents of the predeceased spouse, to the predeceased spouse's surviving parent or parents equally.

(3) If there is no surviving issue or parent of the predeceased spouse but the decedent is survived by issue of a parent of the predeceased spouse, to the surviving issue of the parents of the predeceased spouse or either of them, the issue taking equally if they are all of the same degree of kinship to the predeceased spouse, but if of unequal degree those of more remote degree take in the manner provided in Section 240.

(4) If the decedent is not survived by issue, parent, or issue of a parent of the predeceased spouse, to the next of kin of the decedent in the manner provided in Section 6402.

(5) If the portion of the decedent's estate attributable to the decedent's predeceased spouse would otherwise escheat to the state because there is no kin of the decedent to take under Section 6402, the portion of the decedent's estate attributable to the predeceased spouse passes to the next of kin of the predeceased spouse who shall take in the same manner as the next of kin of the decedent take under Section 6402.

(b) For purposes of distributing personal property under this section if the decedent had a predeceased spouse who died not more than five years before the decedent, and there is no surviving spouse or issue of the decedent, the portion of the decedent's estate attributable to the decedent's predeceased spouse passes as follows:

(1) If the decedent is survived by issue of the predeceased spouse, to the surviving issue of the predeceased spouse; if they are all of the same degree of kinship to the predeceased spouse they take equally, but if of unequal degree those of more remote degree take in the manner provided in Section 240.

(2) If there is no surviving issue of the predeceased spouse but the decedent is survived by a parent or parents of the predeceased spouse, to the predeceased spouse's surviving parent or parents equally.

(3) If there is no surviving issue or parent of the predeceased spouse but the decedent is survived by issue of a parent of the predeceased spouse, to the surviving issue of the parents of the predeceased spouse or either of them, the issue taking equally if they are all of the same degree of kinship to the predeceased spouse, but if of unequal degree those of more remote degree take in the manner provided in Section 240.

(4) If the decedent is not survived by issue, parent, or issue of a parent of the predeceased spouse, to the next of kin of the decedent in the manner provided in Section 6402.

(5) If the portion of the decedent's estate attributable to the decedent's predeceased spouse would otherwise escheat to the state because there is no kin of the decedent to take under Section 6402, the portion of the decedent's estate attributable to the predeceased spouse passes to the next of kin of the predeceased spouse who shall take in the same manner as the next of kin of the decedent take under Section 6402.

(c) For purposes of disposing of personal property under subdivision (b), the claimant heir bears the burden of proof to show the exact personal property to be disposed of to the heir.

(d) For purposes of providing notice under any provision of this code with respect to an estate that may include personal property subject to distribution under subdivision (b), if the aggregate fair market value of tangible and intangible personal property with a written record of title or ownership in the estate is believed in good faith by the petitioning party to be less than ten thousand dollars ($10,000), the petitioning party need not give notice to the issue or next of kin of the predeceased spouse. If the personal property is subsequently determined to have an aggregate fair market value in excess of ten thousand dollars ($10,000), notice shall be given to the issue or next of kin of the predeceased spouse as provided by law.

(e) For the purposes of disposing of property pursuant to subdivision (b), "personal property" means that personal property in which there is a written record of title or ownership and the value of which in the aggregate is ten thousand dollars ($10,000) or more.

(f) For the purposes of this section, the "portion of the decedent's estate attributable to the decedent's predeceased spouse" means all of the following property in the decedent's estate:

(1) One-half of the community property in existence at the time of the death of the predeceased spouse.

(2) One-half of any community property, in existence at the time of death of the predeceased spouse, which was given to the decedent by the predeceased spouse by way of gift, descent, or devise.

(3) That portion of any community property in which the predeceased spouse had any incident of ownership and which vested in the decedent upon the death of the predeceased spouse by right of survivorship.

(4) Any separate property of the predeceased spouse which came to the decedent by gift, descent, or devise of the predeceased spouse or which vested in the decedent upon the death of the predeceased spouse by right of survivorship.

(g) For the purposes of this section, quasi-community property shall be treated the same as community property.

(h) For the purposes of this section:

(1) Relatives of the predeceased spouse conceived before the decedent's death but born thereafter inherit as if they had been born in the lifetime of the decedent.

(2) A person who is related to the predeceased spouse through two lines of relationship is entitled to only a single share based on the relationship which would entitle the person to the larger share.

(Added by Stats.1983, c. 842, § 55. Amended by Stats.1985, c. 982, § 20; Stats.1986, c. 873, § 1.)

§ 11440. Petition to Allocate Debt

If it appears that a debt of the decedent has been paid or is payable in whole or in part by the surviving spouse, or that a debt of the surviving spouse has been paid or is payable in whole or in part from property in the decedent's estate, the personal representative, the surviving spouse, or a beneficiary may, at any time before an order for final distribution is made, petition for an order to allocate the debt.

(Added by Stats.1987, c. 923, § 93.)

§ 11441. Contents of Petition

The petition shall include a statement of all of the following:

(a) All debts of the decedent and surviving spouse known to the petitioner that are alleged to be subject to allocation and whether paid in whole or part or unpaid.

(b) The reason why the debts should be allocated.

(c) The proposed allocation and the basis for allocation alleged by the petitioner.

(Added by Stats.1987, c. 923, § 93.)

§ 11442. Value of Separate and Community Property Affecting Allocation Where No Inventory and Appraisal Provided; Show Cause Order

If it appears from the petition that allocation would be affected by the value of the separate property of the surviving spouse and any community property and quasi-community property not administered in the estate and if an inventory and appraisal of the property has not been provided by the surviving spouse, the court shall make an order to show cause why the information should not be provided.

(Added by Stats.1987, c. 923, § 93.)

§ 11444. Agreement for Allocation; Apportionment of Debts in Absence of Agreement; Determination of Portions

(a) The personal representative and the surviving spouse may provide for allocation by agreement and, on a determination by the court that the agreement substantially protects the rights of interested persons, the allocation provided in the agreement shall be ordered by the court.

(b) In the absence of an agreement, each debt of the decedent shall be apportioned based on all of the property of the spouses liable for the debt at the date of death that is not exempt from enforcement of a money judgment, in the proportion determined by the value of the property less any liens and encumbrances at the date of death, adjusted to take into account any right of reimbursement that would have been available if the property were applied to the debt at the date of death, and the debt shall be allocated accordingly.

(Added by Stats.1987, c. 923, § 93.)

§ 11445. Payment of Allocated Shares; Court Order

On making a determination as provided in this chapter, the court shall make an order that:

(a) Directs the personal representative to make payment of the amounts allocated to the estate by payment to the surviving spouse or creditors.

(b) Directs the personal representative to charge amounts allocated to the surviving spouse against any property or interests of the surviving spouse that are in the possession or control of the personal representative. To the extent that property or interests of the surviving spouse in the possession or control of the personal representative are insufficient to satisfy the allocation, the court order shall summarily direct the surviving spouse to pay the allocation to the personal representative.

(Added by Stats.1987, c. 923, § 93.)

§ 11446. Last Illness and Funeral Expenses

Notwithstanding any other statute, funeral expenses and expenses of last illness shall be charged against the estate of the decedent and shall not be allocated to, or charged against the community share of, the surviving spouse, whether or not the surviving spouse is financially able to pay the expenses and whether or not the surviving spouse or any other person is also liable for the expenses.

(Added by Stats.1987, c. 923, § 93.)

§ 13550. Personal Liability for Debts Chargeable Against Property

Except as provided in Sections 951.1, 13552, 13553, and 13554, upon the death of a married person, the surviving spouse is personally liable for the debts of the deceased spouse chargeable against the property described in Section 13551 to the extent provided in Section 13551.

(Added by Stats.1986, c. 783, § 24.)

§ 13551. Limitation of Liability

The liability imposed by Section 13550 shall not exceed the fair market value at the date of the decedent's death, less the amount of any liens and encumbrances, of the total of the following:

(a) The portion of the one-half of the community and quasi-community property belonging to the surviving spouse under Sections 100 and 101 that is not exempt from enforcement of a money judgment and is not administered in the estate of the deceased spouse.

(b) The portion of the one-half of the community and quasi-community property belonging to the decedent under Sections 100 and 101 that passes to the surviving spouse without administration.

(c) The separate property of the decedent that passes to the surviving spouse without administration.

(Added by Stats.1986, c. 783, § 24.)

§ 13553. Exemption From Liability

The surviving spouse is not liable under this chapter if all the property described in paragraphs (1) and (2) of subdivision (a) of Section 13502 is administered under Division 3 (commencing with Section 300).

(Added by Stats.1986, c. 783, § 24.)

§ 13554. Enforcement of Debt Against Surviving Spouse

(a) Except as otherwise provided in this chapter, any debt described in Section 13550 may be enforced against the surviving spouse in the same manner as it could have been enforced against the deceased spouse if the deceased spouse had not died.

(b) In any action based upon the debt, the surviving spouse may assert any defense, cross-complaint, or setoff which would have been available to the deceased spouse if the deceased spouse had not died.

(Added by Stats.1986, c. 783, § 24.)

§ 13650. Petition for Order of Administration Not Necessary

(a) A surviving spouse or the personal representative, guardian of the estate, or conservator of the estate of the surviving spouse may file a petition in the superior court of the county in which the estate of the deceased spouse may be administered requesting an order that administration of all or part of the estate is not necessary for the reason that all or part of the estate is property passing to the surviving spouse. The petition may also request an order confirming the ownership of the surviving spouse of property belonging to the surviving spouse under Section 100 or 101.

(b) To the extent of the election, this section does not apply to property that the petitioner has elected, as provided in Section 13502, to have administered under Division 3 (commencing with Section 300).

(c) A guardian or conservator may file a petition under this section without authorization or approval of the court in which the guardianship or conservatorship proceeding is pending.

(Added by Stats.1986, c. 783, § 24.)

§ 13656. Order; Determination of Property Passing to Surviving Spouse

(a) If the court finds that all of the estate of the deceased spouse is property passing to the surviving spouse, the court shall issue an order describing the property, determining that the property is property passing to the surviving spouse, and determining that no administration is necessary. The court may issue any further orders which may be necessary to cause delivery of the property or its proceeds to the surviving spouse.

(b) If the court finds that all or part of the estate of the deceased spouse is not property passing to the surviving spouse, the court shall issue an order (1) describing any property which is not property passing to the surviving spouse, determining that that property does not pass to the surviving spouse and determining that that property is subject to administration under Division 3 (commencing with Section 300) and (2) describing the property, if any, which is property passing to the surviving spouse, determining that that property passes to the surviving spouse, and determining that no administration of that property is necessary. If the court determines that property passes to the surviving spouse, the court may issue any further orders which may be necessary to cause delivery of that property or its proceeds to the surviving spouse.

(c) If the petition filed under this chapter includes a description of the interest of the surviving spouse in the community or quasi-community property, or both, which belongs to the surviving spouse pursuant to Section 100 or 101 and the court finds that the interest belongs to the surviving spouse, the court shall issue an order describing the property and confirming the ownership of the surviving spouse and may issue any further orders which may be necessary to cause ownership of the property to be confirmed in the surviving spouse.

(Added by Stats.1986, c. 783, § 24.)

§ 13657. Conclusive Nature of Order

Upon becoming final, an order under Section 13656(1) determining that property is property passing to the surviving spouse or (2) confirming the ownership of the surviving spouse of property belonging to the surviving spouse under Section 100 or 101 shall be conclusive on all persons, whether or not they are in being.

(Added by Stats.1986, c. 783, § 24.)

ESTATE OF COFFEE

Supreme Court of California, 1941.
19 Cal.2d 248, 120 P.2d 661.

EDMONDS, JUSTICE. The Controller has appealed from an order fixing the inheritance tax in the estate of Harry Coffee, deceased, which, in effect, allows his widow to take one-half of their community property without deduction for debts, expenses of administration or inheritance taxes.

* * *

The Controller contends that the entire community property, proportionately with the husband's separate property, is subject to his debts and the expenses of administration, and that the widow is only entitled to take one-half of the community property remaining after the payment of these charges. He also asserts that the commissions of the executrix and of her attorneys should be based upon the value of the community property and the separate property subject to distribution by the probate court. In support of the probate court's order, the respondent argues that upon the death of the husband one-half of the community property is no part of his estate and, further, that it may not be used for any purpose in computing the inheritance tax because of section 1 of the Inheritance Tax Act of 1935, supra, declares "the one-half of the community property which belongs to the surviving spouse * * * shall not be subject to" its provisions.

In 1873, section 1401 of the Civil Code, which was a part of Title VII concerning "Succession," provided that upon the death of the wife, the entire community property, without administration should belong to the surviving husband except such portion of it as had been set aside to her by judicial decree for her support and maintenance. At that time section 1402 of the Civil Code provided: "Upon the death of the husband, one half of the community property goes to the surviving wife, and the other half is subject to the testamentary disposition of the husband, * * *. In case of the dissolution of the community by the death of the husband, the entire community property is equally subject to his debts, the family allowance, and the charges and expenses of administration." Both sections were recast by the legislature of 1923. Section 1401 became: "Upon the death of either husband or wife, one-half of the community property belongs to the surviving spouse; the other half is subject to the testamentary disposition of the decedent, and in the absence thereof goes to the surviving spouse, subject to the provisions of section [1402] of this Code." The following section was amended to read: "Community property passing from the control of the husband, either by reason of his death or by virtue of testamentary disposition by the wife, is subject to administration, his debts, family allowance and the charges and expense of administration * * *." In 1931, these were enacted without substantial change of language as sections 201 and 202, respectively, of the Probate Code.

Because in 1923, says the respondent, the legislature placed a semicolon instead of a comma after the words "belongs to the surviving spouse" in section 1401, only that portion of the community property which is subject to the testamentary disposition of the decedent is liable for the debts and charges which were stated in section 1402 and are now specified by section 202 of the Probate Code. But this argument overlooks the difference in scope between the two provisions. Section 201, like its predecessor, is a statute of succession; section 202 is a legislative declaration that "the community property" is chargeable with the husband's debts and is subject to the general provisions concerning the administration of the property of a decedent. Also, although punctuation may be of some assistance in the construction of a statute, it is not of controlling importance. Certainly, it is reasonable to suppose that if the legislature had desired to change the law relating to the liability of community property for debts, it would have done so by express enactment and not by substituting a semi-colon for a comma in the statute relating to succession. See Estate of Matthiessen, 23 Cal.App.2d 608, 73 P.2d 1267; In re Davis, 18 Cal.App.2d 291, 63 P.2d 853.

Moreover, in construing the enactments of 1923, this court held that they changed the law concerning community property in two particulars. "First, the wife was given the right equal with that of the husband, to make testamentary disposition of the one-half of the community property to which she would be entitled if she survived the husband, a right which she did not before possess; and, secondly, it changed the rule of inheritance by substituting the surviving wife for the husband's descendants as successor to his half of the community property in case he made no disposition thereof up to the time of his death." Travelers' Ins. Co. v. Fancher, 219 Cal. 351, 354, 26 P.2d 482, 483. Although the point now presented was not then before the court, its enumeration of the effects of the new enactments purports to include all of the changes which the legislature had made. It is most significant that no mention was made of any difference between the old and new legislation in other particulars.

For many years, the rule in this state has been that during the lifetime of a husband, the community property is liable for his debts. Grolemund v. Cafferata, 17 Cal.2d 679, 111 P.2d 641; Spreckels v. Spreckels, 116 Cal. 339, 48 P. 228, 36 L.R.A. 407, 58 Am.St.Rep. 170. And section 202 of the Probate Code, said the United States District Court in a recent case, "subjects all community property passing from the control of the husband, by his death or otherwise, to administration, to his debts, and to certain other charges. This is a provision more or less typical of the law in all community property states and should be construed as correlative to the principle that during the husband's life the community property is subject to his debts. Both are apparently corollaries to his right of management and control." Sampson v. Welch, D.C., 23 F.Supp. 271, 281.

It is clear, therefore, that the portion of the community property which belongs to the wife is the one-half which remains after the payment of the husband's debts and the expenses of administration apportioned between the community and separate property in accordance with the value thereof, and this is true even when the husband's share of the community, together with his separate property, is ample to pay those debts and expenses.

The judgment is reversed with directions to the probate court to compute the inheritance tax in accordance with the conclusions which have been stated.

CARTER, JUSTICE (Concurring specially). I concur in the judgment of reversal. In my opinion, the debts of the deceased, expenses and charges of administration, etc. should be first deducted from the gross value of the property subject to administration, including all of the community and separate property. These deductions should be apportioned between the community and separate property in accordance with the value thereof, giving effect to the provisions of section 750 of the Probate Code when applicable. One-half of the net value of the community property belongs to the surviving spouse and is not subject to inheritance taxes. Section 201, Probate Code. The other half which is subject to the testamentary disposition of the deceased spouse, together with the separate property of such deceased, is taxable under the provisions of the Inheritance Tax Act. Stats.1935, p. 1266, Deering's General Laws 1937, Act 8495. Before computing such tax, the widow in the case at bar is entitled to an exemption of $24,000, and the tax should be computed upon the balance remaining after the deduction of such exemption.

Notes

1. In Estate of Haselbud, 26 Cal.App.2d 375, 79 P.2d 443 (1938), the court noted that California courts had not traditionally drawn any distinc-

tion between the debts of a spouse incurred with respect to separate property and those incurred in managing community property, and that no rules had been established requiring either separate or community property to be resorted to for the payment of debts. The court indicated that such a distinction might be appropriate, but that the record in the case before it contained no information as to the nature or origin of the debts proved against the decedent husband's estate.

2. It has been suggested that the general prorata apportionment principle enunciated in Estate of Coffee should obtain only where the debt is not properly allocable to either separate property or community property under established doctrines of community property law. Gutierrez, *Apportionment of Debts, California Continuing Education of the Bar, Handling Disputes in Probate* (1976), 11–68.

3. In 1986 the California Law Revision Commission recognized that the existing allocation rules then contained at Probate Code Section 980 failed "to make clear the substantive basis for the allocation." The Commission proposed new legislation making it apparent that the allocation is to be based on the liability that the spouse would have had for the debt if the death had not occurred. The Commission stated that "[t]his has the effect of incorporating a known body of law governing liability for marital debts and avoids the problems inherent in litigation over 'separate' versus 'community' character of a debt. Whether a marital debt is separate or community in character is highly problematical. Such a determination made after one of the spouses is deceased and no longer able to testify is suspect." *Recommendations Relating to Probate Law,* 19 Cal.L.Revision Comm'n 1, 309 (1986). The current debt allocation rules are contained at Probate Code sections 11440–11446, applicable to all proceedings commenced after July 1, 1988.

ESTATE OF PRAGER
Supreme Court of California, 1913.
166 Cal. 450, 137 P. 37.

Sloss, J. Fannie Prager Cohn, one of the devisees under the will of Charles Prager, deceased, appeals from a decree of settlement of final account and of distribution.

The will, so far as its terms are material here, provides as follows: "Second. I direct that all of the real property owned by me at the time of my death, situate without the corporate limits of the city of Los Angeles, be distributed to the following named persons, share and share alike, to wit: My brother, * * * my nephews * * * and my nieces, * * *." Then follows this provision: "All the rest, residue and remainder of my estate, of every kind and character, including all real property owned by me within the corporate limits of the city of Los Angeles, and mortgages, notes, bonds and other personal property of every description, I give, devise and bequeath unto my wife, Mary J. Prager, absolutely." * * *

Charles Prager died on the 14th day of September, 1911. The total value of the estate, as shown by the appraisement, was $630,321.67.

The real property situate outside of the city of Los Angeles, covered by paragraph second of the will, was appraised at $179,928.50. All of this was community property. There was other community property consisting principally of a note secured by mortgage and two bonds, said note and bonds, together, being of the appraised value of $16,000, also two parcels of land in the city of Los Angeles, appraised at $54,000. The separate property of the decedent consisted of land in the city of Los Angeles, appraised at $380,000.

Very shortly after the testator's death, the widow, Mary J. Prager, through her attorney and coexecutor, Mr. Lawler, informed the devisees named in the second paragraph that she claimed the right to succeed to one-half of the community property, in addition to taking what was given her by the will. Most of the said devisees at once conceded the validity of this claim. * * * Mrs. Fannie Cohn, the appellant, remains as the only one of the devisees now contesting the widow's claim.

* * * The claim of the appellant, Fannie Cohn, is that the widow, by taking under the decree of partial distribution one-half of the community property not devised to her, had manifested her election to forego the benefits given her by the will.

Reading the will by itself or in the light of the circumstances shown by the record, we find no ground for holding that the widow was called upon to surrender either her interest in the community property or the devises and bequests given her. The rules of law governing the question of election in cases like the present have been declared in numerous decisions of this court.

The testator is presumed to have made his will with knowledge that his power of testamentary disposition did not extend to the surviving wife's interest in the community property. The presumption is further that he did not intend to devise or bequeath the one-half of the community property which, upon his death, would vest in his widow irrespective of any attempt that he might make to dispose of it by will. In the absence of anything in the instrument to indicate a contrary intent, the testamentary dispositions must accordingly be understood as intended to cover only the property which the testator had the right to devise or bequeath; i.e., his separate property and an undivided half of the community property.

The mere fact that provision, however liberal, is made in the will for the wife is not enough to justify the conclusion that such provision was intended to be in lieu of her interest as survivor of the community. Beard v. Knox, 5 Cal. 252, 63 Am.Dec. 125; Estate of Silvey, 42 Cal. 211; King v. Lagrange, 50 Cal. 328; Estate of Frey, 52 Cal. 658; Estate of Gwin, 77 Cal. 313, 19 P. 527; Estate of Gilmore, 81 Cal. 240, 22 P. 655; Estate of Smith, 108 Cal. 115, 40 P. 1037; Estate of Wickersham, 138 Cal. 355, 70 P. 1076, 71 P. 437; Estate of Vogt, 154 Cal. 508, 98 P.2d 265. The widow's obligation to elect arises only where the testator has, by the terms of the will, clearly manifested the intention to make the testamentary gift to her stand in lieu of her interest in the community property. The provision may be "declared in terms to be given in lieu of" the right as survivor of the community (Morrison v. Bowman, 29 Cal. 337), or the language of the will may be such as to show clearly an intent to dispose of the whole of the community property in such manner that "the widow cannot take the moiety given her by law without, to that extent, defeating the plain intent of the testator" (Estate of Vogt, supra; Estate of Stewart, 74 Cal. 98, 15 P. 445; Estate of Smith, supra).

The will before us does not declare that the gifts to the widow shall be in lieu of her community right. Neither do its provisions show an intention which would be frustrated by permitting the widow to take both her moiety of the community property and the residue given to her. The property given to the widow included both separate and community estate. Some of the community property (i.e., the land outside the city of Los Angeles) was devised to the persons named in paragraph second. There is nothing to indicate that the latter provision was intended to operate as a gift of more than the share which was subject to the decedent's testamentary disposition. Applying the presumptions of which mention has been made, the will discloses a simple and consistent scheme, which may be carried out in every respect without affecting the widow's right to claim her lawful interest in the community property. In every case in which the widow has been held to be put to her election, the will contained language which, when read in the light of the circumstances, showed plainly that the testator was undertaking to dispose of the entire community property, and that his intention could not be given effect if one-half of such property were withdrawn from the operation of the will. This case presents no such features. On the contrary, it is in every material respect like a number of those, above cited, in which this court concluded that no duty of election arose.

Notes

1. *Estate of Prager* indicates that the preferred construction is against requiring an election, and an intention on the part of the testator to dispose of his wife's community property interest will not be implied. Where, however the testator's will purported to dispose of his own and his wife's share of the community property as his separate property, and left the bulk of the estate to the testator's wife and sister equally, the court held that an election was clearly indicated. "Under the circumstances, the assertion by the wife of her rights under the will and at the same time of her interest in the community property under [former] Probate Code § 201 are inconsistent." Estate of Wolfe, 48 Cal.2d 570, 311 P.2d 476 (1957).

2. In Estate of Kennedy, 135 Cal.App.3d 676, 185 Cal.Rptr. 540 (1982), the deceased wife's will declared that "all property standing in my name and in the name of my husband as joint tenants is our community property. It is my intention by this Will to dispose of all my separate property and my share of our community property * * * ". The will divided the bulk of the estate between the surviving husband and the decedent's daughter. The husband's representative sought to assert the husband's rights as a surviving joint tenant together with the property bequeathed under the will. The trial court held that an election was required. The appellate court affirmed,

noting that "[d]ecedent could not of course bequeath half of any joint tenancy property to Daughter, because upon Decedent's death Husband became sole owner of all joint tenancy property by right of survivorship. However, if decedent for whatever reason nevertheless believed she could make such disposition, and clearly intended to give half of the joint tenancy property to Daughter, she could force Husband to an election."

*

Index

References are to Pages

CLASSIFICATION OF PROPERTY—Cont'd
Tracing, doctrine of, 10–14
Transmutation in form,
    Classification unaffected by, 12

COMMINGLING
Doctrine defined, 265–279
Presumptions, commingling doctrine founded on, 265

COMMUNITY PROPERTY
    See also Classification of Property.
Defined, 10–12
Equitable community property, 177–207
Quasi-community property, 234–255

COMMUNITY PROPERTY SYSTEM
Background material, 1–7
Basic ideas of system, 10
Comparative law,
    Sister state precedents, 10
    Spanish–Mexican system, 6, 10
Contracts, modification of system by, 21–42
Domicile in state required, 226
Dower and Curtesy rejected, 6
Equitable system for putative spouse, 177–207
Historical introduction, 1–10
Marital property law of California, 5
Marriage required, legal, 177
Nature of interests of spouses, 15
Partnership analogy, 2
Property within system, 133–176
Putative spouse,
    Equitable system, 177–207
    Good-faith requirement, 178
    Legal and putative spouses, shares of, 192–207
    Statutory recognition, 180
Separate or community, all wealth classified as, 10
Separation, acquisitions during, 74–75, 81–83
Sui Generis, California system, 10

CONFLICT OF LAWS
Domicile, effect of, 226–227
Interests not changed by change of domicile, 226–227
Reclassification of property on removal to state, 234–255

CONSTITUTION
Community property system recognized, 6–7
Separate property guaranty, 6–7

CONSTITUTIONAL LAW
Doctrine against retroactive operation of amendments, 133–141
Due process, 232–255
Federal supremacy doctrine, 255–264
Privileges and immunities of citizens, reclassification as violation of, 233

CONTRACTS
    See also Classification of Property; Creditors' Rights; Dissolution and Separation.
Actions and recoveries for personal injury, Classification by contract, 333
Antenuptial contracts,
    Statutory conditions, 25–27
Dissolution, contractual division of property on, 491–509
Postnuptial contracts,
    Affirmation of antenuptial contract, 22
    Classifying property,
        General treatment, 22–23
        To be acquired, 22
    Express, 42–58
    Implied in fact, 22
    Oral contracts, 30
Transmutation of property by contract, 21–59

CONTROL AND MANAGEMENT
Conveyances of community real property, restrictions on, 422–423, 402
Dual control from 1951 to 1975, 396
Equal control from 1975, 396–400
Fiduciary spouse in control as, 397
Fraud in management, remedies for, 422–423
General survey, 396–402
Gifts of community property, restrictions on, 396–402
Mortgage of community property, 422–423, 402
Presumption of validity of record-title conveyance, 454–461
Recapture of real property, 437–454
Reimbursement when separate property improved, 410–411
Remedies for wrongful acts of management, 422–423
Single control prior to 1951, 396
Transfer of furniture and wearing apparel, restrictions on, 402

COTENANCY
See Presumptions.

CREDIT ACQUISITIONS
See Classification of Property.

CREDITORS' RIGHTS
Classification of debts,
    Administration in, 599–602
    Dissolution proceedings, in, 534–537
Control and management by debtor required, 462–465
Necessaries, statutory procedure to charge non-contracting spouse for, 464
Premarital debts, 465
Statute,
    Community property available,
        Contractual debts, for, 463
        Tortious debts, for, 464

†

0-314-03491-9

90000

9 780314 034915